GW01418795

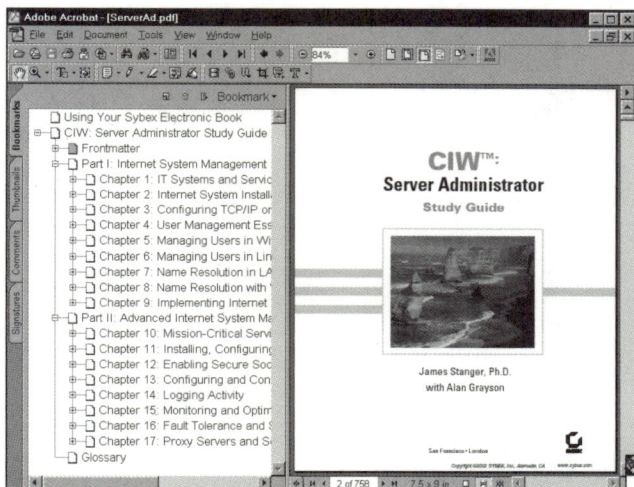

Search through the complete book in PDF!

✔ Access the entire *CIW:Server Administrator Study Guide*, complete with figures and tables, in electronic format.

✔ Search the *CIW:Server Administrator Study Guide* chapters to find information on any topic in seconds.

✔ Use Adobe Acrobat Reader (included on the CD-ROM) to view the electronic book.

CIW™:
Server Administrator
Study Guide

James Stanger, Ph.D.
with Alan Grayson

San Francisco • London

Use the Electronic Flashcards for PCs or Palm devices to jog your memory and prep last minute for the exam!

✔ Reinforce your understanding of key concepts with these hardcore flashcard-style questions.

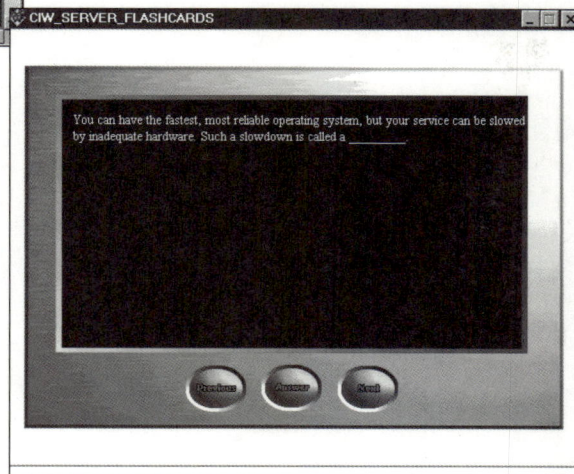

You can have the fastest, most reliable operating system, but your service can be slowed by inadequate hardware. Such a slowdown is called a _____

Prepare for the Server Administrator exam on the go with your handheld device!

✔ Download the Flashcards to your Palm device and go on the road. Now you can study for the CIW Server Administrator exam anytime, anywhere.

CIW: Server Administrator Study Guide

Exam 1D0-450

OBJECTIVE GROUP	CHAPTER
Internet System Management	
Identify common IT services related to various hardware platforms and frequently used operating systems, including but not limited to: mission-critical services, system maintenance, connectivity, platform strategies.	1, 2
Identify TCP/IP configuration parameters, and configure Windows and Linux systems with static IP addresses.	3
Identify various levels of user access, and create password policies and permissions based on standard practice and procedures.	4
Manage users in Windows, Linux, and Novell networks, including but not limited to: Security Accounts Manager, authentication, remote user administration, user rights and settings, remote shares, account creation, password policies, permissions.	5, 6
Define and implement the Domain Name System (DNS), including but not limited to: DNS components, record types, reverse lookup, utilities, DNS servers, NetBIOS.	7
Identify additional name resolution options for LANs and WANs, including but not limited to: Windows Internet Naming Service (WINS), Samba.	8
Implement and control access to Internet services, including but not limited to: FTP, Telnet.	9

SYBEX

OBJECTIVE GROUP	CHAPTER
Advanced Internet System Management	
Select and implement popular Web servers, including but not limited to: Microsoft IIS, Apache Server.	10, 11
Perform advanced Web server administration tasks, including but not limited to: user based authentication, access control, HTML administration, alias creation, error messages.	11
Perform Secure Sockets Layer (SSL) transactions.	12
Configure and manage news servers and e-mail servers.	13
Install and configure proxy servers and Internet servers.	17
Analyze server and service logs.	14
Evaluate system performance, including but not limited to: server monitoring and optimization, maximizing performance, disaster assessment, data recovery.	15, 16
Identify internal and external security risks, including but not limited to: operating system features and vulnerabilities, firewalls, log file analysis.	17

SYBEX

CIW:
Server Administrator
Study Guide

CIW™:
Server Administrator
Study Guide

James Stanger, Ph.D.
with Alan Grayson

San Francisco • London

SYBEX

Associate Publisher: Neil Edde
Acquisitions and Developmental Editor: Maureen Adams
Editor: Pat Coleman
Production Editor: Kelly Winquist
Technical Editors: Andy Barkl, Liam Noonan
Contributors: Liam Noonan, Patrick T. Lane, Jeremy Teitelbaum, Emmett Dulaney, William Sodeman
Book Designer: Bill Gibson
Graphic Illustrator: Tony Jonick
Electronic Publishing Specialist: Jill Niles
Proofreaders: Nancy Riddiough, Dave Nash, Emily Hsuan, Laurie O'Connell, Rich Ganis, Abigail Sawyer, Sarah Tannehill
Indexer: Nancy Guenther
CD Coordinator: Dan Mummert
CD Technician: Kevin Ly
Cover Designer: Archer Design
Cover Photographer: Jeremy Woodhouse, PhotoDisc

This book was developed and published by SYBEX Inc. under a license from ProsoftTraining. All Rights Reserved.

Original Internet System Management training material © 2001 ComputerPREP, Inc.

Library of Congress Card Number: 2002100056

ISBN: 0-7821-4085-8

Manufactured in the United States of America

10 9 8 7 6 5 4 3 2 1

SYBEX

To Our Valued Readers:

The Certified Internet Webmaster (CIW) program from ProsoftTraining™ has established itself as one of the leading Internet certifications in the IT industry. Sybex has partnered with ProsoftTraining to produce Study Guides—like the one you hold in your hand—for the Associate, Master Administrator, and Master Designer tracks. Each Sybex book is based on official courseware and is exclusively endorsed by ProsoftTraining.

Just as ProsoftTraining is committed to establishing measurable standards for certifying IT professionals working with Internet technologies, Sybex is committed to providing those professionals with the skills and knowledge needed to meet those standards. It has long been Sybex's desire to help bridge the knowledge and skills gap that currently confronts the IT industry.

The authors and editors have worked hard to ensure that this CIW Study Guide is comprehensive, in-depth, and pedagogically sound. We're confident that this book will meet and exceed the demanding standards of the certification marketplace and help you, the CIW certification candidate, succeed in your endeavors.

Good luck in pursuit of your CIW certification!

Neil Edde
Associate Publisher—Certification
Sybex, Inc.

Acknowledgments

I wish to thank my family. Sandi, James, Jacob, Joel, and now Joseph, you have shown amazing patience with me as I worked on this book.
—James Stanger

I would like to thank my wife Dianne and our two teacup poodles, Angel and Noel, for their support and encouragement. I would also like to thank Pat Coleman, copyeditor; Kelly Winquist, production editor; Maureen Adams, developmental editor; Andrew Barkl and Liam Noonan, technical editors; Jill Niles, compositor; Tony Jonick, illustrator; Dan Mummert, CD coordinator; Kevin Ly, CD technician; and Nancy Riddiough, Laurie O'Connell, Emily Hsuan, Dave Nash, and Rich Ganis, proofreaders. This team wouldn't rest until their years of experience were carefully blended into a book that reflected their collective wisdom. It was an honor working with this elite group, and I trust that readers will truly appreciate their efforts. Thanks are also due to Emmett Dulaney, who added material, including wonderful anecdotes, and Bill Sodeman, who also supplied additional material. Their insight and vision are clearly reflected throughout this book.
—Alan Grayson

Contents at a Glance

Contents

Table of Exercises

Introduction

The Prosoft CIW (Certified Internet Webmaster) certification affirms that you have the essential skills to create, run, and update a website. These skills are exactly what employers in today's economy are looking for, and you need to stay ahead of the competition in the current job market. CIW certification will prove to your current or future employer that you are serious about expanding your knowledge base. Obtaining CIW certification will also provide you with valuable skills, including basic networking, web page authoring, internetworking, maintaining security, and website design, and expose you to a variety of vendor products made for web design and implementation.

This book is meant to help you prepare for the Certified Internet Webmaster Server Administrator Exam 1D0-450. The Server Administrator Exam is a prerequisite for the following CIW certifications: CIW Certified Instructor (for those teaching CIW Server Administrator content), Master CIW Web Site Manager, and Master CIW Administrator. CIW Associates who pass the CIW Server Administrator exam also achieve the CIW Professional certification.

The Certified Internet Webmaster Program

The CIW Internet skills certification program is aimed at professionals who design, develop, administer, secure, and support Internet- or intranet-related services. The CIW certification program offers industry-wide recognition of an individual's Internet and web knowledge and skills, and certification is frequently a factor in hiring and assignment decisions. It also provides tangible evidence of a person's competency as an Internet professional; holders of this certification can demonstrate to potential employers and clients that they have passed rigorous training and examination requirements that set them apart from non-certified competitors. All CIW certifications are endorsed by the International Webmasters Association (IWA) and the Association of Internet Professionals (AIP).

CIW Associate

The first step toward CIW certification is the CIW Foundations series. A candidate for the CIW Associate certification and the Foundations exam has the basic hands-on skills and knowledge that an Internet professional is expected to understand and use. Foundations skills include basic knowledge of Internet technologies, network infrastructure, and web authoring using HTML.

The CIW Foundations program is designed for all professionals who use the Internet. The job expectations of a CIW Associate, or person who has completed the program and passed the Foundations exam, include:

- Understanding Internet, networking, and web page authoring basics
- Application of Foundations skills required for further specialization

> **NOTE** There are a few prerequisites for becoming a CIW Associate. For instance, although you need not have Internet experience in order to start Foundations exam preparation, you should have an understanding of Microsoft Windows.

Table I.1 shows the CIW Foundations exam and the corresponding Sybex Study Guide that covers the CIW Associate certification.

TABLE I.1 The CIW Associate Exam and Corresponding Sybex Study Guide

Exam Name	Exam Number	Sybex Study Guide
Foundations	1D0-410	*CIW: Foundations Study Guide* (ISBN 0-7821-4081-5)

> **NOTE** CIW accepts score reports from CIW Associate candidates who have passed the entry-level CompTIA i-Net+ exam (IKO-001) and will award Foundations certification to these individuals. For more information regarding the i-Net+ and other CompTIA exams, visit www.comptia.org/.

After passing the Foundations exam, students become CIW Associates and can choose from four Master CIW certification tracks, by choosing a path of interest and passing the required exams:

- Master CIW Designer
- Master CIW Administrator
- CIW Web Site Manager
- Master CIW Enterprise Developer
- CIW Security Analyst

Master CIW Designer

The Master Designer track is composed of two exams, each of which represents a specific aspect of the Internet job role:

- Site Designer

- E-Commerce Designer

Site Designer Exam   The CIW Site Designer applies human-factors principles to designing, implementing, and maintaining hypertext-based publishing sites. The Site Designer uses authoring and scripting languages, as well as digital media tools, plus provides content creation and website management.

E-Commerce Designer Exam   The CIW E-Commerce Designer is tested on e-commerce set-up, human-factors principles regarding product selection and payment, and site security and administration.

Table I.2 shows the CIW Site Designer and E-Commerce Designer exams and the corresponding Sybex Study Guide for each of these steps toward the CIW Master Designer certification.

TABLE I.2   The Master Designer Exams and Corresponding Sybex Study Guides

Exam Names	Exam Numbers	Sybex Study Guide
Site Designer	1D0-410	*CIW: Site and E-Commerce Design Study Guide* (ISBN 0-7821-4082-3)
E-Commerce Designer	1D0-425	*CIW: Site and E-Commerce Design Study Guide* (ISBN 0-7821-4082-3)

Master CIW Administrator

The CIW Administrator is proficient in three areas of administration:

- Server

- Internetworking

- Security administration

After passing each test, you become a CIW Professional in that specific area.

Server Administrator Exam The CIW Server Administrator manages and tunes corporate e-business solutions infrastructure, including web, FTP, news, and mail servers for midsize to large businesses. Server administrators configure, manage, and deploy e-business solutions servers.

Internetworking Professional Exam The Internetworking Professional defines network architecture, identifies infrastructure components, and monitors and analyzes network performance. The CIW Internetworking Professional is responsible for the design and management of enterprise TCP/IP networks.

Security Professional Exam The CIW Security Professional implements policy, identifies security threats, and develops countermeasures using firewall systems and attack-recognition technologies. As a CIW Security Professional, you are responsible for managing the deployment of e-business transactions and payment security solutions.

The Exams in the Master Administrator track are listed in Table I.3.

TABLE I.3 The Master Administrator Exams and Corresponding Sybex Study Guides.

Exam Names	Exam Numbers	Sybex Study Guide
Server Administrator	1D0-450	*CIW: Server Administrator Study Guide* (ISBN 0-7821-4085-8)
Internetworking Professional	1D0-460	*CIW: Internetworking Professional Study Guide* (ISBN 0-7821-4083-1)
Security Professional	1D0-470	*CIW: Security Professional Study Guide* (ISBN 0-7821-4084-X)

Other CIW Certifications

Prosoft also offers three additional certification series in website management, enterprise development, and security analysis.

Master CIW Web Site Manager The Web Site Manager certification is composed of two Internet job role series exams (Site Designer 1D0-420 and Server Administrator 1D0-450) and two additional language exams

(JavaScript 1D0-435 and Perl Fundamentals 1D0-437 from the CIW Web Languages series).

Master CIW Enterprise Developer The Enterprise Developer certification is composed of three Internet job role series (Application Developer 1D0-430, Database Specialist 1D0-441, and Enterprise Specialist 1D0-42) and three additional language/theory series (Web Languages, Java Programming, and Object-Oriented Analysis).

CIW Security Analyst The Security Analyst certification recognizes those who have already attained a networking certification and demonstrated (by passing the CIW Security 1D0-470 exam) that they have the in-demand security skills to leverage their technical abilities against internal and external cyber threats.

For more information regarding all of Prosoft's certifications and exams, visit `www.ciwcertified.com`.

Special Features in This Book

What makes a Sybex Study Guide the book of choice for over 500,000 certification candidates across numerous technical fields? We take into account not only what you need to know to pass the exam, but what you need to know to apply what you've learned in the real world. Each book contains the following:

Objective Information Each chapter lists at the outset which CIW objective groups are going to be covered within.

Assessment Test Directly following this Introduction is an Assessment Test that you can take to help you determine how much you already know about administering Windows 2000 and Linux Internet servers. Each question is tied to a topic discussed in the book. Using the results of the Assessment Test, you can figure out the areas where you need to focus your study. Of course, we do recommend you read the entire book.

Exam Essentials To review what you've learned, you'll find a list of Exam Essentials at the end of each chapter. The Exam Essentials section briefly highlights the topics that need your particular attention as you prepare for the exam.

Key Terms and Glossary   Throughout each chapter, you will be introduced to important terms and concepts that you will need to know for the exam. These terms appear in italic within the chapters, and a list of the Key Terms appears just after the Exam Essentials. At the end of the book, a detailed glossary gives definitions for these terms, as well as other general terms you should know.

Review Questions, complete with detailed explanations   Each chapter is followed by a set of Review Questions that test what you learned in the chapter. The questions are written with the exam in mind, meaning that they are designed to have the same look and feel of what you'll see on the exam.

Hands-on Exercises   Throughout the book, you'll find exercises designed to give you the important hands-on experience that is critical for your exam preparation. The exercises support the topics of the chapter, and they walk you through the steps necessary to perform a particular function.

Interactive CD   Every Sybex Study Guide comes with a CD complete with additional questions, flashcards for use with a palm device or PC, and a complete electronic version of this book. Details are in the following section.

What's On the CD?

Sybex's *CIW: Server Administrator Study Guide* companion CD includes quite an array of training resources and offers numerous test simulations, bonus exams, and flashcards to help you study for the exam. We have also included the complete contents of the study guide in electronic form. The CD's resources are described here:

The Sybex Ebook for the *CIW Server Administrator Study Guide*
Many people like the convenience of being able to carry their whole study guide on a CD. They also like being able to search the text via computer to find specific information quickly and easily. For these reasons, the entire contents of this study guide are supplied on the CD, in PDF format. We've also included Adobe Acrobat Reader, which provides the interface for the PDF contents as well as search capabilities.

The Sybex CIW Edge Tests   The Edge Tests are a collection of multiple-choice questions that will help you prepare for your exam. There are three sets of questions:

- Two bonus exams designed to simulate the actual live exam.

- All the Review Questions from the Study Guide, presented in an electronic test engine. You can review questions by chapter or by objective area, or you can take a random test.

- The Assessment Test.

Sybex CIW Flashcards for PCs and Palm Devices   The "flashcard" style of question offers an effective way to quickly and efficiently test your understanding of the fundamental concepts covered in the exam. The Sybex CIW Flashcards set consists of 150 questions presented in a special engine developed specifically for this study guide series. We have also developed, in conjunction with Land-J Technologies, a version of the flashcard questions that you can take with you on your Palm OS PDA (including the Palm and Visor PDAs).

How to Use This Book

This book provides a solid foundation for the serious effort of preparing for the exam. To best benefit from this book, you may wish to use the following study method:

1. Take the Assessment Test to identify your weak areas.

2. Study each chapter carefully. Do your best to fully understand the information.

3. Study the Exam Essentials and Key Terms to make sure you are familiar with the areas you need to focus on.

4. Answer the review questions at the end of each chapter. If you prefer to answer the questions in a timed and graded format, install the Edge Tests from the book's CD and answer the chapter questions there instead of in the book.

5. Take note of the questions you did not understand, and study the corresponding sections of the book again.

6. Go back over the Exam Essentials and Key Terms.

7. Go through the study guide's other training resources, which are included on the book's CD. These include electronic flashcards, the electronic version of the chapter review questions (try taking them by objective), and the two bonus exams.

To learn all the material covered in this book, you will need to study regularly and with discipline. Try to set aside the same time every day to study, and select a comfortable and quiet place in which to do it. If you work hard, you will be surprised at how quickly you learn this material. Good luck!

Exam Registration

CIW certification exams are administered by Prometric, Inc. through Prometric Testing Centers and by Virtual University Enterprises (VUE) testing centers. You can reach Prometric at (800) 380-EXAM or VUE at (952) 995-8800, to schedule any CIW exam.

You may also register for your exams online at www.prometric.com or www.vue.com.

Exams cost $125 (U.S.) each and must be paid for in advance. Exams must be taken within one year of payment. Candidates can schedule exams up to six weeks in advance or as late as one working day prior to the date of the exam. To cancel or reschedule an exam, contact the center at least two working days prior to the scheduled exam date. Same-day registration is available in some locations, subject to space availability. Where same-day registration is available, registration must occur a minimum of two hours before test time.

When you schedule the exam, the testing center will provide you with instructions regarding appointment and cancellation procedures, ID requirements, and information about the testing center location. In addition, you will receive a registration and payment confirmation letter from Prometric or VUE.

Tips for Taking the CIW Server Administrator Exam

Here are some general tips for achieving success on your certification exam:

- Arrive early at the exam center so that you can relax and review your study materials. During this final review, you can look over tables and lists of exam-related information.

- Read the questions carefully. Don't be tempted to jump to an early conclusion. Make sure you know *exactly* what the question is asking.

- For questions you're not sure about, use a process of elimination to get rid of the obviously incorrect answers first. This improves your odds of selecting the correct answer when you need to make an educated guess.

- Mark questions that you aren't sure of and return to them later. Quite often something in a later question will act as a reminder or give you a clue to the correct answer of the earlier one.

Contacts and Resources

Here are some handy websites to keep in mind for future reference:

Prosoft Training and CIW Exam Information	www.CIWcertified.com
Prometric	www.prometric.com
VUE Testing Services	www.vue.com
Sybex Computer Books	www.sybex.com

Assessment Test

1. Joe needs the best performance he can obtain for the hard drive system for his database server. Which hard drive system should Joe choose?

    A. IDE

    B. ATA 100

    C. SCSI 3

    D. EIDE

2. Jim wants to know the number of users currently accessing his IIS website so that he can adjust bandwidth. Which System Monitor counter should Jim examine?

    A. Processor\Server Work Queues

    B. Processor\Queue Length

    C. Web Service\CGI requests/sec

    D. Web Service\Current Anonymous Users

3. Wendy is an editor for a book publisher. When Wendy goes on the road it takes her a long time to download her e-mail that includes large attachments before she can get to any urgent messages from her boss. What type of server would help Wendy to manipulate e-mail on the server and choose which messages to download first?

    A. SMTP

    B. POP

    C. IMAP

    D. Daemon

    E. Sendmail

4. On the Sources server, Jim has the NTFS Full Control permission and the Read share permission on the `Confidential` folder. Jim needs to delete a memo there that should have gone in the `Top Secret` folder. Which of the following statements are true?

   A. Jim can delete this file if he logs on locally to the Sources server.

   B. Jim can delete this file if he uses the network to access the Sources server.

   C. Jim can do this if he takes ownership of the sources folder.

   D. Jim can do this over the network if he is an administrator.

5. Frank is troubleshooting a second network card that was just added to a Linux server. He wants detailed information on how Linux configured that NIC at startup. Which command would give Jim just the information that he needs?

   A. `ifconfig eth1`

   B. `ifconfig eth2`

   C. `dmesg | grep eth1`

   D. `dmesg | grep eth2`

6. Jim just completed a minimum installation of Red Hat Linux. He needs to do some user account administration, but notices that `linuxconf` has not been installed. How can he add the `linuxconf` program to his current installation of Linux? Choose the best answer.

   A. He must reinstall Linux in server mode

   B. He can use the RPM command to install `linuxconf`

   C. He should boot off the installation CD and choose to repair the installation

   D. He should mount the Linux installation CD and extract the executable for `linuxconf` to the `/bin/bash` working directory

7. Ginger's brand-new Gateway laptop comes with Windows XP pre-installed. Ginger wants to dual boot this computer with Linux. What should Ginger obtain before she installs Linux?

   A. Drivers

   B. DHCP

   C. BIOS updates

   D. Samba software

8. Mark is developing Microsoft Access macros. He encounters a glitch. Where can Mark go for free advice and feedback from peers that might have encountered and overcome similar problems? Choose the best answer.

   A. www.microsoft.com/technet

   B. www.tucows.com

   C. microsoft.public.access.macros

   D. www.whatis.com

9. Jim wants to share files and folders among his five employees while minimizing cost. Which type of network should Jim install?

   A. Peer-to-peer

   B. User-level access model

   C. Active Directory

   D. Domain based

10. George wants to set access permissions on the C:\secret folder on a newly installed Windows 2000 Server. He right clicks the folder and selects Properties from the shortcut menu to open the Properties dialog box, but the Security tab is not available. What might be the problem? Choose two.

    A. Drive C is the system partition.

    B. George isn't logged on as administrator.

    C. Drive C is formatted with NTFS.

    D. Drive C is formatted with FAT or FAT32.

11. Mark wants to automatically make home folders for new users that he will create. What should Mark do first?

A. Use the *%username%* variable

B. Open Active Directory Users and Computers

C. Create and share a `users` folder

D. Open Computer Management

12. George enables auditing on the HR folder. Which utility should George use to view the results?

A. The Audit log of System Tools

B. The Audit log of System Information

C. The Security log of Event Viewer

D. The Application log of Event Viewer

13. Your company's IT department plans to implement an operating system. Your boss is concerned about supportability, the range of applications that must be supported, ease of use, and the available talent pool of IT professionals experienced in the NOS to be chosen. Which NOS should you choose?

A. Windows 2000

B. Linux

C. IBM AIX

D. Novell NetWare

14. Bart modifies the `/etc/passwd` file to add a user account as follows:

`U2:x:101:100:U2 Band:/home/U2:/bin/bash.`

What has been accomplished? Choose all that apply.

A. A user account has been created.

B. A password has been assigned.

C. A home directory has been created.

D. A default shell has been assigned.

15. Frank wants to overcome the failure of a single disk controller. What fault-tolerant hardware should Frank implement?

    A. Disk mirroring

    B. Disk duplexing

    C. SCSI

    D. RAID

16. Jonathan wants to see if all three of his DNS servers are functioning correctly, because some users have reported problems in name resolution and other users have reported that everything is working correctly. After going to a command prompt, typing **nslookup**, and pressing Enter, which command should Jonathan issue to first check ns1.ciw.com?

    A. server=ns1.ciw.com

    B. type=server@ns1.ciw.com

    C. server ns1.ciw.com

    D. type=ns1.ciwcertified.com

17. As part of an unannounced security inspection, there is a bogus emergency meeting. A user logged in as root and a user logged in as gbush walk away from their workstation without logging off. Will either of these users be vulnerable to having their password changed?

    A. No

    B. Only root

    C. Only gbush

    D. Both

18. Jim hosts several high-traffic FTP sites on his IIS 5 server. What can Jim do to increase performance? Choose the best answer.

    A. Add IP addresses

    B. Use round-robin DNS

    C. Add NICs

    D. Add ports

19. Ralph is setting up logging for his web server. What, if anything, should limit how much information he logs? Choose the best answer.

    A. Logging may require additional client-access licenses.

    B. Logging can have legal implications.

    C. Logging can compromise security.

    D. Logging affects system performance.

20. Mike is writing a job description for a new IT position that will be responsible for backbone services. Which of the following are characteristic of backbone services? Choose all that apply.

    A. Operate in the background

    B. Operate in the foreground

    C. Provide naming services

    D. Provide directory services

    E. Provide central logon

21. George wants to get information about local and remote users on his Linux FTP server. Which protocol should George use?

    A. echo

    B. XWindows

    C. finger

    D. TCPWrappers

22. Bill is accessing the Internet. He cannot access his corporate website by host name, but he can access it by IP address. What is the likely problem?

    A. DNS server

    B. Default gateway

    C. NetBIOS over TCP/IP

    D. Proxy server

    E. Firewall

23. Mark wants to make the Projects folder available to network users. What should Mark create?

   A. A global group

   B. A share

   C. A local group

   D. An ACL

24. Jim wants to configure his Apache server as a web proxy server. Which file should Jim edit?

   A. `httpd.conf`

   B. `proxy.conf`

   C. `srm.conf`

   D. `access.conf`

25. Jim is installing a Windows 2000 domain controller that has the DNS name of `server1.northwesttraders.com`. NT 4 workstations need to join this domain. Which domain should these workstations join?

   A. server1

   B. northwesttraders

   C. northwesttrader

   D. com

26. Linda wants works for a web-hosting company that will deploy 200 servers. She needs to minimize licensing costs. Which NOS should Linda choose?

   A. NT 4

   B. Windows 2000

   C. Linux

   D. Novell NetWare 5.2

27. Ralph wants to use the dump command to create a full backup. What number does dump use to denote a full backup?

   A. 0

   B. 1

   C. 2

   D. 3

28. George is setting up name resolution using WINS. He wants clients to use the WINS server first, and if the WINS server is unavailable or cannot resolve a NetBIOS name, he wants the client to broadcast in order to resolve a NetBIOS name. Which node type should George use on his WINS server?

   A. p-node

   B. b-node

   C. h-node

   D. m-node

29. Jim is training a new webmaster, and he wants to emphasize the importance of web servers, database servers, and e-commerce servers that integrate to form his website. How should he categorize these services?

   A. Enterprise

   B. Background

   C. Mission-critical

   D. Foundation

30. Frank is optimizing performance on his web server farm. His boss says that the firewall's intrusion detection alarm went off. What might have set off that alarm?

   A. Use of vmstat by a user other than root

   B. Use of top by a user other than root

   C. Use of port 80

   D. Activation of disk performance counters

   E. A packet sniffer placing a host's NIC in promiscuous mode.

31. Ralph wants to host a second website on his `www.number-one.com` website. He sets up a shared virtual server on port 2222. How can users access this website?

A. `http://www2.number-one.com`

B. `http://www.number-two.com`

C. `http://www2.number-one.com:2222`

D. `http://www.number-one.com:2222`

E. `http://www.number-one.com/2222`

F. `http://www.number-one.com@2222`

32. Mark needs to make a list of the MAC addresses of the computers in his company. Which command can Mark use to gather these statistics without leaving his computer?

A. `ipconfig /all`

B. `ping -a IP_address`

C. `nbtstat -A IP_address`

D. `netstat -A computer_name`

33. Frank is a webmaster. He is concerned that someone is probing his website and poking around to see what directories exist. He reviews the server logs when he comes in on Monday morning. What series of HTTP reply messages would be of greatest interest to Frank?

A. 1xx

B. 2xx

C. 3xx

D. 4xx

E. 5xx

F. 6xx

34. Mark runs out of space on his FTP server. He has additional space on his web server. What can Mark do to use some of the space on the web server for FTP download?

  A. Use port 21 on the web server

  B. Use port 80 on the FTP server

  C. Create an FTP virtual directory that points to a share on the web server

  D. Create an FTP virtual directory on the FTP server

35. Mike is writing a new web-enabled database application. What must he do to enable this application to use SSL?

  A. Compile the application using a block cipher

  B. Nothing

  C. Use ODBC

  D. Download and apply the Netscape SSL API

36. Frank wants to set up a firewall that has minimal impact on network performance and that is a popular choice for high-volume traffic. What type of firewall is Frank talking about?

  A. Packet-filtering firewall

  B. Application-layer gateway

  C. Circuit-level gateway

  D. Proxy server

  E. Intrusion detection system

  F. Encryption

37. Jim has set up an internal CA. He tests the CA using his laptop computer to connect to an ISP and then to his corporate website as if he were a customer. SSL authentication fails. Why?

  A. Jim needs a VeriSign authorization number.

  B. The web server certificate has expired.

  C. Jim's web browser is preprogrammed to recognize only worldwide CAs.

  D. Jim need's to file his CA authorization with the Internet Assigned Numbers Authority.

38. Bart is trying to remember the function of e-mail agents in delivering e-mail. Bart knows that this agent is any e-mail client application with which end users compose, send, and retrieve e-mail. What is the name of the e-mail agent that Bart is trying to recall?

   A. Mail Transfer Agent (MTA)

   B. Mail Delivery Agent (MDA)

   C. Mail User Agent (MUA)

   D. Mail Acceptance Agent (MAA)

39. Mark wants to analyze HTTP server log files. What is the best way to do this?

   A. Online

   B. Offline

   C. In a browser

   D. From the command line

40. Wendy wants her firewall to support FTP, HTTP, and SSL traffic. Which ports should Wendy open?

   A. 21

   B. 25

   C. 80

   D. 119

   E. 443

41. Ralph needs to open ports on his corporate firewall for an e-mail server that uses SMTP to send mail and IMAP4 to deliver mail. Which ports should Ralph open on the firewall for this e-mail server?

   A. 21

   B. 143

   C. 25

   D. 110

42. Mike wants a packet sniffer that will work with both Windows 2000 and Unix/Linux. Which of the following would be a good choice?

    A. tcpdump

    B. Ethereal

    C. Network Monitor

    D. Sniffer Wireless by Network Associates

43. Frank wants to back up all the critical files on his Windows 2000 domain controller. The system partition is on the C drive, and the boot partition is on the D drive. What should Frank back up? Choose three.

    A. System state data

    B. C drive

    C. D drive

    D. Master Boot Record

44. Frank wants to choose a standardized, cross-platform log file format that will work with Apache server and IIS. Which log file format should Frank choose?

    A. W3C Extended Log File Format

    B. NCSA Common Log File Format

    C. ODBC Logging

    D. Microsoft IIS Log File Format

45. On his BIND 9 DNS server, Joe just created a new secondary zone for headquarters.com so that users in his macon.headquarters.com domain will not have to go across a WAN link for name resolution. Joe monitors the WAN traffic, and it is unchanged. Which initialization file does Joe also have to update?

    A. named.boot

    B. named.conf

    C. resolv.conf

    D. rev.headquarters.com

    E. rev.macon.headquarters.com

46. Bart is deciding between buying a block of 254 IP addresses that are valid on the Internet or using NAT and one IP address that is valid on the Internet, while using private IP addresses internally. The benefits of using private network addresses include which of the following?

   A. Requires hosts to access other Internet hosts

   B. Reduces an enterprise's ability to access the Internet

   C. Conserves globally unique IP addresses when global uniqueness is not required

   D. Allows a one-to-one correspondence between the network portion of each client's Internet address

47. Mark runs out of space on his web server. He has additional space on a file server. What, if anything, can Mark do to use some of the file server space for the web server download? Choose all that apply.

   A. Create a virtual directory that points to a share on the file server

   B. Create a virtual IP address that points to a share on the file server

   C. Create a virtual directory that points to the URL of the file server

   D. Create a virtual IP address that points to the URL of the file server

48. George is typing an MX record. Which one of the following fields is *not* required?

   A. Domain name

   B. IN

   C. PTR

   D. MX

   E. Numeric value

   F. Server name

49. Penny and Bill are trying to get information out to a volunteer group that uses their own laptops when they come into work. Their laptops include Windows 98 and Apple PowerBooks. What could they set up so that clients would need only a browser to connect to resources at work?

   A. Internet

   B. Intranet

   C. Extranet

   D. E-commerce

   E. WAN

   F. LAN

50. Which of the following security mechanisms is used most often to detect a security breach as it passes across the network wire?

   A. A host-based IDS

   B. A network-based IDS

   C. A firewall

   D. A proxy server

51. Ginger needs to add a second protocol to her laptop that had been networked using TCP/IP exclusively. She needs to add AppleTalk. She is currently using a built-in NIC. What should Ginger do?

   A. Add a PC Card NIC for AppleTalk

   B. Disable the onboard NIC and install a PC Card NIC for each protocol

   C. Install the second protocol on the same NIC, and set up hardware profiles so that only one protocol is active at a time

   D. Install the second protocol on the same NIC

Answers to Assessment Test

1. **C.** SCSI systems generally provide more reliable service, are faster, and are more scalable than their IDE counterparts. SCSI-3 has a bi-directional data transfer rate of as much as 160Mbps. For information about SCSI systems, please refer to Chapter 2.

2. **D.** The Web Service\Current Anonymous Users counter identifies the number of anonymous users currently on the system. To learn more about System Monitor, refer to Chapter 15.

3. **C.** You can use IMAP to receive e-mail and manipulate e-mail on the server. You can also use POP to receive e-mail, but you can't download headers and then selectively download messages or delete e-mail on the server before it is received on the client computer. To learn more about IMAP, refer to Chapter 1.

4. **A.** Jim is limited by share permissions as well as by NTFS permissions if he attempts to access the file over the network. For information about NTFS permissions in Windows 2000, please refer to Chapter 5.

5. **C.** The first NIC is eth0, and the second NIC is eth1. The dmesg command reports in detail how Linux configured all recognized devices on your system at startup. If you use the command by itself, it will likely give you more information than you need. Instead, use it in combination with a pipe (the | character) and grep. For information on Linux commands, please refer to Chapter 3.

6. **B.** Jim should install linuxconf using the RPM command, which is the quickest and most direct way. For information about Linux administration, please refer to Chapter 6.

7. **A.** Ginger needs the appropriate drivers for each operating system including NIC drivers. For information about NIC drivers, please refer to Chapter 3.

8. C. The newsgroup `microsoft.public.access.macros` has about 150 postings. For information about newsgroups, please refer to Chapter 13.

9. A. Peer-to-peer networks are economical and suitable for workgroups of as many as 10 computers. To learn more about peer-to-peer networks, refer to Chapter 4.

10. B, D. George may not be logged on with an account that has the permission to create shares, or drive C might be formatted with FAT or FAT32 when NTFS is necessary to create file and folder permissions. To learn more about file and folder permissions, refer to Chapter 4.

11. A, C. Mark needs to create and share a `users` folder and designate the `\\users\%username%` variable in each user's home folder during their profile configuration. For information about creating home folders, please refer to Chapter 5.

12. C. The Security log of Event Viewer displays audit events. A key icon represents a successful audit, and a lock icon represents a failure audit. For information about auditing, please refer to Chapter 5.

13. A. Microsoft is the most popular NOS with an established support base, a large pool of available IT professionals skilled in its use, and a wide range of supported applications. For information about network operating systems, please refer to Chapter 2.

14. A, D. You must assign the password separately assigned, and you must create the home directory manually. For information about Linux administration, please refer to Chapter 6.

15. B. Disk duplexing eliminates the problem of a single controller failure. Disk duplexing functions the same way as disk mirroring, but provides a separate controller for each hard disk. For more information on fault tolerance, see Chapter 16.

16. C. The `server ns1.ciw.com` command is the correct `nslookup` command. To learn more about `nslookup`, refer to Chapter 7.

17. D.   At root's workstation, a security inspection team member could, without further ado, change both root's password and any other user's password. If only gbush had left his workstation unattended, a security inspector would have to hack his current password before he could change it. For information about Linux administration, please refer to Chapter 6.

18. C.   Jim should put each FTP site on its own NIC. For information about adding NICs, please refer to Chapter 9.

19. D.   Logging affects system performance. For information on logging, refer to Chapter 14.

20. A, C, D, E.   Backbone services operate in the background and include naming services and directory services, as well as services that provide address management, central logon, and routing. To learn more about background services, refer to Chapter 1.

21. C.   You can use finger to get information about local and remote users. For example, to get information about a user James, use the command `finger james`. For information about using finger, please refer to Chapter 9.

22. A.   DNS provides host name resolution. To learn more about DNS servers, refer to Chapter 7.

23. B.   Mark should create a share. To learn more about shares, refer to Chapter 4.

24. A.   You edit the `httpd.conf` file to configure Apache server as a web proxy server. For information about proxy servers, please refer to Chapter 17.

25. C.   Windows systems allow you to enter 15 characters in a NetBIOS name; the sixteenth character is hidden. For information about Net-BIOS, refer to Chapter 8.

26. C. Linda should use Linux because she will not have to pay a licensing cost for 200 servers. If she had only several servers, the ease of use of NT 4 or Windows 2000 would offset the licensing cost. For information about network operating systems, please refer to Chapter 2.

27. A. The dump command uses the number 0 to denote a full backup. For information about the dump command, see Chapter 16.

28. C. George should use hybrid node on his WINS server so that it will be primary for NETBIOS name resolution and use broadcast node as a backup method by WINS clients. This is the default node type. For information about node types, refer to Chapter 8.

29. C. Jim should categorize these servers as mission-critical. Without any one of them, customers would not be able to order from his website. For more information, refer to Chapter 10.

30. E. Packet sniffers can be used by good guys or bad guys to capture packets as they cross the network. An intrusion detection system could see that a NIC has been placed in promiscuous mode and generate an alarm. To learn more about packet sniffers, refer to Chapter 15.

31. D. Users enter http://www.number-one.com:2222 in their browser. For information on virtual servers, refer to Chapter 11.

32. C. You use the nbtstat -A IP_address command to gather statistics on a remote computer. For information about nbtstat, refer to Chapter 8.

33. D. The 4xx HTTP messages indicate a client error—that the client request contained bad syntax or cannot be fulfilled. Repeated 404 HTTP messages from a website visitor may indicate that a visitor is probing the website. For more information, refer to Chapter 11.

34. D. Mark should create an FTP virtual directory that points to a share on the other server. For information about virtual directories, please refer to Chapter 9.

35. B. SSL sits between the Transport layer and the Application layer of the four-layer TCP/IP model. To learn more about SSL, refer to Chapter 12.

36. A. Frank wants the speed of a packet-filtering firewall that has a small impact on performance. For more information, refer to Chapter 10.

37. C. Web browsers are preprogrammed to recognize only worldwide, third-party CAs such as VeriSign. To learn more about SSL, refer to Chapter 12.

38. B. The MDA agent is any e-mail client application with which end users compose, send, and retrieve e-mail (for example, Outlook Express). For information about e-mail servers and clients, please refer to Chapter 13.

39. B. One major advantage of HTTP server logs is that you can analyze them offline. For information on logging, refer to Chapter 14.

40. A, C, E. FTP uses port 21, and HTTP uses port 80; SSL uses port 443. To learn more about SSL, refer to Chapter 12.

41. B, C. Ralph should open port 25 for SMTP and port 143 for IMAP4. For more information, refer to Chapter 10.

42. B. Ethereal works with many flavors of Unix and Windows 2000. To learn more about packet sniffers, refer to Chapter 15.

43. A, B, C. Frank should back up his C and D drives, plus the system state data. For information on fault-tolerance, refer to Chapter 16.

44. B. Almost all servers produce access log files in a standardized form called National Center for Supercomputing Applications (NCSA). For information on logging, refer to Chapter 14.

45. B. The `named.conf` file is the main initialization file for BIND 8 and 9. It specifies the types, names, and locations of zone files. To learn more about BIND, refer to Chapter 7.

46. C. By using private network addresses, you can conserve global uniqueness by only requiring the addresses be unique within your network. For information about private network addresses, please refer to Chapter 17.

47. A. Mark should create a virtual directory that points to a share on the other server. The file server doesn't have a URL. For information on virtual directories, refer to Chapter 11.

48. C. The five fields of an MX record are domain name, IN, MX, numeric value, and server name. For information about e-mail servers and clients, please refer to Chapter 13.

49. B. Penny and Bill should set up an intranet that provides Internet-based services to browser-based clients within their organization. To learn more about intranets, refer to Chapter 1.

50. B. A network-based IDS is an application that scans all internal network traffic passed over the wire. For information about security, please refer to Chapter 17.

51. D. Multiple protocols can be bound to a single NIC. For information on protocols, please refer to Chapter 3.

Internet System Management

Chapter

1

IT Systems and Services Overview

THE CIW EXAM OBJECTIVE GROUPS COVERED IN THIS CHAPTER:

✓ Identify common IT services related to various hardware platforms and frequently used operating systems, including but not limited to: mission-critical services, system maintenance, connectivity, platform strategies.

In this chapter you will gain an understanding of the duties that systems administrators perform in an *Information Technology (IT)* department. We will look at the tasks that systems administrators perform to maintain and enhance backbone and mission-critical services on local area networks (LANs) and wide area networks (WANs). You will see that these tasks include installing systems, configuring systems, and maintaining systems in order to optimize performance, availability, and responsiveness to users. You will also see that efficiently managing users and groups will allow you to share resources securely in order to maximize the usefulness of your network. This chapter serves as an overview of all these topics, each of which will be developed in later chapters in much greater detail.

The IT department is responsible for administering servers and supporting end users in an organization. As a systems administrator, you may work in an IT department in which each employee is responsible for one specific area, such as installing servers, supporting end users, configuring web servers, configuring e-mail, or maintaining the system. However, it is more likely that you will be required to work in several areas. In a single day, you might install Windows 2000 Server to facilitate file transfer between departments, help an end user check e-mail for the first time, and configure a Linux web server.

The purpose of this chapter is to discuss some of the common systems with which a server administrator will work.

Common IT Tasks and Services

As businesses adopt Internet-based services such as websites and e-mail, IT departments must expand their capabilities to support services and enable businesses to fulfill goals. Therefore, the IT professional's role is to provide the following services:

- Install and configure systems and services
- Support users, which includes troubleshooting applications and managing systems

Table 1.1 lists and describes some of the tasks that an IT department performs. It also lists and describes some of the services you will administer throughout your career as an IT professional.

TABLE 1.1 Common IT Tasks and Services

Task or Service	Description
Install systems	Install and configure an *operating system (OS)*.
Configure a web server	Enable the transfer of information to Internet, intranet, and extranet users via *Hypertext Transfer Protocol (HTTP)*.
Configure and manage an FTP server	Enable the transfer of large files across the Internet using the *File Transfer Protocol (FTP)*.
Configure name resolution	Using the *Domain Name System (DNS)*, the *Windows Internet Naming Service (WINS)*, and *Samba*, provide *local area network (LAN)* and *wide area network (WAN)* naming.
Install and support e-mail servers	Enable communication among users across a LAN or a WAN. Popular e-mail servers include Microsoft Exchange, Unix sendmail, and shareware servers such as EMWAC e-mail server.

TABLE 1.1 Common IT Tasks and Services *(continued)*

Task or Service	Description
Install and support e-commerce servers	Install and maintain settings for services devoted to buying and selling on the Internet using tools such as IBM Net.Commerce and Microsoft Transaction Server E-commerce Edition.
Install and support database servers	Sample database servers include Oracle, Microsoft SQL Server, and IBM DB2.
Manage users	Add, delete, and manage users using Novell, Unix, and Windows 2000 servers. Managing can also include providing (or disabling) user identification services such as finger.
Monitor and optimize servers	Use native programs that help determine optimal usage of CPU, hard drive, and RAM. Such programs include UNIX ps and top and the Performance snap-in in Windows 2000.
Back up files	Use backup programs such as Unix dump and cpio, as well as native Windows 2000 programs such as Disk Administrator, to safeguard against system failure.
Routing	Ensure that messages and packets travel from one user to another in a controlled and timely manner. This function is accomplished with routers, bridges, and switches.
Establish and manage shares	Establishing a share offers space on a server's hard drive to remote users. Unix systems allow access through the use of the *Network File System (NFS)*, whereas Windows 2000 utilizes Microsoft Networking.
Plan LANs and WANs	Network design and planning requires experts in TCP/IP, routing, user management, e-mail addressing, and security.

TABLE 1.1 Common IT Tasks and Services *(continued)*

Task or Service	Description
Manage security	Once the network is operational, qualified individuals must monitor the network for problems. Security issues can include monitoring network routers and servers for various attacks, determining user-level access problems, checking servers for improper permissions, checking logs, and checking the configuration of network servers (e-mail, DNS, web, and so forth).
Manage addressing	Many networks use the *Dynamic Host Configuration Protocol (DHCP)* to ensure that all computers on the network can to communicate on the network. You can configure a special server to assign addresses to client computers.

> The primary difference between a service (that is, a *daemon*) and an application is that a service runs more or less full-time on the "back end" (for example, on a Windows 2000 server or a Unix box). Applications are deployed for specific user tasks, such as checking e-mail, editing a file, or configuring an IP address.

As you can see from Table 1.1, IT departments offer a multitude of services. These services are categorized as either backbone or mission-critical and can be more appropriate for a LAN or a WAN.

Backbone Services

Backbone services provide the foundation for a working LAN or WAN. Because these services generally operate in the background, they are often invisible to users and may be taken for granted until and unless there is a malfunction. That problem may have critical network-wide consequences that must be quickly remedied. Backbone services help organize users by allowing them to work with machines by name rather than by IP address.

Problems with these services can include a failure of client computers to obtain an IP address, the inability to resolve IP addresses to friendly host names, or the inability to locate resources on the network through a central logon to a directory service.

The following is a list of the most essential services:

Naming services   These services include the Domain Name System (DNS), the Windows Internet Naming Service (WINS), and Samba (Samba enables Unix systems to participate in Windows networking). Naming services also include Dynamic DNS (DDNS), which allows DNS automatic name-to-IP address mapping changes. Companies such as TZO (www.tzo.com) offer this service. With the advent of Windows 2000, dynamic DNS has become popular in LANs, as well.

Address management   You can coordinate DHCP servers with naming servers to ensure that all systems have the most current addressing information.

Directory services   These services centralize system resources such as servers, printers, and Internet access. Examples of directory services include Novell Directory Services (NDS), the Windows *NT Directory Services (NTDS)* found in Windows NT 4, and the Windows NT Active Directory found in Windows 2000.

Central logon   This single logon point allows access to additional resources (such as servers, printers, and the Internet). A service of this type lets users maintain a single username and password and yet have access to multiple resources. Examples of central logon services include Windows NT and NIS domains, as well as the *Kerberos* implementations found in Windows 2000 and various Unix flavors (including Linux). Kerberos is a secure method of providing a central logon. Kerberos authentication does not allow passwords to travel across the network and provides granular access to resources on a timed basis.

Routing   Whenever you connect one LAN to another, you can use a bridge, a router, or a switch. A router is the popular connection. You might be asked to configure routers or handle other routing issues.

Mission-Critical Services

Now that we've looked at backbone services, we need to understand mission-critical services. Any service provided by IT is potentially mission critical. Generally, the more visible a system is and the more users depend on it, the more mission-critical the system is. *Mission-critical services* can include the following:

- World Wide Web servers such as Microsoft Internet Information Server (IIS), Apache Server, and so forth

- Database, application, and e-commerce servers (any service designed to collect, gather, and present information across a network)

- FTP servers such as Wu-FTPD and IIS

The best way to identify a mission-critical service is to identify the nature of the business. E-commerce sites focus on web servers and accompanying support servers, including databases and other *middleware*. Middleware is software that extends the capabilities of a web server. Middleware can include Java servlets, application servers, and other servers that let you organize and direct information between an end user and a web server.

For example, when a business wants to provide real-time audio and video, a streaming video server, such as RealServer (www.real.com), becomes mission-critical to that business. You must prioritize the various services your company offers.

E-mail

For many companies, the e-mail server is the ultimate mission-critical service. Mail servers can store, send, and receive e-mail messages using several protocols, including *Simple Mail Transfer Protocol (SMTP), Post Office Protocol (POP)*, and the *Internet Mail Access Protocol (IMAP)*. These three protocols reside at the application layer of the OSI (Open Standards Interconnect) Reference Model. Sometimes, the SMTP and POP3 servers are located on separate machines. Popular mail servers include Netscape Messaging Server and Microsoft Exchange Server. Let's take a look at the e-mail protocols:

SMTP   Is responsible solely for sending e-mail messages. In Unix, for example, the sendmail program activates in response to a command and sends the requested message.

POP   Is the simplest protocol for storing and receiving e-mail messages. It is currently called POP3 because it is in its third iteration. POP responds to a request, asks for the appropriate password, and then downloads the message from the server to the intended recipient, who can then read, delete, or otherwise manage it.

IMAP   Handles messages in a more sophisticated manner than POP by allowing a user to browse and manage files remotely.

End-User Support: Troubleshooting

An often overlooked role filled by IT professionals is that of troubleshooter. An efficient IT professional can assess a problem quickly and has the proper tools to resolve it. Although the IT professional's job is mostly technical in nature, good interpersonal skills are critical for successful interactions with users. Often, in order to isolate the source of a problem, an IT professional must interview a user to find out what changed just before a problem occurred.

User issues can include resetting lost passwords, removing viruses, granting users permissions to resources, and installing, fixing and upgrading software and hardware. We will see that you can use group policy in Windows 2000 to reduce the Total Cost of Ownership (TCO) by standardizing user desktops and automatically installing and upgrading software.

A network administrator must also prioritize tasks based on the number of users affected. Is one user's e-mail down or is the e-mail server down so that all users are affected? If a large number of users are having problems with a certain application, you must isolate, document, and remedy the cause to prevent further incidents.

LAN vs. WAN Services

Many of the services discussed thus far offer a variety of applications depending on the situation. For example, because of security issues, it is not wise to extend NFS or Microsoft shares over Internet connections. Therefore, offer these services from your machine only in a LAN or controlled WAN environment.

In contrast, e-mail, Web, and FTP services apply to almost any environment. You can offer these services within a LAN environment to create an intranet, or you can offer them across the Internet or an extranet. An *intranet* is a network that provides Internet-based services to end users within a specific organization or division within an organization. An *extranet* is a private network shared by organizations or company divisions over a public connection, such as the Internet. An extranet employs a virtual private network (VPN) connection to encrypt transmissions.

System Configuration

As a systems administrator, you must be able to configure both end-user and back-end systems. This configuration includes binding protocols such as TCP/IP to the network interface card (NIC) and checking the status of the communication protocol being used (for example, TCP/IP, NetBEUI, or IPX/SPX). Additional issues include the following:

- Addressing

- Configuring gateways

- Configuring name resolution

- Installing and managing services and applications

- Configuring automated and manual IP addressing

> **NOTE** You can configure clients so that they automatically receive information about addressing, name resolution, and gateways.

These issues permeate the remaining chapters of this book. Chapter 3 is especially helpful to our understanding of IP addressing, and Chapters 7 and 8 focus on how to configure DNS, WINS, and Samba name resolution.

User Management

User management includes adding and removing users from the system and utilizing the applications specific to that operating system. For example, the Computer Management snap-in performs this function in Windows 2000. The Useradd program performs the same tasks in Unix systems. Additional user management issues include the following:

Permissions Can be granted to users over resources that belong to an individual server or over resources that are controlled by a centralized logon server such as a Windows Primary Domain Controller (PDC) or a Kerberos server.

Group membership   The most efficient way to manage user permissions

Password aging   Making a password expire after a certain period of time

Account lockout   Locking out an account permanently or for a certain period of time if a user logon repeatedly fails

Password history   Requiring users not to reuse passwords

Password complexity   Requiring users to use strong passwords

Controlled access   Providing user-level access to directories and files

System Performance

Another IT department function is performance monitoring—determining exactly how a particular system is performing. Performance monitoring involves checking system components, including keeping watch on the following:

- Bandwidth and access rate issues
- System I/O performance, including traffic on the NIC
- Hard drive access statistics, including capacity and access rate
- CPU usage
- Usage of random access memory (RAM)

In Chapter 2, you will learn how to monitor performance in both Windows 2000 and Unix as you implement various internetworking services.

Maintenance and Backup

System maintenance and backup issues are related to performance. Your tasks will include the following:

- Upgrading operating systems
- Installing service packs and hot fixes
- Upgrading services, including web and e-mail servers
- Scanning hard drives for errors
- Upgrading hard drives to provide more storage capacity

A *service pack* is a self-contained, all-inclusive patch designed to bring the Windows 2000 operating system up to the latest vendor-mandated specifications. Most vendors issue service packs regularly (for example, approximately every six months). A *hot fix* is generally a vendor solution for a specific problem. Most vendors issue hot fixes as problems are discovered and solved. Although delivery times vary, hot fixes have been issued within days or weeks of each other. Most of the time, a service pack contains all the relevant hot fixes issued in previous months.

Backup tasks include the following:

- Archiving user-created files, such as Microsoft Word and Excel documents
- Keeping copies of entire operating systems, complete with customized configurations
- Storing changes to databases, as well as other volatile data stores such as human resources and e-commerce databases
- Storing backups offsite to protect data against fires and natural disasters

---

Internet Operating Systems and Platforms

Visit the following sites to learn more about common Internet operating systems and platforms:

www.microsoft.com

www.sun.com

www.redhat.com

www.oracle.com

www.ibm.com

www.apache.org

www.mdaemon.com

www.sendmail.org

www.compaq.com

www.adaptec.com

www.sybex.com

These sites are only a few of those central to deploying Internet servers.

Summary

In this chapter you learned about the services an IT department performs in fulfilling its primary mission of administering servers and supporting end users in an organization. These services include installing and configuring systems and services and supporting users, which includes troubleshooting applications and managing systems.

Among those services, you learned to distinguish backbone and mission-critical services. You learned that backbone services provide the foundation for a working LAN or WAN and that these services include naming services, address management, and directory services. You also learned that mission-critical services are those whose disruption would have an immediate and critical negative impact on the ability of an organization to perform its primary mission. Mission-critical services typically include World Wide Web, database, application, e-commerce, and FTP servers. For many companies, e-mail servers are the ultimate mission-critical server.

Finally, we discussed the IT concepts of system maintenance, including fault tolerance, server optimization, and backup.

Exam Essentials

Be able to identify backbone services, which provide the ability to share, find, and connect to resources. Backbone naming services such as Dynamic DNS, WINS, and Samba provide the ability to find resources by using a host name or a NetBIOS name that is friendlier and easier to remember than an IP address. A central logon to a directory service allows universal access to resources based on permissions. In Windows 2000 and Unix, Kerberos implements security for a central logon.

Specify mission-critical services, the loss of which would immediately disrupt a company's ability to perform key operational tasks. World Wide Web, FTP, database and application services, and e-mail are often key and interdependent elements of a company's business operations.

Key Terms

Before taking the exam, you should be familiar with the following terms:

backbone services	local area network (LAN)
daemon	middleware
Domain Name System (DNS	mission-critical services
Dynamic Host Configuration Protocol (DHCP)	Network File System (NFS)
extranet	NT Directory Services (NTDS)
File Transfer Protocol (FTP).	operating system (OS)
hot fix	Post Office Protocol (POP)
Hypertext Transfer Protocol (HTTP)	Samba
IMAP	service pack
Information Technology (IT)	Simple Mail Transfer Protocol (SMTP)
Internet Mail Access Protocol	wide area network (WAN)
intranet	Windows Internet Naming Service (WINS)
Kerberos	

Review Questions

1. Jonathan is director of Human Resources for Great Escapes. He is advertising for a systems administrator. Which common IT tasks and services will job candidates be expected to perform? Choose the two most common tasks.

   A. Install and configure operating systems and services.

   B. Monitor the contents of user e-mails for appropriateness.

   C. Train and evaluate junior IT personnel.

   D. Design databases.

   E. Support users.

2. Mary runs MostGifts.com, which provides website hosting with a shopping cart for independent gift shops. The independent gift shops must upload their price lists to their individual website and communicate with customers expeditiously. Which services would be mission critical for MostGifts.com? Select all that apply.

   A. Real Player

   B. SQL server

   C. Exchange server

   D. A proxy server

   E. Checkpoint firewall

   F. IIS

3. Edward wants to ensure that his business will survive the failure of a server. When he comes to work in the morning, which element of his system does he always check?

   A. The UPS

   B. The backup logs

   C. Web server configuration

   D. Operating system and service installation and configuration

4. Jason is configuring name resolution for NT 4, Windows 2000, and Linux. Which of the following name servers would Jason configure? Select all that apply.

A. DHCP

B. DNS

C. WINS

D. SMBD

5. Heather's network has grown so that she now has two junior network administrators. Users sometimes complain that they are unable to communicate on the network because they get an error message stating that a duplicate IP address is in use. Which server should Heather implement to minimize IP address conflicts?

A. DNS

B. WINS

C. Active Directory

D. A database server

E. DHCP

6. Jim works as a tutor for eLearning.com. One of his fellow tutors is a principal player in a start-up company and says he could use Jim's talents. He tells Jim that he can't announce what the company does until first-round financing is completed; however he asks Jim if he is familiar with IBM Net.Commerce or Microsoft Transaction Server E-commerce Edition. What can Jim surmise about the startup company?

A. It will be an online training company.

B. It will be well funded.

C. It will be selling a product or a service on the Internet.

D. It will be using Windows XP.

E. It will be using NDS.

7. Jason is concerned about the risk of passwords traveling across the network and the possibility of stolen credentials being reused over a long period of time. Which authentication method will alleviate Jason's concerns?

   A. Kerberos

   B. NTLM

   C. EAP

   D. NDS

   E. IPSEC

8. Mike is part of a large server administration team at Global Interconnect. He is responsible for backbone services. Which of the following statements are true about Mike's duties? Choose all that apply.

   A. His job is secure.

   B. The services he supports operate in the background.

   C. Mike supports naming and directory services.

   D. Mike supports routing.

9. Patrick is looking at third party e-mail servers at www.tucows.com. His boss wants a reasonably priced e-mail server that will not only send mail but allow users to receive mail and manipulate that e-mail on the server. Patrick's boss wants to ensure that if a large message is received before several smaller but more important messages, the large message does not have to be downloaded first. To make this a reality, which e-mail protocols need to be supported on the system? Choose all that apply.

   A. SMTP

   B. POP

   C. IMAP

   D. Daemon

   E. Sendmail

10. Penny and Bill have formed a partnership between their firms and want to exchange encrypted information over a VPN. Which of the following terms describes the secure interchange of information between their companies?

    A. Internet

    B. Intranet

    C. Extranet

    D. E-commerce

    E. WAN

    F. LAN

11. Denise wants to share HR benefits information within her organization with users of diverse computers from manufacturers including Macintosh, Novell, Windows XP, and Linux. All client computers have browsers. Which of the following network technologies should Denise deploy?

    A. Internet

    B. Intranet

    C. Extranet

    D. E-commerce

    E. WAN

    F. LAN

12. Fred wants to administer the access users have to resources and to do so in an organized manner. Which two of the following constructs are most appropriate for this task?

    A. Permissions

    B. Group membership

    C. Auditing

    D. Group policies

    E. Kerberos

13. Rajesh is the only user with administrative rights on his network of 100 Windows 2000 computers. He is concerned about repeated data dictionary attacks against the administrator account in order to hack its password. What should Rajesh do to minimize this risk? Choose the two best answers.

A. Change his password every 60 days.

B. Use a complex password.

C. Rename the administrator account.

D. Set an account lockout duration of 12 hours.

E. Disable the administrator account until needed.

14. Hank's Windows 2000 server has been successfully attacked by a new worm that exploits numerous holes in IIS. What should Hank do to patch these holes?

A. Install a service pack.

B. Apply a hot fix.

C. Use system tools.

D. Use NLM.

15. Jessica just installed Windows 2000 Professional and wants to use Windows Update to fix existing problems and security vulnerabilities. What should Jessica download? Choose all that apply.

A. A service pack

B. A hot fix

C. A driver cache update

D. System tools

E. Driver signing

16. Frank is configuring an Internet server. Users will be downloading large audio files. What server service should Frank set up to enable fast and reliable file download?

A. A file server

B. A web server

C. An FTP server

D. An e-mail server

17. Tom wants the higher security of a central logon using Kerberos, because Kerberos does not allow passwords to travel across the network, and access to resources is granted only for a finite time span. Which servers support Kerberos? Choose all that apply.

A. Unix

B. NT 4

C. Novell

D. Windows 2000

18. Dennis works for a major ISP. He wants a separate set of e-mail servers to send e-mail and a separate set of e-mail servers to receive e-mail in order to distribute the load on the e-mail servers, speed up e-mail processing, and provide scalability for greater e-mail loads. Which services can Dennis separate? Choose two.

A. NNTP

B. POP3

C. SMTP

D. SSL

E. FTP

19. Jessica wants to master the intricacies of the most common web server on the Internet so she can get a position as a Webmaster. What is the most common web server used on the Internet?

A. IIS

B. Apache

C. Netscape

D. Red Hat

20. InternetBank.com wants to create a comprehensive backup policy. Which backup issues of this policy will they address?

A. Offsite storage

B. Archiving user-created files

C. Keeping copies of entire operating systems

D. Storing changes to temporary files

E. Storing changes to databases

Answers to Review Questions

1. A, E.   The IT professional's role is to install and configure systems and services and to support users.

2. B, C, F.   Internet Information Server (IIS) provides a WWW server to offer products for sale on the Internet and an FTP server for gift shops to upload their websites, including price lists, to `MostGifts.com`. The price lists and customer orders would be stored on a SQL database server. Finally, customer orders would be confirmed using a Microsoft Exchange e-mail server.

3. B.   The file backup service provides a disaster recovery method in the event of server disk drive failure.

4. B, C, D.   For name resolution, NT 4 typically uses WINS and DNS. On the other hand, Windows 2000 typically uses Dynamic DNS and can use standard DNS and/or WINS. Finally, Linux and Unix typically use DNS or Dynamic DNS to resolve host names.

5. E.   Heather should implement a Dynamic Host Configuration Protocol (DHCP) server to automatically hand out IP addresses and IP configuration information.

6. C.   E-commerce servers are used to sell products on the Internet. They integrate with web servers and database servers.

7. A.   Kerberos provides a secure central logon. Passwords do not travel over the network, and the access ticket has an expiration time. Kerberos authentication is supported in Windows 2000 and Unix/Linux, but not in NT 4.

8. B, C, D.   Backbone services operate in the background and include naming services and directory services, as well as services that provide address management, central logon, and routing.

9. A, C. SMTP is used to send e-mail, and IMAP is used to receive mail with the additional capability of manipulating e-mail on the server. POP can also be used to receive mail, but without the capability of downloading headers and then selectively downloading messages or deleting mail on the server before it is received on the client computer.

10. C. Penny and Bill have formed an extranet.

11. B. Denise should set up an intranet that provides Internet-based services to browser-based clients within her organization.

12. A, B. Fred should create users, add the appropriate users to groups, and assign permissions to the groups.

13. B, C. Rajesh should rename the administrator account and use a complex password. He wouldn't want to lock this account out for 12 hours at a time. Also, he should change the password more frequently than 60 days. The administrator account cannot be disabled.

14. B. Hank should apply a hot fix downloaded from Microsoft's website. Any patches to disable the new virus have probably not yet been incorporated into a service pack.

15. A, B. Service packs and hot fixes are used to fix known bugs.

16. C. An FTP server enables the reliable transfer of large files across the Internet.

17. A, D. Kerberos authentication is supported in Windows 2000 and Unix.

18. B, C. Dennis should separate the sending service (SMTP) from the receiving service (POP3).

19. B. Apache is the most common web server on the Internet.

20. A, B, C, E. Backup issues include archiving user-created files, keeping copies of entire operating systems, storing changes to databases, and storing backups offsite to protect data against fires and natural disasters.

Chapter

2

Internet System Installation and Configuration Issues

THE CIW EXAM OBJECTIVE GROUPS COVERED IN THIS CHAPTER:

✓ Identify common IT services related to various hardware platforms and frequently used operating systems, including but not limited to: mission-critical services, system maintenance, connectivity, platform strategies.

To administer Internet services, you need to be familiar with the hardware and operating systems that you will be using. You also need to understand the key issues in choosing hardware. Important considerations are memory, I/O card type and quality, network adapter card, RAM, hard drive space, and the speed and number of CPUs.

In this chapter, in addition to looking at how to optimize web servers, we will look at how to provide the sufficient bandwidth to support web server client connections. You will learn the bandwidth provided by common high-speed wide area network (WAN) access methods such as a digital T1 line, a Basic Rate Interface ISDN line, a Digital Subscriber Line (DSL), and cable modems. You will then learn to choose among these options in order to provide the required throughput for users in your organization. Throughput measures how much information must be transferred in a given time in order to satisfy business requirements.

After evaluating server and network hardware including WAN and Internet access devices, we'll explore internetworking operating systems that will affect the nature of services and applications you can use. We'll take a look at network operating systems and hardware vendors, including Microsoft, Unix/Linux, and Novell operating systems installed on Compaq and HP systems. Finally, we'll look at how to configure an installation and how to troubleshoot these network operating systems regardless of the hardware platform.

System Architecture and Hardware

You can have the fastest, most reliable operating system, but your service can be slowed by inadequate hardware. Such a slowdown is called a *bottleneck*. A server connection is only as fast as its slowest component.

In the following sections, you will learn how system architecture affects your ability to provide internetworking services. You will also learn how hardware issues affect your ability to connect to the Internet.

Bus Speed

A computer's motherboard coordinates signals sent from a computer's devices (for example, the hard drive, the network interface card, and so forth). The path on which the data travels is called the bus. *Bus speed* is an important consideration when building an Internet server. Even if you have fast RAM, a fast hard drive, and a fast CPU, the system can still be slowed by the computer's bus.

Motherboards based on Intel Pentium III processors, for example, have bus speeds of 100 and 133 megahertz (MHz); Pentium 4 processors have a bus speed of 400 megahertz (MHz).

System Input/Output

An Internet server's ability to process information internally as well as from the network wire is a paramount concern. An I/O card coordinates the transfer of information among the hard drive, the network interface card, and the motherboard (which houses the CPU). The two most common types of I/O cards are integrated drive electronics (IDE) and Small Computer System Interface (SCSI), each of which we'll discuss next.

Integrated Drive Electronics

An *integrated drive electronics (IDE)* system requires a controller card that interprets instructions processed on the device communicating with it. IDE devices communicate serially. IDE-based systems also require each device, such as a hard drive, to process its own instructions. In other words, IDE devices integrate their ability to process instructions directly on the device.

Enhanced integrated drive electronics (EIDE) is an extension of the original IDE standard that allows faster throughput. Although most of today's computers use EIDE, SCSI is often preferable in high-performance networks.

Small Computer System Interface

Widely used by every system from mainframes to PCs, *Small Computer System Interface (SCSI)* is a parallel interface that allows two devices, such as a hard drive and a scanner, to communicate with the local system simultaneously. The

SCSI computer socket connects SCSI devices such as high-resolution scanners. It supports a transfer rate of up to 160 megabytes per second (MBps), which is significantly faster than the transfer rate of IDE devices.

SCSI allows between 7 and 15 devices to be daisy-chained using one SCSI controller (30 devices can be daisy-chained with two controllers). A SCSI controller is an expansion board that extends SCSI capability to a computer.

SCSI systems generally provide more reliable service, are faster, and are more scalable than their IDE counterparts. However, SCSI systems are more costly. They are also less common, and therefore harder to replace.

Different SCSI standards exist. These include SCSI-1 (standard SCSI) and SCSI-2 (comprising Fast SCSI, Wide SCSI, and Fast/Wide SCSI). The SCSI-3 standard is really a family of standards and is defined in that context. A high-performance server should use Ultra-Wide SCSI I/O cards and hard drives. You can learn more about the SCSI standards at the SCSI Trade Association website (`www.scsita.org`).

Although you may be tempted to buy a less expensive card, purchasing a SCSI I/O card from a reputable vendor is well worth the additional expense.

> **NOTE** Additional connectivity options are available, including Universal Serial Bus (USB) and FireWire. However, these technologies allow you to add peripherals, whereas SCSI and IDE represent fundamental architecture choices.

Ultra Advanced Technology Attainment

Although not a true I/O card, *Advanced Technology Attainment (Ultra ATA)* also referred to as Ultra Direct Memory Access (DMA), is an important extension to IDE devices. Ultra ATA allows higher data transfer speed between a hard drive and the IDE I/O card. Generally, IDE cards communicate at a rate of 16.6 megabits per second (Mbps). Ultra ATA allows data to travel at 33/66/100/133 Mbps. To use Ultra ATA, you must have the following:

- An Ultra ATA–compatible hard drive
- A system BIOS that supports Ultra ATA
- Device drivers that support Ultra ATA
- An IDE card or motherboard IDE controller that supports Ultra ATA

If you have an Ultra ATA hard drive but you do not have a BIOS or an IDE controller that can support it, the drive will default to EIDE or IDE speeds.

The Network Interface Card

As a systems administrator, you will work with different types of networks and *network interface cards (NICs)*. Table 2.1 lists some typical NIC types and their speeds.

TABLE 2.1   NIC Types and Speeds

NIC Type	Speed
Standard Ethernet	10Mbps
Fast Ethernet	100Mbps
Gigabit Ethernet	1,000Mbps
10 Gigabit Ethernet	10,000Mbps
Token ring	Either 4Mbps, 16Mbps, or 100Mbps
100VG-AnyLAN cable	100Mbps

Although high-quality, inexpensive NICs do exist, they can be difficult to find among the many low-end NICs available. Purchasing lower-quality equipment can lead to compatibility and customer service problems, as well as diminished performance. NIC manufacturers include the following:

- 3Com (www.3com.com)
- Intel (www.intel.com)
- Linksys (www.linksys.com)

The Hard Drive

The quality of your hard drive is important. As a systems administrator, you'll need to consider the following hard-drive issues:

- Vendor
- Size
- Search speed
- Access speed

- Caching and buffers

- The number of hard drives you need

For excellent values in hard drives, Maxtor, Seagate, Western Digital, Quantum, and IBM are leading vendors. Seagate's Cheetah hard drives run at 15,000 rpm. Quantum developed the ATA/100 standard. Maxtor has an Ultra ATA/133 drive. Western Digital features a hard drive with an 8MB cache. IBM invented the disk drive and currently distributes an Enterprise Storage Server with an array of hard drives offering a maximum system capacity of more than 22 terabytes.

Hard drive access speed is measured in milliseconds. Generally, the larger the hard drive, the slower the access speed. For example, if you have a 15GB hard drive, a 9-millisecond access time may be acceptable. However, if you have a 100GB hard drive, access speeds will be lower, because the drive will need more time to find data. If you are running a busy web server, increased hard drive access time can lead to overall sluggishness.

If your web server typically transfers many small files, search speed becomes an important indicator of hard drive performance. Caching and buffers significantly decrease both access speed and search speed. Caches typically range from 512KB to 8MB.

You will likely use multiple hard drives. For example, enterprise-strength websites frequently have as many as four drives per host. Utilizing multiple hard drives allows a busy web server to store the paging file and log files on a separate drive or to enable fault tolerance solutions such as RAID (Redundant Array of Inexpensive Disks). In fact, servers dedicated to RAID backup and fault tolerance solutions can have as many as 20 hard drives, but typically web servers will have fewer drives.

Random Access Memory

The amount of random access memory (RAM) your system needs depends greatly on how your system is used. Relevant criteria include the number of users accessing the system, as well as what those users do once they gain access. If they are simply establishing an HTTP (Hypertext Transfer Protocol) connection, they will draw fewer system resources (and therefore need less RAM) than users who launch complex applications.

A web server, for example, might require as little as 64MB of RAM if it hosts a seldom-accessed site (that is, if it gets about 1,000 hits a day). A web server hosting a site that receives 30,000 hits a day might need 256MB of RAM or much more.

Obviously, the amount of traffic you expect will determine the amount of RAM you need. A database server for 1,000 people will require significantly more resources, because the nature of the transaction requires more RAM to process the data. An AS/400 system can be configured with as much as 4,096MB of RAM. However, this case is extreme and suitable only for a high-end e-commerce site or a Lotus Notes server for a large company.

You need to monitor your system's performance and add RAM when necessary. Higher performance may be extracted from newer processors if faster memory is used. If the motherboard is upgraded, a single inline memory module (SIMM) with speeds of up to 133MHz may be replaced with a dual inline memory module (DIMM) with a bus speed of 266MHz or a Rambus DRAM (RDRAM) with a speed of 800MHz.

Moore's Law

Gordon Moore is one of the cofounders of Intel. In 1973, he stated that the number of transistors on integrated circuits doubles every 18 months. This estimate has proven accurate. Consequently, statistics regarding processor speed, RAM, and so forth change rapidly, and you should periodically review the configuration of your servers to insure that they reflect the best available "bang-for-the-buck."

The Central Processing Unit

Two types of CPUs exist: complex instruction set computing (CISC) and reduced instruction set computing (RISC). CISC CPUs include Intel-based systems. RISC CPUs include Sun or Motorola PowerPC chips. Generally, Intel processors are CISC based and use 32-bit memory. The Intel Itanium processor is the company's entry into the 64-bit memory/64-bit internal bus market. You can learn more about these processors at the following URL: http://www.itanium.com. RISC chips use 64-bit memory. As you might suspect, 64-bit chips can process instructions more quickly than 32-bit processors.

In addition, RISC machines cost more. However, this cost is often justified by the efficiency of the system. RISC chips are constructed so that they process instruction sets in a uniform manner. An instruction set contains simple, basic instructions of equal length. Thus, the processor can process simple instructions and then engage in complex tasks. RISC chips generally operate at faster speeds and take only one machine cycle to process instructions (as opposed to several machine cycles in a CISC chip). One of the more popular RISC chips on the market is the Sun SPARC chip. You will learn more about Sun systems shortly.

Additionally, processors differ in the amount of cache memory. A Celeron processor not only has a slower bus speed than a Pentium III processor, but less cache memory. On the other hand, a Pentium III Xeon processor as opposed to a standard Pentium III processor has as much as 2MB of cache memory, so it is an excellent choice for an Internet server that is being pounded with multiple requests for data.

Finally, although AMD K-7 processors may be an excellent value in the desktop market, possible rare incompatibilities with network operating systems limit their use in a server.

> **NOTE** To prevent bottlenecks at the CPU, most production servers have multiple CPUs. Four CPUs is a typical configuration. Multiprocessing allows a busy web server to share tasks, such as database processing or making web transactions, so that the system can handle more requests. You can, of course, have many more than four processors. The IBM NUMACenter platform, for example, handles as many as 64 CPUs.

Bandwidth

*B*andwidth is the total amount of information that can fit on a network wire (sometimes called the network pipe), measured in bits. A company must balance its desire for greater bandwidth for fast data transfers and Internet downloads against its budget. In past years, T1 and fractional T1 lines provided by telephone companies were the overwhelming choices for WAN data transfers. Telephone calls between company locations connected by T-carrier lines could also share this bandwidth, avoiding separate long-distance charges. The downside was the high price collected for these dedicated data lines with guaranteed bidirectional data transfer rates. As companies' interests shifted more toward quickly downloading information from the Internet and providing this ability to many more users in an economical fashion, high-speed, low-cost connectivity options such as cable modems and Asymmetric Digital Subscriber Lines (ASDL) have soared in popularity.

The following section looks at some typical bandwidth speeds, as well as the technologies used to deliver them.

> **NOTE** Do not confuse bandwidth with throughput. Bandwidth describes the total amount of information a specific network connection can carry. Throughput describes exactly how much a network connection is being utilized. For example, a T1 line has a total bandwidth of 1.544Mbps. A particular network, however, might use only a portion of that available 1.544Mbps. When you calculate a network's use of bandwidth, you are calculating throughput. The terms are often used interchangeably, but they are not identical.

Typical Bandwidth Speeds

The following sections discuss standard bandwidth commonly used by businesses and individuals.

T1

T1 is a popular digital leased-line service. It provides a total bandwidth of 1.544Mbps, supporting 24 channels at 64Kbps each (an extra 64Kbps is used for overhead). Each of the channels in a T1 circuit can carry voice and data transmissions.

Fractional T1

Many times, you will need only a portion of a T1 line to obtain sufficient throughput. Fractional T1, also called FT1, allows customers to lease individual channels instead of a full T1 line. Each individual channel is 64Kbps.

To connect a T1 line to your LAN, you need the following systems.

Channel Service Units (CSU) Diagnoses and prepares the signals on the line for the LAN. CSU is the first point of contact for the T1 wires.

Data Service Units (DSU) Connects to the CSU and converts LAN signals to T1 signaling formats.

Multiplexor Provides a mechanism to load multiple voice and data channels into the digital line.

Bridge/router Provides the interface between the LAN and the T1 line.

T2

T2 is an internal carrier specification that is equivalent to four T1 lines. T2 lines provide a bandwidth of 6.3Mbps. T2 is not available to the public.

T3

T3 is equivalent to 28 T1 circuits and provides a total bandwidth of 44.736Mbps. Fractional T3 allows customers to lease less than the full T3 rate.

The digital signal hierarchy used in the United States provides a standard for digital signal levels. Table 2.2 shows this hierarchy with the T-carrier system equivalents.

TABLE 2.2   The Digital Signal Hierarchy Used in the United States

Digital Signal Level	T-Carrier Equivalents	Data Rate
DS0	N/A	64Kbps
DS1	T1	1.544Mbps
DS2	T2	6.312Mbps
DS3	T3	44.736Mbps
DS4	T4	274.176Mbps

Both T3 and DS3 are the equivalents of 28 T1 lines. The seeming discrepancy between the product of 28 multiplied by 1.544Mbps and the product of 672 multiplied by 64Kbps is caused by the frame bit. The frame bit is the overhead required when using the lines for data and voice in multiplexed channels. Once you account for the bandwidth used by the frame bit in each connection, the product is 44.736Mbps.

The European Conference of Postal and Telecommunications Administrations (CEPT) has adopted the E-carrier line speeds as its standard. (See www.cept.org/.) Table 2.3 lists the typical E-carrier speeds that are used in Europe.

TABLE 2.3 E-carrier Line Speeds

Level	Speed
E1	2.048Mbps
E2	8.448Mbps
E3	34.368Mbps
E4	139.264Mbps
E5	565.148Mbps

Integrated Services Digital Network

Integrated Services Digital Network (ISDN) is a digital service that can carry voice, imaging, or data communications. It was intended to replace the Plain Old Telephone Service (POTS) system, using its existing copper wiring, and has since become popular for home and small business use.

ISDN is considered a dial-up service, meaning that each connection must be dialed like a standard analog call. However, because ISDN is a completely digital service, it can provide higher capacity across the phone system's existing wiring.

ISDN offers two service types: Basic Rate Interface and Primary Rate Interface.

Basic Rate Interface (BRI)   Provides three channels of data transfer. Two of the channels carry up to 64Kbps of data and are referred to as B, or bearer, channels. The third channel carries data at 16Kbps and is referred to as a D, or delta, channel. In a typical BRI connection, the two B channels transmit the data, and the D channel manages the link.

> **NOTE** The term *2B+D* is sometimes used to describe a BRI circuit.

Primary Rate Interface (PRI)   Provides a significantly higher amount of bandwidth and divides the equivalent of a T1 line into 24 channels. PRI uses 23 B channels, each capable of carrying 64Kbps, and one 64Kbps D channel to manage the link. ISPs or companies that require multiple ISDN connections normally use PRIs.

ISDN lines require the use of an ISDN terminal adapter (sometimes referred to as an ISDN modem). Connecting an ISDN line (or any other digital phone line) to a standard analog modem might damage the unit.

Digital Subscriber Line

As with ISDN, a *Digital Subscriber Line* (DSL) allows you to transfer data at high speeds over conventional telephone lines. DSL can carry both voice and data, is widely available, and is especially popular with small business and home users. Unlike dial-up connections, DSL connections are always on, which means that incoming and outgoing connections do not have to wait for the modem to build the connection. A DSL modem is not a modem in the technical sense. Whereas a traditional modem converts digital signals from your computer to analog signals to be transmitted over a phone line, a DSL connector transmits digital signals across copper phone lines. Thus, a DSL "modem" is actually a router.

DSL speeds vary much more widely than ISDN speeds. Also, DSL connections are generally discussed in terms of download and upload speed. Common vernacular refers to download speed as downstream speed, whereas upload speed is referred to as upstream." An Asynchronous Digital Subscriber Line (ADSL) allows different download and upload speeds. Download speeds are usually faster than upload speeds, generally due to the nature of the telephone connection used. Also, most users employing DSL spend more time downloading information than uploading it.

Downstream speeds can range from 1.544Mbps to 9Mbps. Remember, upstream speeds are usually slower and typically range from 64Kbps to 768Mbps. The following are some typical DSL speeds:

- 256Kbps downstream, 64Kbps upstream

- 384Kbps downstream, 384Kbps upstream

- 768Kbps downstream, 768Kbps upstream

- 1.5Mbps downstream, 768Kbps upstream

Many other combinations are possible with ADSL. If phone system infrastructure has been upgraded so that ASDL connectivity is available in your area, phone companies and/or ISPs will offer a menu of ASDL speeds and prices tailored to your needs and budget.

One limitation of all varieties of DSL is signal degradation. Although this concept is not unique to DSL, anyone who wants to use DSL must be located within a certain distance of a telephone switch. The distances vary, although with some versions of DSL, a client must be within five to seven miles of a switch. Some DSL variants allow distances greater than seven miles from a DSL-compatible switch. Generally, the DSL provider will conduct a line test to determine whether a business or home can handle a DSL connection. Sites such as www.everythingdsl.com provide connectivity information, as well as bandwidth tests. Generally, such sites provide current databases with real-time information to help you determine whether a home or business can have DSL access.

Many DSL companies require that the computer support a special protocol called *Point-to-Point Protocol over Ethernet (PPPoE)*. Most DSL companies provide their own binaries that enable this protocol. Although most DSL providers will not support Linux systems directly, the Roaring Penguin Software site (www.roaringpenguin.com) provides a binary that allows most Linux systems to become PPPoE clients.

You can learn more about DSL at www.dsl.com.

Cable Modems

Another way to provide bandwidth is through a cable modem. Cable connections are similar to xDSL connections, with the following differences:

- Cable connection speeds generally vary over time. During higher-volume periods, speeds tend to be slower than during lighter times.

- Many cable companies divide their networks into physical segments, which subdivide the large network they manage. Your neighborhood or apartment complex, for example, might have its own network segment. The general rule is that a higher number of connections on a segment can radically slow connection speeds. DSL connectivity does not usually fluctuate in this way.

- The cable modem acts as a router, just like an xDSL modem. However, in this case, the modem uses existing cable connections, rather than the telephone line.

- Cable modems generally do not require PPPoE support.

- This technology does not depend on proximity to xDSL-enabled switches. It does, however, depend on whether the business or home has cable access.

Dynamic Host Configuration Protocol (DHCP)

Most companies that provide high-speed access to businesses and homes use *Dynamic Host Configuration Protocol (DHCP)* to manage IP addresses. DHCP allows networks to conserve IP addresses and exercise more control over services they offer customers. Once one business customer shuts down his system, another customer's computer can receive this now-unused IP address and participate on the network.

Calculating Throughput

You now understand some of the choices concerning bandwidth. Your next step is understanding throughput. *Throughput* determines the amount of bandwidth a network needs to conduct its business. As an IT professional, you will often have to calculate how much of your available bandwidth is in use. You might also have to determine how much bandwidth you will need in the future.

Throughput is the amount of a network connection that is actually being used. Throughput is measured in terms of connection speed (that is, bandwidth), amount of information to be transferred (for example, the size and number of HTML pages, images, and e-mail messages that pass over the connection), and the time available to transfer this information. Once you understand the throughput, you can determine how much bandwidth your network must have to conduct its business efficiently (called bandwidth utilization).

> **NOTE** One analogy that helps differentiate between bandwidth and throughput is a pipe used to transfer water. Bandwidth is the actual size of the pipe. Throughput is the measurement of the amount of water flowing through that pipe over a given amount of time.

Determining Connection Speed and Performance

To determine the required bandwidth and wisely choose the appropriate connectivity device and level of service that is needed to meet business needs, you must accurately determine the throughput required to download a certain amount of data in a given time period. For instance, if your business needs to be able to download the latest 800MB kernel of Red Hat Linux within 4 hours, you need to be able to calculate the required throughput to yield the required download time.

To determine download time, use the following simple formula:

Download time = file size / connection speed

In this formula, the units of measurement above and below the division line must be the same, either bits or bytes. (Remember that 1 byte equals 8 bits.) We'll look at some examples of how to use this formula in the next section.

Converting Kilobytes and Megabytes to Bits Per Second

A 1-kilobit (Kb) connection is 1,000 bits. A 1-megabit (Mb) connection is 1 million bits. You need never convert either of these figures to calculate bandwidth or throughput. However, most connection speeds and document sizes are provided in kilobytes (KB) and megabytes (MB). For example, it is accurate to refer to a standard modem sold at most stores as being a 56-kilobyte (KB) modem.

You calculate most connection speeds in terms of bits per second. You must convert all document sizes and connection speeds, including those measured in kilobytes (KB) or megabytes (MB), into bits.

The following examples show how to convert all units to bits and then determine how long it will take to download a 25MB file over several connection speeds.

NOTE The connection speeds in these examples are theoretical because they do not take into account network latency and congestion.

Example 1

To download a 25MB file over a T1 connection (1.544 Mbps), make calculations as follows:

25MB in bits = $25 \times 1{,}024 \times 1{,}024 \times 8 = 209{,}715{,}200$ bits

1.544Mbps in bits = 1,544,000 bits per second

Download time = 209,715,200 / 1,544,000 = 135.83 seconds

In this example, you must first convert 25 megabytes to bits. To do so, you multiply 25 by 1,024, which is the actual number of bytes in a kilobyte. You then multiply that product by 1,024 again to convert the file size from megabytes to kilobytes. You multiply by 8 because there are 8 bits in a byte.

Example 2

To download a 25MB file over a 256Kbps connection, make calculations as follows:

25MB in bits = 25 × 1,024 × 1,024 × 8 = 209,715,200 bits

256Kbps in bits = 256,000 bits per second

Download time = 209,715,200 / 256,000 = 819.2 seconds

Example 3

To download a 25MB file over a 64Kbps connection, make calculations as follows:

25MB in bits = 25 × 1,024 × 1,024 × 8 = 209,715,200 bits

64Kbps in bits = 64,000 bits per second

Download time = 209,715,200 / 64,000 = 3,276.8 seconds

Assessing Network Bandwidth Needs

In an ideal world, you could download data as fast as your Internet or network connection will allow, and the above formulas would always be valid. In the real world, you are also constrained by the amount of bandwidth that a web server or a network server has to divide among the users. For instance, if you have a cable modem that can download a copy of a 180MB copy of the Microsoft Official Curriculum for a particular course in only two hours, but the download will really take 12 hours, you are being limited by the available bandwidth of the Microsoft web server. You just learned how to determine download times for a given file. However, you also need to determine how much bandwidth your network servers need. Before you begin, it is helpful to categorize your requirements, as follows:

Applications   Remote user logon and database replication (for example, DNS and WINS)

Type of file to download Web and FTP transactions, office documents, database connections, images, and streaming media

As a server administrator, you must determine how much bandwidth your servers need to accommodate the number of connections they must handle. The following factors determine your site's bandwidth requirements:

Type of connection You have already learned about the common connection speeds.

Document complexity A large graphic or streaming video session will take longer to download than a simple text file.

Average and peak number of connections Traffic across a network will be busier at certain times of the day than at others.

> **NOTE** Do not confuse the term *bits per second* with *baud*. Bits per second is the accepted rate of measurement for network bandwidth. Baud is an older term that actually measures the rate at which a carrier signal changes its value; this term should be avoided.

Average and Peak Connections

Connections to Internet, intranet, and extranet servers are not consistent. You will have to examine the web server logs for the average and peak number of users connecting and the average amount of data downloaded in order to create a baseline of activity. This baseline is useful if you know that in the next year the number of users will be doubling and the number of websites hosted will be tripling. You can then make an educated guess about the future needs of your business.

If you administer a web server, for example, you can determine the average number of connections from your site logs. The average hit rate is simply the number of hits in a given day divided by 24 (the number of hours in a day). If you receive 2,000 hits a day, your average hit rate would be 83 an hour. If your site received 1 million hits a day, the rate would average 41,667 hits an hour. You determine the peak hit rate by checking your logs and finding the largest number of simultaneous hits in any given hour. By tracking these figures daily, you can determine peaks and lulls in site usage. These patterns can then help you determine whether you need more powerful servers or more bandwidth.

Impressions vs. Hits

Impression is a term used to describe the process of downloading the contents of a page. An impression is different from a hit because an impression counts all the contents of a particular page as one. Say, for example, a client downloads a page that contains some HTML text plus four images. This page is one impression; however, this single impression counts as five hits, because the client is downloading five separate items.

Calculating Throughput to Determine Necessary Bandwidth

You have already seen how to convert bytes to bits. The next step is only the first in a longer process of estimating necessary bandwidth. The ability to estimate bandwidth is important to network planners because it helps ensure that a company or an organization purchases adequate bandwidth and equipment. However, to estimate bandwidth, you must first calculate throughput. Following is a description of the process.

Suppose your Web site gets 100 impressions in a day. Each user downloads files (HTML, images, and so on) that add up to 46KB. To determine the required bandwidth, follow these steps:

1. Take the total document size (46KB). Because this document is given in kilobytes, you must convert the number of bytes into bits by first multiplying 46 by 1,024 (the number of actual bytes in 46KB), then again by 8 (the number of bits in a byte). The result is 376,832 bits.

2. Multiply 376,832 (the size of the page each user downloads in bits) by 100 (the number of impressions in a day) to get 37,683,200.

3. Divide this figure by 86,400 (the number of seconds in 24 hours). The result is 436.149, which averages 436 bits per second. Using this figure, you can determine the line speed required to handle this traffic volume.

4. According to the calculation in step 3, you can serve this one page to 100 people with a simple ISDN line or even a 56,000Kbps modem.

This example is rather modest. Many websites receive more than 100,000 hits a day. Also, users will download more pages, increasing the total document size. Thus, you may have to calculate for megabytes.

You can alter this formula to calculate the amount of bandwidth required over a particular period. For example, you can use the number of seconds in an eight-hour period (28,800) to determine possible peak times.

These calculations are theoretical in the sense that they do not account for issues that the carrier may encounter, including line noise, router congestion, and overhead imposed by networking protocols such as TCP/IP.

Evaluating and Recommending Connection Speeds

When determining the ideal connection speed for a particular usage, remember to consider the costs against your usage requirements. For example, if you are installing a system that 15 people on 15 separate machines will use to browse the World Wide Web and send and receive e-mail, you probably will not need a T1 line. A simple ISDN or DSL connection would be suitable.

Packet Loss

Whenever a network transaction occurs, some packets are dropped and must be resent. The busier the connection, the greater the loss rate. You calculate this rate as follows:

1. Determine the number of packets you have lost.

2. Divide this number by the number of packets you have sent.

Using the Windows 2000 `pathping` utility, you might see a 5 percent packet loss even on a small LAN. Packet loss rate is one element of determining network latency, which is the time it takes for a transaction to occur. Latency is caused by services and servers that must first process information and then pass it back to the host. For example, if you communicate with a web server, and the web server then communicates with a database, latency results as the packet is transferred between these hosts. Do not confuse latency with congestion, which is a term that applies to overburdened routers.

Internetworking Operating Systems

The type of operating system you use will directly affect its ability to participate on a network. Your operating system will also affect the nature of the services and applications you can use. Of the many different operating systems, Windows, Unix, and Novell systems are the most popular. Each has its own strengths, although Microsoft's Internet Information Server (IIS) and Unix/Linux's Apache web server are currently the most popular Internet servers. In the following sections, we'll briefly discuss each system.

The Microsoft Windows Family

Microsoft Windows New Technology (NT) is a family of network operating systems dating from 1993. It is widely implemented. The current version is Windows 2000; however, the previous version, Windows NT 4, is still in prominent use. Windows XP, an incremental upgrade to Windows 2000, is also available.

Windows NT 4 and Windows 2000 use TCP/IP as the default network protocol, and both have a user interface similar to Windows 9x/Me. Following is a chronology of network-aware Windows operating systems:

- Windows NT 3.1 (1993)
- Windows NT 3.5 (1994)
- Windows NT 3.51 (1995)
- Windows NT 4 (1996)
- Windows 2000 (2000)
- Windows XP (2001)

Whenever you log on to Windows 2000 Server, you run a logon shell called explorer.exe, which you can customize. Once you log on, you can execute programs and services. Figure 2.1 shows an example of the Windows 2000 Server shell.

> **NOTE** Logging on locally is often referred to as logging on interactively. Logging on interactively is the opposite of logging on to a system remotely.

Unix

Unix was first developed in 1969, and its evolution continues today. Many versions have grown from the original *kernel*. A kernel is a part of an operating system that provides basic services and resides within the memory of the operating system. Unix is a multiuser operating system that most non-PC networks today use as a network operating system. Almost all hardware vendors include Unix as a primary or secondary operating system; however, Microsoft Windows dominates the end-user market.

Unix consists of a kernel, a file system, and a *shell*, which is a command-based interface. Because Unix uses more than 600 commands, its programmers developed *Graphical User Interfaces (GUIs)* to simplify Unix operations. (For the same reason, Microsoft Windows was originally developed to simplify command-based DOS operations.) For example, the X Window System, a windowing system used with Unix, is enhanced by the KDE or Motif GUI. Unix uses TCP/IP as its core networking protocol, although it can support additional protocols, if necessary.

Popular Unix versions are Red Hat Linux, Sun Solaris, Digital Unix, Hewlett-Packard HP-UX, Santa Cruz Operation (SCO) UnixWare, and the IBM AIX. Many IBM mainframes run Unix.

FIGURE 2.1 A sample Windows 2000 Server desktop

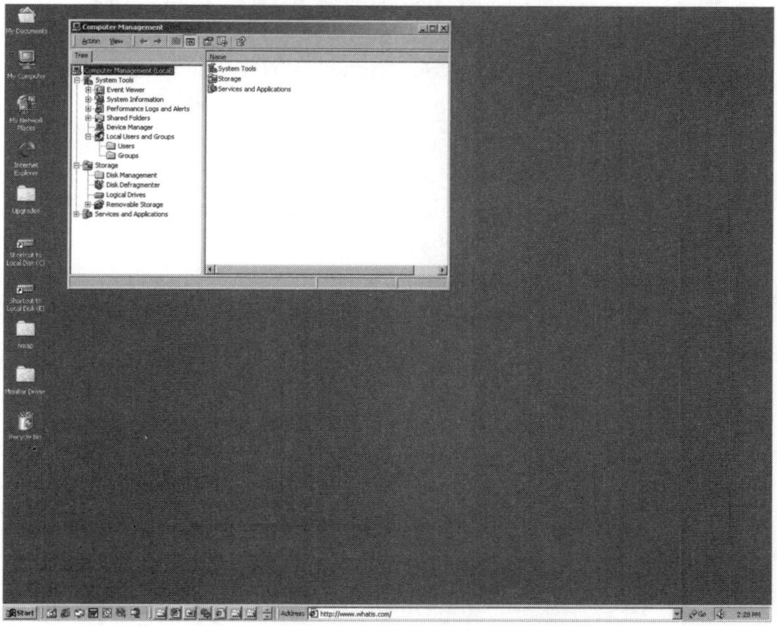

System V and Berkeley Systems Distribution

Over the years, several companies and organizations got involved in Unix development. By the 1980s, two strands of Unix—AT&T and Berkeley—developed in parallel. The Berkeley strand was adopted by Sun Microsystems, which used the Berkeley code as the basis for its SunOS operating system. IBM and Hewlett-Packard (HP) chose the AT&T version. By the late 1980s, several groups of companies (for example, AT&T and Sun versus IBM, HP, and Digital Equipment Corporation) formed associations with the goal of producing a single Unix standard. This effort failed. However, the AT&T and Sun alliance produced Unix System V, which is still in use today. Solaris (www.sun.com) is the most popular example of a System V system. It has become the de facto standard in the Internet space due to its stability and support from vendors such as Oracle (`www.oracle.com`).

Other versions of System V include the following:

- Hewlett-Packard HP-UX

- IBM AIX

Another standard developed around the Berkeley Systems Distribution (BSD). Examples of the BSD implementation include FreeBSD, NetBSD, and SunOS.

FreeBSD has a reputation for stability and security, mainly because its developers made these characteristics a priority during the development process. (You can learn more about FreeBSD at `www.freebsd.org`.) NetBSD is available at `www.netbsd.org`. Both have become popular with Internet Service Providers (ISPs). Each is free and is designed to run on several architectures, including Intel, Alpha, and Sparc.

Although Sun intended Solaris to entirely replace SunOS, both the SunOS and the Solaris operating systems (see `www.ocf.berkeley.edu/solaris/versions`) are still in use today because customer demand continued for the fee-based SunOS.

The main differences between System V and BSD include the following:

Location and name of files Although both use the /etc directory, each Unix version has its own variations.

Command names To print, for example, System V uses the `lp`, `lpstat`, and `lpadmin` commands. BSD systems use `lpr`, `lpq`, and `lpc`.

Packet processing Each operating system processes packets differently. The Berkeley Packet Filter (BPF) system in FreeBSD is the fastest. For this reason, some sites prefer to use FreeBSD rather than System V-based servers, such as Linux.

Additional Unix Distributions

Many additional versions of Unix exist. Varieties include the following:

- IRIX from Silicon Graphics (`www.sgi.com`).

- SCO from the Santa Cruz Organization (`www.sco.com`). SCO has existed for years as an Intel-based version of Unix, but it is not as popular as Linux.

- AIX by IBM (`www.ibm.com`).

- HP-UX by Hewlett-Packard (`www.hp.com`).

Unix Shells

Internet services are configured in the Unix shell. Many Unix logon environments, or shells, exist. The most common include the following:

sh (the Bourne shell)   This shell was the original shell program. It has the smallest feature set, but is the most widely available shell. Because of its universality, the Bourne shell is a good choice for shell programming. Because of its limitations, however, one of the other shells is a better choice for interactive work.

ksh (the Korn shell)   This shell is widely available on machines running versions of System V Unix. The Korn shell is an extension to the Bourne shell, adding command-line editing, job control, and more programming options.

csh (the C shell)   The programming constructs in this shell are intended to resemble the C programming language. Once popular, it is less widely used now with the evolution of System V Unix. Many sites using the C shell also offer an extension called tcsh.

bash (the Bourne Again shell)   This shell was developed by the GNU (GNUs Not Unix) software project and is freely distributed on the Web. It is similar to the Korn shell in most respects and is fully compatible with the Bourne shell. The *bash* shell is distributed with Linux.

Linux

Linux is a hybrid of the System V and BSD systems. Linux is popular for several reasons: it is free, it runs on Intel processors, and it is quite stable. Also, Linux is not supported by any one vendor or company. Linux is an ideal example of the *open source movement*, which is a largely informal group of developers who create freely available applications, services, and operating systems.

Although Linux systems have become increasingly popular over the last few years, they have been the most effective as dedicated DNS (domain name service) platforms or web servers. Oracle and IBM have adopted Linux, however, and have ported their database servers to Linux. Linux promises to become a popular, if not dominant, operating system in IT departments.

You can obtain the Linux kernel for free, although several vendors package and resell it along with a few value-added items. Such distributions include the following:

Red Hat (www.redhat.com)   The most popular distribution of Linux.

Debian (www.debian.org)   This distribution is supported by a non-profit organization led by Deborah and Ian Jacobs.

Caldera Systems (www.calderasystems.com)   This distribution has become popular because it sells specialized Linux versions. For example, its operating system helps implement load clustering, which is the ability to distribute incoming requests among several servers. Such distribution, or clustering, allows several systems to work together as one.

SuSE Linux (www.suse.com)   Popular in Europe, this German-based distribution has also shown its strength in the server space.

Slackware Linux (www.slackware.com)   Considered the "original Linux" in many circles, this distribution has tried to remain close to its Unix roots.

You can learn more about Linux at the Linux System Labs website (www.openlinux.com).

Local Unix Logon and the X Window System

Traditionally, Unix systems have used a command-line interface. However, many GUI desktops have been developed for Unix. These are established through the X Window System. When properly configured, this system allows you to start a server and then access it with a client. Much of the time a client accesses the server locally. You can also start and administer an X Window System over a network.

X Window System interfaces include the following:

K Desktop Environment (KDE)   For more information about this desktop, visit www.kde.org.

Ximian GNOME desktop   Figure 2.2 shows a typical Gnome desktop. For more information, visit www.ximian.org.

BlackBox   A simple desktop, written in the C++ language, that loads quickly. For more information, visit http://draknor.net/kbb/howto/.

AnotherLevel   A generic desktop manager often used as a fallback when others are not working or are not present (`www.redhat.com`).

Common Desktop Environment (CDE)   Also found in Solaris systems, this desktop allows you to conduct remote sessions.

Failsafe mode   A simple command-line interface, and not a GUI. Failsafe mode is universal to Unix systems.

> The full server installation of Red Hat Linux does not provide X Window System support. Therefore, it is vital that you learn how to use the Linux command line.

FIGURE 2.2   The Gnome desktop

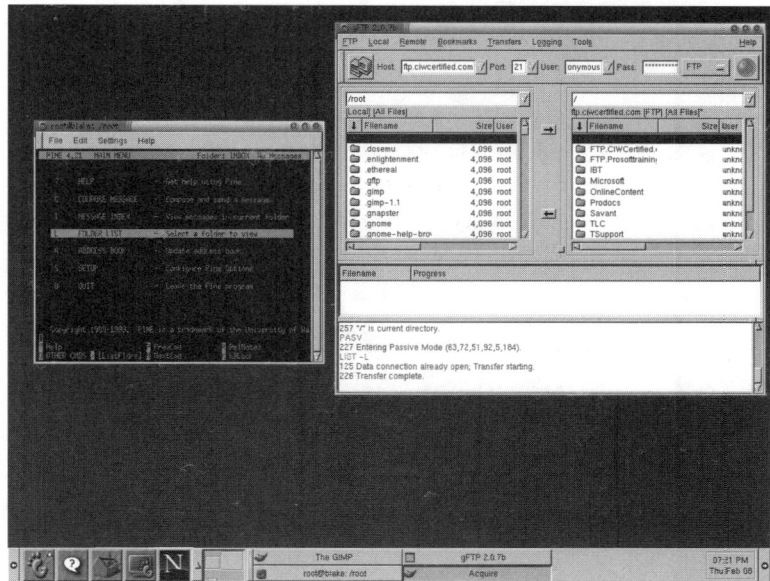

Remote Unix Logon

One of the strengths of the Unix system is that you can administer it remotely. Figure 2.3 shows a logon session in which a user first logs on to a Red Hat Linux server and then assumes root (that is, administrative) privileges.

FIGURE 2.3 Logging on to a Linux server remotely using Telnet

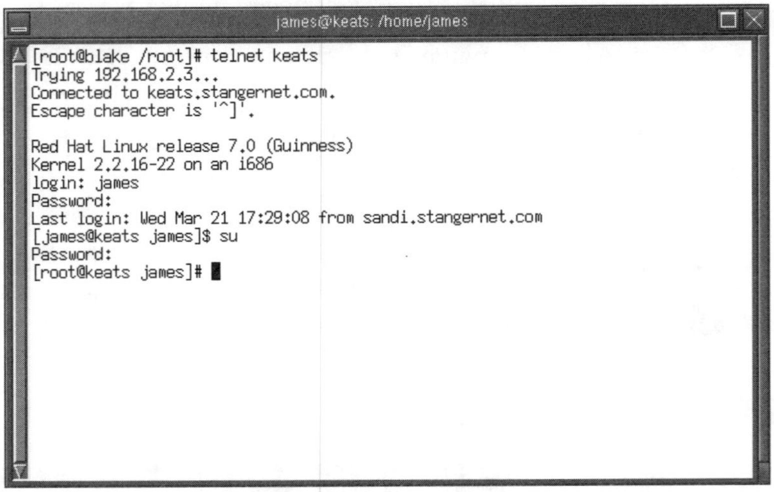

```
[root@blake /root]# telnet keats
Trying 192.168.2.3...
Connected to keats.stangernet.com.
Escape character is '^]'.

Red Hat Linux release 7.0 (Guinness)
Kernel 2.2.16-22 on an i686
login: james
Password:
Last login: Wed Mar 21 17:29:08 from sandi.stangernet.com
[james@keats james]$ su
Password:
[root@keats james]# 
```

In Chapter 9, you will see that Windows 2000 introduced a native Telnet server. A popular and more secure alternative to Telnet is Secure Shell (SSH), which encrypts all data transmissions. You can learn more about Secure Shell at www.secureshell.com and www.openssh.com. Windows 2000 uses its Kerberos-based authentication system to provide a secure Telnet logon. However, a Windows-based SSH server is available at www.ssh.com.

Novell NetWare and NDS

Novell NetWare is a family of network operating systems that began in 1989, and before Windows NT 4 (1996) and Windows 2000 grew in popularity, Novell NetWare was the most widely installed *network operating system (NOS)*. Implementations of NetWare through NetWare 3.*x* required a logon to each individual NetWare server. Later versions of NetWare, starting with NetWare 4.*x*, required only a single logon to Novell Directory Services (NDS), which allows universal access to resources, based on permissions, and single seat administration. The most recent version is NetWare 5. Before NetWare 5, NetWare was a proprietary NOS that communicated using the Internetwork Packet Exchange (IPX) protocol, the Sequenced Packet Exchange (SPX) protocol, and the NetWare Core Protocol (NCP). These protocols were necessary for all network computers to communicate.

NetWare 5 supports TCP/IP (Transmission Control Protocol/Internet Protocol) as its networking protocol and Java as its application language.

Because TCP/IP is the protocol of the Internet, and because Java is a programming language that operates across platforms (for example, Windows, Unix, and so on), NetWare 5 is more flexible than its predecessors.

Novell systems provide an extremely powerful centralized logon service called Novell Directory Services (NDS). Like a good telephone book or directory that tells you where everything is, NDS lets you map out your network. NDS also lets you manage many different server types in an easy-to-browse, hierarchical directory structure. Consequently, IT employees can administer Unix, Windows, and Novell systems from a central point, and end users can access services via one method, such as the Windows Me Network Neighborhood application.

NDS terminology is quite simple. An NDS organization is a company or a division. Several organizations compose an NDS tree. An NDS tree can contain organizational units (OU). An OU can be a specific department, such as human resources or research. A tree can contain several OUs. In NDS terminology, a leaf can be any of several elements, including the following:

- User

- Group

- Server

- Share

- Computer

- Printer and print server

Choosing an Operating System

When choosing a network operating system, you must evaluate performance and benefits against the licensing, training, and support costs. With a consumer operating system, training and end-user support costs may be the most important considerations. With a network operating system that supports a server taking millions of hits a day, these costs are less significant. Performance, stability, scalability, and licensing costs may well be the most important considerations.

Depending on your needs, your choice of a network operating system may well hinge on the following:

Ease of use   Traditionally, Unix systems have required more technical knowledge on the part of systems administrators than other operating systems because much of the administration is based on cryptic commands with multiple switches executed at the command line. Administration is relatively easy in Windows 2000 Server because of the graphical user interface and wizards that step you through common tasks. Because the same desktop layout is used in the Windows family of consumer operating systems and network operating systems from Windows 9*x*/Me through Windows 2000 Professional and Server, finding administrative tools is easy.

Platform stability   Operating system stability is highly desirable; however, it comes at a price. For example, stable platforms are traditionally more difficult to use and more costly than platforms that tend to crash and have other problems.

Available talent pool   Windows 2000 has become popular as a result of the Microsoft Certified Systems Engineer (MCSE) training program and its marketing strength. Consequently, the pool of competent Windows 2000 systems administrators exceeds that of Unix or Linux systems administrators. Linux certification and training programs such as the Red Hat Certified Engineer Program seek to increase the number of available skilled Linux professionals.

Available technical support   Your IT department needs to access technical support information quickly. Companies such as Sun, Hewlett-Packard, Red Hat, Compaq, IBM, and others provide technical support for Unix, but be aware of charges for these services.

Licensing Costs   The cost of Windows 2000 Server licenses is substantially higher than licensing costs for Linux and most Unix network operating systems. As a result, there are almost twice as many Unix/Linux-based Apache web servers as there are Microsoft IIS web servers on the Internet.

Hardware costs   Many operating systems, such as Sun, AIX, and HP-UX, can require more expensive hardware than Windows 2000 or Linux. Although Intel-specific versions of Solaris exist, RISC-based solutions are considered more stable. However, RISC solutions are significantly more expensive.

Some operating systems come preinstalled with certain servers. Carefully consider the type of hardware that best suits your needs, because it may help determine the type of operating system that you use.

Availability of services and applications   Many operating systems will not run the services and applications you need. For example, if you want to use Microsoft IIS, you will need to use Windows 2000. If you want a highly stable operating system that will run a Java virtual machine (JVM) to connect to a database, you might consider Sun, which developed the JVM and seamlessly integrated it with its Solaris operating system.

Purpose of the server   As you weigh costs and other issues, consider the actual purpose of your server. If all you require is a simple DNS server for your LAN, Linux may be sufficient. It is a free, relatively stable operating system. However, if you require a database server for web transactions and Java servlets, a Solaris system may be a better choice.

Company policy may dictate which operating systems the IT department can use. For example, one site may mandate the use of Windows 2000 for all solutions. This, of course, makes your decision much easier!

Popular System Vendors

Now that you've decided which NOS is the perfect fit for your organization, the next step is to select the perfect hardware platform. Although price is often the overriding factor in choosing a personal computer, supportability and stability are often the preeminent concerns in choosing an Internet server platform vendor. You'll probably prefer to work with a mainstream vendor rather than vendor that can provide a custom-built system of unknown reliability. Mainstream platform vendors include Compaq, IBM, Dell, Sun Microsystems, and Hewlett-Packard. Many others exist, including Rave Systems (`www.rave.com`) and VA Linux (`www.valinux.com`). Following is a discussion of two popular platforms.

Compaq

Compaq ProLiant servers are quite popular, including the following:

ProLiant DL590/64   This rack-mounted system runs quad 800MHz Intel Itanium Processors, with at least 4,096MB of RAM with as much as 146GB of SCSI hard drive storage at up to 15,000 rpm.

ProLiant 8000 This tower system runs eight 700MHz Intel Xeon Processors, with at least 1,028MB of RAM with as much as 764GB of SCSI hard drive storage at up to 15,000 rpm.

> **NOTE** You can learn more about Compaq servers by visiting www.compaq.com/products/servers/platforms/#.

IBM

IBM sells systems that use both RISC and CISC (Intel) CPUs. These include the following:

- RS 6000
- AS/400
- NetFinity
- NUMACenter

You can learn more about IBM servers at www.ibm.com.

Installing Network Operating Systems

You can choose a server with a preinstalled network operating system that you can configure for DNS, web, or database utilization For instance, you can buy an IBM WebSphere Application Server with an integrated package of IBM software, scaled to your e-business needs, preinstalled on IBM hardware. More commonly, however, you will have to install the operating system yourself. In the following sections, we'll discuss some of the issues you'll confront when installing your NOS.

Listing System Components

As you prepare to install a system, it is helpful to list all system components on a separate piece of paper. You will then have the information readily available as you continue your installation. Exercise 2.1 demonstrates how you can organize this information.

> Although this particular discussion focuses on installing operating systems, consider writing down relevant information when installing other services as well.

Gathering Information

You can gather information about a system in the following ways:

- By checking the system documentation
- By opening the machine and getting the information from each internal component
- By booting the system into another operating system and using its tools to gather the necessary information

EXERCISE 2.1

Preparing for a System Installation

After determining hardware compatibility, you must determine the best installation method. You will then determine exactly which type of hardware you will install. In this exercise, you will determine the installation method and investigate your hardware.

1. From the following list, choose the installation method best suited for your application.

   Boot disk

   Bootable CD-ROM

   Network (HTTP, FTP, and so on)

2. Do you plan to use a dual-boot configuration (yes or no)?

3. Do you need an MS-DOS disk?

4. If you are installing Linux, will you use a text or GUI installation?

5. In the appropriate blanks, list the devices on your system.

   Device

   Description: _____

   Hard Drive

   Number: _____

   Size: _____

   Type (SCSI, IDE, and so on): _____

   CD-ROM

   Type (SCSI, IDE, and so on): _____

   IDE or SCSI Adapter(s)

   Vendor and model: _____

   Type (SCSI or IDE): _____

   Vendor: _____

   Model number: _____

   NIC

   Vendor: _____

   Model number: _____

   Mouse

   Type (generic, three-button, PS/2): _____

   Monitor

   Vendor: _____

   Model number: _____

   Video Card

   Vendor: _____

   Model Number: _____

EXERCISE 2.1 *(continued)*

Amount of RAM: _____

IP Address(es): _____

Netmask: _____

Default Gateway: _____

Domain Name: _____

Host Name: _____

Kerberos Domain: _____

In Exercise 2.1, you reviewed the essential steps for installing an operating system. If possible, find an extra system and install Windows 2000 and/or Red Hat Linux.

If possible, create a dual-boot system. First, completely format the hard drive so that it is blank. Then, create two partitions: one for Windows 2000 and one for Red Hat Linux.

As you install the systems, identify points when it would become difficult to install the operating system if the operating system did not support the hardware. Also, notice that you apply essentially the same concepts on both operating systems (for example, IP addresses, DNS addresses, default gateways), but in different ways.

Hardware Considerations

As you prepare to install your operating system, you must know all relevant hardware information. This task involves checking your system to determine whether your hardware can support the planned installation. The best way to make this evaluation is to consult the vendor's *hardware compatibility list (HCL)*. This list contains detailed information about entire systems and system components that are compatible with its operating system and/or applications.

If you don't consult the HCL for the operating system you plan to use, you can encounter problems. For example, Red Hat Linux still has a relatively limited HCL concerning network interface cards. If your interface card is not compatible, the Linux installation process will simply skip the networking phase of installation and then require you to manually define an interface.

Even then, you have no guarantee that Linux will properly recognize your interface. Therefore, you must check for compatibility.

EXERCISE 2.2

Consulting Hardware Compatibility Lists

In this exercise, you will consult hardware compatibility lists for Windows 2000 and Linux.

1. Open a web browser. You can use Netscape Navigator, Microsoft Internet Explorer, or Lynx (Unix).

2. Visit the Microsoft HCL page (www.microsoft.com/hcl). If you cannot find the page, enter **hardware compatibility list** in the Microsoft search engine field. You'll see something similar to the page in the following graphic.

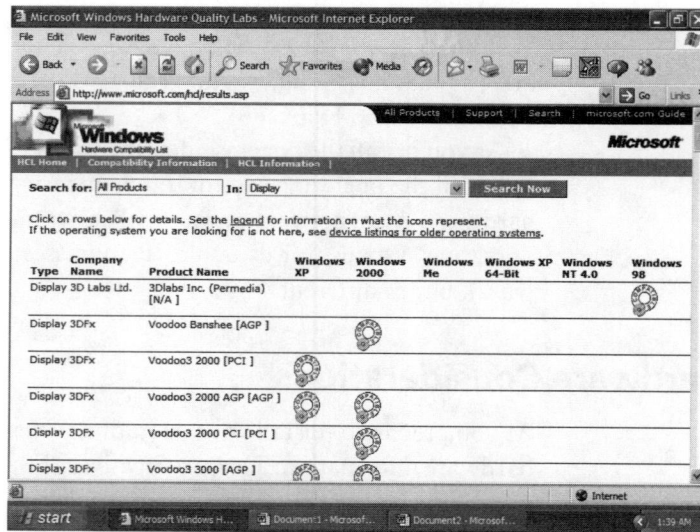

3. In the Search for the Following box, enter **Compaq**.

4. In the Following Types drop-down list box, enter **System/Server Multiprocessor**.

5. In the space provided, list two Compaq systems currently compatible with Windows 2000 Server.

6. Conduct a new search. This time, leave the Search for the Following box blank. In the Following Types drop-down list box, select **Network/Ethernet**.

7. In the space provided, list two NICs that are compatible with both Windows 98 clients and your servers.

8. Go to the Red Hat Web site to view its HCL (`www.redhat.com/corp/ support/hardware`). If this URL is no longer valid, enter **hardware compatibility list** in the Red Hat.com search engine field.

9. Navigate to the HCL link that conforms to the version of Red Hat Linux you are using in this course. Select **HCL**.

10. Scroll down to the **Advanced Search Form**.

11. You can choose from many hardware categories, releases, architectures, and manufacturers. The Search For field allows you to enter the system component in question.

12. Under Hardware Class, select **Network Device/Controller**.

13. In the Release category, select your version of Red Hat.

14. Select the relevant options for Architecture and Manufacturer (for example, Intel x86-based and 3Com).

15. Enter **3c509** in the String field.

16. Click the **Search** button.

17. When the search is complete, scroll down and view the models that Red Hat Linux supports: Red Hat Ready (as shown by the Red Hat icon), Compatible (as shown by the green check), Not Supported (as shown by the red check), and Community Knowledge (as indicated by the yellow question mark). Community Knowledge means that there may be a way to use this NIC in Red Hat Linux, but you will have to search sites such as www.linuxdoc.org for more information. See the following graphic.

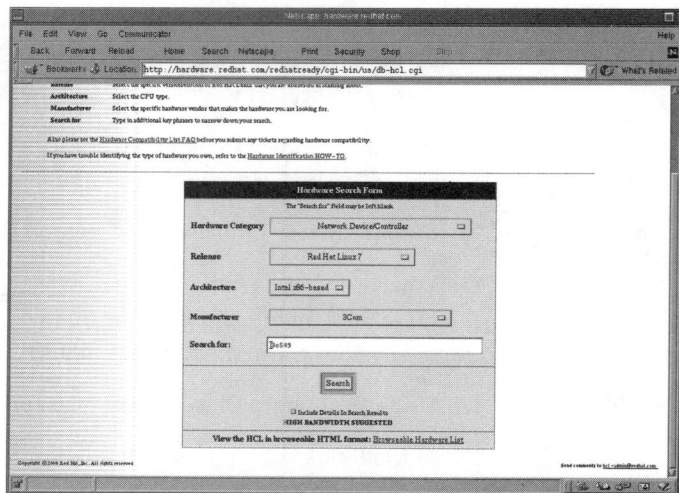

18. You should see several links concerning a specific card. Click one of the links to learn more about how the card is supported. Information includes the name of the Linux module responsible for allowing the operating system to communicate with the NIC. See the following graphic.

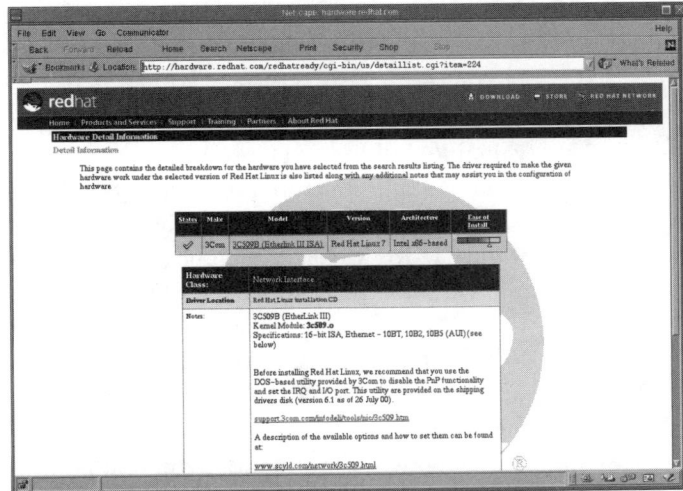

In this exercise, you visited the hardware compatibility sites of Microsoft and Red Hat. You learned how you can plan your hardware purchases and better ensure compatibility between operating systems.

Local and Network Installations

You can install operating systems and services using files located on your computer or media that reside on a remote server. However, you will need a way to boot the system to an installation program in order to make this choice. You can do this in one of the following ways:

Boot from a floppy disk Insert the floppy disk. The installation program will ask how you want to install the system. You can then run an application such as DOS Client to gain access to the network and begin installing.

Although operating systems have become extremely sophisticated, you will have to begin with an MS-DOS floppy disk to install some operating systems.

Boot from a CD-ROM   New CD-ROM devices allow you to boot directly from the device.

Boot from a hard drive   If the drive is bootable, it may contain the appropriate installation files.

The DOS Client application is an older but useful program that lets you boot from a floppy disk and then create a simple network connection to obtain the operating system. Although describing how to use DOS Client is beyond the scope of this chapter, knowing how to use this application is a valuable skill for an IT professional.

In a local installation, the installation files are contained on a local CD-ROM. If the CD-ROM is bootable, the installation starts from the CD-ROM. If the CD-ROM is not bootable, the installation starts from setup disks that allow the computer to see the CD-ROM and start the installation from the CD. If the operating system you are installing will not be able to see the CD-ROM drive once installation is underway, either replace the CD-ROM drive with a compatible CD-ROM or copy the installation files to the hard drive and then proceed with the installation.

In a network installation, you first boot from a disk (floppy, CD-ROM, or hard drive) and then choose from several options, including the following:

- Windows Networking shares

- HTTP

- FTP

- Network File System (NFS)

Each of these methods lets you connect to a remote system and then obtain the operating system.

Red Hat Linux refers to a remote installation as a "kickstart installation." You can learn more about kickstart installations at `www.redhat.com/support/manuals/RHL-7-Manual/ref-guide/s1-kickstart2-howuse.html` or by reading the relevant information at `www.linuxdoc.org`.

Summary

In this chapter, you learned about the relevant components of an Internet server. You learned about bottlenecks and how to choose specific elements. You considered I/O card choice as well as hard drives and RAM. You learned about the importance of bandwidth and throughput to Internet services. You also reviewed various operating systems and their relevant features. Finally, you checked hardware compatibility lists and organized other important information before beginning the installation process.

With this information, you should be able to select the most appropriate operating system, hardware platform, and system components for a given environment. You should now be able to successfully resolve installation issues and troubleshoot bottlenecks.

Exam Essentials

Select the best operating system, hardware platform, and hardware components based on the requirements for a given Internet server. Consider the following: ease of use; platform stability; available talent pool; available technical support; hardware, licensing, and other costs; availability of services and applications; and, finally, the purpose of the server.

Memorize common bandwidth speeds. The definition of bandwidth is the total information that can fit on a network wire. We discussed common bandwidth speeds such as T1 at 1.544Mbps and basic rate ISDN with two B, or bearer, channels at 64Kbps and one D channel for control.

Know the difference between throughput and bandwidth. Bandwidth is the actual size of the data pipe, and throughput is the amount of data that can successfully be moved from one place to another in a given time period. Throughput is often the most telling measurement because it stacks up the data to be moved against the capacity of the channel, yielding a time to move a given amount of data through a channel with a given bandwidth.

Identify common hardware platforms and describe the capabilities of various platform components, including multiple CPUs, I/O issues, and system memory.   You need to configure hardware platforms with Internet server grade CPUs, such as the Pentium 4, Xeon, and Itanium, and RISC CPUs such as Alpha. These CPUs differ in speed, cache memory, and instruction set and can be 32-bit or 64-bit. When even the best single CPU is inadequate, you can deploy multiple CPUs. Also configure Internet servers with adequate memory, a fast hard drive system such as SCSI-3 in a RAID configuration, and single or multiple server-grade, high performance NICs.

Identify common network operating systems and determine the ideal operating system for a given environment.   Internet server operating system choices include Windows NT 4, Windows 2000, Novell NetWare, and the various distributions of Unix and Linux. We discussed operating system selection based on ease of use; platform stability; available talent pool; available technical support; hardware, licensing and other costs; availability of services and applications; and, finally, the purpose of the server.

Discuss system installation issues.   Before you install an operating system, you need to consult the hardware compatibility list to ensure that your system and its components will work with the new operating system. You can then decide on an installation method: booting from the installation CD-ROM or booting from a network installation startup disk and installing from a network share.

Key Terms

Before taking the exam, you should be familiar with the following terms:

Advanced Technology Attainment (ATA)

bandwidth

bash

bottleneck

bus speed

DHCP

Digital Subscriber Line (DSL)

Dynamic Host Configuration Protocol (DHCP)

enhanced integrated drive electronics (EIDE)

Graphical User Interface (GUI)

hardware compatibility list (HCL)

integrated drive electronics (IDE)

Integrated Services Digital Network (ISDN)

kernel

Linux

network interface card (NIC)

network operating system (NOS)

open source movement

Point-to-Point Protocol over Ethernet (PPPoE)

shell

Small Computer System Interface (SCSI)

T1

throughput

Ultra ATA (Advanced Technology Attainment)

Review Questions

1. Jim is shopping for a new web server. He wants to make sure that the server can provide optimal bandwidth and coordinate control signals and data sent from various computer devices. Which hardware should Jim evaluate?

   A. CPU

   B. Motherboard

   C. Bus

   D. I/O cards

2. Mark must select a processor system for a server. His choices are Celeron, Pentium III, Pentium 4, Xeon, Itanium, and AMD K-7 processors. Which of the following statements are true? Choose two.

   A. The Xeon processor has more cache memory than a standard Pentium III, so it would be more suitable for a server.

   B. The Celeron processor has a slower bus speed than a Pentium III, so it would be more reliable than a Pentium III.

   C. The Itanium processor has a 64-bit internal bus as opposed to a 32-bit internal bus on a Pentium 4, so it can process more information each clock cycle.

   D. The AMD K-7 processor has greater compatibility with Windows XP.

3. Brad is upgrading the hard drive system for a server that will house 600GB of frequently accessed financial records. Which hard drive system should Brad choose?

   A. IDE

   B. ATA 100

   C. SCSI 3

   D. EIDE

4. Ann wants to be able to download files as large as 5MB in size in 2 minutes or less. She also wants to pay the lowest price for this service. Which choices will work for Ann? Choose the two best options.

A. ISDN

B. Cable modem

C. DSL

D. T-1

E. Dialup connection

5. Linda works for a bank and wants to be able to transfer files to and from bank branches at a guaranteed speed of 1.5Mbps. What is the best solution for Linda?

A. ISDN

B. T1

C. DSL

D. Cable modem

E. T3

6. Frank works for an ISP that uses a combination of Unix and Linux servers. Which Unix shell should Frank use?

A. The Bourne shell

B. The Korn shell

C. The C shell

D. Bash

7. George wants to use an operating system with the lowest total cost of ownership for a 100-server website. Which NOS should George choose?

A. NT 4

B. Windows 2000

C. Linux

D. Novell NetWare 5.2

8. Sergio is putting together a server from spare parts. Before installing a network operating system, what should Sergio consult?

   A. Orange Book

   B. HCL

   C. Help files

   D. Tucows

9. Wendy is trying to decide how to spend a limited budget to get the highest performance Internet server for the price. Which of the following is an important potential problem to consider when determining how system elements (hardware and software) work together?

   A. Bandwidth

   B. Bottlenecks

   C. Throughput

   D. RAM

10. Hector is trying to explain bandwidth to his assistant. Which of the following explanations is correct?

    A. The total amount of information that can fit on a network wire, measured in bits

    B. The total amount of information that can fit on a network wire, measured in bytes

    C. Network connection utilization at any given moment, measured in bits/sec

    D. Network connection utilization at any given moment, measured in bytes/sec

11. Jerry is looking at a help wanted add at his university and is trying to determine if he is familiar with the operating system that is being used in its computer labs. Which of the following operating systems consists of a kernel, a file system, and the bash shell?

A. Macintosh

B. Microsoft Windows 2000

C. Novell NetWare

D. Unix

12. Your company's IT department plans to implement an operating system. The organization is a Microsoft Solutions Provider. Which of the following operating systems is your best choice?

A. Windows 2000

B. Linux

C. IBM AIX

D. Novell NetWare

13. Jason is evaluating a new database server that will host a mission-critical application. What are the two most important criteria in selecting the hardware?

A. Stability

B. Supportability

C. Scalability

D. Cost

14. Frank is supporting a small business that has one server. The IDE hard drive fails and he replaces it with an Ultra ATA/133 hard drive and then restores the server from tape backup. He does not get the hard drive performance improvement that he expected. What might Frank need to do? Choose two answers.

A. Set the dipswitches

B. Set the jumpers

C. Flash the BIOS

D. Add an IDE controller card

15. Debbie buys a new Ultra ATA 100 hard drive running at 7,200 rpm for a client that owns a small business and has a Pentium II–based server. The client reports that this hard drive is not that much faster than the old hard drive. Debbie runs some benchmarks that confirm the client's suspicion. What can Debbie do that will most likely solve the problem?

   A. Upgrade the processor.

   B. Add more RAM.

   C. Put the hard drive on its own IDE controller.

   D. Add an Ultra ATA 100 I/O.

16. The WebRing.com wants to optimize performance and recoverability of the hard drive systems of its web servers. What advantages could using multiple hard drives have over using one large hard drive?

   A. Faster access speed

   B. Storage of log files on a separate drive

   C. Fault-tolerant systems

   D. Lower mean time between failure (MTBF) for each drive.

   E. Read after write verification

   F. Quicker backup

   G. Storage of the paging file on a separate drive

17. A company's database server supports 1300 users on a quad Pentium 4 server. What is the fastest memory type available for use on this server?

   A. SIMM

   B. EDO

   C. DIMM

   D. RDRAM

18. Cost is no object. Your boss wants the most powerful processor he can get for the workstations of engineers that are designing a new air traffic control system. Which processor should he choose?

    A. Pentium 4

    B. AMD K-7 XP

    C. Itanium

    D. Xeon

19. Even the Itanium processor is not powerful enough for the air traffic control center master server. The CPU can carry only half the required load. What is the most cost effective upgrade that would solve the problem?

    A. Double the amount of RAM.

    B. Quadruple the amount of RAM.

    C. Upgrade to a dual-processor configuration.

    D. Upgrade to a quad-processor configuration.

20. Jim is a salesman for MCI and is presenting to a Fortune 500 CIO the advantages of dedicated T1 lines between regional headquarters. The CIO says that the data bandwidth he needs is only 768Kbps, and not 1.54Mbps between regional headquarters. What should Jim recommend that the CIO do?

    A. Buy a fractional T1.

    B. Buy a T3.

    C. Multiplex voice on the T1 line.

    D. Buy ISDN.

Answers to Review Questions

1. B.   The motherboard coordinates signals sent from a computer's various devices.

2. A, C.   The Xeon processor has more cache memory than a standard Pentium III, so it would be more suitable for a server. If he could afford it, an Itanium processor would be better yet, because it has a 64-bit internal bus as opposed to a 32-bit internal bus on a Pentium 4. Therefore, the Itanium can process more information each clock cycle.

3. C.   SCSI systems generally provide more reliable service, are faster, and are more scalable than their IDE counterparts. SCSI-3 has a bidirectional data transfer rate of up to 160Mbps.

4. B, C.   Cable modem and DSL can handle this throughput at a reasonable price, while T1 is too expensive, and a dialup or ISDN connection is too slow.

5. B.   T1 guarantees a data transfer rate (both upload and download) of 1.544Mbps.

6. D.   Frank should use `bash` (the Bourne Again shell), which is the shell distributed with Linux.

7. C.   George should use Linux because he will not have to pay a licensing cost for 100 servers. If he had only several servers, the ease of use of NT 4 or Windows 2000 would offset the licensing cost.

8. B.   Sergio should consult the appropriate HCL (hardware compatibility list).

9. B.   To gain the highest performance, eliminate bottlenecks.

10. A.   Bandwidth is the total amount of information that can fit on the network wire, measured in bits.

11. D. Unix has these elements.

12. A. Microsoft Solution Providers sell Microsoft solutions.

13. A, B. Stability and supportability are the two most important criteria in choosing a mission-critical server. For most personal computers, price is a very important consideration, but the impact of downtime is much more critical on a server.

14. C, D. If the computer recognizes the hard drive, then the dipswitches and jumpers are set correctly. Frank may need to upgrade to a BIOS and an IDE controller card capable of supporting Ultra ATA.

15. D. Although newer motherboards have a built-in Ultra ATA 100–capable IDE controller, older motherboards require a separate Ultra ATA 100 I/O card. A hard drive is attached to this card.

16. A, B, C, G. Larger hard drives generally have slower access speeds. A RAID array of multiple hard drives allows faster access to data and fault-tolerance. Storage of log files on a separate drive would reduce contention for the first drive and share the workload among the drives. The paging file might also be moved from the first drive in order to increase performance.

17. D. RDRAM runs at 800MHz

18. C. Itanium is the new 64-bit Intel processor.

19. D. The second processor does not double the performance of a server due to the overhead of dividing the tasks and coordinating with the other processor.

20. C. Data and voice can be multiplexed on T-carrier lines.

Chapter

3

Configuring TCP/IP on Internet Servers

THE CIW EXAM OBJECTIVE GROUPS COVERED IN THIS CHAPTER:

✓ Identify TCP/IP configuration parameters, and configure Windows and Linux systems with static IP addresses.

Y ou've chosen the best operating system for your needs, installed it, and now you need to configure it properly to get the best performance possible. In this chapter, you will learn how to configure Internet servers for *Transmission Control Protocol/Internet Protocol (TCP/IP)*. This task involves assigning *Internet Protocol (IP)* information, which includes the address, subnet mask, default gateway, and domain name server (DNS) information. It also involves adding adapters and establishing parameters that help your system operate more efficiently.

The first task is to choose the appropriate *network interface card (NIC)* for your server. An Internet server places a far heavier load on a NIC than a PC. You typically want to select a more expensive, higher-performance NIC from an established manufacturer. One NIC may not be enough; you may need to install multiple NICs. Linux typically doesn't support the newest NICs, so if you are using the Linux operating system, obtain an established NIC.

When you install a NIC, you will be prompted to install a networking protocol. TCP/IP is the protocol used on the Internet, and it has become the default wide area networking protocol for the current versions of all the major network operating systems. On the client side, you can configure TCP/IP with a static address, subnet mask, and default gateway. You must ensure that the address you assign is on the appropriate subnet and does not duplicate and conflict with another TCP/IP address on the subnet. You can eliminate conflicts if the client has been set to obtain an address automatically and you have configured a Dynamic Host Configuration Protocol (DHCP) server to hand out IP addresses and configuration information to requesting client computers.

Whether you configure TCP/IP manually or automatically, you can use a command to display TCP/IP information. In Windows NT 4, you use the `ipconfig` command. In Windows 9*x*/Me, you use the `winipcfg` command.

And in Unix/Linux, you use the `ifconfig` command. To troubleshoot a network configured with TCP/IP, you use the `ping` command, and you can trace IP packets using the `traceroute` in Unix/Linux and `tracert` Windows operating systems.

In this chapter, we'll look at how to configure TCP/IP in detail. With this information, you will be able to network Internet servers using TCP/IP and then effectively and efficiently share information locally and globally.

Adapters and Drivers

The first step in configuring TCP/IP involves the lowest layer of the protocol stack: the physical layer of the *Open Standards Interconnect (OSI)* Reference Model. If you are accustomed to the four-layer TCP/IP model, this layer corresponds to the Network layer, in which communication between the host computer and the network is handled by the NIC. The interface card is a hardware element, located either on the system's motherboard or in an expansion card on the main bus.

The next step is to provide the proper driver for the NIC. The device driver, which operates at the Data-Link layer, helps process information up the IP stack (that is, up the layers of the OSI Reference Model). The network interface device driver is software that mediates the passage of data between network adapter hardware and TCP/IP software in the host computer's operating system. Device-driver software is hardware dependent; each type of Ethernet card requires its own device driver code.

Internetworking servers often have more than one NIC. Multiple NICs help divide the load (for example, on a web server) or can turn a standard computer into a routing device that connects two separate networks. Multiple NICs help serve multiple websites at the same time and balance the load for one web server.

Whether you add one or multiple NICs to a computer, the software that allows the computer to recognize and use the NIC hardware is a NIC driver. Drivers are specific to the computer's operating system. The procedure for adding these drivers is also specific to the operating system. Mastering these procedures is essential for administering networking Internet servers. We'll look first at how to add drivers in the Unix/Linux operating system and then in NT 4 and Windows 2000.

Adding Network Adapter Device Drivers in Unix/Linux

In Linux, managing I/O tasks is the responsibility of either the operating system kernel or a *module* that the kernel accesses. In Linux, a module is code meant to act as a driver for a device (for example, a NIC, a sound card, or a video driver). Device drivers of all sorts, including disk, keyboard, mouse, and network, can be incorporated into the kernel or loaded as modules using the `insmod` or `modprobe` commands.

Discovering where device drivers are located in a particular Linux kernel can be difficult. This information is displayed on screen while the kernel boots, or the user can enter the `lsmod` command to display it. The messages include reports on many of the device drivers installed in the booting kernel.

Modules vs. Recompiling

Adding a device driver to a Linux machine requires either extending the Linux kernel by incorporating device driver code or by installing a new module. Extending the Linux kernel requires recompiling the kernel executable to include support for the NIC. Generally, using a module is easier than recompiling kernel code. However, the benefit of recompiling the kernel is that it will be more efficient in processing information from the network.

> **NOTE** If you install multiple identical NICs (for example, two 3c509 cards), you will need only one module. The easiest way to add the second NIC is to use the `linuxconf` program.

Suppose you install a NIC, and Linux does not recognize it automatically. To determine which type of interface you have, you can use the *modprobe* command. For example, if you have a 3c509 adapter, you can issue the following command, which displays information about the IRQ (interrupt request) and memory address:

```
modprobe 3c509
```

If the NIC you are installing is a Peripheral Component Interconnect (PCI) card, you can also use the `lspci -v` command to display information about how the system recognized the PCI card.

> **NOTE** If you purchase a NIC that is not on the Linux HCL, installation could be difficult or impossible.

Adding Network Adapter Device Drivers in Windows 2000

As in other operating systems, I/O in Windows 2000 is managed at a low level (by the I/O manager in the Windows 2000 Executive). But Windows 2000 provides a strong facility for extending the operating system by adding device drivers without having to relink or recompile the operating system kernel. In this way, the Windows 2000 system resembles the loadable kernel module approach to adding device drivers under Linux.

When adding a NIC, Plug and Play will take care of any issues, including software installation. Nevertheless, you should always consult the Microsoft HCL.

NOTE You can add an unlimited number of protocols to your NIC.

Assigning IP Addresses

Your home or apartment is able to receive regular mail, including packages, because it has a street address. In order for your computer to receive IP packets, it must have an IP address. An IP address consists of a network portion, similar to street, and a host portion, similar to your house number. You can assign IP addresses manually or dynamically. In this section, we'll look at how to configure your systems manually and at how to use the Dynamic Host Configuration Protocol (DHCP) to manage IP addresses from a central location.

Whether you configure IP addresses manually by individually entering TCP/IP addressing information on each computer or automatically by creating configuration information on a DHCP server with a pool of IP addresses and then pushing that information out to client computers, you must enter certain parameters. For instance, to communicate on a subnet, you need enter only an IP address and a subnet mask. To communicate with hosts on other subnets, a default gateway is required. To find hosts by friendly names, a pointer to a DNS server is required. We'll discuss these and other IP configuration parameters in the next section.

The following list describes normal configuration parameters for a server or a workstation on a TCP/IP network.

Computer name   The name you assigned your computer, paired with your IP address. Windows 2000 and other systems also allow you to identify your workgroup name. In Windows 2000, you must carefully specify proper DNS information along with the computer name. Otherwise, the system will not function properly.

IP address   The 32-bit number sequence that is unique to your workstation on the network.

Subnet mask   The 32-bit number that distinguishes the network and host portions of your IP address. The subnet mask is also used to calculate whether a destination address is local or remote.

Default gateway   A local computer's IP address. If your computer determines that a destination address is remote, your computer sends the packet to the default gateway. The router then sends the packet to the remote network.

DNS information   Data that you can use to query DNS servers for name resolution.

DHCP client information   The easiest way to configure clients on a network (you will learn about DHCP clients and servers in detail later in this book). If you are a DHCP client, your TCP/IP configurations will automatically be sent to your computer when you initialize your system.

WINS   Primarily a legacy protocol. In Windows NT Server 4 and Windows 2000 Server, you can use a WINS server to provide name resolution.

Static Addressing

Although TCP/IP is universal, you implement it using operating system-specific tools. In this section, we'll configure Windows 2000 and Linux servers to set static IP information. The universality of TCP/IP enables the global Internet with communication between Microsoft, Unix/Linux, Novell, and Apple systems. Although TCP/IP was initially developed for Unix platforms as an add-on component, Microsoft was the first to incorporate the TCP/IP protocol stack into the core of an operating system.

Configuring Windows 2000 for Static Addressing

The *ipconfig* command displays the Windows 2000 IP configuration; the ipconfig command performs functions similar to the Unix/Linux ifconfig command. The ipconfig command displays only the IP address, subnet mask, and default gateway. The command format is as follows:

```
ipconfig    options
```

To view all the IP-related configuration information, use the /all option. This option displays additional information, such as the hardware address. Following is an example of using the ipconfig command with the /all option:

```
ipconfig  /all
```

This command yields the following results:

```
Windows 2000 IP Configuration:
Host Name              student13
Primary DNS Suffix
Node Type              Hybrid
NetBIOS Scope ID
IP Routing Enabled     No
WINS Proxy Enabled     No
DNS Suffix Search List classroom.com
Ethernet adapter Local Area Connection:
Description . . .      3Com 10/100 PCI (3C905C-TX)
Physical Address       00-00-1C-3A-62-BD
DHCP Enabled           No
IP Address             192.168.3.13
Subnet Mask            255.255.255.0
Default Gateway        192.168.3.1
DNS Servers            192.168.1.1
```

You can also use the ipconfig command to renew and release IP addresses from a DHCP server. If you don't specify an adapter name, all IP leases are released and/or renewed. For example:

```
ipconfig /release adapter
ipconfig /renew adapter
```

EXERCISE 3.1

Identifying IP Configuration and Hardware Address Information in Windows 2000

In this exercise, you will locate your Windows 2000 Server IP address configuration and hardware address.

1. Choose Start ➢ Programs ➢ Accessories ➢ Command Prompt to open the Command Prompt window.

2. Enter the following command to display the Windows IP configuration and NIC information:

   `ipconfig /all`

3. Write the following information in the spaces provided.

   Host name: _____

   Primary DNS suffix: _____

   DNS suffix search list: _____

   IP address: _____

   Subnet mask: _____

   Default gateway: _____

   DNS servers: _____

   Physical (that is hardware) address: _____

You can use the *winipcfg* command to display your network card's Ethernet address in Windows 9*x*/Me. Choose Start ➢ Run to open the Run dialog box, and then enter **winipcfg** in the open box to open the IP Configuration dialog box, as shown in Figure 3.1.

NOTE   You can also enter **winipcfg** at the MS-DOS prompt.

FIGURE 3.1 Windows 9x/Me Ethernet address and network configuration

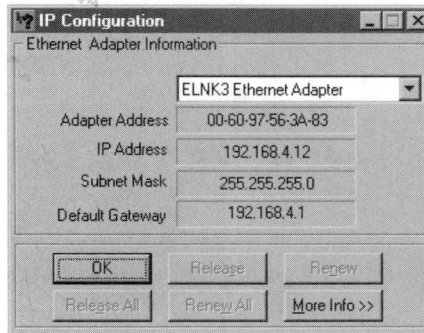

Configuring Linux for Static Addressing

You can use the following commands to configure static IP addresses in Linux.

/sbin/ifconfig Works similarly to ipconfig. This command checks the configuration of an interface or changes the IP address of an interface. However, you must specify the name of the interface. Linux defaults to calling the first interface eth0. This command can take many arguments, including the interface name (for example, eth0), the netmask, and the broadcast. Therefore, to configure this interface with the IP address of 192.168.4.20 and a standard subnet mask, enter the following:

```
/sbin/ifconfig eth0 192.168.4.20 netmask 255.255.255.0
↪broadcast 192.168.4.255
```

Additional arguments such as down and up also exist, as you will see in the next exercise. In Linux, ifconfig will not permanently change a system's IP configuration. When you reboot, settings revert to their original configuration.

/sbin/ifup and ifdown Opens or closes the specified interface up or down.

/sbin/linuxconf Can be used to configure many system elements, including host name, IP address, subnet mask, default gateway, and so forth. You can issue the *linuxconf* command at any prompt, locally or via Telnet, and run linuxconf either in the X Window System or directly from a root prompt.

/sbin/yast or **DrakeConf** Similar to linuxconf. The yast program is used primarily on SuSE systems. DrakeConf is used primarily on Linux-Mandrake systems. Each allows you to set system parameters, including how the Linux system uses TCP/IP. The name yast is an acronym for "yet another setup tool."

/usr/bin/netcfg Must be used in an X Window System. As root, activate a terminal and enter *netcfg*.

/usr/sbin/netconfig An ASCII-based tool that you can use to configure your system for networking. The linuxconf command is generally preferable.

One of the easiest ways to configure a Linux host is to use linuxconf, as shown in Figure 3.2. This utility is available in all X Window System desktops, including KDE, *Gnome*, and NextLevel.

The linuxconf utility is also available via the command line and through remote connections. Figure 3.3 shows how you can access linuxconf via a Telnet client.

FIGURE 3.2 The linuxconf in the X Window System

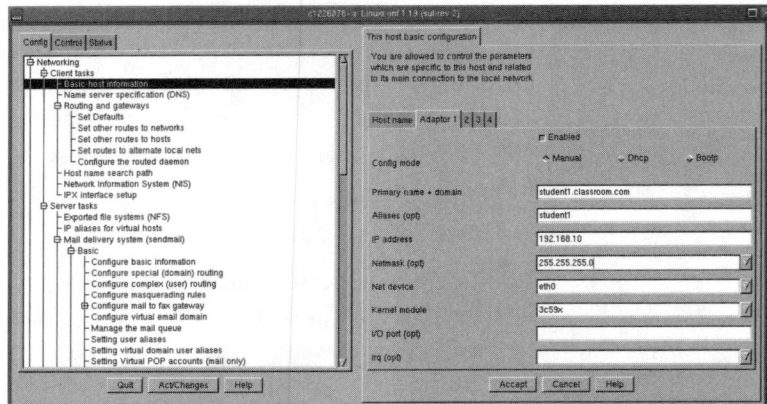

FIGURE 3.3   Using linuxconf via Telnet

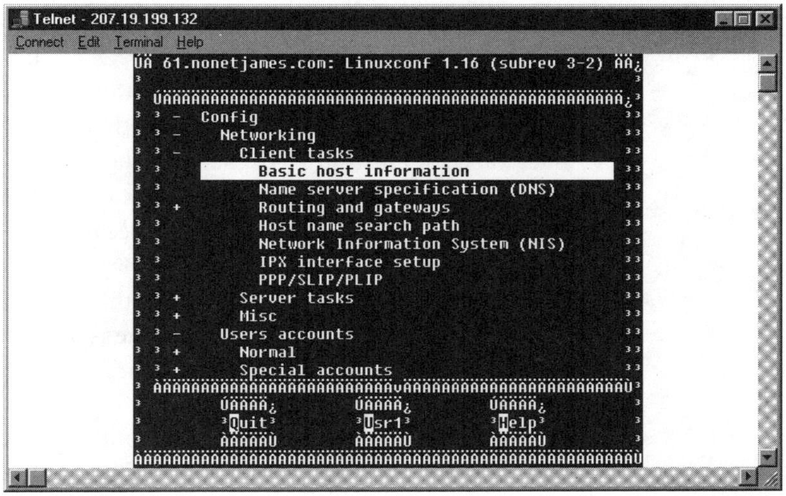

You can navigate to the basic host information section by using your keyboard. Simply use the arrow keys, navigate to the Basic Host Information section, and press Enter. You will see the screen shown in Figure 3.4.

FIGURE 3.4   The basic host configuration menu in linuxconf

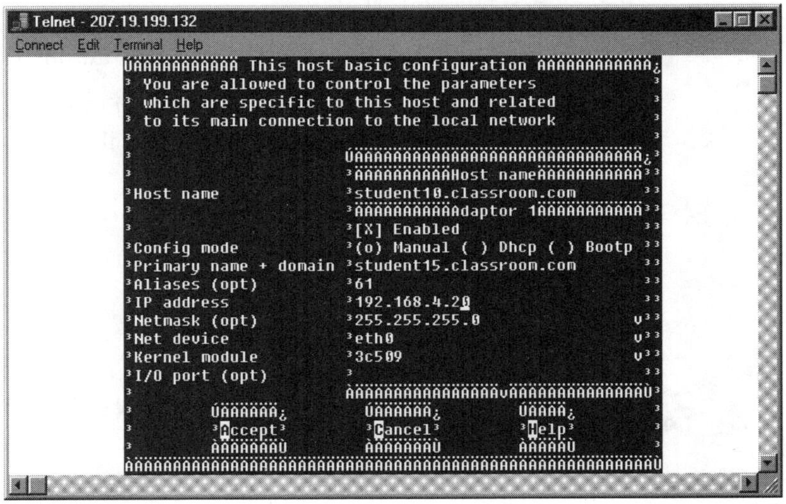

The benefit to using linuxconf is that the changes you make are permanent.

Manual Interface Configuration in Linux

It is not always possible to use the X Window system. In fact, many server administrators prefer not to install the X Window System. Because Linux and Unix use a cryptic language that has great power at the command line, some administrators, particularly those with programming backgrounds, revel in their ability to master the intricacies of Unix/Linux commands without resorting to pointing at pictures. Also, because Unix/Linux is economical in its use of resources, a graphical interface may be viewed as an unnecessary drain on resources. Whether you share this opinion or not, you should still be able to administer your Linux server if there is a problem with the X Window System and the graphical linuxconf utility is not available. If this happens, you might have to create an interface from scratch if you have added an additional NIC. Note that changing your configuration using ifconfig does not change the IP interface permanently. To administer your Linux server without using linuxconf, you need to edit certain files that Linux reads to configure the NIC.

For example, assume that you want to do the following:

- Change the IP address to 192.168.4.20.

- Change the subnet mask to 255.255.255.0.

- Use only TCP/IP.

- Specify that the network activate automatically.

To manually make these changes, edit the /etc/sysconfig/network-scripts/ifcfg-eth0 file to read as follows:

```
IPADDR="192.168.4.20"
NETMASK="255.255.255.0"
ONBOOT="yes"
BOOTPROTO="none"
```

Additional entries exist. Those listed here are pertinent to standard TCP/IP.

Next, you must do the following:

- Turn on networking.
- Indicate whether you want IP forwarding.
- Provide a host name and a gateway, and then specify the device.

To do this, edit the /etc/sysconfig/network file to read as follows:

```
NETWORKING=yes
FORWARD_IPV4="no"
HOSTNAME="student10.classroom.com"
GATEWAY="192.168.4.1"
GATEWAYDEV="eth0"
```

You would then edit the /etc/hosts file so that it knows your IP address.

If you want name resolution, you must edit resolv.conf. You will learn more about resolv.conf when we discuss DNS in Chapter 7.

If you want to the eth0 device to run automatically, use either linuxconf or edit the files in the /etc/rc.d directory.

If you want to learn more about the particular NIC you are using, you can use the *dmesg* command. The dmesg command reports in detail how Linux configured all recognized devices on your system at startup. If you use the command by itself, it will likely give you more information than you need. Instead, use it in combination with a pipe (the | character) and *grep*. In the following example, grep sifts through all the dmesg output and returns only those messages relevant to the eth0 interface.

```
[root@student15 user1]# /bin/dmesg | grep eth0
eth0: 3c509 at 0x300 tag 1, 10baseT port, address   00 a0
↳24 55 29 e8, IRQ 9.
eth0: Setting Rx mode to 1 addresses.
[root@student15 user1]#
```

This command reports that the eth0 interface is using an Etherlink 3c509 adapter. The command also gives the interface's memory address, network type, MAC address, and IRQ. In addition, it shows that the NIC is using one IP address.

You can use the pipe and grep with many other applications.

Configuring Static IP Addresses in Linux Using *ifconfig*

In this exercise, you and a partner will configure the Linux network interface.

1. Connect to the console or start a terminal window as user root. Your password is password. If you do not log on as root, you will not be able to use ifconfig.

2. Using the ifconfig command, enable the eth0 network interface as 198.246.244.*x*; *x* represents your original IP address plus 10. Also, use the following netmask and broadcast arguments:

/sbin/ifconfig eth0 192.168.4.20 netmask 255.255.255.0
↳broadcast **192.168.4.255**

3. Check the status of the interface using the -a option with the ifconfig command:

/sbin/ifconfig -a

You can use either ifconfig by itself *or* ifconfig –a. In some Unix systems, ifconfig –a provides additional information.

4. Close the network interface using the following command:

/sbin/ifconfig eth0 down

5. Reopen the network interface by entering the following command:

/sbin/ifconfig eth0 up

6. The changes you have made are still valid.

7. Restart your system by entering the following command:

/usr/bin/shutdown -r now

You can also use the /usr/bin/reboot command or type sbin/init 6.

8. After the system restarts, at the LILO prompt, indicate that you want to enter Linux.

9. Log back on as root.

EXERCISE 3.2 *(continued)*

10. Issue the ifconfig command. Notice that you are back to your original TCP/IP configuration, even though you made the changes using ifconfig.

EXERCISE 3.3

Configuring Static IP Addresses in Linux Using *linuxconf*

In this exercise, you will configure IP addresses in Linux using linuxconf in the X Window System.

1. As root, type **linuxconf** to launch the linuxconf program. You may have to enter the entire path of linuxconf: /sbin/linuxconf.

2. Use your mouse to navigate to the Networking section.

3. Expand the Networking section by clicking the x icon.

4. You should now see entries for client tasks, server tasks, and Misc. Click the Client Tasks icon and expand it. Highlight the Basic Host Information button. You set the host name in this section. Leave this information as it is.

5. Click the Adaptor 1 tab. Note the entries, including Config mode, Primary name + domain, and aliases. Especially note the IP address and netmask entries.

6. Change the IP address so that it conforms to the scheme used in Exercise 3.2 (see Figure 3.2). If your Linux machines are already configured as shown in that figure, increase your current IP address by one.

7. Click the Accept button, and then click the Act/Changes button, which is at the bottom of the linuxconf program.

8. Linux display a Status of the System dialog box, telling you that the state of the system is not "in sync" with the current/updated configuration. Click the Activate Changes button.

9. Quit linuxconf by clicking the Quit button. You may have to activate the changes again before you can exit linuxconf.

10. Use `ifconfig` to verify that you have changed this system's IP address.

11. Restart your system. Make sure that you choose Linux at the LILO prompt.

12. Log back on as root. Use `ifconfig` to check your changes. Notice that the information has changed permanently.

13. If you want, take a look at the X Window System and run `linuxconf`. Note that this program configures the entire system, not only TCP/IP.

You have just used `linuxconf` to configure TCP/IP. You can also change your IP address configuration by editing the relevant files in the `/etc/sysconfig/` directory.

Additional TCP/IP Issues and Commands

Now that you have looked at basic TCP/IP configuration and trouble-shooting using `ipconfig`, `ifconfig`, and `winipcfg`, you are ready to look at advanced TCP/IP utilities that are powerful troubleshooting tools in particular situations. In this section, we'll explore the **netstat**, **route**, **traceroute**, and **pathping** commands.

As you troubleshoot a network, you will need to know the connections made between systems. You can use the *netstat* command, for example, to view the existing connections to a server, as shown in Figure 3.5.

FIGURE 3.5 Viewing the results of the netstat command

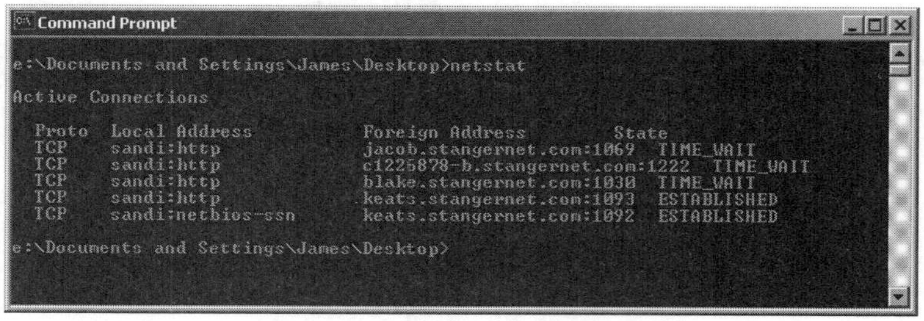

In Figure 3.5, the machine named sandi has received four connections to its web (that is, HTTP) server and one Windows networking connection. The machines connected to sandi are named jacob, c1226878-b, blake, and keats.

The machine named keats has established both an HTTP and Windows networking connection. Only two connections are still established. Whenever a TCP/IP connection has completed, the server first reports that the connection is being discontinued by displaying the TIME_WAIT field. When the connection is almost finished, the server reports a CLOSED field. When there is no connection, `netstat` reports nothing.

You use the `route` command to determine the static and dynamic routes that exist between you and other hosts. In Linux systems, you can use `route` to add and edit your default gateway:

```
[root@61 james]# /sbin/route
Kernel IP routing table
Destination     Gateway        Genmask        Flags
↳Metric Ref     Use Iface
192.168.4.20  *  255.255.255.255 UH  0    0       0 eth0
192.168.4.0   *  255.255.255.0   U   0    0       0 eth0
127.0.0.0     *  255.0.0.0       U   0    0       0 lo
default 192.168.4.1 0.0.0.0    UG  0    0       0 eth0
[root@61 james]#
```

This output shows the current machine's IP address (192.168.4.20), subnet mask, and interface number. It also provides the network address (192.168.4.0), the loopback address information, and the default gateway (192.168.4.1).

To change this information, you can use `linuxconf` or enter the following command:

```
/sbin/route add default gw 192.168.4.1
```

NOTE On Linux systems, you can also use the `netstat -nr` command to view routing information.

traceroute

If wide area communications are slow or fail, you will sometimes want to trace the route that a packet takes to a destination though a series of routers that exist between you and a particular server in order to see if the packet is being held up at a slow or congested router or being dropped at a router before reaching its destination. For this task, you can use the `traceroute` program. The `traceroute` program is similar to the `ping` program, but provides more details: It queries a destination host and counts the number of routers needed to get from your computer to the remote host. You can also use `traceroute` to determine where a connection point fails in a WAN. When `traceroute` is counting the connection points, it is said to be counting the "hops" between networks. Therefore, using `traceroute`, you can learn the hop count between your computer and a specific host. In NT 4/Windows 2000, the equivalent of the `traceroute` command is *tracert*. Here is an example in Windows 2000:

```
tracert www.microsoft.com
```

pathping

New in Windows 2000 is the *pathping* command. This command combines the features of `tracert` and `ping`. The `pathping` command sends packets to each router on the way to a final destination over a period of time in order to locate congested or malfunctioning routers. For example:

```
pathping www.ciwcertified.com
```

Additional Protocols

As you learn more about routing IP, consider that a router also has an operating system. Although routing is beyond the scope of this book, you should note that routers must be configured and must produce data and that they have traffic limitations. You can use a standard Windows NT or 2000 server as a router, as long as you use multiple NICs and enable IP forwarding. For such a system to communicate with other routers, it must use protocols such as the *Routing Information Protocol (RIP)* or the *Open Shortest Path First (OSPF)* protocol.

The arp program is helpful when determining which hosts have connected to your computer. This program determines how your host has resolved IP addresses to MAC addresses and can edit this information.

Dynamic Host Configuration Protocol (DHCP) Addressing

*D*ynamic Host Configuration Protocol (DHCP) is a protocol designed to assign IP addresses dynamically on a TCP/IP network. It allows a central server to govern IP addressing issues. DHZP is defined in RFCs 2132, 1534, 2131, and 1542. You can view these RFCs at www.rfc-editor.org or www.cis.ohio-state.edu. Managing IP addresses and defining an enterprise subnet design are two important tasks in any TCP/IP-based computing environment.

DHCP is a critical protocol in a client/server node configuration. With DHCP, client systems do not require manual TCP/IP configuration. A client system receives its TCP/IP configuration parameters dynamically at startup. If the client system is removed from one subnet and connected to another, it will automatically relinquish its old IP address and be assigned a new one when connected to the new segment. DHCP is based on BOOTP, but also includes automatic allocation of reusable network addresses and additional configuration options. DHCP users can communicate with BOOTP systems. (BOOTP, short for Boot Protocol, is a protocol that is used for booting diskless workstations and is defined in RFCs 951 and 1084.)

> **NOTE** Because DHCP automatically assigns IP addresses, it has become a central part of large enterprise LANs and WANs. DHCP can save a great deal of time for the IT department.

At startup, the client system sends a DHCP message, referred to as a *discover message*. This broadcast message is processed by all nodes on the local segment and can be forwarded to all DHCP server systems on the private enterprise network. It is then in the *initializing state*.

Each DHCP server that receives this message responds with an *offer message*, which contains an IP address and valid configuration information for the specific client that sent the request. Each DHCP server reserves the address it offers so that another client will not be given the same address. At this point, one or more DHCP servers may have *outstanding offers*.

The client system collects all configuration offerings from DHCP servers and enters a *selecting state*. The client chooses one configuration and sends a request message that identifies the DHCP server for the selected configuration. This process is known as the *requesting state*. Each DHCP server that received the original discover message also receives the request message.

The selected DHCP server then sends a DHCP *acknowledgment message*. This message contains the address sent earlier to the client, the TCP/IP configuration parameters, and a valid *lease* for the address. Other DHCP servers return the offered addresses to their free address pools. The client receives the acknowledgment and enters a *bound state*. It can now complete its startup process and communicate with other nodes on the TCP/IP network. The lease includes an expiration date and time for the information.

Figure 3.6 shows a diagram of the DHCP lease process.

FIGURE 3.6 The DHCP lease process

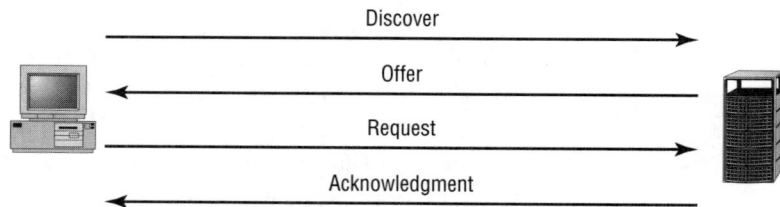

The DHCP lease process is similar to the process for leasing an automobile. You first make your request to the salesperson, who, in turn, offers you a car. You then accept the car offered. The final step is the transaction, or the signing of the lease.

NOTE Both Linux and Windows 2000 can serve as DHCP servers and clients.

For a greater understanding of TCP/IP, DCHP, and common routing protocols, visit **www.rfc-editor.org**, **www.cis.ohio-state.edu** or another site and search the RFCs for the following protocols:

- TCP
- IP
- ARP
- DHCP
- RIP
- OSPF

Summary

As an internetworking professional, one of your basic tasks is configuring the server's IP address. In this chapter, you learned how TCP/IP is bound to the NIC in both Windows 2000 and Linux. You also learned how to configure static IP addresses in both operating systems. Finally, you learned more about DHCP and how you can use it to automatically configure addresses.

You should now have the prerequisite skills to network Windows 2000 and Linux machines using key TCP/IP parameters that are configured either statically or dynamically.

Exam Essentials

List key TCP/IP configuration parameters. To communicate in a routed environment, you need to configure an IP address, a subnet mask, and a default gateway. To resolve host names, you need to configure the address of the DNS server. The computer name and the IP address that you select should be unique if TCP/IP communication is to function properly. If you can't communicate with another subnet by IP address, the default gateway might not be configured correctly. On the other hand, if you can communicate with hosts on another subnet by IP address, but not by host name, the DNS server may not be configured correctly.

Add NICs in Windows 2000 and Linux. Install the appropriate NIC driver and configure multiple NICs when required for load balancing or routing. You can add an unlimited number of protocols to your NIC. Adding a device driver to a Linux machine requires either extending the Linux kernel by incorporating a device driver code or by installing a new module. Be able to filter the `dsmesg` command with `|grep eth0` in order to learn more about the IP configuration of just the first NIC. Be able to use the `traceroute` or `tracert` commands to troubleshoot router congestion or failure.

Configure Windows 2000 with static IP addresses. Examine IP addresses using the `ipconfig` command to obtain the IP address, subnet mask, and default gateway. You can use additional `ipconfig` switches such as `/all` for all addressing information, `/release` to release an IP address, and

/renew to renew an IP address. The Windows *9x*/Me equivalent command is winipcfg.

Configure Linux with static IP addresses. Examine IP addresses using the ifconfig command. Use additional Linux commands to configure networking, including ifup, ifdown, linuxconf, netcfg, netconfig, and dsmesg. In Unix/Linux, you can use ifconfig to temporarily change interface configuration information. The changes will not survive a reboot. To permanently change IP configuration, use linuxconf. You can also run linuxconf on a remote client using Telnet.

Describe how DHCP works. You configure client computers to obtain an address automatically and broadcast to find a DHCP server. A DHCP server hands out TCP/IP configuration parameters from an address pool so that each DHCP client is leased a unique IP address. In this manner, DHCP reduces IP address conflicts and administrative workload.

Key Terms

Before you take the exam, be certain you are familiar with the following terms:

dmesg	netstat
Dynamic Host Configuration Protocol (DHCP)	network interface card (NIC)
Gnome	Open Shortest Path First (OSPF)
grep	Open Standards Interconnect (OSI)
Internet Protocol (IP)	pathping
ipconfig	Routing Information Protocol (RIP)
linuxconf	tracert
modprobe	Transmission Control Protocol/ Internet Protocol (TCP/IP)
module	winipcfg
netcfg	

Review Questions

1. Jim just installed Red Hat Linux on his workstation, and he wants detailed information on how Linux configured his 3Com NIC at startup. Which command gives Jim only the information he needs?

    A. `linuxconf`

    B. `ifconfig eth0`

    C. `dmesg | grep eth0`

    D. `ifup eth0`

2. Mark administers a mixed network with Linux and Windows 2000 servers that have been assigned static IP addresses. Windows XP, Windows 2000 Professional, and Red Hat Linux client computers receive their IP addresses from DHCP and can talk to one another and to hosts on the Internet, but can't see the local Linux and Windows 2000 servers. What should Mark do to solve this problem?

    A. Use DHCP for all computers including servers.

    B. Configure an `lmhosts` file.

    C. Use a WINS server.

    D. Add DNS records for the servers.

3. Brad is upgrading a Linux web server to quad Itanium processors and upgrading the NIC to 100Mb/s Ethernet. He wants the highest performance possible from this server. How should Brad install the NIC?

    A. By using `linuxconf`

    B. By using `netconfig`

    C. By using `dmesg | grep eth0`

    D. By extending the Linux kernel

    E. By using `ifconfig eth0`

4. Joshua wants to add a second NIC to a DNS server for load balancing and higher performance. The second NIC is identical to the first. How should Joshua add this NIC? Choose two.

    A. By using `linuxconf`

    B. By using `netconfig`

    C. By using `dmesg | grep eth0`

    D. By extending the Linux kernel

    E. By using `ifconfig eth0`

5. Mandy installs a NIC in Linux, and it is not automatically recognized. Which commands could Mandy use to enable Linux to recognize the NIC? Choose two.

    A. `tracert`

    B. `pathping`

    C. `modprobe`

    D. `lspci-v`

    E. `arp`

6. Frank is upgrading a server from NT 4 to Windows 2000. The NIC is not automatically recognized. Which of the following could NOT be the problem? Choose the best answer.

    A. The BIOS has not been reset to Plug and Play.

    B. The NIC is not Plug and Play.

    C. The NIC is not on the HCL.

    D. The operating system is not Plug and Play.

7. For practice, on his home computer, Scott is configuring a Windows 2000 server with Gateway Services for Netware that uses the NWLink protocol and configuring this server to talk on the Internet using TCP/IP. He is also configuring this server to act as a router between three local TCP/IP subnets. What is the minimum number of NICs that Scott can use?

A. 1

B. 2

C. 3

D. 4

E. 5

8. Tony's computer is unable to talk to any computers on remote networks by host name, but it can talk to computers on his local subnet. What might be the problem? Choose two.

A. If Tony can ping remote computers by IP address, the default gateway might be at fault.

B. If Tony cannot ping remote computers by IP address, the default gateway might be at fault.

C. If Tony can ping remote computers by IP address, DNS might be at fault.

D. If Tony cannot ping remote computers by IP address, the DNS might be at fault.

9. Peter's Windows 2000 Professional computer is set to obtain an IP address automatically. It is unable to connect to the Windows 2000 server to log on. Which commands might be helpful to troubleshoot and fix this problem? Choose three.

A. `ipconfig`

B. `ipconfig /release`

C. `ipconfig /renew`

D. `ipconfig /flushdns`

10. Ralph sets up Easy Proxy on a Windows 98 computer connected to the Internet with a cable modem and wants to network an Me computer on the same subnet. Which command can he use to obtain the IP address and subnet mask of the Windows 98 computer?

    A. `ipconfig`

    B. `ifconfig`

    C. `winipcfg`

    D. `netconfig`

11. Users in Rochester, N.Y., complain that it takes a long time to connect to company headquarters in Boston. On your Windows 2000 Professional computer, which commands could you execute to locate the problem? Choose two.

    A. `pathping`

    B. `tracert`

    C. `ping -a`

    D. `ping -t`

12. Mark administers a mixed network with Linux and Windows 2000 servers. He is installing a new NIC in each of his servers. What does Mark need first before he can proceed?

    A. Drivers

    B. DHCP

    C. DNS

    D. Samba

13. Brad installs Linux on an old computer. The installation is successful, except that the legacy 3c509 NIC is not automatically recognized. Which command should Brad issue?

    A. `linuxconf`

    B. `netconfig`

    C. `dmesg | grep eth0`

    D. `modprobe 3c509`

    E. `ifconfig eth0`

14. Because of budget cutbacks, Joshua's company has consolidated locations. Now twice as many users share a file server, and users complain about slow response times. What should Joshua do to improve response time? Choose the two best answers.

    A. Upgrade to Token Ring.

    B. Add a second NIC and segment the network.

    C. Upgrade the processor.

    D. Add memory.

    E. Add a second server.

15. Mandy installs a NIC in a Linux machine, and it is not automatically recognized. Her efforts to manually configure the NIC also fail. What might Mandy not have checked?

    A. HCL

    B. Readme

    C. FAQs

    D. HowTo's

16. In his practice lab, Frank is configuring an NT 4 server to dual boot with Windows 2000. He receives a warning that the NTFS file system on NT 4 must be upgraded if NT 4 is to be able to read the Windows 2000 partition. What could Frank download and install to fix this problem? Choose two.

    A. Swap file

    B. BIOS update

    C. Hot fix

    D. Service pack

17. Scott's file server supports the TCP/IP, NetBEUI, AppleTalk, and NWLink protocols. What is the minimum number of NICs required?

A. 1

B. 2

C. 3

D. 4

E. 5

18. On a Window's 98 computer, Tony is unable to access his company's website. What are some useful troubleshooting steps? Choose those that apply.

A. Try to access the company's website by IP address

B. Type **ipconfig /all**

C. Try to access other websites by host name

D. Try to access his company's website by NetBIOS name

19. Peter's Windows 2000 Professional computer is set to obtain an IP address automatically, and he is unable to log on to the network. Peter checks that his network cable is connected and sees a green flashing light on the NIC. He now wants to check his IP address. Which command should Peter type from a command prompt?

A. `ipconfig`

B. `ifconfig`

C. `winipcfg`

D. `netconfig`

20. Ralph is unable to talk to other computers by host name. Which command can Ralph use to check his Windows 2000 computer's DNS server configuration?

A. `ipconfig /flush DNS`

B. `ipconfig`

C. `winipcfg /all`

D. `ipconfig /all`

Answers to Review Questions

1. **C.** The `dmesg` command reports in detail how Linux configured all recognized devices on the system at startup. If you use the command by itself, it will likely give you more information than you need. Instead, use it in combination with a pipe (the | character) and `grep`.

2. **D.** The servers also must have DNS records if client computers are to resolve their host names.

3. **D.** Adding a device driver to a Linux machine requires either extending the Linux kernel by incorporating device driver code or installing a new module. Extending the Linux kernel requires *recompiling* the kernel executable to include support for the NIC. Generally, using a module is easier than recompiling kernel code. However, the benefit of recompiling the kernel is that the kernel will be more efficient in processing information from the network.

4. **A, B.** If you install multiple identical NICs (for example, two 3c509 cards), you will need only one module. The easiest way to add the second NIC is to use the `linuxconf` program, however, `netconfig` would also work.

5. **C, D.** You use `modprobe` and `lspci -v` to configure NICs in Linux that are not automatically recognized.

6. **D.** Windows 2000 is a Plug-and-Play operating system.

7. **A.** Multiple protocols and even multiple IP addresses can be bound to a single NIC.

8. **B, C.** If Tony can ping remote computers by IP address, DNS might be at fault. If Tony cannot ping remote computers by IP address, the default gateway might be at fault.

9. **A, B, C.** Peter would see that his IP address is set to 0.0.0.0 using `ipconfig`. He would then release and renew his IP address using `ipconfig /release` and `ipconfig /renew`.

10. C.   You use `winipcfg` is used to determine IP addressing information for Windows 9*x*/Me.

11. A, B.   In NT 4 and Windows 2000, you use the `tracert` command to find congested or malfunctioning routers. In Windows 2000, the `pathping` command combines the features of `tracert` and `ping`.

12. A.   Mark needs the appropriate drivers for each operating system.

13. D.   Issuing the `modprobe` command will allow Brad to learn the IRQ and memory address that this card is using.

14. B, D.   Adding a second server would cost too much, as would upgrading to Token Ring. A file server does not require the latest processor. Adding memory would support the additional users. Adding a second NIC and segmenting the network would reduce contention for the network wire.

15. A.   Mandy might not have checked the HCL, which would have indicated that the NIC she's trying to install is not compatible with Linux.

16. C, D.   Major improvements to Windows 2000 are distributed through service packs. Critical smaller updates are initially distributed as hot fixes. Hot fixes are incorporated into service packs.

17. A.   Multiple protocols can be bound to a single NIC.

18. A, C.   If Tony can access other websites by host name, his DNS server is working. This means that either his company's Internet server is down or the DNS record for his company's Internet server has been deleted. If Tony can access his company's website by IP address, his company's Internet server is working but there is a problem with DNS. The command to view IP configuration information on Windows 9*x* computers is `winipcfg`.

19. A.   Peter would check his IP address using the `ipconfig` command. If his IP address is set to 0.0.0.0, he did not obtain an IP address from a DHCP server. The DHCP server may be offline, or it may not have any remaining IP addresses to lease.

20. D.   The `ipconfig /all` command would return this information. If this were a Win9*x*/Me computer, then `winipcfg /all` would return full TCP/IP configuration details.

Chapter
4

User Management Essentials

THE CIW EXAM OBJECTIVE GROUPS COVERED IN THIS CHAPTER:

✓ Identify various levels of user access, and create password policies and permissions based on standard practice and procedures.

t's important that systems administrators develop the ability to work effectively with people and be able to respond to user problems. To prevent network outages and work slowdowns, systems administrators need to establish good user management protocols and security policies. By securing a network and communicating to users the reasons for security policies, systems administrators ensure that the right information will be available to the right people so that they can do a first-rate job.

So far, you have learned about network topologies and protocols. You know how to provide a host with an address so that it can participate in a network. In this chapter, you will learn how to manage user communication by adopting a security model (also called a security context), and by enhancing the operating system's logon security. By studying several operating systems, you will learn how to define, modify, and delete user accounts, as well as create well-formed passwords. Each of these elements enables strong authentication, which is essential for Internet servers.

You will also learn how to assign permissions and rights to users based on their ability to authenticate. By utilizing the tools necessary to define users and assign permissions, you will create a working network that fosters well-organized communication. The security tools that you will use depend on the underlying security models as implemented by the respective network operating system whether it is NT 4, Windows 2000, NetWare, Unix, or Linux. All these security models employ the common concepts of user and group, file, folder, and share permissions based on user authentication. Therefore, we will start with a look at user authentication.

Security Models and Authentication

*A*uthentication is the ability to determine a user's or computer's true identity. You have already learned that networks consist of clients and servers. These networks include resources that users access, such as printers, files, and databases. Every network manages these resources through a security model, which determines exactly how and when users can access resources based on authentication. The two basic security models are peer-to-peer and user-level. Which you implement depends on the situation.

Peer-Level Access

A *peer-to-peer network security model* does not require dedicated resources such as file servers; all computers are, in effect, both servers and clients. Any host can share resources with other systems on the network and can effectively become a type of server.

In a peer-to-peer network, each user becomes the administrator of his or her own computer. Therefore, control over resources is decentralized. As long as each workstation is available on the network through sharing, it can participate as a member. No other restrictions exist.

Figure 4.1 shows a peer-to-peer network. Each computer in this network has a name: Athena, Aphrodite, Hermes, Apollo, and Ares. These computers can access the printer attached to Apollo as long as the user administering Apollo has established a *share* for the printer on the network. A share is the method of making a computer's resources available to a network. Such resources can include files, folders, or printers.

FIGURE 4.1 The peer-to-peer network security model

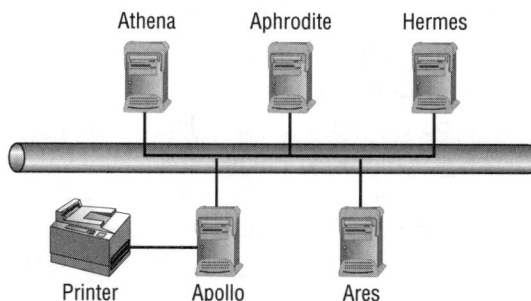

Each computer user can choose whether to participate in the network. A peer-to-peer network does not regulate user access from a central point.

You can set up a peer-to-peer network using the following operating systems:

- Novell NetWare Lite

- Microsoft Windows for Workgroups

- Microsoft Windows 9*x*/Me

- Apple AppleTalk network for Macintosh

- Windows NT 4, Windows 2000 Professional, and Windows XP

Advantages and Disadvantages

Peer-to-peer networks tend to be less expensive and easier to implement than networks that enforce user-level access. Therefore, a small business that initially has a few stand-alone computers can easily, with your help, network these computers by simply adding networks cards and a hub without having to buy a high-priced server. However, peer-to-peer networks have the following weaknesses:

- They do not centralize access control, tend to be difficult to administer, and may not be as secure, unless you take special measures.

- They offer less control over file and resource management than user-level access networks. Because each user can move files and establish and revoke shares at will, such networks require a high level of communication among their users.

- They are not as scalable as user-level access networks. Peer networks support only a small number of users. For example, Microsoft recommends fewer than 10 users for its peer-to-peer solution.

Establishing a Share in a Peer-to-Peer Setting

Regardless of the operating system you are using, you run the proper services if your system is to participate in a network. A *service* is program that runs on a server or a client. For example, to place a Windows 9x or Me system on a network, you must first install Client for Microsoft Networks, as well as File and Printer Sharing for Microsoft Networks. Other operating systems use different services to make a resource available across a network.

Although you generally will not establish shares to provide access to resources over the Internet, shares are a good place to begin understanding how to provide and control access to information from remote systems. After you verify the services on your computer, you can establish a share. A share is a file, folder, or disk on a host that can be accessed over the network. In Microsoft Windows 9*x*/Me, you establish a share using Windows Explorer. Open Windows Explorer, and then follow these steps to share a folder:

1. Right-click the folder you want to share, and then choose Sharing from the shortcut menu to open the Properties dialog box for the folder at the Sharing tab, as shown in Figure 4.2.

FIGURE 4.2 The Sharing tab in the Backup Properties dialog box

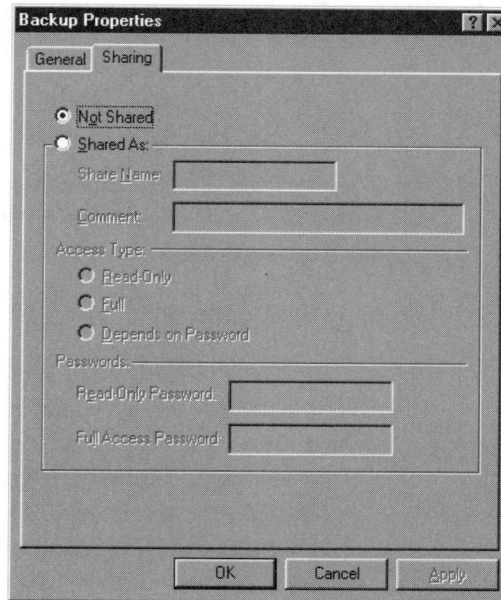

2. Click the Shared As radio button, and enter any name you want in the Share Name field. Make sure the name is no more than 12 characters and does not include invalid characters such as /, \, *,?, + or =. This name will become the share name on the network.

In Windows 95, you also use Windows Explorer to establish a share.

3. In the Comment box, enter a description of the share so that users will know what the share contains. On many networks, share names are limited to a specified number of characters. This limitation presents a problem if, for example, you must create a share for the accounting department with the share name `acntdpf1`. A description in the Comment box could clarify the share by stating "Accounting Department Files."

4. Click the Access Type radio button for the type of access you want to allow. Windows 9x or Me offers you three choices: Read-Only, Full, and Depends on Password. You can establish a read-only share, which allows users to only open and view a file or copy it to another file. If you allow full access, users can read, copy, and modify the file. Users can even delete the file or replace it, because they have the right or permission to do so.

> **NOTE** Many network and operating system vendors use the terms "right" and "permission" interchangeably. However, some vendors, such as Microsoft, apply specific meanings to the two terms. In Windows operating systems, a *right* applies to the user's ability to perform actions on a system. A *permission* describes a rule applied to an object, such as a folder or file.

5. To limit access to your share by establishing a password, click the Depends on Password radio button, and designate passwords for the types of access, as shown in Figure 4.3. If a user enters the password you designate in the Read-Only Password field, they are allowed only read permission. By entering the password you designate in the Full Access Password field, the user gains full permissions. The Depends on Password feature creates a password-protected share, providing a limited amount of security.

6. When you have selected all your options, click OK to close the Properties dialog box for the selected folder.

   You will learn more about permissions with user-level shares using Windows 2000 Server later in this chapter.

FIGURE 4.3   Creating a password-protected share

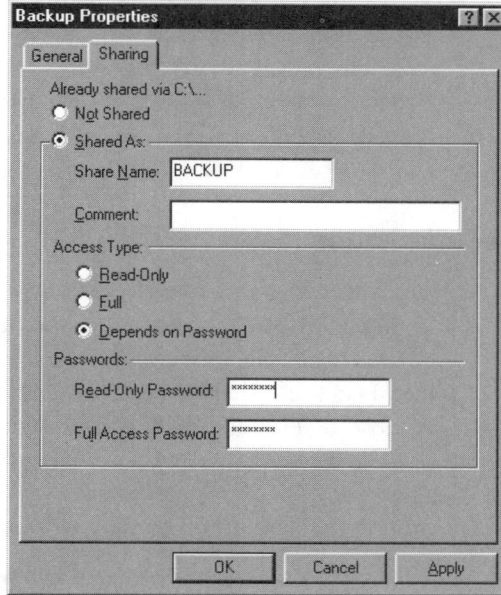

Identifying a Share

Once you establish a share in a Windows environment, Windows Explorer informs you of this share by displaying a hand icon under the folder, as shown in Figure 4.4.

FIGURE 4.4   A Backup share viewed in Windows Explorer

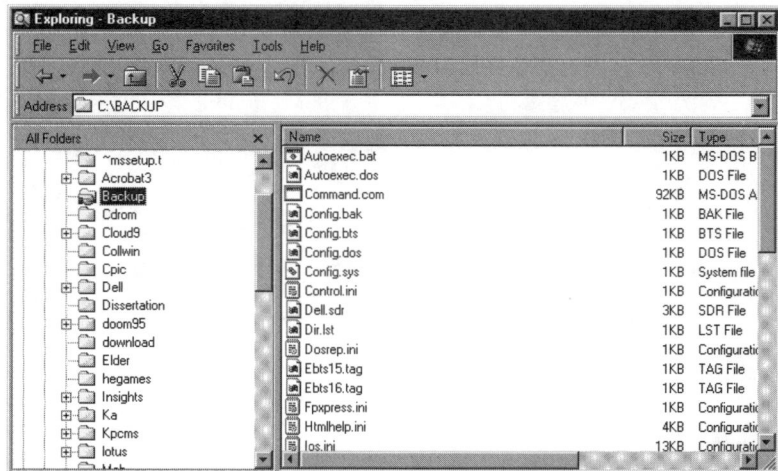

Notice that the steps for establishing a peer-to-peer share do not include asking for a user name. The password is the only feature that protects your resources. Anyone can connect to your system if he or she knows the share's location and password. No user-level protection is available.

The concept of a share is not Microsoft-specific. Network vendors, such as Novell, also allow you to create shares. Unix systems participate in Windows-based networks through the Samba service to share files with Windows.

Workgroups

Most peer-to-peer networks are organized in logical units of operation called *workgroups*. All members of a workgroup have equal access to all shares depending on the password. This access is the reason that the workgroup members are called peers. The computers shown in Figure 4.1—Athena, Aphrodite, Hermes, Apollo, and Ares—can configure themselves to belong to a workgroup, as shown in Figure 4.5.

FIGURE 4.5   Setting the workgroup name in Windows 98

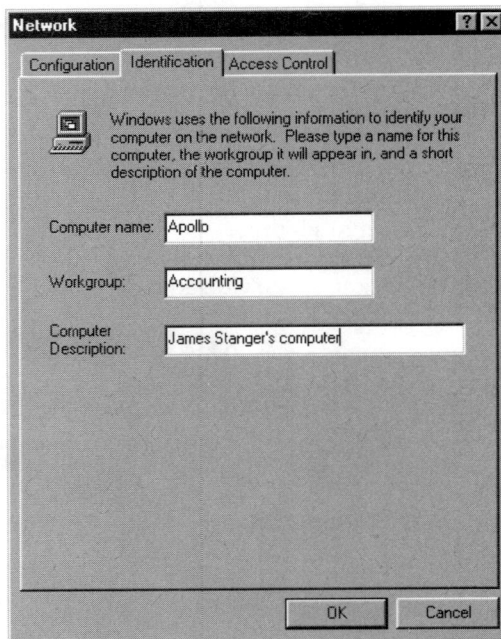

For convenience, many Internet servers are placed either into a workgroup security model or into no security model at all. In both cases, the administrator must secure the server's logon process as much as possible through encryption, strong passwords, stringent account and network security policies, and an alternative authentication model such as public key encryption. *Public key encryption* is the use of a pair of keys that allows two or more systems to encrypt transmissions to each other. The resulting encryption is difficult to unencrypt without the key and allows systems to communicate with confidence.

User-Level Access

A network using the *user-level access security model* allows users to obtain access to resources only if they belong to a centralized access list. This access list can be central to a particular server or to an entire network. User-level access is quite different from share-level access because it can be used to authenticate specific users.

An *access control list (ACL)* is a list of individual users and groups associated with an object and the permissions they have when accessing that object.

User accounts database is the standard term for an access list in the user-level access security model. A user accounts database is also an application of an access control list (ACL).

> **NOTE** Depending on the operating system, you can establish password-protected shares as well as shares based on user names. For example, on a Windows 98 system, you can establish only password-protected shares. On a Windows NT system, you can establish shares meant only for certain users and/or workgroups.

Operating systems that provide both centralized and local user-level server access include the following:

- Microsoft Windows 2000 Server and NT 4 Server
- Novell NetWare
- Digital Equipment Corporation's DECnet
- Unix, including Solaris, System V, Free BSD, and all Linux variants

> **NOTE**
>
> Many other client/server operating systems exist, including AppleTalk.

Centralized User Accounts Database

Figure 4.6 shows a network that employs a centralized user accounts database on a server. Any system that wants to access resources associated with this server must first authenticate with this database. If a computer is not in the database, it cannot connect to resources on that network server.

FIGURE 4.6 A user-based network

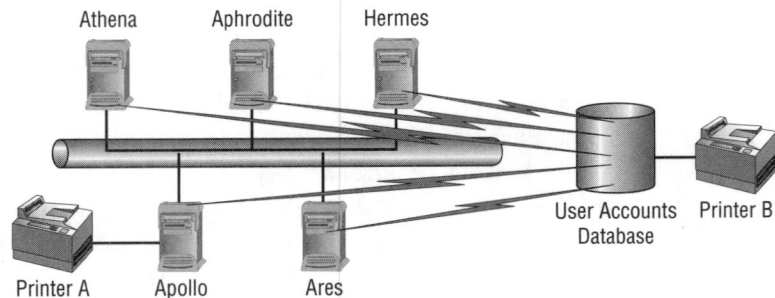

Because they belong to a user-level network with a centralized database, Athena, Aphrodite, Hermes, Apollo, and Ares must authenticate with the user accounts database before they can work together efficiently. If the user for Ares, for example, fails to provide the correct password, they will not be able to communicate with the rest of the network. This inability is not due to a physical break in the line or in the network transport protocol. The user cannot communicate because that computer has failed authentication and can no longer participate in the network. The only remedy for this problem is to enter the correct password (the one that corresponds to that user in the user accounts database) and become authenticated.

> **NOTE**
>
> Regardless of the network operating system (NOS), a centralized user accounts database resides on a server available to the rest of the network.

Local Accounts Database

All servers have local accounts databases as well that you can use to create user-level workgroups. For example, all users shown in Figure 4.6 can access Printer A provided that they authenticate with the user accounts database.

Windows 2000 servers work most effectively within a Windows 2000 domain structure that enforces the use of a centralized database. However, you can also create a workgroup between stand-alone 2000 servers. These servers still use strong, user-level authentication, while offering user organization options. Often, Internet system administrators do not configure their servers to participate in the Microsoft Kerberos domain model and choose the Workgroup model instead.

You will see how to work with a local accounts database later in this chapter.

Establishing a User-Level Share

As mentioned previously, permissions are not limited to local shares. They apply to remote shares as well.

A share is established in a user-level access network almost the same way as in a peer-level network. However, one key difference exists: Any resource you decide to share in a user-level network can be tied to a specific user or group of users.

For example, in Windows 2000, you can use Windows Explorer to establish a share and its permissions, as well as grant or limit access to users. In Windows 2000, you establish a share using Windows Explorer. Open Windows Explorer, and then follow these steps to share a folder:

1. Right-click the folder you want to share, and then choose Sharing from the shortcut menu to open the January Reports Properties dialog box at the Sharing tab, as shown in Figure 4.7.

2. Click the Share This Folder radio button, and enter any name you want in the Share Name field. In Windows 2000 share names can be a maximum of 30 characters. Make sure the name does not include invalid characters such as /, \, *, ?, + or =. This name will become the share name on the network.

3. In the Comment box, enter a description of the share so that users will know what the share contains.

FIGURE 4.7 The Properties dialog box for the January Reports folder

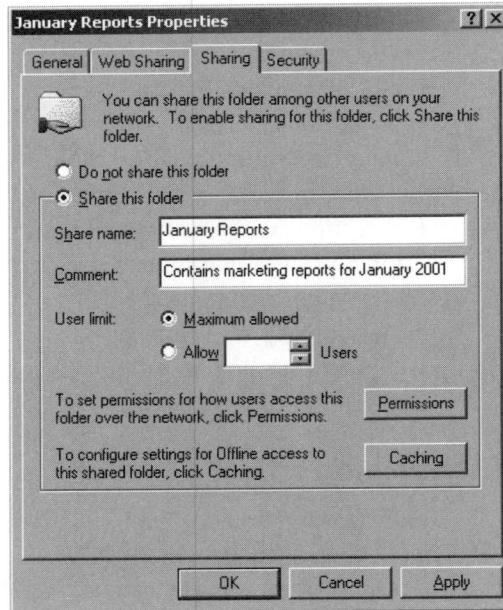

4. Click the Permissions button to open the Permission for January Reports dialog box, as shown in Figure 4.8.

5. Click the Add button to add the Administrators group. Click the Full Control check box, and then click OK.

6. Click the Permissions button to open the Share Permissions dialog box.

7. Highlight the Everyone group, and click Remove. Click OK twice. We have now restricted access to the January Reports share.

This particular share will allow access to Administrators of the server in which the share was created. Later in this chapter, you will see how a server can use directory services to allow access to many different servers across a network.

You will learn more about establishing individual user accounts shortly. The first exercise in this chapter will show you how to establish user accounts and user-level shares in a Windows 2000 network.

FIGURE 4.8 The Permissions for January Reports dialog box

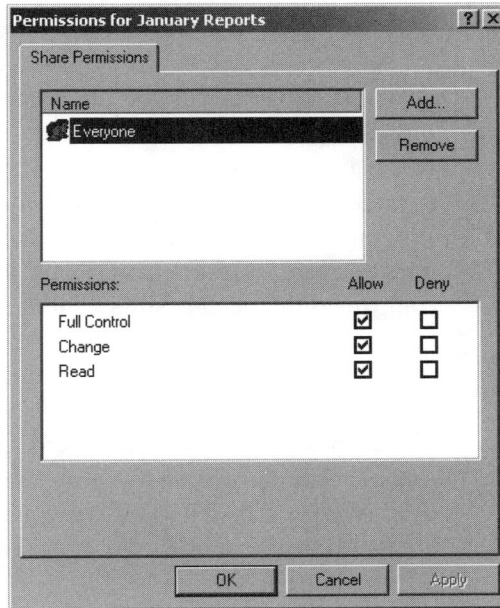

Advantages and Disadvantages

As a company's business grows and it acquires more than 10 computers, the disadvantages of buying one or more dedicated servers and supporting a sophisticated network operating system are overcome by the strengths of user-level access.

The strengths of user-level access include the following:

- Increased security

- Support for more users

- Increased control over access to resources

- The ability to monitor access to resources through system logs

- The ability to grow in response to an organization's needs

If you are planning on a low-security network for a small number of users, a peer-level solution may be the better choice. However, if you plan to create a higher security network for more than 10 people, consider a user-level network.

Creating User Accounts

In a peer-to-peer network, you can password protect shares (for example, in Windows 9*x*/Me), or you can create local user accounts on each computer (for example, in Windows NT 4 Server, Windows 2000 Server, Windows XP Professional). For example, if your company has a Windows 2000 Professional peer-to-peer network, and it has 10 employees with 10 Windows XP computers, each with a need to access files on all the other computers, you will need to create 100 local accounts and 100 passwords. Now imagine that your company is doubling in size within the next year. By implementing a server-based network with user-level access, you will need to define user accounts only once on a central user accounts database allowing universal access to resources on all computers based on permissions.

The most important element of a user-level network is the *user logon account*. Before you can establish a user-level share, you must specify the users who are allowed to use that resource. With a logon account, you have access to certain resources local to your system as well as certain resources on a LAN or WAN.

A logon account establishes an individual's identity. You can use this identity locally on an individual computer or over a network. A logon account is also tied directly to rights and permissions, which determine exactly what a user can (and cannot) do.

To a user, a logon account consists of a user name and a password. For example, in Linux systems, a user is presented with a screen that asks for a user name and a password, as shown in Figure 4.9.

FIGURE 4.9 Logging on to a Linux system with a user account

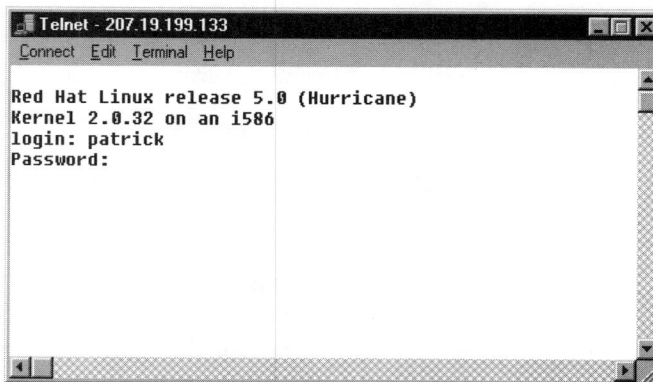

However, to a systems administrator, a logon account represents a more complete understanding of how a network operates. A logon account generally contains the following attributes:

- User name
- Password
- Group associations
- Permissions
- Additional options, such as logon scripts and a home directory

These attributes apply to all networks, including Windows NT, Novell NetWare, and Unix. The following sections explore each of these attributes.

User Name

A user name must be unique. Many administrators choose to create a user name that closely resembles a user's real name. For example, if your name were John Smith, your user name could be smithj. However, if more than one John Smith worked in your organization, you might be smithj, and the other John Smith could be jsmith or smithj2. As you plan a large network, you must consider such issues and alternatives.

Figure 4.10 shows how a systems administrator can take people's proper names and convert them into user names for the user accounts database.

FIGURE 4.10 Creating user names

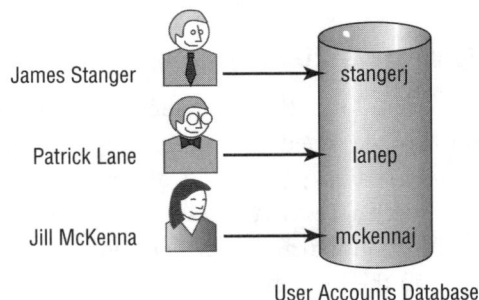

User Accounts Database

Unix

Unix systems assign a user identification number (UID) to each user name. These numbers are stored in 32-bit fields and can be any size. UIDs are stored in text files read by the operating system.

Windows 2000 and NetWare

Windows 2000 stores all account information in a central user accounts database. Each user account is assigned a unique security identification number (SID).

NetWare provides a similar logon structure, although older NetWare networks require a separate user name and password for each server.

Password

As you learned earlier, a password is the primary means for authentication on a network because a password is linked directly to a user name. Each operating system has its own requirements and suggestions for passwords. For example, some operating systems have reserved characters that you cannot use.

You will learn how to create well-formed passwords later in this chapter.

Group Associations

Most enterprise-grade operating systems allow you to place users into groups. For example, Windows 2000 includes a default Administrators group that contains all users who are able to control every aspect of the system. Unix systems have at least one user who is part of the root group. You can administer users more easily when you use groups.

For example, you can create a group called users. You can then assign permissions to that group. Next, you can place individual user accounts inside the users group. The result of this process is that any account you place in the users group assumes all permissions—and restrictions—given to that group.

Windows 2000

Windows 2000 provides two group types: global and local. *Global groups* are designed to contain users. *Local groups* contain resources. You can place global groups into local groups, which provides anyone in the global group with access to the resources in the local group. Figure 4.11 shows an example of a global group, which contains users who can access a printer and a server in the local group.

The purpose of this particular scheme is to differentiate between users (global groups) and resources (local groups). This scheme can also help organize a network more efficiently.

FIGURE 4.11   Placing a global group into local group

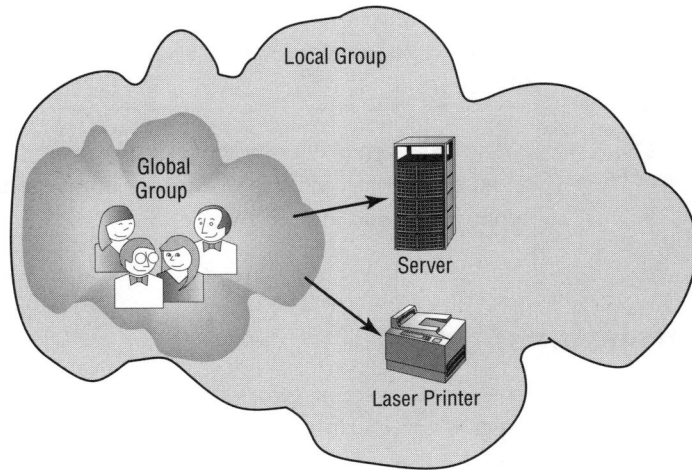

Often, administering Windows 2000 involves the use of the Microsoft Management Console (MMC). The MMC contains several *snap-ins*, which are tools you can use to administer network applications and to control elements of the system, including the following:

- Adding and managing users

- Configuring logon and security policies

- Limiting and managing user access to the system (for example, controlling access to shares)

- Controlling Internet services, such as HTTP, FTP, and SMTP servers

> **NOTE** In Windows NT Server 4, the MMC was invoked by the Internet Services Manager (ISM).

Unix

Unix systems provide the model for Windows groups. Whenever you create a user, you must place that user in a group. Using the `/etc/group` file, you can place specific users into groups. These users will then have the right to access the resources defined for the group.

NetWare

Like the other two major network vendors, NetWare uses groups to organize users into manageable units.

NOTE Many other types of networks exist, including Macintosh networks. However, most enterprises include Macintosh computers as part of the major network types discussed in this chapter.

Permissions

In a server-based network, you must grant or deny permissions to specific users. These permissions can be either local or share-based. A local permission grants or denies access to users who are logged on locally. A share-level permission applies only across a network.

As illustrated in Figure 4.12, permissions are generally granted through the user accounts database. Users are authenticated by the database and then assigned certain permissions.

FIGURE 4.12 User permissions are granted through user accounts database

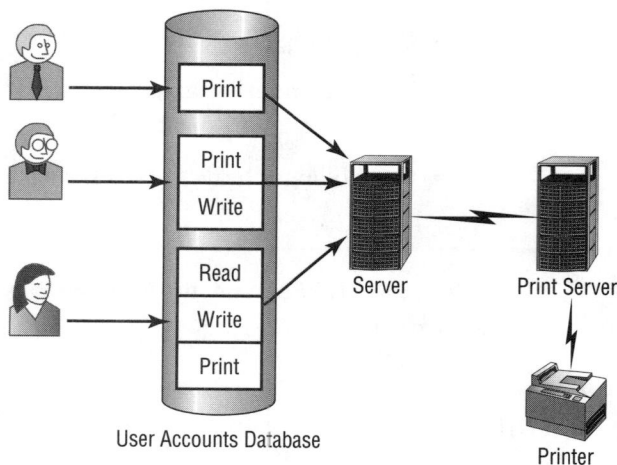

In Figure 4.12, each user is assigned different permissions. In this case, all users can use the printer because each has been authenticated and granted

print permission. Windows NT and 2000 servers, for example, will not let a user connect to a share unless that user has been defined on the system.

Some operating system permissions imply other permissions. For example, in Windows NT, the built-in Users group has print permissions.

You should not assume that simply creating an account allows a user to access a particular resource. Depending on the operating system, the user might have full access permissions or none at all. Therefore, you will often need to modify the accounts you create so that they have the appropriate permissions.

Additional User Account Options

Following are some additional terms you will encounter as you create logon accounts.

Logon Scripts

A *logon script* is a special application designed to customize a user's work environment. Generally, a logon script runs specific programs that enable an individual user to work more efficiently.

Home Directories

All three of the network operating systems discussed in this chapter allow you to establish a *home directory*. A home directory is a directory on a server in which, by default, all work is saved. This function helps organize files. Home directories are important because they allow a server administrator to back up user files easily. A home directory can exist on a local drive or on a remote drive.

In addition to simplifying fault tolerance (discussed later in this book), a home directory can also help users manage files. Such organizational tools will minimize confusion for new users and save administrative time.

Local and Roaming Profiles

A *local profile* connects a user's permissions to a computer's interface. In Windows 2000 systems, you can create a local profile that restricts user access to certain areas of the operating system. For example, most users do not need access to network configuration commands. You can, therefore, create a local profile that forbids access to this element of the operating system.

Profiles do not simply limit access. They are also helpful in organizing a user's files, thereby increasing productivity. However, what happens if a user gains access to another computer and logs on? Given that most networks employ user-level security, a user can log on from several locations.

Many network operating systems allow you to create a *roaming profile*. This profile type is the same as a local profile, except that a roaming profile travels with the user. For example, you assign a roaming profile to an employee named Joel. As soon as Joel authenticates, regardless of the location, the server downloads his profile.

File and Folder Permissions

In the previous section you learned to create user accounts. The purpose of creating user accounts is to give users the level of access to resources to do a super job without stepping on work that is not their business. In this section you will learn how to set file and folder permissions based on user logon accounts and group associations. Whereas share permissions only affect a user's ability to connect to a resource over the network, file and folder permissions further limit what a user can do once they connect. File and folder permissions also limit the permissions of users that log on locally to a computer. It is important that an administrator limit permissions on sensitive files and folders such as human resource and payroll records. Most operating systems provide the capability to permit users to read, write, and execute, and print files. Table 4.1 describes these permissions.

TABLE 4.1 Universal Permissions

Permission	Description
Read	Allows users to access a file in a folder using a specific program. For example, users can open and read the info.txt file with a word processor. Users can also copy the file to their own systems. However, they cannot modify or delete the original file, nor can they create a new file or add a file to that folder.

TABLE 4.1 Universal Permissions *(continued)*

Permission	Description
Write	Allows users to write information to the hard disk in most operating systems. Write implies read permission. Write permission allows users to modify the file. They can, for example, open the info.txt file and add content to it. They can also delete information from that file. In fact, they can even delete the entire file.
Execute	Allows users to run, or execute, a specific application residing in a specified folder.
Print	Allows users to send files to a printer. Some operating systems, such as Windows 2000, treat this as a right. Others, such as Unix, treat the ability to print as an additional set of permissions.

When a user creates a file or folder, they become its owner. A user with full permissions can read, write, and execute the individual file or the files in the folder. In Windows 2000 all users can print any file they can read, although permissions may be set on specialized printers such as plotters or check printers. Unix allows more granular control of print permissions. Generally, administrators assume ownership of a file or a folder. In the following sections, we'll briefly look at the major network operating systems and their approach to permissions.

> **NOTE** Each operating system discussed in this section has additional policies and permissions. A detailed discussion of permissions and rights specific to each operating system is beyond the scope of this book and the CIW Server Administrator exam.

Windows 2000 Permissions

In NT 4 and Windows 2000, all user accounts are a member of the Everyone system group that by default has full access to every file and folder. As the administrator, you will remove these permissions from the Everyone group for sensitive files and folders and grant the appropriate permissions to users and groups that you will create. For instance, you might create an HR group and give that group access to HR files. On the other hand, you might create a folder with Microsoft Office XP installation files and give users only read access to these files so that they do not delete them, while retaining full control for the Administrators group so that they can update these files and grant others permissions to use them.

Table 4.2 describes the access permissions allowed for Windows NT-based systems (Windows NT Server 4, Windows NT Workstation 4, Windows 2000 Server and Professional, and so forth). More specific permissions (listed in Table 4.3) are allowed only on partitions formatted with the *New Technology File System (NTFS)*. NTFS is the Windows NT and 2000 file system that provides added security and recovers dynamically from hard-drive crashes. (NT 4 supports FAT16 and NTFS. Windows 2000 supports FAT16, FAT32, and NTFS.) Notice how these permissions combine with the universal permissions discussed in the previous section.

TABLE 4.2 Windows NT/2000 Access Permissions

Permission	Description
Full Control	Allows a user to write to the hard disk and to change the permissions of a file or a folder. Also allows a user to change the file or folder owner.
Change (NT 4)/Modify (Windows 2000)	Allows a user to write to the hard drive; the same as the universal write permission. Also allows a user to delete, modify, or create a file.
Read	Allows a user to view a file or folder and to execute any application that lies within it.
No Access	Prohibits all access to a file or a folder. A user will not be able to open or read anything marked with the No Access permission.

NOTE Microsoft Windows 2000 calls the permissions described in Table 4.2 "access permissions." These permissions, which are granted to network users, determine the privileges a user has for a network resource, such as a shared folder. Note the difference between user-level security and access permissions: user-level security manages user accounts, whereas access permissions determine the privileges a user has to a particular resource.

Windows 2000 and Effective Permissions

Permissions can be combined. When permissions are combined in a Windows 2000 network share, the principle of least restrictive permissions applies. For example, your user account could belong to a group that has Read permission and to another group that has Full Control. Your effective share permissions would be Full Control because such permissions are cumulative.

NTFS Permissions

You can apply additional permission if hard drives are formatted with NTFS. These permissions apply differently for files and folders, as shown in Table 4.3.

TABLE 4.3 NTFS Permissions

NTFS Permission	Folder Permission	File Permission
Read (R)	Allows a user to display the contents of a folder, including the owner and the permissions.	Allows a user to display the file's properties, including the owner, size, and permissions.
Write (W)	Allows a user to add files and folders and to see the contents of a folder. Also allows a user to read the permissions associated with the folder.	Allows a user to display the same data as the Read permission and to create data within a file. Also allows a user to merge one file with another.

TABLE 4.3 NTFS Permissions *(continued)*

NTFS Permission	Folder Permission	File Permission
Execute (X)	Allows a user to see the contents of a folder. Also allows a user to read the permissions associated with the folder.	Grants all Read permissions; allows a user to run an application.
Delete (D)	Allows a user to delete the folder.	Allows a user to delete any file not in use by the system.
Change Permission (P)	Allows a user to change the permissions, even though they were set by another user or an administrator.	Allows a user to change a file's permissions, even if they were set by another user or an administrator.
Take Ownership (O)	Allows a user to take ownership of a folder, even though ownership was set by the creator or administrator.	Allows a user to take ownership of a file, even though ownership was set by the creator or administrator.

Windows 2000 also provides the Read and Execute permission, which allows you to list and view files. These permissions allow you to exercise granular control over all files and folders on a hard drive. For example, you can mark a folder as executable without making it readable. This capability is desirable in certain situations, such as when you have a folder that is storing an executable file. For example, if you are using a CGI script, you want it to be executable, but you do not want anyone to see it on the network. In this case, the file is both usable and secure.

NTFS and Share-Effective Permissions

If you combine share and NTFS permissions, the most restrictive permission applies. This principle is different from situations in which only share permissions are involved. For example, if you create a share and assign full control share permissions but only read NTFS permissions, the effective permission of this share will be read. Finally, NTFS permissions apply to both local and remote access. Share permissions apply only across a network connection.

Windows 2000 Administrative Utilities

In Windows 2000, you create accounts on the system using Computer Management. Choose Start ➤ Programs ➤ Administrative Tools ➤ Computer Management to open the Computer Management window, which is shown in Figure 4.13. Use the Users folder in the Users and Groups section to create user names and groups and to assign permissions.

FIGURE 4.13 Administering users through the Computer Management window

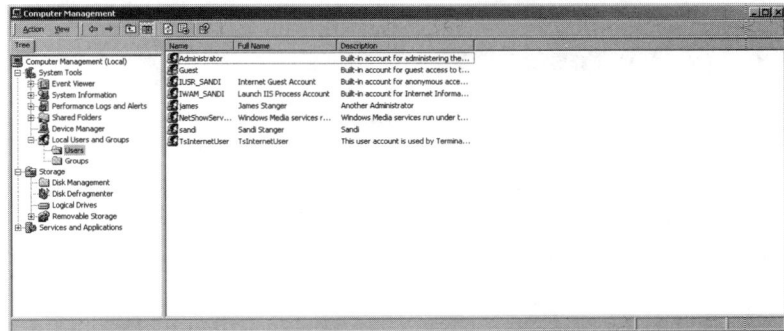

To manage your computer's shares, you use the Shared Folders folder. To view active sessions, expand the Shared Folder folder, and then select the Sessions folder, as shown in Figure 4.14.

FIGURE 4.14 Managing shares in the Computer Management window

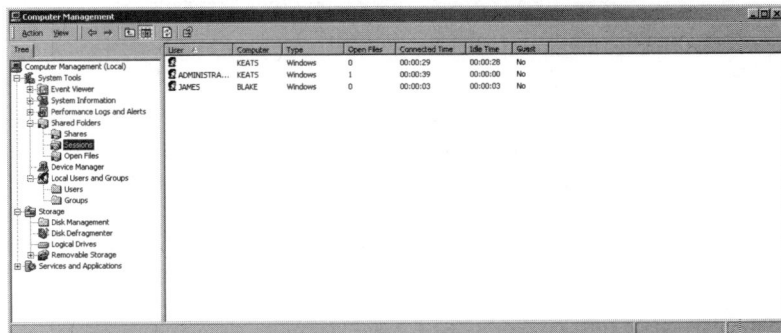

Figure 4.14 shows that the Keats and Blake machines are attached to the local machine. The Keats machine has established a null session, which means the session has no specific user. There is also a user-based session from the user named Administrator. The user on the Blake machine is named James. You can see which files and folders are being accessed by selecting the Open Files folder.

> **WARNING** Do not confuse the ability to monitor and manage shares with the ability to create shares. When you want to create a share, use Windows Explorer as explained earlier in this chapter.

Unix Permissions

Unix appends certain values called *access bits* to all files and directories (that is, folders). These bit values control access to files and directories at three levels: the user level, the group level, and the "everyone" or "other" level. Windows NT and 2000 use a similar permissions model that involves access control entries based on a user's individual and group permissions including membership in the Everyone system group. By default, in Windows NT and 2000, the Everyone group has full control NTFS and share permissions until permissions are reassigned in order to selectively control access to resources.

When you view a long file by using the ls -l command in Unix, the permissions granted on your files and directories are displayed as a block of letters and dashes:

```
drwxr-xr-x (sample, for a directory)
-rw-r--r-- (sample, for a file)
```

The ls -l listing also shows the file's owner and the group to which it belongs and may show additional information. (See http://bit.csc.lsu.edu/~mbowler/unixfs.html for a discussion of SUID, SGID, and sticky bit information that may be disclosed by an ls-l listing.)

To read basic permission information, you need to know the following:

- The character in the first position is d for a directory or a hyphen (-) for a file.

- The next nine positions, or characters, are organized in three groups of three. The first group pertains to the file owner, the second group to the file's group, and the third group to all other users (everyone).

- The permissions are Read (r), Write (w), and Execute (x). If the permission is granted to the level in question, the corresponding letter appears. A hyphen indicates that the permission is denied.

For files, Read, Write, and Execute permissions mean the same as the universal permissions discussed earlier in this chapter. For directories, Write permission allows you to create files in that directory, Read permission allows you to read file names in that directory, and Execute permission allows you to change to that directory (using cd) and modify file attributes in that directory.

> **NOTE**   In Unix, everything is a file; this means that data files, directories, device entries, and links are all considered files. The very first letter in a file's ls -la listing indicates its file type. For example, files beginning with a hyphen (-) are regular files (also called plain files), and files beginning with the letter *d* are directories. For details, see http://www.onlamp.com/pub/a/bsd/2000/09/06/ FreeBSD_Basics.html.

Following are some examples of each permission type:

- -rwxr--r-- describes a regular file whose owner can read, write, or execute it. Members of the file's group and everyone else can only read the file.

- -rwxr-xr-x describes a regular file whose owner can read, write, or execute it. Members of the file's group and everyone else can read or execute it, but not write to it.

- -rw------- describes a regular file whose owner can read it or write to it. No one else has access to the file.

- drwx------ describes a directory to which its owner has full access. No one else has access to this directory.

- drwxr-xr-x describes a directory to which its owner has full access. Others (the group and everyone else) can read the directory, but cannot create or delete files in the directory.

Numeric Equivalents

Table 4.4 summarizes the numeric values for access bits.

TABLE 4.4 Access Value Bits

Access Value (octal form)	Read/ Write/ Execute	Meaning of Access Value Bits (additive in nature)
7	4/ 2/ 1	Read, write, and execute
6	4/ 2/ -	Read and write
5	4/ -/ 1	Read and execute
4	4/ -/ -	Read only
3	-/ 2/ 1	Write and execute
2	-/ 2/ -	Write
1	-/ -/ 1	Execute
0	-/ -/ -	No mode bits (that is, access absent)

The default permissions for a plain file are usually 666 (that is, read and write to the file's owner, group, and others). Each bit pattern (or octal value) is assigned to each component of the file's three values (owner, group, and others). The default permissions for a directory and an executable program are usually 777 (that is, read, write, and execute for the directory's owner, group, and others).

Unix Administrative Utilities

Table 4.5 describes some of the commands you can use to create user accounts and alter permissions in Unix. As you know, many different versions, or flavors, of Unix exist. Some versions have commands that are slightly different from those in the table.

TABLE 4.5 Unix Administrative Utilities

Utility	Description
linuxconf useradd/adduser usermod userdel	These commands add and modify new user accounts and assign group membership. The linuxconf command opens the linuxconf utility, which you can use to configure the entire system. You can use the linuxconf utility either from the command line or in the X Window System. The useradd command is especially effective because it automatically adds all the necessary parameters for using the X Window System, among other elements. The adduser command is another name for the useradd command.
chown chgrp	These commands change the user and group ownership of a file. The chgrp command is older and is only found in certain Unix versions.
chmod	This command changes the permissions on a file or a directory.
chage	This command sets passwords so that they become invalid after a certain time, a process called *password aging*. You will learn more about this concept shortly. The linuxconf command can also modify password age.

Many versions of Unix exist. Although most of these versions share many commands and other attributes, you should still familiarize yourself with the details of your particular operating system.

NetWare Rights

Unlike the other major network operating systems, NetWare uses the word *rights* to refer to files and systems permissions. Table 4.6 describes the rights found in NetWare systems.

TABLE 4.6 NetWare Rights

Right	Description
Supervisor	Similar to administrator access in NT or root access in Unix
Read	Same as read access in NT, Windows 2000, or Unix
Write	Same as Unix write access or change permission in Windows 2000
Erase	Same as Unix write access or change permission in Windows 2000
Modify	Same as Unix write access or change permission in Windows 2000
Create	Same as write access in Unix; no equivalent NT or Windows 2000 permission
File Scan	Allows you to list a file. No equivalent Unix or Windows 2000 permission
Access Control	Same as write access in Unix or change permission in Windows 2000
No Access	Same as no access in Unix or Windows 2000

NetWare Administrative Utilities

Table 4.7 describes the most commonly used Novell NetWare administrative utilities.

TABLE 4.7 NetWare Administrative Utilities

Program	Description
NWAdmin	Allows you to create user accounts and assign permissions. Allows you to assign policies for the entire network. The primary tool used for administering networks, NWAdmin replaces an earlier management tool called Syscon.

TABLE 4.7 NetWare Administrative Utilities *(continued)*

Program	Description
NDS Manager	Allows you to manage Novell Directory Services (NDS).
Rconsole	Allows you to administer the network remotely (requires IPX/SPX). In a TCP/IP environment, it must operate in compatibility mode.

Administrative Privilege

To create, delete, or modify user accounts, you must have privileged access to the operating system. For example, if you want to assign permissions or exercise control over an operating system's processes and programs, you must be an administrative user. This concept of privilege and administration is expressed in different ways, depending on the operating system. In Unix systems, the name for such an account is root. In Windows NT and 2000 systems, it is called the Administrator account. In NetWare systems, the Supervisor account administers the network.

Table 4.8 summarizes the names of privileged accounts. Each account has access to all functions in the operating system.

TABLE 4.8 Privileged Account Names

Operating System	Name	Universal Privilege
Unix (including System V, Solaris, Free BSD, and all Linux variants)	root	Full
Windows NT, 2000	Administrator	Full
NetWare 3	Supervisor	Full
Netware 4, 5, and 6	Admin	Full

Standard Password Practices

You have already learned the importance of passwords to authentication. Because they provide a key link in the authentication process, passwords should be as strong, or well formed, as possible. In this section, we'll take a look at how to set strong password policies and, perhaps more important, how to convey this information to network users so their accounts and your network are safe.

The Computer Emergency Response Team (CERT) and various industry leaders such as Microsoft, Sun, and IBM developed standards for determining a well-formed password. A strong password contains the following:

- At least six characters
- Both uppercase and lowercase letters
- At least one Arabic numeral
- At least one symbol, such as the plus sign (+), the dollar sign ($), or the percent sign (%)

Implementing a Password Policy

Many users have difficulty remembering passwords and thus often choose easy-to-remember but ineffective passwords. Some people use their spouses' names as passwords, whereas others use their pets' names, the name of their favorite television show or bands, or even the names of the companies for which they work. Still others use "password" as the password. As a network administrator, you must create network-wide policies that will ensure the use of strong passwords.

As a network administrator, be sure that all your users understand the password policy. Creating a strong password policy that everyone can understand and use requires that you comply with the following procedures.

Plan the password policy.   Determine how simple or complicated the passwords should be, depending on your network needs.

Write and publish the policy.   Closely document the policy so that all employees, including temporary workers, can understand and follow it.

Create a balanced policy.   The policy must be as simple to implement as possible. If it is too strict, users will find ways to circumvent the password practice, leaving you with an ineffective security policy. If your policy is not strict enough, you will defeat the purpose of using passwords at all.

After planning a reasonable and secure password policy, you must implement it through a server's operating system. For instance, you can use `linuxconf` to require complex passwords in Unix. In Windows 2000, set group policy at the domain level to require a complex password. In either case, any new account passwords or password changes that do not meet this policy will be rejected. (We'll look at password policies in more detail in Chapter 5.)

Training Users

Implementing effective passwords involves training both server administrators and users. Because users affect password usage, you must always consider their ability to adhere to the policies you set. Here are some guidelines to follow when training users:

- Train users in short group meetings.

- Conduct one-on-one user training sessions, if feasible.

- Include a written description of the policy in the new employee pamphlet.

- Discuss the policy with new employees.

- Send the policy (as well as other key network security issues) via e-mail occasionally as a reminder to all employees.

- Place the password policy on a workplace bulletin board.

Each option has its own use in specific situations. For example, an announcement on a workplace bulletin board might go unnoticed, but most employees read their e-mail.

Network Security Policies

In addition to training users on password security, you should educate users on additional network security policies such as account lockout. Most networking vendors allow you to establish network-wide policies. You set these policies through a network operating system, such as Linux or Windows 2000 Server. Many of these policies focus on password usage because a password is generally the first line of defense in a network security scheme. However, some policies focus on other aspects of network management.

Table 4.9 describes a few of the more commonly applied policies.

TABLE 4.9 Network Security Policies

Policy	Description
Password aging	Allows you to make a password valid for only a certain amount of time. After this time, the usual procedure is to require the user to choose another password. A specific form of password aging includes requiring a user to change their password after initially logging on.
Password length	Allows you to specify the minimum or maximum number of characters in each password.
Password history	Lists previously used passwords. If you associate this list with a user account, that user will not be able to choose a password on this list.
Uniqueness	A password should not be a standard word from a dictionary. If you want to use a dictionary word, alter it by substituting non-standard characters (~ ! @ # $ % ( ) ^ & *) for certain letters and by using capital and lowercase letters.
Account lockout	Allows you to lock out a specific account if a user repeatedly fails to provide the proper password. This method is often necessary because hackers will try to guess a password until they discover the correct one.
Share creation	Allows additional users beyond Administrators, Server Operators, and Power Users. Allows you to create shares on a computer.
User creation	Allows you to create users. Except in certain circumstances, this right should be reserved for administrators.
Local logon	Allows you to sit in front of a computer and log on. Most servers limit a user's ability to log on locally. Only specific administrative accounts should have such a privilege. Another name for local logon is "interactive logon." Local logon is the opposite of logging on remotely.

A moderate administrative approach is important when establishing a network security policy. As stated previously, a strict policy may prove ineffective if it requires too much from users, who will attempt to find ways to circumvent it. For example, if you require constant password renewal, and program the operating system to disallow users from reusing old passwords, you may decrease your network's overall security. Some users will leave the password in a desk drawer or write it on a note attached to their monitor.

Therefore, carefully balance your security needs with your users' abilities and motivation to follow the policy.

Standard Operating Procedures

A *standard operating procedure (SOP)* is any written policy on which the IT department and management agree. SOPs usually apply to IT employees rather than to users. For example, you might want to establish an SOP directing all internetworking personnel to use the reserved class C address (192.168.0.0) when creating additional networks. You might also want to establish an SOP that defines the procedures in case an IT employee discovers a virus or detects hacker intrusion. Most networks implement several SOPs for a variety of activities, including the following:

- Stipulations concerning vendors for operating systems, hardware, and software
- Procedures for upgrading, replacing, and maintaining hardware
- Procedures for upgrading software, including operating systems and applications
- Procedures for responding to power outages, building evacuation, and hacker intrusion
- Documentation for an acceptable use policy

Acceptable Use Policy

The rules applied to users are often collected in documentation called an *acceptable use policy (AUP)*. Such documentation typically discusses the following issues.

- Internet privileges, including web access and e-mail

- Supported applications (such as e-mail clients, web browsers, word processors, and antivirus programs), operating systems, and hardware

In order to better understand AUPs, you will create a logon account policy for a company in Exercise 4.1. In Exercise 4.2 you will practice adding and deleting user accounts that will comply with the logon policy you created in Exercise 4.1.

EXERCISE 4.1

Creating a Logon Account Policy

In this exercise, you will write a simple logon account policy for a small company. You must create a policy that users can understand and follow. If your policy is too complex or strict, users will become confused. First, you will create an SOP for user names. You will then create a policy for passwords. Be sure to follow the instructions for each step.

1. Use the following naming convention for the three user names you will create: full last name and first letter of first name with no spaces. (For example, John Smith's user name would be smithj.)

   Write the user names for the following three people in the spaces provided.

   John Smith: _____

   Jane Smith: _____

   Bill Evans: _____

2. Already, you have encountered a conflict. There are two smithj user names. To resolve this problem, use the following policy.

   If another user name duplicates an existing user name, place a numeral at the end of the duplicate name, beginning with number 2. (The first user name assigned will not have a numeral.) Consider an alternative policy you can implement.

   Use a consistent policy to write Jane Smith's user name in the space provided: _____

3. The password Tr$ning1 contains a non-standard character, uses more than six characters, and includes a capital letter and a number. This password is sufficiently altered so that it is not a dictionary word. It is an example of a strong password. You will use this password in subsequent exercises.

4. Consider the following policy training options with regard to password usage:

   Train users in short group meetings.

   Conduct one-on-one user-training sessions.

   Include a written description of the policy in the new employee pamphlet.

   Discuss the policy with new employees.

   Periodically send the policy via e-mail as a reminder to all employees.

   Place the password policy on a workplace bulletin board.

   How will you ensure that users can implement both the account and password policies? Describe at least three delivery methods.

   In this exercise, you implemented three key concepts: You defined a password naming convention, you defined a strong password, and you delineated a network policy for users.

EXERCISE 4.2

Adding and Modifying User Accounts

In this exercise, you will create user accounts and add them to the Windows 2000 user accounts database. You will then place users into groups. You will work with local accounts databases, not with any Domain Controller (DC). The permissions are similar, except the local accounts databases provide security only for your computer and not the entire network.

1. To manage users, choose Start ➤ Programs ➤ Administrative Tools ➤ Computer Management to open the Computer Management window.

2. To add a user, expand System Tools and then expand Local Users and Groups icons by clicking on the plus sign next to each.

3. Click the Users folder to display a list of users in the right pane.

4. To add a user, right-click in the right pane and choose New User from the shortcut menu to open the New User dialog box:

5. In the User Name field, enter **smithj**.

6. In the Full Name field, enter John Smith's full name, and in the Description field, enter **New Administrator**.

7. In the Password field, enter the password **Tr$ning1**. (For the purpose of this exercise, you will use this password for all users.)

8. In the Confirm Password field, enter **Tr$ning1** again to confirm the password.

9. Clear the User Must Change Password at Next Logon check box, because you will be using this account. If another user will be using this account, leave the check box selected so the user will have a secret password. To create the new user, click the Create button.

10. Click the Close button to return to the Computer Management window.

11. Right-click the smithj account and select Properties from the short-cut menu to open the Properties dialog box for this account.

12. To remove smithj from the Users groups, click the Member Of tab, highlight the Users group, and click the Remove button.

13. Click the Add button to open the Select Groups dialog box.

14. Add John Smith's account to the Administrators group by high-lighting Administrators and clicking Add. When you are finished, your screen should resemble the following:

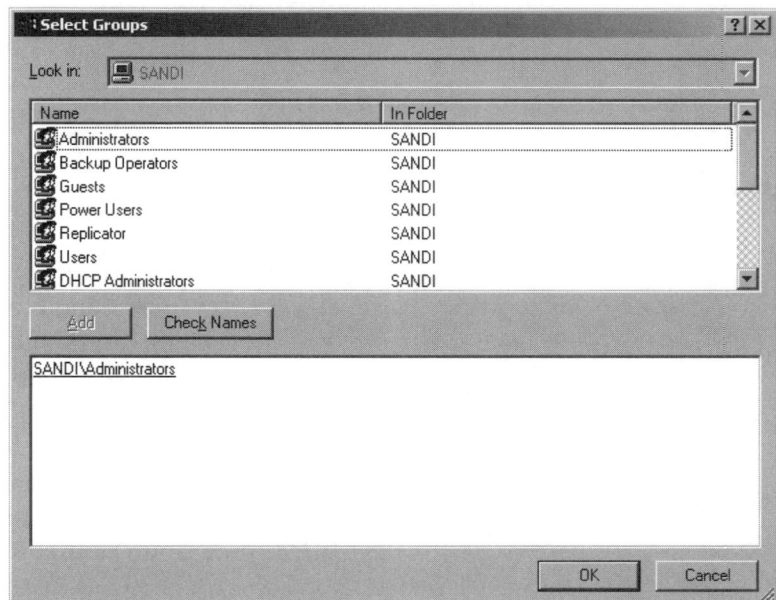

As you can see, smithj has been added to the local computer's Administrators group. The local computer's name is SANDI.

15. Click OK, click Apply, and then click Close to return to the Computer Management window.

16. Add the two users you defined in the previous exercise (smithj2 and evansb). Make smithj2 a member of the Power Users group, which has most of the privileges of the Administrator group. Make sure that you clear the User Must Change Password at Next Logon check box. Create the evansb account, making sure that you clear the User Must Change Password at Next Logon check box. Do not modify this account any further. Follow the logon account policy you established in the previous exercise. Also, be sure to use the same password for each: Tr$ning1.

Be sure to create all these users. Otherwise, you will have to create them in future exercises.

17. When you have finished, review your work.

Summary

In this chapter, we explored the basics of user management, and looked at network security models: peer-to-peer and user-level. We discussed user accounts, password practices and procedures, and network resources such as network shares. We explained the universal permissions to read, write, execute, and print, including details about Windows 2000, Unix, and NetWare. Finally, we discussed SOPs and how to create a logon account policy, user accounts, and shares.

With these skills you will be able to implement share-level and user-level access security models. You should also be able to use administrative utilities for specific networks and operating systems. With these utilities, you should now be able to create users and groups, assign the users to groups, and assign permissions to groups.

Exam Essentials

Define authentication and how it is implemented in share level and user level access security models.   Authentication is the process of identifying a user for the purpose of granting access to local computer or network resources. In a high-security environment, you can authenticate by combining what you know (username and password), what you have (Smart Card), and who you are (biometrics). In a workgroup, which uses share-level security, only the location of a share and a password may be required. In a domain, which uses user-level security, besides the location of the share, a valid username and password authenticated against a central user accounts database are required

Identify the purposes of logon accounts, groups, and passwords in granting access to resources by setting permissions, and be able to discuss permission issues, including the permissions needed to add, delete, or modify user accounts.   In a user-level security environment, a logon account with a secure password grants universal access to resources based on permissions. To make permissions easier to track and to facilitate administration, you add logon accounts to groups that are assigned permissions. In Windows 2000, you add accounts to global groups that are used to aggregate users. You then add global groups to Domain Local groups that are used to aggregate permissions. Finally, you assign permissions to the Domain Local groups. In Unix/Linux, you use the ls -l command to display permissions for the file or directory owner, group, and others. The administrative account that can create users and groups and grant permissions is the Administrator account in NT 4 or Windows 2000, the root account in Linux/Unix, and the Supervisor account (NetWare 3.*x*) or the Admin account (NetWare 4.*x* and later).

Be able to use administrative utilities in Windows 2000, NT 4, Linux, and NetWare to add, delete, or modify user accounts, groups, and permissions.   The major administrative utilities in Windows 2000 and NT 4 include User Management (workgroup environment) and User Manager for Domains. In Novell NetWare, Syscon (NetWare 3.*x*) and NWAdmin (NetWare 4.*x* and later) are the primary administrative tools. In Linux, the primary administrative utilities are linuxconf, adduser, and useradd. In Unix/Linux, you use chown to change ownership, and you use chage for password aging.

Be able to create a secure and stable user environment by developing a network password policy that uses standard practices and procedures and by creating user home directories and user profiles. Complex passwords have six or more characters and include three of the following: uppercase letters, lowercase letters, numbers, and other symbols including punctuation. A network password policy should include password complexity requirements, password aging, and password uniqueness requirements. Once users have logged in using their username and password, create a home directory to allow user access to their files. Create a roaming profile to allow user access to their desktop settings no matter which workstation on the network they are using.

Key Terms

Before you take the exam, be certain you are familiar with the following terms:

acceptable use policy (AUP)

access control list (ACL)

authentication

global groups

home directory

local groups

local profile

logon script

New Technology File System (NTFS)

peer-to-peer network security model

public key encryption

roaming profile

service

share

snap-in

standard operating procedure (SOP)

user accounts database

user logon account

user-level access security model

workgroups

Review Questions

1. Jim just installed Windows 2000 Professional on seven computers at work. He has these computers networked in a peer-to-peer network. Under what circumstances should Jim seriously consider upgrading to a server-based network?

    A. The number of computers will double in size in the next six months.

    B. He will be doing defense-contracting work on forensic accounting.

    C. He wants his users to have individual control of shares based on passwords.

    D. He wants a single logon with universal access to resources based on permissions and single seat administration.

2. Mark owns a small engineering design business that has seven computers that need access to a central database. His business is fairly stable in size, and his budget for hardware is limited. Which type network if any should Mark install?

    A. A peer-to-peer or workgroup network

    B. A hybrid network

    C. A server-based or user-level access network

    D. A Samba network

3. Brad wants to set up a peer-to-peer network on four Windows Me computers. When users need access to shares on Brad's network, what must users on client computers do? Choose two.

    A. Locate the share

    B. Provide a valid username

    C. Provide a valid password

    D. Ensure that the netlogon service is started

    E. Ensure that the sharing service is enabled

4. Andrea is administering a Unix Apache web server. What permissions should she set on the directory that holds CGI scripts?

   A. drwerwe_r_

   B. dr_er_e__e

   C. drwerw_rw_

   D. drwer_x__x

   E. drw_rw__wx

   F. drw_rw_r_x

   G. dr_er_x__x

5. Joshua wants to set up a user-based network on 20 Windows 2000 Professional computers joined to a domain. When users need access to shares on Joshua's network, what must users on client computers do? Choose three.

   A. Locate the share

   B. Provide a valid local username to the computer that has the share

   C. Provide a valid password

   D. Provide a valid domain username to a Windows 2000 Domain Controller

   E. Ensure that the sharing service is enabled

6. Frank wants to share some files between two Windows 98 computers. What must Frank do? Choose two.

   A. Install Windows Client32

   B. Install File and Print Sharing for Microsoft Networks

   C. Upgrade to Windows 2000 Professional

   D. Install Client for Microsoft Networks

7. From a Windows 2000 Professional computer, Frank wants to create a network share. Which of the following tools would he use to share a folder?

A. Server Manager

B. NW Admin

C. Windows Explorer

D. Disk Administrator

E. netconfig

8. Andrea wants to know how Unix sets permissions on files and directories. Which of the following statements are true?

A. Unix controls permissions using access bits.

B. Unix controls permissions using a shadow file.

C. Unix controls permissions using a centralized access database.

D. Unix controls permissions at three levels.

E. Unix controls permissions at the two levels.

9. Peter is a Linux systems administrator. He wants to add new user accounts and assign group membership. Which of the following utilities can perform both tasks?

A. linuxconf

B. chmod

C. useradd

D. chown

E. chgrp

F. adduser

G. chage

10. Ralph is using Extensible Authentication Protocol (EAP) on his Windows 2000 Professional laptop. He is using a thumbprint scanner and a Smart Card to which he must authenticate with a PIN. By what means is Peter authenticating? Choose all that apply.

    A. What he knows

    B. What he has

    C. Who he is

    D. Where he is

11. Frank sets a policy that users must use strong passwords. He then creates a user with the password of HeresSam. His password is rejected, so Frank must try another password. Which of the following passwords meet strong password complexity requirements? Choose all that apply.

    A. HeresSamantha

    B. Here'sSam

    C. Here'sSamantha

    D. #here'samantha!

12. Mark administers a mixed network with Linux and Windows NT 4 servers. Tom asks Mark what authenticates his users and allows their access to resources in Linux and Windows NT. Mark replies that _____ performs these tasks. Fill in the blank.

    A. The name service

    B. The user accounts database

    C. The directory service

    D. The routing service

13. Brad asks Tim what are the names of the administrative accounts in Linux, NetWare, and Windows 2000. Tim replies that these accounts are _____in Linux, _____ in NetWare, and _____in Windows 2000. Fill in the blanks.

A. SU, Supervisor, Admin or Administrator

B. Root, Supervisor, Admin or Administrator

C. Admin, Supervisor or SU, Root

D. SU or Supervisor, Root, Administrator

E. Root, Supervisor or Admin, Administrator

14. Ben is a Windows 2000 administrator. He wants to give Wendy, Bill, and John, who are managers in the `Corp.com` domain, access to the Pilot Projects folder in the `Development.Corp.com` domain. How should Ben do this? Choose three.

A. Add Wendy, Bill, and John to the Managers Global group in the `Corp.com` domain

B. Add Wendy, Bill, and John to the Managers Global group in the `Development.Corp.com` domain

C. Add the Managers Global group to the Pilot Access Local group in the `Corp.com` domain

D. Add the Managers Global group to the Pilot Access Local group in the `Development.Corp.com` domain

E. Assign permissions for the Pilot Projects folder to the Managers Global group

F. Assign permissions for the Pilot Projects folder to the Pilot Access Local group

15. Mandy is a member of the Server Operators group in Windows 2000. She wants to change a report on abnormal server activity in the Weekly Update folder for which she has Full Control NTFS permissions and Read share permissions. The report is located on the Database1 server. How can Mandy do this?

    A. From her workstation she can change the file over the network.

    B. She can change the file locally at the Database1 server.

    C. She cannot change the report.

    D. She must be removed from the Server Operators group before she can change the report.

16. Frank is a Unix systems administrator. He is trying to overwrite a file in the /usr/bin/readme directory and is denied access. He types ls -l and receives the following output: drwxr-xr-x. Why can't Frank overwrite the file in the /usr/bin/readme directory?

    A. He is not in the group that owns the file.

    B. He does not own the file.

    C. He is not logged on as Administrator.

    D. The file is archived.

17. Peter is a Linux systems administrator. For higher security, he wants to change the permissions on a directory and to make sure that users reset their passwords on a regular basis. Which two utilities are devoted to these two tasks?

    A. linuxconf

    B. chmod

    C. useradd

    D. chown

    E. chgrp

    F. adduser

    G. chage

18. Andrea wants to use her desktop settings, including wallpaper, short-cuts, mapped drives, and mapped printers, from any computer on the network. What should be created for Andrea to accomplish this goal?

A. Local profile

B. Roaming profile

C. Home directory

D. Administrative tools

E. Cached directory

19. Peter wants to make sure that his users periodically change their passwords and cannot change their passwords back to their original password. Which password policies should Peter implement? Choose two.

A. Password complexity

B. Password history

C. Password aging

D. Password length

20. Ralph wants to add users in Linux. Which administrative utilities could Ralph use?

A. useradd

B. adduser

C. chown

D. chage

E. linuxconf

Answers to Review Questions

1. A, B, D.   Peer-to-peer networks are suitable for workgroups of as many as 10 computers. Server-based networks offer more security and centralization of the user accounts database.

2. A.   Mark should install a peer-to-peer network to save the expense of additional hardware.

3. A, C.   Users must locate the share and provide a valid password.

4. D.   The other group used for anonymous access needs the execute permission but not the read or write permission to CGI scripts. The owner of the directory also needs the read and write permission.

5. A, C, D.   Joshua's users must have a domain user account and password valid for the Windows 2000 domain. They must also locate the share.

6. B, D.   Frank must install Client for Microsoft Networks, and he must install and enable File and Print Sharing for Microsoft Networks.

7. C.   Frank should use Windows Explorer.

8. A, D.   Unix controls access to directories and files using access bits that are set at the user, group, and other levels.

9. A, C, F.   Peter can use `linuxconf` and `useradd/adduser` to add new accounts and assign group membership.

10. A, B, C.   Ralph must prove what he knows (PIN), what he has (Smart Card), and who he is (biometric thumb print scanner).

11. B, C.   Strong passwords need to contain at least six characters and three of the following four character types: uppercase letters, lowercase letters, numbers, and symbols including punctuation.

12. B. The user accounts database performs these tasks.

13. E. In Novell NetWare 3.*x*, Supervisor is the administrative account; in NetWare 4.*x* and later, Admin is the administrative account.

14. A, D, F. Accounts are added to Global Groups in the users' home domain. Global Groups are added to Local Groups that reside in the domain to which users need access. Local Groups are assigned permissions.

15. B. Mandy will not be restricted by Read share permissions if she accesses the file locally.

16. D. Only the permissions for the file owner rwe allow the file to be modified.

17. B, G. Peter can use chmod to change the permissions on a file or folder and chage to require passwords to be changed after a certain period of time.

18. B. A roaming profile will allow Andrea to access her desktop setting from anywhere on the network.

19. B, C. Peter should implement password aging so that users will have to change their passwords. He should also implement password history so that users cannot change their passwords back to the original passwords.

20. A, B, E. Ralph could add users with useradd, adduser, or linuxconf. He could change the owner or group of a file with chown. He could set password aging with chage.

Chapter

5

Managing Users in Windows 2000 Server

THE CIW EXAM OBJECTIVE GROUPS COVERED IN THIS CHAPTER:

✓ Manage users in Windows, Linux, and Novell networks, including but not limited to: Security Accounts Manager authentication, remote user administration, user rights and settings, remote shares, account creation, password policies, permissions.

Y ou have already learned how to add users and groups in three operating systems: Windows 2000, Unix, and Novell NetWare. In this chapter, we'll look in detail at how to manage users and user policies in Windows 2000 in a domain and in a workgroup.

Managing users is a fundamental part of managing Internet servers for two reasons:

- You might need to add standard user accounts for either the Windows 2000 operating system itself or for the services that its server offers (web servers, e-mail servers, and so forth).

- Internet services, such as Web, File Transfer Protocol (FTP), and Remote Access Service (RAS), must access a user account in order to operate. You might need to modify or troubleshoot these types of user accounts.

Active Directory Users and Computers

I n Windows 2000, in a workgroup environment, you add users locally using the Computer Management snap-in to manipulate the local Security Accounts Manager (SAM) database. If you have 20 servers, each with 200 users, you would have to create 4,000 user accounts, and each user might have to remember 20 passwords. This process would be tedious and prone to errors.

To solve this problem, you can install Windows 2000 as a *domain controller (DC)* so that you have to create users only once. In Windows 2000, the domain database of users, computers, and other objects used to manage them is called *Active Directory (AD)*. If you install Active Directory, you create a domain that you can centrally manage so that users have a single logon with universal access to resources based on permissions.

If you create an additional DC in an existing domain, it will copy Active Directory from an existing DC. All DCs will then act as peers, so you can make changes to Active Directory, such as creating a user, on any DC, and those changes will be replicated to the other DC(s) using multimaster replication.

In this section, we'll install Active Directory and use Active Directory Users and Computers to manage users in a domain.

Installing Active Directory

Creating a Windows 2000 domain controller is a two-step process. First you install a Windows 2000 server and then you run the Active Directory Installation Wizard:

1. Choose Start ➢ Run to open the Run dialog box.

2. In the Open box, type **dcpromo** and press Enter to start the Active Directory Installation Wizard:

3. At the Welcome screen, click Next to open the Domain Controller Type screen:

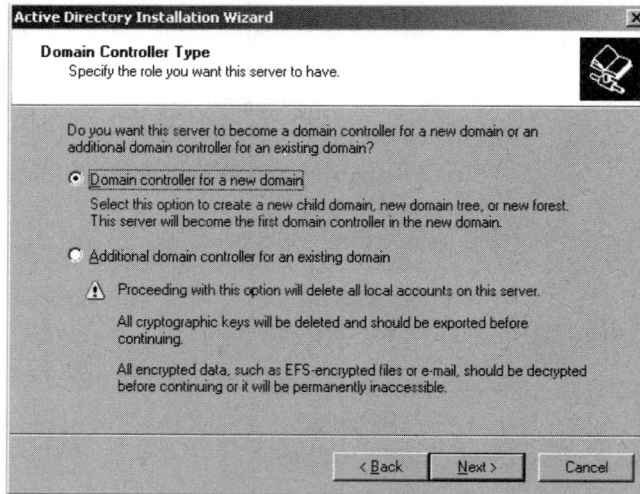

4. Be sure that the Domain Controller for a New Domain option is selected, and then click Next to open the Create Tree or Child Domain screen.

5. Accept the default Create a New Domain Tree option, and then click Next to open the Join or Create Forest screen.

6. Accept the default Create a New Forest of Domain Trees option, and then click Next to open the New Domain Name screen:

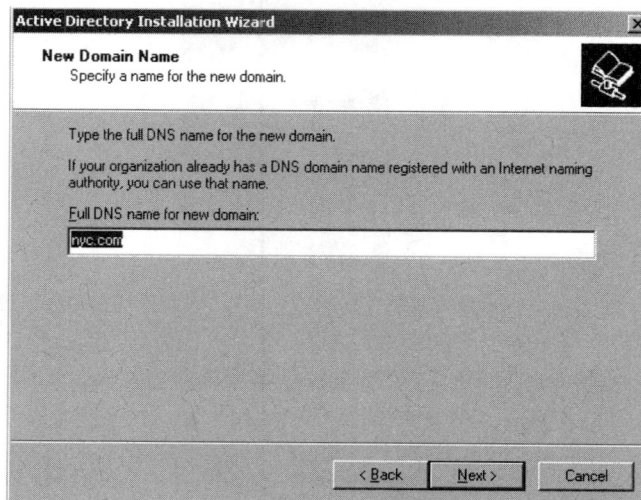

7. In the Full DNS Name for New Domain box, enter the full DNS name for your new domain such as nyc.com, and then click Next to open the NetBIOS Domain Name screen.

8. Accept the Domain NetBIOS name that was automatically derived from the FQDN you entered in the previous screen, and then click Next to open the Database and Log Locations screen:

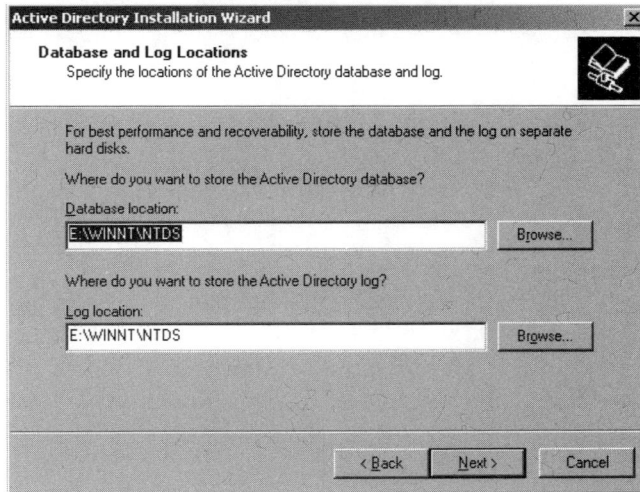

> **Active Directory Installation Wizard**
>
> **Database and Log Locations**
> Specify the locations of the Active Directory database and log.
>
> For best performance and recoverability, store the database and the log on separate hard disks.
>
> Where do you want to store the Active Directory database?
>
> Database location:
> `E:\WINNT\NTDS`   Browse...
>
> Where do you want to store the Active Directory log?
>
> Log location:
> `E:\WINNT\NTDS`   Browse...
>
> < Back   Next >   Cancel

9. Accept the default storage locations, and click Next to open the Shared System Volume screen.

10. Accept the default folder location for the Sysvol folder, which stores the server's copy of the domain's public files. Click Next.

If the wizard displays the following error message:

> **Active Directory Installation Wizard**
>
> The wizard cannot contact the DNS server that handles the name "nyc.com" to determine if it supports dynamic update. Confirm your DNS configuration, or install and configure a DNS server on this computer.
>
> OK

you need to install and/or configure a DNS server with a forward lookup zone for your new domain. Follow these steps.

1. Click OK to open the Configure DNS screen:

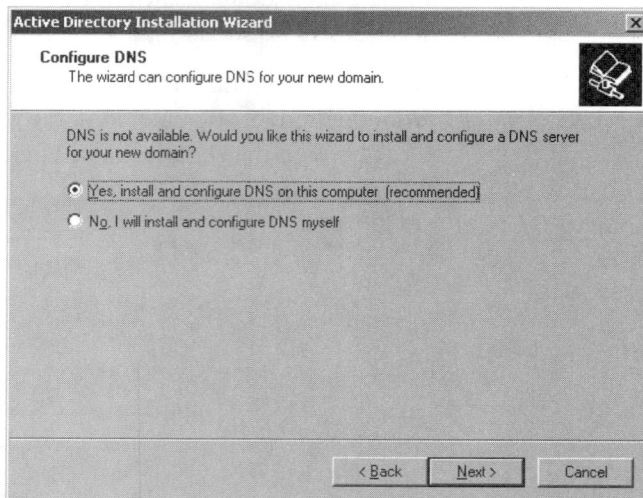

2. Click the Yes, Install and Configure DNS on This Computer (recommended) option, and then click Next to open the Permissions screen.

3. Accept the default Permissions Compatible with pre-Windows 2000 Servers option, and then click Next to open the Directory Services Restore Mode Administrator Password screen.

4. Enter a password in the Password field and in the Confirm Password field, and then click Next to open the Summary screen.

5. Confirm the options you selected, and click Next. The Active Directory Installation Wizard will now install and configure the Active Directory database, \winnt\ntds\ntds.dit.

If you are prompted for the Windows 2000 installation CD, insert it in the CD-ROM drive. When the Completing Active Directory Installation Wizard screen appears, click Finish. Restart the computer and you are up and running as a domain controller. Congratulations!

Managing Users and Groups in Active Directory

Now that Active Directory is installed, you have several important administrative tools available for creating and managing users and groups. The primary tool is Active Directory Users and Computers. We will use it to create users and add those users to groups. We'll then use Windows Explorer to assign permissions to groups.

In Windows 2000, global groups aggregate users, and domain local groups aggregate permissions. Following the steps of the abbreviation AGDLP, you will give users permissions to resources:

- Accounts get added to
- Global groups that get added to
- Domain
- Local groups that are assigned
- Permissions

Creating User Accounts and Resetting Passwords

To create user accounts and reset passwords, follow these steps:

1. Choose Start ➤ Programs ➤ Administrative Tools ➤ Active Directory Users and Computers to open the Active Directory Users and Computers dialog box:

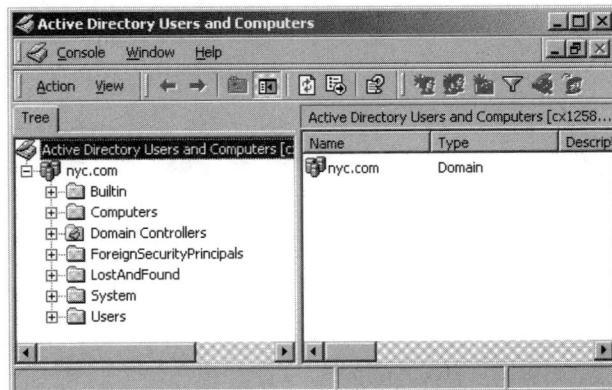

2. Expand your domain name (click the plus sign), right-click the Users folder, and choose New ➤ User to open the New Object - User dialog box:

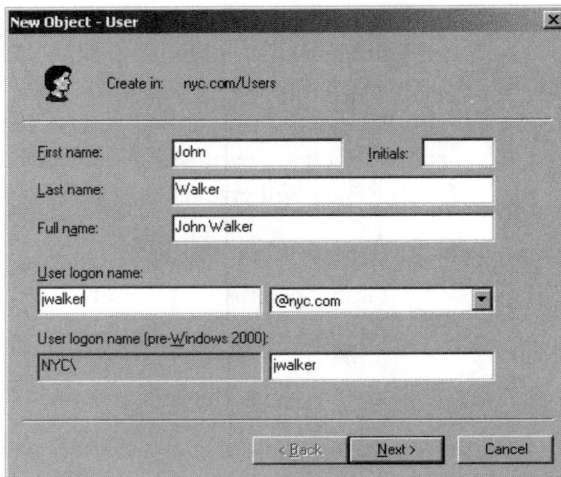

3. Enter the information for a new user John Walker, and then click Next to open the second New Object - User dialog box:

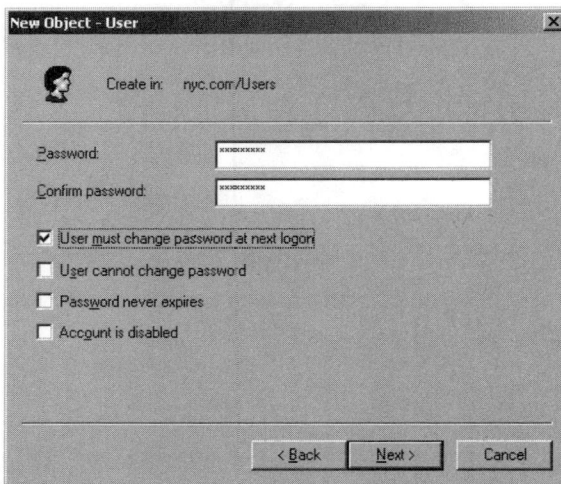

4. In the Password field, enter a password for this user, and then in the Confirm Password field, enter the password again. Click the User Must Change Password at Next Logon check box, and then click Next.

5. Click Finish. Back in the Active Directory Users and Computers dialog box, you should now see John Walker in the list of your users:

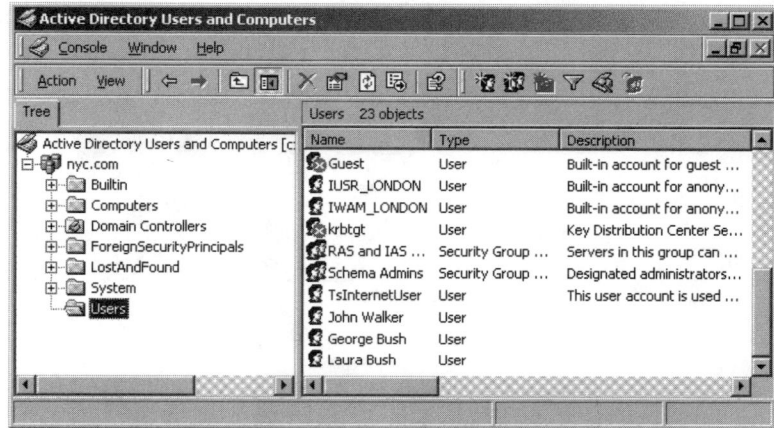

6. If you need to reset John Walker's password, open the Active Directory Users and Computer's MMC. Expand your domain. Open the User's folder. Right-click John Walker, and from the shortcut menu, choose Reset Password to open the Reset Password dialog box:

7. For practice, use a password of newpass. Enter and confirm the new password, and then click OK to open the Active Directory dialog box, which confirms that John Walker's password has been changed. Click OK.

8. Repeat the previous steps in this section to create two more users, gbush and lbush. Also practice resetting their passwords.

Creating Groups and Adding Members

In this section, we'll create a global group and add users to this group. We'll then create a local group and add the global group to this local group. In the next section, we'll assign permissions to the local group. Let's start by creating the Americans global group. Follow these steps:

1. In the Active Directory Users and Computers dialog box, right-click the Users folder, and choose New ➤ Group from the shortcut menu to open the New Object - Group dialog box:

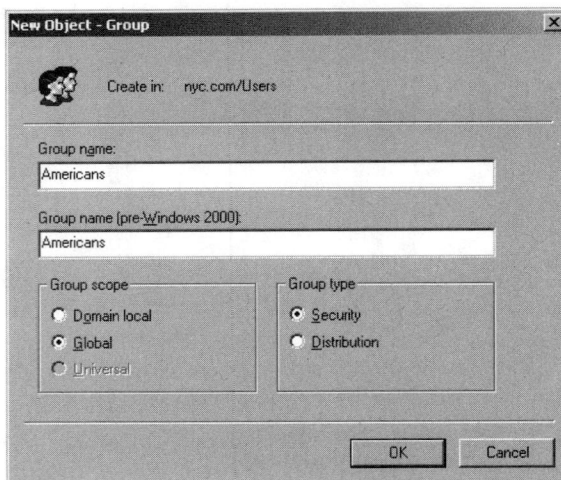

2. In the Group Name box, enter **Americans**, and then be sure that the Global option and the Security option are selected. Click OK.

3. Back in the Active Directory Users and Computers dialog box, expand the Users folder, and then double-click the Americans global group to open its Properties dialog box.

4. Click the Members tab, and then click the Add button to open the Select Users, Computers, or Groups dialog box.

5. Add the users you created earlier to the group by double-clicking jwalker, gbush, and lbush. Click OK to return to the Americans Properties dialog box. Click OK to close the American Properties dialog box.

6. Back in the Active Directory Users and Computers dialog box, create a Rights and Responsibilities domain local group. Right-click the Users folder, and choose New ➤ Group from the shortcut menu to open the New Object - Group dialog box.

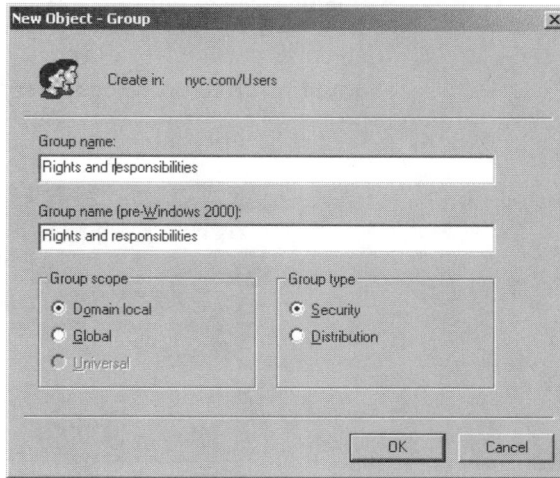

7. In the Group Name field, enter the name for the group (Rights and Responsibilities), and select the Domain Local option and the Security option. Click OK.

8. Back in the Active Directory Users and Computers dialog box, expand the Users folder, and double-click the Rights and Responsibilities group to open its Properties dialog box.

9. Click the Members tab, and then click the Add button to open the Select Users, Computers, or Groups dialog box.

10. Add the Americans global group by double-clicking it. Click OK to return to the Rights and Responsibilities Properties dialog box. Click OK to close the Rights and Responsibilities Properties dialog box.

Now, also add the Americans global group to the Backup Operators local group that is in the Builtin folder. Members of this group have to log on locally at the domain controller, rather than being restricted to logging on over the network. This will be important in a later exercise in this chapter.

Assigning Permissions to Groups

The final step in AGDLP is to assign permissions to domain local groups. We'll use Windows Explorer for this task. Follow these steps:

1. Right-click the Desktop, and choose New ➢ Folder from the shortcut menu.

2. Name this folder Constitution.

3. Right click the Constitution folder, and choose Properties from the shortcut menu to open the folder's Properties dialog box.

4. Click the Security tab:

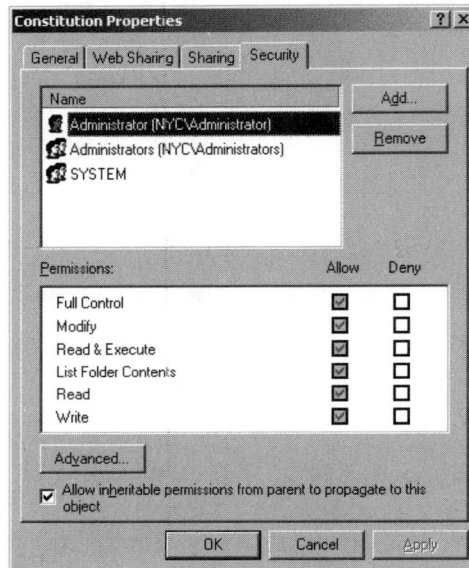

5. Clear the Allow Inheritable Permissions from Parent to Propagate to This Object check box to open the Security dialog box.

6. Click the Remove button to remove permissions on this folder inherited from parent folders and to return to the Constitution Properties dialog box.

7. Click the Add button to open the Select Users, Computers, or Groups dialog box.

8. Double-click the Rights and Responsibilities local group. Double-click the Administrators local group, and then click OK to return to the Constitution Properties dialog box.

9. Select the Administrators group, and click the check box in the Allow column next to the Full Control permission. This will place a check-mark in all the permissions in the Allow column. Click Apply.

10. Select the Rights and Responsibilities group, click the check box in the Allow column next to the Read & Execute permission. This will also place a checkmark in the Allow column next to the List Folder Contents and Read permissions. Your dialog box should resemble the following graphic:

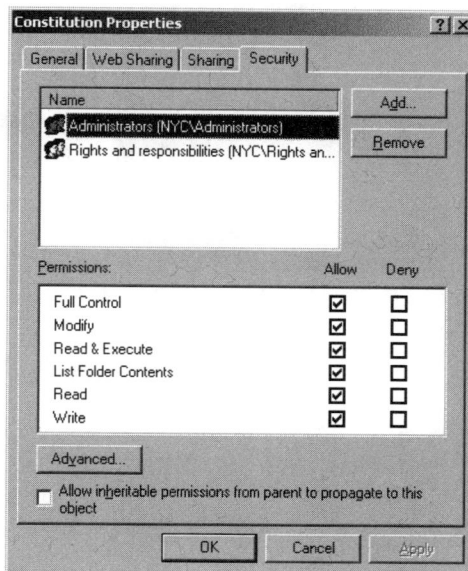

Click OK. You have completed all the steps of AGDLP. In so doing, you modified the Active Directory file \winnt\ntds\ntds.dit. You performed single seat administration and gave users a single logon with universal access to resources based on permissions. These advantages are not available in a workgroup.

The Microsoft Management Console (MMC)

The *Microsoft Management Console (MMC)* is an interface that accepts management snap-ins to perform various administrative tasks. You can use standard MMCs (located in the Administrative Tools folder) to perform common tasks, or you can customize an MMC to perform advanced tasks and/or to combine different administrative tools into a common MMC that can be used for administration of the local computer or even multiple remote computers. In this example you will create a custom MMC in order to practice adding snap-ins to the MMC and to integrate various administrative tools into a single interface. First you will open a blank MMC and then you will add snap-ins. To open a blank MMC, follow these steps:

1. Choose Start ➢ Run to open the Run dialog box.

2. In the Open box, enter **mmc**, and press Enter to open the Console:

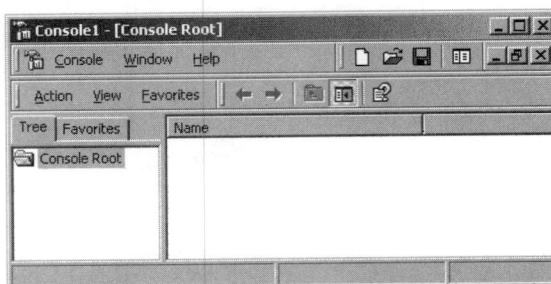

3. Choose Console ➢ Add/Remove Snap-in to open the Add/Remove Snap-in dialog box. Click the Add button to open the Add Standalone Snap-in dialog box.

4. Double-click Active Directory Users and Computers. Double-click DNS. Double-click Computer Management to open the Computer Management screen. Click Finish to return to the Add Standalone Snap-in screen. Click Close to return to the Add/Remove Snap-in screen. Click OK to return to Console1.

5. Choose Console ➢ Save As to open the Save As dialog box. In the File Name text box, enter **My Tools** and click Save.

6. Experiment using this custom MMC. When finished, close the My Tools MMC. If you want to use it again, choose Start ➢ Programs ➢ Administrative Tools ➢ My Tools.

You have created and used a customized MMC. Most of the MMCs that you will use have been pre-configured. Active Directory Users and Computers is a standard MMC, as is Computer Management.

To administer web servers that are members of a workgroup instead of a domain, you use the Computer Management MMC to create users and add them to local groups. Finally you will use Windows Explorer to assign permissions to local groups. For practice, you will create a user and add that user to a local group and then asign the local group permissions. To do this, follow these steps:

1. On the Desktop, right-click My Computer and then choose Manage from the shortcut menu to open Computer Management:

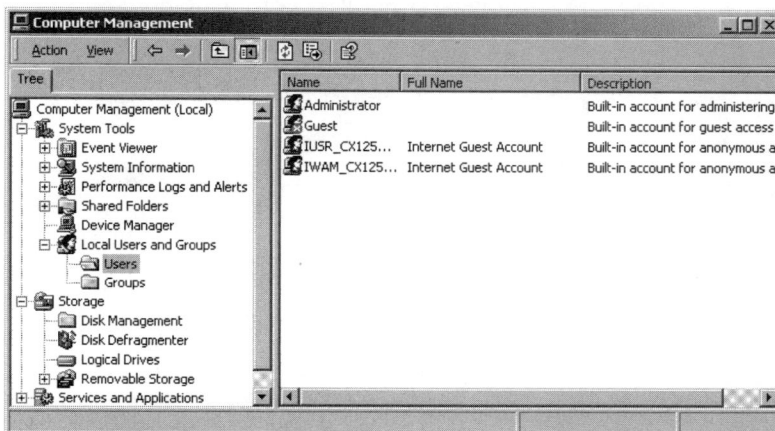

2. Expand System Tools, and then expand Local Users and Groups. Right-click the Users folder, and choose New User from the shortcut menu to open the New User dialog box.

3. Enter a username, the user's full name, a description (optional), and a password, and then confirm the password. Click the Account Is Disabled

check box, and click Create. Repeat the process to add another user. Click Close to return to the Computer Management MMC.

4. If you need to change the password of any user at a later date, right-click the user, and choose Set Password from the shortcut menu to open the Set Password dialog box:

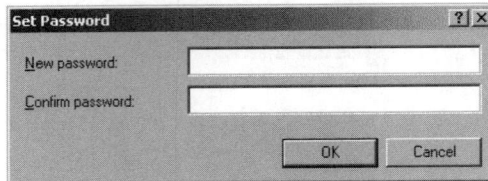

Enter and confirm a new password, and then click OK to return to the Computer Management MMC.

5. To create a local group, right click the Groups folder, and choose New Group from the shortcut menu to open the New Group dialog box:

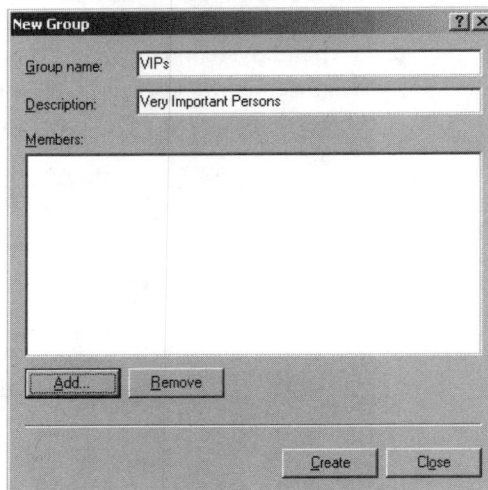

6. Click the Add button to open the Select Users or Groups dialog box:

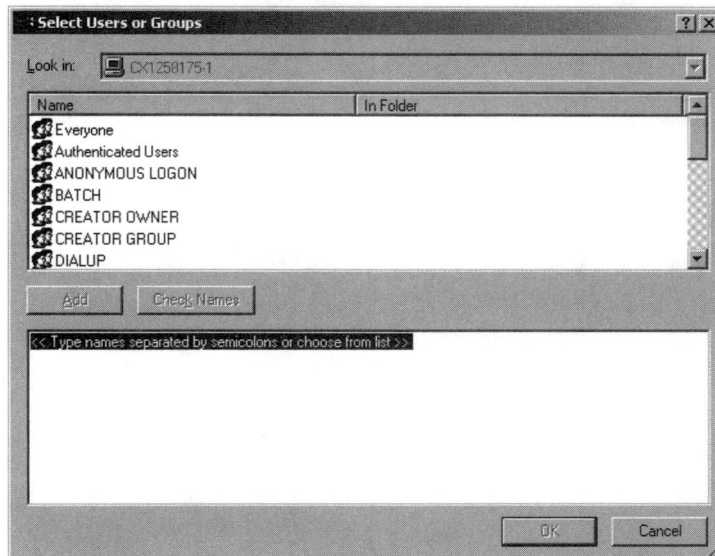

7. Double click the users that you just created in order to add them to the local group. Click OK to return to the New Group dialog box. Click Create. Click Close to return to the Computer Management MMC. Close this MMC. You have just created two users, and added them to a local group. The last step will be to assign permissions to this local group.

8. Right-click an empty area on your Desktop, and choose New ➢ Folder. Name the folder Perks. Right-click the Perks folder, and choose Properties from the shortcut menu to open the Perks Properties dialog box. Click the Security Tab. Clear the Allow Inheritable Permissions from Parent to Propagate to This Object check box to open the Security dialog box. Click Remove to return to the Perks Properties dialog box. Click Add to open the Select Users, Computers, or Groups dialog box. Double-click the local group that you previously created. Click OK to return to the Perks Properties dialog box.

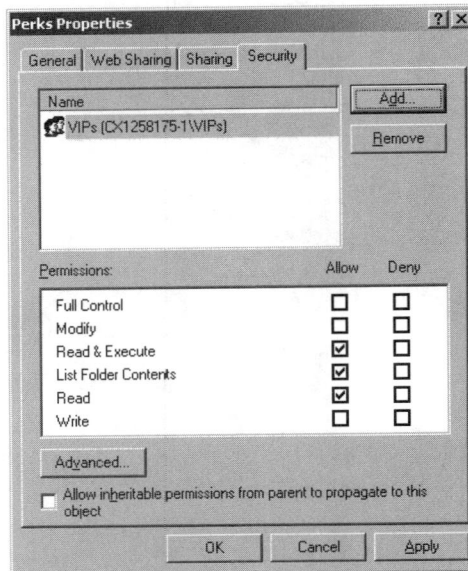

9. Click Add to open the Select Users or Groups dialog box. Double-click the Administrators local group. Click OK to return to the Perks Properties dialog box. Next to the Full Control permission, click the check box in the Allow column. This will place a checkmark in all the check boxes in the Allow column. Click OK. You have just completed the AGP process:

   - Accounts were added to local
   - Groups that were assigned
   - Permissions

You just modified the local Security Accounts Manager (SAM). The *Security Accounts Manager (SAM)* is a collection of processes and files that Windows 2000 uses to authenticate local users. If you have a Windows 2000 system installed on your C drive, by default the SAM file is in C:\winnt\system32\config. When you use the AGP process, these security changes are recorded in the SAM.

> **NOTE** Just about all the administrative and diagnostic tools that come with Windows 2000 can be used both locally and remotely. For example, to manage another Windows 2000 computer in your workgroup, open Computer Management. Choose Action ➤ Connect to Another Computer, and then specify the computer to manage. You can then administer user and groups on the remote computer.

Domain and Local Security Settings

In a domain, you use the Group Policy MMC to configure security settings, and in a workgroup, you use the Local Security Settings MMC snap-in. Other than the interface used, the steps are virtually the same. You can establish the local security settings on any computer in a domain as well as in a workgroup; however, group policy set at the domain level takes precedence.

To set the group policy for a domain, follow these steps:

1. Choose Start ➢ Programs ➢ Administrative Tools ➢ Active Directory Users and Computers to open the Active Directory User and Computers dialog box.

2. Right-click your domain, and choose Properties from the shortcut menu to open the Properties dialog box for the domain.

3. Click the Group Policy tab:

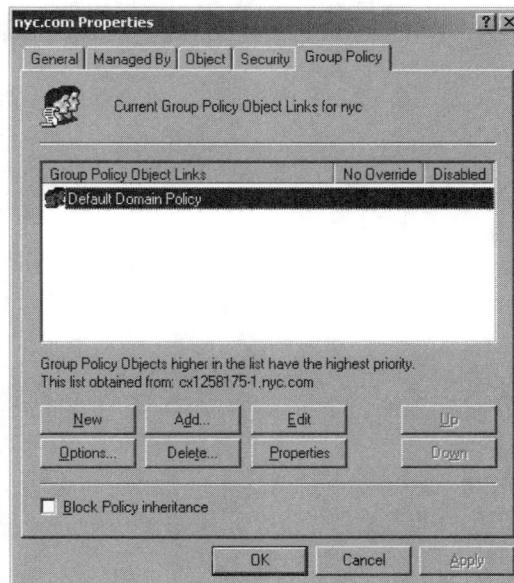

4. Double-click Default Domain Policy to open the Group Policy window.

5. Expand Computer Configuration, expand Windows Settings, and then expand Security Settings, as shown in the following graphic:

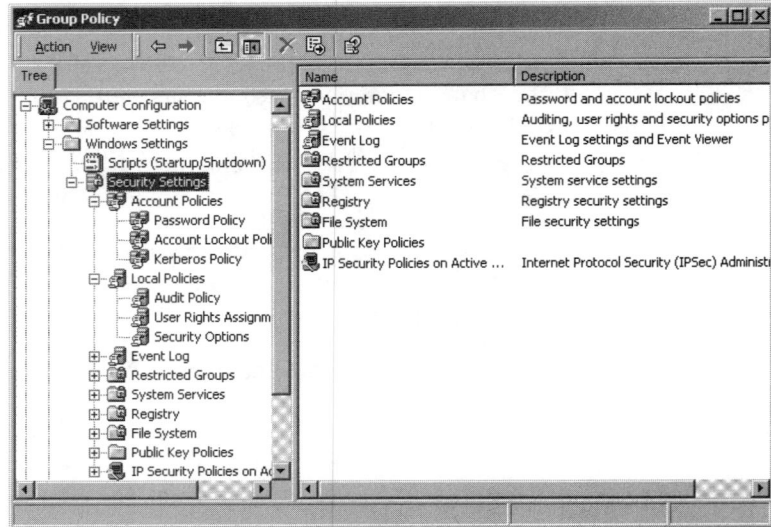

6. For practice, let's set a password policy so that the minimum password length for all users is 8 characters. Expand Account Policies, and then select Password Policy. In the pane on the right, double-click Minimum Password Length to open the Minimum Password Length dialog box:

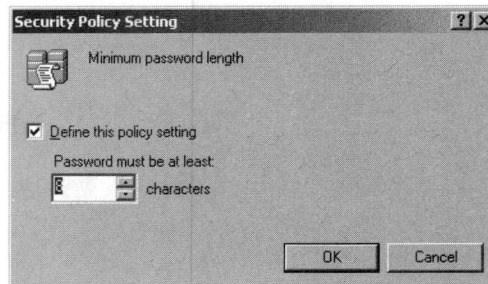

7. Click the Define This Policy Setting check box, and then enter 8 in the Password Must Be at Least *x* Characters spin box. Click OK.

You will have further practice setting policy later, but first let's look at how to configure these same settings in a workgroup. To configure local security settings for a workgroup, choose Start ➤ Programs ➤ Administrative Tools ➤ Local Security Policy to open the Local Security Settings window.

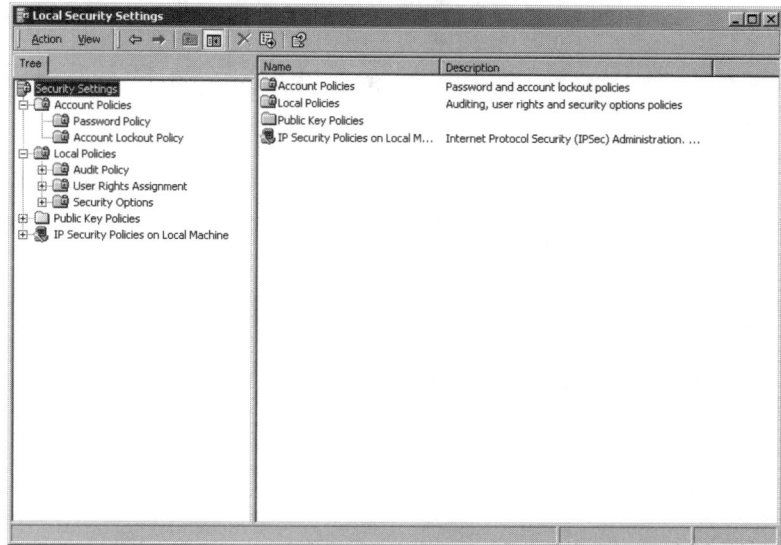

From this window, you can do the following:

- Configure account policies, including altering the system's password policy and setting a lockout policy to help prevent password-guessing attacks.

- Establish auditing for your local system.

- Change default user-rights settings for various accounts and groups.

- Alter default settings that configure restrictions over system peripherals (printers, removable drives, and so forth), auditing options, and additional security features (renaming accounts, logon message options, and various logon options).

- Determine public-key encryption and IP security policies. Further discussion of these features is beyond the scope of this book.

All the local security settings described previously apply without exception to all users that access the local computer. If your system happens to be a domain controller, any policies you configure apply to the entire domain. Let's begin by looking at password policies.

Password Policy

Whether you define account policies for your own computer or for the entire network, you need to plan them just as you planned your user names. We'll start by looking at what you need to consider before you establish password policies, and then we'll look at how you implement the policies you develop.

You'll need to decide the following before you begin setting password policies:

- The length of time users must wait before using a previously used password
- The length of time a password can be used before it expires
- The minimum number of characters a password must contain
- How complex a password must be
- How you will implement account lockout
- How the SAM will count login attempts

Password History

Many users become attached to favorite passwords and prefer to use the same one or the same few over and over again. For security reasons, this is obviously not a good idea. To set the number of passwords that a user must use before reusing a password, follow these steps:

1. Choose Start ➤ Programs ➤ Administrative Tools ➤ Local Security Policy to open the Local Security Policy window.

2. Expand the Account Policies folder, and then select the Password Policy folder to display the policies in the pane on the right.

3. Double-click Enforce Password History to open the Enforce Password History dialog box:

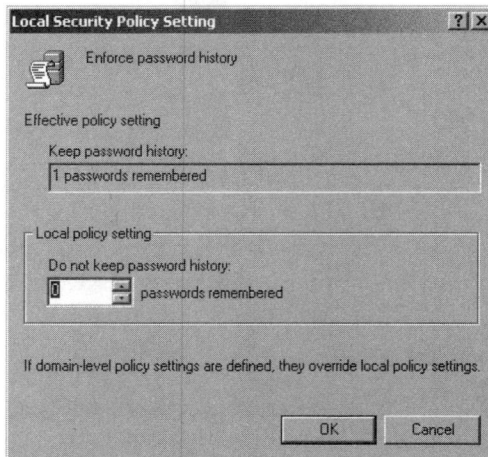

4. In the Passwords Remembered spin box, select the number of passwords that must be used before reusing a password, and then click OK.

Password Aging

Password aging concerns how long a user can use a password before it expires. You may want to enforce minimum and maximum aging limits. A minimum limit requires the user to keep a password for a certain period of time before being allowed to change it. A maximum limit requires that a user change a password after a certain period of time. Having no password-aging policy can pose security risks, but your policy should not be too rigid. If your password policy requires users to change passwords too often, users will become annoyed or confused and may resort to writing down passwords and placing them in obvious places. Enforcing a password change every 60 to 90 days is considered reasonable.

To set a maximum aging limit, follow these steps:

1. In the Local Security Settings window, expand Account Policies, and then select Password Policy.

2. Double-click Maximum Password Age to open the Maximum Password Age dialog box:

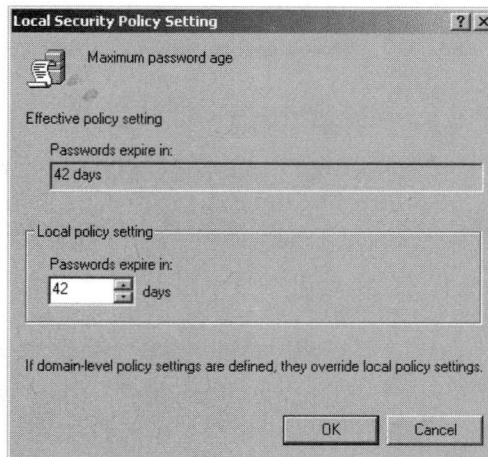

3. In the Passwords Expire in *x* Days spin box, enter the number of days before passwords will expire, and then click OK.

To set a minimum aging limit, follow these steps:

1. In the Local Security Settings `window`, expand Account Policies, and then select Password Policy.

2. Double-click Minimum Password Age to open the Minimum Password Age dialog box:

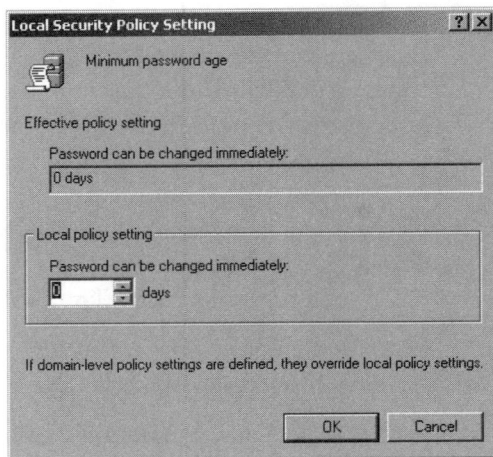

3. In the Days spin box, enter the minimum number of days that a user must use a password before changing it, and then click OK.

Password Length

This setting requires all users to enter a minimum number of characters. A short minimum password length invites hacking. A very long minimum password length invites users to write their passwords on a sticky note attached to their computer. In a medium security environment, six to eight characters is a reasonable compromise.

To set the minimum password length limit, follow these steps:

1. In the Local Security Settings window, expand Account Policies, and then select Password Policy.

2. Double-click Minimum Password Length to open the Minimum Password Length dialog box.

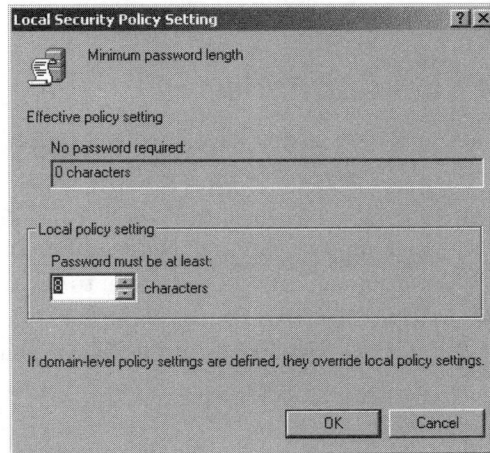

3. The No Password Required box will change to the Password Must Be at Least *x* Characters box. Click OK.

Password Complexity

When this option is enabled, all newly defined passwords must be at least six characters and contain mixed characters. Password complexity helps defeat hacker programs that try to guess a password by using a list of words in the dictionary.

To set password complexity, follow these steps:

1. In the Local Security Settings window, expand Account Policies, and then select Password Policy.

2. Double-click Passwords Must Meet Complexity Requirements to open the Passwords Must Meet Complexity Requirements dialog box:

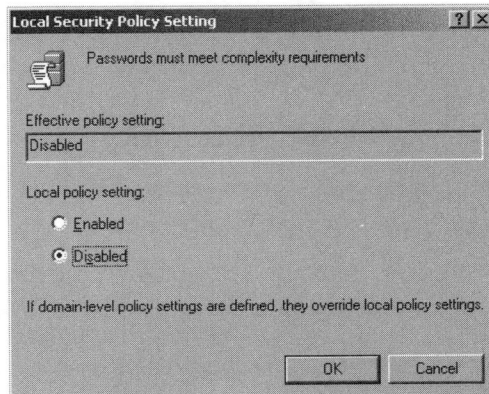

   3. Click the Enabled option, and then click OK.

Account Lockout Policy

You establish an account lockout policy to defeat hackers who attempt to guess passwords through high-speed, repeated logons. You should be aware, though, that account lockout can penalize employees who have difficulty logging on. Although some administrators prefer to manually unlock an account, allowing the lockout to end after five minutes may be more practical.

To establish your account lockout policy, in the Local Security Settings window, expand Account Policies, and then select Account Lockout Policy to display the policies in the pane on the right, as shown in Figure 5.1.

FIGURE 5.1 The Account Lockout Policy settings

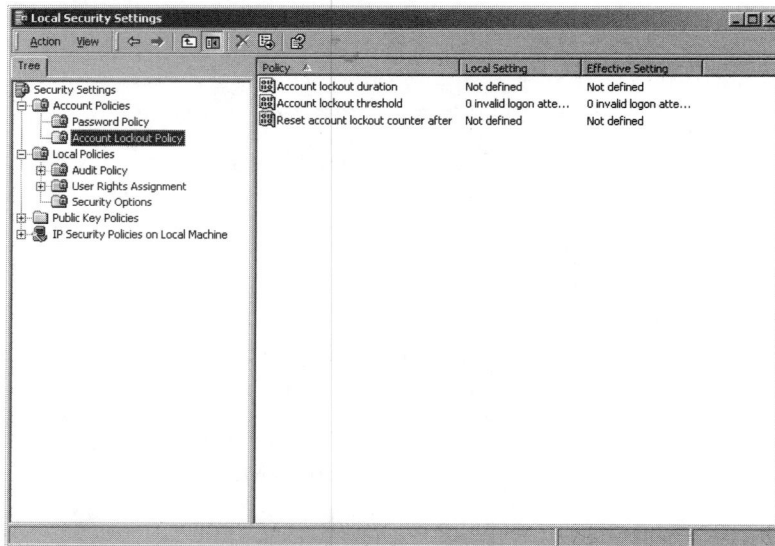

Account Lockout Duration

In most cases, it is reasonable to set the duration of the account lockout to a short period, such as 30 minutes. To set the duration, follow these steps:

   1. Double-click Account Lockout Duration to open the Account Lockout Duration dialog box.

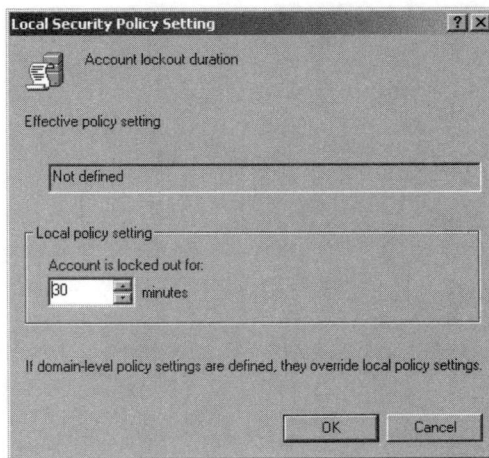

2. In the spin box, select the number of minutes that you want accounts to be locked out, and then click OK.

Account Lockout Threshold

Setting the threshold specifies when an account will be locked out. For example, if you set the threshold to 3, the account will be locked out after the third failed logon attempt. Follow these steps to set the threshold:

1. Double-click Account Lockout Threshold to open the Account Lockout Threshold dialog box:

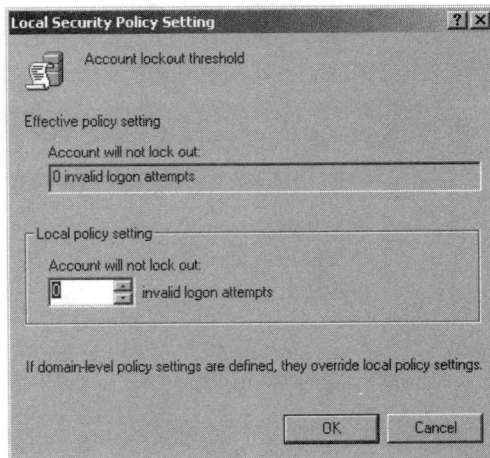

2. In the spin box, select the number of invalid logon attempts after which the account will be locked out, and then click OK.

Reset Counter

The Reset Account Lockout Counter After setting determines how long the counter will store failed logon attempts. If the counter is set to five minutes and the account lockout threshold is set to three logon attempts, any three bad logon attempts within any five-minute period will lock out the user. To set the counter, follow these steps:

1. Double-click Reset Account Lockout After to open the Reset Account Lockout Counter After dialog box:

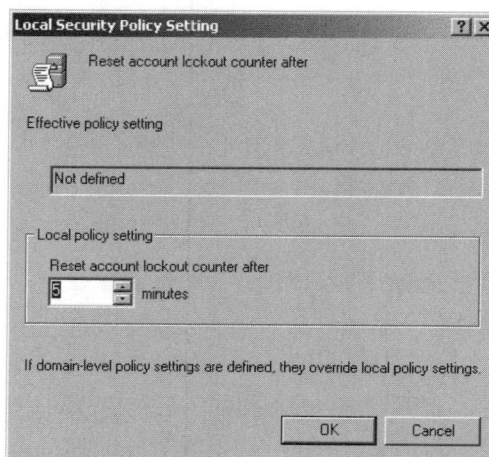

2. In the spin box, select the number minutes after which invalid logon attempts will be purged, and then click OK.

EXERCISE 5.1

Creating an Account Policy

You have already created users and established user-based shares. In this exercise, you will create an account policy and enforce it for all users. You will do this at the domain level using Group Policy.

1. Establish an account policy using the following suggestions (or establish your own and write notes in the spaces provided).

   Maximum password age: 60 days or

   Minimum password age: zero or

EXERCISE 5.1 *(continued)*

Minimum password length: six characters or

Password history: three previously used passwords or

Require an account lockout. Choose the following settings:

Account lockout threshold: three invalid attempts or

Lockout duration: 30 minutes or

Lockout count reset: 30 minutes or

2. Enact your policy. First, open the Active Directory Users and Computers snap-in. Choose Start ➢ Programs ➢ Administrative Tools ➢ Active Directory Users and Computers. Right-click your domain, and choose Properties from the shortcut menu to open the Properties dialog box for you domain. Click the Group Policy tab:

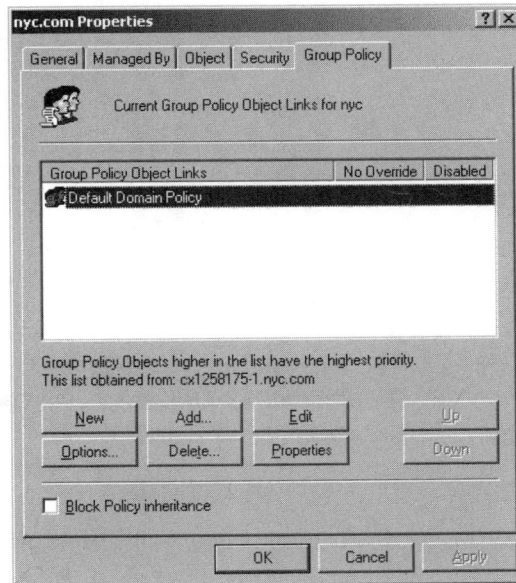

3. Double-click Default Domain Policy to open the Group Policy window. Expand Computer Configuration, expand Windows Settings, expand Security Settings, expand Account Policies, and then select Password Policy to display the password policies in the right pane.

4. Double-click Enforce Password History to open the Enforce Password History dialog box, and change the value to 3.

5. Click OK.

6. Follow similar procedures to set the policies for maximum password age, minimum password age, and minimum password length. Follow the policy outlined in Step 1.

7. You are now ready to leave the Password Policy section and to set account lockout policies. Click the Account Lockout Policy folder.

8. Double-click and set the Account Lockout Threshold value to three invalid attempts, as suggested in the policy above, or follow the policy you created.

9. Click OK to open the Suggested Value Changes dialog box:

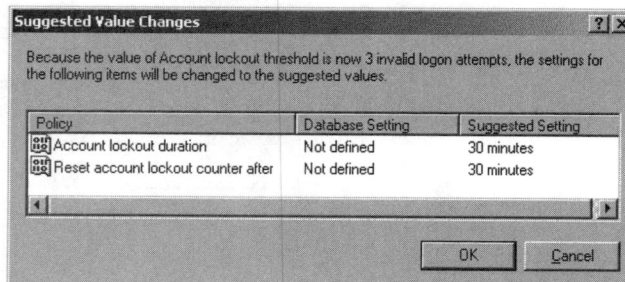

10. The suggested settings are 30-minute values for Account Lockout Duration and Reset Account Lockout Counter After. Click OK to accept these values.

11. Log off as administrator.

12. As jwalker, log on incorrectly one more time than your policy allows (four times, if you followed the instructions in Step 1). On the fourth try, this account is locked out. An error message will inform you that the account is locked out, in contrast with a message informing you that the password is incorrect.

13. Log back on as administrator and unlock the jwalker account. Open the Active Directory Users and Computers snap-in by choosing Start ➤ Programs ➤ Administrative Tools ➤ Active Directory Users and Computers. Expand your domain, and open the Users folder.

14. Double-click the jwalker account to open the Properties dialog box for this user. Click the Account tab.

15. Notice that the Account Is Locked Out check box is selected. To allow the jwalker account to work again, clear this check box and click OK.

16. Log off and log back on as jwalker. You should see that this account is no longer locked out.

17. Log off and log back on as administrator.

18. Add a new user. Use any name you want. Select a password that is shorter than the minimum password length required by the password account policy you created. What error message do you receive?

19. Open the Active Directory Users and Computers snap-in. Choose Start ➤ Programs ➤ Administrative Tools ➤ Active Directory Users and Computers. Right-click your domain, and choose Properties from the shortcut menu to open the Properties dialog box for your domain. Click the Group Policy tab. Double-click Default Domain Policy to open the Group Policy window. Expand Computer Configuration, expand Windows Settings, expand Security Settings, expand Account Policies, and then select Password Policy to display the password policies in the right pane. Change the Minimum Password Length option to 0, click OK, close the Group Policy window, and click OK in your domain Properties dialog box.

20. Create a new user account using Active Directory Users and Computers. This time, use a one-letter password. You should see that you are allowed to use a short password.

21. After you create the new user, use the Group Policy snap-in to change the Minimum Password Length setting back to the value suggested by your security policy. Notice that if you set the Minimum Password Length option after creating the password, the SAM will not check older passwords.

Creating NTFS Partitions

Unless you are dual-booting your computer in order to practice on different operating systems, you should always install Windows 2000 on an NTFS (New Technology File System) partition. You can also install Windows 2000 on a disk formatted with FAT (File Allocation Table). The FAT, however, is an older standard that does not provide much security or stability, features that are paramount for a web server. You have already learned how NTFS allows you to set file permissions on local files and folders, as well as on remote shares. In addition, you must install Windows 2000 on NTFS in order to access many services and servers. For example, Microsoft Proxy Server requires NTFS.

NTFS offers several additional benefits:

- Drives formatted with NTFS fragment less often.
- NTFS provides native data compression.
- NTFS provides for larger hard disk formats.
- NTFS provides a separate Recycle Bin for each user you create.
- NTFS gives you granular control over files inside directories. NTFS is the only file system that allows you to place permissions on a file that are different from the permissions on the directory that contains it. Unix and Novell NetWare systems have offered this feature for years. For example, suppose you place a file in the `c:\files` directory. You can assign the directory full write permissions, which means you can delete and add files. In addition, you can assign read-only permissions to the file, making it possible only to read it.

Windows 2000 uses NTFS 5, which supports features such as disk quotas, disk sharing between systems, and on-the-fly dynamic disk encryption. For more information go to `http://support.microsoft.com/support/kb/articles/Q184/2/99.ASP`. Table 5.1 describes the Windows file formats.

> **NOTE**
>
> The FAT16 file system in supported in Windows 2000 for backward compatibility with legacy operating systems. You might use FAT16 if you were dual booting with another operating system that could read FAT16 but not NTFS. If you are dual booting with Windows 9*x*/Me (except the earliest versions of Windows 95), you can use FAT32 on your system partition. FAT32 is designed for larger hard disks.

TABLE 5.1 Windows File Formats

Asset	FAT	FAT32	NTFS 5
Partition size	4GB.	Microsoft does not recommend partitions of more than 32GB.	A maximum of 2 terabytes.
Permissions	Directory-level security on established shares; security applies only to users accessing shares remotely.	Directory-level security on established shares; security applies only to users accessing shares remotely.	User-level and file-level security on both local and remotely accessed shares.
Additional security options	Password-protected shares.	Password-protected shares.	Enhanced auditing.
Removable media	Yes.	Yes.	Yes.
Forbidden filename characters	/ \ [ ] : ; | = ^ * ?	/ \ [ ] : ; | = ^ * ?	/ \ | " < > * ?
Overhead	Less than 1MB.	Less than 1MB.	50MB.
Additional issues	Once you convert FAT to FAT32, you cannot convert back unless you use third-party software.	NTFS 4 and FAT drives cannot access local FAT32 partitions. Windows 95 OEM Service Release 2 and Windows 98 support FAT32 drives. FAT32 is not supported by Windows NT, but is supported by Windows 2000.	Not suitable for smaller drives (less than 400 MB). This file system now supports disk quotas, file encryption, and the ability to mount foreign file systems.

> **NOTE**
>
> It is generally good practice to avoid using any forbidden file name characters, regardless of the file system you are using. Such avoidance will help ensure compatibility between FAT and NTFS partitions.

Converting From FAT and FAT32 to NTFS

You can convert FAT partitions to NTFS by first switching to the partition you want to format and then typing the following command at a command prompt:

```
convert c: /fs:ntfs
```

You will then see the following messages:

```
e:\Documents and Settings\James\Desktop>convert c: /fs:ntfs
The type of the file system is FAT32.
Determining disk space required for file system conversion...
Total disk space:            3196903 KB
Free space on volume:         703280 KB
Space required for conversion:  57407 KB
Converting file system
```

After some time, the partition will complete conversion.

If Windows 2000 is currently using this drive, the system will schedule the drive for conversion on the next startup. Thus, to finish the job, you must shut down and restart your system.

Once you convert from FAT to NTFS and reboot, you cannot revert to FAT unless you use third-party software. However, if you have only scheduled a conversion and not rebooted, you can cancel this conversion. For more information, see the following URL: http://support.microsoft.com/support/kb/articles/Q130/9/13.asp?.

Auditing in Windows 2000

Once you enable NTFS, you can establish auditing policies. Auditing policies help keep everyone honest, and you can use them to detect attempted or successful security breaches. The role of a computer in a Windows 2000 network determines where auditing is configured. For member or standalone servers, you establish an audit policy locally for each individual computer. To set local auditing policies, follow these steps:

1. Choose Start ➢ Programs ➢ Administrative Tools ➢ Local Security Policy to open the Local Security Settings window.

2. Expand the Local Policies folder.

3. Select the Audit Policy folder to display the policies in the pane on the right, as shown in Figure 5.2.

FIGURE 5.2 Viewing auditing options in Windows 2000

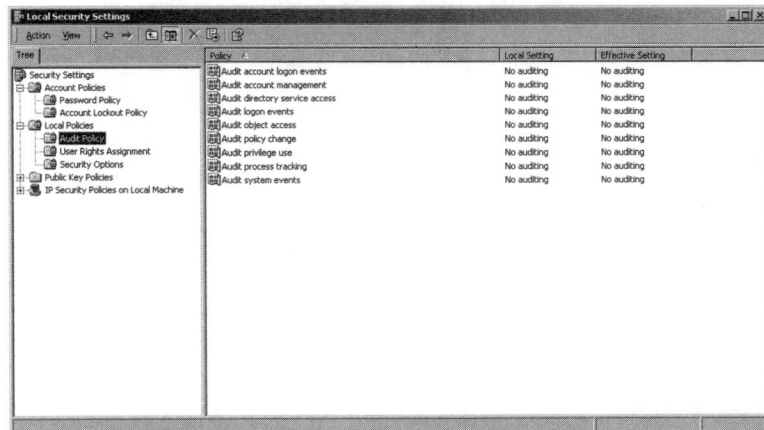

You configure the auditing policies by double-clicking an individual policy to open its Local Security Policy Setting dialog box and configure that particular audit policy. Enabling an audit policy allows the system to track the success or failure of various events, such as a user logging on and off or a user accessing a file or a folder. Exercise 5.2 will walk you through the steps involved in enabling a local audit policy. Once you navigate to the Audit Policy folder, the steps will be the same as the following for domain controllers.

To set an audit policy that tracks all failed account logon events for all domain controllers, follow these steps:

1. Choose Start ➢ Programs ➢ Administrative Tools ➢ Active Directory Users and Computers to open the Active Directory Users and Computers dialog box.

2. Expand your domain folder.

3. Right-click Domain Controllers OU, and choose Properties from the shortcut menu to open the Domain Controllers Properties dialog box.

4. Click the Group Policy tab.

5. Double-click Default Domain Controllers Policy to open the Group Policy window.

6. Expand Computer Configuration, expand Windows Settings, expand Security Settings, and then expand Local Policies.

7. Click Audit Policy to display the audit policies in the pane on the right:

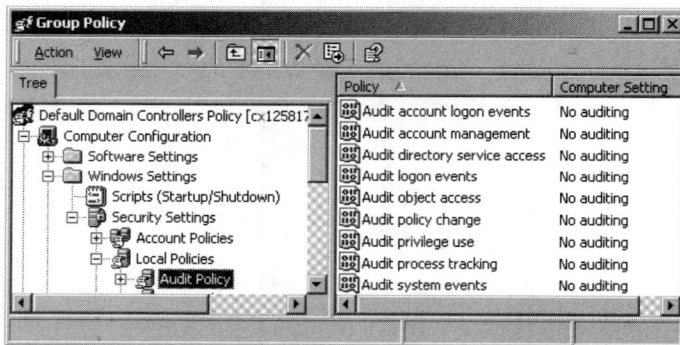

8. Double-click Audit Account Logon Events to open the Audit Account Logon Events dialog box:

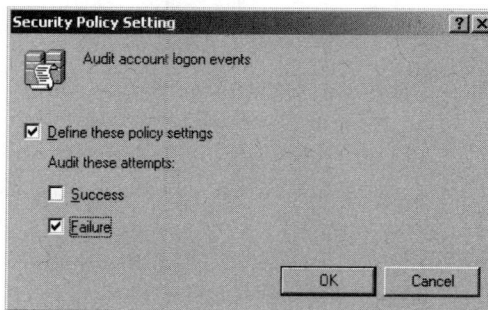

9. Click the Define These Policy Settings check box, click the Failure check box, and then click OK.

WARNING   Use care when establishing auditing settings. Auditing, especially on a busy system, can consume system resources and create log files that could fill the hard drive.

You can view the results of your audit settings using Event Viewer. To open Event Viewer, choose Start ➢ Programs ➢ Administrative Tools ➢ Computer Management. Expand System Tools, and then select Event Viewer to display the logs of audited events in the pane on the right. As Figure 5.3 shows, you'll see the following logs:

FIGURE 5.3   Selecting logs in Event Viewer

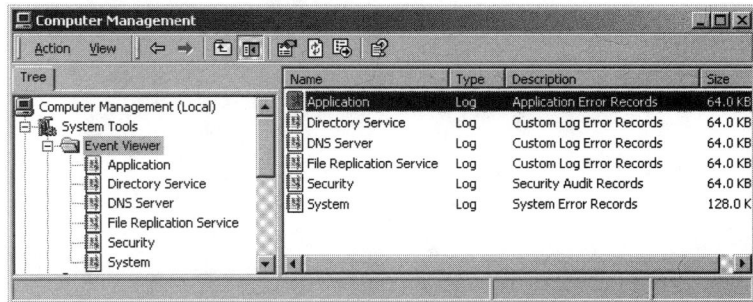

- Application, which contains errors warnings and information generated by programs such as e-mail or database programs. Errors generally prevent the program from functioning. Warnings point to problems that either currently impair but do not disable the program or that might prevent the program from functioning in the future if the condition is not corrected. Information events are nice-to-know data.

- Security, which reports events relevant to security, including system shutdowns, logged-in users, processes created, and privilege usage. You can audit security events for success and failure. A lock icon indicates failures, and a key icon indicates success.

- System, which reports service and system restart events.

- Directory Service, which reports events relevant to Active Directory on domain controllers.

- DNS Server, which reports events associated with the DNS server.

- File Replication Service, which reports replication events on domain controllers.

To display details about an event, double-click it to open the Event Properties dialog box. Figure 5.4 shows a sample Event Properties dialog box. As you can see, it shows that on 1/2/2002 at 19:48 (7:48 PM), an error occurred on the DHCP server on computer CX1258175-1 with an Event ID of 1051. The description shows that the DHCP server has not been authorized to service clients.

FIGURE 5.4 Viewing Event properties

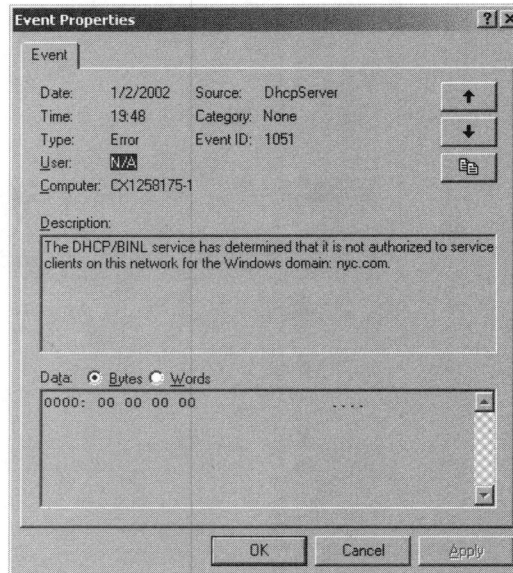

You can also use Event Viewer to view logs on remote servers. In the Computer Management MMC, choose Action ➢ Connect to Another Computer to open the Select Computer dialog box:

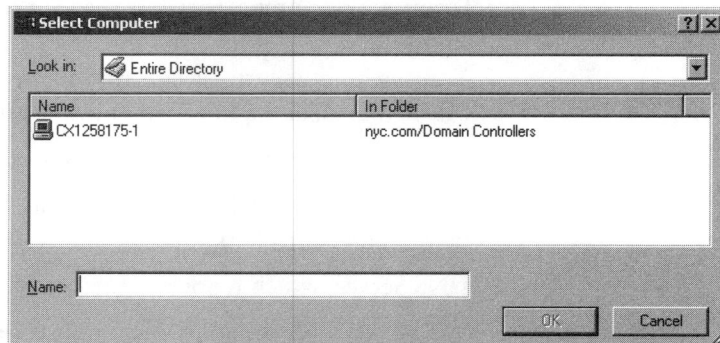

Enter the name of a remote computer, and then open Event Viewer and view the server's logs.

NOTE

As with all remote connections, you must have the proper user name and password on both systems to remotely administer any aspect of a system.

EXERCISE 5.2

Enabling Auditing in Windows 2000

In this exercise, you will enable auditing for a Secret folder that you will create. You will see that auditing files and folders is a two-step process. First you must enable auditing of object access. Second, you must enable auditing on the particular folder or file. But first, before you can enable auditing, if necessary, you must convert your system from FAT to NTFS.

1. If you don't know how a hard drive or a partition on your system is formatted, open Windows Explorer, right-click the drive or partition, and choose Properties from the shortcut menu to open the Properties dialog box for the drive or partition:

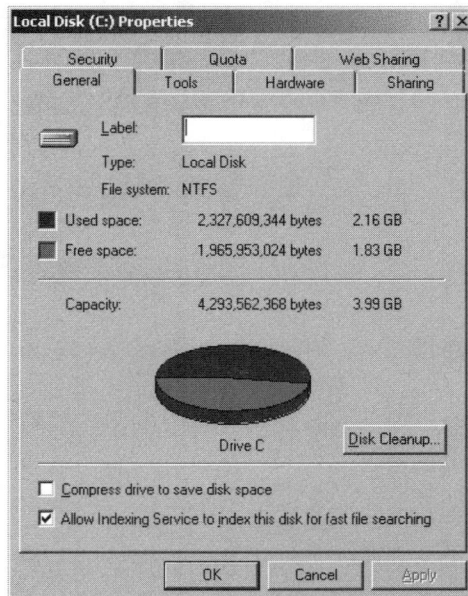

2. This graphic shows that the partition is already formatted as NTFS. If this is not the case on at least one of your computer's partitions, convert at least one partition to NTFS using the instructions in the sidebar in this chapter.

3. Choose Start ➤ Programs ➤ Administrative Tools ➤ Domain Security Policy to open the Local Security Settings window. Expand Local Policies, and then select Audit Policy. In the pane on the right, double-click Audit Object Access to open the Audit Object Access dialog box:

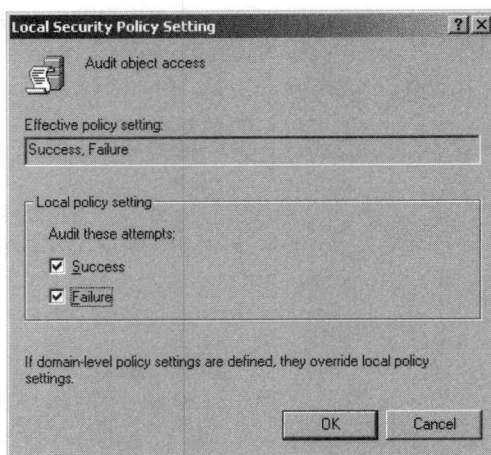

4. Click the Success check box, click the Failure check box, and then click OK.

5. Close the Local Security Settings window.

6. Next you will create a Secret folder and enable auditing. Right-click an empty area of the Desktop, and choose New ≻ Folder from the shortcut menu. Type **Secret** as the name of this folder. Right-click the Secret folder, and choose Properties from the shortcut menu to open the Properties dialog box for the folder. Click the Security tab. Click the Advanced button to open the Access Control Settings for Secret dialog box. Click the Auditing tab.

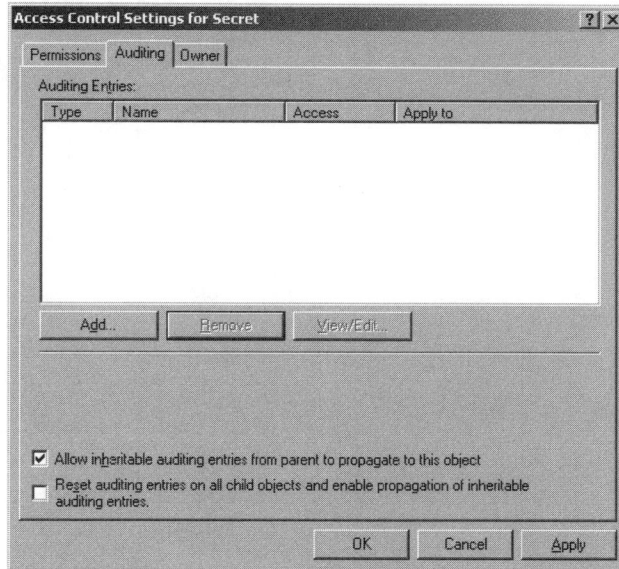

7. Click Add to open the Select User, Computer, or Group dialog box.

EXERCISE 5.2 *(continued)*

8. Double-click the Everyone group to open the Auditing Entry for Secret dialog box:

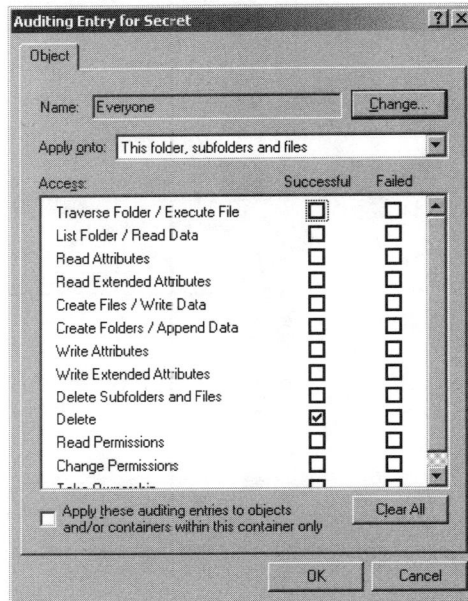

9. Click the check box in the Successful column for the Delete entry in the Access list, and then click OK.

10. Click OK twice more.

11. Right click the Secret folder and delete it.

12. Choose Start ➢ Programs ➢ Administrative Tools ➢ Event Viewer to open Event Viewer. (You can also open Computer Management and then open Event Viewer.)

13. Select Security Log.

14. In the right pane, double-click the first Success Audit security event to open the Event Properties dialog box. You should see a window similar to the one shown in the following graphic:

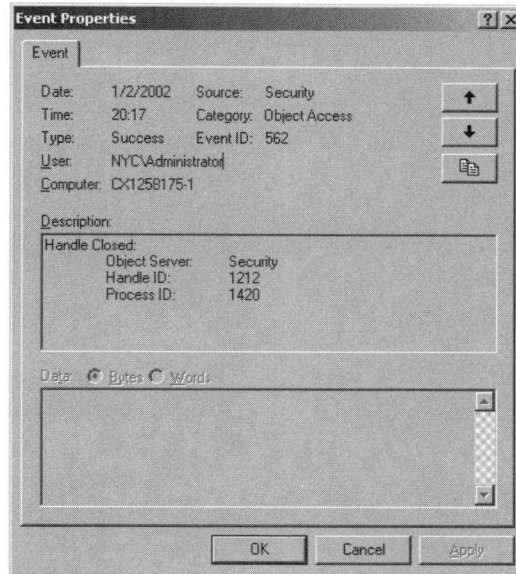

15. If you want, you can view previous entries by clicking the down arrow, as shown in the previous graphic.

In this exercise, you converted all drives from FAT to NTFS to ensure proper auditing. You then generated an event and viewed it in the Event Manager. Now, you can find out who deleted a file or folder.

NTFS Permissions and Internet Users

You learned earlier that share permissions limit network access to shared folders. However, share permissions do not limit local access to files and folders. On the other hand, NTFS permissions limit access to files as well as folders whether they are accessed locally or over the network. Understanding these permissions is vital if you want to limit access to files on Internet systems. You have already learned about the available NTFS permissions. Now let's look at how to set those permissions on a folder and on a file using Windows Explorer. Follow these steps to set permissions on a folder:

1. In Windows Explorer, right-click the Secret folder that you created earlier, and select Properties from the shortcut menu to open the Properties dialog box for the Secret folder.

2. Select the Security tab:

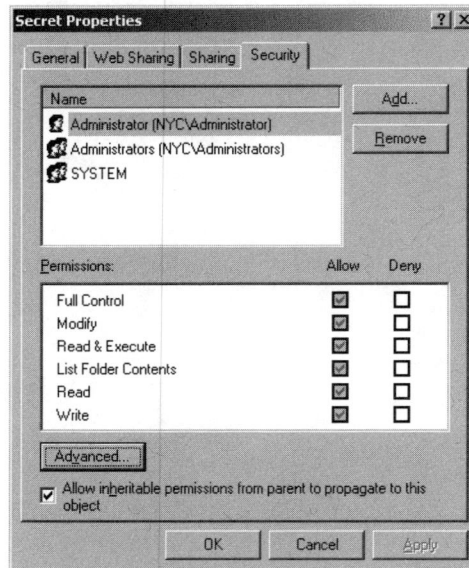

3. Clear the Allow Inheritable Permissions from Parent to Propagate to This Object check box, and then click OK to open the Security window.

4. Click Remove to return to the Security tab.

5. Click Add to open the Select Users, Computers, or Groups dialog box:

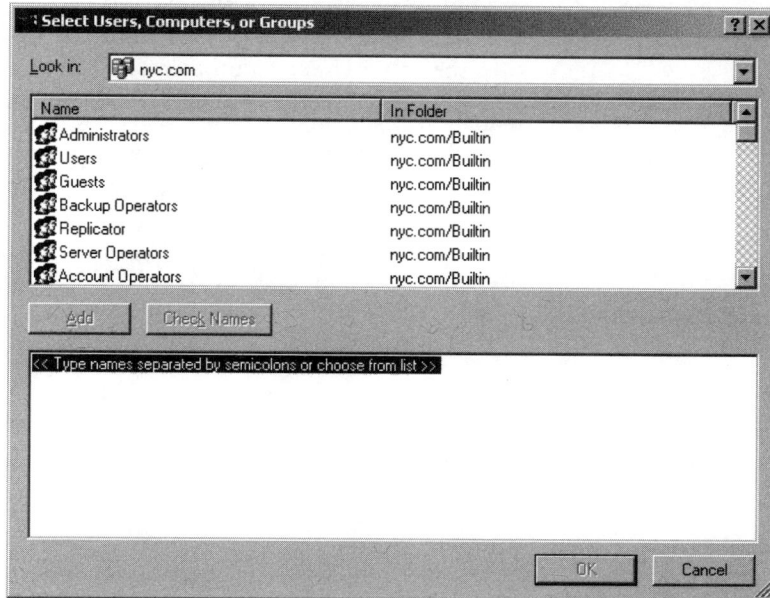

This Select Users, Computers, or Groups dialog box is more complex than it looks. Consider the following warnings:

- When you want to add a group or username, you can either double click the user, group, or computer or first highlight the username and then click the Add button. Many inexperienced administrators falsely assume that highlighting the name and clicking OK will add the user. This is not true.

- As you saw earlier, when you add a group or a user, the access permissions default to Read Only. If you want to set a different permission, you must change it.

- Adding groups to or removing groups from a system-defined directory can cause inheritance issues. Inheritance refers to permissions established on a directory higher up in the drive hierarchy. Thus, if you change permissions on the C:\inetpub\ftproot directory, you must first disable the inherited permissions gained from the C:\inetpub directory.

1. Double-click Administrators to add Administrators to the bottom window of the Select Users, Computers, or Groups dialog box, and double-click Account Operators to also add this group to the bottom of the Select Users, Computers, and Groups dialog box. Click OK to return to the Secret Properties dialog box.

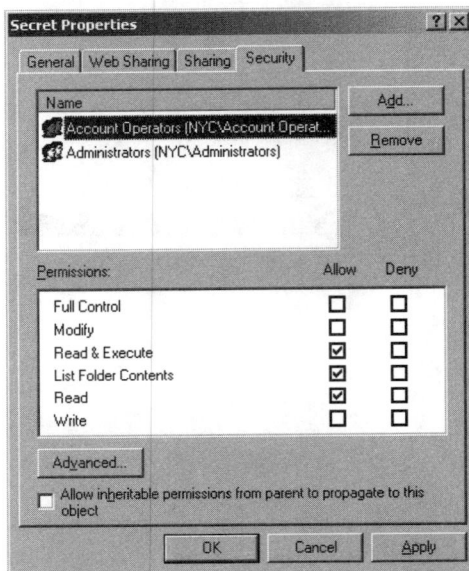

2. Leave the Account Operators at the default permissions of Read and Execute, List Folder Contents, and Read.

3. Select Administrators, and click the check box in the Allow column for Full Control permission. Click OK.

You have successfully given Administrators the Full Control permission on this folder and given Account Operators Read permission, while removing NTFS permissions from everyone else.

Ownership

Whenever a user creates a file or a folder on an NTFS partition, they own it. If a user in the Administrators group, for example, creates a folder or file, this folder or file remains owned by that group. This is the case even if the Administrators group does not have permission to read the file or folder. In other words, a user can retain ownership of a file or a folder even though they do not have permissions to read it.

To can change ownership of a folder or a file, follow these steps (we'll work with the Secret folder created earlier):

1. In Windows Explorer, right-click the Secret folder to open its Properties dialog box.

2. Click the Security tab, and then click the Advanced button to open the Access Control Settings for Secret dialog box. From this dialog box, you can do the following:

   - Set specific user and group-permissions for the folder

   - Audit events on a user or group level

   - Change ownership

3. Click the Owner tab:

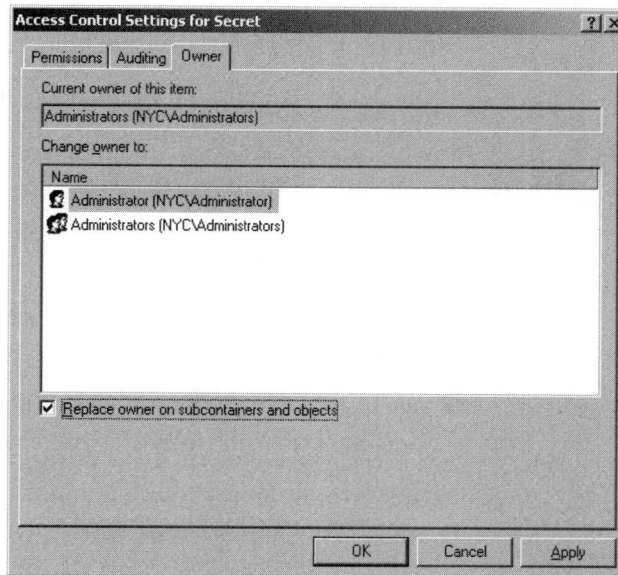

4. Select the Administrator account, click the Replace Owner on Subcontainers and Objects check box, and click OK.

5. In the Secret Properties dialog box, click OK.

You have now changed or have at least made sure that the Administrator account and the Administrators local group have ownership of the `Secret` folder. Administrators can now grant permissions to this folder.

Ownership is a key concept, and it is a separate issue from access permissions: Users who own a file or a folder but who do not have permission to read it can use Windows Explorer to regain all permissions. For example, suppose User1 and User2 are in a group named Managers. Both User1 and User2 are working in an NTFS folder that only they have permission to use. User1 creates a file named `user1.txt` and thus owns this file.

However, as far as permissions are concerned, both User1 and User2 can read the file if User1 does not alter the default permissions. By default, anyone in the Managers group can read any new file that is created in this folder. Suppose User2 decides to remove the Managers group from `user1.txt` and add only himself. When User1 tries to access user1.txt, he or she will be locked out. However, remember that User1 still owns the file. Because User1 still has ownership, User1 can use Windows Explorer to get permissions back. All he or she has to do is access the Properties dialog box of `user1.txt`.

If you are User1, follow these steps to regain permissions on `user1.txt`:

1. In Windows Explorer, right-click `user1.txt`, and choose Properties from the shortcut menu to open the Properties dialog box for the file.

2. Click the Security tab.

3. Click the Add button to open the Select Users, Computers, or Groups dialog box.

4. Double-click your account to move it to the bottom panel of the Select Users, Computers, or Groups dialog box, and then click OK.

5. Back in the Properties dialog box for `user1.txt`, select your account, and click the Full Control check box.

6. Select the account of User 2, and then clear the Full Control, Modify, and Write check boxes.

7. Click OK.

User1 can then take ownership of the file using the steps given previously in this section. Now User2 cannot regain permissions on this file and lock User1 out again.

Testing NTFS Permissions

In this exercise, you will control access to a file in a shared folder using NTFS permissions.

1. Create a new folder named `ntfsdir`. Double-click My Computer to open the My Computer folder. Double-click on Local Disk (C:) to open the Local Disk (C:) folder. Right-click a blank area of the Local Disk (C:) folder and choose New➤ Folder from the shortcut menu. Type the name **ntfsdir**.

2. Create a new file named `secret.txt` in the `ntfsdir` folder. You can do this much like creating a new directory. Double-click the `ntfsdir` folder to open it. Inside the `ntfsdir` window, right-click a blank area and choose New ➤ Text Document from the shortcut menu Type the name **secret.txt**.

3. Double-click the Secret file to open the file in Notepad and enter the following text: **This is secret**. Close the file and select Yes to save your changes.

4. Create a subfolder in the `ntfsdir` folder named `subfolder` and populate it with a text file named `notsecret.txt`.

5. Now, share the `ntfsdir` folder and all its contents as `ntfsdir`. Leave the default permissions (Full Control to Everyone).

6. Right-click the `secret.txt` file and choose Properties from the shortcut menu to open the Properties dialog box for the file. Click the Security tab.

7. Select the Everyone group and remove it. You will see that removing it is impossible because this file is inheriting permissions from the folder that contains it.

8. To get past this inheritance issue, clear the Allow Inheritable Permissions from Parent to Propagate to This Object check box. Doing so allows the file to assert its own permissions, rather than rely upon the parent object (the `ntfsdir` folder).

9. In the Security dialog box, which warns you about your change, click Remove.

10. You will see that the Everyone group has been removed. Click Add to add only the user under whom you are currently logged. For example, if you are logged on as Administrator, click this user (not the group), click Add, then click OK.

11. In the Security tab of the Properties dialog box for the secret.txt file, give Administrator full control, click Apply, and then click OK.

12. If you haven't already created a user named gbush, create that user and make him a member of the Backup Operators group, using Active Directory Users and Computers. Log on to your computer as gbush, and then try accessing your system's ntfsdir share. Choose Start ➢ Run to open the Run dialog box. In the Open box, enter **\\127.0.0.1\ntfsdir**, and click OK. As gbush, you should be able to read the folder's contents, but you should not be able to access the secret.txt file. However, notice that gbush can access and manipulate all other files and the subfolder. The gbush account can even create additional files and subfolders, but cannot read or otherwise use the secret.txt file.

13. Now, log on as Administrator, and right-click the secret.txt file to open its Properties dialog box.

14. Change permissions on the file so that your account is no longer listed, and add the gbush account. The Administrator account should no longer have permission to read the file. Test this by trying to open the file while logged on as Administrator. You should not be able to open this file, even though you are the system's administrator.

15. However, you still own this file. Right-click the file again, add yourself to the file, and give yourself full permissions. If you were not the owner, you would be unable to do this. Instead, as Administrator, you would have to take ownership of the file from the user.

16. Test your work by reading the file.

EXERCISE 5.3 *(continued)*

17. Change the Share Permissions on the `ntfsdir` folder to Read Only. Right-click the `ntfsdir` folder and choose Properties from the shortcut menu to open the `ntfsdir` Properties dialog box. Click the Sharing tab. Click the Permissions button to open the Share Permissions dialog box. Select the Everyone group and clear the Full Control and Change check boxes. Click OK.

18. Access the `ntfsdir` folder. Choose Start ➢ Run to open the Run dialog box. In the Open box, type **\\127.0.0.1\ntfsdir**, and click OK Attempt to delete `secret.txt`. You should be unable to do this due to share permissions.

19. Access the `secret.txt` file locally and delete it. You should be able to do so because share permissions do not affect local access to a file or folder.

Managing User Rights

A subtle difference exists between permissions (that is, privileges) and rights. A *permission* grants the ability to access a resource, such as a file or a printer. A *right* is the ability to determine how an operating system functions. To take a look at the rights you can alter, follow these steps:

1. Choose Start ➢ Programs ➢ Administrative Tools ➢ Active Directory Users and Computers to open the Active Directory Users and Computers dialog box.

2. Expand your domain.

3. Right-click the Domain Controllers OU and choose Properties from the shortcut menu to open the Domain Controllers Properties dialog box.

4. Click the Group Policy tab.

5. Double-click Default Domain Controllers Policy to open the Group Policy window.

6. Expand Computer Configuration, expand Windows Settings, expand Security Settings, and expand Local Policies.

7. Select User Rights Assignment. You'll see the rights you can alter in the right pane, as shown in Figure 5.5.

FIGURE 5.5 Viewing User Rights in Windows 2000

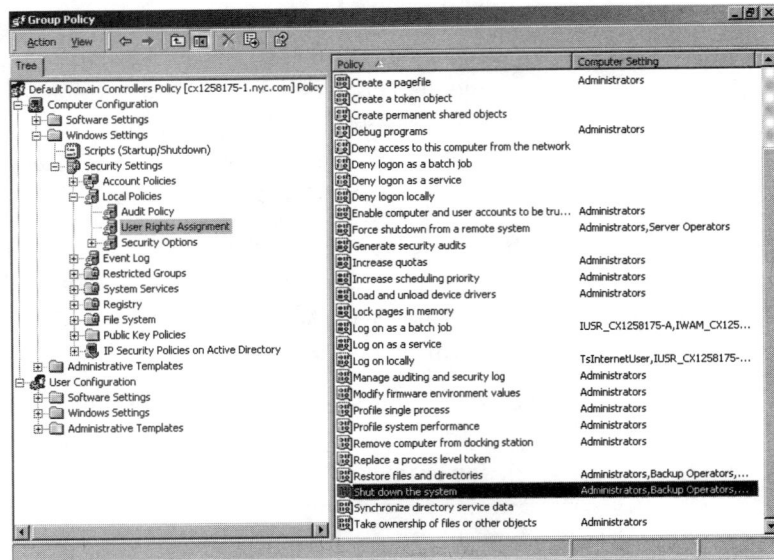

The Computer Setting column lists who has permission to alter a specific right. For example, on a domain controller, the Administrators, Backup Operators, Server Operators, Account Operators, and Print Operators groups have the right to shut down the system, whereas only the Administrators group has the right to take ownership of a file, increase quotas, or manage the auditing and security logs. The User Rights Assignment section, shown in the preceding figure, allows you to view and customize the rights that belong to particular user groups.

To give gbush the right to restore files and directories, follow these steps:

1. Choose Start ➤ Programs ➤ Administrative Tools ➤ Active Directory Users and Computers to open the Active Directory Users and Computers window.

2. Expand your domain.

3. Right-click the Domain Controllers OU, and choose Properties from the shortcut menu to open the Domain Controllers Properties dialog box.

4. Click the Group Policy tab.

5. Double-click the Default Domain Controllers Policy to open the Group Policy window.

6. Expand Computer Configuration, expand Windows Settings, and then expand Local Policies.

7. Select User Rights Assignment to display user rights in the pane on the right:

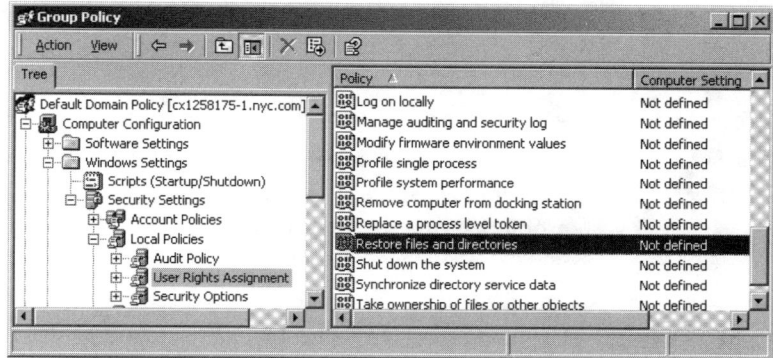

8. In the right pane, double-click Restore Files and Directories to open the Security Policy Setting dialog box:

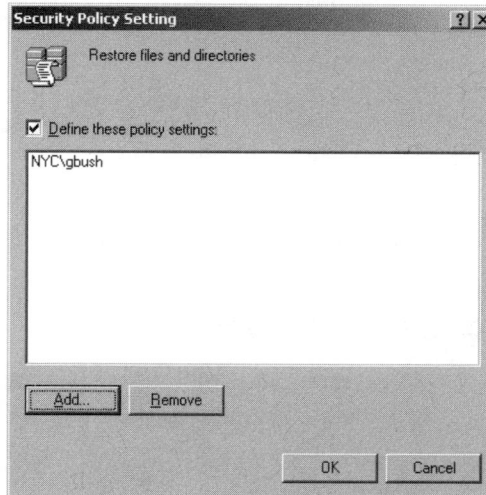

9. Click the Define These Policy Settings check box.

10. Click the Add button to open the Add User or Group dialog box.

11. Click the Browse button to open the Select Users, Computers, or Groups dialog box.

12. Double-click gbush.

13. Click OK three times, and then close the Group Policy window. Click OK in the Domain Controllers Properties dialog box and in the Active Directory Users and Computers dialog box. Gbush now has the Restore Files and Directories right.

For a stand-alone or a member server you use Local Security Policy to assign user rights. Be careful when editing these settings because changes can cause problems for your Internet services.

Editing and Customizing User Accounts

You will likely need to customize user accounts. For example, you might need to edit user accounts so that each user gets a default folder of your choosing. You can customize the following user account parameters:

- Groups
- User environment, including home folder, logon scripts, and user profiles
- Dial-in options

You have already seen how to customize groups in a previous section. In this section, we'll look at how to customize the user environment and dial-in options.

Home Folders and Logon Scripts

You create home folders for your users so that they have a central place to store their files that is backed up and is accessible from wherever they log on. You might also want to create a logon script for your users to customize their environment. In a domain, follow these steps to change these user settings:

1. Choose Start ➤ Programs ➤ Administrative Tools ➤ Active Directory Users and Computers to open the Active Directory Users and Computers dialog box.

2. Expand your domain.

3. Select the Users folder.

4. In the right pane, double-click gbush to open the gbush Properties dialog box:

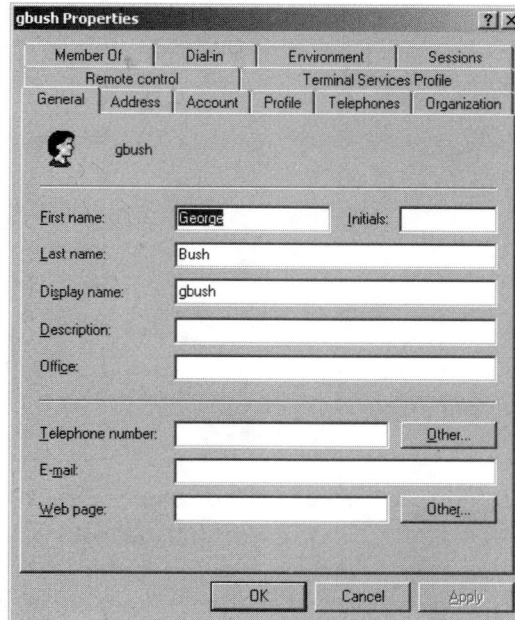

You use the Profile tab in the gbush Properties dialog box to create a home folder and to point toward a logon script for gbush. First, though, create and share a users folder. Follow these steps:

1. Right-click an empty area of your Desktop, and choose New ➢ Folder from the shortcut menu.

2. Name this folder users.

3. Right-click the users folder, and choose Sharing from the shortcut menu to open the Properties dialog box for this folder at the Sharing tab.

4. Select the Share This Folder option, and click OK.

Now you can create a home folder for gbush. Follow these steps:

1. Following the steps given earlier, open the gbush Properties dialog box.

2. Click the Profile tab.

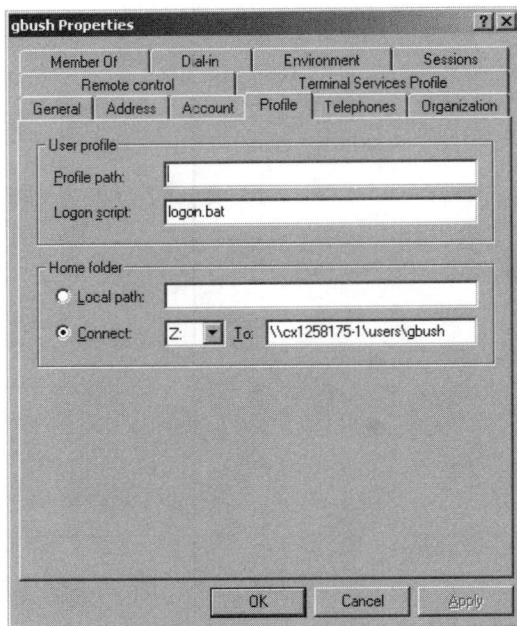

3. In the User profile section, enter **logon.bat** in the Logon Script box In the Home Folder section, select the Connect option. If desired, use the drop-down list box to change the mapped drive letter. Enter **\\127.0.0.1\ users\%username%** in the To box. (Instead of \\127.0.0.1, you can enter your server name.) Click OK.

4. Close the Active Directory Users and Computers dialog box

5. Log on as gbush.

6. Double-click My Computer to open the My Computer folder and confirm that you have created gbush's home folder and mapped a drive to it.

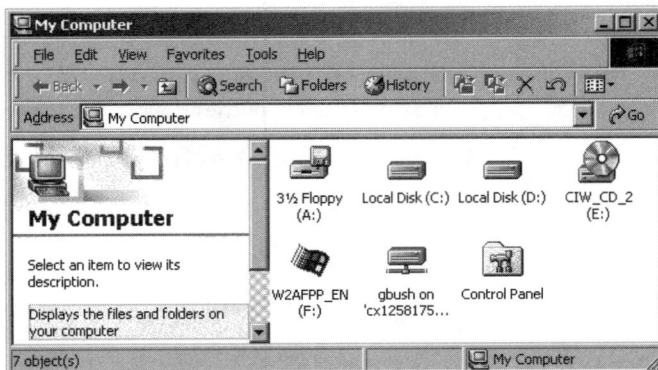

Now, although you have a pointer to gbush's logon script, you have not yet created it. Follow these steps to do so:

1. Create the logon script using a simple text editor, such as Windows Notepad. The following logon script customizes a user's logon shell so that each time they log on, the system gathers statistics about workstation connections and places them in the c:\statistics file and gathers statistics about the current route of the host and places them in the c:\users.txt file. The script then connects the user to a remote share named drivers on a system named keats, under the user name gbush, with the password of newpass.

```
@echo off
net statistics workstation >> c:\statistics.txt
net user >> c:\users.txt
net use j: \\keats\drivers newpass /USER:gbush
```

Many options are available when creating logon scripts. These options include using the net use commands, launching programs such as the Windows Calculator (calc.exe), and so forth.

2. Name the logon script file. The name of the logon script in this example is logon.bat. However, any name is suitable, as long as you end it with either the .exe or .bat filename extension. For greater compatibility with legacy DOS systems, use the .bat extension.

3. Place the logon script file in the scripts folder on a domain controller. If you have a default installation on a drive C, this location is C:\winnt\sysvol\sysvol\domain_name\scripts.

> **NOTE** The next time this gbush logs on, he will have a customized user environment. For practice you can create a logon.bat file with a single-line calc.exe and save this file in the scripts folder. Log back on as gbush, and confirm that the Calculator program launches. In a workgroup, you use the Local Users and Groups folder of Computer Management to customize a user's environment.

Dial-in

In a domain, if you are creating a Windows 2000 server that allows remote dial-in, you must create your Routing and Remote Access Server (RRAS) settings as well as explicitly designate each user that can use dial-in access — or set a policy that applies globally

Routing and Remote Access is installed by default in Windows 2000, but not enabled. To enable RRAS, follow these steps:

1. Choose Start ≻ Programs ≻ Administrative Tools ≻ Routing and Remote Access to open the Routing and Remote Access dialog box:

2. Right-click your server, and choose Configure and Enable Routing and Remote Access from the shortcut menu to open the Routing and Remote Access Server Setup Wizard.

3. At the Welcome screen, click Next to open the Common Configurations screen:

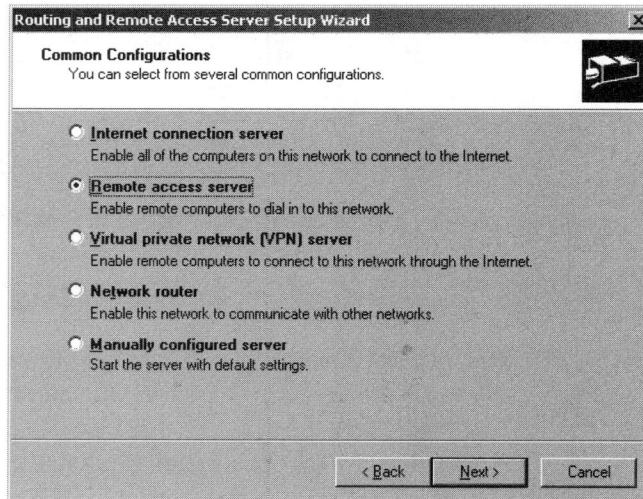

4. Select the Remote Access Server option, and then click Next to open the Remote Client Protocols screen.

5. Ensure that TCP/IP is installed, and click Next to open the IP Address Assignment screen.

6. Ensure that Automatically option is selected, and then click Next to open the Managing Multiple Remote Access Servers screen.

7. Click Next to open the Completing the Routing and Remote Access Server Setup Wizard, and then click Finish.

8. Return to the Routing and Remote Access dialog box, expand your server, and select Remote Access Policies. In the pane on the right, you should see the default policy, Allow Access If Dial-In Permission Is Enabled.

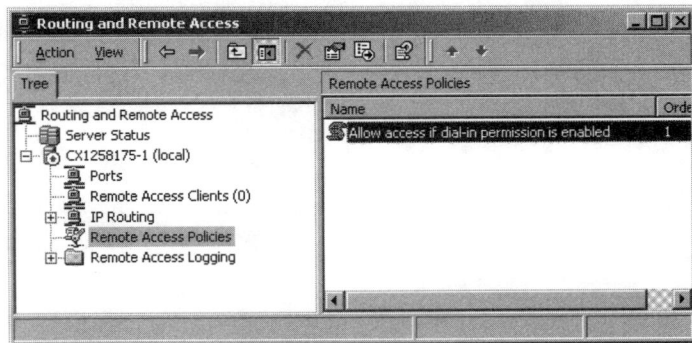

To enable gbush to dial in, follow these steps in a domain:

1. Choose Start ➤ Programs ➤ Administrative Tools ➤ Active Directory Users and Computers to open the Active Directory Users and Computers dialog box.

2. Expand your domain.

3. Select the Users folder.

4. In the right pane, double-click gbush to open the gbush Properties dialog box.

5. Click the Dial-in tab:

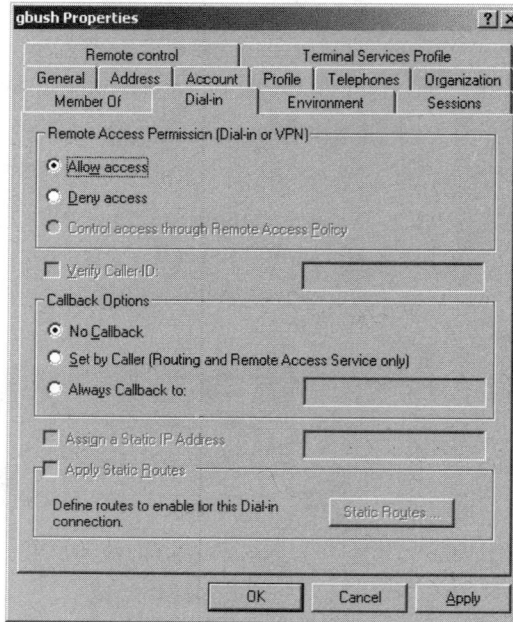

6. In the Remote Access Permission (Dial-in or VPN) section, select the Allow Access option, and click OK.

You can set additional options in the Callback Options section.

- Select No Callback to prevent the server from calling the user back.

- Select Set by Caller to allow the user to determine whether the computer should call them back. Organizations that allow long-distance charges might want to select the Set by Caller option, which also allows the user to use any callback number.

- Select Always Callback To predetermine the callback number, regardless of what the caller requests.

If required, you can also specify that IP addresses and routing information be given to dial-in users.

Windows 2000 Services and User Accounts

When you installed Windows 2000, you automatically created an Administrator account, the Guest account (disabled by default), and at least three additional system accounts used for remote guest access to your web server (IUSR_COMPUTERNAME), remote administration (IWAM_COMPUTER-NAME) of your Internet server, or remote access to Terminal Services through the Internet (TSInternetUser).

These accounts can be useful, or they can be a security hole. Protect the IWAM_COMPUTERNAME account with a strong password or disable it. If you want to deny access to folders on your web server to anonymous clients, set NTFS permissions on the IUSR_COMPUTERNAME account, the Internet guest account for your IIS server. Follow these steps:

1. In Windows Explorer, navigate to the C:\Inetpub\wwwroot_private folder.

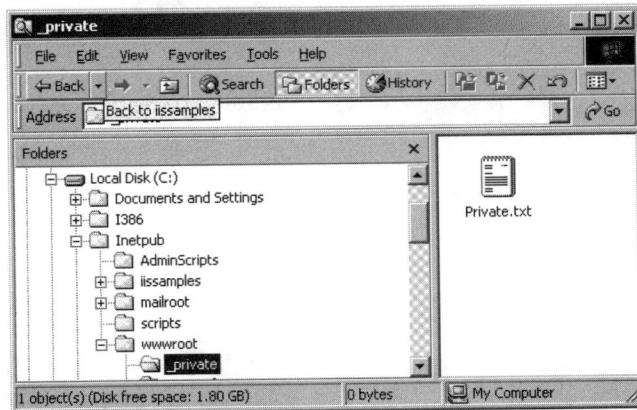

2. Right-click the _private folder, and choose Properties from the short-cut menu to open the _private Properties dialog box.

3. Click the Security tab:

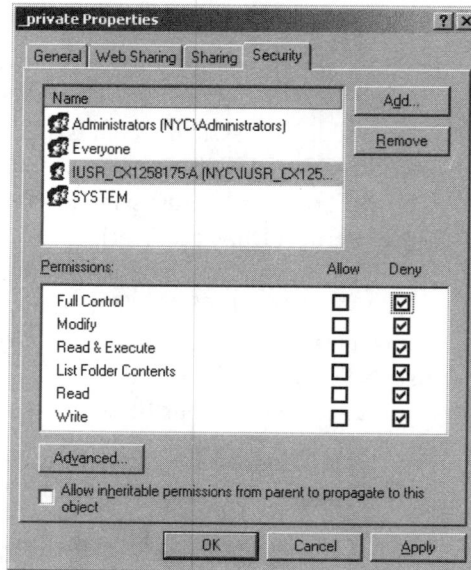

4. Click the Add button to open the Select Users, Computers, or Groups dialog box.

5. Double-click the IUSR_COMPUTERNAME account to add it to the bottom panel.

6. Click OK to return to the _private Properties dialog box. Make sure that the IUSR_COMPUTERNAME account is selected. Click the Deny Full Control checkbox, and then click OK.

7. When you see the following warning, click OK.

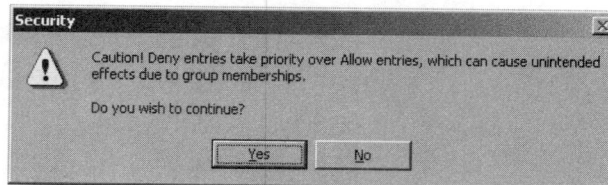

For NTFS permissions, Deny entries take precedence over Allow entries.

Table 5.2 lists some important service accounts in Windows 2000 Server.

TABLE 5.2   Windows 2000 Services and User accounts

Service	Account Name
IIS	IUSR_COMPUTERNAME
Remote Management	IWAM_COMPUTERNAME
Terminal Services	TsInternetUser

Additional user accounts may exist, depending on the services installed on your Windows 2000 system. For example, if you install SQL Server or Exchange Server, you will find additional accounts. You must ensure that these accounts have the appropriate rights, such as to log on as a service or act as part of the operating system or back up files and directories as appropriate for the specific system account, and that their passwords are set to never expire.

Summary

In this chapter, you learned about how various services installed on the operating system use special accounts and how you can use groups to limit access to users who connect over the Internet.

You learned to use the Active Directory Users and Computers dialog box in a domain or the Computer Management snap-in in a workgroup to create user accounts and assign passwords and password properties. You noticed that the user account used for anonymous web server access, the IUSR_ COMPUTERNAME account, has limited access because it is in the Guests group. You learned to place selected user accounts into groups that you created using the Groups icon in the Computer Management snap-in, and you learned to assign permissions to these groups by adding them to the access list for the appropriate files or folders. In this way, you can enable higher levels of web server access for selected groups.

In this chapter, you also learned about the SAM database and administered local and remote SAM databases. You discovered the importance of access control and authentication when you created accounts that allowed users to log on and control the system. You instituted system-wide policies, managed user rights, and implemented NTFS and auditing. Using Event Viewer, you viewed local and remote events. You also customized user environments using logon scripts and custom home folders. Finally, you learned about NTFS permissions and ownership.

Exam Essentials

Be able to identify the purpose of the Windows 2000 Security Accounts Manager.   The Security Accounts Manager (SAM) is a collection of processes and files that Windows 2000 uses to authenticate users.

Be able to convert a FAT drive to NTFS.   To impose security on files and folders in Windows 2000, the drive on which the files and folders reside must be formatted with NTFS. To convert a drive from FAT to NTFS, you use the `convert c: /fs:ntfs` command.

Be able to administer local and remote Windows 2000 systems and users.   You use the Computer Management snap-in to administer both local and remote systems. You can also use Computer Management to enforce systemwide policies such as account lockout settings, password policies, and auditing. In addition, you use Computer Management to create users, set their passwords, home folders, and user profiles. From Computer Management, you can view specialized system accounts used for remote access, such as the web server Guest account, IUSR_COMPUTER-NAME. You use Event Viewer to monitor event logs on local and remote computers. Finally, you use Windows Explorer to manage NTFS and share permissions on files and folders.

Key Terms

Before taking the exam, you should be familiar with the following terms:

Active Directory (AD)	Microsoft Management Console (MMC)
dcpromo	Security Accounts Manager (SAM)
domain controller (DC)	

Review Questions

1. Jim wants to create shares on seven computers that he administers. Three of those computers are in a remote city. What is the easiest way for Jim to create these shares?

   A. Visit each computer.

   B. Visit the local computers and create a script for the other computers.

   C. Create a customized MMC and e-mail it to the administrator in the other city.

   D. In Computer Management, select Connect to Another Computer.

2. Mark owns a small engineering design business that has seven computers that need access to a central database. He is concerned that hackers might try to guess the administrator password or the password of another user. What should Mark do to enhance security? Choose all that apply.

   A. Configure an account lockout policy.

   B. Enable auditing for failed logon attempts.

   C. Use NTLM authentication instead of Kerberos.

   D. Configure a complex password policy.

3. Brad wants to set account policies so that users must use a strong password, must change that password regularly, and must not reuse that password. Which three of the following password policies is sufficient to meet these needs?

   A. Password history

   B. Password aging

   C. Password length

   D. Complexity requirements

   E. Account lockout

4. Joshua owns Furniture South. He has four Windows 2000 computers in a workgroup. His computer has pricing data; his wife's computer has accounting data; his warehouse manager's computer has shipping and repair data; and the sales manager's computer has sales data. Joshua and his wife should have access to all of the data. The warehouse manager only needs access to his own data, and the sales manager needs access to both sales and shipping data. How should you set the appropriate access permissions? Choose all that apply.

    A. Use Active Directory Users and Computers to add users to global groups.

    B. Use Computer Management to add users to global groups.

    C. Use Computer Management to add users to local groups.

    D. Use Active Directory Users and Computers to add users to domain local groups.

    E. Joshua adds MMC snap-ins to manage all the computers from a central MMC.

    F. Each user must create additional users locally.

5. Joshua is dual-booting his home computer between Windows 98 and Windows 2000. He sets up auditing and is able to audit files and folders on his D: drive but not his C: drive. What is the problem?

    A. Windows 98 files cannot be audited.

    B. The system and the boot partitions cannot be audited.

    C. The file system.

    D. The operating system.

    E. The patch level.

6. Frank wants to dual-boot between NT 4 and Windows 2000, so he installs the latest NT 4 service pack that, among other things, upgrades the NTFS file system to NTFS 5. Which features of this file system will only be available in Windows 2000?

A. Disk mirroring

B. Disk quotas

C. Compression

D. Encrypting File System (EFS)

E. NTFS permissions

7. Frank initially installed Windows 2000 on a FAT32 partition. He wants to increase the security and enhance the stability of the file system. What should Frank do? Choose the best answer.

A. Install the latest Service Pack.

B. Apply the hisecdc security policy.

C. Install another hard drive. Format it as NTFS. Move the system and boot partitions to the other hard drive.

D. Use the `convert C: /fs:ntfs` command to convert drive C to NTFS.

E. Back up data, reformat the drive to NTFS, and then restore data.

8. The HR director leaves for another position. Before assuming the new position, she goes on a vacation to Nepal and leaves her cell phone at home. Mark, the network administrator, needs to grant the new HR director access to the folders to which only the old HR director has access. How can Mark accomplish this goal? Choose two.

A. Take ownership of the folders and grant the new HR director the right to take ownership.

B. Directly make the new HR director the owner of the folders.

C. Directly give the new HR director Full Control of the HR folders.

D. Rename the old HR director's account to the new HR director's account and change the password. Ask the new HR director re-change the password.

9. Peter is the webmaster for Cletus, a Windows 2000 server hosting an IIS 5 website, www.pending-legislation.com. Users with logon IDs pay a subscription fee for the latest news on pending legislation. First-time visitors can tour the website without a logon. These guest users will be granted rights within the security context of which user?

   A. Cletus users

   B. IUSR_Cletus

   C. IWAM_Cletus

   D. TSInternet User

10. Ralph needs to add a user to the Windows 2000 nwtraders.com domain. On which computers can Ralph add this user?

    A. Any DC

    B. PDC

    C. BDC

    D. Any PDC

11. Frank starts work at a new company and upon initial logon to a Windows 2000 domain is prompted to change his password. He tries to change the password to the one he used at his old company, and that password is rejected. What might be the problem?

    A. Password uniqueness

    B. Minimum password age

    C. Minimum password length

    D. Password complexity requirements

12. Sarah comes back to work after a vacation in Hawaii. She attempts to log on and is immediately prompted to change her password. She attempts to change it from Hilo2You back to her last password of Maui4Me but is unable to do so. What is the most likely problem? Choose the best answer.

    A. Password history

    B. Password length

    C. Password complexity

    D. Maximum password age

13. While Brad was on a road trip, a temp used his computer to type a memo. Brad attempts to log on, but his password is rejected. What is the most likely cause?

    A. Caps Lock.

    B. Password expired.

    C. Temp changed his password.

    D. Network cable disconnected.

    E. Brad forgot his password.

14. Ben needs to complete an expense report for his last trip before he goes out on his next trip later in the afternoon. After repeated unsuccessful logon attempts, Ben receives a message that his account has been locked out. Ben calls the help desk, but all members are in a meeting with the network manager. What could Ben do to get access as quickly as possible? Choose three.

    A. Disengage Caps Lock and immediately try again.

    B. Disengage Caps Lock, wait, and then try again.

    C. Wait until the meeting is over.

    D. Log on to the domain using the guest account if it is enabled.

    E. Log on to his local computer.

    F. Disconnect the network cable and attempt to log on.

15. Mandy is a member of the Server Operators group in Windows 2000. She is reviewing the event logs for the domain controller, BuzzLightYear. She looks at the Security Log, and it is empty. What is the likely cause?

    A. It has been set to overwrite changes.

    B. The size of the log needs to be increased.

    C. The Administrator has not set up auditing.

    D. It's been a quiet week.

16. Frank starts his Windows 2000 Professional computer and receives an error message that a service failed to start. How should Frank troubleshoot this message? Choose two.

    A. Use the Last Known Good option.

    B. Check Event Viewer.

    C. In Computer Management check the services that have not started.

    D. Enable promiscuous logging in the HKey Local Machine Registry tree.

17. Andrea receives a help desk call that a user's Windows 2000 Professional computer had an error on startup. The user cannot remember the exact message. How should Andrea troubleshoot this problem? Choose the best answer.

    A. Ask the user to restart the computer and write down the message verbatim.

    B. Visit the remote computer and check the System Log.

    C. Ask the user to check the System Log.

    D. Connect to the remote computer using Computer Management.

18. Willy creates a network share on which to install Office XP. How should Willy configure permissions? Choose three.

    A. Remove the Everyone group.

    B. Grant Read permissions to the Domain Users group.

    C. Grant Full Control to Administrators.

    D. Deny the Everyone group Full Control.

    E. Grant the Modify permission to the Domain Users group.

19. Jim suspects that someone is trying to guess the Administrator password, so he is looking for failed logon attempts using Event Viewer's Security log. Which icon indicates a failed logon attempt?

A. A check mark

B. An exclamation point

C. A lock

D. A key

20. Ralph is installing an application that needs the _____ to log on locally, back up files and folder, and act as a part of the operating system. Fill in the blank.

A. Right

B. Permission

C. Privilege

D. Ability

E. Policy

Answers to Review Questions

1. D. Jim can use Computer Management to connect to the other computers in order to administer them and create shares.

2. A, B, D. Windows 2000 uses Kerberos authentication, which is more secure than NTLM authentication, which was used in NT 4, so choice C is incorrect. The rest of the choices are excellent security measures.

3. A, B, D. Complexity requires that passwords contain mixed characters. Password history prevents the reuse of a password, and password aging ensures that users change passwords periodically.

4. C, F. Joshua should create a custom MMC that has computer management snap-ins for the four computers and you should create users and local groups on each computer.

5. C. Auditing files and folders requires the NTFS file system.

6. B, D. Disk quotas and encryption are new features of NTFS 5 that are available on Windows 2000 but not on NT 4.

7. D. Frank should convert the hard drive to NTFS. The data will be preserved.

8. A, D. Mark cannot grant permissions on the folders without first taking ownership. Once Mark takes ownership, he can give the new HR director the Full Control right or the right to take ownership, but he cannot assign ownership. Mark can also rename the old HR director's account and reset the password.

9. B. The IIS guest account is IUSR_COMPUTERNAME.

10. A. In Windows 2000, domain controllers are peers, each with a read-write copy of the Active Directory database. Changes to this database are replicated using multi-master replication.

11. C, D.   Frank's proposed password might be too short or might not be complex enough for his new organization's domain.

12. A.   Keeping a password history and enforcing unique passwords increase security. If Sarah's old password was long enough and complex enough before, it probably still meets those requirements, but she must choose a password that was not previously used.

13. A.   The temp probably engaged Caps Lock. Passwords are case sensitive.

14. B, D, E.   If the lockout duration has been set to a short period such as five or ten minutes, Ben can just wait and try again. If the guest account has been enabled, Ben can log on using that account while he is waiting for his account to be reset, or Ben can log on to his local computer provided he has permissions.

15. C.   The Administrator must set up auditing in order for the logs to display tracked events.

16. B, C.   Frank should check the System Log in Event Viewer. He can also try to restart the service using Computer Management.

17. D.   Andrea should connect to the remote computer using Computer Management and check the System Log herself. She can then use Computer Management to remotely restart any service that failed to start.

18. A, B, C.   By default, the Everyone group has Full Control. Remove this group, substitute Domain Users, and give this group only Read permissions, while giving the Administrators group Full Control.

19. C.   A lock indicates a failure audit.

20. A.   A permission grants the ability to access a resource; a right is the ability to determine how the operating system functions.

Chapter

6

Managing Users in Linux

THE CIW EXAM OBJECTIVE GROUPS COVERED IN THIS CHAPTER:

✓ Manage users in Windows, Linux, and Novell networks, including but not limited to: Security Accounts Manager, authentication, remote user administration, user rights and settings, remote shares, account creation, password policies, permissions.

Although Windows 2000 is a powerful operating system, it is not the only one. Unix systems have dominated Internet space for years, and Linux has recently become a popular choice. The Linux source code is distributed for free, and tens of thousands of programmers have reviewed the source code to improve performance, eliminate bugs, and strengthen security. Linux has no vendor lock-in and runs on a wide range of hardware, from supercomputers to Personal Digital Assistants (PDAs, such as Palm Pilot). In addition, Linux is exceptionally stable.

In this chapter, you will learn how to add users and implement security on the Linux operating system. You will learn about Pluggable Authentication Modules (PAMs), the associated encryption utilities, and the `/etc/passwd` and `/etc/shadow` files that work transparently to constitute the equivalent of the Windows 2000 Security Accounts Manager (SAM). You will also learn about some of the utilities that you can use to automate Linux services, including `linuxconf` and `ntsysv`.

> **NOTE** In this chapter, we'll use Red Hat Linux in the exercises.

Adding Accounts in Linux

When you install Linux, you create the root user account that has the rights and privileges to administer the system. This all-powerful user account has complete access to all files and directories regardless of the owner or permissions. The root user controls user account administration by creating users, setting their passwords, adding users to groups, and assigning user, group, and other permissions to files and directories.

When logged on as the root user, you can add users in Linux in the following ways:

- Manually by directly editing Linux system files and creating directories

- With the aid of the following utilities:

  - /usr/sbin/useradd

  - /usr/sbin/adduser

  - linuxconf (in the X Window System)

We'll look first at how to add users manually, and then we'll look at how to use utilities to add users.

Creating Accounts Manually

In Linux everything is a file. The most common file type is simply called a regular file, which stores information. Regular files include executables and data files. Another type of file is a directory, which contains a list of other files and their locations. Other files include block devices, such as hard drives, and character devices, such as keyboards.

Given the emphasis that Linux places on files, you should not be surprised that you add users, add groups, add users to groups, and assign permissions by directly modifying the appropriate files using a text editor.

Table 6.1 lists and describes the files that you use to perform these administrative tasks.

TABLE 6.1 Important Files for Adding Linux Users

File	Description
/etc/passwd	Public user database; contains usernames, user IDs, logon shells, and home directories.
/etc/shadow	Shadow password file; contains encrypted passwords that only root can read. May also contain password aging information.

TABLE 6.1 Important Files for Adding Linux Users *(continued)*

File	Description
/etc/logon.defs /etc/default/useradd /etc/skel/	Contain default values for newly created accounts.
/etc/group	Group file; contains group names, group IDs, and lists of group members. Everyone can read this file.

Creating a user account on a Linux computer is a two-step process. First, you enter the new account in the system user database (also called the password database), and then you create the resources that the account needs, such as a home directory and default logon configuration files.

Entering the New Account in the User Database

You are already familiar with the universal properties of a user account. On Linux systems, a user account is defined by the following properties.

A username   Usually the first item of information used to log on to a system. A username must not contain spaces, but otherwise it can be a general ASCII string (the length limit is long enough to be irrelevant). Most organizations devise a system to create and assign usernames. As you saw in earlier chapters, one convention is to use the user's last name, first initial, and maybe a number (to allow for smithj1, smithj2, and so on).

A user ID number (UID)   Identifies the user on the system. A *user ID number (UID)* is stored in the file system to identify a file's owner, and it's stored in the kernel's process table to identify the owner of a process. The UID is stored internally in 32-bit fields, so it can be any reasonable size.

A primary group ID number (GID)   A *primary group ID number (GID)* is the default group for a given user. This group owns files that the user creates.

A home directory   The initial directory for the user's logon shell.

A shell program   The program that is executed when the user logs on. Usually, the *shell program* is the user's preferred interactive environment

(/bin/sh, /bin/ksh, /bin/csh, or /bin/bash, for example), but it can also be a special-purpose shell with limited capabilities.

A password   The user's logon password. All the complications in user account management come from the need to protect this field.

All Linux account information is stored in the system user database. This database is stored in two files: the password file (/etc/passwd) and the shadow password file (/etc/shadow). In this section, we'll look first at how to edit the /etc/passwd file to create a user, assign a user ID, and assign a primary group ID. Because passwords are encrypted and reside in the /etc/shadow file, you cannot manually assign a password but must use one of the utilities to do so. We'll look at these utilities later in this chapter.

The password file, /etc/passwd, holds all account information that everyone on the system can read. All properties except the encrypted password data are stored here; the file is necessary because processes must be able to convert UID numbers to usernames and vice versa, as well as determine a user's home directory.

Each line of the /etc/passwd file represents a user and has seven fields separated by colons:

- username
- x
- UID
- GID
- Full Name
- Home Directory
- Shell

To create a user account, you use any text editor to add a line with these fields to the /etc/passwd file. For example, the following line:

```
wolf1:x:100:100:Wolfman Jack:/home/wolf1:/bin/bash
```

creates a user with the username wolf1, a UID of 100, a GID of 100, the full name Wolfman Jack, the home directory /home/wolf1, and the logon shell /bin/bash. The x in the second field indicates that the password is encrypted in the shadow passwords file, /etc/shadow, which only root can read. The Full Name field is sometimes called the GECOS field, after an outdated operating system.

Let's look at another example. To create a new user named Laura Craft with a logon name of raider1 that has the next available user ID, a primary group ID of 100, a home directory of /home/laura, and a logon shell of /bin/bash, add the following line to the etc/passwd file:

```
raider1:x:101:100:Laura Craft:/home/raider1:/bin/bash
```

If Laura Craft were out of country for a long period of time, you should disable her account for security purposes. To do so, replace x in the second field with another letter, for example, y, as follows:

```
raider1:y:101:100:Laura Craft:/home/raider1:/bin/bash
```

Although most current versions of Linux (including Red Hat 7) enable shadow passwords by default, you need to ensure that shadow passwords are enabled if you are using an early version of Linux. As root, issue the following command to find out if the file /etc/shadow exists:

```
host# ls -l /etc/shadow
```

If this file exists, your system uses shadow passwords. If it does not, run the pwconv program as follows:

```
host# /usr/sbin/pwconv
```

Now verify that the /etc/shadow file exists as shown:

```
host# ls -l /etc/shadow
-r-------- 1 root root 825 May 27 08:46 /etc/shadow
```

Also for security, consider using Pluggable Authentication Modules (PAMs). PAMs govern user authentication and set limits on certain applications. For example, by default a non-root Linux user can reboot the system. You can use PAMs to change this behavior. For details on PAMs, see www.linuxdoc.com.

Creating Resources for the New Account

After you create a new user account, you need to create resources for that account, including a home directory and default configuration files. A home directory stores a user's files on a server, which allows them to be accessed from any computer on the system. A home directory also stores the user's default logon configuration files, which are used to customize a user's environment.

When you create the user account in the /etc/passwd file, you create a pointer to their home directory. You must create the home directory manually, however, and you must also assign permissions to the user and copy the default configuration files into the home directory.

To create a home directory for the new user raider1, open a terminal window, change to the /home directory (CD /home), and create the raider1 directory (mkdir raider1). Next, make Laura Craft the owner of her home directory (chown craftl /home/raider1), and give Laura exclusive control of her home directory (chmod 700 /home/raider1).

You also need to provide the user with a basic set of logon initialization files. All users need at least a .bashrc and .bash_profile file to set up their environments. They may also need other configuration files to set up applications such as Emacs and the X Window System.

The default system profile files (usually stored in the /etc directory, for example, as /etc/profile) can be used as default logon initialization files. As time passes, you can customize these files to better reflect user preferences. You should keep these default files in a convenient location. (Linux looks for them in the /etc/skel directory.)

Using Utilities to Create an Account

Although understanding all the steps involved in creating an account is worthwhile, Linux provides utilities that automate the process. These utilities fall into two categories:

- Utilities that create accounts. The two main account creation utilities are linuxconf, which is graphical, and /usr/sbin/useradd, which is a command line utility. You use these utilities to enter the necessary information into the /etc/passwd and /etc/shadow files. You can also use them to create a home directory and the necessary logon configuration files for the user account.

- Utilities that set account defaults by modifying the /etc/logon.defs file. A default value is a parameter that is automatically entered if no other value is specified. Default values specified in the /etc/logon .defs file include userlogon shell, home directory naming convention, and account characteristics such as the default umask for the new account. These default rules are applied no matter which account creation utility is subsequently used. They fill in unspecified parameters of a new user account so that if you merely specify the username and password, the defaults will fill in the home directory, default shell, and other information such as the maximum password age.

The `useradd` command falls into both of the above categories. You can use it to create accounts and to set defaults for accounts.

Setting *useradd* Account Defaults

You should follow the apocryphal "Lazy Administrator's Guide to Success" and set account defaults first, because doing so will reduce the effort that it takes to create subsequent users and reduce errors in entering user information. The `useradd` utility operates in two modes. In the first mode, it sets defaults; in the second, it creates a user account. For the first mode, the default modification is signaled with –D, as described in Table 6.2.

> **NOTE** The Unix and Linux operating systems use case-sensitive commands and switches.

TABLE 6.2 Setting Defaults for Use with useradd

Option (with *–D*)	Meaning	Purpose
–g	Group	Defines the default primary group
–b	Path	Defines the default initial path for home directories
–e	Date	Sets the default account expiration date (default: no expiration)
–f	Number	Sets the default for the number of days an account can be inactive before it is disabled (default: no limit)

For example, the following command:

```
host# useradd -D -g users -b /home
```

by default sets user directories to be stored in /home, sets the default group for new users as `users`, and does not set an expiration date or an inactivity limit.

Creating User Accounts with *useradd*

After you set account defaults with `usr/sbin/useradd`, you can create user accounts. When creating accounts, you omit the –D option and supply a username. Table 6.3 lists the options for this form of `useradd`.

TABLE 6.3   Options for useradd without -D

Option	Meaning	What It Does
-u	UID	Specifies a UID. If you do not specify a UID, the next available UID is used.
-g	Group	Specifies the primary group for the user. If you do not specify a group, the default is used.
-G	Groups	Updates the /etc/group file; a comma-separated list of secondary groups.
-d	Home directory	Specifies a path name for the home directory; if a default base has been set with the –b option for the defaults, you can omit this option, and the home directory will be base/username.
-m	Home directory/user	Creates the home directory and gives the user ownership, or if the directory exists, changes ownership to the user.
-s	Shell	Specifies the logon shell; the default is /bin/sh, the Bourne shell.
-k	Dir	Specifies the skeleton directory where initialization scripts are located; defaults to /etc/skel (used with the –m option).
-c	Full name	Enters the user's full name in the password database.
-e	Date	Specifies the account expiration date.

TABLE 6.3 Options for useradd without -D *(continued)*

Option	Meaning	What It Does
-f	Number	Specifies the number of days the account can remain unused before being disabled.

For example, if the defaults have been set, the following command:

```
host# useradd -m -s /bin/bash -c 'Jeremy Teitelbaum' jeremy
```

creates an account with the user name jeremy, the full name Jeremy Teitelbaum, the logon shell /bin/bash, home directory /home/jeremy (using the –b default), and group users (using the –g default). It also creates the home directory and copies files from /etc/skel to it with the correct ownership and permissions.

The usermod command takes the same options (except –k) and can be used, for example, to change a user's logon shell. To change the previous user logon shell to /bin/ksh instead of /bin/bash, you use the following command:

```
host# usermod -s /bin/ksh jeremy
```

The userdel command deletes a user and (depending on options) that user's home directory. The userdel –r command removes the home directory automatically.

Creating Accounts Using *linuxconf*

The linuxconf program provides a graphical interface that you can use to create user accounts and take care of many other administrative tasks. As mentioned earlier, one version of linuxconf runs from the command line, and another runs under the X Window System.

To install the command line version, insert and mount the second Red Hat installation CD, open a command line prompt, enter the following case-sensitive command, and press Enter:

```
Host# rpm -ivh /mnt/cdrom/RedHat/RPMS/linuxconf-1.24r2-
↳10.i386.rpm
```

If this command doesn't work in your version of Red Hat Linux, enter the following auto complete command and then press Tab to complete the entry:

Host# rpm -ivh /mnt/cdrom/RedHat/RPMS/linuxconf-

To install the Gnome X Window System version of `linuxconf`, enter the following at a command line prompt:

Host# rpm -ivh /mnt/cdrom/RedHat/RPMS/gnome-linuxconf-
↳0.64-1.i386.rpm

If this command doesn't work in your version of Red Hat Linux, enter the following auto complete command and then press Tab to complete the entry:

Host# rpm -ivh /mnt/cdrom/RedHat/RPMS/gnome-linuxconf-

To add a user using `linuxconf` in the X Window System, follow these steps:

1. Choose Gnome ➢ Programs ➢ System ➢ Linuxconf to open `linuxconf`.

2. Expand Users Accounts, expand Normal, and then select User Accounts, as shown in Figure 6.1.

FIGURE 6.1   Adding a user in `linuxconf`

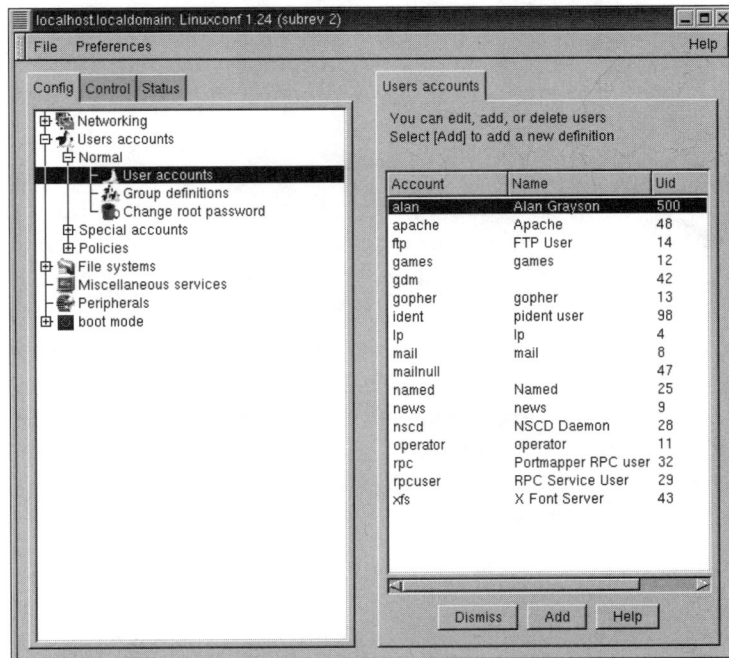

3. Click the Add button to open the User Account Creation tab, as shown in Figure 6.2.

FIGURE 6.2 The User Account Creation tab in `linuxconf`

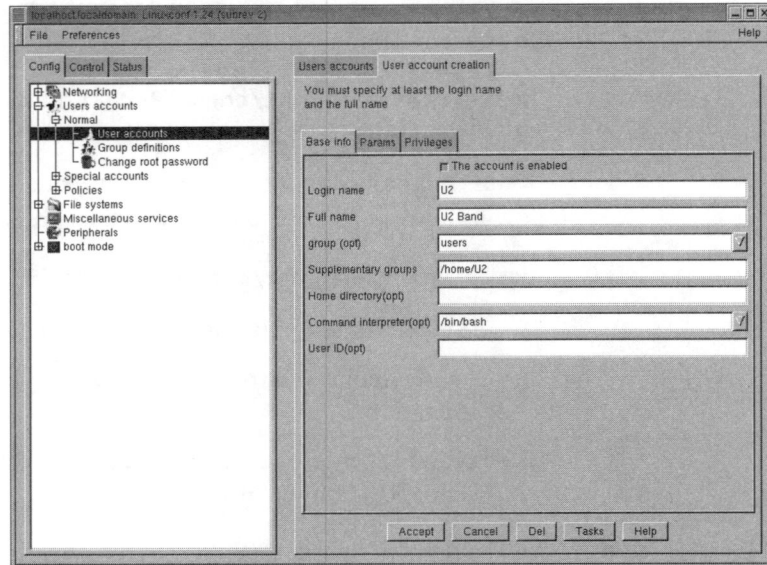

4. Enter user account information similar to that in Figure 6.2, and then click the Accept button to create the user.

When using either the command line (ASCII text) version or the X Window System version of `linuxconf`, be sure to activate your changes before closing the application.

As you can see, adding users with the Gnome X Window System version of `linuxconf` is really easy. Unfortunately, you may not be able to administer remote Internet systems using this version. For example, firewalls prevent the use of the X Window System version of `linuxconf`. You can conduct remote X Window System sessions, but most administrators don't do so for security reasons.

Remember also that many Linux systems do not have the X Window System installed in the first place. In the following exercise, you will practice adding users with the command line version of linuxconf.

EXERCISE 6.1

Adding Users with *linuxconf*

In this exercise, you will learn how to add users with linuxconf.

1. Log on as root, or use the su command to assert root privileges.

2. As root, open linuxconf (/sbin/linuxconf).

3. Press Enter to expand the Config icon.

4. Scroll down to Users Accounts.

5. If necessary, press Enter to expand the Users Accounts tree.

6. Scroll down to Normal, press Enter, scroll down to User Accounts, and press Enter to display the contents of the user accounts database (the /etc/passwd file).

7. Tab to the Add button, and then press Enter to create a new user. Your screen should resemble that shown in the following graphic:

8. Enter the logon information for John Smith as suggested in Exercise 4.1 in Chapter 4. Fill in the Login Name and Full Name values, using the down and up arrow keys to navigate through the fields. Remember that your policy is to use the full last name plus the first letter of the first name. Add John Smith to the users group. Leave the supplementary groups and the home directory empty because linuxconf will automatically create the /home/smithj directory. Leave the user ID field blank as well. Linux will create a user ID automatically.

9. Press Tab to highlight Accept, and then press Enter to display a screen that asks for a password for smithj.

10. Enter **Tr$ning1** as the password, and then confirm this password.

11. The linuxconf program will display a message informing you that it added the username smithj and changed the password from blank to Tr$ning1.

12. As root, create the /romantics directory. Add three more users: William Blake, William Wordsworth, and John Keats. This time, choose a custom home directory—romantics—by entering **/romantics/username** into the Home Directory(Opt) field. Follow the policy you defined earlier. For example, when adding William Blake's home directory, enter **/romantics/blakew**. You do not have to create this subdirectory; linuxconf will do it for you. Give Tr$ning1 as the password for two users. For the third user, use the password training. You'll receive a warning that the password might be easy to guess. You can still use this password, despite the warning. As root, you can use any password you wish. However, other users will have to choose more difficult passwords when this original password ages.

13. After adding the last three users, return to the Users Accounts window. Press Tab to highlight Quit, and then press Enter to display the main linuxconf window.

14. Press Tab to highlight Quit, and then press Enter.

Adding users generally does not require you to activate any changes. Making other changes, such as altering IP address information, does require you to save changes. If you do not activate such changes, linuxconf will not enable the settings you requested. Still, if you are required to activate changes, highlight Activate the Changes, then press Enter. (Do not use the Tab key to access the Quit button.) After a short delay, linuxconf will return you to the command prompt.

15. Test the last three accounts you created. Log on to each. Notice that the home directory for each is now filed in the /romantics/ directory, rather than in the /home/ directory.

EXERCISE 6.2

Deleting a User Account using *linuxconf*

In this exercise, you will learn how to delete a user account with linuxconf.

1. Open linuxconf, expand Config, expand Users, expand Normal, select User Accounts, and press Enter.

2. Highlight smithj, and press Enter to display the smithj account.

3. Press Tab to navigate to the Del button, and then press Enter.

4. The linuxconf program will ask you to confirm that you want to delete the user account. The confirmation screen offers three choices, but defaults to archiving the deleted account for later use, as shown in the following graphic:

```
ÚÄÄÄÄÄÄÄÄÄÄ Deleting account blowdown ÄÄÄÄÄÄÄÄÄÄ¿
³ You are deleting an account.                   ³
³ The home directory and the mail inbox folder   ³
³ may be archived, deleted or left in place      ³
³                                                ³
³    ÚÄÄÄÄÄÄÄÄÄÄÄÄÄÄÄÄÄÄÄÄÄÄÄÄÄÄÄÄÄÄÄÄÄÄÄÄ¿       ³
³    ³(o) Archive the account's data     ³       ³
³    ³(_) Delete the account's data      ³       ³
³    ³( ) Leave the account's data in place³     ³
³    ÀÄÄÄÄÄÄÄÄÄÄÄÄÄÄÄÄÄÄÄÄÄÄÄÄÄÄÄÄÄÄÄÄÄÄÄÄÙ       ³
³    ÚÄÄÄÄÄÄ¿      ÚÄÄÄÄÄÄ¿       ÚÄÄÄÄ¿           ³
³    ³Accept³     ³Cancel³       ³Help³           ³
³    ÀÄÄÄÄÄÄÙ      ÀÄÄÄÄÄÄÙ       ÀÄÄÄÄÙ           ³
ÀÄÄÄÄÄÄÄÄÄÄÄÄÄÄÄÄÄÄÄÄÄÄÄÄÄÄÄÄÄÄÄÄÄÄÄÄÄÄÄÄÄÄÄÄÄÄÄÄÄÙ
```

5. Choose to completely delete the account by using the down arrow key on your keyboard to place the cursor in the parentheses next to Delete the Account's Data. Press the space bar once to select this option. A lowercase *o* should appear next to the option.

6. Press Tab to move to Accept, and then press Enter to return to the Users Accounts window.

7. Press Tab to navigate to the Quit button, and then press Enter.

8. Again, press Tab to navigate to the Quit button, and then press Enter.

9. Exit linuxconf by pressing Tab to access the Quit button and then pressing Enter.

10. Tab to the Quit button again, and press Enter.

11. Enter the following command to see if the smithj account is still in the /etc/passwd database:

    more /etc/passwd

12. List the /home/ directory. You should not see any directory for the smithj account. You should see all the user accounts. Notice, however, that the smithj account no longer has an entry.

The linuxconf program sometimes has problems deleting account information. If linuxconf does not delete the information, use vi or any other text editor to edit the /etc/passwd file. Open the file, and place the cursor in front of the account information. If you are in command mode (press the Esc key if you are unsure), enter **dd** to delete the entire line. To exit vi, press Esc, and then enter **q!**.

Managing Passwords

You can establish the following password policies in Linux:

- Changing passwords
- Password aging
- Password checking

Changing Passwords

The root user can change passwords for all users defined on the system, and users can change their own passwords. As root, you can change passwords using the command line or using `linuxconf` in the X Window System. At a command line prompt, enter the `passwd` command with a username argument to set the password for any user. The following graphic shows root changing the password for a user:

To change a user's password using `linuxconf` in the X Window System, follow these steps:

1. Choose Gnome ➤ Programs ➤ System ➤ Linuxconf.

2. Expand User Accounts, expand Normal, and then select User Accounts:

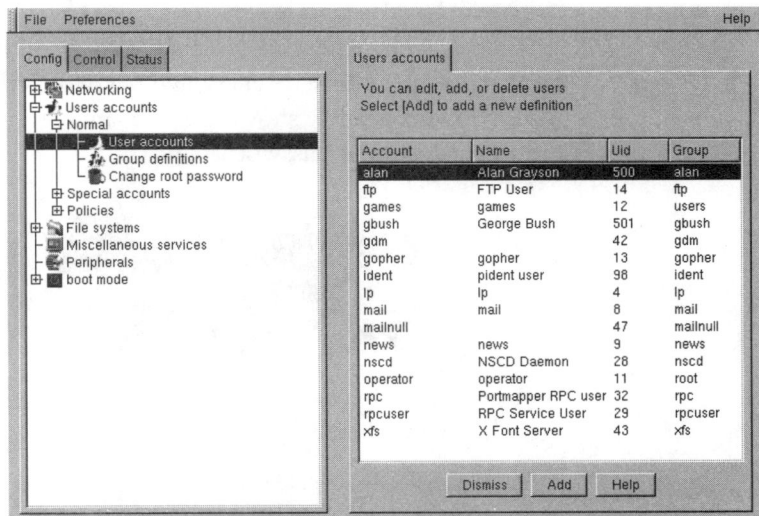

3. Double-click the user account for which you want to change the password to display a screen similar to the following:

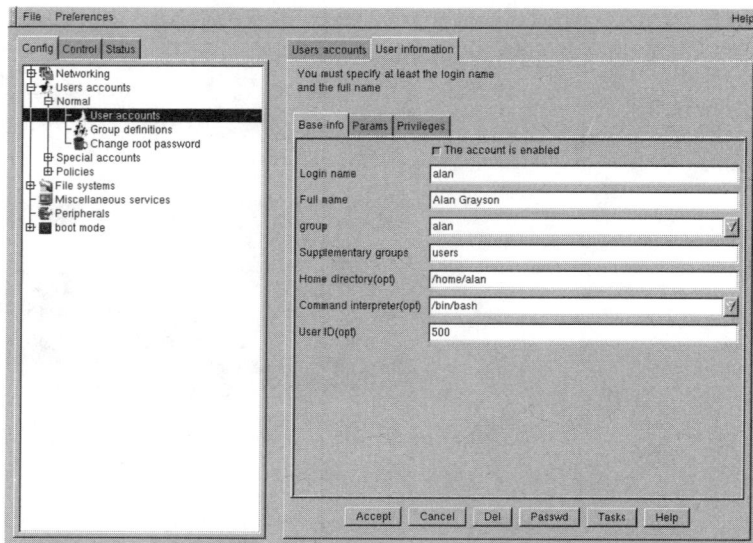

4. Click the Passwd button to open a window in which you can change the user's password.

Users can change their own password using the `passwd` command. The `passwd` command inserts encrypted passwords into the `/etc/shadow` file. The following graphic shows a user changing to a new password after providing their current password.

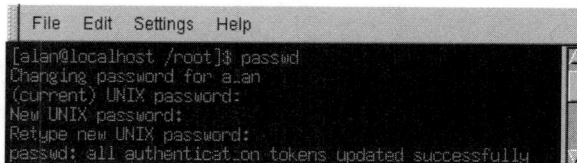

A user can also change their password using the X Window System interface, following these steps:

1. Choose Gnome ➤ System ➤ Change Password Utility to open the New Unix password input box.

2. Enter the new password, and press OK. In the Retype Unix Password input box, retype your password and press OK. In the Information Updated message box, press OK.

Password Aging

The administrator can set maximum and minimum periods of time between password changes. Password aging can also involve setting an account to expire on a certain date, expiring an account if it remains inactive for some time, and setting grace periods for the time restrictions. Exercise 6.3 walks you through the steps involved in password aging.

In addition to the encrypted passwords, the shadow password file contains password-aging information. This information is used to mandate that users change their passwords under certain conditions. We will discuss this aspect of the shadow file later.

Under the default PAM configuration, Linux stores password-aging values for individual users in the /etc/shadow file. Each record in the /etc/ shadow file is a colon-separated list of fields, as shown:

```
name:password:when_changed:min:max:warn:inactive:expires:
```

This example includes the following fields.

- name (the username)

- password (the encrypted password)

- when_changed (the day the password was last changed, given as the number of days since the beginning of the Unix epoch on January 1, 1970)

- min (the minimum number of days allowed between password changes)

- max (the maximum number of days allowed between password changes)

- warn (the number of days before the user is warned of a required password change)

- inactive (the number of days beyond the password expiration date that the account will be disabled)

- expires (the date on which the account will be disabled)

You manipulate these values using the chage command, which has the following syntax:

```
host# chage [options] user
```

Table 6.4 summarizes the chage command options.

TABLE 6.4 Options to the chage Command

Option	Meaning	Purpose
-m	Number	Sets min in the shadow file
-M	Number	Sets max in the shadow file
-W	Number	Sets warn in the shadow file
-d	Number	Specifies the date when the password was last changed (when_changed), measured in days since January 1, 1970, or as MMDDYY
-E	Number	Sets the date when the password expires (expires), measured in days since January 1, 1970, or as MMDDYY
-l	User	Displays information from the password database for the user
No option		Displays a help screen

For example, the following command will require user jeremy to wait at least one day before changing his password. It further requires him to change his password every 150 days.

```
host# chage -m 1 -M 150 jeremy
```

EXERCISE 6.3

Using Password-Aging Commands

In this exercise, you will learn how to use password-aging commands.

1. Create an account named phillip with a non-blank password. Test this account to make sure you can log on.

2. For the examples in this exercise, the account name is phillip. Acquire root permissions. Begin by listing the current password aging parameters:

```
host# chage -l phillip
```

Minimum:	0
Maximum:	99999
Warning:	7
Inactive:	-1
Last Change:	Apr 21, 2002
Password Expires:	Never
Password Inactive:	Never
Account Expires:	Never

3. Set the account to expire in one week. Require 1 day between password changes, and require a change every 28 days. Give the user a warning three days before the change is required. Use the following command to establish these parameters, substituting next week's date in place of /06/04/02:

```
host# chage -m 1 -M 28 -W 3 -E 06/04/02 phillip
```

4. To force Phillip to change his password immediately, use the following command:

```
host# chage -d 0 phillip
```

In this command, the -d option sets the last date of password change to day 0 (January 1, 1970), sufficiently long ago that the password has expired and must be changed.

5. Try to log on using the account name, and verify that the system requires a password change.

Password Checking

You can test passwords to verify that they are well formed. Some systems require that passwords contain a certain number of non-alphabetic characters or that they be a minimum number of characters. Others check passwords against standard cracking programs to see if they can be defeated by a dictionary attack.

Creating Groups

Just as you did in Windows 2000, you use groups in Linux to manage users who have common access requirements. You can give permissions to one group of 100 users just one time, rather than using the tedious process of individually modifying 100 user accounts.

You create groups in much the same ways that you create user accounts. You can create groups manually by directly modify the underlying /etc/group file, or you can do so safely and automatically with a command line or a graphical utility. We'll look at both methods in the following sections.

Editing the */etc/group* File to Create a Group

You manage groups by using two files:

- /etc/passwd, which, as you know, contains a default group ID (GID) for every user

- /etc/group, which contains a list of group names, group ID numbers, and the names of the group members

Like the other configuration files you have seen, /etc/group is a text file, in which each line is a record consisting of comma-separated fields. A typical record has the following format:

```
group_name:*:GID:user_list
```

In this format, group_name is the name of the group, * is a placeholder, GID is the numeric group identifier, and user_list is a list of usernames separated by commas. For example, the following record defines the group orange, with GID 508, and members user1, user2, user3, and user10:

```
orange:*:508:user1,user2,user3,user10
```

By default, Linux creates a special group for each user, with the same name as the user's name.

> **NOTE** The field containing an asterisk (*) placeholder was used at one time to hold an encrypted group password. Although encrypted group passwords are no longer in use, the field is still there. You can place any character you want into the field, but * is a traditional choice.

If you want to add a group named managers with a GID of 501, and members alan and gbush, edit the /etc/groups file as shown in the following graphic.

Using Utilities to Create Groups

Before discussing how to use linuxconf to create groups and add users to groups, let's take a look at the groupadd and the gpasswd commands. You use the /sbin/groupadd command to add groups. For example to add an appellate group with a GID of 602, execute the following command:

```
host # groupadd -g 602 appellate
```

You use the /sbin/gpasswd command to add users to groups. For example to add judgej to the appellate group, execute the following command:

```
host # gpasswd -a judgej appellate
```

To add groups using linuxconf in the X Window System, follow these steps:

1. Choose Gnome ➢ Programs ➢ System ➢ Linuxconf.

2. Expand Users Accounts, expand Normal, and select Group Definitions to display the User Groups tab:

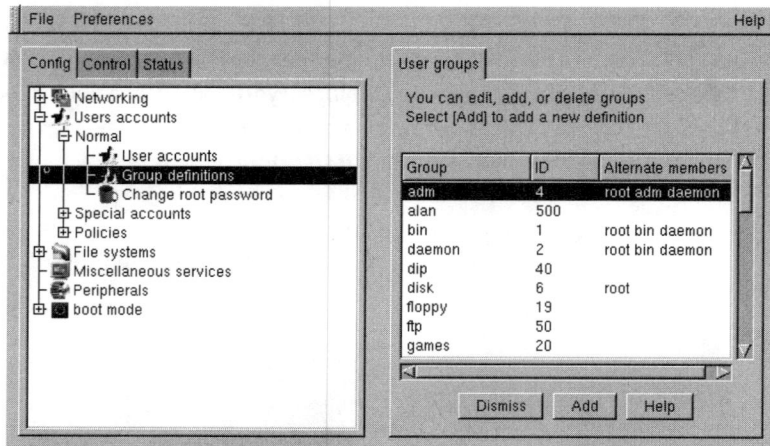

3. Click the Add button to open the Group Specification tab:

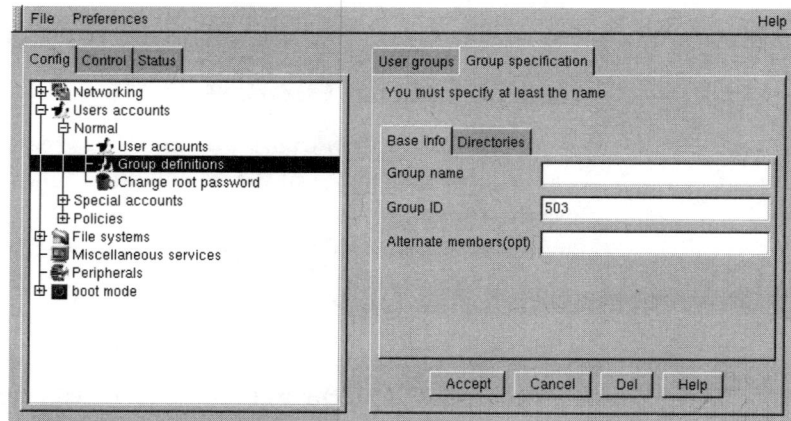

4. In the Group Name field, enter the group name. Optionally, you can add members to this group by adding the member names separated by commas in the Alternate Member's field. Click Accept. With a few short keystrokes, you have created a group and populated it.

Using Run Levels to Maintain the System and to Shut Down or Reboot Linux

As you probably know, you can choose to run Windows 2000 in Safe Mode, which loads a minimal set of drivers in order to perform system maintenance. Windows 2000 also provides an easy way to shut down a computer or reboot it. In Linux, you run levels to halt a system, reboot it, allow networking, run a GUI, or put the computer in maintenance mode. Linux systems generally have seven run levels (0 through 6). A *run level* describes the current state of the system, including the number of services the system can run. Lower run levels start minimal services and accommodate few or no additional users, whereas higher run levels can start additional services. For example, run level 3 usually starts networking services so that the system can operate on a network. However, run level 3 requires the use of a command line interface. Other services, such as Samba, `httpd`, and FTP, are often started at run level 3.

The `/etc/inittab` file governs the services that are activated at various run levels. It tells the system to run certain scripts that reside in the subdirectories of `/etc/rc.d/`. Any script in one of these subdirectories can be run automatically. These subdirectories are named `rc1.d`, `rc2.d`, and so forth.

Table 6.5 provides an overview of the run levels.

TABLE 6.5   Run Levels

Run Level	Description
0	Halts the system. To reboot the system, use the `/sbin/init 0` command.
1	Places the system into maintenance mode. This run level is also called single user mode.
2	Provides additional file system support, but still does not allow networking. This run level is also called multiuser mode.

TABLE 6.5 Run Levels *(continued)*

Run Level	Description
3	Supports all common Internet services (SMTP, POP3, HTTP, FTP, and so on) and log on using the command line interface. This run level is called full multiuser mode and is often used by Internet-addressable services.
4	User defined. Typically unused and undefined in many Linux and Unix operating systems, including Red Hat. For a laptop, you can use it as a power-saving mode and change some settings to minimize power use.
5	Identical to run level 3, although with the addition of a graphical logon interface.
6	Reboots the system. To reboot the system use the `/sbin/init 6` command.

In Linux, you will usually spend most of your time starting services at run levels 3 and 5. Run level 5 often starts the X Window System service, which provides a graphical user interface.

NOTE Run levels are not necessarily cumulative. When a daemon is started at run level 3, this daemon will not necessarily remain running when the system goes to run level 5. Usually, when a system shifts from run level 3 to run level 5, certain daemons are shut down only to be started again at run level 5. It is possible, however, that run level 5 may not start these daemons again unless you use ntsysv command to modify how these daemons start. (We'll discuss the ntsysv command later in this chapter.

Determining the Current Run Level

You use the `runlevel` command to return your current run level:

```
host# /sbin/runlevel
N 5
Host#
```

In this example, the system is at run level 5. If a malfunction occurs, a system can be in two run levels:

```
host# /sbin/runlevel
5 3
Host#
```

If it is important to be in only one run level (otherwise some services may not work as intended), use the /sbin/init command to first bring the system down to level 1, single-user maintenance mode, and then bring the system up to the level you want. Using this process is much quicker than rebooting the system and can be thought of as a soft reboot.

```
host# init 1 going into single user mode . . .
host# init 3
Entering run level 3 . . .
```

When your system is in run level 5, you may find it necessary to change to run level 3. However, if you simply type **init 3** at the command line, you will be dropped into both run level 3 and run level 5, which can cause problems when troubleshooting your X Window System display. To go into only one run level, drop your current run level all the way down to run level 1, and then use the init command to go back up to the run level you want to use.

You can set your system to go to a default run level by opening the /etc/ inittab file and editing the id:3:initdefault: line. By changing the default level to 5, for example, the system will automatically enter run level 5, instead of 3.

The *ntsysv* Command

The ntsysv command determines the run level where services (that is, daemons) will run the next time the system reboots. The ntsysv command does this by manipulating the numerous symbolic links in the /etc/rc.d/ subdirectories that specify which daemons will start in what order at what run level. You can use ntsysv as a one-time command, complete with arguments and options, or you can use it without any arguments. Run without arguments, ntsysv displays a simple ASCII-based GUI, as shown in the following graphic:

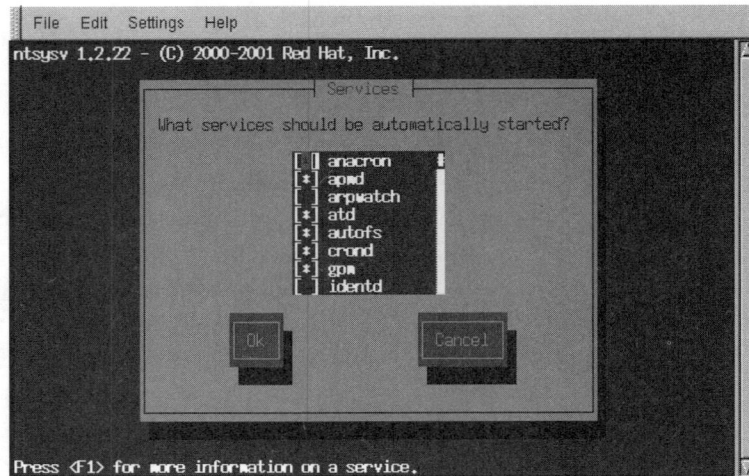

This GUI shows a list of daemons for only the current run level. If, for example, you open ntsysv without arguments in run level 3, you will be shown a list of daemons to be started only during that run level. If you start ntsysv while in run level 5, it is possible you will see a different list of daemons. If you start ntsysv in run level 1, you will see that very few daemons can be started.

It is possible to use ntsysv to modify different run levels. The following command, for example, allows you to ensure that ntsysv alters scripts only for run level 3, regardless of the current run level:

```
host# ntsysv --level 3
```

> **NOTE**   Improper use of ntsysv can disable systems for the next startup. Use this command carefully.

The *chkconfig* Command

The chkconfig command is similar to ntsysv, except that it does not provide a GUI. Using chkconfig, you can list all available daemons and their current run levels as shown:

```
host# chkconfig --list
[root@blake james]# /sbin/chkconfig --list |less
crond    0:off   1:off   2:on    3:on    4:on    5:on    6:off
syslog   0:off   1:off   2:on    3:on    4:on    5:on    6:off
network  0:off   1:off   2:on    3:on    4:on    5:on    6:off
httpd    0:off   1:off   2:off   3:on    4:on    5:on    6:off
named    0:off   1:off   2:off   3:off   4:off   5:off   6:off
gpm      0:off   1:off   2:on    3:on    4:on    5:on    6:off
innd     0:off   1:off   2:off   3:off   4:off   5:off   6:off
host#
```

The chkconfig command will also list the settings for individual daemons:

```
host# chkconfig --list httpd
httpd 0:off 1:off 2:off 3:on 4:on 5:on 6:off
host#
```

Configuring Run Levels

Daemons are the Linux equivalent of Windows 2000 services. In Windows 2000 services, you can start, stop, pause, or restart an individual service using the Computer Management MMC. For example, in Windows 2000, if the print spooler is stalled, you can stop and restart this service to fix this problem. This granular control over the equivalent system functions is available in Linux. If a particular Linux daemon is malfunctioning or needs to be brought down for maintenance or an upgrade, you can use the chkconfig command to individually control that daemon. Using chkconfig, you can alter the run level for a particular daemon. The following command removes the httpd service from run levels 3 and 5:

```
chkconfig --level 35 httpd off
```

The following command adds this service to run levels 3 and 5 again:

```
chkconfig --level 35 httpd on
```

Improper use of chkconfig can disable systems for the next startup. Use this command carefully.

EXERCISE 6.4

Viewing System Accounts and Using the *ntsysv* Command

In this exercise, you will view the system accounts that are marked to run at boot time.

1. Log on as root.

2. Use the less command to display the /etc/passwd file:

   Host# less /etc/passwd

   You can open the accounts using a text editor such as vi or pico. If you use a text editor, be careful not to change any account information.

3. View the information on the FTP account. Use the up and down arrow keys to navigate around using the less command. This account is necessary for the FTP server to operate correctly.

4. Scroll down by pressing the down arrow key on your keyboard to view the information for the nobody account. This account is used by several services, including Apache Server (httpd).

5. Press the q key to quit the less command.

6. Issue the following command:

   host# runlevel

7. What run level are you in?

8. At your command prompt, enter the following command:

   host# /usr/sbin/ntsysv

Remember that the ntsysv command does not stop and start services. Rather, it shows which daemons are marked to run the next time the system is booted into that particular run level.

9. Your screen should appear similar to the following graphic:

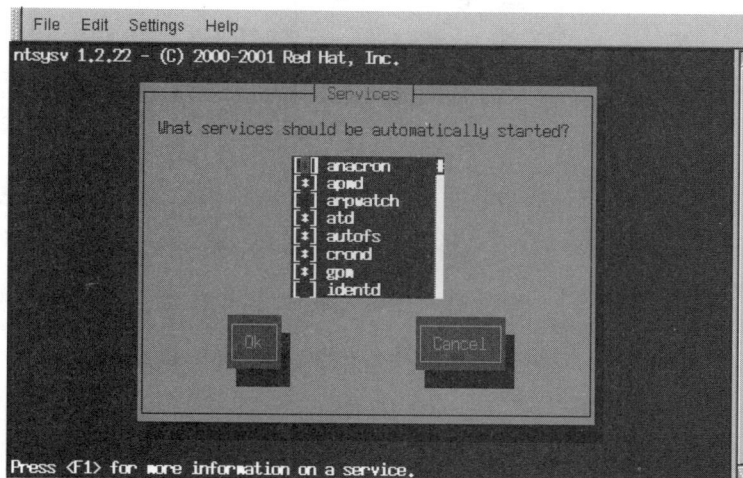

10. Scroll up and down the ntsysv screen.

11. Make no changes to the services. When you are finished viewing the services for this run level, press Tab to access the Cancel button, and then press Enter to return to the command prompt.

12. Now, issue the following command:

/sbin/init 1

13. You will immediately be logged out, all services will shut down, and you will be placed into single user mode. You may have to press Enter to see the prompt for single user mode.

14. Once in single user mode, enter ntsysv again.

15. Scroll down and notice that the screen may have a few services enabled.

EXERCISE 6.4 *(continued)*

16. Enter the following command:

    `/sbin/init 3`

17. You will see the system's services activate, and you will be presented with a logon prompt.

18. Log on as root.

19. Now, use the `less` command to view `/etc/inittab` as follows:

    `host# less /etc/inittab`

20. Scroll down the file and look for the `id:x:initdefault:` line.

21. What is the current default run level?

22. Press the q key to quit `less`.

23. Now, issue the following command:

    `/sbin/init 6`

24. The system will reboot. When the system reboots, log back on as root.

In this exercise, you viewed accounts and became familiar with the `ntsysv` and `chkconfig` programs, and you learned more about run levels.

Summary

In this chapter, you learned how to add and manage users in Linux. You learned about the essential programs to use as well as the files these programs manipulate. You implemented users and groups and controlled access to specific files. You learned about the system accounts that Linux services use in order to access the system. You also used the `ntsysv` and `chkconfig` commands to control which services start at boot time. Finally, you learned how to determine and change a system's run level.

With this information you should be able to create, modify, and delete accounts on Linux systems by directly editing the appropriate files or by using useradd, adduser, or linuxconf. You should also be able to add users to groups, reset user passwords, and set minimum and maximum password age, account expiration, home directory, and a default shell.

In addition to controlling users, you now should be able to control your Linux computer using the init command to set the run level for maintenance, graphical logon, or reboot, and the ntsysv and chkconfig commands to control the services that start, such as named and httpd.

Exam Essentials

Be able to create new accounts on Linux systems.   You should be able to create new accounts manually by editing the /etc/passwd file. In this file, you enter the username, UID, GID, full name, home directory, and default shell. Existing entries in this file include system accounts such as daemon, nobody, and ftp. Using PAMs and shadow passwords will enhance the security of these accounts. Shadow passwords live in the /etc/shadow file. If shadow passwords are not enabled, use the pwconv command to enable shadow passwords. Setting minimum and maximum password age using the chage command also increases password security. You can change passwords using the passwd command or by using linuxconf, a graphical utility. You can also use linuxconf to add users to groups, or you can add users to groups by directly editing the /etc/ groups file.

Be able to control the run level and the services that start automatically on Linux systems.   You use the init command to set the Linux computer in single user maintenance mode (Init 2), to set up the Linux computer for a text-based logon (Init 3), to set up the Linux computer for graphical logon (Init 5), or to reboot the Linux computer (Init 6). On reboot, the GUI utility, ntsysv, or the text-based utility, chkconfig, controls the services that will start, such as named, dhcpd, and httpd. Alternately, you can directly edit the /etc/inittab file to specify which services will be activated at different run levels.

Key Terms

Before taking the exam, you should be familiar with the following terms:

ntsysv	shell program
primary group ID number (GID)	user ID number (UID)
run level	

Review Questions

1. Jonathan is Director of Human Resources for Great Escapes Theme Park. He just hired 100 employees for the summer, and these 100 employees need accounts on the system. Meanwhile, the Linux systems administrator sprained his neck testing the new roller coaster and can't come to work, so he asks Jonathan to create these accounts. Jonathan is told to edit the `/etc/passwd` file. He is told that each line represents a different user. The last line of the file has the following information:

   `jackw:x:323:100:Jack Washington:/home/jackw:/bin/bash`

   For users that Jonathan creates, which number needs to be incremented?

   A. 100

   B. 323

   C. Neither

   D. 100 and 323

2. Jonathan is Director of Human Resources for Great Escapes Theme Park. He just hired 100 employees for the summer, and these 100 employees need accounts on the system. Meanwhile, the Linux systems administrator sprained his neck testing the new roller coaster and can't come to work, so he asks Jonathan to create these accounts. Jonathan is told to edit the `/etc/passwd` file. He is told that each line represents a different user. The last line of the file has the following information:

   `bush_g:x:323:100:George Bush:/home/bush_g:/bin/bash`

   To create a new user named Lisa Reese, which of the following is the best line?

   A. `reese_l:x:324:100:Lisa Reese:/home/reese_l:/bin/bash`

   B. `lisa:x:323:101:Lisa Reese:/home/lisa:/bin/bash`

   C. `lisa_r:x:323:101:Lisa Reese:/home/lisar:/bin/bash`

   D. `reese_l:x:323:101:Lisa Reese:/home/reese_l:/bin/bash`

3. Brian works at Red Hat. He must change the logon shell for all 125 developers from `/bin/bash` to `/bin/ksh`. The Group ID of all the developers is 200. What is the quickest way to make these changes?

   A. Directly edit Linux system files.

   B. Use `/usr/sbin/useradd`.

   C. Use `/usr/sbin/adduser`.

   D. Use `linuxconf`.

4. Jason is concerned about limiting the rights of ordinary users to install programs and reboot the Linux servers on his network. What can Jason use to tighten security? Choose the best answer.

   A. Samba

   B. SAM

   C. PAM

   D. Tango

5. Heather is a security consultant to many clients that use many versions of Unix and Linux. She is at the office of a new client and wants to see if their passwords are somewhat secure. Which command should Heather execute?

   A. `host# ls - l /etc/pwconv`

   B. `host$ ls - l /etc/pwconv`

   C. `host$ ls - l /etc/shadow`

   D. `host# ls - l /etc/shadow`

6. In Linux, Jim wants to create a user and his home directory. Which of the following commands would work?

   A. `host# useradd -h -s /bin/bash -c 'Jeremy Morning'`
   `↳jeremy`

   B. `host# useradd -d -s /bin/bash -c 'Jeremy Morning'`
   `↳jeremy`

   C. `host# useradd -m -s /bin/bash -c 'Jeremy Morning'`
   `↳jeremy`

   D. `host# useradd -f -s /bin/bash -c 'Jeremy Morning'`
   `↳jeremy`

7. Jason was at a training seminar for a day and wants to know if his assistant who is out to lunch has added three user accounts as requested. Which commands could Jason execute to see these accounts? Choose two.

   A. `linuxconf`

   B. `ls-lart /etc`

   C. `usermod -s /bin/ksh jeremy`

   D. `useradd -D -g users -b /home`

   E. `more /etc/passwd`

8. Mike is on the road at a branch location. He needs to create a new account on his home server for the new CFO of his company. He tries to log on as root to his corporate Linux server using Telnet. This account will not work, so Mike logs on with a regular user account. Mike must have root privileges in order to use administrative utilities. Once logged in using his regular user account, which command should Mike execute to log in as root?

   A. `root`

   B. `su`

   C. `login`

   D. `usermod`

   E. `admin$`

9. Mike wants to change his own password on a Linux system to match the password he uses on a Windows 2000 system. Which command should Mike use?

   A. `secedit`

   B. `setpass`

   C. `chpass`

   D. `passwd`

   E. `chmode`

10. Mike is a Unix systems administrator. Hank Williams calls to say that while he was on a long road-trip his password expired. How can Mike change Hank's password?

   A. Mike must know Hank's old password.

   B. Mike must use the `passwd hwilliams` command.

   C. Mike must use the `passwd` command.

   D. Mike must use the `setpass hwilliams` command.

   E. Mike must use the `setpass` command.

   F. Mike must re-create Hank's account.

11. Because of recent hacker activity, Denise wants to ensure that the account for the director of Human Resources, Jenny Craig, is more secure. Denise wants the password changed every 30 days with a minimum of 1 day between password changes. What command should Denise execute?

   A. `host# chage -m 1 -M 30 jcraig`

   B. `host# chage -M 1 -m 30 jcraig`

   C. `host# Passwd -m 1 -M 30 jcraig`

   D. `host# Passwd -M 1 -m 30 jcraig`

12. Because of recent hacker activity, Denise wants to ensure that the account for the director of Human Resources, Jenny Craig, is more secure. Denise wants Jenny to change her password immediately. What command should Denise execute?

   A. `host# chage -m 1 -M 30 jcraig`

   B. `host# chage -M 1 -m 30 jcraig`

   C. `host# chage -d 0 jcraig`

   D. `host# chage -M 0 jcraig`

13. Rajesh wants to ensure that the user accounts for a summer intern cannot be used after the end of the summer of 2002. What command should Rajesh enter?

A. `host# chage -m 1 -M 30 intern1`

B. `host# chage -d 0 intern1`

C. `host# chage -E 09/09/02 intern1`

D. `host# chage -M 09/09/02 intern1`

14. Hank wants to add 10 interns (intern1 through intern10) to the Temp group. How can he do this?

A. Edit the `/etc/group` file.

B. Edit the `/root/home/group` file.

C. Edit the `etc/passwd` file.

D. Use the `host# cat /etc/groups` command.

15. Jessica wants to reboot her Linux computer. How can she do this?

A. Use the `/sbin/init 6` command.

B. Use the `/sbin/init 1` command.

C. Use the `/sbin/init 2` command.

D. Use the `/sbin/init 3` command.

E. Use the `/sbin/init 5` command.

16. Jessica wants to place her Linux computer in maintenance mode. Which command can she use to do this?

A. `/sbin/init 6`

B. `/sbin/init 1`

C. `/sbin/init 2`

D. `/sbin/init 3`

E. `/sbin/init 5`

17. Tom wants to a graphical interface each time he logs on to his Linux computer. How can Tom accomplish this?

    A. Edit the `/etc/inittab` file to change the default run level to 5.

    B. Edit the `/etc/inittab` file to change the default run level to 3.

    C. Use the `/sbin/init 3` command.

    D. Use the `/sbin/init 5` command.

18. Dennis wants to prevent the DNS service from starting automatically on a Linux server. Which commands could Dennis execute? Choose two.

    A. `chkconfig`

    B. `init 3`

    C. `linuxconf`

    D. `/etc/services disable dns`

    E. `ntsysv`

19. Jessica is accustomed to using a graphical interface to create user accounts in Windows 2000. Which graphical Linux utility could Jessica use to create user accounts?

    A. `ntsysv`

    B. `linuxconf`

    C. User Manager

    D. Server Manager

    E. `useradd`

20. Willy wants to remotely change user accounts on a Linux system. Which utility can Willy use?

    A. Telnet

    B. Rconsole

    C. Computer Management

    D. `ntsysv`

    E. Drake

Answers to Review Questions

1. B. The User ID (UID) needs to be unique, but the Group ID (GID) can be the same. In this example the GID of 100 represents the users group.

2. A. The naming convention of the last name followed by an underscore followed by first initial is preserved. The user ID is incremented, but the group ID can stay the same.

3. A. The fastest way to change the logon shell of all the developers is to directly edit the /etc/passwd file. Search in turn for a GUI of 200 and paste over the logon shell.

4. C. For higher security, Jason should install a Pluggable Authentication Module (PAM).

5. D. While logged in as root (host#) as opposed to being logged in as another user (host$), Heather should check for the existence of the /etc/shadow directory. If this directory does not exist, she should execute the host# /usr/sbin/pwconv command in order to enable shadow passwords.

6. C. In useradd, the -m switch creates the home directory.

7. A, E. The linuxconf command or the host# more /etc/passwd command will display the user accounts.

8. B. The su (substitute user/super user) command allows Mike to change to root. It will prompt him for the root password.

9. D. Mike should use the passwd command.

10. B. The command is passwd username. Mike doesn't need to know the old password.

11. A. Denise should use the `host# chage -m 1 -M 30 jcraig` command. This will set the minimum age to 1 day so that Denise cannot immediately change back to her original password. It will also set the maximum password age to 30 days so that any password that is compromised will not be valid indefinitely.

12. C. The command `host# chage -d 0 jcraig` will force Jenny to change her password immediately.

13. C. Rajesh should use the command `host# chage -E 09/09/02 intern1` in order to expire the intern account at the end of the summer.

14. A. Hank should edit the `/etc/group` file. The `cat` command only allows you to see the contents of a file.

15. A. The `/sbin/init 6` command reboots a Linux computer.

16. B. The `/sbin/init 1` command places a Linux computer in maintenance mode.

17. A. In order to get a graphical interface each time he logs on, Tom should edit the `/etc/inittab file` to change the default run level to 5.

18. A, E. Dennis could use the `ntsysv` or the `chkconfig` command to change the default startup behavior of applications.

19. B. You use the `linuxconf` graphical utility to create users in Linux.

20. A. You use Telnet to connect to remote Linux or Unix computers.

Chapter 7

Name Resolution in LANs with DNS

THE CIW EXAM OBJECTIVE GROUPS COVERED IN THIS CHAPTER:

✓ Define and implement the Domain Name System (DNS), including but not limited to: DNS components, record types, reverse lookup, utilities, DNS servers, and NetBIOS.

n a previous chapter, you learned about foundation services offered by IT departments. The Domain Name System (DNS) is one foundation service. Without proper DNS resolution, your FTP, web, and e-mail servers would not function properly. In this chapter, you will learn about DNS structure. You will learn how to implement DNS in a LAN using Windows 2000 and Red Hat Linux. (In this chapter, we'll use Red Hat Linux in examples; other versions of Linux are similar.) You will see how Windows 2000 and Red Hat are configured as caching servers by default, and then you will create master and slave servers, as well as forward and reverse zones, for each. You will also see how Windows 2000 uses *Dynamic DNS (DDNS)*. As you implement DNS in this chapter, you will understand the importance of name resolution in a LAN. You will also investigate issues relevant to creating DNS on specific servers.

DNS converts host names and domain names (such as `www.ciwcertified.com`) into their corresponding IP (Internet Protocol) addresses (such as 207.19.199.245). This conversion is performed in a distributed database that helps organize hosts, and consequently the Internet, in a hierarchical fashion. You can implement DNS locally, or you can attach your own DNS structure to DNS servers on the Internet. DNS can be compared to a directory assistance service for IP networks. Just as a phone book correlates a name with a phone number, DNS resolves user-friendly names into corresponding IP addresses.

NOTE Standard DNS resolution involves resolving names to IP addresses. Reverse DNS resolution resolves IP addresses to names.

The Domain Name Space

To divide the workload on DNS servers, DNS is organized in a hierarchical structure. Each part of the structure is called a *domain*. Whenever you create or edit a domain, you participate in the domain name space. A DNS domain is an entity that controls the naming of all network resources by resolving names to IP addresses. The hierarchical naming system consists of three levels:

Root   This level is at the top of the hierarchy. Root uses a null label that is expressed by a period (called a dot). This trailing period is usually removed from domain names.

Top   This level contains organizations (.org), businesses (.com), universities (.edu), and so forth. Most Internet users are familiar with this level.

Second   This level is one level below the *top-level domain*. Second-level domains are usually named after the organization (for example, W3C) or business (for example, CIW).

Figure 7.1 shows how the DNS hierarchy works.

FIGURE 7.1   The DNS hierarchy

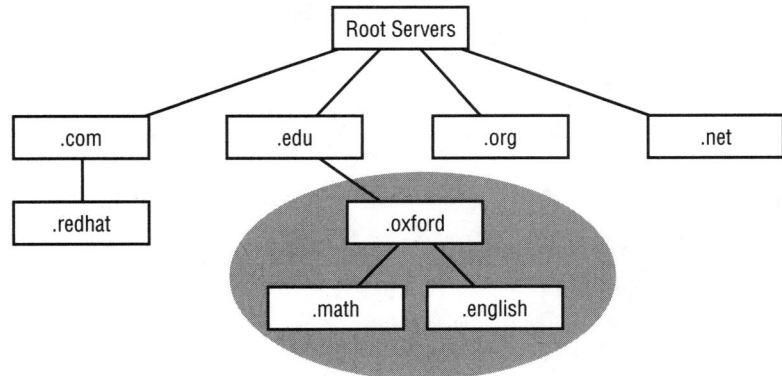

If the system named wordsworth.english.oxford needs to contact the www.redhat.com server, then wordsworth will contact its local DNS server. If this server has not previously resolved this query and does not have this information in its cache, then it will pass the query up the hierarchy to one of the root DNS servers and then down the hierarchy to the DNS server responsible for the `redhat.com` domain. This server will pass the IP address for `www.redhat.com` back to `wordsworth`'s local DNS server, which will pass the information to `wordsworth`. The gray area in Figure 7.1 denotes the `oxford` zone. The DNS administrator for this zone has complete control over its contents. They can add any system or subdomain to this zone, as you will see later in this chapter.

Table 7.1 lists and describes the top-level Internet domains. These domains are the original domains that were available on the Internet. However, the majority of top-level domains are country codes. Each country assigns domain names using its own standards. Additional top-level domains have been proposed. To search for available domain names, go to `www.netsol.com`.

TABLE 7.1   Top-Level Internet Domains

Domain	Description
com	Commercial businesses
edu	Educational institutions
gov	U.S. civilian government institutions
mil	Military organizations
net	Network support centers (ISPs)
org	Other non-profit organizations
int	International organizations (rarely used; country codes are used instead)

Table 7.2 shows several ISO (International Organization for Standardization) country codes that are used to categorize top-level domains by country.

TABLE 7.2   Top-Level Domain Country Codes

Code	Country
au	Australia

TABLE 7.2 Top-Level Domain Country Codes *(continued)*

Code	Country
ca	Canada
ch	Switzerland
fr	France
ie	Ireland
mx	Mexico
tv	Tuvalu
uk	United Kingdom
us	United States

Second-level domains include the businesses and institutions that register domain names with top-level domains (through their respective registrars). Second-level domains include registered names such as iso.ch and amazon .com. Second-level domains can also be categories of top-level domains. For example, the United States domain (us) is categorized into a second-level domain for each state, such as California, as ca.us. Companies and academic institutions in the United Kingdom (and most countries) are also categorized using second-level domains:

- co.uk (for companies)
- ac.uk (for universities)

Second-level domains can be divided into subdomains. For example, a subdomain of company.com might be sales.company.com. A host computer of that subdomain might be identified as user1.sales.company.com.

You can use a subdomain if you want your network structure to imitate the structure of your business. For example, suppose the ciwcertified.com company has a division called sales. You can create a DNS subdomain to name all the hosts in the sales division. Therefore, you can create a

sales.ciwcertified.com subdomain. You can further dissect the sales
.ciwcertified.com subdomain name into the two domains and one host
name, as follows:

com	Commercial (secondary)
ciwcertified	Second level
sales	Host name

Network domains are similar to city and county names and organizations. Just as a county can contain several cities and a city can contain many communities, a network domain can contain several LANs, each of which has at least one server.

Accessing Hosts by DNS Name

DNS names are commonly used to access hosts because they are easier to remember than the associated IP addresses. In a DNS name, reading from left to right, the information moves from specific to general. For example in www.ciwcertified.com, www refers to the server in the ciwcertified subdomain of the com domain. Subdomains may have many levels. For example, in dns1.dnsresearch.research.ciwcertified.com, dns1 is the server in the dnsresearch subdomain of the research subdomain of the ciwcertified subdomain of the com domain.

If you were addressing the dns1 server from another host in the dnsresearch.research.ciwcertified.com domain, then you could address that server by the short name of dns1. On the other hand, if you were addressing dns1 from another domain on the Internet, you would have to distinguish which dns1 server you wanted to address, among all the dns1 servers on the Internet, by using the FQDN of dns1.dnsresearch.research .ciwcertified.com.

DNS Terminology

DNS consists of the following two key components:

Name server   A server application that supports name-to-address translation. Typically, the system on which the *name server* resides is called the name server system or DNS server. Many types of name servers exist. You will learn about each type in this chapter.

Name resolver   Commonly called a DNS client. Technically, a *name resolver* is the client software component that uses the services of one or more name servers. Each client must know how to contact at least one name server so that the name resolver software can exchange query packets with the DNS server. In Unix, the resolver is actually a group of routines that resides in the C library `/usr/lib/libc.a`. In Windows 2000, NT, and *9x*, the resolver is built into the various applications that use DNS. That is, the web browser and the FTP client have built-in resolvers. In Windows systems, the resolver is not part of the operating system kernel, as are the TCP/IP suite protocols. When the client software needs to send a DNS query to look up an IP address for a given name, the resolver sends that query to the name server.

DNS Server Types

DNS follows the standard client/server model: the client makes a request and the server fulfills that request. DNS servers can fill several roles, depending on the needs of an organization. Regardless of which role the server takes, the client must specify the domain name or IP address of the name server. The following server types are included in the DNS model:

- Root
- Master (or primary)
- Slave (or secondary)
- Caching-only
- Forwarding

Root servers can identify all top-level domains on the Internet. Root servers provide authoritative information for the location of authoritative top-level domains (`.com`, `.edu`, `.tv`, and so forth). The primary duty of a root server is to ensure that all the top-level servers are connected and can communicate with one another. They generally fulfill thousands of requests per second and send these requests to the authoritative servers for top-level domains. No name resolution would be possible on the Internet if all Internet root servers were to become inaccessible.

The InterNIC determines which systems act as root servers. You can find the list of Internet servers at `ftp.rs.internic.net/domain/named.ca`. Following is a partial root server list:

- `a.root-servers.net.` (formerly `ns.internic.net`)
- `b.root-servers.net.` (formerly `ns1.isi.edu`)
- `c.root-servers.net.` (formerly `c.psi.net`)
- `d.root-servers.net.` (formerly `terp.umd.edu`)
- `e.root-servers.net.` (formerly `ns.nasa.gov`)
- `f.root-servers.net.` (formerly `ns.isc.org`)

The period at the end of each root server name specifies that it is the absolute domain name, also called an FQDN. Without the period, the server name becomes relative to the current domain. As you configure your own domains, you will discover the importance of using periods to indicate a fully qualified domain name.

A *master server* loads its database from a file on a local disk. This server is used for adding the master domain, subdomains, and hosts for those domains. Another name for a master server is a primary server. Microsoft, for example, uses the term "primary" as opposed to master.

A *slave server* receives its authority and database from the master server. The slave server provides fault tolerance and load distribution. When the slave server first starts, it requests all the data for a given zone from the master server. The process of pulling information from the master server is called a *zone transfer*. The slave server then periodically checks with the master name server to determine whether it needs to update its data. Another name for a slave server is "secondary server," which is the term Microsoft uses.

> **NOTE**
>
> You need both a master and a slave DNS server for full DNS registration with the InterNIC. If your company is configuring a DNS server for internal use only, a slave DNS server is not absolutely necessary. It is wise, however, to place the master and the slave servers on different subnets and even on networks serviced by different ISPs. This strategy provides fault tolerance. If one network fails, your organization still has DNS resolution.

A *caching-only server* acts much like a master or a slave server, with two important differences:

- A caching-only server does not maintain its own database files (called zone files).

- A caching-only server gathers information from client requests that it fulfills.

Caching-only servers fulfill requests by asking other servers for information, and they store the name to host-name resolution information until the data expires. Data expires according to a special field called Time To Live (TTL). You will learn how to configure TTL fields for various DNS servers shortly.

> **NOTE** The DNS servers for Windows 2000 and Red Hat Linux both ship with caching-only servers installed.

Also referred to as a forwarder, a *forwarding server* sends any request that cannot be resolved locally to a remote server you specify. A forwarding server is effective when you want to reduce network traffic, mainly because forwarding servers process recursive requests that master and slave servers cannot resolve locally.

Recursion occurs when the DNS server receives a request for an FQDN, but cannot provide all the information. The DNS master or slave server then contacts other servers on behalf of the client until the client receives this information. The DNS server can reject recursive requests. This type of configuration can help improve the server's performance but can also cause unnecessary DNS errors for clients that rely upon recursive requests.

You can also configure a DNS server with its own zones and enable forwarding. A *forwarding-only server* is a DNS server that has no other zones and offers no caching.

Zone Files and DNS Records

A zone file helps define a branch of the DNS name space under the administrative control of a master DNS name server. Many IT professionals use the terms "domain" and "zone" interchangeably; however, they are not the same. A *zone* is a specific file that resides on a server. A company that registers the domain name `ciwcertified.com` gains administrative control of the `ciwcertified.com` domain.. To exert control over that domain, the company must create zone files. In Windows 2000, you use GUI applications to create and manage these zone files. In Linux, you generally edit zone files manually, although you can use GUI devices, such as `linuxconf`.

When you create a DNS server, you generally populate it with the following zone file types:

- Forward, which contains entries that map names to IP addresses.

- Reverse, which contains entries that map IP addresses to names. A reverse zone is also known as the loopback network.

- Hint, which provides the root-name servers. In many cases, the root-name servers are called hint servers.

- Local, which is a simple zone file informing the DNS server of its own loopback interface.

Usually, you must create and edit each of these files. However, Windows 2000, Windows NT 4, and Red Hat Linux provide the hint and local files automatically. You will learn shortly about how today's DNS operates dynamically.

Every domain zone file consists of DNS entries (also called records). A DNS record is an entry in a DNS database that provides resolution (and sometimes routing) information. Microsoft Windows 2000 refers to these records as resource records. You can configure many types of records, but only a few are essential for full address resolution routing. Table 7.3 lists the most common DNS records.

TABLE 7.3 Common DNS Records

DNS Record	Function
Internet (IN)	Identifies Internet records; precedes most DNS record entries.
Name Server (NS)	Identifies DNS servers for the DNS domain. This record is automatically created when you create a new master zone.
Start of Authority (SOA)	Identifies the DNS server with the best source of information for the DNS domain. Because several backup DNS servers may exist, this record identifies the master server for the specified DNS domain.

TABLE 7.3 Common DNS Records *(continued)*

DNS Record	Function
Address (A)	Associates a host with an IP address. This is the most commonly used record. For example, you can establish an association between an IP address and a web server by creating an address record.
Canonical Name (CNAME)	Creates an alias for a specified host. For example, suppose the name of a web server is server1.company .com. A CNAME record can create an alias to the server1.company.com host so that it is known as www.company.com.
Mail Exchanger (MX)	Identifies a server used for processing and delivering e-mail for the domain.
Pointer (PTR)	Helps map IP addresses to names (the opposite of a standard, "forward" lookup).
AAAA	Used for resolving names to IPv6 addresses.

NOTE Do not confuse the idea of a forward and reverse zone file with a master or slave server. A master or slave server contains forward and reverse zones. Zone files make it possible to populate a DNS server (either master or slave) with individual host information.

Besides converting domain names to IP addresses, the DNS system can do the reverse: convert IP addresses into domain names. This conversion is performed by associating a domain name with a network address and placing this domain name in the top level in-addr.arpa domain. You simply create *reverse zone files* and populate them with PTR records.

Suppose that your company has the class C network address 196.175.34.0. The associated in-addr.arpa domain name is 34.175.196.in-addr.arpa. You create this zone name and file by reversing the order of the bytes in the network address and adding in-addr.arpa at the end.

With this naming convention, suppose you want to create the host name of the computer with IP address 135.175.34.143. You simply extract the network portion of this standard class B IP address (135.175.34.143),

135.175, then reverse it, and then create the following `in-addr.arpa` domain:

```
175.135.in-addr.arpa
```

You then enter the host IP address of 143.34 in the reverse lookup file.

At the very least, a company gains control of the `in-addr.arpa` zones corresponding to the company's network addresses. For example, if `company.com` has two class C network addresses, 197.132.14.0 and 197.132.15.0, `company.com` will have control over the `company.com` zone and the two reverse zones: `14.132.197.in-addr.arpa` and `15.132.197.in-addr.arpa`.

Probing DNS with *nslookup*

The *nslookup* program is a standard TCP/IP utility that probes and queries DNS databases. It is the primary DNS troubleshooting tool. You can use it to view examples of DNS record types. Also, it generates name server queries on command. The `nslookup` program is free and available in all TCP/IP systems.

> **NOTE**   Some operating systems, such as Red Hat Linux, have begun to deprecate `nslookup` in favor of the `dig` and `host` applications.

The `nslookup` program operates interactively. When started, `nslookup` uses the `/etc/resolv.conf` file on a Unix server (or the setting entered for DNS servers in Windows NT/2000) to locate a name server. After a name server is found, `nslookup` directs its initial queries at that server.

```
host$ nslookup
Default Server: dns.class.com
Address: 196.241.12.122
>
```

To look up the IP address for a host name or the host name for an IP address, simply type the name or address at the prompt:

```
host$ nslookup
Default Server: dns.class.com
Address: 196.241.12.122
> www.microsoft.com
```

```
Server: dns.class.com
Address: 196.241.12.122
Name: www.microsoft.com
Addresses: 207.68.156.58, 207.68.156.61, 207.46.130.14
>
```

The results indicate that Microsoft operates many computers under the name www.microsoft.com.

> **NOTE** You may see the phrase "non-authoritative answer" in the output from nslookup. This phrase means that nslookup obtained the information from a server cache rather than by consulting an authoritative source such as a master or a slave server.

In its simplest form, nslookup extracts the A and PTR records from the DNS database. However, it can be useful to read the SOA, HINFO, and other record types as well. To direct nslookup to extract other kinds of records, use the set type command (at the nslookup prompt). The syntax is as follows:

```
>set type=SOA
>ciwcertified.com
Server: dns.class.com
Address: 196.241.12.122
ciwcertified.com
    origin = ns1.portal.ca.ciwcertified.com
    mail addr = hostmastter.portal.ca
    serial = 10
    refresh = 10800 (3 hours)
    retry = 3600 (1 hour)
    expire = 3600000 (41 days 16 hours)
    minimum ttl = 86400 (1 day)
ciwcertified.com nameserver = ns1.portal.ca
ciwcertified.com nameserver = ns2.portal.ca
ciwcertified.com nameserver = ns3.portal.ca
ciwcertified nameserver = ns4.portal.ca
ns1.portal.ca internet address = 204.174.35.18
ns2.portal.ca internet address = 204.174.35.49
```

```
ns3.portal.ca internet address = 204.174.19.17
ns4.portal.ca internet address = 204.174.35.51
```

In this output, you have obtained the full SOA record. You can now see, for example, that the authoritative server for the `ciwcertified.com` organization is `ns1.portal.ca.ciwcertified.com`, and the responsible party is `hostmastter.portal.ca`.

The entry `hostmastter` is probably a typographical error in the zone file.

In this example, `nslookup` has also extracted other information from the database. The following are NS records:

```
ciwcertified.com nameserver = ns1.portal.ca
ciwcertified.com nameserver = ns2.portal.ca
ciwcertified.com nameserver = ns3.portal.ca
ciwcertified.com nameserver = ns4.portal.ca
```

The following are the A records for the name servers:

```
ns1.portal.ca internet address = 204.174.35.18
ns2.portal.ca internet address = 204.174.35.49
ns3.portal.ca internet address = 204.174.19.17
ns4.portal.ca internet address = 204.174.35.51
```

The previous example shows that the `ciwcertified.com` domain has four name servers. The A records beneath the authority data inform you of the IP addresses for each of these DNS servers.

Following is one more example, this time with an HINFO query:

```
> set type=HINFO
> raphael.math.uic.edu
Server: dns.class.com
Address: 196.241.12.122
raphael.math.uic.edu CPU = Intel OS = linux
math.uic.edu nameserver = newton.math.uic.edu
math.uic.edu nameserver = dns2.math.uic.edu
math.uic.edu nameserver = uic-dns1.uic.edu
math.uic.edu nameserver = uic-dns2.uic.edu
math.uic.edu nameserver = uic-dns3.uic.edu
newton.math.uic.edu internet address = 131.193.278.229
uic-dns1.uic.edu internet address = 128.248.2.50
```

```
uic-dns2.uic.edu internet address = 128.248.7.50
uic-dns3.uic.edu internet address = 128.248.171.50
```

Notice the HINFO record describing the machine `raphael.math.uic.edu`, together with the authority records and additional information.

By default, `nslookup` uses the DNS server specified in `/etc/resolv.conf`. However, you can instruct `nslookup` to use a different name server with the server command. In the following example, `nslookup` is asked to communicate with the server at `ns1.portal.ca` (which is the master server for `ciwcertified.com`):

```
>server ns1.portal.ca
Default Server: ns1.portal.ca
Address: 204.174.35.18
> ciwcertified.com
Server: ns1.portal.ca
Address: 204.174.35.18
ciwcertified.com
origin = ns1.portal.ca
mail addr = hostmaster.portal.ca
serial = 10
refresh = 10800 (3 hours)
retry = 3600 (1 hour)
expire = 3600000 (41 days 16 hours)
minimum ttl = 86400 (1 day)
```

You can use `nslookup` to list an entire zone. To perform this task, `nslookup` pretends to be a slave server for the zone and requests a zone file transfer. The command to list a domain is `ls`, the same command used in Unix. For this command to work, you must set `nslookup` to use that site's master server as its default server. Many sites will not allow this procedure for security reasons.

```
> server ns1.portal.ca
> ls ciwcertified.com
[ns1.portal.ca]
*** Can't list domain ciwcertified.com: Query refused
```

A query could be refused for one or more of the following reasons:

- The DNS server has used the allow-transfer directive in `named.conf` to restrict transfers to only certain servers.

- The DNS server is using public-key algorithms to limit zone transfers. Limiting zone transfers is often preferable, because DNS information can be used to map a network. Limiting zone transfers also defeats DNS poisoning. In DNS poisoning, a hacker places bogus entries in the DNS cache to trick clients into connecting to a bogus website or an e-mail server.

These settings are configured on a zone-by-zone basis.

Configuring DNS in Windows 2000

Windows 2000 server relies on DNS as its primary name resolution option. This feature is a change from NT 4, which favors the Windows Internet Naming Service (WINS).

The DNS component of Windows 2000 runs as a service. By default, Windows 2000 installs a caching-only server. Creating your own forward and reverse zones is relatively simple. The service is a fully functional DNS server and can be easily implemented for an intranet. It can also function as a master DNS server that can be registered with InterNIC.

Windows 2000 uses GUI tools to create DNS zone files. Each time you use the DNS service interface wizards and dialog boxes, you are creating a new zone file, or you are creating entries within a zone file. You create and modify entries within zones by manipulating the standard Windows text boxes and radio buttons. (You'll work with these items in the exercises in this chapter.)

Windows 2000 Server allows you to use its standard version of DNS or its new DDNS server. Essentially, DDNS allows the DNS server to update itself automatically whenever a DDNS client's host name and/or IP address changes. Microsoft has, in essence, made its DNS similar to WINS, in that its DNS server can dynamically update itself. The client must have the compatible DNS client software installed in order for it to update the DNS server's records. All flavors of Microsoft Windows 2000, for example, have built-in DDNS clients. All clients are automatically configured to search for a DDNS server so that they can participate in DDNS. However, the DDNS feature is not activated by default.

DDNS is documented in RFCs 2535, 2136, and 3007.

Linux systems do not have a DDNS client installed by default. However, even systems that are not compatible with DDNS can benefit. For example, suppose that a Windows 2000 server named james.ciwcertified.com changes its IP address and reports to a Windows 2000 DNS server with DDNS properly configured. A simple Linux client will still be able to query the Windows 2000 DNS server and get the updated IP information about james.ciwcertified.com. However, suppose that the Linux client now changes its IP information. This unmodified Linux client will not be able to report its changed IP address information to the Windows 2000 server unless it is configured with third-party DDNS software.

As you will see in the next section, you use the Allow Dynamic Updates setting to activate your DNS server so that it participates in a DDNS environment. It is available in the General tab of the Properties dialog box of any zone configured in Windows 2000.

Two features of DDNS are record aging and records scavenging. Each DNS entry (that is, resource record) receives a timestamp entry. The Windows 2000 server then uses the record-timestamp value to determine when it will remove a stale record. The record receives a new timestamp value every hour. When the client system shuts down, the record can be deleted. Microsoft calls the process of deleting DDNS records scavenging. Without scavenging, the DNS server's database could become crowded with invalid entries. Microsoft calls such entries stale records. Too many stale records can negatively affect the DNS server's performance.

The default value for scavenging is seven days, which means that an entry that is not refreshed in seven days will be removed automatically. Manual entries (that is, entries that you add using the New Host Wizard) have the value of 0, which excludes them from the scavenging process.

As discussed earlier, you use the SOA field to establish settings for the entire zone. These settings are always authoritative, unless overridden by the DNS server's global settings. Table 7.4 explains some of the individual settings available in the SOA field when configuring a zone in Windows 2000.

TABLE 7.4 Windows 2000 Zone Parameters

Parameter	Explanation
Serial number	Used for notifying the slave (that is, secondary) servers that the master (that is, primary) server has been updated. The value should be incremented each time a change is made to the primary server. Therefore, if you make a change to a primary DNS server zone file (such as adding a host), you must also increment the serial number. Otherwise, your secondary server will not be updated. As a technique, the date, hour, and minute may be entered as the serial number instead of a generic number whenever you manually update a primary DNS server zone file.
Responsible person	The e-mail address of the person responsible for the DNS server. The e-mail address is administrator.ciwcertified.com, not administrator@ciwcertified.com, because in DNS syntax, the @ symbol is reserved to specify the DNS domain name.
Refresh interval	Determines how often the secondary servers need to contact the primary servers for updates. Do not confuse this entry with the serial number.
Retry interval	If the secondary server fails to contact the primary server, it will wait a specified period of time before attempting to contact the primary server again.
Expires after	Determines how long the secondary server will store its DNS records, after which time they are discarded.
Minimum default TTL	In Windows 2000, the default setting is one hour. It is also possible to set a default TTL for each record.
TTL for this record	Individual records can also receive their own TTL. Record-specific TTLs take precedence over all other values.

Although WINS has largely been deprecated, Windows 2000 supports coordinating DNS records with other WINS servers.

You have already learned that a zone transfer involves transferring the records from one server to another. By default, all systems can obtain a zone transfer. Windows 2000 allows you to lock down your DNS server and determine exactly which servers are allowed to conduct a zone transfer from your DNS server.

EXERCISE 7.1

Preparing Windows 2000 for DNS and Reviewing the System

You can use whatever computer name and domain name you choose. In the exercises in the chapter, we'll use student10 for the computer name and student10.com for the domain name. You can substitute your actual computer name and domain name wherever you see student10 or student10.com.

Windows 2000 installs the DNS server service by default. The server is a caching-only server. In this exercise, you will review DNS settings and configure your system to act as a master DNS server. You will then review the Windows 2000 DNS interface to become more familiar with it.

1. Log on as administrator.

2. Open Notepad, and then open the C:\Winnt\system32\drivers\ etc\hosts file.

3. Remove all entries except the loopback address entry (127.0.0.1 localhost).

4. Exit this file, click Yes to save any changes, and close Notepad.

5. Choose Start ➤ Programs ➤ Administrative Tools ➤ DNS to open the DNS MMC snap-in. You will see only your computer, as in the following graphic:

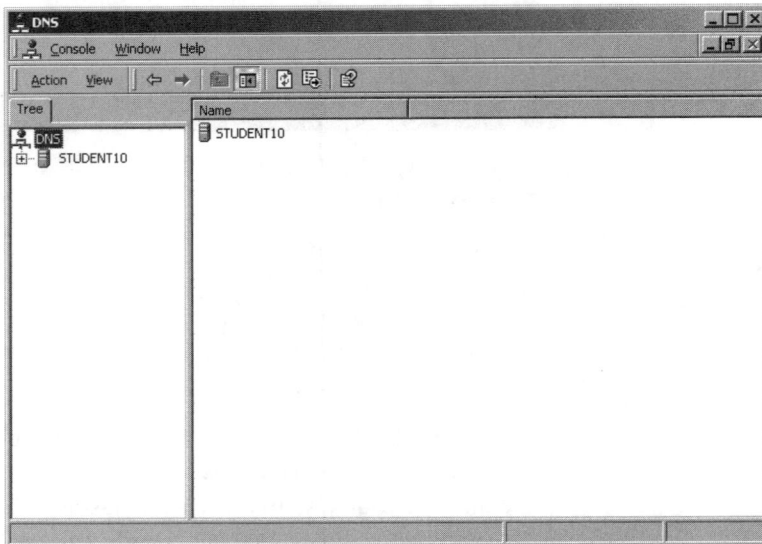

Before you can configure the primary zone, you must add your server to the list. If you do not see your own host, right-click the DNS icon, and select Connect to Computer from the shortcut menu. Be sure that the This Computer radio button is selected and that the Connect to the Specified Computer Now check box is selected, and then click OK. You will then see your computer listed.

6. In the DNS MMC snap-in, right-click the icon that represents your computer to open the Properties dialog box for your system. It will resemble the following graphic. Each setting is applied to individual zones and zone records. However, any zone or zone file entry overrides any setting you establish here.

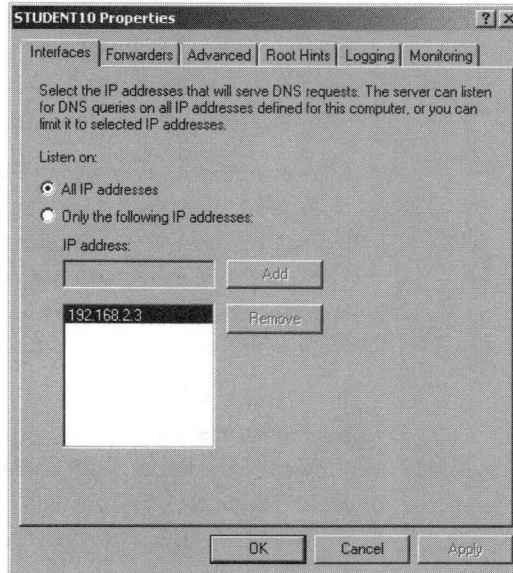

7. Select the Interfaces tab (if it is not already selected by default). Remember that Windows 2000 systems can use multiple addresses on one NIC (network interface card). This tab governs the local interfaces that will accept DNS requests. Make no changes.

8. Select the Forwarders tab. Using this tab, you can specify that this server forward DNS requests to another server.

9. Select the Advanced tab. From here, you can configure additional parameters, including whether your server will act recursively, check its own zone data, and protect itself against DNS zone poisoning.

10. Select the Root Hints tab. You use the options on this tab to add additional hint servers.

11. Select the Logging tab. You use the options on this tab to log DNS transactions. For example, if you select the Query text box, the server logs all DNS queries made by your clients. Normally, you choose to log such sessions only to troubleshoot the DNS server, because your logs would soon become inordinately large.

12. Select the Monitoring tab. You use the options on this tab to test your server's configuration. Because you have not yet created a zone, you cannot test the server effectively, so click Cancel to return to the DNS main window.

13. Click the plus sign next to the icon that represents your computer to display the Forward Lookup Zones, and Reverse Lookup Zones icons. Clicking either the Forward Lookup Zones icon or the Reverse Lookup Zones icon starts a wizard that steps you through adding specific zone files (if no zones were previously configured). We'll work with these wizards in the next exercise.

In this exercise, you ensured that your system is ready to be configured as a master DNS server, and you viewed the effective settings and windows for the entire DNS server. You learned how these settings affect all zones, unless specifically overridden by an individual entry in a zone. Right now, your DNS server has not been configured with any authoritative zone files. In the next exercise, you will configure a master zone.

Creating a Master (Primary) DNS Server in Windows 2000

In this exercise, you will create a master DNS server on your system.

1. Create a separate, unique DNS domain. Write the domain name in the space provided: _____

2. Write your IP address in the space provided: _____. This IP address is the address of your master (that is, primary) DNS server.

Configuring DNS in Windows 2000 **295**

3. Expand the icon that represents your computer to display the Forward Lookup Zones, and Reverse Lookup Zones icons. In the right pane, you should see a message entitled Configure the DNS Server.

4. Right-click Forward Lookup Zones, and then choose New Zone from the shortcut menu to start the New Zone Wizard, as shown in the following graphic:

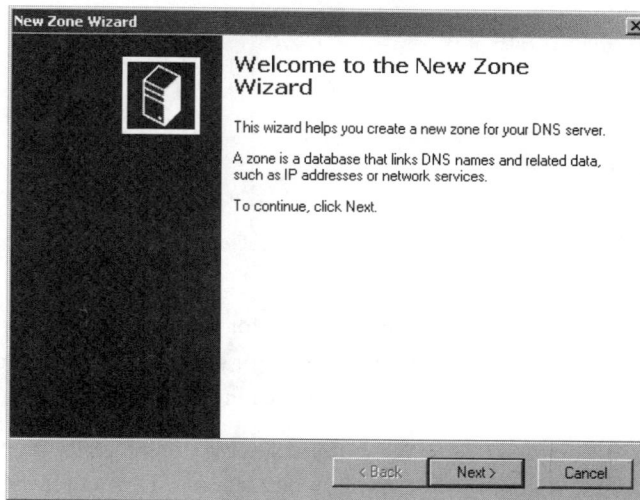

5. Click Next.

6. Select the Standard Primary radio button if it is not already selected by default.

7. Click Next to open the Zone Name screen.

8. Enter the name of the domain you created in Step 1 (for example, student10.com), and click Next to open the Zone File screen.

9. Notice that the name of the zone file is already in the Create a New File with This File Name field. Leave this default, and click Next.

10. You will be informed that the zone is complete. Review the settings, and then click Finish.

11. You will return to the DNS MMC snap-in. You should now see the new zone you created, as shown in the following graphic. This graphic shows the `student10.com` zone added to the server1 machine.

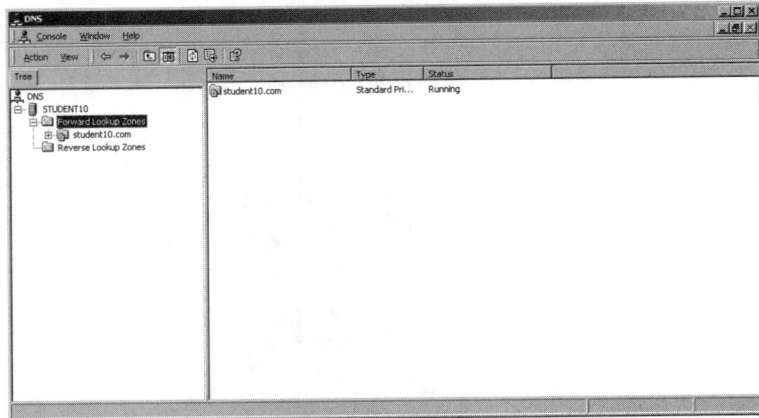

12. Click the icon for the zone you just created. Use your own DNS information. For example, if you used the `student10.com` domain, select the `student10.com` icon.

13. You should see two new files in the pane on the right, as shown in the following graphic. These files inform you of how this zone is configured. The first file is the Start of Authority record. The second is the NS (name server) record for this zone.

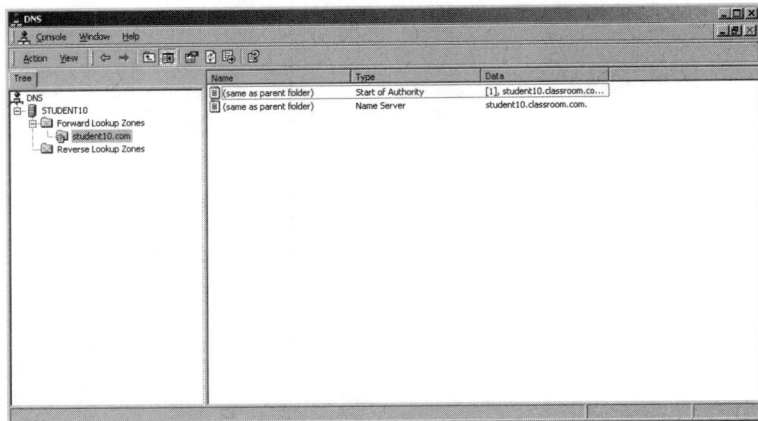

14. Double-click the Start of Authority (SOA) entry to open its Properties dialog box. You will see a dialog box similar to the following graphic.

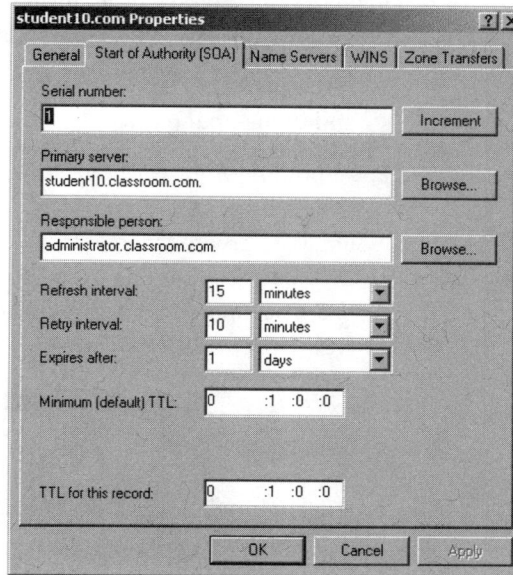

15. You will see your own zone information. From here, you can customize any of the values, including the refresh and retry intervals, the expiration date, and the TTL information. Notice the additional tabs. Each is designed to let you specify how this particular zone operates. Leave all default settings for now.

16. Select the General tab. You can use the options on this tab to further configure universal settings for the zone. These settings override the global settings you viewed in the previous exercise. Notice the Allow Dynamic Updates? drop-down list box. You can use the settings in this drop-down list box to specify that your zone use DDNS. Leave this setting at No (the default) for now.

17. Click Cancel.

In this exercise, you created a primary zone and viewed the available settings. In the next exercise, you will create host entries.

EXERCISE 7.3

Creating DNS Records for the Forward Zone on the Primary Server

In this exercise, you will create static DNS records on the primary Windows 2000 DNS server, beginning with a record for your own system.

1. In the DNS MMC snap-in, expand the icon for your computer name, and then expand the Forward Lookup Zones icon.

2. Although Windows 2000 DDNS will create a dynamic entry for all DDNS-compliant clients in your zone with DDNS enabled, it is still useful to create static entries for the machine that is the primary DNS server. Right-click the zone you created in the preceding exercise, and select New Host from the shortcut menu to open the New Host dialog box:

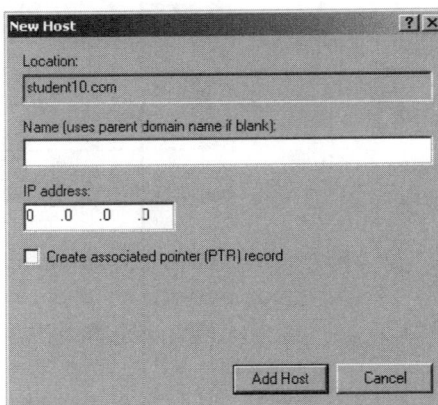

3. In the Name box, enter the name for your server, which is also your Primary DNS server. Do not add the domain part of the name when creating the address record. The domain is automatically appended to the host name.

4. In the IP Address box, enter the IP address of your computer. Do not select the Create Associated Pointer (PTR) Record entry. You have not yet created a reverse DNS lookup zone, and Windows 2000 will return an error.

5. Click the Add Host button to open the DNS message box, which will tell you that the host record record_name was successfully created.

6. Acknowledge that you have created the host entry by clicking OK.

7. Click Done to enter the record into the DNS database.

8. Right-click your zone icon again, and choose Other New Records from the shortcut menu to open the Resource Record Type dialog box.

9. Scroll down the list and click the Alias option.

10. Click the Create Record button to open the New Resource Record dialog box.

11. Enter **www** in the Alias Name (Uses Parent Domain If Left Blank) text box.

12. In the Fully Qualified Name for Target Host field, enter your FQDN (for example student10.student10.com).

13. Click OK.

14. Click Done. You will see that a new Alias record has been created.

15. Repeat the relevant steps to create a record for another system on your network (real or fictitious), as well as Alias records for at least two other systems (real or not).

16. After you add records for three additional systems, create an alias (that is, a CNAME entry) called ciw for one of the hosts.

You can assign the alias to a host name that is not part of the current domain. For example, you can assign the alias to the host name server1.company.com.

EXERCISE 7.4

Configuring a Windows 2000 Server As a DNS Client

In this exercise, you will configure your server as a client to itself so that you can test your master server.

1. Log on as an administrator.

2. On the Desktop, right-click the My Network Places icon, and choose Properties from the shortcut menu to open the Network and Dial-up Connections dialog box.

3. Right-click the Local Area Connection icon, and choose Properties from the shortcut menu to open the Local Area Connection Properties dialog box.

4. Highlight the Internet Protocol (TCP/IP) icon, and then click the Properties button to open the TCP/IP Properties dialog box.

5. Make sure the Use the Following DNS Server Addresses radio button is selected.

6. Enter your own server's IP address in the Preferred DNS Server field.

7. Click the Advanced button to open the Advanced TCP/IP Settings dialog box.

8. Select the DNS tab.

9. Make sure that the Append These DNS Suffixes (In Order) check box is selected.

10. Select the entry in the Append These DNS Suffixes (In Order), and click the Add button to open the TCP/IP Domain Suffix dialog box.

11. Enter the domain name you selected in an earlier exercise. If, for example, you are in the student10.com domain, enter **student10 .com** in this field.

12. Click Add.

13. In the DNS Suffix for This Connection field, enter the same domain name (for example, student10.com, if this is your assigned domain name).

14. Click OK, and then click OK twice more to return to the Network and Dial-up Connections window. Minimize this window.

15. On the Desktop, right-click My Computer, and choose Properties from the shortcut menu to open the System Properties dialog box.

16. Select the Network Identification tab.

17. Your full computer name should read student10.student10.com, and your domain should read student10.com. The Properties dialog box should be grayed out, and you should see the message "Note: The Identification of the computer cannot be changed because - The computer is a domain controller."

18. Click OK.

19. Open a command prompt and ping your own system by using its FQDN (for example, student10.student10.com) and then its CNAME entry of www.

20. You should be successful. If not, review the data you entered in the DNS server configuration. Retrace the steps of this exercise and the previous exercise. Have you configured the DNS server as a DNS client?

21. Open a command prompt window, and enter **ping ciw** to ping the remote host named ciw (you created this CNAME alias earlier).

22. Choose Start ➤ Programs ➤ Administrative Tools ➤ Event Viewer to open the Event Viewer window.

23. Select the DNS Server log. View any messages that have been generated by double-clicking them. You should see entries concerning the records you have created. If any problems exist, the system will notify you about these, as well.

EXERCISE 7.4 *(continued)*

24. Exit Event Viewer.

In this exercise, you configured a master DNS server in Windows 2000. However, you cannot use nslookup efficiently yet because you need to add a reverse lookup zone.

EXERCISE 7.5

Creating a Reverse Lookup DNS Zone and Associated Records for the Primary Server

In this exercise, you will create reverse lookup DNS records on your Windows 2000 DNS server. To create these records, you will need to create a primary zone called *<network>* in-addr.arpa, in which *<network>* is the reverse of the network portion of the server's IP address.

1. Open the DNS MMC snap-in.

2. Select the Reverse Zone, right-click Reverse Lookup Zone, and then choose New Zone from the shortcut menu to start the Welcome to the New Zone Wizard.

3. Click Next to open the Zone Type screen. Select the Standard Primary radio button, and then click Next to open the Reverse Lookup Zone screen.

4. The Zone name will be the network portion of your IP address in reverse order. For example, if your IP address is 192.168.4.10 and the subnet mask is 255.255.255.0, the network portion is 192.168.4. You enter 192.168.4. The server will reverse the numbers and add the in-addr.arpa extension automatically.

When adding the in-addr.arpa numbers, do not reverse them yourself. Windows 2000 will do this for you. Unlike Windows NT 4, Windows 2000 expects you to simply enter the network portion of your IP address in forward order (192.168.4).

5. Click Next twice, and then click Finish.

6. Once you are back in the DNS snap-in, expand the Reverse Lookup Zone and click the new reverse zone. Now, create a new PTR record for your own server. Right-click the new reverse zone you just created, and choose New Pointer from the shortcut menu to open the New Resource Record dialog box:

7. In the Host IP Number text box, enter only the host portion of your master DNS server's IP address. If, for example, your IP address is 192.168.4.10, enter **10**. As you will remember, reverse DNS maps IP addresses to names. The trick of reverse DNS is creating a zone for each network, with individual entries for the host IP address.

8. In the Host Name text box, enter the FQDN for your master DNS server. If, for example, you created this server on student10.student10.com, you enter **student10.student10.com** in this text box. This step is vital for troubleshooting purposes. The nslookup program, for example, will not work properly unless you create a reverse DNS lookup entry for the DNS server. This is because nslookup conducts a reverse DNS lookup search when connecting to the DNS server.

9. Click OK. You will see a new entry in the reverse DNS lookup zone you created, as shown in the following graphic:

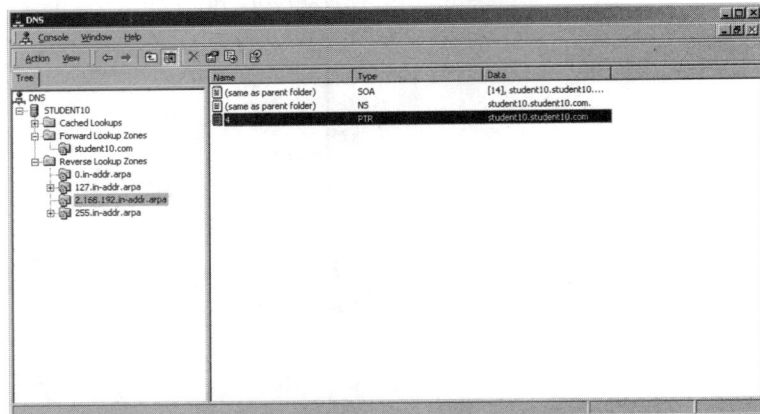

10. Open a command prompt and use nslookup to query your server. When you are finished, type **exit** to quit nslookup. Minimize the command prompt.

11. Now that you have created a reverse DNS zone for your network, it is much easier to add a PTR record for any host you subsequently add. All you have to do is select the Create the Associated Pointer (PTR) Record check box. If the proper reverse DNS zone exists, the system will create the reverse entry automatically. This feature works only for hosts you add after creating the proper reverse DNS zone.

Remember that reverse DNS zones are specific to the network IP address. If, for example, you need to add a record for the system named sandi, and this host has an IP address of 192.168.4.4 in a standard class C network, you create a new reverse lookup zone for the 192.168.4.0 network range.

12. Click the Forward Lookup Zones icon.

13. Right-click the Student10 forward lookup zone, and choose New Host from the shortcut menu to open the New Host dialog box.

EXERCISE 7.5 *(continued)*

14. In the Name (Uses Parent Domain If Blank) text box, enter a bogus new host (such as Student11).

15. In the IP address box, enter an IP address that is on your subnet.

16. Now, select the Create Associated Pointer (PTR) Record check box.

17. Click Add Host to open the DNS dialog box.

18. Click OK to acknowledge that you have added this host.

    If you receive an error message informing you that the proper reverse DNS zone must be present, check your work to make sure you entered the correct information when creating the reverse DNS zone. The most common mistake is reversing the network IP address, because Windows 2000 does this automatically.

19. Click the Done button.

20. Repeat the relevant steps to create additional entries for each forward entry you manually created in the previous exercise.

Propagating Changes from the Primary Server to the Secondary Server

The standard method for propagating any changes in your zone is to set the Refresh Interval in the SOA record. You can do so by double-clicking the SOA record for your zone in the DNS MMC.

If you need to change the SOA values, you must change them on the primary DNS server. Any changes you make on the secondary server are overwritten by the primary server during the subsequent zone transfer. Unlike Linux, Windows 2000 will automatically increment the serial number by one, whereas you must increment the value yourself in most Linux systems.

> If you change the SOA record on the primary DNS server, the primary server will not write the changes to the secondary server until the original refresh value has expired, not the new refresh value.

Controlling Zone Transfers in Windows 2000

It is important to limit zone transfers. If, for example, an unauthorized party obtains a zone transfer from your system, this user could map your entire network. To limit zone transfers in Windows 2000, open the SOA file, and then select the Zone Transfers tab, which shown in Figure 7.2. Follow these steps:

1. Choose Start≻ Programs ≻ Administrative Tools ≻ DNS to open the DNS snap-in.

2. Expand the Forward Lookup Zones folder, and expand the Reverse Lookup Zones folder.

3. Right click a forward or a reverse zone (such as nyc.com or 24.37.132.xSubnet), and from the shortcut menu choose Properties to open the Zone Name Properties dialog box.

4. Click the Zone Transfers tab.

FIGURE 7.2 The Zone Transfers tab

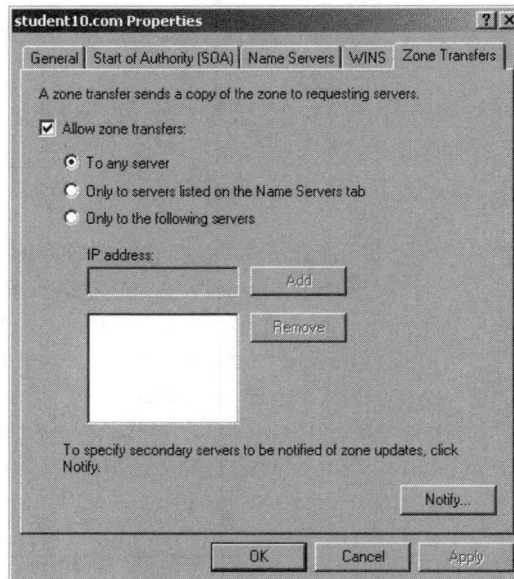

By default, Windows 2000 and most other servers allow zone transfers to all systems. You can limit transfers by doing the following:

- If you select the Only to Servers Listed on the Name Servers Tab button, you must select the Name Servers tab, and then add the servers that are allowed to obtain zone transfers from your system.

- If you select the Only to the Following Servers button, you must enter the IP address of any server(s) allowed to obtain a zone transfer from your system.

Understanding BIND

Berkeley Internet Name Daemon (BIND) is the daemon (that is, service) used by many Unix systems to provide DNS. BIND has been through many iterations.

- BIND 4 is found in many Unix systems, including Red Hat Linux version 5.2 and earlier.

- BIND 8.*x* is a more recent version, current through Red Hat 7.

- BIND 9.*x* is the latest version, available in Red Hat 7.1 and newer.

You can download the latest version of BIND from `www.isc.org/products/BIND/`. Many distributions, including Red Hat Linux, include a BIND distribution. In Linux, the BIND daemon is referred to as named.

Many Unix DNS servers still use BIND 4, mainly because systems administrators tend to establish DNS and then never check it again unless it malfunctions. BIND 4 uses an older initialization file, which is called `named.boot`. This file holds the initialization parameters required for the named daemon.

Following is an example of the contents of a `named.boot` file. This syntax shows the information for the `ciwcertified.com` domain. All IP addresses in this domain are of the format 192.168.120.X.

```
domain ciwcertified.com
directory /var/named
primary ciwcertified.com ciwcertified.hosts
primary 120.168.192.in-addr.arpa.rev. ciwcertified.hosts
primary 0.0.127.IN-ADDR.ARPA
```

```
named.local
cache named.ca
```

Table 7.5 explains the entries in `named.boot`.

TABLE 7.5 The Contents of `named.boot`

Entry	What It Does
Domain	Refers to the domain name; in this example, `ciwcertified.com`.
Directory	Indicates the location of all the DNS files required by the named daemon; in this example, `/var/named`.
Primary (`ciwcertified.com ciwcertified.hosts`)	Identifies the file to be used for host-name-to-IP-address resolution.
Primary (`120.168.192 .in-addr.arpa.rev. ciwcertified.hosts`)	Identifies the file to be used for IP-address-to-host-name resolution (note that 120.168.192 is the reverse of the IP address 192.168.120.*X*).
Primary (`0.0.127.in-addr .arpa named.local`)	Identifies the file to be used for the loopback address.
Cache	Identifies the file that holds information on the root servers; in this example, `named.ca`.

Newer versions of BIND use a boot file that is called `named.conf`. This file has a different format than the one you just reviewed. You will learn more about `named.conf` in the next section as you learn about configuring DNS in Linux.

Setting Up DNS in Linux

You are already familiar with DNS concepts. However, implementing DNS in Linux requires different tools. You can use vi or any text editor to edit the following files.

- `/etc/named.conf` (BIND 8 and 9 use this file to launch.)

- `/var/named/named.ca` (contains the root server file)

- `/var/named/named.local` (provides information about the loop-back network)

- `/var/named/forward` (often called *domain_name*.hosts, in which *domain_name* is the first part of the file name)

- `/var/named/reverse` (often called *rev.domain_name*.hosts, in which *domain_name* is the middle part of the file name)

- `/etc/resolv.conf` (contains information that configures the Unix system as a DNS client; usually located in the `/etc/` directory)

The preferred way to start the server is to use the `/etc/rc.d/init.d/named` script. The following command, for example, will start BIND:

```
host# /etc/rc.d/init.d/named start
```

You can also use the `stop, restart,` and `status` commands for this script.

In addition, you can verify whether the daemon has started by issuing the following command:

```
ps aux | grep named
```

This command helps you determine if `named` is running. You can restart the named process (and any other, for that matter) by using the following command:

```
kill -HUP [PID]
```

If you insert the proper process ID (PID) number, this command will stop and restart the service to make sure DNS rereads any changes in your DNS file.

You must use a program such as `ntsysv` to specify that the DNS service (usually BIND) start automatically at the appropriate run level(s).

Following is a discussion of each file.

The `named.conf` file holds the initialization parameters required for the named daemon. Red Hat Linux 5.2 through 7.0 use the BIND 8 initialization file, which is called `named.conf`. Red Hat 7.1 and later use BIND 9.

The `named.conf` file resembles the following, which is an example of the master DNS server for the `ciwcertified.com` zone. All IP addresses in this example are of the format 192.168.120.X.

```
options {
directory "/var/named"; // The BIND 8 location for named
};
zone "ciwcertified.com" in {
type master;
```

```
file "ciwcertified.hosts";
};
zone "120.168.192.in-addr.arpa" in {
type master;
file "rev. ciwcertified.hosts";
};
zone "0.0.127.in-addr.arpa" in {
type master;
file "named.local";
};
zone "." in {
type hint;
file "named.ca";
};
```

The in statement in front of the first bracket for each zone tells the DNS server that this zone will resolve IP addresses.

Also, notice that this particular file supports the # character as a comment. Any text that follows this character will not be read by the computer. Additional commenting methods include /* comment text */ (for multiple lines) and // comment text. In this particular file, never use the semicolon character (;) to begin a comment, because it is reserved to end option and zone statements.

Table 7.6 explains the entries in the previous example.

TABLE 7.6 The Contents of named.conf

Entry	What It Does

options {
 directory /var/named";
 };
	Indicates the location of all the DNS zone files required by the named daemon. To change this location, edit the file.

zone "ciwcertified.com" in {
 type master;
 file "ciwcertified.hosts";
 };
	Identifies the file to be used for host-name-to-IP-address resolution.

TABLE 7.6   The Contents of `named.conf` *(continued)*

Entry	What It Does

zone "120.168.192.in-addr.arpa" in {
type master;
file "rev. ciwcertified.hosts";
};
	Identifies the file to be used for IP-address-to-host-name resolution (note that 120.168.192 is the reverse of the IP address 192.168.120.X).

zone "0.0.127.in-addr.arpa" in {
type master;
file "named.local";
};
	Identifies the file to be used for the loopback address.

zone "." in {
type hint;
file "named.ca";
};
	Identifies the file that holds information on the root servers.

The `named.ca` file contains information about the root servers. This file is used to initialize the cache of internal domain name servers. It is located in the `/var/named` directory. To ensure that your file is up-to-date, check the InterNIC root server file at `ftp.rs.internic.net/domain/named.ca`. Visit this site and update this file every six months.

The following is a small portion of the `named.ca` file.

```
; formerly NS.INTERNIC.NET
;
. 3600000 IN NS A.ROOT-SERVERS.NET.
A-ROOT-SERVERS.NET. 3600000 A 198.41.0.4
;
;
```

As you can see, this file is the counterpart to the Root Hints tab of a Windows 2000 server DNS Server Properties dialog box. Notice the use of the semicolon (;). All actual zone files support only the semicolon (;)as a comment. Do not use any other method for adding comments.

The `named.local` file is required to cover the loopback network. You use the loopback network when you ping the local host.

```
; Contains local host name information
$TTL 86400 ; Default TTL is one day.
```

```
@ IN SOA webserver.ciwcertified.com. root.ciwcerified.com. (
94073101 ; serialnumber, date & edition
36000 ; refresh time in seconds (10 hours)
3600 ; retry after one hour
3600000 ; expire after 1000 hours - roughly 41.5 days
    IN NS server.ciwcertified.com.
1 IN PTR localhost.
```

The default $TTL 86400 is placed at the top of the file, rather than beneath the In SOA field. Also, the indention is important for this file. Notice that the IN NS server.ciwcertified.com. entry is indented more than the others and that the 1 IN PTR localhost. entry is not indented at all.

Table 7.7 explains the entries in the previous example.

TABLE 7.7 The Contents of named.local

Entry	Explanation
TTL (time-to-live)	The time that a DNS entry obtained from another server will remain in cache so that subsequent queries for the same information will be handled locally, increasing efficiency.
@	A variable defined in the named.boot and named.conf files. The domain is assigned to this parameter. In this example, @ has the value ciwcertified.com. The value of ciwcertified.com is derived from the /etc/named.boot file.
server.ciwcertified.com	Name of the server that holds the DNS records. This entry must be defined in the hosts file.
root.ciwcertified.com	The e-mail address for the person responsible for the DNS server. The e-mail address is root.ciwcertified.com, not root@ciwcertified.com, because the @ symbol is reserved, as explained in the first entry of this table.

TABLE 7.7 The Contents of named.local *(continued)*

Entry	Explanation
Serial	Used for notifying the secondary servers that the primary server has been updated. The value should be incremented each time any change (such as adding a host) is made to the primary server. Otherwise, your secondary server will not be updated.
Refresh	Determines how often the secondary servers need to contact the primary servers for updates. Do not confuse this entry with the serial number.
Retry	If the secondary server fails to contact the primary server, it will wait a specified period of time before attempting to contact the primary server.
Expire	Determines how long the secondary server will store its DNS records, after which time they are discarded.
IN NS server.ciwcertified.com	Identifies the authoritative name server as `server.ciwcertified.com`.
1 IN PTR localhost	Reverse lookup for localhost address, which is 127.0.0.1. An entry for localhost must be in your hosts file, as well.

Do not confuse the serial entry with the refresh entry.

Sometimes called the *domain*.hosts file, the *forward zone file* contains the host-name-to-IP-address entries and follows the same patterns as the named.local file. Notice the absence of the period at the end of the NS entry for server and also the entry for router and printer. If no period exists, the domain name is appended. For example, the DNS server will falsely report server.ciwcertified.com. The domain ciwcertified.com is defined in the boot file as named.boot/named.conf.

```
$TTL 86400 ; Default TTL is one day.
@ IN SOA server. ciwcertified.com. root. ciwcertified.com.
↳(
94073101 ; serialnumber - increment after changes
36000 ; refresh time in seconds (10 hours)
3600 ; retry after one hour
3600000 ; expire after 1000 hours - roughly 41.5 days
IN NS server.ciwcertified.com.
router IN A 192.168.120.1
printer IN A 192.168.120.2
```

Sometimes called the *rev.domain*.hosts file, the reverse zone file contains the IP-address-to-host-name entries. If you compare this file with the *domain*.hosts file, you will notice that the entries in *rev.domain*.hosts contain the FQDN. These entries also end with the period, which means that the domain name ciwcertified.com (which is defined in the boot file named.boot/named.conf) will not be added to the end of the name.

```
$TTL 86400 ; Default TTL is one day.
@ IN SOA server. ciwcertified.com. root. ciwcertified.com. (
94073101 ; serialnumber - increment after changes
36000 ; refresh time in seconds (10 hours).
3600 ; retry after one hour
3600000 ; ; expire after 1000 hours - roughly 41.5 days
IN NS server.ciwcertified.com.
1 IN PTR router.ciwcertified.com.
2 IN PTR printer.ciwcertified.com.
```

Troubleshooting DNS

You have already used nslookup, the primary DNS troubleshooting tool. The Ping program is also helpful, because you can use it to test resolution on hosts. For example, if you cannot ping a host by its name but can still ping it by its IP address, there is likely a problem with DNS. However, you must still determine whether the problem lies with the client or with the server.

On the client side, your client might be referencing the wrong DNS server, or the entry might be incorrect. On the server side, many problems could exist. Here are some suggestions for tracking the source of the problems:

- View the message logs. In Windows 2000, use Event Viewer. In Linux systems, view the log messages in the `/var/log/` file. The `tail -f` command is useful, because it allows you to see the last 10 messages generated in real time.

- If you created your DNS zones by hand, trailing periods (or the lack thereof) could be the source of your problems.

- The DNS server might not have been explicitly told whether it is a primary or secondary server in the `named.conf` file (in older versions, `named.boot`).

- When checking your Linux system's `/var/log/message` file, you might see an error message indicating that the default TTL has not been set. Newer versions of BIND ignore the default TTL value unless it is placed as the very first line of the forward, reverse, and `named.local` files. The value, which is usually `$TTL 86400`, should be at the very front of the file, on its own line. It should precede the `@ IN SOA` line.

To limit zone transfers, use the allow-transfer entry. For example, if you want to limit transfers to a host with the IP address of 192.168.2.4, enter the following code into `/etc/named.conf`:

```
options {
 directory "/var/named";
 allow-transfer {
  192.168.2.4;
     };
   };
```

When troubleshooting zone transfers to slave servers, be sure you have incremented the serial number after each change to a zone file. If you do not increment the serial number for the zone file, your slave server will not conduct a zone transfer and gain the new information. Windows 2000 should automatically update the serial number. You will have to change the serial number yourself in Unix systems.

The Ask Mr. DNS Archive is a useful site to keep you informed about DNS issues. You can access it at www.acmebw.com/askmrdns.

You might also find the following Windows troubleshooting utilities helpful:

- DNS Professional (`www.menandmice.com/infobase/mennmys/vef-sidur.nsf/index/2.1`)

- CyberKit Professional (`www.cyberkit.net`)

- Ping Plotter (`www.nessoft.com/pingplotter`)

- WS_FTP Ping ProPack (`www.ipswitch.com`)

In addition to `nslookup`, `ping`, and `traceroute`, Unix troubleshooting utilities include the following:

- `dig`, which you can use to query name servers and determine usage. This product is included with Red Hat Linux 6.2.

- `host`, which provides detailed information about the host, as well as its name servers. This product is included with Red Hat Linux 6.2.

- `dnswalk`, which is a Perl script that conducts zone transfers and analyzes output. This utility runs with the latest version of Perl only.

Many other Unix utilities exist, including automated scripts that help you create the DNS files you just created manually.

Many websites will check domains at no cost to you. These include the Men and Mice site, where you can have its utility check your DNS infrastructure. Visit `www.menandmice.com` for more information.

For more information about DNS concepts, visit the InterNIC site at `http://rs.internic.net` and view the FAQ files you find. Although DNS is a well-defined protocol, its implementation is constantly changing. Visit the Microsoft site at `http://www.microsoft.com` to learn more about DDNS. Once there, enter **Windows 2000 DNS** in the site's search field. View the various URLs to learn more about Microsoft's perspective. Then visit the BIND site at `http://www.isc.org/products/BIND` and view the latest developments about this popular open source DNS platform.

Summary

In this chapter, you learned how to create master and slave DNS servers on two of the most popular platforms, Windows 2000 and Red Hat Linux. You learned about DDNS, and you also picked up some troubleshooting hints that can help you work with various platforms and versions of BIND.

With this information, you should understand the Domain Name System (DNS) and the relationship of the DNS components, including zones, name server types, and resolvers. You should know how to enter the appropriate DNS record types into forward and reverse lookup zones, including A, NS, SOA, MX, CNAME, and PTR records. PTR records are used for reverse DNS lookup in order to resolve IP addresses to host names, whereas forward DNS lookup resolves host names to IP addresses.

Finally, after completing the exercises and working through this chapter, you should be able to implement DNS in Linux and Windows 2000 including Dynamic DNS (DDNS). In addition to configuring master and slave DNS servers, you should be able to configure caching servers and forwarders and to trouble-shoot these DNS servers using nslookup and other troubleshooting tools.

Exam Essentials

Be able to explain the Domain Name System (DNS) and identify DNS components, including zones, name server types, and resolvers.   DNS resolves user-friendly host names to IP addresses. Reverse DNS resolves IP addresses to host names. The Domain Name Space is a hierarchy with root-level, top-level, and second-level domains. Name resolvers are DNS server clients. Resolvers generally access hosts by a fully qualified domain name (FQDN).

Be able to implement DNS in Linux and Windows 2000 including Dynamic DNS.   This essential includes creating forward and reverse lookup zones and creating common DNS record types, including A, NS, SOA, MX, CNAME, and PTR records (used for reverse lookup). This essential also includes configuring the following DNS server types: mas-ter, slave, caching-only, and forwarding. You enter records on master servers and then copy them to slave servers via zone transfers. Caching-only servers have no records to start with, but forward requests to other DNS servers and cache the answers in order to directly answer future requests.

Be able to troubleshoot DNS using nslookup and additional trouble-shooting tools. The nslookup program is a standard TCP/IP utility that probes and queries DNS databases. Understand how to use this program to change servers and list domain records.

Key Terms

Before taking the exam, you should be familiar with the following terms:

caching-only server	nslookup
Canonical Name (CNAME) record	Pointer (PTR) record
Dynamic DNS (DDNS)	reverse zone file
forwarding server	root server
forward zone file	slave server
Mail Exchanger (MX) record	Start of Authority (SOA)
master server	top-level domain
name resolver	zone transfer
name server	

Review Questions

1. Jonathan is the IS director of Great Escapes. His DNS infrastructure includes a master DNS server and two slave DNS servers. The master DNS server fails. What will be the impact on his business?

    A. Name resolution will fail.

    B. Jonathan will not be able to add DNS records.

    C. Fault tolerance will be lost.

    D. Load balancing will be lost.

    E. Caching will be lost.

2. Jonathan is the IS director of Great Escapes. His DNS infrastructure includes a master DNS server and a slave DNS server. The slave DNS server fails. What will be the impact on his business? Choose two.

    A. Name resolution will fail.

    B. Jonathan will not be able to add DNS records.

    C. Fault tolerance will be lost.

    D. Load balancing will be lost.

    E. Caching will be lost.

3. Jonathan is the IS director of Great Escapes. His DNS infrastructure includes a master DNS server and a slave DNS server. He has just installed an additional DNS server at a remote location without creating any master or slave, forward or reverse lookup zones. He has, however, enabled the additional DNS server as a forwarder to the master DNS server, and he has configured the clients at the remote location to use the additional DNS server. What benefit does this new DNS server provide?

    A. None so far.

    B. It serves as a caching-only DNS server.

    C. It serves as a secondary DNS server.

    D. It serves as a primary DNS server.

    E. It serves as an additional slave DNS server.

4. Jason bought the right to register Internet names for a country that has the .tv domain. He hoped that businesses would pay a premium for such domain names as www.hollywood.tv. What level DNS name is .tv?

    A. Primary

    B. Secondary

    C. Root

    D. Top

5. Jason bought the right to register Internet names for a country that has the .tv domain. He is using one of the domain names himself, and one of his most popular websites is www.inside.hollywood.tv. Which three levels of the DNS name space does this website span?

    A. First

    B. Second

    C. Root

    D. Top

6. Jim enters www.compaq in his browser window and is unable to connect to Compaq's website. What can Jim do to connect? Choose two options.

    A. Press F5 to refresh his display.

    B. Use the FQDN.

    C. Clear his browser cache.

    D. On the DNS tab of the Advanced TCP/IP Settings dialog box, add com to the Append These DNS Suffixes (In Order) text box.

    E. Ensure that his DNS server is functioning by using nslookup.

7. Jason sets up a forward lookup zone but not a reverse lookup zone for www.citylights.com. What will be the effects of omitting the reverse lookup zone? Choose two.

   A. Name resolution will not function for citylights.com.

   B. Using nslookup to find the IP address of a host name in citylights.com will not work

   C. Using nslookup to find the host name of an IP address in citylights.com will not work

   D. Secured websites that require the domain name of the host requesting service may refuse the connection.

8. Mike uses Internet Explorer in Windows 2000 and uses Netscape with Linux 7 to surf the Internet. What is the name of the function that these browsers serve with regard to DNS?

   A. Name server

   B. Name resolver

   C. Caching-only client

   D. Slave-client

   E. Browse master

9. Mike wants to schedule late-night updates from a master DNS server in Chicago to a slave DNS server in London. What are these updates called?

   A. Zone transfers

   B. Snapshot replication

   C. Active Directory updates

   D. Scheduled daemons

   E. Push replication

10. Jordan needs to add DNS records for `server1.birdwatcher.edu` that is the web server and the master DNS server that hosts the `birdwatcher.edu` domain. She wants users to be able to address this server as `www.birdwatcher.edu`. Which DNS records should Jordan create in the forward lookup zone of `birdwatcher.com`? Choose four.

    A. Address (A)

    B. Name Server (NS)

    C. Start of Authority (SOA)

    D. Canonical Name (CNAME)

    E. Mail Exchanger (MX)

    F. Pointer (PTR)

11. Jordan needs to add a DNS record for `server1.birdwatcher.edu` to show that it is the e-mail server for `birdwatcher.edu`. Which record type does Jordan need to enter?

    A. Address (A)

    B. Name Server (NS)

    C. Start of Authority (SOA)

    D. Canonical Name (CNAME)

    E. Mail Exchanger (MX)

    F. Pointer (PTR)

12. Fred is told to add PTR records to the `stockwatch.com` domain that spans the 200.30.4.0 network with a subnet mask of 255.255.255.0. Fred will create a reverse lookup zone. What should he name this zone?

    A. `200.30.4.0.in-addr.arpa`

    B. `0.4.30.200.in-addr.arpa`

    C. `30.4.0.in-addr.arpa`

    D. `4.30.200.in-addr.arpa`

13. The only DNS server for the LAN fails. While it is being repaired, Brian wants to point to an authoritative DNS server on the Internet in order to resolve Internet domain names. Which DNS file will contain information about root servers on the Internet?

   A. Cache

   B. Directory

   C. Primary

   D. Boot

14. Hank's company has an NT 4 DNS server and a Linux BIND 4 DNS server. He is considering upgrading the NT 4 DNS server to Windows 2000 DNS and upgrading the BIND 4 DNS server to BIND 9. Why should he complete the upgrade? Choose the most important new feature that BIND 9 and Windows 2000 DNS have in common.

   A. Host records

   B. AAAA records

   C. Multicast zones

   D. Dynamic DNS

15. Hank wants to troubleshoot a DNS problem. Which TCP/IP utility should Hank use?

   A. path ping

   B. ifconfig

   C. nslookup

   D. tracert

   E. ping

16. Hank has set up an internal DNS server inside the company firewall that receives dynamic updates from internal computers. Corporate users will talk to this DNS server exclusively, and if a host name on the Internet needs to be resolved, this DNS server will talk to a DNS server on the Internet once this is configured. What needs to be configured on the internal DNS server?

A. Secondaries

B. Forwarders

C. Slaves

D. Reverse Lookups

17. Tom wants to see which records are in the `mostgifts.com` domain. He knows that the DNS server for that domain is a Windows 2000 server with an IP address of 192.168.4.3. He uses `nslookup`, changes the server to 192.168.4.3, and issues a command to list the records in the `mostgifts.com` domain. The DNS server refuses this request. What is a likely reason?

A. It is offline.

B. It is incompatible with `nslookup`.

C. Zone transfers have been set to Only Servers Listed on the Name Servers tab or to Only to the Following Servers.

D. This is a caching-only DNS server, and it does not contain any original records in its forward or reverse lookup zone.

18. Dennis wants to edit the file that boots a BIND 9 DNS server that hosts the `greatdogs.com` domain, and he wants to make that DNS server a DNS client of itself. Which two of the following files should Dennis edit?

A. `/etc/named.conf`

B. `/var/named/named.ca`

C. `/var/named/greatdogs.com`

D. `/etc/resolv.conf`

19. Users complain to Jessica that the Linux DNS server is not functioning. Jessica wants to see if the DNS daemon has started, and if it hasn't started, she wants to start it. Which two commands should Jessica issue?

A. host# /etc/rc.d/init.d/dns start

B. host# /etc/rc.d/init.d/named start

C. ps aux | grep named

D. ps aux | grep dns

20. Willy looks at the following file:

```
$TTL 86400 ; Default TTL is one day.
@ IN SOA server. ciwcertified.com. root.
⤷ciwcertified.com. (
94073101 ; serialnumber - increment after changes
36000 ; refresh time in seconds (10 hours)
3600 ; retry after one hour
3600000 ; expire after 1000 hours - roughly 41.5 days
IN NS server.ciwcertified.com.
router IN A 192.168.120.1
printer IN A 192.168.120.2
```

What type of file is it?

A. Forward zone file

B. Reverse zone file

C. Cache file

D. Boot file

E. SOA file

Answers to Review Questions

1. **B.** You make changes to the DNS database on the master DNS server. Slave DNS servers have a read-only copy of the DNS database. Slave DNS servers provide fault tolerance and load balancing.

2. **C, D.** You make changes to the DNS database on the master DNS server. Slave DNS servers have a read-only copy of the DNS database. Slave DNS servers provide fault tolerance and load balancing.

3. **B.** DNS servers, without zones that are configured to forward requests for clients, serve as caching-only DNS servers that can conserve bandwidth on slow links by providing additional referrals to resolved host names to clients from the local cache.

4. **D.** Examples of top-level domains are .com, .edu, .tv, .ca, and .us.

5. **B, C, D.** The three levels are root, top, and second. The root level domain is the understood dot after tv, tv is the top level domain, hollywood is the second level domain, inside is a subdomain, and www is the server name.

6. **B, D.** Jim needs to use the fully qualified domain name or add com to the Append These DNS Suffixes (In Order) text box. This acts like a path statement.

7. **B, D.** Name resolution is still possible, except that name resolution of the IP address to the domain name will not function for either nslookup or for a website that for security purposes wants to limit by domain the hosts that can connect.

8. **B.** Mike's browsers are functioning as DNS clients or name resolvers.

9. **A.** The process of pulling information from a master DNS server is called a zone transfer. Zone files are the DNS database files that contain the records for a DNS domain or subdomain. Zone transfers update these files on the slave server.

10. A, B, C, D.   Jordan will have an A, an NS, an SOA, and a CNAME record for `server1.birdwatcher.edu`. The CNAME record aliases `www.birdwatcher.edu` to `server1.birdwatcher.edu`.

11. E.   Jordan needs to add a Mail Exchanger record.

12. D.   For the reverse lookup zone, only the network portion of the IP address counts. In this case, the first three octets count. Also, these octets need to be reversed.

13. A.   The cache file contains the names and IP addresses of the root DNS servers on the Internet. The name of the file depends on the operating system. In Linux, it is `named.ca`, and in NT 4 and Windows 2000, it is `cache.dns`.

14. D.   Hank should upgrade these DNS servers to take advantage of dynamic DNS.

15. C.   You use `nslookup` to troubleshoot DNS servers.

16. B.   You must configure the internal DNS server as a forwarder and point it to one or more DNS servers on the Internet that will be used to resolve queries that the internal DNS server cannot resolve.

17. C.   For security, zone transfers have been restricted to authorized servers.

18. A, D.   Dennis should edit the boot file `/etc/named.conf` and the DNS client file `/etc/resolv.conf`.

19. B, C.   The `ps aux | grep named` command will show if the `named` daemon responsible for DNS has started. The `host# /etc/rc.d/init.d/named start` command will start the `named` daemon.

20. A.   This is a forward zone file. It is authoritative for `ciwcertified.com`. It has IN A (Internet Address) records; a reverse zone file would have IN PTR (Internet Pointer) records.

Chapter

8

Name Resolution with WINS and Samba

THE CIW EXAM OBJECTIVE GROUPS COVERED IN THIS CHAPTER:

✓ Identify additional name resolution options for LANs and WANs, including but not limited to: Windows Internet Naming Service (WINS), Samba.

n the previous chapter, you learned that the Domain Name System (DNS) is the primary means of providing name resolution on the Internet, as well as on intranets and extranets. However, DNS is not the only system for performing name resolution. In this chapter, you will learn about the *NetBIOS (Network Basic Input Output System)* naming convention and how it relates to the *Server Message Block (SMB)* protocol. SMB is the networking protocol used in DOS, Windows, and OS/2 networks that allows the sharing of printers and files across networks. SMB can run on top of many different protocols, including *TCP/IP (Transmission Control Protocol/Internet Protocol)*. In Windows networking, TCP/IP establishes and manages the connection, and SMB provides access to shares and operating-system–specific information across that connection. SMB provides a common *applications programming interface (API)* between two different server types. When used with TCP/IP, SMB allows many different systems to share information.

In this chapter, you will see how the SMB protocol is supported by the *Windows Internet Naming Service (WINS)* and Samba. WINS' past popularity was largely based on its ability to automatically update friendly NetBIOS names to IP address mappings at a time before a similar capability existed with Dynamic DNS. Although WINS is an older system, it is nevertheless important because many legacy intranets and networks still use WINS to resolve names.

SMB is somewhat similar to the Network File System (NFS) found in Unix. However, whereas NFS uses UDP (User Datagram Protocol), SMB under TCP/IP uses TCP.

NetBIOS over TCP/IP

NetBIOS is an interface that allows systems to communicate on a LAN, and it runs over TCP/IP much the same way that SMB runs over TCP/IP. NetBIOS Enhanced User Interface (NetBEUI) is a protocol and an extension of NetBIOS that uses a different format for data frames. Windows 2000 and earlier versions of Windows used the NetBEUI protocol and used NetBIOS to transfer the NetBEUI information. NetBIOS defines a software interface, not a protocol. Although there is no official NetBIOS service standard, the IBM PC-Network version is the most popular.

> **NOTE** Windows 2000 systems support NetBIOS by default, although you can disable this support, if necessary.

RFC 1001 states that the NetBIOS "namespace is flat and uses 16 alphanumeric characters." It further states that "names cannot start with an asterisk (*)." Windows systems, however, automatically supply one hidden hexadecimal character and allow you to enter only 15 characters.

NetBIOS uses UDP ports 137 and 138 and TCP port 139. Port 137 supports the NetBIOS name service, port 138 carries the NetBIOS datagram service, and port 139 carries the NetBIOS session-layer protocol. Collectively, these three ports support the SMB protocol. Running the `netstat -a` command on a network server will show these services listening on these ports.

> **NOTE** You can read more about NetBIOS over TCP/IP in RFC 1001 and RFC 1002.

Using the *nbtstat* Command

The Windows *nbtstat* command (NetBIOS over TCP/IP statistics) is essentially the NetBIOS equivalent of the `nslookup` command. You can use the `nbtstat` command to display NetBIOS names when only an IP address is available. This command also displays protocol statistics and TCP/IP connections on networks running NetBIOS over TCP/IP.

The command format is as follows:

```
nbtstat options
```

Table 8.1 lists and describes the options commonly used with the
nbtstat command in Windows 2000.

TABLE 8.1 Windows 2000 nbtstat Options

Option	What It Does
-a remote_name	Lists the name table of a remote computer given its NetBIOS name.
-A remote_IP_address	Lists the name table of a remote computer given its IP address.
-n	Lists the local name cache of your computer, which contains statistics about your computer.
-c	Lists the remote name cache of your computer, including IP addresses. The remote name cache contains statistics about remote computers.
-R	Purges your remote name cache and reloads the remote cache name table.

Entries in the remote cache name table can be entered in the lmhosts file,
which you will learn about later in this chapter.

By itself, the nbtstat command displays the help file. To use an option,
enter the option code after the command, such as -A to list statistics on a
remote computer, as follows:

```
nbtstat –A 192.168.10.9
```

This option yields the following output:

```
NetBIOS Remote Machine Name Table
Name    Type  Status
STANGER  <00>  UNIQUE  REGISTERED
COURSEWARE  <00>  GROUP  REGISTERED
STANGER  <03>  UNIQUE  REGISTERED
```

```
STANGER  <20>  UNIQUE  REGISTERED
STANGER  <1E>  GROUP   REGISTERED
STANGER  <03>  UNIQUE  REGISTERED
MAC Address = 00-AA-00-38-E7-C3
```

From this information, you can determine that the NetBIOS name STANGER exists at the IP address 192.168.10.19 and is a member of the workgroup courseware. Workgroups are specific to Windows and are used to logically group computers in a Windows network.

EXERCISE 8.1

Using *nbtstat* to Locate NetBIOS Names

1. In Windows 2000, open the Command Prompt window. To locate your own computer name and domain or workgroup, enter **nbtstat -n** and press Enter.

2. Write your computer name and domain or workgroup in the space provided: _____

3. Create a share on your computer named nbtstat. Right-click the Desktop, and from the shortcut menu, choose New ➢ Folder. Name the folder nbtstat. Right-click the nbtstat folder, and from the shortcut menu, choose Sharing to open the nbtstat Properties dialog box at the Sharing tab. Click the Share This Folder option, and then click OK.

4. Connect to this share. Choose Start ➢ Run to open the Run dialog box, and in the Open box, enter *your_computer_name*\nbtstat, and then press Enter. You should connect to your own computer's nbtstat share. If this share were on another computer, you could use it to transfer files.

5. Experiment with the remote names. At a command prompt, enter **ipconfig** and press Enter to display your own IP address. To display your own name, enter the following at a command prompt and then press Enter:

   nbtstat –A *your_own_IP_address*

6. Close the command prompt.

Resolving NetBIOS Names in Windows

You can resolve NetBIOS names to IP addresses in Windows networks using the following tools:

- An lmhosts file
- A hosts file
- Broadcasts
- DNS
- WINS

This chapter focuses on how WINS resolves names.

Windows 2000 WINS supports four node types. Table 8.2 explains these node types.

TABLE 8.2   NetBIOS Node Types

Node Type	Name	Description	Configuration Information
p-node	Peer-to-peer node	Instead of using broadcasts, a p-node system directly queries a WINS server for name resolution when its cache does not have the proper name-to-IP-address mapping. This WINS server can be a Windows-based system or a Unix system using Samba.	This type of node relies on a NetBIOS name server. If that name server fails, the host will not be able to participate on the network. This is because a p-node sends requests directly to the server, not to other systems on the network.

TABLE 8.2   NetBIOS Node Types *(continued)*

Node Type	Name	Description	Configuration Information
b-node	Broadcast node	NetBIOS names are broadcast only on the network.	The most common node type for Windows systems. NetBIOS broadcasts cannot pass through routers. Also, these broadcasts can generate undue amounts of traffic and cause certain systems to become confused (for example, browsing lists may not be updated correctly). Windows 2000 systems are b-node by default, unless they have a WINS server installed.
h-node	*Hybrid node*	When trying to resolve a name, an h-node first resorts to a p-node method and then resorts to a broadcast method, b-node.	A common node type for Windows systems; Windows 2000 servers with the WINS service installed are h-nodes. If you remove the WINS server, the Windows 2000 server will become a b-node server.
m-node	Mixed node	This type of system configuration relies on b-node broadcasts first and then resorts to p-node methods.	Although this type of system can generate a large amount of broadcast traffic, it is still quite functional.

Windows servers resolve names for h-node systems, the default for Windows 2000, in a particular order. If DNS, WINS, and lmhosts are all configured, your Windows 2000 system will search for names in the following order:

1. The system searches its *NetBIOS name cache*, if present.

2. It then searches for a WINS server, if configured.

3. A b-node broadcast is generated.

4. The system then uses its lmhosts file.

5. The hosts file is then consulted.

6. The system then queries a DNS server.

> **NOTE** You can find more information about name order at http://support
> .microsoft.com/support/kb/articles/Q142/3/09.asp.

If NetBIOS name resolution is disabled, and the system is configured to use DNS, the system searches the hosts file first and then queries its DNS server. If these methods fail, the source host must specify an IP address for the destination host.

Just as DNS uses a *hosts* file, the Microsoft NetBIOS-over-TCP/IP solution uses a text file, *lmhosts*, to resolve NetBIOS names to IP addresses. As with the hosts file, you can find the lmhosts file in the %systemroot%\ system32\drivers\etc\ folder. The file is not correctly named by default. To use the lmhosts file, you must rename it from lmhosts.sam to just lmhosts. Figure 8.1 shows a sample lmhosts file.

Like the hosts file, the lmhosts file will override the WINS server entries. Locate and view your computer's lmhosts file.

> **NOTE** The name lmhosts stands for LAN Manager hosts. Microsoft's older networking
> operating system was called LAN Manager.

By default, Windows 2000 uses a simple NetBIOS server that communicates via broadcasts. This NetBIOS server allows you to perform name resolution instantly.

Because the NetBIOS server uses broadcast, it consumes a high percentage of bandwidth on Ethernet networks. If the host resides on the other side of a router, the NetBIOS server cannot resolve NetBIOS names. More efficient methods exist for discovering and resolving server names on Windows networks, especially on large networks. One such method uses WINS servers.

FIGURE 8.1 A sample lmhosts file

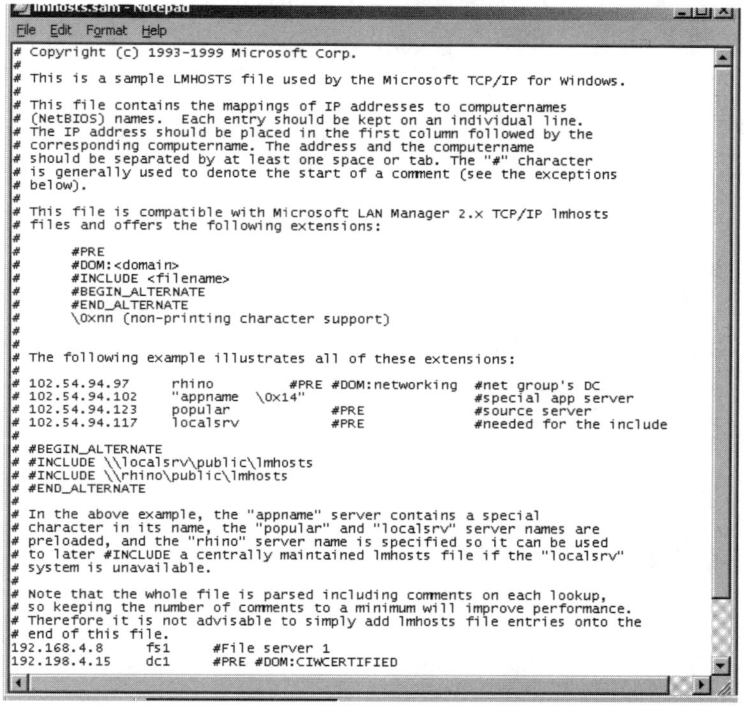

```
lmhosts.sam - Notepad
File  Edit  Format  Help
# Copyright (c) 1993-1999 Microsoft Corp.
#
# This is a sample LMHOSTS file used by the Microsoft TCP/IP for Windows.
#
# This file contains the mappings of IP addresses to computernames
# (NetBIOS) names.  Each entry should be kept on an individual line.
# The IP address should be placed in the first column followed by the
# corresponding computername. The address and the computername
# should be separated by at least one space or tab. The "#" character
# is generally used to denote the start of a comment (see the exceptions
# below).
#
# This file is compatible with Microsoft LAN Manager 2.x TCP/IP lmhosts
# files and offers the following extensions:
#
#      #PRE
#      #DOM:<domain>
#      #INCLUDE <filename>
#      #BEGIN_ALTERNATE
#      #END_ALTERNATE
#      \0xnn (non-printing character support)
#
#
# The following example illustrates all of these extensions:
#
# 102.54.94.97     rhino         #PRE #DOM:networking  #net group's DC
# 102.54.94.102    "appname  \0x14"                    #special app server
# 102.54.94.123    popular            #PRE             #source server
# 102.54.94.117    localsrv           #PRE             #needed for the include
#
# #BEGIN_ALTERNATE
# #INCLUDE \\localsrv\public\lmhosts
# #INCLUDE \\rhino\public\lmhosts
# #END_ALTERNATE
#
# In the above example, the "appname" server contains a special
# character in its name, the "popular" and "localsrv" server names are
# preloaded, and the "rhino" server name is specified so it can be used
# to later #INCLUDE a centrally maintained lmhosts file if the "localsrv"
# system is unavailable.
#
# Note that the whole file is parsed including comments on each lookup,
# so keeping the number of comments to a minimum will improve performance.
# Therefore it is not advisable to simply add lmhosts file entries onto the
# end of this file.
192.168.4.8     fs1     #File server 1
192.198.4.15    dc1     #PRE #DOM:CIWCERTIFIED
```

The Windows Internet Naming Service

As we mentioned earlier, WINS is now considered a legacy service because Microsoft switched to DNS as its primary name resolution method. WINS is similar to a standard DNS server, except for the following characteristics:

- The WINS database is dynamic rather than static. DDNS, however, shares this similarity with WINS.
- No hierarchy of computers exists within the WINS namespace. A WINS server can replicate with another WINS server, but the WINS structure is not similar to a DNS domain.
- WINS processes NetBIOS names; DNS does not.
- WINS uses an `lmhosts` file; DNS uses a `hosts` file.

WINS clients register their names and IP addresses with the server when they initialize and connect to the network. When a computer changes its NetBIOS name and reregisters with the WINS server, the WINS server automatically changes the NetBIOS name of that computer's WINS entry. This feature demonstrates the dynamic nature of the WINS service.

WINS also permits NetBIOS-name-to-IP-address mapping from a central location. When a WINS client initializes, the WINS system expects the machine to register its NetBIOS name and IP address with a WINS server. The WINS system also permits static NetBIOS-name-to-IP-address mapping for clients that do not support this registration procedure.

You can distribute the WINS database among primary and secondary WINS servers. This distribution is not a hierarchy. The servers exchange their database updates at periodic intervals. Data can be replicated by a server-push method or a server-pull method, as you will see later in this chapter.

Windows-based WINS clients register their names and IP addresses with the server automatically when they start.

WINS also allows you to manage NetBIOS-name-to-IP-address mapping from a central location, browse the Windows 2000 domain across routers, and match dynamically assigned IP addresses to resource names. The last point is the most significant. When clients receive their IP addresses dynamically (for example, when a DHCP server is used), the problem of matching resource names to IP addresses must be solved. The WINS system expects a machine to register its NetBIOS name and IP address with a WINS server, whether this address is statically assigned or comes from a DHCP server. However, the WINS system also permits static NetBIOS-name-to-IP-address mapping for clients that do not support WINS registration procedure.

The name registration process works as follows.

Name registration   When a WINS client starts, it sends its NetBIOS name and IP address to the WINS server with which it is registered. Once the name-and-IP mapping is registered, the WINS server grants a lease.

Name query and resolution   After registration, a WINS host can then obtain IP address information from a server for other WINS clients on the network from the WINS server.

Name renewal and release   Each client is responsible for maintaining its own lease. When a client wants to renew its lease or shut down, it sends the appropriate message to the WINS server.

Because WINS is a dynamic database, you can review and edit the entries as they appear. To work with local and remote WINS servers, follow these steps:

1. Choose Start ≻ Programs ≻ Administrative Tools ≻ WINS to open the WINS snap-in:

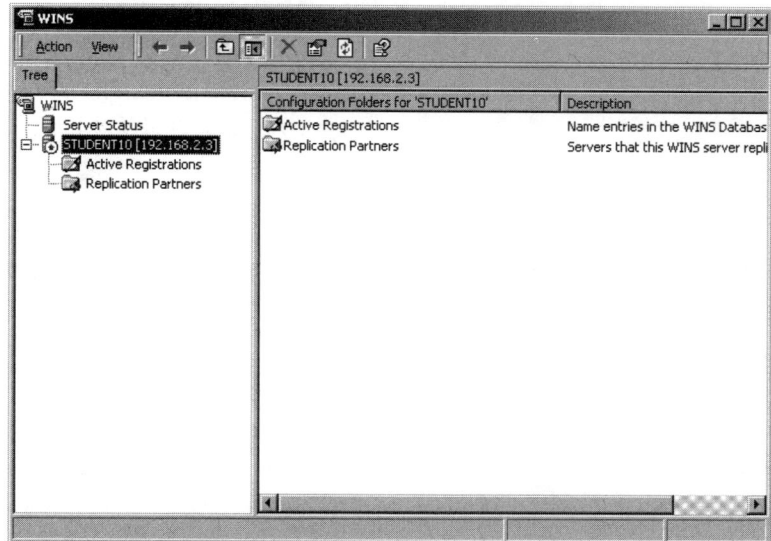

2. To view the existing database entries in your WINS server, expand your server, right-click the Active Registrations folder, and choose Find by Name from the shortcut menu to open the Find by Name dialog box.

3. Enter the NetBIOS name you want to find in the Find Names Beginning With field, and click Find Now. The WINS server will report the name if the name is registered in its database.

You can schedule the WINS database to remove old entries. As with DDNS, cleaning out the database is referred to as scavenging. You can schedule scavenging on a server-by-server basis. Follow these steps:

1. Choose Start ≻ Programs ≻ Administrative Tools ≻ WINS to open the WINS snap-in.

2. Right-click your WINS server icon, and from the shortcut menu choose Scavenge Database to open a WINS message box stating that "The request Scavenge Database has been queued to the server. Check

the Windows event log for status on when this operation is completed." Click OK to close this message box and return to the WINS snap-in.

You can also back up your WINS database. Follow these steps:

1. From the WINS snap-in, right-click on your WINS server icon, then choose Backup Database from the shortcut menu to open the Browse for Folder dialog box.

2. Select any device you want (such as a tape drive or another place on your own hard drive) and click OK.

3. When you see the message "The database back up was completed successfully," click OK.

EXERCISE 8.2

Configuring a WINS Server and Client

In this exercise, you will configure a WINS server and become a client.

1. Make sure the WINS server is installed. Choose Start ➢ Programs ➢ Administrative Tools ➢ WINS to open the WINS snap-in.

   If WINS is not installed, on the Desktop right-click My Network Places, and from the shortcut menu, choose Properties to open the Network and Dial-up Connections dialog box. Choose Advanced ➢ Optional Networking Components to start the Windows Optional Networking Components Wizard. In the Windows Components screen, double-click Networking Services to open the Networking Services dialog box. Click the Windows Internet Naming Service (WINS) check box, and click OK. Click Next. Close the Network and Dial-up Connections dialog box.

2. Configure your computer to be a WINS client. On the Desktop, right-click My Network Places, and from the shortcut menu, choose Properties to open the Network and Dial-Up Connections dialog box. Right-click the Local Area Connection icon and choose Properties from the shortcut menu to open the Local Area Connection Properties dialog box.

3. Select the Intenet Protocol (TCP/IP) icon, and then click Properties to open the Internet Protocol (TCP/IP) Properties dialog box.

4. Click the Advanced button to open the Advanced TCP/IP Settings dialog box, and then select the WINS tab.

5. Click the Add button to open the TCP/IP WINS Server dialog box, enter your IP address in the WINS Server field, and then click Add to return to the Advanced TCP/IP Settings dialog box.

6. Leave all additional settings at their defaults, and then click OK three times to return to the Network and Dial-Up Connections window.

7. Open the WINS snap-in.

8. Search for yourWINS record. Right-click the Active Registrations icon for your server, and from the shortcut menu, choose Find by Name to open the Find by Name dialog box.

9. In the Find Names Beginning With field, enter your own computer name and click the Find Now button.

10. You will see a message informing you that no records are found.

11. Restart your system. Upon restarting, your system will register with your WINS server.

12. After your system reboots, use the Find by Name dialog box to find your WINS records. When you are successful, you should see a listing of your system, similar to the following:

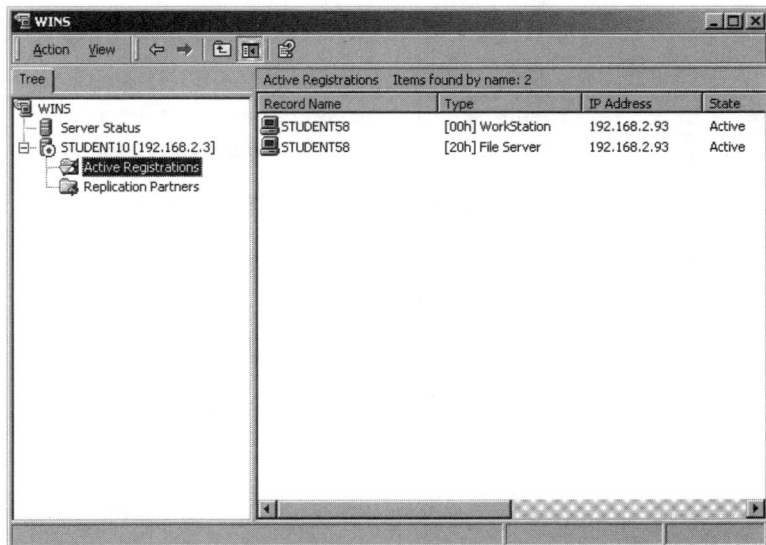

Record Name	Type	IP Address	State
STUDENT58	[00h] WorkStation	192.168.2.93	Active
STUDENT58	[20h] File Server	192.168.2.93	Active

Backing Up the WINS Database

1. If you are not already, become a client to your own WINS server following the the steps in Exercise 8.2. (Becoming a WINS client to yourself is not necessary for backup, but it is absolutely necessary for future exercises.)

2. Open Windows Explorer, and create a new folder on drive C named \winsbackup.

3. Open the WINS snap-in.

4. Right-click your WINS server entry, and choose Back Up Database from the shortcut menu to open the Browse for Folder window.

5. Select the C:\winsbackup folder, and click OK to start the backup.

6. Click OK to acknowledge that the backup was completed successfully.

7. Use Windows Explorer to view the C:\winsbackup folder. You should see a folder named wins_bak. Double-click this folder to view your WINS records.

8. Exit Windows Explorer.

Static Mapping

You can produce entries in the WINS database to accommodate non-WINS clients (such as Unix systems not running Samba) by creating a *static mapping*. To produce these entries, follow these steps:

1. Open the WINS snap-in and expand your server.

2. Right-click Active Registrations, and then choose New Static Mapping from the shortcut menu to open the New Static Mapping dialog box:

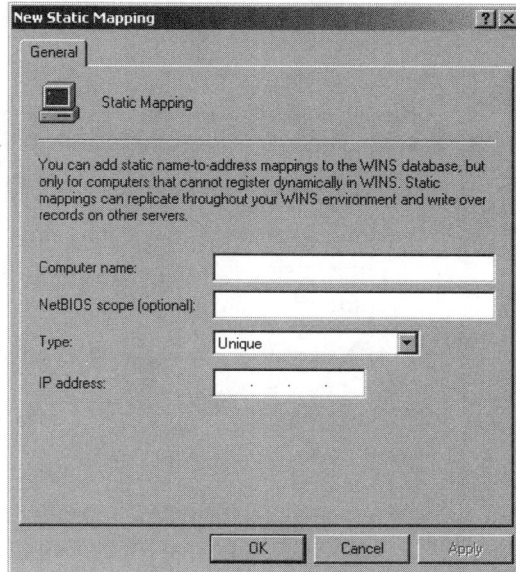

In the New Static Mapping dialog box, you have the following options:

- In the Computer Name box, enter the name you want to give to this static client. Generally, if a Unix system has a DNS name, use it.

- In general, leave the NetBIOS Scope (optional) box blank. This value makes the NetBIOS name, in conjunction with its scope identifier, a valid domain system name.

- In the Type drop-down list box, you can select from the following options to specify how WINS processes this name.

  - Unique is the most common type; it maps a name to an IP address.

  - Group maps addresses of workgroup members to a group name.

  - Domain Name lets you specify a group of names and IP addresses.

  - Internet Group specifies a group using NetBIOS names with a different byte value from that of standard Windows clients.

  - Multihomed allows you to specify one name but multiple IP addresses.

- In the IP Address box, enter the IP address of the system to become a WINS client.

Once you configure a static mapping, you can view the entry as you would any other WINS client.

EXERCISE 8.4

Creating a Static Mapping Entry

In this exercise, you will implement static mapping for your own computer to simulate making a static mapping for a non–WINS-registering computer such as a Linux server.

1. Make sure you are a WINS client to your own system.

2. Open the WINS snap-in

3. Expand your WINS server.

4. Right-click the Active Registrations folder, and choose the New Static Mapping option from the shortcut menu to open the New Static Mapping dialog box.

5. Enter **ciwstudent** in the Computer Name field.

6. Leave the NetBIOS Scope text box blank and leave the Type setting at Unique. Then, enter your own IP address in the IP Address field.

7. Click OK, and then minimize the WINS snap-in.

8. Test your work by using your WINS server to view the active registrations for the ciwstudent.

9. To further test your static mapping, run a ping test from the client computer. At a command prompt, enter **ping ciwstudent** and press Enter.

In this exercise, you created static entries in your WINS database. As you will see later in this chapter, if a Unix system is using Samba, you will not need to use a static mapping entry, if the Samba system is configured as a client to your WINS server.

Replicating a WINS Database

You can distribute a WINS database among two or more WINS servers. WINS uses primary and secondary servers, similar to DNS. You configure the servers to exchange their database updates at periodic intervals. As mentioned earlier in this chapter, you can replicate data using either a server-push method or a server-pull method. By default, whenever you create a replication partner in Windows 2000, the server becomes both a push and a pull client.

A WINS push partner is a server that is configured to notify another WINS server when its database has changed or when the WINS service has started. Once the WINS push partner notifies its pull partner of a change, the push partner then passes on its database.

To replicate a WINS database, follow these steps:

1. Open the WINS snap-in.

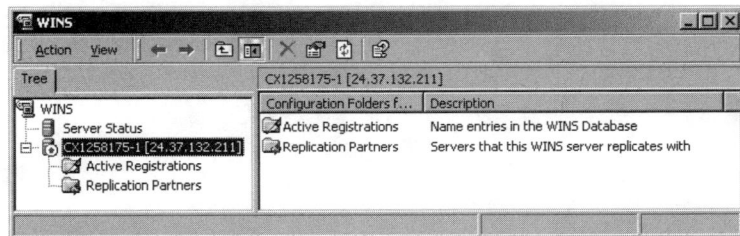

2. Expand your server. Right-click Replication Partners, and chose New Replication Partner from the shortcut menu to open the New Replication Partner dialog box.

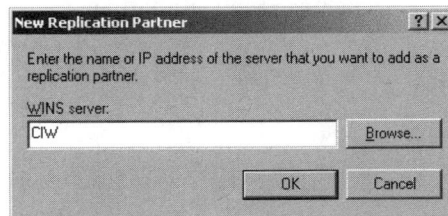

3. In the WINS Server text box, enter your replication partner's IP address or name. Click OK.

4. Your replication partner will appear in the right pane of the WINS snap-in. Double-click your replication partner to open your replication partner's Property dialog box. Click the Advanced tab.

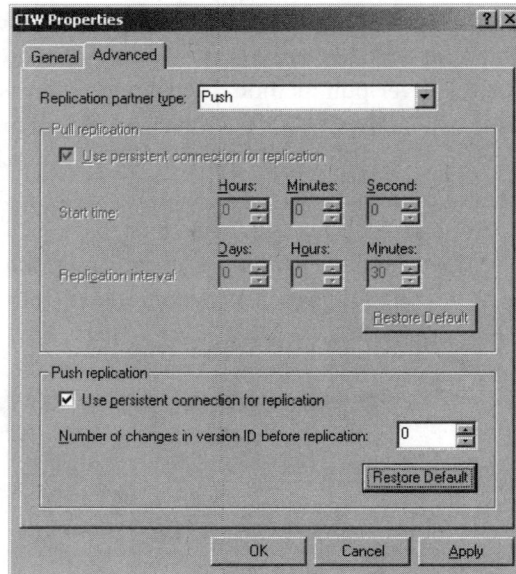

5. In the Replication Partner Type drop-down box, select Push. Leave the Use Persistent Connection for Replication check box selected, and leave the spinner at zero for Number of Changes in Version ID before Replication.

The push replication that you just set up would work well in a LAN with high bandwidth to keep the WINS servers tightly synchronized. In push replication, the WINS server with the changes pushes those changes to its WINS replication partners.

In a WAN with less bandwidth, you might want your WINS servers to replicate their changes in batches to conserve bandwidth. A pull partner contacts other WINS servers at certain times and requests copies of their data. In Figure 8.2, notice that you can set the time when replication will start, as well as the interval between replication periods. By default, your WINS server will begin the pulling service and will retry a pull three times before it abandons the function. A persistent connection means that WINS will use TCP to obtain WINS information from a partner.

FIGURE 8.2   Setting replication options

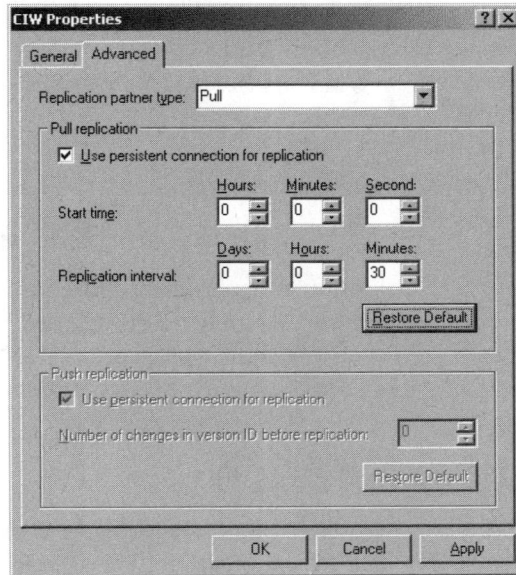

In the Replication Partner Type drop-down box, select Pull. Leave the Use Persistent Connection for Replication check box selected, and leave the spinners at the default Replication Interval of 30 Minutes with a Start Time of midnight.

Server Message Blocks

You have already used SMB without realizing it. Every time you establish a share, you are using the SMB protocol. SMB is a Microsoft-specific protocol for communicating across networks. Microsoft uses SMB to establish file and print shares, as well as execute commands and named pipes using TCP-based connections.

Using a *named pipe*, a process on Machine A, for example, can communicate information to a process on Machine B. The primary benefit of a named pipe is that any process on a remote or local system can access this information without regard to how the original process on Machine A was created. As long as a process knows the name of the named pipe, it can access the information. Named pipes are also known as first in, first out (FIFO) processing.

Microsoft uses SMB to perform name resolution. One of the benefits of SMB is that it allows many different network types to communicate, including the following:

- Windows 9x, Me, NT, 2000, and XP
- DEC networks
- Samba servers (Linux systems)
- Client/server IBM networking, including IBM's Warp products

Microsoft has publicized SMB as Common Internet File System (CIFS). The only difference between CIFS and SMB is that you do not establish printer shares with CIFS.

The Samba Service

The *Samba* service allows Linux systems to participate in all elements of Windows networking. It is the premier service for interoperability between Linux and Windows systems. The name Samba indicates that this service allows Linux to communicate via SMB. Using Samba, you can do the following:

- Configure your Linux system to act as a WINS client or server.
- Configure a Linux system to act as a Windows 2000–compatible file and print server.
- Enable your Linux systems to participate in a Windows NT or 2000 domain authentication scheme.
- Deploy Linux systems to obtain backups of Windows systems.

In this section, you will learn how to configure Samba for a Linux system. Let's begin by taking a look at the files you will be working with.

Samba Files

Samba consists of two daemons and several files. The two daemons are as follows.

Installing Samba

If Samba is not installed during the system setup of Red Hat Linux, you will need to install several packages. For example, if you are installing version 2.2.2-10, you will need to install the following:

- samba-common-2.2.2-10 (files used by the Samba server and by the client)

- samba-client-2.2.2-10 (software such as smbclient and smbmount)

- samba-2.2.2-10 (the actual Samba server)

- samba-swat-2.2.2-10 (installs SWAT)

Some versions of Samba install SWAT automatically. Many newer versions of Samba require that you install the SWAT package separately. See www .samba.org for detailed Samba installation instructions such as the following: Look at your /etc/services. What is defined at port 139/tcp? If nothing is defined, then add a line like this: netbios-ssn 139/tcp. Similarly for 137/udp you should have an entry like netbios-ns 137/udp.

- /usr/sbin/nmbd, which provides NetBIOS names over the network

- /usr/sbin/smbd, which provides services, such as shares and printing, over the network

You'll find the Samba configuration files in the /etc/samba/ directory. They include the following:

- /etc/samba/smb.conf, which is the main configuration file. You can edit this file directly, or use a utility such as Samba Web Administration Tool SWAT. (We'll look at SWAT in the next section.)

- /etc/samba/smbusers, which provides the names of those who are allowed to administer Samba.

- /etc/samba/smbpasswd, which contains the names of users to which smbd refers when asked to enforce user-level access control. Samba will generate this file if it is not already present.

- /etc/rc.d/init.d/smb, which is an initialization script found in many Linux flavors. Instead of starting and stopping the system using /usr/ sbin/nmbd, /usr/sbin/smbd, and the kill command, you can use the

/etc/rc.d/init.d/smb script. For example, to start all Samba dae-mons, you can issue the following command: /etc/rc.d/init.d/ smb start. To stop Samba, you can issue the following command: /etc/rc.d/init.d/smb stop.

All Linux and Unix flavors use these daemons and files, though they may store them in different locations.

The Samba Web Administration Tool (SWAT)

One of the services you can use to configure Samba is the *Samba Web Administration Tool (SWAT)*. This service resides on the computer running Samba and provides a convenient GUI interface for configuring Samba. You can use any web browser to access SWAT. Once you access the GUI, you can use your mouse and keyboard to enter desired values in the text fields that SWAT provides. SWAT will then accept your commands, interpret them, and update the /etc/samba/smb.conf file accordingly. If you do not use SWAT, you will have to edit the /etc/samba/smb.conf file directly using a text editor such as vi, pico, or emacs.

> **NOTE** SWAT can update all files in the /etc/samba/ directory, except for the smbusers and smbpasswd files.

To access SWAT on a particular host, enter the system's IP address or host name in a web browser, making sure to specify the proper port. By default, SWAT is configured to use port 901. For example, to access SWAT on the host named james.ciwcertified.com, enter the following URL in any web browser:

http://james.ciwcertified.com:901

Before you can access SWAT, however, you will have to configure it to accept connections.

Configuring SWAT to Accept Connections

Although SWAT comes with Samba installation files, you must edit two files to allow it to accept connections. First, you need an entry in the /etc/ services file, which is used to pair ports to services used on Linux systems, that tells your system which port SWAT will use. The default port for Swat is TCP port 901, although you can use any port not in use by another service.

If port 901 is already used by some other service, choose another port number higher than 1023. The default entry should read as follows:

```
swat 901/tcp
```

Once you have confirmed that the /etc/services file is using port 901 (or any other port you want to use), you then need to edit the /etc/xinetd.d/swat file, which is a file that is used by the xinetd daemon. You will learn more about xinetd later in this book. For now, it is important to understand that xinetd is used to run various daemons, including FTP, POP3, IMAP, and of course SWAT. Because xinetd is used to start other daemons, it is often called the "super daemon." The contents of this file should appear exactly as in the following example:

```
# description: SWAT is the Samba Web Admin Tool. Use SWAT \
#      to configure your Samba server. To use SWAT, \
#      connect to port 901 with your favorite web browser.
service swat
{
    disable = no
    port  = 901
    socket_type    = stream
    wait  = no
    only_from = localhost
    user  = root
    server = /usr/sbin/swat
    log_on_failure = USERID
}
```

The key entries in this file are read disable = no and only_from. If the disable entry reads disable = yes, no one can access SWAT. The second entry should read only_from = localhost, not because it limits access to everyone but the local system, but because this entry allows the SWAT binary (/usr/sbin/swat) to function locally on the system. You can edit the /etc/xinetd.d/swat file using any text editor. It is vital to understand, however, that once you edit this file, you must restart `xinetd` so that it will re-read all the files in the `/etc/xinetd.d/` directory. If you fail to restart `xinetd`, your changes will not be read, and you will not be able to use SWAT.

Finally, notice that the `/etc/xinetd.d/swat` file contains the following line:

```
only_from = localhost
```

If this line is present, you will be able to use Samba only from the local system. To allow all hosts to access SWAT, simply comment the line out by placing a # in front of it. Do not forget to restart `xinetd` after commenting out this line. If you want to allow only a certain host to connect to SWAT, you can enter an IP address or host name in the `only_from =` entry.

SWAT and *inetd*

Older systems do not use the `xinetd` superdaemon. Rather, they use `inetd`. Unlike `xinetd`, you configure `inetd` by editing only one file, `/etc/inetd.conf`. Open the file using a text editor, and then search for a line that references SWAT:

```
swat stream tcp nowait.400 root /usr/sbin/swat swat
```

The details of this line are not important to this discussion. However, you need to make sure that this line is not commented out (that is, that it does not have a # in front of it). If the line is commented out, remove the # character, save your changes, and then restart `inetd`:

```
/etc/rc.d/init.d/inetd restart
```

You will then be able to access SWAT so that you can then use it to configure Samba.

Using SWAT

Now that you know to configure SWAT so that it accepts connections, you can use it to configure Samba. Using any web browser, begin the authentication process, as shown in Figure 8.3.

Once you authenticate properly, you can use SWAT to edit the files in the `/etc/samba/` directory. Figure 8.4 shows SWAT's introductory screen.

FIGURE 8.3   The SWAT configuration interface in Netscape Navigator

FIGURE 8.4   Using SWAT to configure Samba

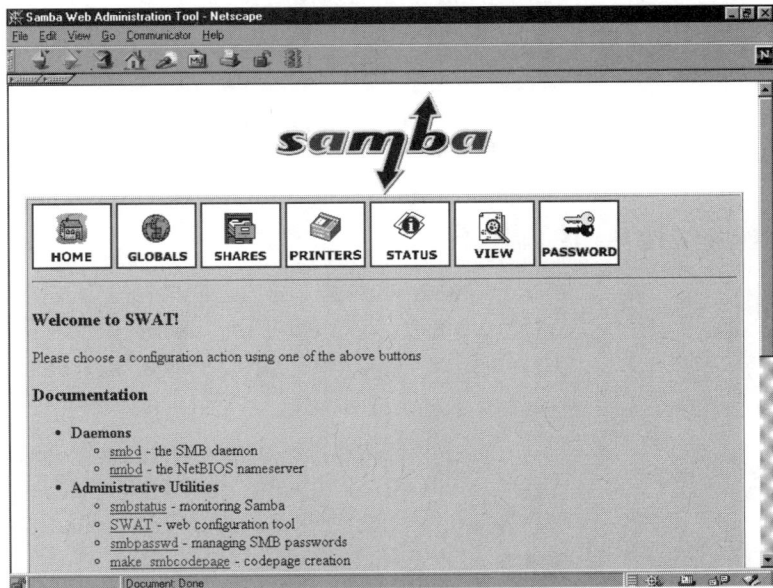

Clicking an icon on this introductory screen opens a new screen that you can use to configure Samba:

- Clicking Home displays documentation that helps you use SWAT to configure Samba.

- Clicking Globals displays a screen on which you can configure the workgroup name, as well as configure the server to become a WINS server or client. On this screen you can also set security options, create guest accounts, and configure logging.

- Clicking Shares opens a screen on which you can create and define shares. You can also specify which users will be allowed to access the shares you create.

- Clicking Printers opens a screen on which you can set options to share printers with Windows systems.

- Clicking Status opens a screen on which you can stop and restart smbd and nmbd. You can also monitor access to the system from this screen.

- Clicking View opens up a screen that displays the raw contents of the /etc/samba/smb.conf file.

- Clicking Password opens a screen on which you can create a new user name and password for Samba administrators. By default, when you authenticate with Samba, you use the user name and password for the root account.

Now, let's see how you can configure Samba so that it can participate in a WINS network.

Samba and WINS

Using Samba, you can configure a Linux host as either a WINS server or a WINS client. To create a WINS server, you simply add the following line to the global section of the /etc/samba/smb.conf file:

```
wins support = Yes
```

To do the same thing in SWAT, first authenticate with SWAT, and then click Globals. Scroll down to the WINS Options section and change the WINS Support drop-down box to Yes. Your system will then act as a WINS server.

A LAN can have only one Linux Samba server running WINS on it. This rule also applies to a WAN. Although a Microsoft WINS server can have more than one server, the Linux server is more powerful. If you have more than one WINS server, resolution will fail.

After making this change, scroll to the top of the Globals section, and click the Commit Changes button. After doing so, your Linux host will begin to act as a WINS server.

You can then configure your Samba server so that it belongs to the company workgroup. By default, all Samba servers are configured to belong to the MYGROUP group. It is likely that your company will have its own workgroup name. Remember, after you make any changes you will have to click the Commit Changes button.

By default, Linux servers refer to the /etc/hosts file. Once you modify the /etc/samba/smb.conf code, you can change the Name Resolve Order value as shown:

`name resolve order = wins lmhosts host bcast`

Remember that whenever you make a change to the /etc/samba/smb .conf file, you will have to restart Samba. This change makes it possible for the server to use WINS first, rather than referring to a text file or to NetBIOS broadcasts.

To change the Name Resolve Order value in SWAT, make sure that you are still accessing the Globals section, and then click the Advanced view button. You will see that many more options are now available. Scroll down to the Protocol Options section to find the Name Resolve Order section, and enter the appropriate values. When you are finished, commit your changes so that the /etc/samba/smb.conf file is re-read.

The benefit of making a Linux host a client to a WINS server is that a Linux system can engage in name resolution to legacy networks running Windows NT and 2000 that do not use DNS. In short, with Samba, a Linux server can behave like a standard Windows system, which will automatically inform the WINS server that it is on the network.

As you saw earlier in this chapter, without Samba, an administrator must assign a static mapping in the Windows WINS server in order to get a Linux system to participate in WINS. If a system is constantly moved from one subnet to another, you can begin to see how inconvenient a static mapping can be.

Configuring a Linux Server as a WINS Client

You can configure your Linux system as a WINS client by directly editing the /etc/samba/smb.conf file and adding the IP address of your WINS server. For example, if your WINS server has the IP address of 192.168.4.2, you can add the following line in the global section of smb.conf using any text editor:

```
wins server = 192.168.4.2
```

After adding this line, restart Samba so that it recognizes the change.

In SWAT, you simply access the Globals section again, and enter the proper IP address in the WINS server section. Click the Globals button, and then scroll down to the WINS Options section. Enter the IP address of the WINS server in the WINS Server section.

> You can also change the Name Resolve Order value for your WINS client using the exact same steps as those given earlier for the WINS server.

Troubleshooting WINS in Linux Systems

When configuring a Linux host to become a WINS server or client, you will very likely have to determine if Samba is working properly. Primarily, you will have to query WINS servers to ensure that name resolution is occurring as you expect. To help you do this, Samba provides the /usr/bin/nmblookup command. It is designed to map WINS names to IP addresses. You can also use it to display a list of all the WINS clients and servers on your network:

```
host# nmblookup \*
10. 10.199.130 *<00>
10. 10.199.137 *<00>
10. 10.199.65 *<00>
10. 10.199.245 *<00>
10. 10.199.66 *<00>
10. 10.199.251 *<00>
10.10.199.200 *<00>
10.10.199.67 *<00>
```

This example uses nmblookup to query all hosts on the network. The asterisk (*) is a "wildcard" character that tells nmblookup to query all hosts on the network. The backslash (\) is necessary so that the Linux shell does not interpret the wildcard as a local shell command, which would have `nmblookup` read all files in the system's local directory, instead of all hosts on the local network

You can also use `nmblookup` to query the database of a server. Suppose, for example, you have a server named `wins1` that has `sandi` as a client, but you do not know the IP address. You could query the WINS database of `wins1` to find the IP address:

```
host# nmblookup -U wins1 -R 'sandi'
10. 10.199.137 sandi<00>
```

Linux Samba Clients

All Windows systems have built-in support to act as Samba clients: In Windows 2000 and XP systems, this client is used whenever you double-click the My Network Places icon. Similarly, this client is used when you use the Windows Explorer Map Network Drive utility. Linux systems have several Samba clients. The following are the most reliable:

- `smbclient` is a text-based, interactive program that operates much like an FTP client. You can use it to connect to a system and then navigate through directories and download files.

- `smbmount` is an application you can use to access SMB-based shares on remote systems. However, `smbmount` does not behave like an FTP client. Rather, `smbmount` accesses a remote share and makes it appear as if it actually resides on the local hard drive.

Using *smbclient*

The `smbclient` program begins an interactive session with a Windows system or a Linux system running Samba. To establish a connection with a remote Windows system (or remote Linux/Unix system running Samba, for that matter), you must use smbclient and specify the host name, share name, and your user name, using a modified form of the Universal Naming Convention (UNC). Whereas the standard Windows-based UNC requires the use of backslash characters, `smbclient` uses forward-slash characters. You can then specify a Linux user name by using the -U option. Success is indicated by a specific prompt provided by Samba (for example, `smb: \>`). Following is a sample `smbclient` session that accesses a system named student10.

```
host# /usr/bin/smbclient //student10/ddrive -U james
Added interface ip=192.168.4.1 bcast=192.168.4.255
↳nmask=255.255.255.0
Password:
Domain=Stanger OS=[Windows 5.0] Server=[Windows 2000 LAN
↳Manager]
smb: \>
```

The –U option allows you to specify a Windows 2000 or Samba-based username, which will likely be different from the username under which you are currently logged.

While in smbclient, you can use the following commands:

- get retrieves a file.
- mget retrieves multiple files in a directory.
- put places a file.
- dir and ls list files and directories.
- cd changes directories.
- quit ends a session.
- help *command* lists information for a specific topic.

You can specify your password using the % character. Doing so excuses you from entering your password:

```
host# /usr/bin/smbclient //student10/files -U
↳james%password
Added interface ip=192.168.4.1 bcast=192.168.4.255
↳nmask=255.255.255.0
Domain=Stanger OS=[Windows 5.0] Server=[Windows 2000 LAN
↳Manager]
smb: \>
```

The smbclient command mounts the //student10/files share using the username of james and the password of password.

Using *smbmount*

The smbmount application is not interactive; as discussed earlier, you use it to mount an SMB share onto a local directory. Whenever a remote share is mounted onto a local directory, the local directory is called a *mount point*. A mount point can be any directory on your system, although it is wise to create an empty directory, rather than using one that contains content. For example, you never want to use the /etc/ or /root directory as a mount point. Instead, create an empty directory off the system root (/) that you can use. For example, create a directory named /samba, and use it only when you want to mount a remote directory.

Using smbmount is relatively straightforward. For example, if you have a local directory named /samba, you can issue the following command to mount a remote share:

```
host# /usr/bin/smbmount //student10/ddrive /samba -o
↳username=james%password
Added interface ip=192.168.4.1 bcast=192.168.4.0
↳nmask=255.255.255.0
host#
```

This command sequence shows that the user has executed smbmount so that it accesses a host named student10 and mounted its drive share. This drive is now accessible through the local /samba mount point. Remember, the /samba directory must first exist, because smbmount requires a local directory to mount the remote share. Also, the /samba directory should have permissions only for specific users on your system. Notice that the -o option is used. This option tells smbmount to accept the username and password pair as parameters. If you are accessing Linux systems using Samba, you do not need to use this option. However, when accessing Windows-based SMB shares, you will need to use it. If you do not use it, the mounting attempt will fail.

Once the directory is mounted, any user with the proper permissions to access the directory can then use the standard cd command and access the local mount point. Thus, using smbmount can be somewhat more convenient for local Linux users; instead of having to initiate an FTP-like session with smbclient, users can instead simply refer to the remote share as if it were a local resource.

To unmount a directory that has been mounted by smbmount, use the umount command. For example, to unmount the /samba directory, issue the following command:

```
host# umount /samba/
```

If a user is currently accessing the /samba directory, you will not be able to unmount it, even as root. However, you can forcibly remove a user using the fuser command. For example, to forcibly remove all users from the /samba directory, issue the following command:

```
fuser -k /samba
```

Levels of Access in Samba

Samba can imitate all functions of a Windows NT primary domain controller and most of the functions of a Windows 2000 domain controller. You can configure Samba in any number of ways. Because Samba is so scalable, it is also rather complex. Accordingly, its creators realized that they needed to provide certain basic levels of access in order to simplify administration. The most common levels of access in Samba are share, user, server, and domain.

Share   Establishes a password-protected share similar to a share on a Windows 9x or Me system. This access level is the least secure, because it provides no user-level access control at all. Nevertheless, this level of access is quite common, because it is the easiest to use. After all, no users have to be created; all the systems administrator has to do is use SWAT to create a share, and all users who can access the network will be allowed access to it. The primary limitation of this level of access is that it does not allow you to limit access to resources by username and password.

User   Allows the creation of shares that provide access only to certain users. A user-based Samba server (described previously) keeps its own user database in the /etc/samba/smbusers and /etc/samba/smbpasswd files. As with almost any more secure solution, this option is more difficult to configure. First, you must synchronize the /etc/passwd and /etc/shadow files with the /etc/samba/smbuser and /etc/samba/smbpasswd files. If you set user-level access in Samba, you will also have to encrypt transmissions. You will learn more about user-level access and encryption later in the "Samba and Windows Systems" section. The user-level option is quite popular, because it allows a Samba server to imitate a stand-alone Windows NT or 2000 server, which is one that authenticates users using its own user database, rather than accessing a central stand-alone server.

Server   Allows authenticating a user. This remote server can be another Linux system or a Windows NT or 2000 server. Encryption must be enabled on your Samba system in order for your Windows 2000 server to communicate in this access level. Server-level authentication is useful because it allows users to be centralized on a stand-alone server, yet allows resources (for example, files and printers) to be distributed across multiple servers.

Domain Queries a Windows NT primary domain controller (PDC) or Windows 2000 domain controller (DC) to obtain passwords. Encryption must be enabled on your Samba system in order for your Windows 2000 server to communicate in this access level. This level of access is quite similar to server-level access, except that instead of querying another member server, a PDC or domain controller is queried.

Samba and Windows Systems

Samba defaults to using unencrypted passwords, which immediately limits its usefulness. Systems such as Windows NT and Windows 2000 require the use of encrypted passwords in order to connect to your user-based Samba shares. You can, as discussed earlier, create simple password-protected shares. However, it is very likely that you would not feel comfortable placing sensitive information in such weakly protected shares.

In order to allow Samba to work with Windows NT and 2000 servers, for example, you can do one of two things:

- Configure Samba to expect encrypted passwords.

- Change the Registry values in your Windows systems so that they send unencrypted passwords.

> **NOTE** Whenever a system sends unencrypted passwords, they are said to send cleartext passwords.

The second option is clearly problematic because sending passwords in cleartext will degrade your network's security. Also, editing all the Registries in all your Windows systems can be somewhat daunting, especially if you are working in a large organization. The best solution is to configure Samba to encrypt passwords.

To encrypt Samba transmissions so that Windows 2000 systems can access shares on Linux systems, you must do the following:

- Add two lines about password encryption to the /etc/samba/ smb.conf file.

- Synchronize the host's logon account database files (/etc/passwd and /etc/shadow) with the /etc/samba/smbpasswd file using the /usr/sbin/smbpasswd program.

To add support for encryption, edit /etc/samba/smb.conf so that the two values exist exactly as shown:

```
encrypt passwords = yes
smb passwd file = /etc/samba/smbpasswd
```

You will have to scroll down the file until you find these values.

The smbadduser command maps Linux user information found in /etc/passwd and /etc/shadow to Samba usernames and passwords, which are compatible with Windows 2000. This program works only on accounts that are defined in /etc/passwd and /etc/shadow. If, for example, you want to ensure that the administrator account of a Windows 2000 system can log on to your system, you can issue the following command:

```
host# /usr/bin/smbadduser administrator:administrator
```

The name preceding the colon must be the Linux account name. The name following the colon must be the Windows 2000 account name. This command adds the user administrator to /etc/samba/smbpasswd. You must then use smbpasswd to add a password to the account you have just created using smbadduser.

As with smbadduser, the smbpasswd command works only on accounts defined in /etc/passwd and /etc/shadow. For example, after you add the user sandi to your system using useradd or adduser, you can issue the following command:

```
host# /usr/bin/smbpasswd -a sandi
New SMB password:
Retype new SMB password:
Added user sandi.
Password changed for user sandi.
host#
```

The -a option adds the username to the /etc/samba/smbpasswd file. After you add the name, you need not use the -a option again. Once the sandi account is synchronized with Samba, Windows 2000 users can access shares on your Linux system.

NOTE If you use the -a option with smbpasswd, you need not use smbadduser. For example, the smbpasswd -a james command adds the name james to /etc/samba/smbuser and also places a password in /etc/samba/smbpasswd.

Linux File Sharing in Samba

Samba ships with a default share called homes, which allows users who have already been defined to use smbclient or smbmount to access their home directories via SMB. As soon as Samba is successfully started, the home directories for all users (including root) are automatically shared. For example, the user named james will have his /home/james directory automatically shared. However, this share will not appear on browser lists.

To access a home share for a specific user, you specify the name and password of that user. Samba will then automatically log the user on to the appropriate home directory. For example, suppose you want to use smbclient to log on to a system named blake as a user named james, who has the password Tra$ning1. You issue the following command:

```
host# /usr/bin/smbclient //blake/homes -U james%Tra$ning1
```

Because Samba has created the homes share, you will automatically be logged on to blake as james and be able to access any files in that user's home directory. Notice that you didn't specify the share of /home/james. If you are using a Windows 2000 system and are logged on as james with the password of Tra$ning1, choose Start ➢ Run to open the Run dialog box, enter \\blake\homes in the Open box, and press Enter. You will then be logged on to the james home directory. If you are logged on to the local system as another user, you will be asked to provide the correct username and password.

Creating a New Share in Samba

When creating a share in Samba, you must carefully consider the permissions imposed by the Linux operating system. Perhaps an example will help. Samba can impose its own permissions onto a share, but it must work in concert with directory permissions. This arrangement is no different from making sure that your NTFS permissions do not conflict with the share permissions you set on a Windows 2000 system. Just as in a Windows system, if Samba permissions and Linux directory permissions conflict, the most restrictive combination applies. For example, if a directory has full permissions (for example, 777), and a Samba share has read-only permissions, the share will not allow anyone to write to the directory.

Suppose you want to share a directory named /share on the network. You will give this share a truly original name: share. Furthermore, you will allow only the user named alan access to that share (that is, no one else will be allowed access to that directory). To do so, follow these steps:

1. Create the /share directory on your Linux system using the mkdir command.

2. Give the /share directory adequate permissions so that the user named alan can access it and write to it. To do so, you must do the following:

   a. Make sure that the /share directory is owned by the user named alan using the chown alan /share command.

   b. Make sure that the /share directory is owned by the group named alan using the chgrp alan /share command.

   c. Use the chmod 660 /share command to change permissions on the directory so that only alan can read it. Adequate permissions include read and write permissions for alan's user and group name, but no permissions for any other user:

Now, the directory is secure, in the sense that only alan can read and write to it.

You are now ready to configure Samba so that it will allow alan (and no other user) to write to the /share directory. Remember, you have only configured Linux permissions for the /share directory. You have not yet configured Samba to allow write access. To configure Samba, follow these steps:

1. Access SWAT, and click the Shares icon to open the Share Parameters screen.

2. Enter the share name of share in the text field next to the Create Share button. This name represents only the share name. It does not represent the directory you will use (/share). Enter **alan** in the text field, and click the Create Share button to open a new Share Parameters screen.

3. This screen contains various options that allow you to choose the specific directory to share, as well as determine if the share is writeable. Find the Base Options section, and enter the /share directory path.

4. In the Security Options section, find the Writeable drop-down box. By default, it reads No. To allow the user named alan to write to the share, change it to Yes.

5. Specify the path to the /share directory, and then click the Commit Changes button to create the share. There is no need to restart Samba. The share will be made immediately. Assuming that you have configured the Samba system to encrypt passwords and allow user-based access, you can now use any system to access this share. However, only the user named alan will be able to access and write to this share.

Figure 8.5 shows what the SWAT screen looks like when creating this share.

FIGURE 8.5 Changing share parameters in SWAT

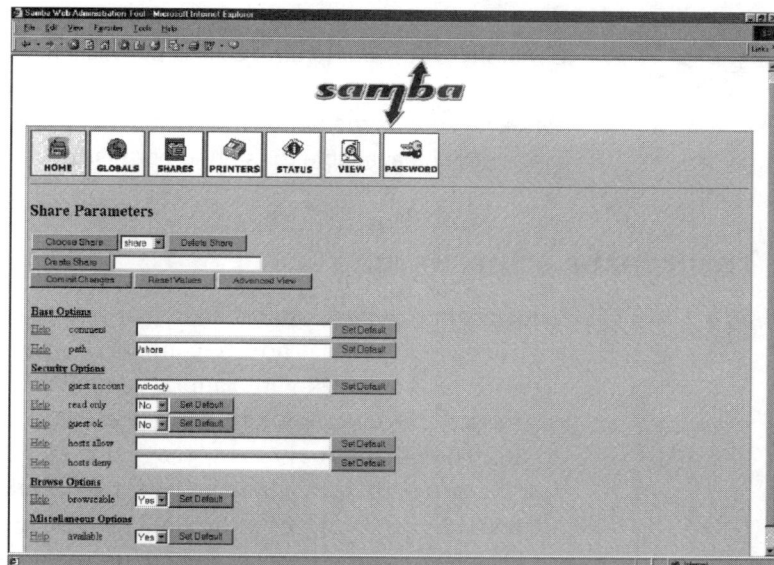

Additional Options for Creating Shares

Additional options are available when creating a share. For example, by default, all shares are readily seen by any SMB client. However, you could decide to hide a share so that it does not appear in browsing lists. To do so, change the Browseable option on the Share Parameters screen so that it reads No. The share created in Figure 8.5 is, in fact, browseable.

Now, consider what happens if you change the Guest OK drop-down box to Yes. Doing so tells Samba to allow all users to access the share. If Linux directory permissions allow, this one change would allow all users to access the share. However, remember that in our example the share you created allows access only to alan, because the Linux directory permissions forbid all users but alan to access the /share directory. In this case, the Linux directory permissions are the most restrictive, and it wouldn't matter if you changed the Read Only drop-down box from No to Yes.

However, suppose you use the chmod command to give full access to the /share directory. If the Read Only drop-down box reads Yes, everyone is allowed access to the share. Finally, consider what would happen if you change the permissions again. Now, suppose that you change the Read Only drop-down box to No, but you use your Linux directory permissions to allow access to all users. In this case, access is still denied to all users, because the Samba daemon overrides the Linux directory permissions.

> Generally, you want to limit access permissions to defined users only. You also want only certain users and/or groups to be able to read or write to the share. Of course, the options you set depend on the situation, and you have many options available for setting permissions.

Troubleshooting Samba

You now have a basic understanding of how to configure Samba in a WINS environment, as well as how to configure Samba to provide shares across a network. As you work with Samba, you will want to troubleshoot it and ensure that all your changes are being read by the nmbd and smbd daemons. To do this, you use the /usr/sbin/testparm utility. This application reads the /etc/samba/smb.conf file and reports how Samba is currently configured. It is a text-only utility, which means that no GUI interface is provided. You will simply see the output of the command on your screen. The program's output will inform you about shares and printers defined on the system. You can also use the output to discover problems.

Using testparm is usually quite straightforward, as shown in the following syntax:

```
host# testparm
```

As testparm runs, it will present its output on two separate screens. The first screen will contain a list of existing shares that the system is configured to present on the network. The second screen, which displays after you press enter, shows all the current Samba settings. Samba entries can be long and complex, so it is best to run testparm as follows:

```
host# testparm > testparm.txt
```

Press Enter twice. You have now saved all the output into the `testparm`
`.txt` file. You can now open this file in a text editor and learn more about how
the daemon is configured. You can use various options with `testparm`, but
they are not tested on the CIW Server Administrator exam. You must, however, remember its usefulness as a troubleshooting tool.

Summary

In this chapter, you used WINS and Samba to resolve and manage names.
You learned how the NetBIOS naming convention works, as well as how SMB
allows systems to share resources over networks. You learned how to configure WINS using the Linux-based Samba service using the SWAT configuration
tool. You also used SWAT to create and manage Samba shares.

We also explored some additional name resolution options for LANs and
WANs. With this information, you can now implement and manage WINS
and use Samba to create a WINS server in Linux. You should also be able to
configure Samba systems to use Windows 2000 authentication and to create
and manage shares using Samba.

In sum, using these new skills, you can now integrate Linux with
Windows 2000.

Exam Essentials

**Be able to explain the basics of the NetBIOS naming convention and Net-
BIOS name resolution in LANS and WANs, including the use of WINS.**
A NetBIOS name can be a maximum of 16 characters and resolves a
friendly name to an IP address. In NT 4 and Windows 2000, the sixteenths
character identifies the services or workgroup/domain membership of the
computer. The first 15 characters identify the NetBIOS name of the computer. This name must be unique on the network. Other computers resolve
this name by using in turn previously resolved NetBIOS names in the Net-
BIOS cache, a WINS server, a broadcast on the local subnet, an `lmhosts`
file, and a `hosts` file and finally by querying a DNS server. Among these
NetBIOS name resolution methods, a WINS server and the `lmhosts` files
are primary. Clients configured to use a WINS server automatically register
their names when they boot up and deregister their names during normal

shutdown. By querying the WINS server, clients can find computers on local and remote subnets, including domain controllers used for logon. WINS clients on other subnets can locate non–WINS-registering clients such as Linux guests, if a static mapping for that host is entered in the WINS database.

Be able integrate a Linux server into a Windows 2000 domain using Samba and SWAT to allow the Linux system to become WINS clients or servers, to authenticate to a Windows 2000 domain, and to create file and print shares that are available to Windows 2000 clients. Samba also uses the SMB protocol to create shares. Samba consists of the nmbd daemon that provides NetBIOS names over the network and the smbd daemon that provides file and print shares. The smb.conf file is the main configuration file in the etc/samba directory. The smbpasswd file contains authorized Samba users, and the smbusers file contains authorized Samba administrators. You administer Samba using the Samba Web Administration Tool (SWAT). By default, Samba administrators connect to SWAT by entering the URL for the server plus the port in a browser, for example, http://www.greenderby.com:901.

Key Terms

Before taking the exam, you should be familiar with the following terms:

lmhosts file	rpm command
named pipes	Samba
nbtstat command	Samba Web Administration Tool (SWAT)
NetBIOS names	Server Message Block (SMB) protocol
NetBIOS cache	smbd daemon
netstat command	static mapping
nmbd daemon	testparm command
nmblookup command	WINS

Review Questions

1. Jonathan is director of IS for Great Escapes Theme Park. He uses a legacy NetBIOS accounting application on Windows 2000. He also is deploying Exchange 2000, an application that is integrated with Active Directory, and he has Windows 98 dial-in RRAS (Routing and Remote Access Services) clients. For which of these elements, might Jonathan want to use WINS to support name resolution? Choose two.

   A. Active Directory

   B. Exchange 2000

   C. Windows 98

   D. Legacy application

2. Jonathan is director of IS for Great Escapes Theme Park that uses Windows 2000 and TCP/IP for networking. His company just bought Asteroid World, which has been networking using NetBEUI and using NetBIOS applications and WINS. When Jonathan initially integrates their networks so that he can centrally manage both, which protocol can Jonathan shed?

   A. NetBEUI

   B. TCP/IP

   C. NetBIOS

   D. WINS

3. Brian need to resolve NetBIOS names to IP addresses in order to connect to SMB shares on an NT 4 server. Which two of the following would be the most useful?

   A. WINS server

   B. DNS server

   C. hosts file

   D. lmhosts file

4. Jason has a Linux system with Samba installed. He would like to configure this system as a WINS client. How can he do this? Choose the best two answers.

   A. By using My Network Places

   B. By using SWAT

   C. By editing the `/etc/drivers/samba.conf` file directly

   D. By editing the `/etc/samba/smb.conf` file directly

5. Heather has a Linux server that needs to share resources of an NT 4 WAN. What can members of the NT 4 WAN use to find the Linux server?

   A. Static mapping in WINS

   B. Reverse DNS lookup zone

   C. WINS replication

   D. WINS proxy agent

6. Heather supports a pure Windows 2000 network that has been upgraded from NT 4. To reduce network traffic, which protocol and service can she remove? Choose two.

   A. SMB

   B. NetBIOS over TCP/IP

   C. WINS

   D. DNS

7. Jason wants to tighten security on his firewall so that Internet clients outside the firewall cannot access SMB shares inside the firewall. Which NetBIOS ports should Jason disable?

   A. TCP 80 and 21

   B. TCP 25 and 110

   C. UDP 137 and 138, and TCP 139

   D. UDP 53 and 119, and TCP 443

8. Jason wants to tighten security on his firewall so that Internet clients outside the firewall cannot access SMB shares on his web server. What can he use to see which ports are active on the web server?

   A. nbtstat -R

   B. ping

   C. ipconfig /all

   D. tracert

   E. nbtstat -a

9. Mike updates the lmhosts file on an NT 4 server to point toward a new domain controller. Without rebooting the server, Mike wants to purge the remote NetBIOS name cache and reload new information from the updated lmhosts file. Which command should Mike execute?

   A. nbtstat -R

   B. ping

   C. ipconfig /all

   D. tracert

   E. netstat -a

10. Mike is trying to troubleshoot an NT 4 Exchange 5.5 server. He issues the ipconfig command to determine that the server's IP address is 192.168.10.9. He issues the nbtstat -A 192.168.10.9 command. What information can Mike gain from this command? Choose three.

   A. The status of the IS, DS, and MTA services on the Exchange server

   B. The NetBIOS name of the Exchange server

   C. The MAC address of the Exchange server

   D. The workgroup or domain of the Exchange server

11. Mike has an NT 4 routed network that uses WINS but not DNS for name resolution. A Unix server has just been added to subnet A. What should be configured to allow clients on subnet B to find the Unix server? Choose the best option.

    A. lmhosts file on the Unix server

    B. hosts file on the Unix server

    C. A static mapping on the Unix server

    D. lmhosts file on the WINS server

    E. hosts file on the WINS server

    F. A static mapping on the WINS server

12. A Windows 2000 Professional computer on a Windows 2000 network is trying to map a network drive using the Net Use f: \\london\ common command. The net use command uses NetBIOS names. Which of the following will the Windows 2000 Professional computer use in turn to attempt to resolve NetBIOS names?

    A. NetBIOS cache, WINS, broadcast, lmhosts file, hosts file, DNS server

    B. NetBIOS cache, WINS, broadcast, lmhosts file

    C. NetBIOS cache, broadcast, WINS, lmhosts file, hosts file, DNS server

    D. WINS, broadcast, lmhosts file, hosts file, DNS server

13. Because of limited bandwidth between Calcutta and Redmond, Rajesh is scheduling replication between WINS servers in India and the United States to take place only at 5 A.M. Greenwich mean time (GMT). Which type of replication is Rajesh scheduling?

    A. Push

    B. Pull

    C. Snapshot

    D. Transactional

14. Hank has a Linux system that he wants to integrate into a Windows 2000 network. Using Samba, which of the following are possible?

   A. Configure the Linux system to act as a WINS client or server.

   B. Configure the Linux system to act as a file and print server for the Windows 2000 clients.

   C. Enable the Linux system to authenticate to a Windows 2000 domain.

   D. Use the Linux system to administer the Windows 2000 domain.

15. Jessica looks at the /etc/xinetd.d/swat file on the www.tango.com Linux server. It is as follows:

```
 # description: SWAT is the Samba Web Admin Tool. Use
SWAT \
#      to configure your Samba server. To use SWAT, \
#      connect to port 901 with your favorite web
browser.
service swat
{
     disable = no
     port  = 901
     socket_type   = stream
     wait  = no
     only_from = localhost
     user  = root
     server = /usr/sbin/swat
     log_on_failure = USERID
}
```

What URL should SWAT administrators enter in their browser in order to administer the Samba server?

   A. www.tango.com/root

   B. www.tango.com:80

   C. www.tango.com/swat

   D. www.tango.com:901

16. Jessica wants to find out whether Samba has been installed and if it hasn't been installed to install it on her Red Hat Linux computer. Which two commands should Jessica issue?

A. `rpm -qa | grep samba`

B. `vi services`

C. `rpm -ivh samba-2.0.7.21ssl.i386.rpm`

D. `vi swat`

17. Jessica wants to ensure that Samba is using TCP port 901 and that this port is enabled. Which two files should Jessica edit?

A. `ntsysv`

B. `services`

C. `inetpub`

D. `swat`

18. Jessica just edited the `swat` and the `services` file to change the SWAT port from 901 to 1100. Before this new port can be used, which two commands must she issue?

A. `host# nmbd restart`

B. `host# smbd restart`

C. `host# startx`

D. `host# ntsysv`

19. Jessica wants to see which directories and printers are currently shared on a Linux computer running Samba. Which command should Jessica issue?

A. `ntsysv`

B. `linuxconf`

C. `testparm`

D. `linuxshare`

E. `smbserver`

20. Willy wants the Public directory on the RedHat1 server to be accessible to Samba users. He creates this folder and assigns the Linux permissions 660 using chmod. Using SWAT, he then sets the share to Guest OK and Read Only. Anonymous users still cannot access the share. Which of the following Linux permissions should he change to fix this?

A. drwxrwe---

B. dr--r-----

C. drwer----we

D. drw-rw-r--

Answers to Review Questions

1. **C, D.** WINS is used for NetBIOS application support and for legacy clients such as NT 4 and Windows 9x.

2. **A.** Jonathan needs a routable protocol, TCP/IP, but he can shed NetBEUI, a non-routable protocol that cannot be used to tie the two networks together. He needs WINS and NetBIOS for the NetBIOS applications.

3. **A, D.** You use WINS servers and lmhosts files to map NetBIOS names to IP addresses.

4. **B, D.** You can use SWAT to configure Linux as a WINS client, or you can create an entry in the etc/samba/smb.conf file that points toward a valid WINS server.

5. **A.** On the WINS server a static mapping pointing toward the Linux server will allow the NT 4 WINS clients to find the Linux server.

6. **B, C.** NetBIOS over TCP/IP and WINS are no longer needed if legacy clients are no longer supported on a pure Windows 2000 network.

7. **C.** NetBIOS uses UDP ports 137 and 138 and TCP port 139. These should be disabled for inbound packets.

8. **E.** Use the nbtstat -a command to show the active ports on the web server. You can also use a third-party port scanner from outside the firewall.

9. **A.** Mike should use the nbtstat -R (NetBIOS over TCP/IP -Reload) command.

10. **B, C, D.** Mike can determine the NetBIOS name, the MAC address, and the workgroup or domain of the Exchange server.

11. F. Without a static mapping on the WINS server for the Unix server, clients on subnet B will be unable to find the Unix server on subnet A. Routers do not forward NetBIOS broadcasts.

12. A. In turn, the client will try to resolve NetBIOS names using the Net-BIOS cache, WINS server, broadcast, `lmhosts` file, `hosts` file, and DNS server.

13. B. If the available bandwidth is low, use pull replication to schedule WINS replication at slow times.

14. A, B, C. Using Samba, Hank can configure the Linux system as a WINS client or server. The Linux server can also authenticate to the Windows 2000 domain and act as a file and print server.

15. D. In order to connect to the Swat server, administrators should include the port number as part of the URL. Administrators will be limited to connecting locally from the SWAT server itself.

16. A, C. Jessica can find out whether Samba is installed by using the `rpm -qa | grep samba` command. If Samba is not installed, she can install it using the `rpm -ivh samba-2.0.7.21ssl.i386.rpm` command.

17. B, D. Jessica needs to edit the `/etc/services` file and the `etc/xinetd.d/swat` file.

18. A, B. The two Samba daemons are `nmbd`, which provides NetBIOS names over the network, and `smbd`, which provides file and print sharing over the network. When you restart these daemons, the configuration files are re-read.

19. C. The `testparm` command reads the `/etc/samba/smb.conf` file and display a list of existing file and print shares.

20. D. The Other/Nobody user/group used for anonymous access has to be given read access either with a `chmod 661` or with the `r` permission in the third triplet of permissions that represents the Other/Nobody user/group.

Chapter

9

Implementing Internet Services

THE CIW EXAM OBJECTIVE GROUPS COVERED IN THIS CHAPTER:

✓ Implement and control access to Internet services, including but not limited to: FTP and Telnet.

ou now have experience setting up name resolution for your LAN using DNS, WINS, and Samba. This chapter will discuss some other services you can implement and configure, including File Transfer Protocol (FTP), Telnet remote access service, and finger.

FTP is the simplest way to exchange files between computers on the Internet. For example, you can use FTP to upload files to a remote website. You can access FTP from a command line or from a browser, or you can use a third-party graphical program such as WS_FTP Pro (available from www .ipswitch.com). WS_FTP Pro uses side-by-side windows to represent your computer's hard drive and the file structure of the FTP server.

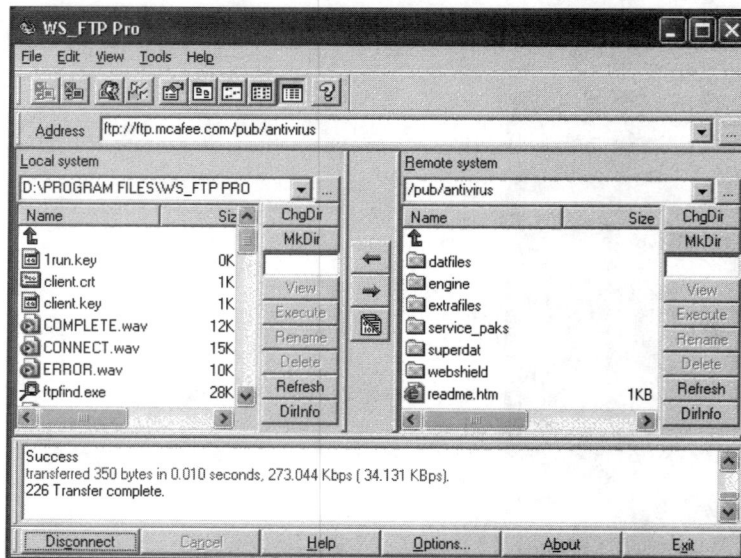

WS_FTP Pro also saves logon information for multiple FTP servers. If you are administering multiple websites, you can easily upload information using the stored addresses and logon information for each website.

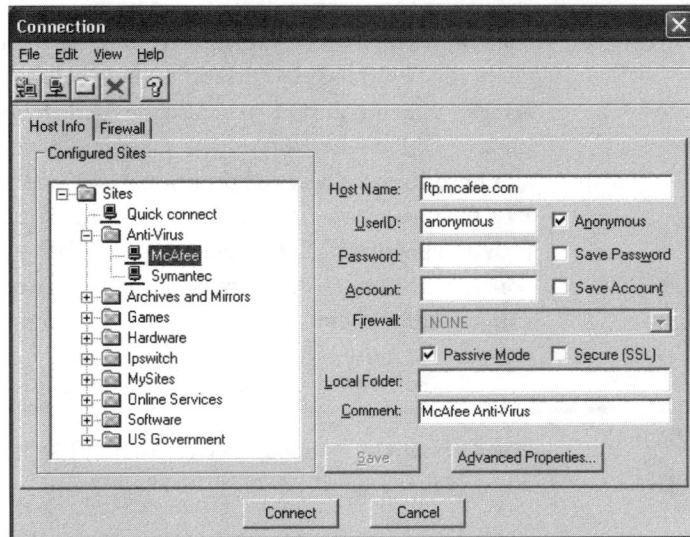

Telnet is another Internet service that you can use to configure a router or to connect to and administer a remote Linux/Unix computer or an NT 4 or Windows 2000 server.

Finger is a Linux/Unix program that you use to request information about a specific user. On some systems, finger reports whether a user is logged in and the user's full name, address, and telephone number.

File Transfer Protocol Servers

FTP exists in two modes—traditional and passive. *Traditional mode* FTP uses two ports: TCP 20 and TCP 21. Port 20 is the data connection (it transports the file you have requested); port 21 is the control connection for the FTP session (it allows commands such as LIST, DIR, PUT, and GET). In traditional mode, the FTP client opens two ephemeral ports. Ephemeral ports are temporary, operating-system assigned ports that the FTP server can detect. The FTP client uses one ephemeral port to connect to the server's port 21 and uses the PORT command to establish the command connection on port 20. The server then connects to the client's second ephemeral port using its own port 20 to transfer data.

In *passive mode*, which has become the industry standard, the FTP client opens two ephemeral ports and then connects to port 21 of the server to create the control connection. Embedded within this connection is a PASV command that allows a passive-enabled FTP server to open an ephemeral port. The FTP client then establishes a connection between its second ephemeral port and the server's ephemeral port to create the data channel. The server then creates a passive TCP connection on an ephemeral port back to the client.

One difference between traditional and passive connections is that in passive FTP the server does not use port 20 for the data connection. Another difference is that in passive FTP, the client initiates both port connections. Passive FTP is considered firewall friendly because many firewalls prohibit a server from using a non-ephemeral port to initiate a connection to an ephemeral port outside the network.

> You can learn more about firewall-friendly FTP from RFC 1579, which is available at www.faqs.org.

Most of today's FTP servers default to passive mode, including servers running Windows 2000 and Red Hat Linux. However, many older clients do not support passive mode FTP, and some clients support only passive mode. Thus, when troubleshooting an FTP connection, consider the client type. The FTP client for Netscape Navigator, for example, uses only passive mode FTP, as does the standard Linux FTP client. Microsoft Internet Explorer and the FTP client for Windows 2000, for example, default to passive mode, but will use traditional FTP connections if necessary.

File Transfer Protocol Clients

Users can access FTP sites anonymously using the default port, and they can access FTP sites using a non-standard port and/or a user login and password. We'll discuss the easiest and most common way to access FTP sites first—anonymous login.

Just as users generally access websites anonymously, they can access FTP sites anonymously using either a browser or the command line. For example, connecting to ftp.mcafee.com using a browser is as easy as opening a browser and entering ftp://ftp.mcafee.com in the Address field.

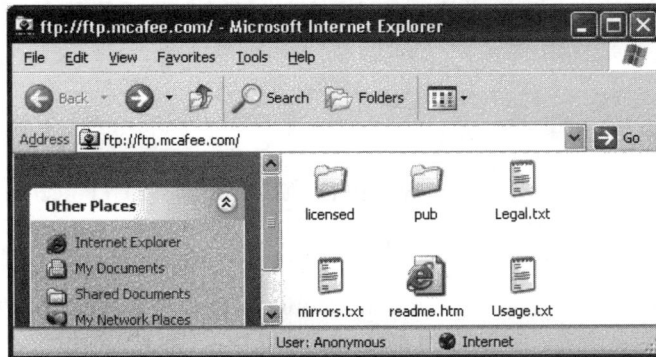

Connecting via the command line is a little more involved as the following graphic illustrates:

User-based FTP generally logs users on to their home directory. When the client accesses an anonymous FTP account, the FTP server applies three restrictions to the session:

- The user is logged on using the system's anonymous account (for example, the FTP account in Linux systems).

- The working directory for the session is a controlled subdirectory of the root directory. This arrangement greatly limits the number of accessible files.

- The file system permissions enforce the anonymous account's privileges on the files it can see.

For example, consider a system with the following directory tree:

```
/var/ftp/pub
/bin
/usr
```

This system has the following FTP account logon home directory:

```
/var/ftp
```

This logon account can see only the pub, bin, and usr directory trees. The /var/ftp directory appears as the / directory. An attempt by the user to change the working directory to the / (root) directory changes to the /home/ftp directory instead.

This design allows the administrator to manage and protect the system from unauthorized access while providing a secure way for files to be extracted and written to the server's disk resources.

Once logged on to an FTP server, you can issue many commands, including the following.

- ls, which lists files

- cd, which changes directories

- get, which downloads a file

- put, which uploads a file

- mget, which allows you to download multiple files or directories

- mput, which allows you to upload multiple files or directories

- ascii, which sets the mode of file transfer to ASCII (this is the default and transmits seven bits per character)

- binary, which sets the mode of file transfer to binary; it transmits all eight bits per byte, thus providing a lesser chance of transmission error, and must be used to transmit files that are not ASCII

- help, which displays all available FTP commands

- bye, which allows you to exit the FTP program (same as quit)

- quit, which allows you to exit the FTP program (same as bye)

You have already seen how Windows 2000 creates an anonymous user account named IUSR_COMPUTERNAME, which has a randomly generated password. This account handles requests from all users. By default, the anonymous account is restricted to the server root, which is C:\inetpub\ ftproot on a system that has Windows 2000 installed on the C:\ drive. The NTFS file system permissions enforce access under the server root folder.

In Linux, the anonymous user account is created as *user name* ftp in the /etc/passwd file. The home directory of the FTP account determines the sub-directory to which the anonymous account will be restricted. Set the password field for the ftp account to * to ensure that no one can access the account except from an ftp client. The Unix file system (ext2fs on Linux), permissions enforce access under the anonymous account's home directory.

Anonymous access using a default port is not the only way to connect to an FTP server. For security, an FTP server can require a username and a password and/or use a non-standard port. In this case, the easiest way to connect is using a third-party FTP client. Many third-party FTP clients allow you to pre-specify a port number so that the clients can work with proxy servers and firewalls. Figure 9.1 shows the configuration screen in the WS_FTP Pro client discussed earlier in this chapter. Each client has its own particular interface, but the principle of specifying alternative ports applies to all.

FIGURE 9.1   Specifying ports in WS_FTP Pro client

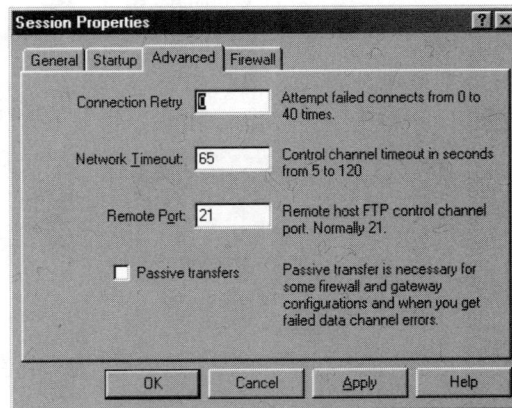

When standard FTP is used, but user authentication is required, you can connect from the command line just as you did for anonymous access, but you must supply a valid username and password, as shown in the following graphic:

You can also connect through a browser. The fourth generations of Microsoft Internet Explorer and Netscape Navigator (in both Windows and Linux) support user-based authentication. The syntax is as follows:

```
ftp://username:password@hostname
```

For example, suppose you want to use a compatible browser to access your own FTP server with the IP address of 127.0.0.1, and your administrator account password is password. You enter the following:

```
ftp://administrator:password@127.0.0.1
```

Of course, the FTP server must be configured to allow user-level access.

Even if you do not specify a password, your browser will prompt you for one. Figures 9.2 and 9.3 show the logon screens for Linux versions of Netscape Navigator and Internet Explorer.

FIGURE 9.2 The Netscape Navigator password prompt

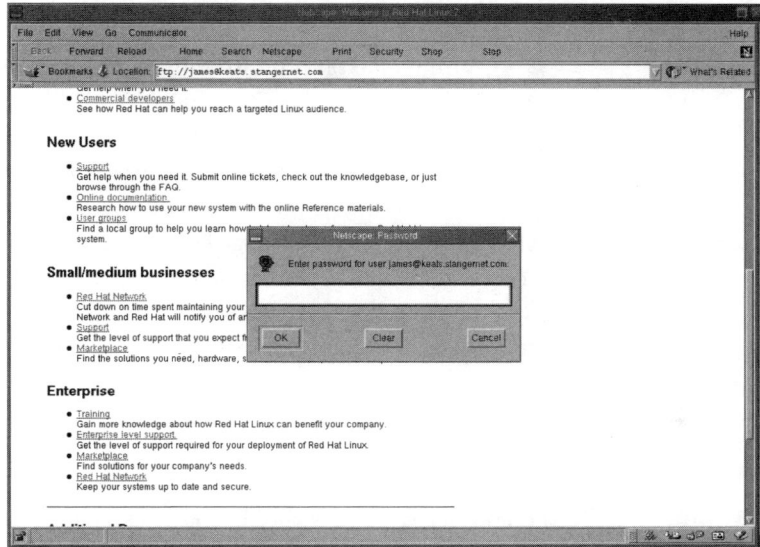

FIGURE 9.3 The Internet Explorer 5 Login As screen

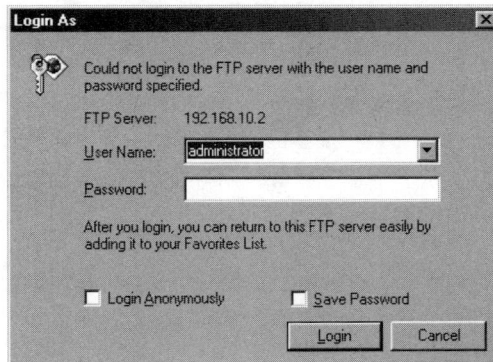

It is possible to conduct a user-based logon for your Linux systems. The Linux PAM, however, does not allow the root account to log on to an FTP server.

Implementing Windows 2000 FTP

In Windows 2000, Internet Information Services (IIS) includes an FTP server. IIS ships with the Windows 2000 installation disks, and default installation includes IIS. With IIS installed, you can administer your FTP server from the Internet Services Manager (ISM) snap-in. Choose Start ➤ Programs ➤ Administrative Tools ➤ Internet Services Manager to open the ISM snap-in, as shown in Figure 9.4.

You can administer many services from the ISM, including your HTTP service, the newsgroup service, and others. Using IIS, you can control almost every aspect of your FTP server.

Configuring an FTP Site

Figure 9.5 shows the Default FTP Site Properties dialog box, which you use to configure your FTP site. In the ISM, right-click your FTP server, and choose Properties from the shortcut menu to open this dialog box.

FIGURE 9.4   The ISM snap-in

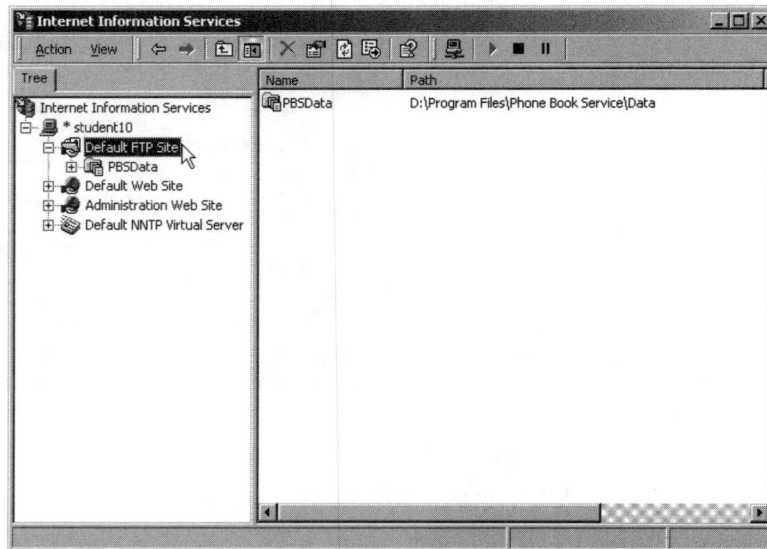

FIGURE 9.5   The Default FTP Site Properties dialog box, open at the FTP Site tab

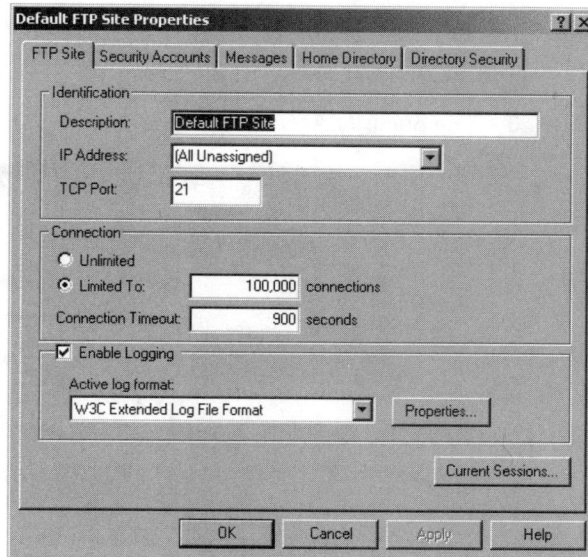

The FTP Site Tab

Using this tab, you can determine or change which IP addresses the FTP server uses (notice the default), as well as the port. Use the Description field to change the display name of the FTP site in the Internet Information Services MMC. (To use a DNS name for your FTP server's IP address, enter a host record in the appropriate domain name server.) You can also limit connections and select logging formats on this tab.

For example, if you want to name your FTP site Developers, use an IP address of 24.37.132.211, use a port number of 2100, limit connections to two with a connection timeout of 300 seconds, enter these parameters on the FTP Site tab. The only prerequisite is that to change the IP address, you use the drop-down list box, which will show only IP addresses that exist for your computer.

From the FTP Site tab, you can also see who is connected to your FTP server by clicking the Current Sessions button to open the FTP User Sessions dialog box. From this dialog box, you can select a user and click the Disconnect button to disconnect only that user, or you can click the Disconnect All button to disconnect all users from your FTP server. Click Close to return to the Default FTP Site Properties dialog box.

The Security Accounts Tab

You use the options on the Security Accounts tab, shown in Figure 9.6, to specify which account you can use to allow IIS to provide FTP.

FIGURE 9.6 The Security Accounts tab

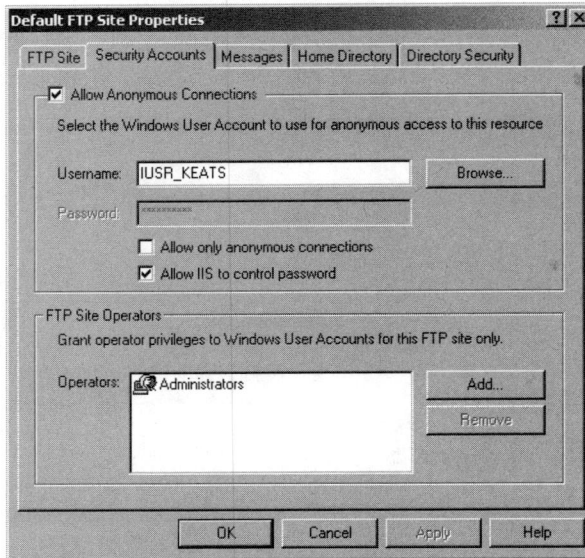

From this tab, you can configure your FTP server to allow anonymous connections or require user-level authentication. Let's look at anonymous connections first.

The Allow Only Anonymous Connections check box is checked by default. If you allow only anonymous connections, users cannot use their user names to access the site. Instead, they must use one of the following sequences to log on anonymously:

```
C:\Windows>ftp 207.19.199.130
Connected to 207.19.199.130.
220 student10 Microsoft FTP Service (Version 5.0).
User (207.19.199.130:(none)): ftp
331 Anonymous access allowed, send identity (e-mail name)
↳as password.
```

```
Password:
230-Welcome to Stanger's Web site.
230 Anonymous user logged in.
ftp>
```

Using the following code sequence, users can log on to an FTP site anonymously or with their user name:

```
C:\Windows>ftp 207.19.199.130
Connected to 207.19.199.130.
220 student10 Microsoft FTP Service (Version 5.0).
User (207.19.199.130:(none)): anonymous
331 Anonymous access allowed, send identity (e-mail name)
↳as password.
Password:
230-Welcome to Stanger's Web site.
230 Anonymous user logged in.
ftp>
```

If you clear the Allow Only Anonymous Connections check box, users can either log on anonymously or with their user names as follows:

```
C:\Windows>ftp 207.19.199.130
Connected to 207.19.199.130.
220 student10 Microsoft FTP Service (Version 5.0).
User (207.19.199.130:(none)): administrator
331 Password required for administrator.
Password:
230-Welcome to Stanger's Web site.
230 User administrator logged in.
ftp>
```

The FTP Site Operators section of the Security Accounts tab is important if you want to grant a group control of their FTP site. For example, to grant the Developers group administrative control, follow these steps:

1. Click the Add button to open the Select Users or Groups dialog box.

2. Double-click the Developers group to add it to the bottom section of this dialog box and click OK.

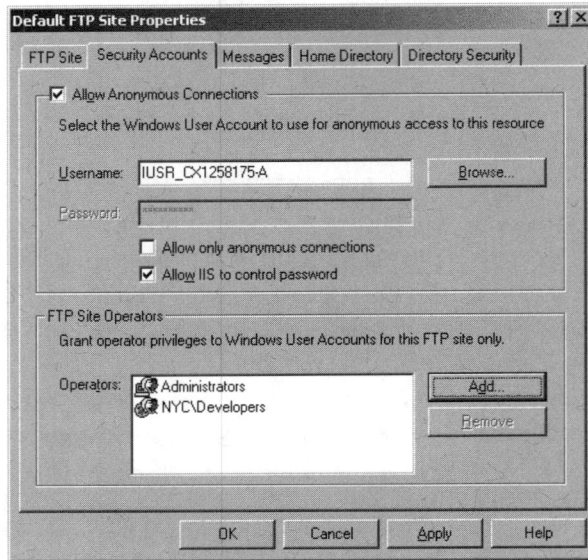

The Messages and Home Directory Tabs

You use the Messages tab, shown in Figure 9.7, to configure Welcome, Exit, and Maximum connections messages.

To enter a message, type it in the appropriate box. The Maximum Connections message displays if a user is unable to connect to your FTP site because of traffic. The Welcome message displays when a user connects to your site. The Exit message displays when a user logs off. After entering messages, click OK. The following graphic shows a user receiving a Welcome and an Exit message.

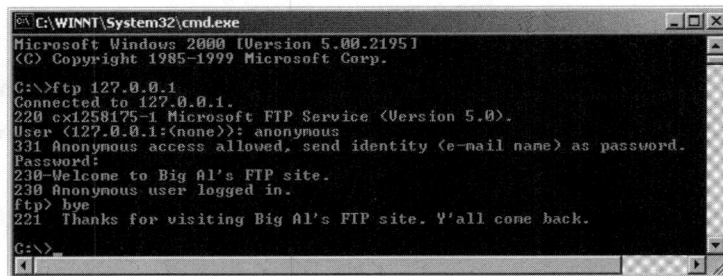

FIGURE 9.7   The Messages tab

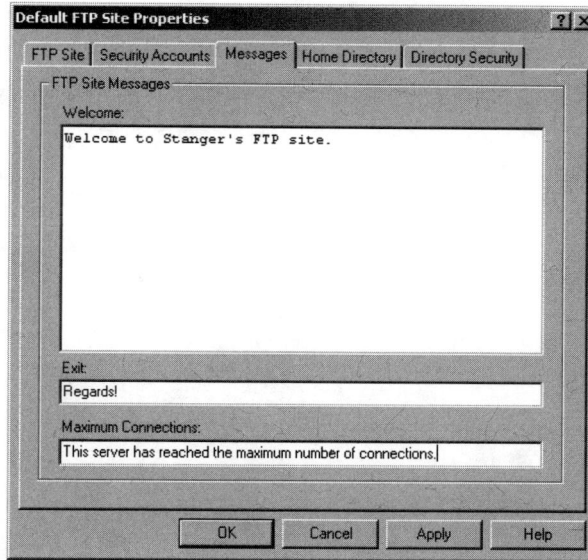

You use the options on the Home Directory tab, shown in Figure 9.8, to specify a local or remote directory. Notice the default directory name. Changing a directory is as easy specifying a local path or a share in the Universal Naming Convention (UNC) format of `\\server\share` or specifying another URL. Each virtual server has a different path. If you run out of space on your hard drive, you might have to add a hard drive and change the local path. For disaster recovery, you might have backup files at a remote directory and need to change the path if the local drive with the files has a problem. If you run a business and for advertising purposes have multiple websites selling the same thing, you might point them all to the same directory. If you buy the FTP site of a competitor that goes out of business you might redirect their FTP site to yours. You can change the home directory to any directory you want, provided that you create it first; IIS will not create it for you.

FIGURE 9.8 The Home Directory tab

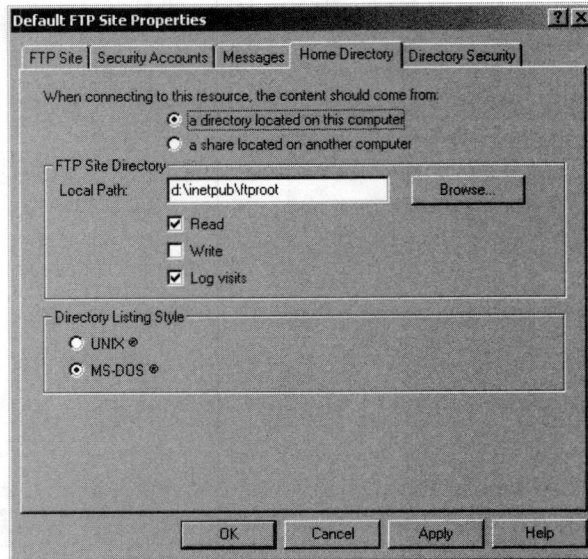

The Directory Security Tab

You use the Directory Security tab, shown in Figure 9.9, to forbid access to your FTP server based on the client's IP address. By default, all users are allowed access to the FTP server.

You have two choices for forbidding access based on IP address:

- Grant access to all but specific hosts. You might use this option to restrict hackers from your FTP site.

- Forbid access to all but specific hosts. You might use this to allow only specific hosts access to your FTP site.

To grant access to all but specific hosts, follow these steps:

1. In the TCP/IP Access Restrictions section, select the Granted Access option.

2. Click the Add button to open the Deny Access On dialog box.

3. Select Single Computer, and enter IP Address. Optionally, click DNS Lookup; or select Group of Computers and enter the Network ID and Subnet Mask; or select Domain Name, and enter the domain name.

4. Click OK.

FIGURE 9.9 The Directory Security tab

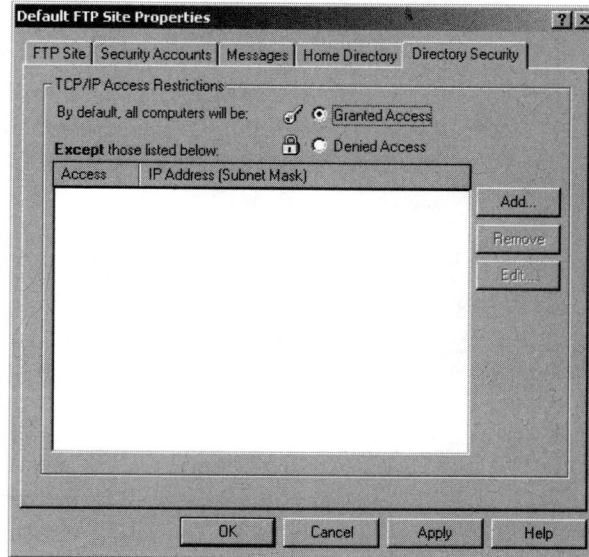

To forbid access to all but specific hosts, follow these steps:

1. In the TCP/IP Access Restrictions section, select the Denied Access option.

2. Click the Add button to open the Grant Access On dialog box.

3. Select Single Computer, and enter IP Address. Optionally, click DNS Lookup; or select Group of Computers and enter the Network ID and Subnet Mask; or select Domain Name, and enter the domain name.

4. Click OK.

Creating Virtual FTP Servers

IIS creates one FTP server by default. If the FTP server exists on a host with more than one IP address, the server will bind to all addresses. You have the option of binding the FTP server to a specific IP address. You can also create more than one FTP server on one host. Additional FTP servers are called *virtual FTP servers.* You can create several types of virtual FTP servers such as the following.

Dedicated virtual FTP servers   Your Windows 2000 server may have more than one NIC, each with its own IP address. If you have two NICs with their own IP addresses, you can create a virtual server for each. Be sure to bind each server to only one IP address.

Simple virtual FTP servers   Your server may have only one NIC, but the NIC may have more than one IP address assigned to it. Therefore, you can create a second virtual FTP server and assign it to only one IP address. As a result, you can have two FTP servers that are bound to each IP address on the NIC. With this option, each FTP server can use port 21. You can, of course, create additional FTP servers that listen on ports greater than 1023 (the ephemeral port numbers).

Shared virtual FTP servers   Even if your server has only one IP address, you can share this IP address by defining a new virtual server that uses an ephemeral port for FTP to listen on. For example, instead of defining port 21, you can define port 2100 or any other port above 1023.

Exercise 9.1 walks you through the steps to create a virtual FTP server.

EXERCISE 9.1

Creating a Simple Virtual FTP Server

In this exercise, you will use the MMC to create a new FTP server. This server will use a separate IP address. If you already have two IP addresses, of course, you don't need to add another. To find out what your IP address(es) are, enter **ipconfig /all** at a command prompt. To add a second IP address of 192.168.0.2 with a subnet mask of 255.255.255.0, follow these steps:

1. On the Desktop, right-click My Network Places, and choose Properties from the shortcut menu to open the Network and Dialup Connections window.

2. Right-click your Local Area Connection icon, and choose Properties from the shortcut menu to open the Local Area Connection Properties dialog box.

3. Select Internet Protocol (TCP/IP), and then click the Properties button to open the Internet Protocol (TCP/IP) Properties dialog box:

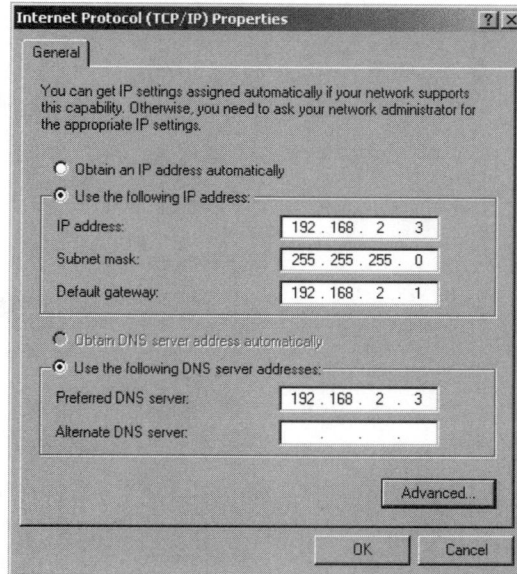

4. Click the Advanced button to open the Advanced TCP/IP Settings dialog box:

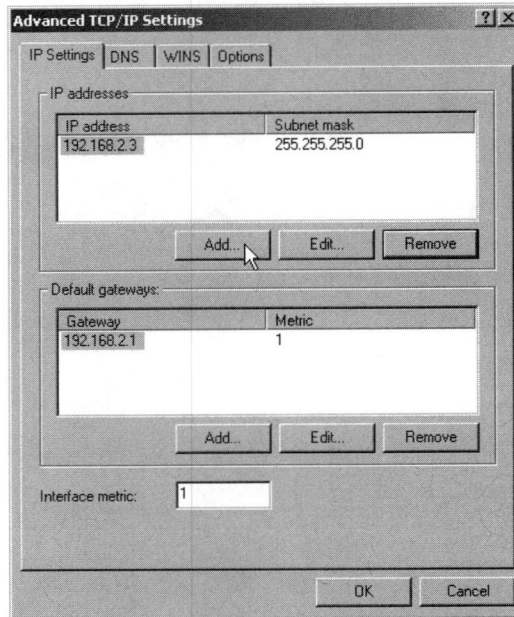

5. In the IP Addresses section, click the Add button, to open the TCP/IP Address dialog box.

6. In the IP Address field, enter **192.168.0.2**, and in the Subnet Mask field enter **255.255.255.0** if it is not added automatically.

7. Click Add, and then click OK three times.

8. Ping both of your IP addresses to make sure that all IP addresses are valid. At a command prompt, enter **ping 192.168.0.2** and press Enter. Look for successful replies. Now ping your other IP address.

Now you are ready to create a virtual FTP server. Follow these steps:

1. Ensure that the FTP service is installed. Choose Start ➤ Settings ➤ Control Panel to open Control Panel. Click Add/Remove Programs to open the Add/Remove Programs window, and then click Add/Remove Windows Components. Select Internet Information Services (IIS), and then click Details. Be sure that the File Transfer Protocol (FTP) check box is selected, and click OK.

2. In Windows Explorer, create a new directory C:\secondsite. You will use this directory as the root directory for the new virtual FTP server.

3. In the C:\secondsite directory, create a new file virtualftp.txt. This file will help you differentiate between your new FTP server and the default FTP server.

4. Choose Start ➤ Programs ➤ Administrative Tools ➤ Internet Services Manager to start the MMC snap-in. Right-click Default FTP Site, and from the shortcut menu, choose New ➤ Site to start the FTP Site Creation Wizard

5. At the Welcome screen, click Next to open the FTP Site Description screen.

6. In the Description box, enter **Second Site**, and then click Next to open the IP Address and Port Settings screen.

7. In the IP Address drop-down list box, select 192.168.0.2, and then click Next to open the FTP Site Home Directory screen.

8. Enter **C:\secondsite** as the path (this is the directory you created earlier in this exercise). You can enter it manually, or click the Browse button and then locate your directory.

9. Click Next to open the FTP Site Access Permissions screen. Select both the Read and Write check boxes, then click Next to open the You Have Successfully Completed the FTP Site Creation Wizard screen.

EXERCISE 9.1 *(continued)*

10. Click the Finish button.

In this exercise you created a simple virtual FTP server. In the next exercise, you will test it.

EXERCISE 9.2

Connecting to a Simple Virtual FTP Server

1. At a command prompt, enter **ftp 192.168.0.2**. At the User prompt, enter **administrator**, and at the Password prompt, enter the administrator password.

2. Transfer some of the files from your own default site to your own host using the get *file name* command. By default, your FTP client uses your Desktop as its initial directory. Therefore, you can upload any file that exists on your desktop.

3. Place a file from your computer onto your own site by entering put *file name*. (If you do not know what files are in the directory from which you started the FTP session, log off, determine the files, and then log back on.)

4. Log off of your own second site.

5. Use your FTP client to log on to your own default site. At a command prompt, enter **192.168.0.1**. At the User prompt enter **anonymous**, and at the Password prompt, enter your e-mail address.

6. Try to upload another file to this site. You will not be able to because, by default, Windows 2000 does not allow write access to the anonymous FTP server.

7. Close your FTP connection.

Creating Virtual FTP Directories

FTP servers always have a root directory. You have already seen how IIS specifies a root directory by default. When it is installed, IIS makes this choice automatically; therefore, if you have a server with only a C:\ drive, IIS defaults to creating a directory named C:\inetpub\ftproot. Every user that logs on via FTP has access only to the C:\inetpub\ftproot directory or any subdirectory you create. Users have no other way to access additional directories.

A *virtual directory* is an FTP directory that does not reside in the FTP root directory. A virtual FTP directory allows you to provide access to FTP on any directory you choose. For example, you can create a directory named C:\ftpstuff and then direct IIS to use this directory as one of its virtual directories. You can create as many of these directories as you need.

Whenever you create a virtual directory, you must assign it an alias. Thus, for your C:\ftpstuff virtual directory, a likely alias might be ftpstuff.

In IIS 5 and later and many other FTP servers, clients cannot display virtual directory aliases; they are hidden from any listing. However, if they have permissions, clients can change to a virtual directory by using the standard change-directory command (cd). Because these directories are hidden, they provide a limited amount of security.

> **NOTE**
>
> When you create a new virtual directory, you can provide read-only or write access. If you don't specify permissions, the directory defaults to read-only permission.

Whenever you create an FTP virtual directory, you must do the following:

- Create a new directory on the hard drive that will become a virtual directory for your FTP site.

- Select an alias for the directory. An alias is simply the name that the FTP server will use to refer to the directory. The alias does not have to be the same name as the directory on the hard drive. For example, if you create a directory named C:\stanger, you can create an FTP alias of another name, such as ciw.

EXERCISE 9.3

Creating a Virtual Directory

In this exercise, you will create a new virtual directory, not a new virtual server.

1. Open Windows Explorer, and create the directory C:\ciw. Create a new file named ciw.txt.

2. Minimize Windows Explorer.

3. Start the Internet Information Services MMC snap-in. Right-click the virtual server you created in a previous exercise, and choose New ➢ Virtual Directory from the shortcut menu to start the Virtual Directory Creation Wizard screen.

4. At the Welcome screen, click Next to open the Virtual Directory Alias screen:

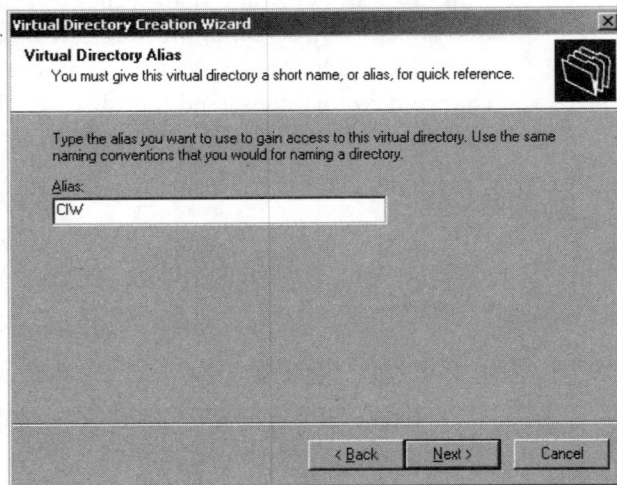

5. In the Alias box, enter **ciw**, and then click Next to open the FTP Site Content Directory screen:

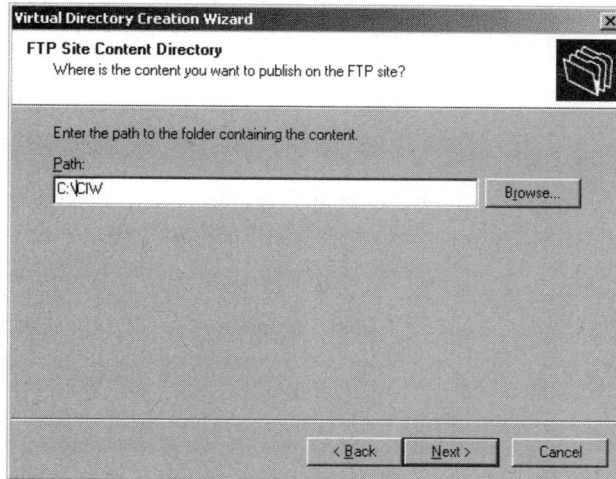

6. Enter **C:\ciw** as the path for this new virtual directory, and then click Next to open the Access Permissions screen:

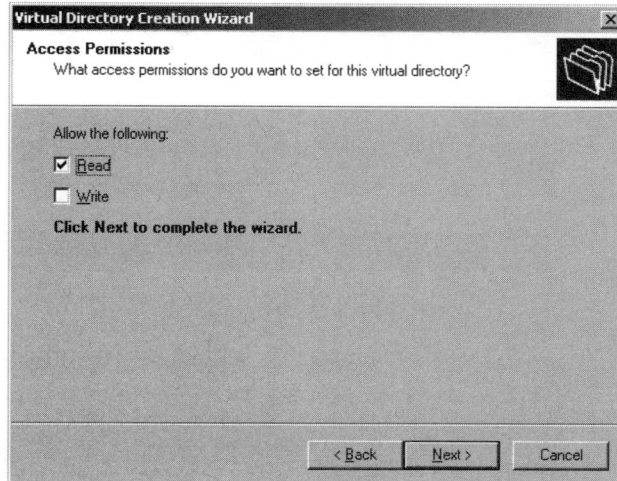

7. Make sure that the Read check box is selected (the default), and then click Next.

8. Click Finish.

9. At a command prompt, log on to your FTP site by entering **FTP 192.168.0.2**.

10. List all the directories using either the dir or the ls command.

11. Notice that the ciw directory does not appear. IIS does not list virtual directories by their aliases.

12. Change to the ciw directory by entering **cd** and then pressing Enter.

13. Transfer some files into the ciw directory. Try to write to the directory. You should not be able to write to the ciw directory because you made this directory read-only. Remain logged on.

14. Give yourself write access to this virtual directory. Open the Internet Services Manager MMC snap-in, right-click the ciw virtual directory, and choose Properties from the shortcut menu to open the ciw Properties dialog box. Select the Write option in the FTP Site Directory section, click Apply, and then click OK. You do not have to restart the server in this instance.

15. Try again to write to the remote server's virtual directory. This time, you will be successful because you now have write access. Log off.

16. Minimize the Internet Services Manager MMC snap-in.

EXERCISE 9.4

Setting Logon Limits for Your IIS FTP Server

In this exercise, you customize settings for your Windows 2000 FTP server.

1. Set a logon limit for your IIS FTP Server. In the Internet Services Manager MMC snap-in, right-click your default FTP server, and choose Properties from the shortcut menu to open the Default FTP Site Properties dialog box.

EXERCISE 9.4

2. Select the FTP Site tab.

3. In the Connection field, make sure that the Limited To radio button is selected, and change the value in the textbox to 1. Apply your settings.

4. Make two connections to your system. Make the first connection using a browser window. In the Address bar, enter **ftp://127.0.0.1**.

5. Attempt to make the second connection from the command prompt. Open a command prompt, and enter FTP 127.0.0.1. What happens?

6. Now, set the Limited To value to 1000 and apply your changes.

Creating an FTP Server in Linux

nix/Linux FTP servers rule the Internet. They outnumber Microsoft servers and offer many of the same features on an extremely stable platform while reducing or eliminating licensing costs. The installation files that come with Red Hat Linux allow you to use the Washington University FTP server (wu-ftpd), which is the industry standard FTP server. If you do not have an FTP server installed and are using Red Hat Linux, the best option is to obtain the Red Hat Package Manager (RPM) for the wu-ftpd server. You can obtain the RPM from the distribution disks or from www.rpmfind.net.

To install and configure an FTP server using the wu-ftpd RPM, you edit the following files:

- /etc/ftpaccess (the main server configuration file)

- /etc/ftphosts (lists host names that are denied access to the server)

- /etc/ftpconversions (automates compression for files stored by the server)

- /etc/ftpusers (bars any listed user, such as root, from logging on)

- /etc/ftpgroups (allows group-based, encrypted access to additional files)

Using the wu-ftpd RPM installs only user-based FTP. You must create your own anonymous FTP configuration. You can do so manually or by using the anonftp RPM, which is available at various RPM sites on the Internet, including www.rpmfind.net.

Setting FTP Logon Limits

Linux FTP servers provide granular control over who can connect. You might want to prevent hackers from connecting to your FTP server, or you might want to limit connections to conserve bandwidth so that file can be downloaded expeditiously. Access to various servers, including FTP, is controlled by xinetd. It can limit the rate of incoming connections, the number of incoming connections from specific hosts, or the total number of connections for a service. It is likely that you have tried to log on to an FTP service, only to be told that the server's logon limit has been reached. The primary way to set logons is to edit the /etc/ftpaccess file. In so doing you can limit logons granularly by classes of users that you define. For example, you can create a class for developers in your company and a class for anonymous users. FTP users with a developer's logon might be assigned a higher connection limit than anonymous users.

The /etc/ftpaccess file allows you to customize various elements of your FTP server. Once you define a class, you can control its behavior.

Following is an example of a standard class found in a default ftpaccess file:

```
class   all   real,guest,anonymous   *
```

This line creates a class named all. The members of this class include all users defined on this system. Real users are those defined in the /etc/passwd and /etc/shadow files. The guest user account is treated separately to allow limited privileges when logging on. You can find additional information about the guest account by reading the `ftpaccess` man page. Man is a utility that displays online manual pages. For more information, see `http://linux.man-pages.net`.

Anonymous users are those who use the word anonymous to log on and who then supply generic information, such as e-mail addresses (usually in the form of `username@domainname.com`, as stipulated in RFC 822). Finally, the asterisk is a wildcard that allows you to specify the origin of the connection. You can list more specific DNS domain names.

The file also supports the creation of multiple classes, as shown:

```
class   all   real,guest   *
class   anon anonymous    *
```

The first line creates a class named `all`. Notice that it does not include anonymous users. The second line creates a new class named **anon**, which includes the anonymous group.

To limit the two classes in the previous example, you can use the following lines:

```
limit   all   2   Any   /etc/limitdocs/user.limit
limit   anon 1   Any   /etc/limitdocs/anon.limit
```

These lines limit the `all` class to only two logons and limits the **anon** class to one. The word Any indicates that this rule applies to any and all logon times. You can specify days by using two-letter indicators (Su, Mo, Tu). The final field contains the path of a message that informs users the limit has been reached. You must, of course, create the directory and the file and then populate the file with appropriate content.

A more reasonable policy enforces a limit of 100 logons for real users and 50 logons for anonymous users as follows:

```
limit   all   100   Any   /etc/limitdocs/user.limit
limit   anon 50   Any   /etc/limitdocs/anon.limit
```

Additional examples of `ftpaccess` files exist in the `/usr/docs/wu-ftpd*` directory.

Using Telnet

Administrators, program developers, and users who need access to data and applications at a specific computer from a remote location can use Telnet. *Telnet* is a terminal emulation protocol that is part of the TCP/IP suite of protocols. Telnet operates on port 23. Windows 2000 and Red Hat Linux include native Telnet servers and clients.

> You can read more about Telnet in RFCs 854 and 855, which are available at www.rfc-editor.org.

A Telnet client allows a user to log on to a remote computer, provided they have permission to do so. As an administrator, you can troubleshoot problems remotely without having to travel to the server location. Once you log on to a computer, you have all the privileges granted to your account. We will discuss Telnet clients and servers specific to Windows 2000 and Unix/Linux in the following sections.

Using Telnet in Windows 2000

The Telnet client is used in Windows 2000 primarily to connect to Unix/Linux systems at the command line. You can also use the Telnet client to configure routers. Windows 2000 includes a Telnet server as well as a Telnet client. The Telnet server service that comes with Windows 2000 can be used by Unix/Linux systems to connect to Windows 2000 systems at the command line. For example, you might use Telnet to connect one Windows system to another in a WAN environment, in order to provide a command line connection that is thrifty with bandwidth. The Telnet server service is installed as part of the default installation of Windows 2000 Server, but you must enable and configure it. You will do that in the following exercise.

EXERCISE 9.5

Configuring Telnet on Windows 2000

1. Enable the Windows Telnet service. Choose Start ➤ Programs ➤ Administrative Tools ➤ Telnet Server Administration to open the Telnet Server Administration window:

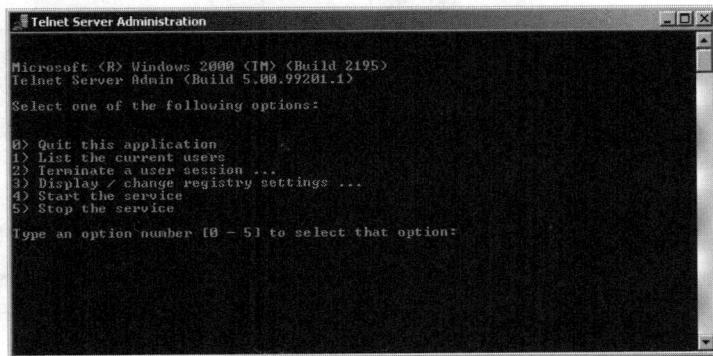

2. You can administer all elements of the Telnet service from this window, which requires you to enter text commands, rather than use your mouse. To start Telnet, press 4, and then press Enter. If the Telnet service is already started, you'll see the following message:

```
Starting Microsoft Telnet Service ...
```

```
Error: StartService
```

```
Error number: 0
```

By default this service tries to use a Windows domain controller (DC) to authenticate connections. Your system is acting as a domain controller for itself. This means that only Windows 2000 clients will be able to access your server and only if they can authenticate with your DC. This option also means that only Windows 2000 clients can access your Telnet client.

3. Begin to verify these settings by entering **3** and pressing Enter. You will see the following list of options, which you use to change the Registry settings for the Telnet service.

4. Enter **7**, and press Enter. You will be informed of the current NTLM setting (2), and you will be asked if you want to change this value. Press y, and then press Enter to change it. (NTLM stands for NT LAN Manager authentication. NTLM is backward compatible with NT and requires a Microsoft domain controller.)

5. You have the following three options:

   - 0, which checks the local server's SAM and uses no encryption to transfer data. This option sends all information—including passwords—in cleartext. Select this option to be compatible with all Telnet clients.

   - 1, which uses a Windows 2000 DC for authentication and encrypts data by default. If no DC is present, your server then reverts to level 0 behavior. This option is best in a heterogeneous environment (for example, if you have Unix systems as well as Windows 2000 servers that use a DC to control authentication).

   - 2, which uses only DC-based authentication. Once authentication occurs, all information is encrypted between the client and the server. This option is best if you have a Windows 2000 Server network that uses a DC to control authentication. Be aware, however, that this option will not allow universal Telnet communication, which is not an ideal Internet-based solution.

EXERCISE 9.5 *(continued)*

6. Enter **1**, and press Enter.

7. You will be asked to confirm this setting. Enter **y**, and press Enter. This option allows your system to participate in a Windows 2000 authentication scheme then resorts to standard Telnet authentication and operations so that Unix clients can attach.

8. You will be returned to the Registry editing menu. Enter **0**, and press Enter to exit this menu and return to the main menu.

9. You now need to stop and restart the Telnet service to make your Registry changes take effect. Enter **5**, and press Enter to stop the Telnet service.

10. Enter **4**, and press Enter to restart the Telnet service.

EXERCISE 9.6

Changing System Settings with the Windows 2000 Telnet Service

In this exercise, you will use Telnet to administer your Windows 2000 system as a model for administering remote Windows 2000 systems.

1. Log on to your own Windows 2000 server as administrator

2. Start the Telnet client program and connect to your own system. At a command prompt, enter **Telnet 127.0.0.1** and press Enter. You should see the following screen:

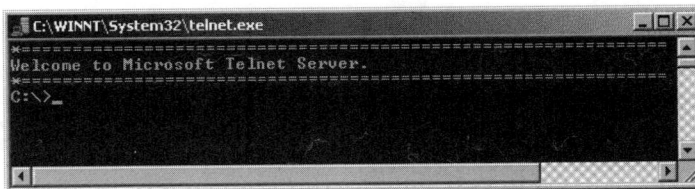

```
C:\WINNT\System32\telnet.exe
*=================================================================
Welcome to Microsoft Telnet Server.
*=================================================================
C:\>_
```

3. Once logged on to your system as administrator, issue the following command, including the quotation marks:

```
net stop "ftp publishing service"
```

You'll see the following message:

4. Open a command prompt and try to access your own FTP server using the Windows 2000 FTP client. You should not be able to, because you disabled it.

5. Start the FTP publishing service using the following command:

`net start "ftp publishing service"`

6. This command will return the following message:

`C:\WINNT\system32>net start "ftp publishing service"`

`The FTP Publishing Service service is starting.`

`The FTP Publishing Service service was started successfully.`

7. Find out which shares exist on your system by entering the following command:

`net share`

You should now see a list of shares for your system.

8. Enter the **c:** command to change to the root directory of the C:\ drive.

9. Create a directory named remote by entering the following command:

`mkdir remote`

10. Share this directory under the share point of `print`:

`net share print=C:\remote`

11. When you are successful, you will see a message similar to the following:

`print was shared successfully.`

12. Open the My Network Places folder to view the share you created. Remember, this share is on your system.

13. Delete this share by entering the following command:

`net share print /delete`

14. You should see the following message:

`C:\ >`

`print was deleted successfully.`

15. Experiment with the following commands:

- `ipconfig /all`

- `net stats server |more`

- `net stats workstation |more`

- `net user username` (username is a user defined on that machine)

- `net user username password` (changes the password of the user you specify)

- `net user username password /ADD` (adds a user)

Using Telnet in Unix

Unix/Linux servers run a Telnet daemon and a Telnet client, which is used to connect to other Unix/Linux servers at the command line. You enter a Telnet client request as follows:

`telnet [remote host IP address or Fully Qualified Domain`
`↳Name (FQDN)]`

The result displays a logon screen with a user account and password prompt. Once you log on to the computer, you have all the privileges of that user account.

Most Unix systems run Telnet as a default daemon, although SSH has become increasingly popular. A daemon in Unix/Linux is the equivalent of a service in Windows 2000. A daemon is a program that runs continually in the background to provide a service. A daemon called Secure Shell (SSH) is a more secure replacement for Telnet. SSH is the standard for secure file transfer and remote logins over the Internet. All traffic, including terminal emulation traffic, is encrypted and optionally compressed. Although configuration of SSH is beyond the scope of this book, you can find out more about SSH at www.ssh.com.

You can enable or disable Telnet in Linux using the /etc/xinetd.d/ telnet script file which controls the Telnet function of the xinetd daemon. You can forbid access to Telnet by editing the /etc/xinetd.d/telnet file, or you can edit the hosts.allow and hosts.deny files. You will learn about using these files later in this chapter.

You can control access to Telnet in three ways:

- You can enable or disable Telnet using the xinetd script.

- You can edit the PAMs (Pluggable Authentication Modules) to modify how Telnet operates.

- You can edit the /etc/hosts.allow and /etc/hosts.deny files, which are part of the TCPWrappers package.

The next sections explain how xinetd, PAM, and TCPWrappers function to control access to your IP services.

Using the *xinetd* Daemon

The *xinetd* daemon is, in essence, a super daemon because it controls how other daemons operate. Following is a partial list of the other daemons that xinetd controls:

FTP	Telnet
finger	SWAT
TFTP	chargen
daytime	POP3
BOOTP	echo

The /etc/xinetd.conf file controls the behavior of the /usr/sbin/xinetd daemon. Generally, you do not need to edit this file.

You control xinetd by editing the files in the /etc/xinetd.d/ directory. Figure 9.10 shows the files that populate the /etc/xinetd.d directory of a default Red Hat Linux installation.

FIGURE 9.10 The configuration files in the /etc/xinetd.d/ directory

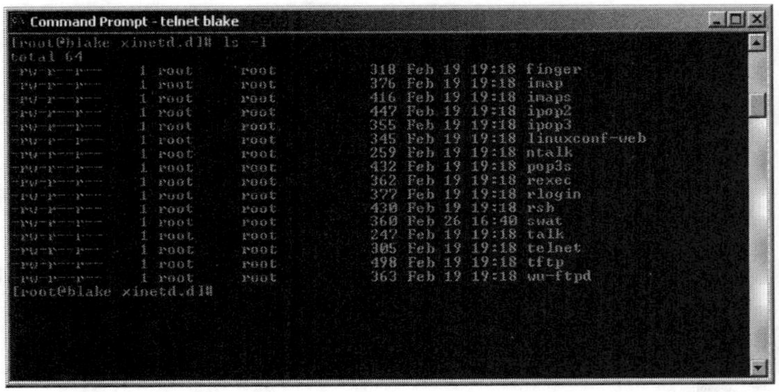

The xinetd daemon reads these files every time it restarts. Whenever you change any of these files, you must restart xinetd by using the /etc/rc.d/init.d/xinetd script. You have already found this to be true when working with DNS and SWAT.

Understanding *inetd*

The xinetd daemon has become the standard for Internet super servers. The previous standard was inetd. This daemon used the /etc/inetd.conf file to configure all daemons it started. The inetd service was used by Red Hat Linux until version 7. If you upgrade from Red Hat Linux 6.2 to 7.x, for example, you will have both inetd and xinetd on your system.

The standard behavior in this case is for inetd to handle finger, Telnet, FTP, POP3, and IMAP requests and for xinetd to handle others. Even though the /etc/xinetd.d/ directory contains scripts for finger, Telnet, FTP, and other services, you will have to control these services from the /etc/inetd.conf file if inetd was previously installed. You will then need to restart inetd using the /etc/rc.d/init.d/inetd restart command. Thus, if a particular service continues to run even though you disabled it in xinetd, check to see if inetd is also running. You can then ensure that you are working with the correct configuration files.

If you want to completely uninstall inetd after an upgrade, the best practice is to disable one service in inetd and then enable it in xinetd. Test each service you disable and enable to ensure that xinetd is handling it correctly. This way, you are migrating each daemon in a controlled, verifiable way. Once you have completely migrated all the daemons to xinetd, you can uninstall xinetd.

Using PAM and TCP Wrappers

Pluggable Authentication Modules (PAM) allow integration of various authentication technologies such as Unix, Kerberos, RSA, smart cards, and DCE into system entry services such as login, passwd, rlogin, telnet, ftp, and su without changing any of these services. Pluggable means that you do not have to recompile the operating system to use the technology.

> **NOTE**
>
> See http://www.kernel.org/pub/linux/libs/pam/modules.html for more information on PAM.

On the other hand, with the *TCP Wrappers* package you can monitor and filter incoming requests for the SYSTAT, FINGER, FTP, TELNET, RLOGIN, RSH, EXEC, TFTP, TALK, and other network services. The package provides tiny daemon wrapper programs that can be installed without any changes to existing software or to existing configuration files. The wrappers report the name of the client host and of the requested service; the wrappers do not exchange information with the client or server applications and impose no overhead on the actual conversation between the client and server applications.

> **NOTE**
>
> For more information on the TCP Wrappers package, see http://www.acm.uiuc.edu/workshops/security/wrap.html.

As mentioned, you can also control access to Telnet by editing the /etc/hosts.allow and /etc/hosts.deny files, which are part of the TCPWrappers package. The TCPWrappers package is included with most Linux systems, and you use this package to limit access to Telnet based on a client's IP address.

TCPWrappers uses a daemon called tcpd, which you start by running xinetd. The tcpd daemon is the first service to accept requests for other daemons, such as ftpd, telnetd, and the logon shell.

The `tcpd` daemon filters client requests to Unix/Linux servers before passing them on to other services rather than letting the other services handle the requests directly. Part of the filtering service includes the use of the `/etc/hosts.allow` and `/etc/hosts.deny` files, which act as access control lists. You can edit these files to limit specific hosts or entire subnets. You can also edit them to limit remote access to all the system's services or only to specific services. Any name listed in the `hosts.deny` file is denied access. The `tcpd` daemon first considers the `hosts.allow` file, which takes precedence over the `hosts.deny` file.

The syntax for the `hosts.allow` and `hosts.deny` files can get quite involved. Following are some examples:

```
in.ftpd: ALL EXCEPT student10.classroom4.com
in.telnetd: ALL
in.telnetd: 192.168.2.4
```

The first line limits access to the wu-ftpd daemon for all systems except one host named `student10.classroom4.com`. The second line prevents all systems from accessing Telnet, whereas the third line limits Telnet access to one host with a specific IP address of 192.168.2.4.

You can use TCPWrappers to enforce a security policy. For example, you can establish a policy that no external clients can access Telnet unless they are explicitly granted permission in the `/etc/hosts.allow` file.

For example, to create an access control policy, create the `file /etc/hosts.deny` and place in it a single line such as `ALL: ALL`. This line states that all external clients are refused access unless an explicit grant is made via the `/etc/hosts.allow` file. You can then explicitly allow access to a service by editing the `/etc/hosts.allow` file. For example, to grant Telnet access to a trusted host, create the file `/etc/hosts.allow` and place `in.telnetd: trusted.host.com` inside it. You can add services as you need, but understand that TCPWrappers control only services offered by xinetd. Stand-alone services, such as named and Apache server, are not controlled by these files.

The Trivial IP Services

The trivial IP services include finger, daytime, echo, and chargen. They are nice to have services that provide information or supplementary services.

The loss of any of these services won't disable a Unix or Linux server; however, these are useful tools that you should master.

Using *finger*

You can use the finger protocol to find out about users on local and remote Windows 2000 and Unix systems. For example, you can use finger to get more information about a user on a Linux/Unix system such as the full name of the user, the user's home directory, whether the user is logged in, and if so, since when.

Both Unix/Linux and Windows 2000 come with a finger client, but only Unix/Linux is packaged with a finger server. The syntax of finger in both Windows 2000 and Linux is as follows:

```
finger user
```

For example, to learn about a user with the user name of james, enter the following command:

```
finger james
```

You receive the following output:

```
[root@student10 sandi]# finger james
Login: james        Name: James Stanger
Directory: /home/james     Shell: /bin/bash
On since Wed Mar 22 18:07 (PST) on pts/0 from 192.168.4.10
 22 minutes 49 seconds idle
On since Wed Mar 22 18:17 (PST) on pts/2 from 192.168.4.12
 8 minutes 48 seconds idle
On since Wed Mar 22 18:28 (PST) on pts/3 from 192.168.4.10
On since Wed Mar 22 17:44 (PST) on pts/1 from student10
 43 minutes 8 seconds idle
Last login Wed Mar 22 18:28 (PST) on 3 from 208.205.77.249
No mail.
No Plan.
```

As you can see this output tells you that the user logon james is James Stanger with a home directory of /home/james and a default /bin/bash shell.

His last logon times, durations, and logon IP addresses are shown. James has no mail and no published plan of work to do.

If you want to finger a remote user, use the following syntax:

```
finger user@hostname
```

For example, to finger the user james on a remote host, enter the following command:

```
finger james@student10
```

Finger is available in many systems, and you control its use by editing its script in the /etc/xinetd.d directory. Many systems administrators disable finger for two reasons: First, finger has a long history of security problems. Second, it tends to reveal too much information about various users.

To disable this file, edit the /etc/inetd.conf configuration file. Comment out the following line by preceding it with a number sign (#):

```
finger stream tcp nowait nobody /usr/sbin/in.fingerd
↳in.fingerd.
```

You can retain the ability to finger users on your system when you are logged on locally, while disabling remote finger queries that would compromise the security of your system by editing the /etc/xinetd.d/finger script.

Using the *daytime, echo, chargen,* and NTP Protocols

Daytime, echo, and chargen are utility protocols associated with specific ports usually used for troubleshooting. The daytime protocol reports the time of day. The echo protocol repeats back any characters sent to it. The chargen protocol generates random characters. These tests are sometimes helpful when troubleshooting a network server.

Although no dedicated client exists to access daytime, echo, or chargen, you can use Telnet to access them by specifying the following ports.

- daytime: port 13

- echo: port 7

- chargen: port 19

If you connect to the chargen port, press Ctrl+C to quit the connection. If you connect via the Windows Telnet client, you may have to disconnect abruptly.

You can use the Network Time Protocol (NTP) to ensure that all systems on your networks are set to the same time. This protocol is important for implementing services such as Kerberos, which require that all systems have a uniform time setting to function properly.

> You can learn more about NTP at www.eecis.udel.edu/~ntp/ or by reading RFC 2030 available at www.rfc-editor.org.

Hackers can use these trivial protocols for denial of service attacks. For instance, echo, chargen, and daytime can be spoofed into sending data from one service on a computer to another service. The solution is to comment out these services by putting a number sign (#) before their line in the /etc/ inetd.conf configuration file. For more information, see xforce.iss.net/ static/400.php.

Summary

In this chapter, you learned how to install and configure FTP, Telnet, and the trivial IP services such as finger. You also learned how to control access to various services by invoking security features native to both Windows 2000 and Linux. This includes using IIS 5 restriction settings and using hosts.allow and hosts.deny files in Linux.

You should now understand the differences between standard FTP and firewall-friendly, passive FTP. You should also be able to set up FTP servers in Windows 2000 and Linux and set these servers for user-level access and/ or anonymous access. Because passwords are not encrypted in FTP, anonymous access prevents only the sniffing of passwords. You should also be able to log on to an FTP server using a command line interface or a browser, and you should understand the benefits of using a third-party FTP client with a graphical interface.

Additionally, you should understand the benefits of using Telnet to remotely administer a Linux or Windows 2000 server. For security, when using Telnet in Linux, you cannot directly log in as root, but must log in as a regular user and then use the su (Super User/Substitute User) command to log in as root. For security, the finger daemon that provides information about a host is often disabled. Finally, for security, you can edit the hosts.allow and hosts.deny files to limit the hosts that can access services in Linux.

With these skills, you should now be able to upload content to remote web servers using FTP and to securely configure remote web servers using Telnet.

Exam Essentials

Be able to configure and troubleshoot FTP servers   If clients outside a firewall cannot talk to an older FTP server, you'll need to upgrade that server to passive FTP. Know that the standard FTP port for control is 21. Know in what circumstances and how to configure dedicated, simple, and shared FTP servers. Know FTP security measures, such as how to limit access to only anonymous logins so that the login user account and password are not sent in cleartext. Know that the anonymous FTP account in Windows 2000 is IUSR_*YourServerName*. Also for security and performance, be able to limit FTP logins by the number of simultaneous logins, by host name/IP address, or by username.

Be able to connect to and download or upload files to an FTP server. Be able to connect to an FTP server by using a command line login such as ftp 192.168.0.100 or ftp austin.ciw.com or by using a browser login such as ftp://192.168.0.100, ftp://austin.ciw.com, or even ftp://administrator:password@austin.ciw.com. Know the ls, get, mget, put, and mput commands used to list files and get or put either single files or multiple files or directories from or on an FTP server.

Be able to configure a Telnet client, to connect to a Telnet server and to manage servers and users from a Telnet command prompt.   In Windows 2000, the Telnet server is installed by default, but the Telnet service must be started. The command you use to connect to a Telnet server is similar to Telnet 192.168.0.100 or Telnet austin.ciw.com. Once connected to a Windows 2000 Telnet server, the following Net series of commands are useful: Net Start, Net User, and Net Share. Once connected to a Linux Telnet server with a standard user account, use the su command to log in as root.

Understand how Linux and Unix limit access to their servers with various files and daemons. The xinetd daemon is a super daemon because it controls how other daemons operate, including FTP, Telnet, and finger. You control xinetd by editing the files in the /etc/xinetd.d directory. Other important access files are the /etc/hosts.allow and etc/hosts .deny files.

Key Terms

Before taking the exam, you should be familiar with the following terms:

dedicated virtual server	simple virtual FTP server
finger	TCP Wrappers
get	Telnet
ls	virtual FTP directories
put	Xinetd
shared virtual FTP server	

Review Questions

1. Jim is using an older, traditional FTP server and a newer firewall. What is the major problem that might occur?

   A. Clients inside the firewall might not be able to download content from FTP servers outside the firewall.

   B. Clients outside the firewall might not be able to download content from the FTP server inside the firewall.

   C. Clients inside the firewall might not be able to download content from the FTP server inside the firewall.

   D. Clients from outside the firewall will not be able to use an anonymous login to the FTP server.

2. Mark administers a Linux FTP server. It has the following directory tree structure: /var/ftp/pub, /bin, /usr, and /home. Which directory or directories can FTP users access?

   A. /var

   B. /var/ftp

   C. /var/ftp/pub

   D. /usr and /home

3. Brad connects to an FTP server. He wants to see which files are available for download and to download a particular file. Which two commands should Brad use?

   A. dir

   B. ls

   C. put

   D. get

   E. copy

4. Brad connects to an FTP server, and he wants to upload a single directory to his website. Which command should Brad use?

   A. get

   B. mget

   C. put

   D. mput

   E. dcopy

5. Joshua wants to restrict what anonymous users can download from his IIS 5 FTP server SantaClaus. Which Windows 2000 account should Brad restrict?

   A. guest

   B. anonymous

   C. IUSR_SantaClaus

   D. SantaClaus

   E. IWAM_Guest

6. Frank wants to make an Excel expense report template file (expense.xls) available for download from an IIS 5 server. The default FTP directory has not been changed. Where should Frank place the file?

   A. C:\winnt\system32\ftp

   B. C:\ftproot

   C. C:\ftp

   D. C:\inetpub\ftproot

7. Frank wants to make a series of Word 2000 files available for FTP download as a unit and to increase the efficiency of the download. What should Frank do?

   A. Place all the files in the same subdirectory.

   B. Compress the files on an NTFS partition.

   C. Use a third-party disk compression utility.

   D. Use Disk Administrator

8. Tony is the administrator of Delta Hospitals. He wants to authenticate to the `data.delta-hospitals.com` FTP server using the Tonym account with a password of GiveIt2Me. What should Tony put in his browser?

   A. `ftp://data.delta-hospitals.com:tonym/GiveIt2Me`

   B. `ftp://tonym:GiveIt2Me/data.delta-hospitals.com`

   C. `ftp://tonym:GiveIt2Me@data.delta-hospitals.com`

   D. `ftp://tonym:GiveIt2Me@data.delta-hospitals.com:80`

9. Peter is concerned that FTP user accounts and passwords are not encrypted and that these accounts could be hacked. What should Tony do?

   A. Allow only anonymous FTP access.

   B. Use a Black Ice firewall.

   C. Use a shadow password file.

   D. Log suspicious activity using Web Trends.

10. Ralph wants to host multiple FTP sites on his IIS 5 server. Which of the following options does Ralph have?

    A. Use host headers

    B. Use multiple IP addresses

    C. Use multiple port numbers

    D. Use multiple virtual directories

11. Frank wants to host multiple low-traffic FTP sites on his company's intranet. He wants to spend as little money as possible and make it easy for users to connect to his FTP sites. How should Frank do this?

    A. Add ports to a single NIC

    B. Add multiple NICs

    C. Add multiple IP addresses to a single NIC

    D. Use host headers

12. From a command prompt, using the default FTP file transfer mode, Mark downloaded a graphic file from the corporate FTP server. It was corrupted. What should Mark do next?

   A. Ask headquarters to upload an uncorrupted graphics file using the put command.

   B. Ask headquarters to upload an uncorrupted graphics file using the gput command.

   C. Ask headquarters to upload an uncorrupted graphics file using the mput command.

   D. Try downloading the file in ASCII format.

   E. Try downloading the file in binary format.

   F. Try downloading the file in graphics format.

13. Because of a security breach, Brad has just been fired as the systems administrator of a Linux FTP server operated by a defense contractor. Brad had been downloading files from this server from his home computer Darkact.2follow.com. In which two ways can Brad's access to the FTP server be denied?

   A. Add Brad's hostname to the /etc/ftphosts file.

   B. Delete Brad's hostname from the /etc/ftphosts file.

   C. Add Brad's name to the etc/ftpusers file

   D. Delete Brad's name in the etc/ftpusers file

14. Ben wants to limit access to his Unix FTP server to 100 logons for real users and 50 logons for anonymous users. Which file should Ben modify?

   A. /etc/ftpaccess

   B. /etc/ftphosts

   C. /etc/ftphosts

   D. /etc/ftpconversions

   E. /etc/ftpusers

   F. /etc/ftpgroups

15. Mandy needs to open ports on her corporate firewall to permit Telnet and FTP traffic. Which ports should Mandy open?

A. 21

B. 23

C. 25

D. 80

16. Frank upgrades his corporate server to Windows 2000 from NT 4. He wants to use his corporate server as a Telnet server. What must Frank do?

A. Install the Windows 2000 native Telnet server in Add/Remove Programs.

B. Install a third-party Telnet server.

C. Enable the Microsoft Telnet service.

D. Reboot the server.

17. Mark has been called at home and asked to create a user account for the CEO of a partner organization. Mark wants to use his Windows 98 laptop to connect to his Windows 2000 server at IP address 191.168.0.100 and add the account for WendyJ with a password of burger$. Mark has a VPN connection to his corporate server. Which two steps should Mark take?

A. `telnet 191.168.0.100`

B. `finger 191.168.0.100`

C. `ftp 191.168.0.100`

D. `adduser wendyj burger$ /GO`

E. `net user wendyj burger$ /ADD`

18. For added security, Andrea wants to disable the finger service. Which file should Andrea modify?

A. /etc/startx

B. /etc/ntstartd

C. /etc/services

D. /etc/xinetd.d/finger

E. /etc/xinetd

19. Peter wants to limit the access of various hosts and various subnets to specific services on a Linux server. Which two files should Peter modify?

A. /etc/access

B. /etc/tcpwrapper.allow

C. /etc/hosts.allow

D. /etc/hosts.deny

20. Ralph wants to deny FTP access to a system named james.badcompany .com. What text string does Ralph need to enter in the /etc/hosts .deny file?

A. in.ftpd : DENY james.badcompany.com

B. in.ftpd ALL DENY EXCEPT james.badcompany.com

C. DENY in.ftpd : james.badcompany.com

D. DENY james.badcompany.com : in.ftpd

Answers to Review Questions

1. **B.** In this case, the clients outside the firewall are of greatest concern. The FTP server should be upgraded to support passive FTP.

2. **B, C.** The `/var/ftp` directory will appear as the root directory to FTP users. Only files in that directory and files under that directory will be accessible to FTP users.

3. **B, D.** The `ls` command lists files, and the `get` command downloads a file.

4. **D.** The `mput` command uploads multiple files or directories.

5. **C.** Joshua should set NTFS permissions on the IUSR_SantaClaus account.

6. **D.** Frank should place the file in `C:\inetpub\ftproot`, which is the default FTP directory that IIS creates.

7. **C.** Frank should zip the files to compress them into one unit using Pkzip or WinZip (`www.winzip.com`).

8. **C.** Tony should use `ftp://tonym:GiveIt2Me@data.delta-hospitals.com`. If the IP address of data.delta-hospitals.com was 192.168.3.2, Tony could use `ftp://tonym:GiveIt2Me@192.168.3.2`.

9. **A.** Peter should allow only anonymous access.

10. **B, C.** Host headers are available only for websites. Ralph can use multiple IP addresses or multiple ports. If the additional FTP server's IP address 192.168.0.100 is using port 2100, use ftp://192.168.0.100:2100 to connect to this server.

11. **C.** Frank can add multiple IP addresses to a single NIC. Multiple NICs would be more expensive. Multiple ports would make the Uniform Resource Locator (URL) of the FTP server longer.

12. E. The default file transfer mode is ASCII. Mark should try to download the file in binary format, which is more reliable and must be used for non-ASCII files.

13. A, C. The `/etc/ftphosts` file lists host names that are denied access, and the `etc/ftpusers` file list user names that are denied access

14. A. Ben should modify the `/etc/ftpaccess` file, which is the main FTP server configuration file.

15. A, B. Mandy should open port 21 for FTP and port 23 for Telnet.

16. C. The Microsoft Telnet server is already installed. It needs to be enabled.

17. A, E. Mark should use Telnet to create Wendy's user account with the `net user` command.

18. D. Andrea should edit the Finger file in the `/etc/xinetd.d` directory.

19. C, D. Peter should edit the following TCPWrappers files: `/etc/hosts.allow` and `/etc/hosts.deny`.

20. D. Ralph should enter the following text string in the `/etc/hosts.deny` file: `DENY james.badcompany.com : in.ftpd`.

Advanced Internet System Management

## PART II

Mission-Critical Services

THE CIW EXAM OBJECTIVE GROUPS COVERED IN THIS CHAPTER:

✓ Select and implement popular web servers, including but not limited to: Microsoft IIS, Apache server.

In earlier chapters, you learned about various kinds of software that you can use to deploy client-server systems. In this chapter, we'll take a fresh look at how foundation services and mission-critical services interoperate and become more than the sum of their parts. We will also discuss how to monitor performance and optimize server and security issues. In addition, we'll look at foundations services, which form an essential part of computer networking, including name resolution, databases, and others.

Mission-Critical Services

A *mission-critical service* is one that an organization requires for its ongoing success and survival. Such a service must operate constantly, consistently, and without interruption, regardless of the operating conditions. If a mission-critical service fails, any processes, systems, and organizations that interact with the service may face intolerable interruptions.

Although each business or organization may have different priorities, certain services are considered mission-critical to most organizations. Managers can choose to develop these services internally, purchase them from an outside organization, or blend the two approaches.

Mail and package delivery are examples of mission-critical services that most companies obtain from outside organizations. Only the largest firms can afford to handle their own mail and shipping, and they might support only internal transactions between their own employees and departments. Any external shipments are routed to the post office, a courier, a package shipper, or another organization that has purchased and developed their own mission-critical services to support the delivery process.

Accounting services are an excellent example of a mission-critical service that can be developed internally or purchased from an outside vendor. Companies must satisfy financial and legal requirements for maintaining an accurate record of the company's transactions and financial condition at all times. Some of the earliest applications of computing technology in corporations were the enhancement and eventual replacement of paper-based accounting records. Although many companies handle their own accounting, managers sometimes choose to outsource these functions to external companies that specialize in various areas of accounting practice.

We can use manufacturing as a more general example of mission-criticality. Most mass-produced items are manufactured using computer-based equipment. The loss of a single machine might slow or shut down operations, causing delays that require considerable time and money to resolve.

With the widespread adoption of computer networks in the corporate workplace, more network services and applications have gained mission-critical status. Many companies depend on e-mail as an essential and timely communications tool. When e-mail is disrupted by a server crash, a network problem, or a communications outage, work can grind to a halt as employees choose other, less efficient methods to send their messages. In a company that requires employees to save files to servers, any server outage can also disrupt work. If employees do not have a local file or paper backup of their work, the company will suffer productivity losses until the server is repaired.

Foundation Services

A foundation service provides the bedrock upon which you can build any subsequent Internet service, including a mission-critical service. Foundation services include name resolution services such as:

- Domain Name System (DNS), the standard IP naming service that is available on many different operating systems and computing platforms
- Windows Internet Naming Service (WINS), using Windows 2000
- Samba, for Unix and Linux systems

Foundation services also include the ability to share data and resources such as applications, databases, printers, files, and directories or folders across a network. Examples of these services include the following:

Server Message Blocks (SMB)   SMB is a command message format that is supported by many network operating systems. On the OSI (Open Standards Interconnect) Reference Model, SMB occupies the Application and Presentation layers. Once a client and server establish a connection, the client sends commands formatted as SMBs to the server. These commands provide access to network files, directories or folders, and devices.

SMB rose to prominence in the late 1980s, when Microsoft and IBM included SMB support in DOS and Windows. SMB is also widely supported in Unix. Samba uses SMB, and SMB is the default choice of Linux server administrators when interconnecting with Windows workstations and servers.

NetBIOS over TCP/IP   NetBIOS is a refinement of SMB. The messaging blocks are called Network Control Blocks (NCBs), but they provide the same features as SMBs. Unlike SMB, NetBIOS works at the Session layer of the OSI Reference Model and supports connection-oriented and connectionless sessions. Almost all LANs for PCs were based on NetBIOS until TCP/IP became the dominant LAN protocol in the late '90s. NetBIOS is discussed in RFCs 1001 and 1002.

Network File System (NFS)   Network File System is a client/server application that was originally designed by Sun Microsystems. NFS allows all network users to access shared files stored on computers of different types, through an interface called the Virtual File System (VFS). VFS runs on top of TCP/IP. With NFS, computers connected to a network operate as clients while accessing remote files, and as servers while providing remote users access to local shared files. These features can also work through properly configured firewalls. RFC 3010 describes version 4 of NFS, including new features such as international language and strong security support.

HTTP Server

An HTTP or web server uses the Hypertext Transfer Protocol (HTTP) to transmit documents to web clients. Its advantage over other file servers is the wide range of clients and services that it supports with a minimum of configuration on the client side. In general, any browser will have at least basic functionality, including navigation features, an address field, and a display window for text. Newer versions of browsers have more capability, such as image display, FTP and Gopher client emulation, and integrated e-mail clients.

Web browsers can handle many other kinds of data by using small applications called plug-ins. A plug-in application is a helper program that a browser automatically recognizes, and its function is integrated into the main HTML file that is being presented. One popular example of a plug-in is Adobe Acrobat Reader, which reads PDF (Portable Document Format) files. PDF files maintain the printed appearance of a file, including fonts and graphics, and can be compressed for faster transfer.

Streaming media players are another example of plug-ins. There are several competing brands, including RealNetworks RealOne Player, Microsoft Windows Media Player, and Apple QuickTime Player. All three of these applications handle popular formats such as MP3. Each player also supports at least one proprietary streaming media format.

HTTP servers use the default port 80 of the IP address to deliver documents and files. Additional ports may be required to support Secure Sockets Layer (SSL) or database connectivity. Chapter 12 discusses SSL in greater detail. We will discuss database connectivity methods later in this chapter.

An HTTP server can download any file type to a browser. However, the web browser must be preconfigured to accept each file type. The *Multipurpose Internet Mail Extensions (MIME)* system allows HTTP and e-mail attachments to identify the files they must use. A version of MIME that encrypts MIME data, called *Secure MIME (S/MIME),* is used for secure transmissions.

The different MIME types are classified under broad headings (text, image, application, audio, and video) and then subclassified by exact type. For example, an HTML document has MIME type text/html, whereas a plain text document has type text/plain.

Whenever data is passed between a web server and a browser, the data is labeled with its MIME type. The recipient uses the MIME type to render the information. For example, when a web server sends an HTML document to a browser, it labels the document with its MIME type (text/html) so that the browser can display the document properly. When a web server sends an Adobe Acrobat file (application/x-pdf) to a browser, the browser opens the correct plug-in (Adobe Acrobat Reader) to view the file.

When a web browser requests a server resource, the server deduces the resource's MIME type from the extension part of the document name. For example, the server understands that a request for the URL `http://www.ciwcertified.com/default.asp` refers to a document of type text/html and labels the document with that type when it returns the document to the browser. The MIME type is included in the HTTP header, which is contained in a TCP/IP packet.

The correspondence between file name extensions and MIME types can be preprogrammed into the web server or configured by the server administrator. In most cases, the preprogrammed MIME types are used, to maintain a standard set of MIME types that are supported by popular web browsers and operating systems.

Database Server

Another server type that integrates well with a web server is a database server. A website that includes a database server can offer a catalog of products, provide a shopping cart to customers, and track their orders. A *database* is a file or a series of files that can be used to organize information. It stores information in a consistent format so that users can search the files for specific information. A sample database is illustrated in Table 10.1.

TABLE 10.1 Example of a Database Table

Record number	First_name	Last_name	Telephone	Email
1	Zosia	Kitty	716-555-3492	zk@niagara.com
2	Ricky	Bell	813-555-2648	runner@tbo.com
3	Kalin	Wegrzyn	512-555-7587	kalin@msn.com
4	Hal	Jordan	707-555-4567	2814@oa.net

A database is composed of several important components, the *field*, *record*, *table*, and *index*:

Field A space allocated for the storage of a particular item of information. Fields are usually the smallest unit of information in a database. A field has several attributes, such as the type of data (text, numeric, or object) and length or size (number of characters, significant digits, or object size). A field can also be calculated or determined by other fields. Each field in a specific database has its own unique name by which it is identified. In a spreadsheet, an individual field is represented as a cell.

Record   A single, complete set of information composed of fields. A record can represent an individual customer, an account, or some other unit as appropriate to the business processes that the database supports. Records are sometimes assigned numbers to aid in identification. In a spreadsheet, a record is represented as a row. In relational databases, records are also called *tuples*.

Table   A file or a unit in which records are stored. Database tables are often represented as having rows of records and having columns made up of individual fields.

Index   A list of unique identifiers, or *keys,* that identify each record. In a relational database table, unique keys help maintain the integrity of the data table. The index is also used by a database management system to provide faster searches of the data table.

Database software usually includes additional features for maintaining reliability. For example, SQL is based around individual database transactions. A programmer can use SQL features to lock a database record that a user is changing. This record lock prevents other users from changing that record until the database finalizes or commits the transaction. If the database detects a record error, another SQL command can roll back a record to its previous state. Many database systems use SQL features to provide an additional software level of database reliability.

Database systems provide the architecture and methods for working with data. The most popular model for database management systems is the *relational* model, in which data is stored in a series of related tables. You can create small tables, called lookup tables, which are a list of entries that can be used in a particular field. For example, the State/Province field in a customer's address can be linked to a short table that lists the U.S. states and Canadian provinces, along with their two-letter abbreviations. The two-letter code is entered in the customer's State field, rather than the complete name of the state or province. Using lookup tables helps enforce *referential integrity*, or the consistent entry of data across related tables. You can also create tables that contain the details for a particular record, such as an order. The details are related or linked to the order by a unique order number. Relational databases have pre-defined types of data that must be used, such as numbers and strings of text.

Regardless of the type of database you are using, you need software that will allow you to view or change the data. A database management system (DBMS) lets authorized users store, access, or manipulate the data in an organized, secure way. A relational database management system, or RDBMS, works only with relational databases. Rather than using static links between information, a relational database uses tables that are indexed or tagged so users can access the information by issuing queries. These queries do not reorganize the table itself. They simply allow the information within the tables to be presented differently.

The RDBMS model supports a data retrieval language called *SQL (Structured Query Language)* that translates human-readable language into machine-readable code. SQL allows users to construct queries that can be understood by the RDBMS. Requesting data from a server in SQL involves the following process:

1. The user requests data.
2. The client machine translates the request into SQL.
3. The client sends the request to the server.
4. The server processes the request, which might involve communicating with a remote database or server.
5. The server delivers the response to the client.
6. The client delivers the response to the computer screen.

As a server administrator, you may be asked to support an RDBMS. Table 10.2 lists various enterprise RDBMS providers and their products. An enterprise RDBMS is designed for high-volume transaction processing environments, using dedicated database servers to store and retrieve information.

TABLE 10.2 Relational Database Management Systems

Developer	Product	URL
Borland	Interbase	www.borland.com
IBM	DB2	www.ibm.com
iPlanet	IPlanet Application Server	www.iPlanet.com

TABLE 10.2 Relational Database Management Systems *(continued)*

Developer	Product	URL
Microsoft	SQL Server 2000	www.microsoft.com
Oracle	Oracle 9i	www.oracle.com

Another database model that has recently gained acceptance is the object-oriented database. In this model, users and developers can easily define their own types of data, called *objects*. Objects may also be defined on other, more basic objects. This model works well with object-oriented programming languages, which let developers use complex data types. This model requires an ODBMS, which in turn has its own technologies such as Object Query Language (OQL) and various schemes for defining and managing objects.

E-commerce Server

Electronic commerce, or *e-commerce* as it is often called, is the use of networked computer systems to sell, buy, and distribute products and services. Integrating a SQL server, a web server, and other servers in a cohesive package that will create a fully functional e-commerce website is a daunting task. E-commerce servers often consist of several tightly integrated software packages. For example, two of the most popular e-commerce products are Microsoft Site Server E-commerce edition and IBM Net.Commerce. Microsoft SiteServer uses Internet Information Services (IIS), Active Server Pages, Microsoft SQL Server, Microsoft Transaction Server, and other servers. The idea behind these product packages is to integrate e-commerce as precisely as possible with specific operating systems and their services.

You can use an e-commerce server to do the following:

- Create web storefronts and conduct business securely

- Create a web storefront by using wizards, reducing the need to write code and learn various languages

- Distribute information over multiple systems

- Organize information through an indexing or catalog system that supports a search engine for the site

News Server

You can also use a news server to extend the functionality and reach of your website by increasing its interactivity. The more clients interact with your website, the greater their comfort level and loyalty. A news server uses the Network News Transfer Protocol (NNTP) to store messages you can view over the Internet or an intranet. NNTP is the Internet protocol for managing postings to Usenet articles in newsgroups. You can learn more about standard NNTP in RFC 977. RFC 2980 explains some of the ways to extend NNTP so that connection, listing, and error messages, for example, are more descriptive.

A news server allows clients to create newsgroups. For example, you can enable clients to communicate via short notes that remain on the news server for a period of time. New users can review older postings, store messages on their local hard drives, and post messages.

> **NOTE** Do not confuse a news server with a list server (a.k.a., mailing server). A list server uses SMTP and POP3 to automatically forward e-mail to people on a list. A news server, on the other hand, uses NNTP and stores a list of messages, called threads, that allows users to keep track of conversations over time.

You can start a newsgroup for your own company or participate in a Usenet newsgroup. A newsgroup of your own is called a private newsgroup.

Many Usenet newsgroups exist. Newsgroups are organized in a loose hierarchy somewhat similar to DNS. For example, many newsgroups exist underneath the alternative (.alt) group. The .alt newsgroup domain contains groups that discuss topics ranging from the occult to specific musicians, for example. Additional newsgroup domains include science (.sci), computers (.comp), and society (.soc).

Newsgroups store information by subject. For example, an organization named ciwcertified might have a private newsgroup called development. You could access this server by entering `development.ciwcertified.com` in the news server dialog box of your chosen newsgroup client.

> **NOTE** In Chapter 13, we'll look at how to configure and manage a news server.

E-mail Server

E-mail is the primary user service of the Internet. In recent years, only HTTP has rivaled e-mail in terms of total network data transmissions. On a typical TCP/IP network, establishing an e-mail presence has meant creating Simple Mail Transfer Protocol (SMTP) and Post Office Protocol version 3 (POP3) servers. However, using the Internet Mail Access Protocol (IMAP) has recently become popular with corporate server administrators.

Some of the elements involved in deploying e-mail include:

Simple Mail Transport Protocol (SMTP)   An Application layer protocol that delivers e-mail from one host to another, SMTP listens on TCP port 25. The Unix sendmail server, for example, is an SMTP mail delivery agent.

Post Office Protocol (POP)   This Application layer protocol retrieves stored e-mail messages from a mail server. The current version is called POP3. POP3 also provides a limited logon shell that allows users to download e-mail messages from a central server. POP3 listens on TCP port 110. Using POP3, you must first download e-mail to your client application before managing the messages.

Internet Message Access Protocol (IMAP)   Like POP3, this Application layer protocol provides a limited logon shell that allows users to manage e-mail. However, this protocol also permits users to first read a list of their messages before downloading them. For example, you can conduct keyword searches. Because users can fully manage messages on the server, IMAP servers allow greater flexibility and use less bandwidth. Users do not need to store messages on a client application, although they can use an IMAP-aware client to manage, read, and view messages. IMAP servers listen on port 143. You can learn more about IMAP in RFC 2060. The current version is IMAP4.

Chapter 13 discusses how to configure and connect to an e-mail server.

Security Services

In addition to mission-critical servers that provide a fully functional e-commerce website, there are mission-critical security services that protect your website from unauthorized users who are attempting to gain entry to the server or access restricted data. If an organization wants to participate with other networks, the organization must differentiate itself from others. This differentiation is done mainly through network security devices, services, and systems.

The *firewall* is an important security tool. We can define a firewall as a collection of hardware, software, and corporate policies that protect a LAN from the Internet. On one side of a firewall is your company's production network, which you supervise, control, and protect. The other side contains a public network, such as the Internet, over which you have no control.

In computer networking, a network firewall acts as a barrier against potential malicious activity, while still allowing a door for people to communicate between a secured network and the open, unsecured network. The most common location for a firewall is between a corporate LAN and the Internet.

A firewall is intended to do the following:

- Restrict unauthorized users

- Retain control of private information

- Prevent unauthorized export of proprietary data and information

A firewall controls access to your private network. It can also create secure intranet domains. Furthermore, it is the primary means of enforcing your security policy, which can help a systems administrator detect threats and take countermeasures.

A firewall defaults to one of two settings: It can deny all first traffic except that which is expressly permitted, or it can allow all traffic except that which is expressly denied. Many security professionals consider the first setting the most secure.

There are several kinds of firewalls, including the following:

Packet-filtering firewall   A packet-filtering firewall inspects packets, and forbids or allows access based on source and destination IP addresses and ports. This type of firewall is a popular choice for a website that has high-volume traffic. Packet-filtering firewalls operate at the Network layer of the OSI Reference Model.

Application-layer gateway   This type of firewall can be more secure than a packet-filtering firewall because it operates at the Application layer of the OSI Reference Model. It can delve deeper into the IP packet, inspecting transmitted data in its original format. It can also inspect the way a host connects to the firewall because all Application-layer gateways employ services, or daemons, that behave as proxies.

Circuit-level gateway   The primary purpose for a circuit-level gateway is Network Address Translation (NAT), in which a single computer can convert or translate privately used, internal IP addresses into addresses suitable for use on the Internet. A circuit-level gateway requires special, modified clients, as well as modified behavior on the part of end users because circuit-level gateways can only read packets addressed to them. An example of a circuit-level gateway is the SOCKS gateway used by many organizations, such as IBM.

We can also use other tools in combination with firewalls. Suppose an attacker manages to break through a firewall on our network. An *intrusion detection system* can identify, log, and even stop suspicious activity. Such a system can also alert or page a server administrator to attend the system during an attack.

A *proxy server* acts for or on behalf of other hosts by accepting requests and applying rules and filters that either allow or reject requests. Proxy-oriented firewalls, however, cannot handle as many requests as packet-filtering firewalls. For example, they can engage in a web proxy in which all client HTTP traffic passing from the inside network to the outside network is first inspected by the proxy server. Most enterprise-grade proxy servers also provide NAT and packet filtering. Application-layer and circuit-level gateways are also used in proxies.

System Logging

Auditing server and security logs is also an important tool that server administrators can use to maintain server security and optimize server performance. All enterprise operating systems provide logging and auditing services that record activities and events on the network. Figure 10.1 shows a log file generated by a Linux system.

Figure 10.1 shows the /var/log/messages file, which provides information about all logons as well as error messages reported by the system. Such error messages might report problems with the DNS server or sendmail or report that the file system is full. Services operating on top of the operating system, including web, FTP, and database servers, have their own logging facilities.

FIGURE 10.1 The /var/log/messages file in Linux

The following example is a log file generated by an IIS 5 HTTP server as it transmitted a web page to a Windows 98 computer running the Netscape 4.5 web browser. Notice that IIS recorded a time/date stamp, IP address, HTTP protocol, and method for each file requested by the browser. The server administrator can load this server log into an analysis program such as WebTrends to generate usage statistics.

```
#Software: Microsoft Internet Information Server 5.0
#Version: 1.0
#Date: 2001-01-05 02:49:18
#Fields: date time c-ip cs-username s-ip cs-method cs-uri-
⮑stem sc-#status cs-version cs(User-Agent)
2001-01-05 02:49:18 10.100.100.1 - 10.100.100.7 GET /
⮑index.html 200 HTTP/1.0 Mozilla/4.5+[en]+(Win98;+U)
2001-01-05 02:49:18 10.100.100.1 - 10.100.100.7 GET /
⮑iissamples/default/SQUIGGLE.GIF 200 HTTP/1.0 Mozilla/
⮑4.5+[en]+(Win98;+U)
```

```
2001-01-05 02:49:18 10.100.100.1 - 10.100.100.7 GET /
↳iissamples/default/MSFT.GIF 200 HTTP/1.0 Mozilla/
↳4.5+[en]+(Win98;+U)

2001-01-05 02:49:18 10.100.100.1 - 10.100.100.7 GET /
↳iissamples/default/nav2.gif 200 HTTP/1.0 Mozilla/
↳4.5+[en]+(Win98;+U)

2001-01-05 02:49:18 10.100.100.1 - 10.100.100.7 GET /
↳iissamples/default/IISSide.GIF 200 HTTP/1.0 Mozilla/
↳4.5+[en]+(Win98;+U)

2001-01-05 02:49:18 10.100.100.1 - 10.100.100.7 GET /
↳iissamples/default/IISTitle.gif 200 HTTP/1.0 Mozilla/
↳4.5+[en]+(Win98;+U)

2001-01-05 02:49:18 10.100.100.1 - 10.100.100.7 GET /
↳iissamples/default/IE.GIF 200 HTTP/1.0 Mozilla/
↳4.5+[en]+(Win98;+U)
```

Many services do not have logging turned on by default. Even those services that log by default may not capture the events that you want to know about. There are a variety of reasons for these default settings, but one of the most important is system performance. Given the comprehensive logging options offered by some operating systems and server applications, it is possible to automatically record a massive amount of detailed log information. In a research or an evaluation setting, information is our friend. We might tolerate the slower system response that occurs when logs are recording every detail of a transaction.

In a production environment, managers demand high network performance. A server administrator must balance system performance with log detail. As a result, you will have to customize your logging environment. You will learn about log configuration options in Chapter 14.

Monitoring Performance and Optimizing a Server

Monitoring system processes is usually the first step in optimizing server performance. Figure 10.2 shows the System Monitor application in Windows 2000, which you can use to monitor system processes.

FIGURE 10.2 The Windows 2000 System Monitor

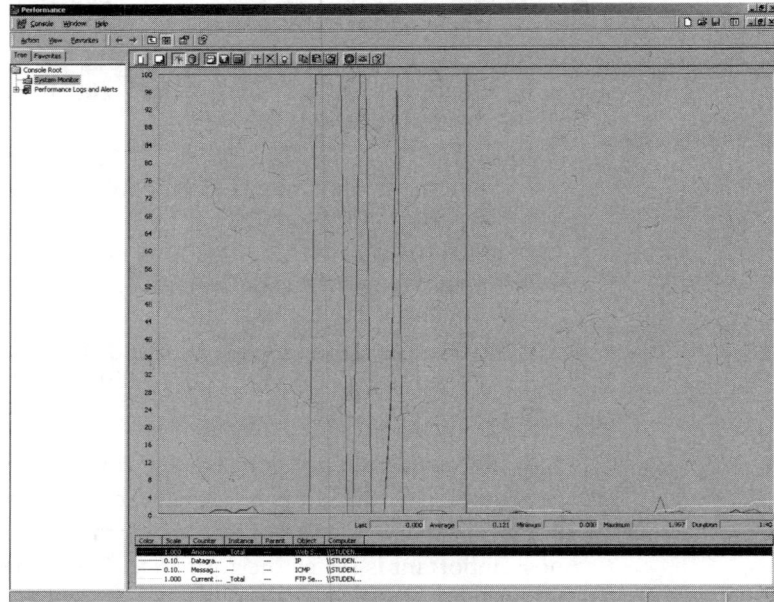

In this example, you can see that this particular system is sustaining five FTP connections and one HTTP connection. It is also currently experiencing a burst of IP datagrams, due to repeated failed connection attempts.

After you check the log files and determine the purpose of your particular server, you can adjust your server. Of course, obtaining the optimal settings depends greatly on the operating system and service vendor, as well as the types of connections made to the server.

The following strategies can help improve server performance.

Make adjustments to the software. Improperly configured operating system and server software can sap system resources. Server administrators should become familiar with performance features that can assign and prioritize the computer's processing power to different applications.

Upgrade existing hardware on your system. Repeated connection failures and timeouts might be caused by a lack of system resources on the server computer. Adding RAM can alleviate these symptoms, if the hardware can support the extra memory modules. Upgrading the system processor to a faster model can also improve overall performance.

Obtain additional systems to help distribute the load.   A load-balancing strategy employs two or more computers to process client requests. This approach is particularly helpful for sites, such as shopping sites, that experience extreme changes in traffic at different times of the year. You can add and remove load-balanced servers as needed. We will discuss load balancing in more detail later in this chapter.

Fault Tolerance

Fault tolerance is the ability of a system to respond gracefully to an unexpected hardware or software failure. This ability should be transparent to the end user. *Transparency* means that the user should not be aware that an error has occurred. The server administrator should be notified in some manner of the error. Depending on the magnitude of the error, this notification can be in a log file, it can be a system warning, or it can be some other feedback mechanism. For obvious reasons, fault tolerance is an indispensable feature for network devices.

There are many levels of fault tolerance, the lowest being the ability to continue operation in the event of a power failure. At a network level, a fault-tolerant system might monitor network connectivity and traffic and help reroute connections if one server in the system is unreachable. We have already discussed how fault tolerance is built into robust network protocols such as TCP. TCP is designed to provide a reliable continuous connection between two computers. The recipient computer can determine if a packet has been damaged in transit and can automatically request a replacement packet from the sender.

An example of a system failure at the host level is the loss of a hard drive. *Redundant Array of Inexpensive Disks (RAID)* is the main strategy for implementing fault tolerance in storage systems. RAID technology uses multiple hard disks and I/O controllers to distribute information that would normally be contained on one hard drive among several drives. This process is completely transparent to the end user. The user accesses data as if it resides on one hard drive. In most forms of RAID, the user does not notice the failure of a single hard disk drive because the remaining disks safely store and provide the requested information. The operating system or hardware diagnostics inform the server administrator of the failure and support continued operations until repairs or replacements can be made. You will learn more about RAID later in this book.

Load Balancing and Clustering

High-availability clustering provides a higher level of fault tolerance. Cluster servers do most of the load balancing work on the Internet. Load balancing is the practice of distributing connections between several systems. A cluster server is a dedicated server that fields requests and then distributes them to additional systems.

Distributing requests provides a smooth service to the end user. Although the connections and resources are distributed among several computers and protocols, the client application thinks that it is connecting to only one resource. One of the key features of high-availability clustering is its ability to automatically sense hosts that have failed or become too busy. Once such a problem occurs, a *load- balancing* scheme can direct subsequent end-user requests to other servers, thus giving IT professionals time to correct the problem.

The benefits of load balancing include the following:

- Available resources can be read faster.

- Network latency is reduced.

- Administration is centralized.

- The systems can be scaled to accommodate increased demand.

You can create a primitive form of load balancing simply by designating two systems to use different protocols. For example, if you have a web server that provides downloads, you can use the web server to provide the initial HTML documents and use an FTP server to provide subsequent downloads. Your HTTP server must then provide only web pages, whereas the FTP server manages the file-downloading tasks.

One of the most popular load-balancing schemes is the use of cluster servers, such as Microsoft Cluster Server (MSCS). Red Hat Linux can also operate as a cluster server. Other cluster server products include Sun Cluster (`www.sun.com/clusters`) and Apcon POWERSWITCH (`www.apcon.com`).

You can also use clustering to increase performance. Sometimes called parallel-processing clustering, this form of clustering is quite different from high-availability clustering. Parallel-processing clustering involves using one computer that takes a single task, such as the process of working out a complex mathematical problem, and then distributes parts of that single task among multiple computers. The ability to distribute a process among multiple computers allows you to effectively create a supercomputer using relatively inexpensive network equipment.

Backing Up Resources

If fault tolerance fails, a well-designed backup process can help server administrators create and maintain data archives for restoring lost files. These archives can include backups of entire operating systems, hard drives, or essential directories and files that change every day. As you prepare to back up resources, you must consider the following issues and options:

- The backup of critical host operating systems and files, including firewall hosts, file servers, and web servers.

- Offsite file storage.

- Unix and Windows 2000 backup programs, including cpio, dump, restore, and the Windows Backup MMC snap-in.

- Backup devices, including tapes, CD-ROM (rewritable as well as write-once) options, and *jukeboxes*. A jukebox is a device that stores multiple writable or rewritable CD-ROMs for use as backups.

- Backup types, including full, incremental, and differential backups.

Another way to back up data is with a *Storage Area Network (SAN)*. A SAN is a dedicated, centrally managed computer network that is accessible via redundant, high-speed connections. Generally used for backing up data in busy networks, SAN solutions have become central to organizations such as eBay, which have found it necessary to back up hundreds of gigabytes of data every day.

> **NOTE** We'll discuss backup in detail in Chapter 16.

Summary

In this chapter, we identified mission-critical services. We also identified various server types, including web, e-mail, and proxy servers. Because servers require constant maintenance, we discussed the concepts of logging, performance monitoring, and optimization. Finally, we described fault tolerance, load balancing, and backup.

With this information, you should be able to identify foundation services, including DNS, WINS, and Samba, which provide name resolution, and other foundation services such as SMB, NetBIOS over TCP/IP, and NFS, which provide sharing across a network. You should also be able to list mission-critical services, including web servers, databases, e-commerce servers, news servers, streaming media servers, e-mail servers, and proxy servers.

For these foundation and mission-critical services, you should also be able to provide security, optimization, fault tolerance, and disaster recovery. Security is provided by firewalls, intrusion detection systems, encryption using SSL, and auditing of server logs. Log files are also inspected to monitor server errors that require corrective action in order to keep your Internet servers fully functional. System processes are also analyzed by such utilities as System Monitor in order to optimize server performance.

As a systems administrator, beyond securing, monitoring, and optimizing Internet servers, you should provide for fault tolerance and disaster recovery. Hard disks are mechanical devices that will eventually fail. RAID is the main strategy for implementing fault tolerance for your hard drives. Backups are also essential, because your hard drives may be intact but have corrupt data, or data may have been intentionally or accidentally deleted. To provide fault tolerance for your mission-critical servers, server clustering is the right solution.

Exam Essentials

Be able to identify foundation services and mission-critical services. DNS, WINS, and Samba are foundation services that provide name resolution. SMB, NetBIOS over TCP/IP, and NFS are foundation services that provide the ability to share information over a network. Mission-critical services are those services whose interruption would cripple your website. Because many services interoperate to create a fully functional website, these services might well include HTTP servers, database servers, e-mail servers, and other servers depending on what your website provides.

Understand that e-commerce servers integrate software packages such as web servers, database servers, and transaction servers. E-commerce servers allow you to create secure and scalable web storefronts using wizards. They also provide for indexing of content distributed over multiple systems.

Know the types of e-mail servers and their ports. SMTP servers are used to send e-mail and use port 25. POP3 servers are used to download mail and use port 110. IMAP servers are more sophisticated in that they allow you to manipulate messages on the server and decide which messages to download using port 143.

Understand the services provided by various types of firewalls, by a proxy server, and by an intrusion detection system. A packet-filtering firewall inspects packets and forbids or allows access based on source and destination IP addresses and ports. A circuit-level gateway provides NAT. A proxy server provides NAT plus caching plus packet filtering. SSL provides security through encryption.

Know how fault tolerance for hardware is achieved using RAID, and clustering. Backups protect against loss of data. Jukeboxes are devices that store multiple writable CD-ROMs for backup of larger networks. Gigantic networks can be backed up online using SANs.

Key Terms

Before you take the exam, be certain you are familiar with the following terms:

database	objects
e-commerce	proxy server
electronic commerce	record
fault tolerance	Redundant Array of Inexpensive Disks (RAID)
field	referential integrity
firewall	relational
index	Secure MIME (S/MIME)
intrusion detection system	SQL (Structured Query Language)
jukebox	Storage Area Network (SAN)
keys	table
load balancing	transparency
mission-critical service	tuples
Multipurpose Internet Mail Extensions (MIME)	

Review Questions

1. Jim is training a new webmaster, and he wants to emphasize the importance of DNS, WINS, and Samba. How should he categorize these services?

   A. Enterprise

   B. Background

   C. Mission-critical

   D. Foundation

2. Mark is rewriting his job description in order to justify a raise. He just read that the DNS, WINS, Samba, SMB, NetBIOS over TCP/IP, and NFS services that he supports on an enterprise level are foundation services. He wants to explain the importance of the foundation services under his control. What do foundation services do? Choose two.

   A. Organize resources

   B. Log security and performance information

   C. Take care of name resolution

   D. Provide sharing across a network

3. Brad wants to support a new type of XML document on his web server. What does Brad need to define?

   A. File association

   B. Document type

   C. MIME type

   D. Host program

   E. Embedded file type

4. Brad's boss wants to know what makes steaming media servers much more efficient at delivering video than downloading a file. What should Brad answer?

 A. UDP

 B. TCPv2

 C. IPv6

 D. IPv4

 E. TCP

5. Joshua wants to extract information from a relational database that contains information about the buying habits of his website's customers. What should Joshua do?

 A. Query the database using SQL

 B. Install Server-Side Database Includes (SSDI)

 C. Install the appropriate plug-in in his browser

 D. Query the ODBC connector

6. Joshua's boss tells him that he will be installing the latest version Microsoft Site Sever E-Commerce Edition. Which Microsoft servers are integrated into Microsoft Site Server E-Commerce Edition?

 A. SQL

 B. Exchange

 C. IIS

 D. Transaction Server

7. Tony is evaluating various e-commerce servers for purchase and deployment. What features should Tony look for?

   A. Stability and durability

   B. Ability to create web storefronts

   C. Security

   D. Use of wizards

   E. Ability to distribute information over multiple systems

   F. Ability to index content

8. Tony's organization is project based with a strong mix of engineers and scientists from around the world who have diverse interests and abilities to contribute to ongoing multidisciplinary projects. How can Tony foster collaboration and knowledge sharing based on interests? Choose the best answer.

   A. Publish the company directory of e-mail addresses

   B. Set up newsgroups

   C. Set up a database of the expertises available

   D. Use a proxy server

9. Peter's mobile e-mail users complain that it takes them a long time to download long messages with large attachments before they can get to critical messages from their boss. What type of e-mail server should Peter consider implementing in order to solve this problem? (Choose the best answer.)

   A. SMTP

   B. POP3

   C. IMAP4

   D. NNTP

10. Ralph needs to open up ports on his corporate firewall for an e-mail server that uses SMTP to send mail and POP3 to deliver mail. Which ports should Ralph open on the firewall for this e-mail server?

   A. 21

   B. 80

   C. 25

   D. 110

11. Frank wants to set up a firewall on his corporate router that is used for Internet access. This firewall should operate at the Network layer and forbid or allow inbound or outbound traffic based on source and destination IP addresses and ports. What type of firewall is Frank talking about?

   A. Packet-filtering firewall

   B. Application-layer gateway

   C. Circuit-level gateway

   D. Proxy server

   E. Intrusion detection system

   F. Encryption

12. Frank wants to set up a firewall on the perimeter of his network. This firewall should also provide Network Address Translation and cache user requests for web content in order to enhance performance. What type of firewall is Frank talking about?

   A. Packet-filtering firewall

   B. Application-layer gateway

   C. Circuit-level gateway

   D. Proxy server

   E. Intrusion detection system

   F. Encryption

13. Frank wants to set up a firewall on the perimeter of his network. He wants this firewall to hide internal network addresses and allow access to the Internet for all internal network clients; while using only one registered Internet address rather than buying a block of Internet addresses. He doesn't want to pay for any additional features. What type of firewall should Frank install?

    A. Packet-filtering firewall

    B. Application-layer gateway

    C. Circuit-level gateway

    D. Proxy server

    E. Intrusion detection system

    F. Encryption

14. Kerry wants to provide encryption for website customers placing their orders. What should Kerry implement?

    A. Packet-filtering firewall

    B. Application-layer gateway

    C. Circuit-level gateway

    D. Proxy server

    E. Intrusion detection system

    F. SSL

15. Mandy is the systems administrator in charge of 40 Linux servers. What should Mandy check in the morning to find any problems that occurred overnight with any of these servers?

    A. Backup logs

    B. Event Viewer

    C. `/var/log/messages` file

    D. `/system32/drivers/etc` file

16. George's Internet security business was run on one Windows 2000 Small Business Server. In the last year, George's business has tripled in size, and his server has slowed considerably. What options does Frank have to restore performance?

    A. Upgrade the existing hardware on his system

    B. Implement server-throttling

    C. Obtain additional systems to distribute the load

    D. Make adjustments to the software

17. Mark administers a medium-sized network of 25 servers. What is the main strategy he should use to implement fault tolerance?

    A. Backups

    B. UPS

    C. RAID

    D. Clustering

    E. SAN

18. Mark administers a medium-sized network of 24 Windows 2000 Advanced Servers. These servers support mission-critical applications that automate patient monitoring at a large metropolitan hospital complex. What should Mark implement so that the failure of one server does not crash a critical service?

    A. Backups

    B. UPS

    C. RAID

    D. Clustering

    E. Warm standby servers

    F. Virtual online backups

19. Peter wants to cut the cost of backup media and automate the backup of many servers. What should Peter install?

A. FireWire based backup

B. Jukeboxes

C. Transaction-based backup

D. Incremental backups

20. Ralph administers the backups for a network of 1000 servers. He cannot physically visit each server and is having a hard time keeping track of all the backups. He wants to centrally manage the backups and provide redundancy. What should Ralph implement?

A. FireWire based backup

B. Jukeboxes

C. Transaction-based backup

D. Incremental backups

E. SAN

Answers to Review Questions

1. D. DNS, WINS, and Samba are foundation services.

2. C, D. DNS, WINS and Samba provide name resolution; SMB, Net-BIOS over TCP/IP, and NFS provide the ability to share information across a network.

3. C. Multipurpose Internet Mail Extensions (MIME) is a protocol that encodes the file using the file type and decodes it properly at the receiving end.

4. A. Although TCP packets have acknowledged, guaranteed delivery, UDP packets are not acknowledged, but they are up to ten times faster at delivering data. For this reason, they are perfect for streaming media servers that must for a given bandwidth present the most detail in a simultaneous broadcast to multiple clients.

5. A. Joshua should query the database using Structured Query Language (SQL).

6. A, C, D. Joshua should study Microsoft IIS, SQL, and Transaction Server because these servers are included in Microsoft Site Server.

7. B, C, D, E, F. Tony should look for the ability to easily create web storefronts using wizards and the ability to securely conduct business, while allowing users to search his website even when information is distributed over multiple systems.

8. B. Tony should setup newsgroups, the only one of the four choices that supports a discussion forum that can be used for collaboration and knowledge sharing. A company directory of e-mail addresses is a less-efficient method, because it provides little information about each individual's interests.

9. C. Peter should implement an IMAP4 server that would allow users to download message headers and select which messages to download or delete.

10. C, D. Ralph should open port 25 for SMTP and port 110 for POP3.

11. A. Frank wants the speed of a packet-filtering firewall that has a small impact on performance.

12. D. Frank wants to install a proxy server.

13. C. Frank wants to install a circuit-level gateway, which does Network Address Translation (NAT).

14. F. Kerry should implement encryption through Secure Sockets Layer (SSL) that uses HTTPS (Hypertext Transfer Protocol Secure).

15. C. Mandy should check the Linux log files in /var/log/messages. To see the latest messages, she should use the tail command.

16. A, C, D. In order to improve performance, George can upgrade the hardware, obtain additional systems, or make adjustments to the software such as disabling features of Small Business Server that are not being used but are using system resources.

17. C. Redundant Array of Inexpensive Disks (RAID) is the main strategy for implementing fault tolerance.

18. D. Clustering of servers with fall-over support would provide fault tolerance and load balancing.

19. B. Peter should use a jukebox of multiple writable or rewritable CD-ROMs.

20. E. Ralph should implement a Storage Area Network (SAN). A SAN is a centrally managed computer network that is accessible via redundant, high-speed connections. It is commonly used for backing up data in a busy network.

Chapter

11

Installing, Configuring, and Integrating a Web Server

THE CIW EXAM OBJECTIVE GROUPS COVERED IN THIS CHAPTER:

- ✓ Select and implement popular web servers, including but not limited to: Microsoft IIS, Apache server.

- ✓ Perform advanced web server administration tasks, including but not limited to: user-based authentication, access control, HTML administration, alias creation, error messages.

You have a great business idea, and your startup Internet company wants to create a fully functional e-commerce website. One of your first tasks is to select the software that you'll use to create your website. The two most popular choices are Microsoft Internet Information Services (IIS) and the Apache web server. IIS is popular because it can be configured using a graphical user interface, and Apache is popular because it sits on top of Unix or Linux and therefore is essentially free. You might even be surprised to know that even though IIS is growing in popularity, Apache is currently almost twice as popular. (See www.netcraft.com/survey for the latest statistics.)

After you choose a web server, you must install and configure it so that your users can connect. You will need to register the host name and IP address of your web server with Internic, and you'll need to configure what users see when they connect. They might see a default document or a directory listing. If the URL is incorrect, or if the client cannot connect to the web server, the client might display an error message. You will choose the document root directory for your website and the default document that will be displayed, and you will choose to enable directory browsing.

If you want to host multiple sites, you'll need to create additional virtual web servers on the same server by using additional IP addresses or additional ports. To increase the size and functionality of your website, you can create virtual directories that are shortcuts to directories that live in one of three places: on your web server, on a network share, or at another URL.

To secure your website and provide the appropriate level of access, you will configure security, including authentication methods such as anonymous access, basic authentication, or integrated Windows authentication (Microsoft). You will also need to restrict or permit access to your Internet servers by IP subnet or DNS domain.

Once users are allowed to connect to your Internet server, they may well expect a website that is rich in content and features. Common Gateway Interface (CGI) scripts and Active Server Pages (ASP) programming are two popular choices for expanding the functionality of your website. A database server integrated with your web server allows users to buy items by placing them in a shopping cart. Streaming media content can be provided using software such as RealNetworks RealServer.

Installing, configuring, and integrating these servers and implementing their services is the focus of this key chapter.

Web Servers and Directories

The World Wide Web is a collection of computer systems running web servers. Together, these servers act as a document delivery system. Documents are delivered to systems that run web browsers, or clients. These client systems request documents from servers. The documents can be from a disk archive, or they can be created dynamically when the client requests them. The Web operates on HTTP (Hypertext Transfer Protocol), a TCP Application-layer protocol. The web server and the web browser are prime examples of client/server communications.

Websites are organized around web server processes, which run as daemon processes on Unix computers and as services on Windows 2000 computers. The server process binds to TCP port 80 and listens for incoming requests from clients. These requests are formed using HTML (Hypertext Markup Language). The applications that web servers use to create documents dynamically in order to present server resources are called Common Gateway Interface applications, or CGI scripts.

The most basic aspect of this relationship between URL paths and true file names involves root directories. The document root directory for a web server is the one referred to by the URL root path /. The server interprets other paths relative to this root directory. For example, Apache web server defaults to the following directory as its document root: `/var/www/html/`. The server also refers to a file named `index.html` by default. Therefore, the URL `http://www.yourhost.com/index.html` refers to the following place on your system's hard drive: `/var/www/html/index.html`.

On Windows 2000 systems in which IIS 5 is installed on a C:\ drive, the default directory is `C:\inetpub\wwwroot`. You must place all files in this folder or create an alias to another folder; otherwise, the web server cannot read them (see Figure 11.1). An *alias* is the part of a URL that tells the server not to use the default document root directory but to provide content from a specified part of the hard drive.

FIGURE 11.1 The web server root directory

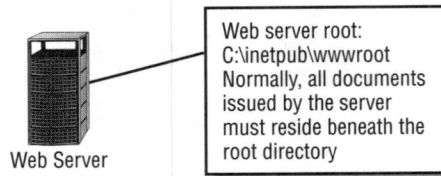

Web server root:
C:\inetpub\wwwroot
Normally, all documents issued by the server must reside beneath the root directory

Web Server

You are not limited to the system root. Most web servers let you configure flexible mapping of URL path names to file names. This kind of mapping is possible with virtual directories that use aliases as FTP does. The primary advantage of creating virtual directories is that you can serve files and information anywhere on a disk or even on another system. You can also create an alias that points to a directory on another system.

For example, suppose you want a server to supply a collection of documents called `doc1.html` and `doc2.html`, located in the directory `/sales/docs`. The server root directory is `/var/www/html/`, but you want to serve the files from `/sales/docs/` instead. To allow this access, you configure the server to map the URL path `/sales/` to the file path `/sales/docs`, instead of to `/var/www/html/docs/sales/doc1.html`. As you will see later in this chapter, the way you do this depends on whether you are using IIS 5 or Apache server.

Directory Browsing and Default Documents

When a server receives a request for a URL that refers to a directory rather than to a specified document, the server can proceed in one of the following ways, depending on its configuration:

- It can generate an error and refuse the request.

- It can return a formatted directory listing to the browser. In most cases, the server constructs an HTML document that associates an

HTML link with each file. By clicking the corresponding link, the browser user can obtain the listed file.

- It can return a default document that is stored in that directory.

Of the preceding three modes of operation, the third is the most common. For example, a request for the URL `http://www.machine.com/` usually returns the default document, or home page, from the server resource root directory on the machine `www.machine.com`.

If a web server permits directory browsing, the server operates in much the same way as an FTP server. Figure 11.2 shows an example of the browser view of a server directory listing.

FIGURE 11.2 A server directory listing

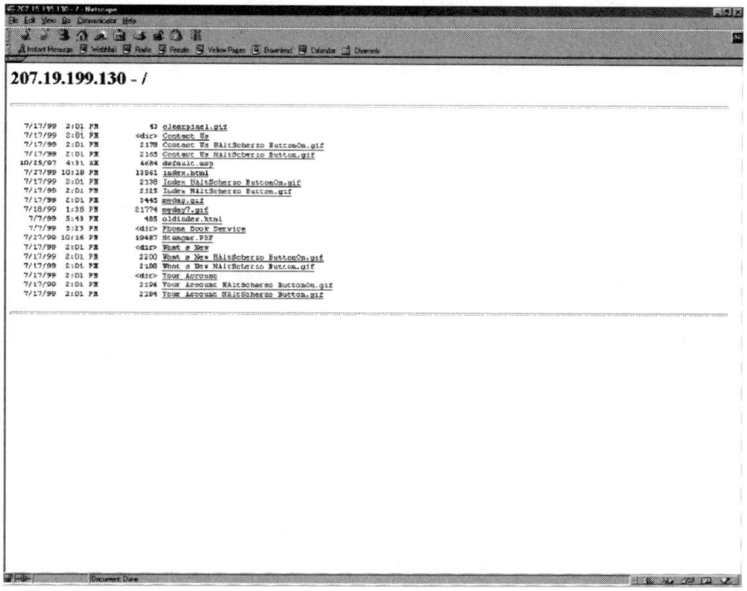

Popular Web Browsers and Servers

The Web allows computers using any operating system to communicate using TCP/IP. The Web is a standard client/server model, with servers running any of several dozen web server software packages. Clients can be running any one of more than 100 web browsers, although the most popular are the following:

- Microsoft Internet Explorer (available for Windows and Macintosh systems)

- Netscape Navigator (available for Windows, Unix, and Macintosh systems)

- Lynx (a text-based browser for Unix systems)

- HotJava (for Solaris systems)

Web server software is available from several companies and for many operating systems; the cost ranges from none (that is, free) to thousands of dollars.

> For information about types of web servers, go to www.serverwatch.com.

The most popular web servers in use today include the following:

- Apache server (www.apache.org).

- Microsoft IIS (www.microsoft.com).

- Netscape Enterprise Server (www.netscape.com).

- Zeus web server (www.zeus.com).

This chapter focuses on IIS 5 and the Apache web server.

Configuring IIS

You can configure any IIS 5 server using the Internet Information Services (IIS) snap-in, which is shown in Figure 11.3. To open the snap-in, choose Start ➤ Programs ➤ Administrative Tools ➤ Internet Services Manager.

Using the Internet Information Services snap-in, you can do the following:

- Connect to a local or remote web server

- Create virtual directories and servers and implement web applications

- Control access to a web server

- Change default settings

FIGURE 11.3   The Internet Information Services snap-in window listing the default website

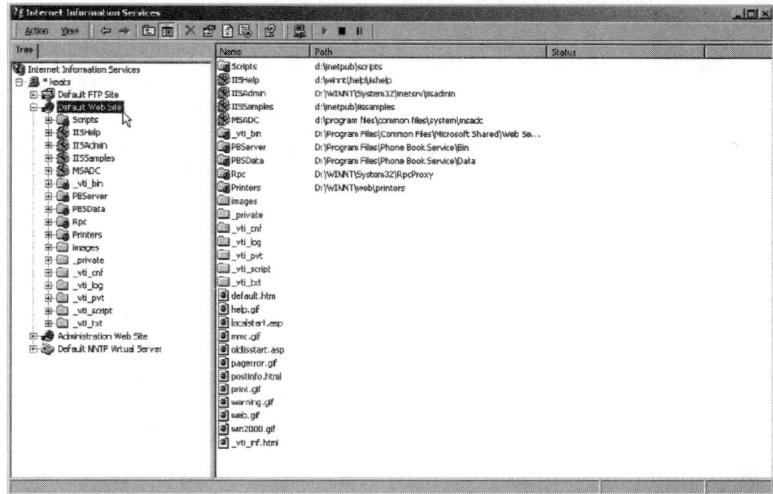

Administering a Web Server

The ISM snap-in defaults to opening IIS 5 on the local server. You can, however, administer any web server you want. In the Internet Information Services snap-in, right-click Default Web Server, and choose Properties from the shortcut menu to open the Default Web Site Properties dialog box, which is shown in Figure 11.4.

FIGURE 11.4   The Default Web Site Properties dialog box, open at the Web Site tab

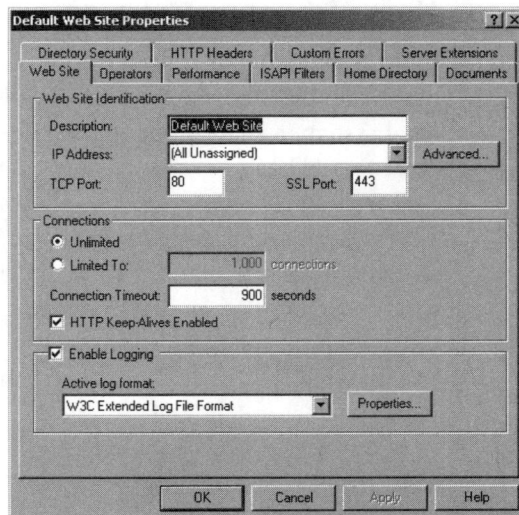

The Web Site Tab

This tab presents basic information about your site, including the site name (in this case, Default Web Site), its IP address, its port, and so forth. You can also limit connections and adjust connection timeout on this tab.

HTTP is a stateful protocol; the Connection Timeout setting determines the length of time in seconds that this connection will remain valid. You can change any of these settings. Consider the following when changing Connection Timeout settings:

- If you set the Connection Timeout value too high, IIS (or any other server) will waste resources keeping a connection alive even after a user has left the site.

- If you set the Connection Timeout value too low, IIS will waste system resources re-establishing a connection when a user decides to visit another page.

Notice that you can also determine log settings from this window, including the log format, and how often you will create a new log file (on a daily, weekly, or monthly basis). In addition, you can set the file to grow to an unlimited size or grow to a fixed threshold (in megabytes).

You can also use this dialog box to change the default log file directory. Click the Properties button to open the Microsoft Logging Properties dialog box. You can set a number of options in this dialog box, such as logging to a database, a flat file, and so on. For the exam, know that the W3C Extended Log File Format is often the most useful for auditing purposes.

The Home Directory Tab

In the first section of this tab (shown in Figure 11.5), you specify the location of the root directory for your IIS 5 web server. You can use a directory on the local system, a share from another computer (via SMB), or a remote web server via HTTP.

The Home Directory tab also allows you to determine access permissions. Access permissions are particularly important because they determine whether this particular server or directory is allowed to execute web applications such as Perl and ASP scripts. Using the Application Protection drop-down list box, you can specify that web applications run in their own memory spaces, which can provide more system stability and security.

FIGURE 11.5 The Home Directory tab

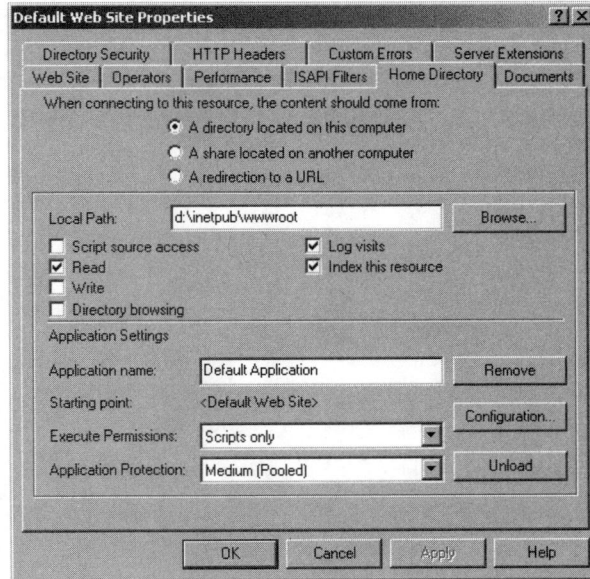

Do not confuse granting read access to the directory with allowing script execution. Read access to the directory allows users to view the contents of the directory. Script execution allows web applications to execute.

If you do not place any documents in the directory, users will see an error message. As you work through the exercises in this chapter, be sure that you place HTML files into the directories you create before you troubleshoot the web server.

The Documents Tab

A web server serves a default document if the web browser does not specify a particular HTML file. On the Documents tab, which is shown in Figure 11.6, you specify the HTML document for which IIS will search first. The default for IIS is `Default.htm`. You can add others, including `index.html`. In this example, IIS will look for `Default.htm` first, then `Default.asp`, and then `iisstart.asp`.

FIGURE 11.6 The Documents tab

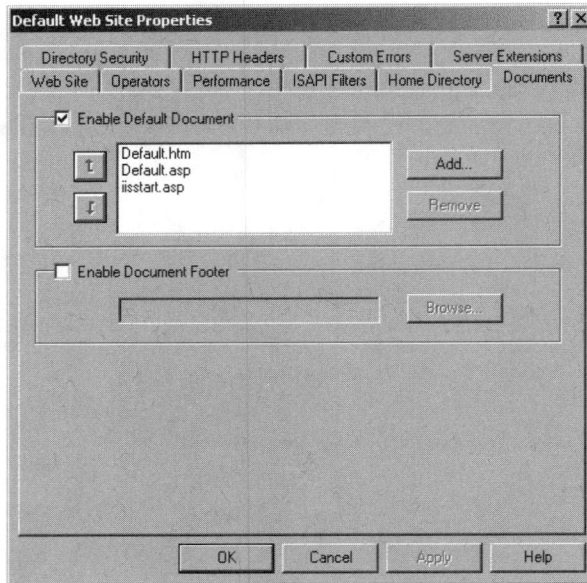

Default Web Site Properties dialog box showing the Documents tab selected. The tabs shown are: Directory Security, HTTP Headers, Custom Errors, Server Extensions, Web Site, Operators, Performance, ISAPI Filters, Home Directory, Documents. The "Enable Default Document" checkbox is checked with a list containing Default.htm, Default.asp, iisstart.asp, and buttons Add... and Remove. The "Enable Document Footer" checkbox is unchecked with a Browse... button. Buttons at bottom: OK, Cancel, Apply, Help.

NOTE Although you can enter any default document name you want, be sure that the actual document is in the home directory. For example, the inetpub\wwwroot directory does not contain the Default.htm file. Rather, it contains the iisstart.asp file.

EXERCISE 11.1

Editing the Root Directory

In this exercise, you will edit the default root directory (that is, the local path) on your computers and add a default document type in IIS 5.

1. Open Windows Explorer and create a new directory named C:\labfiles\newroot. This will be your new web directory.

2. Chose Start ➤ Programs ➤ Administrative Tools ➤ Internet Services Manager to open the IIS snap-in.

3. Your IIS snap-in should already be connected to your local IIS server. If not, connect to your own web server by right-clicking the Internet Information Services icon and taking the necessary steps.

4. Double-click the icon with your computer name so that you can view the web, FTP, and administrative servers that reside on it.

5. Right-click Default Web Site, and choose Properties from the shortcut menu to open the Default Web Site Properties dialog box.

6. Click the Home Directory tab.

7. Write the Local Path value in the space provided: _____

8. In the Local Path box, change the value to C:\labfiles\newroot.

9. Open your browser and connect to your site (http://localhost).

10. You should see a Directory Listing Denied message, because the directory is empty.

11. Populate the site with some simple HTML files. From the CD included with this book, copy the contents of the Chapter11\webcontent folder to the C:\labfiles\newroot directory. Do not copy the entire folder to the C:\labfiles\newroot directory; copy only the files themselves. If you place the entire webcontent folder in the C:\labfiles\newroot directory, the following step will not work properly, because the web server will be looking for HTML files and will see only the webcontent folder.

12. Connect to your system again. You should now be able to view some content.

Many web browsers cache information. One way to make sure that you are reading current information is to close and reopen your browser.

The Directory Security Tab

You use the Directory Security tab, shown in Figure 11.7, to specify who is allowed to access your site. You can also limit access based on IP addresses and configure SSL settings on this tab. By default, IIS allows anonymous access.

FIGURE 11.7 The Directory Security tab

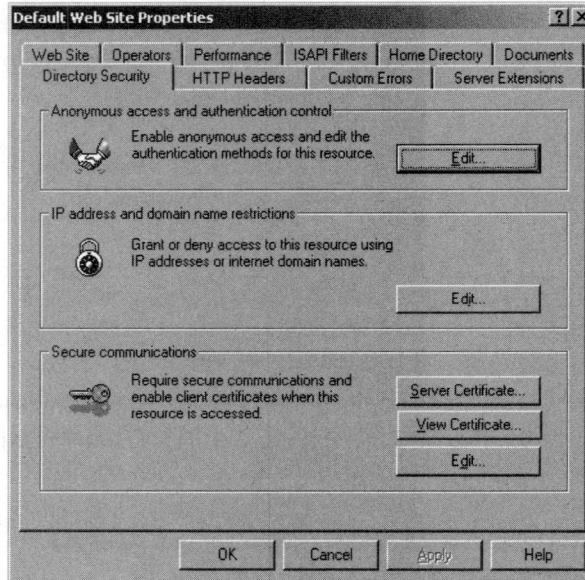

Most websites allow anonymous connections. Whenever you surf the Web and visit a public site, you are logging on as an anonymous user. However, you can also create areas of your site that require authentication.

Figure 11.8 shows the Authentication Methods dialog box. To open this dialog box, click the Directory Security tab in the Web Site Properties dialog box, and then click the Edit button in the Anonymous Access and Authentication Control section. Using this dialog box, you can specify exactly which users can log on to your site. You can also specify exactly how they can log on.

FIGURE 11.8   The Authentication Methods dialog box

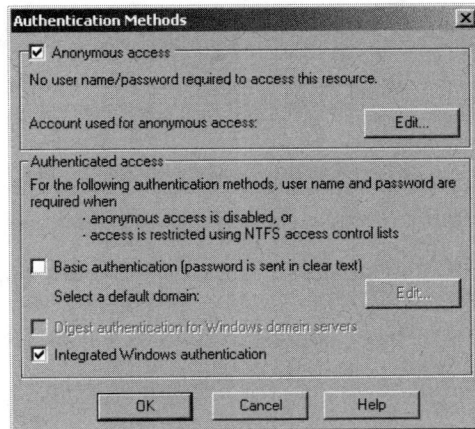

Controlling Access by User Account

Following is a summary of the access methods in IIS 5.

Anonymous Access   Allows any anonymous user access to resources. IIS uses the Windows 2000 IUSR account to provide a limited logon shell that allows users to access web server files. You can change this account, if you want.

Basic Authentication   Requires that users first authenticate. You must use NTFS permissions with this option, which requires IIS to first check with the Windows 2000 SAM. The danger of the Basic Authentication setting is that it allows user names and passwords to be transmitted across networks in cleartext. The benefit to Basic Authentication is that anyone with a browser can authenticate with IIS and gain access to a directory.

Integrated Windows Authentication   You must use NTFS permissions with this option, which is different primarily in how users connect to the site and authenticate. Instead of sending information in cleartext, Windows 2000 detects a connection request, and then issues an encrypted challenge to the browser. The browser then decrypts the challenge, allowing you to respond with a password. The details of Integrated Windows (Challenge/Response) encryption are beyond the scope of this book.

Controlling Access by IP Address

IIS 5 allows you to control access by IP address, domain name, or subnet. You can control access using the IP Address and Domain Name Restrictions dialog box. This access control option is based on IP address and/or domain name. The access control option offers two choices:

- Granting access to all, then denying access to individual hosts or subnets.

- Denying access to all, then granting access to individual hosts or subnets.

Figure 11.9 shows the IP Address and Domain Name Restrictions dialog box.

FIGURE 11.9 The IP Address and Domain Name Restrictions dialog box

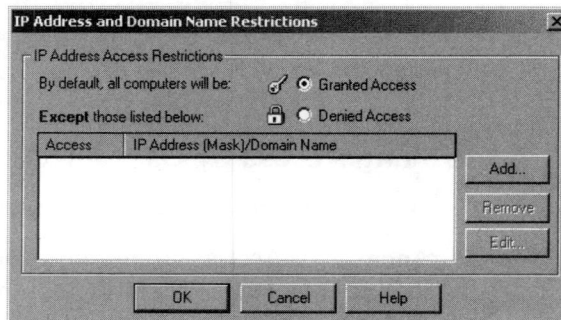

Following are some considerations about establishing restrictions:

- This dialog box does not deny TCP, HTTP or UDP connections. It simply denies access to the web server directories. Users can still connect to the host.

- Hackers can still spoof IP addresses and/or domain names, by altering packet headers and inserting incorrect information. Therefore, this restriction option is only part of a more comprehensive strategy to deny access to unwanted visitors.

- You can use this dialog box to deny access to particular hosts or subnets that are causing security problems. In an intranet setting, you can use this dialog box to limit access to particular departments and/or users.

- You may want to combine user-based access control with IP-address control and name-access control. Doing so may be appropriate in certain settings; however, combining these options may cause problems for users who access a resource from multiple computers.

The Performance Tab

You use the options on the Performance tab, shown in Figure 11.10 to adjust the web server's performance. Customizing the settings reduces the time the server must spend waiting for connections to be made and also improves performance time.

FIGURE 11.10 The Performance tab

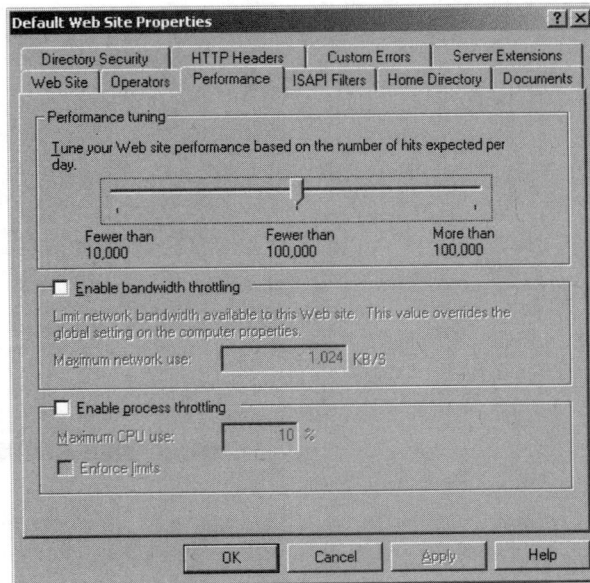

Bandwidth throttling controls the amount of bandwidth a web server can use, measured in kilobits per second (Kbps). Bandwidth throttling is useful in the following scenarios:

- You have several separate web servers on separate hosts, and you want to make sure each receives a certain amount of bandwidth.

- You want to control bandwidth allocated to separate web servers on the same host.

Bandwidth throttling or QoS rate limiting restricts how much of the CPU a web application can use. The server administrator can control the amount of bandwidth allocated to each application.

Custom HTML Error Messages in IIS 5

HTML error messages can be quite helpful in troubleshooting a problem with your server. When IIS 5 receives an invalid request from a client, IIS sends back an HTML error message. You can customize these error messages by accessing the Custom Errors tab in the Web Site Properties dialog box, highlighting an entry, and then editing its properties, as shown in Figure 11.11.

FIGURE 11.11 The Default Web Site Properties dialog box, open at the Custom Errors tab

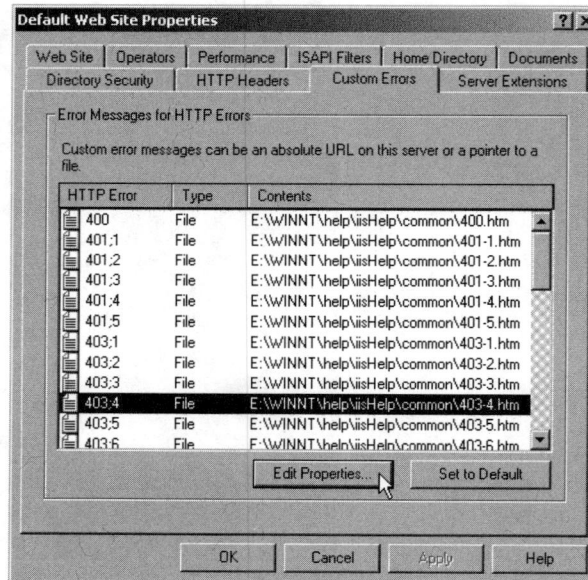

In IIS 5, you can create new error messages or edit existing ones. You cannot edit the error message files from the Custom Errors tab. To edit these files, you must navigate to the `C:\WINNT\help\common` directory, if your system is on the C:\ drive. You can then open the error message files using any text editor such as Notepad.

Some web browsers, especially Internet Explorer 5 and later, do not report the error messages sent by the server by default. Rather, the browsers themselves generate friendly error messages. The individual user must disable the friendly error messages in Internet Explorer, by following these steps:

1. In Internet Explorer, choose Tools ➢ Internet Options to open the Internet Options dialog box.

2. Click the Advanced tab:

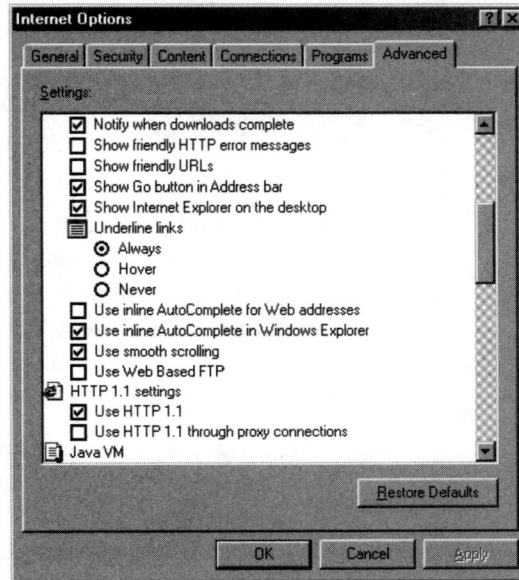

3. In the Settings list, clear the Show Friendly HTTP Error Message check box.

4. Click OK.

Many organizations create customized messages that explain errors better than default error messages do. They direct users to the home page or to a another, more informative page. Custom error messages can be very helpful when troubleshooting problems with your server.

Virtual Servers

IIS, Netscape, and Apache HTTP servers allow you to set up a website by creating one instance of a web server on a machine. This process is standard. However, you can also use each of these products to create multiple instances of a web server. Rather than having to install IIS or Apache web server multiple times, you can simply have IIS or Apache create another instance of itself. This practice saves time and system resources.

Any second server instance created by the same program (such as IIS) is called a virtual server. Implementing the virtual server concept allows you to use one computer to contain multiple websites. Users accessing these servers think that they are accessing completely separate computers. Of course, you must have a relatively powerful machine to support traffic for multiple sites. Once you define a virtual server, you have several options. Following are three of the most common.

Dedicated virtual servers   You can place an additional NIC and IP address on the computer and then bind your virtual server to this added NIC and IP address. You can repeat this process as necessary, depending on the capabilities of the system and the bandwidth of the connecting line. Dedicating each virtual server to its own NIC or IP address is preferable for high-volume, production websites.

Simple virtual servers   Several operating systems, such as Unix and Windows 2000, allow one NIC to have multiple IP addresses. You can bind each IP address to its own virtual server. However, this option may not provide needed throughput because one NIC must perform all the work at the physical layer.

Shared virtual servers   You can create multiple virtual servers using only one NIC and IP address, provided you specify different port numbers for each virtual server. The second (virtual) server can safely use any port higher than 1023. A common port option for virtual servers is 8080. You can then use port 8081 for an additional virtual server, and so forth.

> **NOTE**   A less common method of configuring virtual servers on IIS web servers using host headers is described in the following article from Technet: http://www.microsoft.com/technet/treeview/default.asp?url=/TechNet/prodtechnol/comm/proddocs/cs2000/cs_dp_deploy_waff.asp. Please note that host headers cannot be used with SSL.

When clients use a standard Internet browser to access a shared virtual server, they need to modify the URL. For example, suppose a server has an IP address of 192.168.3.4 and its DNS name is page.zep.com. Suppose further that this computer has two web servers: one default web server and a second server we will refer to as the virtual server. The first server uses port 80, the default port for HTTP. The virtual server uses port 8080. To access the default server, enter `http://page.zep.com` or its IP address (`http://192.168.3.4`). To access the second (virtual) server, enter `http://page.zep.com:8080` (or `http://192.168.3.4:8080`). This URL refers not only to the IP address, but also to the port.

Many HTTP servers allow you to create virtual servers. This list includes Netscape Enterprise Web Server, Microsoft IIS, IBM Domino Web Server, NCSA httpd, CERN httpd, Zeus, Oracle Web Server, and Apache server, among others. Of course, each product implements virtual servers differently.

Whenever you create a virtual server tied to a different IP address on the same computer, you need to update the local and remote DNS servers. Otherwise, all users will need to access the virtual server website by its IP address. Nevertheless, DNS configuration is not essential to the creation of a virtual server.

For example, suppose that instead of having a virtual server use an alternative port, you want it use one NIC with the following IP addresses: 192.168.3.4 and 192.168.3.5. Bind the first server only to 192.168.3.4, and then bind the second server only to 192.168.3.5. You can then access each server by its IP address without specifying a port. However, if clients enter `http://page.zep.com`, they access only the HTML pages at the 192.168.3.4 IP address, even though another IP address (192.168.3.5) resides on the system. To get the new IP address to work with DNS, you need to create a new DNS entry for this IP address. Suppose that you were able to add the following DNS entry:

```
plant.zep.com IN A 192.168.3.5
```

After restarting the Windows 2000 DNS service, you then access the virtual server at 192.168.3.5. Again, you need not create DNS entries to create a virtual server.

Virtual Servers in IIS 5

A *virtual server* is not a dedicated server. The entire computer is not dedicated to running the server software. Instead, the web server is configured to direct requests from different IP addresses to different directories of a single web server. When preparing a virtual server, consider the following issues.

- Determine whether you want to create a dedicated, simple, or shared virtual server.

- Use the appropriate tools to create the actual directory that the virtual server will use. The directory you create on the hard drive need not have the same name as the alias you will create.

- Populate the directory you created with at least one file. If the directory or server is empty, you will receive an error message when you access the server or directory through a browser.

EXERCISE 11.2

Creating a Simple Virtual Server on Windows 2000

Before you begin this exercise, in which you add a new IP address to your server, you need to choose a second IP address to ensure that no IP address conflicts occur. Write your second IP address here:

_____

1. On the Desktop, right-click My Network Places, and then choose Properties from the shortcut menu to open the Network and Dial-up Connections window.

2. Right-click Local Area Connection, and choose Properties from the shortcut menu to open the Local Area Connection Properties dialog box.

3. Highlight Internet Protocol (TCP/IP), and then click Properties to open the Internet Protocol (TCP/IP) Properties dialog box

4. Click the Advanced button.

5. In the IP Addresses section, click Add.

6. Enter the new IP address you selected, and then click the Subnet Mask section. The proper subnet mask will be added automatically.

7. Click Add, and then click OK three times. You have added a new IP address.

8. Open Windows Explorer and create the C:\LabFiles\iisvirtserv directory

9. Copy the contents of the Chapter11\iisvirtserv folder from the CD included with this book to the directory you just created. Be sure that you copy only the contents of iisvirtserv folder to the C:\LabFiles\iisvirtserv directory. Do not copy the folder itself.

10. Open the IIS snap-in.

11. Right-click Default Web Server, and choose New ➢ Web Site from the shortcut menu to start the Web Site Creation Wizard.

12. Click Next.

13. Enter a description of your new website (for example, `serverx.com`). Click Next to open the IP Address and Port Settings screen.

14. Click the Enter the IP Address To Use for This Web Site drop-down list, and select the new IP address, as shown in the following graphic:

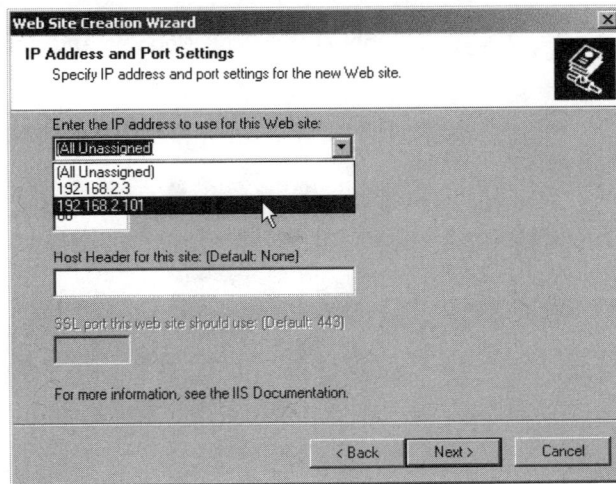

15. Click Next to continue.

16. Enter `C:\LabFiles\iisvirtserv` (the name of the directory you created earlier in this exercise), and then click Next.

17. Accept the default options for access to your new virtual website and click Next. Click Finish. Your new virtual website will appear in the IIS snap-in.

18. Select your new website and make sure it has started.

19. To test your virtual server, open a web browser and enter the new IP address in the Address field. Your new virtual website should appear in the browser.

20. Once you have finished testing the virtual server, delete it.

EXERCISE 11.3

Creating a Virtual Directory

So far, you have only manipulated files directly off the server root. In this exercise, you will create a virtual directory.

1. Open Windows Explorer and create a new directory named C:\labfiles\iisvirtdir. (You can create a new directory on any partition if C:\ is not available.)

2. Right-click Default Web Site, and choose New ➤ Virtual Directory from the shortcut menu to start the Virtual Directory Creation Wizard.

3. Click Next to open the Virtual Directory Alias screen:

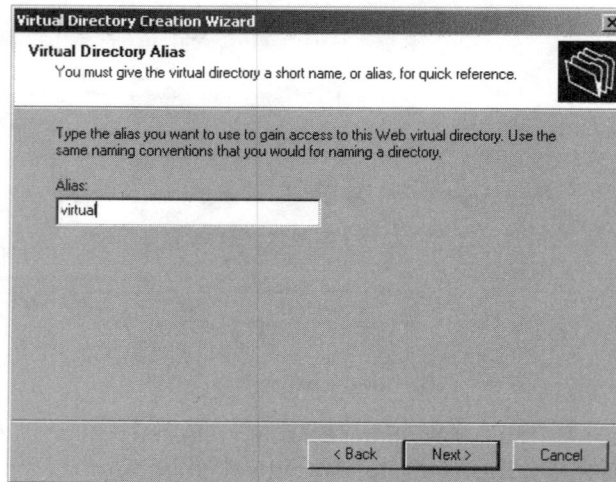

4. In the Alias box, enter the word **virtual** as an alias.

5. Click Next, and then enter the path you created in Step 1 of this exercise.

6. Click Next.

7. Accept the default access permissions (including read and script access) and click Next.

8. Click Finish to close the wizard.

9. Open your browser, and in the Address field enter **http:// localhost/virtual** to access your virtual directory by its alias. You should see an Access Denied message because you have not populated this directory with any HTML files.

10. From the CD included with this book, copy the contents of the folder Chapter11/iisvirtdir to your new virtual directory. (You must use Windows Explorer, not the IIS snap-in, to copy the files.)

11. Right-click the virtual directory, and choose Properties from the shortcut menu to open the Properties dialog box for your virtual directory.

12. Select the Documents tab. Make sure that the default document is Default.htm.

    The standard for HTML files is to use index.htm or index.html. Microsoft defaults to using default.htm. When you create a virtual directory, it inherits the values as the main server. Therefore, if you change the name to index.html, for example, all virtual directories you subsequently create will use index.html as the default.

13. Test your work. You should see the following page:

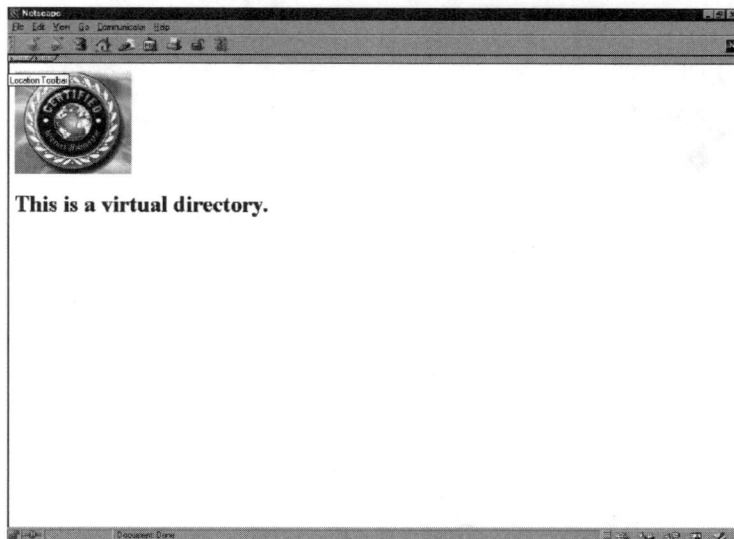

Administering IIS 5 Using Internet Explorer

You can use Internet Explorer to administer IIS. You do so by specifying the port for the Administration Web Site. This port is different for each server. You can learn this port number by right-clicking Administration Web Site and viewing the Web Site tab. The TCP port is listed there. Figure 11.12 shows how to authenticate users with the administration site.

FIGURE 11.12 Authenticating using Internet Explorer 5

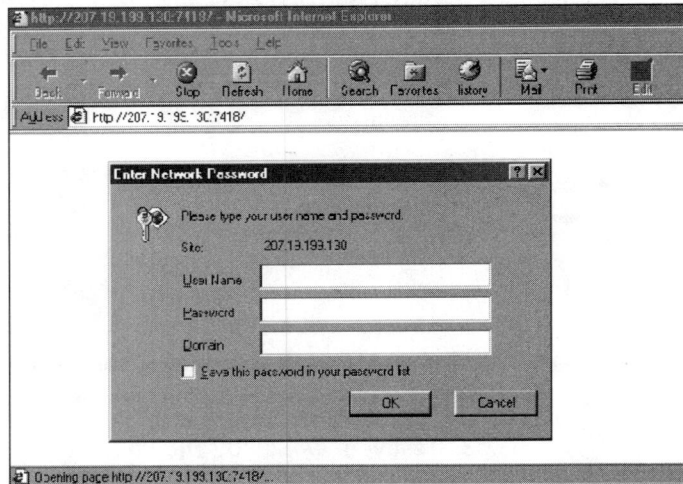

Because of the way IIS 5 authenticates users, you must use Internet Explorer 2 or later.

Figure 11.13 shows the HTML ISM interface you can use after you authenticate.

Using this service, you can administer IIS 5 as if you were actually located at the computer. You must, however, make sure that you have installed the HTML version of the IIS service upon installation.

The HTML ISM interface

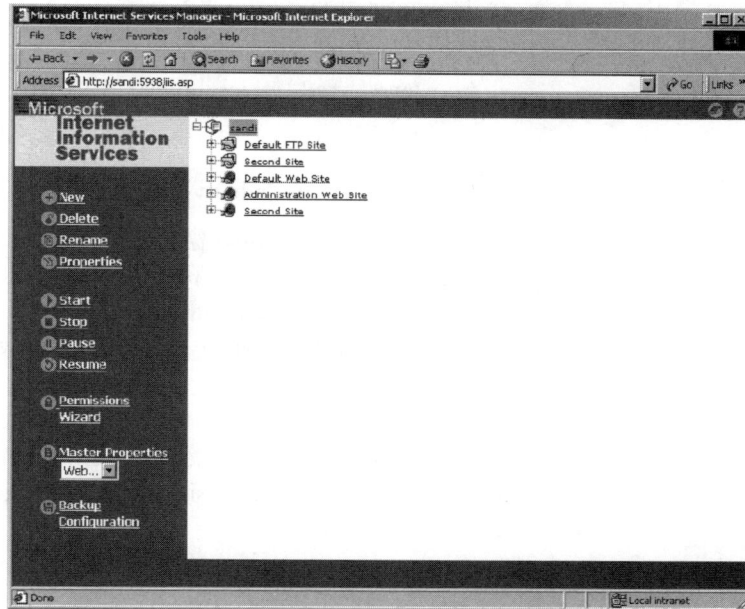

The Apache Server

The Apache server has become the standard web server for Linux. Source files for Apache server are available on the Red Hat Linux 7.*x* CD and at the Apache Software Foundation site (www.apache.org). Apache keeps its files in two main locations, the server root and the document root:

- The server root stores the configuration files. The default server root for Apache server in Linux 7.*x* is /etc/httpd.

- The document root stores the HTML and CGI files. In Linux 7.*x*, the default document is /var/www/.

In addition to this, there are two other files, and their locations, to be aware of:

/usr/sbin/httpd   The location and name of the httpd daemon.

/etc/rc.d/init.d/httpd   The script used to stop, start, and restart the server. You can also use this script to check the server's status.

You can create virtual servers, aliases, and virtual directories in Apache server. However, if you do not declare any aliases or virtual servers, you must place your web files in the following directories:

- /var/www.html, which holds HTML files
- /var/www.cgi-bin, which holds executable files
- /var/www.icons, which contains images used by the server

Red Hat Package Manager (RPM) files are precompiled services and applications created especially for Red Hat Linux. You can use the RPM program to install and delete individual RPM packages. To find out whether an RPM is installed for Apache, enter the following:

```
rpm -qa | grep apache
```

If you get no response, the Apache server package is not installed.

You can also install RPMs using the following command (RPM_*NAME* is the name of the RPM you want):

```
rpm -ivh RPM_NAME
```

To install the RPM for Apache server 1.3.9.4, be informed about any problems, and display a progressive tally of hash marks (#) during installation, enter the following:

```
rpm -ivh apache-1.3.12-25.i386.rpm
```

Administering Apache Server

Apache server does not support a GUI inherently. Generally, administering Apache server involves editing various text files. You can administer Apache server locally or remotely. Local options include the following:

- The command line
- The linuxconf program (either in the X Window System or from the command line)

Remote options include the following.

- Using Telnet or SSH and editing the text files

- Using Telnet or SSH and the `linuxconf` program
- Invoking a remote X Window System session

Apache Server Processes

When the Apache service starts, it does so as a root process with the daemon name httpd. That process then starts a number of child processes, which for security reasons are owned by the user nobody. The following listing shows the four related processes owned by the user nobody:

```
host# ps aux | grep httpd

host#
root 5807  0.0  2.6  2572 1224 ?  S Jan15  0:00 /usr/sbin/
↪httpd s
apache 7071 0.0 2.9 2748 1364 ?  S    12:03   0:00 /usr/
↪sbin/httpd s
apache 7072 0.0 2.9 2748 1364 ? S   12:03   0:00 /usr/
↪sbin/httpd s
apache    7073  0.0  2.9  2748 1364 ?       S    12:03
↪0:00
```

Using child processes is efficient because Apache server does the following:

- Uses fewer system resources.

- Only runs once as root, which is more secure. All child processes run under the permissions of apache.

- Allows you to stop and start the server without terminating existing sessions. If you do, existing sessions will continue, even though httpd has been restarted and is spawning new child processes. The ability to stop and start without terminating existing session is enabled when you issue the `httpd restart` command. Unless you completely stop and restart httpd (`killall httpd`, then `httpd start`), existing sessions will not be terminated. As a result, you may encounter problems when troubleshooting httpd.

You have several options when stopping and starting httpd. These options apply because Apache server is designed to create child processes that run off the main process. When you stop and start httpd, you may not be stopping all the child processes.

You can cause httpd to restart and reread its configuration files using the following command:

```
/etc/rc.d/init.d/httpd restart
```

The benefit of this command is that it causes httpd to create new child processes that use the new configuration file settings found in `httpd.conf`. If you want to stop the server, issue the following commands:

```
killall httpd
/etc/rc.d/init.d/httpd stop
```

Configuring Apache Server

You configure Apache server using several simple text files. The pertinent files for configuring Apache server reside in the `/etc/httpd/conf` directory and include the following:

httpd.conf   Allows you to determine the port number, declare the server's name and type, and declare the user under which all processes will run. Apache server reads this file first when it starts.

access.conf   Allows you to create virtual hosts, set error documents, and configure access to the server's files.

srm.conf   Allows you to configure the document root (in conjunction with `access.conf`), as well as aliases and other settings.

magic   Allows you to specify advanced MIME settings. (This book does not discuss this file any further.)

Current versions of Apache server, including Red Hat Linux, merge the `srm.conf` and `access.conf` files with `httpd.conf`.
Using the files in the `/etc/httpd/conf` directory, you can do the following:

- Declare the server type

- Declare the port the server uses (the default is 80)

- Specify the user account and group under which the server runs

- Specify the e-mail address of the person to contact in case of an emergency

- Declare the server root (the default is `/home/httpd`)

- Specify the server log location

- List modules for Apache server to load

- Configure log format and reporting options

- Declare the name of the server on which Apache server resides

- Specify timeout and keepalive values, as well as related parameters concerning Apache server performance

- Create aliases and virtual directories

- Create virtual servers

Creating Virtual Servers in Apache

The process of adding a virtual server in Apache server is different from adding a virtual server in Windows 2000. Apache server can use one IP address to serve multiple sites on port 80, whereas with Windows 2000, you have to add multiple IP addresses. Apache server listens on port 80 for DNS names rather than IP addresses.

The process for adding virtual servers in Apache server is as follows:

1. Add `NameVirtualHost` and `VirtualHost` directives to the `/etc/httpd/conf/httpd.conf` file. You will learn more about these entries shortly.

2. Add multiple DNS entries that have the same IP address. You must ensure that your web server is properly configured to use this DNS server.

3. Create a separate document root directory for the new virtual server.

Once you complete these steps, clients can use their browsers to access both of your sites on the same port, even though your Linux host uses only one IP address. For example, suppose you have a server named `james.allennet.com`, with the IP address of 192.168.4.10 that currently serves up pages to the network. You can add a DNS record of, say, `sandi.allennet.com` and use the same IP address (192.168.4.10).

When a web browser then makes a request to `sandi.allennet.com`, Apache server presents a completely different website, as long as the second site has been configured to serve up files from a different document directory.

Before you can serve multiple sites from the same IP address, you must use the NameVirtualHost directive. This directive tells Apache server to listen for and process requests for additional servers at this IP address. For example, if your IP address is 192.168.0.10, enter the following directive at the bottom of the httpd.conf file:

```
NameVirtualHost 192.168.0.10
```

Now, the Apache server knows that it will be serving additional sites. You can then add VirtualHost entries.

The first VirtualHost entry must be the same name as your Linux server. For example, if your server name is james.allennet.com, the first entry after the NameVirtualHost directive should be as follows:

```
<VirtualHost james.allennet.com>
        ServerName james
        DocumentRoot /home/httpd/html
        <Directory /home/httpd/html >
           Options Indexes Includes
           AllowOverride All
        </Directory>
</VirtualHost>
```

This repeated VirtualHost entry tells Apache server to listen for requests on james.allennet.com. The ServerName directive tells Apache server that its virtual server name is james. The DocumentRoot and Directory directives tell the server where to find default documents.

In the previous example, the Options field tells Apache server to look for files with the extension of .html and allows for CGI server-side includes. The AllowOverride All directive allows the use of .htaccess files. If you want to deny customization, specify none.

> **NOTE** If you do not include this first virtual server entry, the default server you define will no longer be accessible.

Once you add this first entry, you can then make additional entries.

The VirtualHost directive should have the FQDN of the new server. The ServerName should have only the host name of the server.

```
VirtualHost apache1.server1.com
ServerName apache1
```

If you configure your server this way, users can access this server in their browsers by entering either apache1 or the FQDN.

You can specify many additional server directives, including the following:

```
ServerAdmin root@apache1 # The administrator's e-mail
↳address.
ErrorLog logs/error_log.apache1 # The log file for server
↳errors.
TransferLog logs/access_log.apache1 # Lists accessed
↳pages.
```

Hypertext Transfer Protocol (HTTP)

Hypertext Transfer Protocol (HTTP) is the Application-layer protocol that supports the World Wide Web. The HTTP service uses TCP to carry its commands, and HTTP server processes connect to TCP port 80 (as with all Internet services, although other ports can be used).

Webmasters should learn how HTTP operates at a detailed level. For example, the log files generated by web servers are expressed in terms of HTTP operations; therefore, understanding these files requires a fundamental knowledge of these primitive operations. In addition, a webmaster must frequently arrange for the proper operation of HTTP script files and gateway processes; configuring these features often requires working with HTTP at a low level. Finally, knowledge of HTTP enables the webmaster to see the output that their server is producing before a browser interprets it, which can be a powerful aid in debugging.

HTTP Requests

Each HTTP request made by a client has a specific three-part structure: command, headers, and body.

- The COMMAND portion specifies the type of request being made, the resource or document to which the request refers, and the version of HTTP being used. The list of possible commands is shown in Table 11.1.

- The HEADERS portions specifies additional information about the request. A request can also have no header. Each header line uses the following syntax:

  HEADER-TAG: HEADER-VALUE

  The headers are separated from the body by a blank line.

- The BODY portion is the message's data.

TABLE 11.1 HTTP 1.1 Request Commands

Command	What It Does	RFC 2616 Section
OPTIONS	Inquires about options available on the server	9.2
GET	Retrieves the specified resource	9.3
HEAD	Retrieves headers only for the specified resource	9.4
POST	Passes the body to the resource for further action	9.5
PUT	Stores the body in the location specified by the resource	9.6
DELETE	Deletes the resource	9.7
TRACE	Echoes the outgoing message back to the sender	9.8

The syntax of the HTTP request is as follows:

COMMAND RESOURCE HTTP?VERSION

RESOURCE is the path portion of the resource URL. HTTP versions are specified as 1.0 or 1.1.

HTTP Replies

HTTP replies have a similar three-part structure: status, headers, and body.

- The STATUS portion is a message indicating the status of the request. This message uses the following syntax:

  `HTTP/VERSION STATUS-CODE MESSAGE`

  STATUS-CODE is a numeric value specifying the status of the reply. MESSAGE is a description of the status. The general status codes are shown in Table 11.2.

- The HEADERS portion is a sequence of headers containing information about the reply. These headers use the same syntax as the headers in the request message. Headers are separated from the body by a blank line.

- The BODY portion is the message's data. For example, if an HTML document is requested, the document is returned in the body.

TABLE 11.2 HTTP 1.1 Reply Status Codes

Status Code	Interpretation
1xx	Informational: The request was received; processing is continuing.
2xx	Success: The action was successfully received, understood, and accepted.
3xx	Redirection: Further action must be taken to complete the request.
4xx	Client Error: The request contains bad syntax or cannot be fulfilled.
5xx	Server Error: The server failed to fulfill an apparently valid request.

Following is an example of how HTTP presents information in response to a valid request. In this case, the valid request is for HTTP 1.1. Apache server responds to this request by delivering the HTML to the web browser (or any other user agent, such as a Telnet client querying port 80 on a web server).

```
host$ telnet 192.168.0.40 80

GET /index.html HTTP/1.1

HTTP/1.1 200 OK
Date: Tue, 11 Jan 2002 03:07:17 GMT
Server: Apache/1.3.9 (Unix) (Red Hat/Linux)
Last-Modified: Tue, 21 Sep 2001 14:46:36 GMT
ETag: "32e22-799-37e79a4c"
Accept-Ranges: bytes
Content-Length: 1945
Connection: close
Content-Type: text/html

<!DOCTYPE HTML PUBLIC "-//W3C//DTD HTML 4.0 Transitional//
↵EN">
<HTML>
<HEAD>
<TITLE>Welcome to the CIW Certified website
</TITLE>
```

The server, of course, must have the file named `index.html`. In IIS 5, you may have to specify `default.htm`.

Web Applications and E-Commerce

A web application is an executable file that enhances the normal function of a web server. A web application can be a simple script, or it can be a complex set of files and programs. Among other capabilities, a web application can do the following:

- Process information sent from an HTML form on a web browser to a server
- Count hits on a page

- Create HTML quickly

- Enable communication between a website and a database

- Enable electronic commerce

Two types of web applications exist:

Client-side   These applications are downloaded by the client from the server and executed by the client's browser or operating system. Client-side applications include JavaScript and VBScript embedded into HTML pages, as well as ActiveX controls and Java applets.

Server-side   These applications reside on the server itself, and the server must execute them.

> In this section, we'll discuss server-side web applications. Do not confuse these applications with client-side applications, such as JavaScript or Java applets.

A server-side web application can be a simple file that contains instructions to execute certain commands. A server-side application can also be part of a complex system called an n-tier solution. IIS 5 allows the use of many web applications, including CGI scripts (written in Perl), Internet Database Connector (IDC) files, and Internet Server Application Programming Interface (ISAPI) applications. An *Internet Database Connector (IDC)* is a file that accesses a database to give users requested information; an *Internet Server Application Programming Interface (ISAPI)* is a set of APIs for use with IIS that developers can utilize when creating web applications. More advanced solutions include ASP (Active Server Pages), ColdFusion, and PHP (Hypertext Preprocessor). You can use a web application to enhance the function of Internet and intranet sites.

Implementing a web application is a two-step process. The first step involves developing or coding the program. The second step involves installing and configuring the application.

> In this chapter, we'll focus on installilng and configuring web applications. We won't discuss how to create a web application.

An application server is an advanced method for enabling communication between web servers, clients, and databases. As such, it is called a *three-tier* solution. A three-tier solution is a client/server communication scheme that involves a web browser, a web server, an interpreter/application server, and a database. Examples of application servers include the following:

- Macromedia ColdFusion (`www.macromedia.com`)

- IBM WebSphere Application Server (`www.ibm.com`)

- Microsoft Transaction Server (`www.microsoft.com/NTServer/appservice/exec/overview/Trans_Overview.asp`)

- Microsoft IIS 5 Active Server Pages (`http://support.microsoft.com/default.aspx?scid=kb;en-us;Q297943`)

- PHP: Pre Hypertext Processor (`www.php.net`, or `www.php3.org`)

E-Commerce Web Servers and Perl

The Practical Extraction and Report Language (Perl) has a long, successful history as a scripting language. Perl was originally developed as a report creation tool, but has been adopted as a CGI scripting tool. Whenever people refer to CGI, they generally mean scripts written in Perl. Although other methods for writing CGI files exist (including ColdFusion, PHP, ASP, and JavaServer Pages), Perl for CGI is an almost-universal way to attach web servers to databases. As a systems administrator, you need to understand the following about Perl:

- All Perl-based scripts require an interpreter. An interpreter is an executable program that you install on the system. This interpreter updates the MIME settings for the web server (for example, IIS or Apache server) and then handles incoming requests.

- The Perl interpreter is nearly universal. It is available for Windows 2000, Windows NT, Linux, Solaris, HP-UX, and so forth. Developers enjoy using Perl because they can move scripts from one platform to another with a minimum of code changes.

- All CGI and Perl-based scripts must be executable.

- All CGI and Perl scripts must be owned by the proper user. If you want a web server process owned by nobody to execute the script, make sure that the script is also owned by nobody.

- Older versions of Perl interpreters require that the application execute its own process on the server whenever the application is launched. As a result, older Perl-based CGI can overwhelm a busy web server.

- Because of advances in web server technology, newer CGI applications tend to be much more efficient. Apache server, for example, contains modules that enable Perl to open up child processes of the main Perl interpreter. Effectively, newer Perl-based applications can operate on a single thread as opposed to an entire process.

- Current versions of the ActiveState product ActivePerl automatically update the MIME extensions with the `.pl` file name extension.

- In Linux, all Perl scripts must specify the correct location of the Perl interpreter. The default for Linux 7, for example, is `/usr/bin/perl`.

Most servers currently in use rely on CGI, and most programs executed by servers are written in Perl, but any language can be used.

> You can obtain the latest Perl interpreter, ActivePerl, free of charge from www.activestate.com.

All web servers must map their applications. For some types of CGI applications used with IIS 5, you must manually create an application mapping, which is similar to a file association in Windows. The mapping contains a set of commands that IIS will issue when it receives a request for a particular file extension. For example, Perl files are often saved with the `.pl` extension.

Figure 11.14 shows the Application Configuration dialog box. You can access this dialog box by clicking the Configuration button in the Application Settings section of the Home Directory tab for any virtual server or directory.

Sometimes, a service or an application you install will perform this mapping for you. For example, the latest Perl interpreters from ActiveState will map automatically.

If your site is running an older version of Perl, you must manually map an application. To create a manual mapping, create an application mapping that associates the `.pl` extension with the Perl executable called `perl.exe`. The application mapping enables IIS to execute `perl.exe` in a separate process whenever a file with the `.pl` extension is requested.

FIGURE 11.14 The Application Configuration dialog box

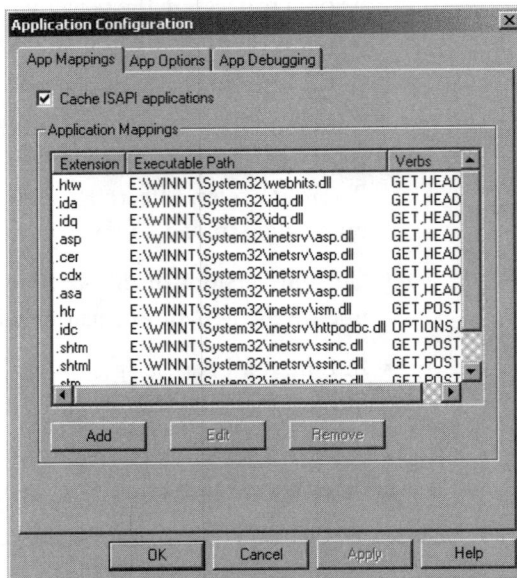

Executing Scripts in IIS 5

Before IIS can run a web application, you must specify the directory in which the application resides. For security purposes, directories that contain HTML documents are normally not flagged as executable. However, all web applications need execution capabilities to function properly.

In IIS, you can apply two types of execution rights. These rights are found in the Application Settings section, as follows:

- Scripts Only allows execution of ASP applications.

- Scripts and Executables allows execution of CGI scripts.

Script permission allows only files associated with a scripting engine to execute. The Script setting is good for allowing only ASP files to execute while restricting other types of executables that may be contained within the application's root directory or subdirectories. Scripts and Executables permission allows any script to run, as well as any other type of application that resides in the application's root directory or subdirectories. This permission is normally used when dealing with CGI applications written in Perl or PHP.

Server-Side Includes and Application Mapping in Windows 2000

Server-side includes (SSI) also extend server functionality. An SSI can consist of any command, such as a command that inserts an image, additional HTML, or code into a web page. An SSI helps improve server response time and customizes web pages. Using an SSI improves response time because it enables the server to preprocess content before delivering it to the client.

If you use `.asp` or `.shtml` endings for all web pages, you do not need to create an application mapping. However, in Windows NT and Windows 2000, you will need to create a mapping for pages ending in `.html` and `.htm` so that they can use server-side includes.

Apache Server and Perl

Apache server uses specific modules to help serve documents. Specifically, Apache server uses a Perl module. Other modules exist, including those that extend Apache's capabilities. For example, some enable authentication.

When determining whether Perl is present on a Linux or a Unix system, you can use the `rpm` command, as follows:

```
host# rpm -qa| grep perl
host# perl-5.00503-6
```

You can also use the `whereis` command, as follows:

```
host# whereis perl
perl: /usr/sbin/perl5.00503 /usr/bin/perl /usr/man/man1/
↳perl.1
```

The output of the `whereis` command shows that Perl is in fact installed, complete with its manual pages.

E-Commerce Web Servers and Gateways

Now that businesses are adopting e-commerce as a standard tool, the ability to connect websites to databases has become a valuable asset. A web application can act as a gateway between the web server and a database. The database can reside on a local or a remote host.

The following process is required when a web server communicates with a database:

1. A web browser passes a data request to the web server.

2. The web server receives the data request and maps it to a web application.

3. The web server executes the application.

4. The application executes and launches either a process or a thread. If the web application is an older Perl interpreter, it will launch a new process with each request. More recent web application servers (for example, newer Perl interpreters, Allaire ColdFusion, Microsoft Active Server Pages, JavaServer Pages, and PHP Hypertext Processors) will open threads. A thread runs within a program and allows one process to handle multiple requests. A thread is the smallest executable on a server; using threads instead of system processes requires less demand on system resources.

5. The web application passes the client's data to the operating system of the server. The operating system then passes the client's data to a database (via ODBC, for example).

6. The web application receives the information from the database driver.

7. The web application then returns the database output and any additional formatting (such as dynamically generated HTML) to the client's browser.

Remember that older gateways, such as the widespread Common Gateway Interface, ask the server to execute a co-process and then return the output from the process to the client. This process is responsible for constructing a correctly formatted HTTP reply. More recently, server developers have designed web applications that act as gateways and use dynamically loaded object libraries. In this type of web application, the server generates the reply document by calling a dynamically loaded subroutine and returning the subroutine's output to the client. Using dynamically loaded libraries eliminates the substantial overhead involved in starting a new process on the host, and it improves performance.

Because CGI and other gateways permit remote users to execute programs on local computers, the use of web applications (either as gateways or as simple dynamic HTML generators) has important security consequences. You must know who is responsible for developing the CGI script or web application that you place on a server.

Active Server Pages (ASP)

Active Server Pages (ASP) is Microsoft technology that implements web applications. ASP allows programmers to use a variety of scripting languages, including VBScript and JavaScript. To create an ASP file, you simply use one of the scripting languages and add an .asp file name extension. The file extension tells IIS to use its own built-in interpreter when executing ASP files.

ASP employs threading, making it more efficient than older CGI applications. ASP is primarily used with IIS; third-party ASP interpreters developed by Sun Chili!Soft are available for other web server platforms, including Apache and iPlanet, and a variety of Unix operating systems, including Solaris, Linux, HP-UX, AIX, and Cobalt. You can find detailed information about Chili!Soft at www.chilisoft.com. In many cases, a web application consists of several files as well as subdirectories. Before creating any application, it is essential to create a virtual directory that will hold all the files and subdirectories for the entire web application. Good practice dictates that you isolate the web application in its own directory. After you create a virtual directory, you click the Create button under the virtual directory's Application Settings field. Once you name the application, all the files and subdirectories will be associated with that web application.

> **NOTE** ASP files and applications need not be created as web applications. However, creating a web application does allow additional configuration parameters for the entire directory, which we'll discuss later in this chapter.

Open Database Connectivity (ODBC)

Open Database Connectivity (ODBC) provides a way for ASP to transfer data between a client and a database. The main purpose of ODBC is to provide a consistent method for an application programming interface (API) to interact with as many databases as possible. Although it purports to be a universal standard, ODBC development was overseen primarily by Microsoft.

When using ODBC, you must do the following:

- Register the database with the operating system. For example, you can create a system data source name (system DSN) so that the operating system can map the ASP request to the database.

- Obtain a valid driver for the database. To read and/or update the database, you must have the proper driver.

Choose Start ➢ Programs ➢ Administrative Tools ➢ Data Sources (ODBC) to open the ODBC Data Source Administrator dialog box, as shown in Figure 11.15.

FIGURE 11.15   The ODBC Data Source Administrator dialog box

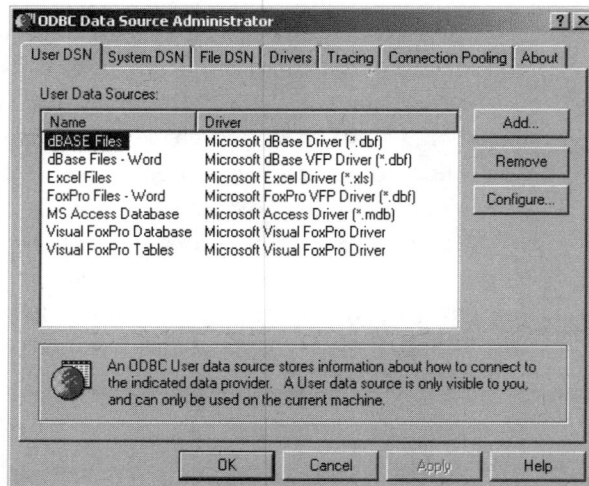

Use the options on the User DSN tab to assign a database to a specific user. Generally, you will work with the System DSN tab, because this tab allows you to create a database connection that all system services can use.

> **NOTE** One of the problems with the Windows NT Server 4 Option Pack was that the installation program for the Microsoft Certificate Server occasionally created a User DSN instead of a System DSN. As a result, the Certificate Server would not issue certificates.

Streaming Media Servers

E-commerce increasingly demands the use of media servers. Multimedia requires a great deal of bandwidth. A digitized movie can consume as much as 1MB per second. It is therefore necessary to reduce the size of the multimedia, but in such a way that quality is not compromised. One way to reduce the size is through smart compression; however, smart compression requires special clients. Therefore, using this option can severely limit the size of your audience. Streaming media servers allow websites to deliver multimedia content such as audio and video while conserving bandwidth.

Selection of your streaming server is critical. Among other factors, you need to choose a format for which most of your visitors will have players.

A few years ago, no standard existed for streaming multimedia content. In 1997, RealNetworks released RealVideo, a free plug-in that allowed users to create and stream multimedia content. Currently, RealNetworks occupies the majority of the market.

The minimum hardware requirements for streaming servers are as follows:

- Pentium class system with 64 to 128MB of RAM.

- Soundcard, with microphone and speaker inputs/outputs.

- At least 100MB of spare disk space. Hard disk access speed is also an issue, so RAID 0 (for example) is also recommended.

- Audio and/or video editors. An editor's cost can range from freeware to professional music industry pricing standards. As you might suspect, price greatly depends on the quality and number of features.

The minimum software requirements for streaming media capability are:

- Encoding/publishing software, which converts your audio/video files to a streaming format
- Streaming server software to serve the streaming media content
- A streaming media player to view the streaming media content

Media content falls primarily into two categories:

On-demand   The media clip can be played at any time. It can be played from the beginning, paused, fast-forwarded, and rewound.

Live streaming   Similar to live television, this media clip can be played only as it is being broadcast. The clip cannot be rewound, paused, fast-forwarded, or rewound.

Depending on the type of streaming media that you are serving, you will probably use different URLs to serve the content. When creating a link in a web page, you are not directly connecting to the media file. Rather, you are linking to a metafile that can then reference the media file. The format for all links that reference media stored on the RealServer streaming server product is as follows:

```
protocol://address:port/MountPoint/path/file
```

Table 11.3 shows a list of streaming server components and their descriptions for RealNetworks RealServer.

TABLE 11.3   RealServer Streaming Server Components

Component	Description
Protocol	The protocol used for accessing the media: RealTime Streaming Protocol (RTSP), Progressive Network Audio (PNA), Progressive Networks Media (PNM), or HTTP
Address	Can be either the IP address or the domain name
Port	The port number at which RealServer listens for requests
Mount point	Indicates how the media should be served

TABLE 11.3 RealServer Streaming Server Components *(continued)*

Component	Description
Path	Optional; used if the RealMedia is stored in a subdirectory of the mount point
File	Refers to the name of the media file; must also contain the extension

Web pages that contain links to RealMedia use HTTP. The default port number is 8080. You can change the port number, which might be necessary if you are running multiple instances of RealServer or using a virtual server on the RealServer port.

RealServer uses mount points to determine which feature will be handling the request. Table 11.4 shows the mount points relevant to RealServer.

TABLE 11.4 RealServer Mount Points

Mount Point	Description
/	Used for on-demand content located in the content directory, which is stored in a subdirectory of RealServer.
/encoder	Used to refer to live content.
/ramgen	RealMedia is contained in a RAM file. This mount point will be used if you are linking to RealMedia inside a web page. The default location for the /ramgen mount point is %systemroot%\Real\RealServer\Content\. If, for example, you have Windows 2000 installed on your C:\ drive, the location is C:\Winnt\Real\RealServer\Content\.

Consider the following scenario: You want to create a link to a RealMedia file that is a live broadcast called concert.rm. You are hosting the concert on a server named www.ciwcertified.com. Your URL appears as follows:

http://www.ciwcertified.com:8080/ramgen/encoder/concert.rm

Suppose further that you want to create a link to a RealMedia file that is an on-demand recording of a speech called speech.rm. The speech is hosted on a server called www2.ciwcertified.com. Your URL appears as follows:

http://www2.ciwcertified.com:8080/ramgen/speech.rm

Summary

In this chapter, you studied advanced site administration issues. You learned about web server configuration, including how to prepare for an installation; how to modify the server root directory; and how to control access based on user names and IP addresses. You practiced creating virtual servers and virtual directories. You also learned how to administer and troubleshoot websites locally and remotely and to identify HTTP error messages and even create custom HTTP error messages. You learned how to apply and configure web applications to extend your web server's functionality. You studied issues associated with CGI and Perl. You learned how to a register a DSN for a database, and you saw how ASP and ODBC allow the web server to pass information between a client and a database. You learned how to address a series of files and subdirectories as one complete web application. Finally, you learned to implement a streaming media server.

With this information and the skills you have gained, you should now be able to install and configure a web server, including creating a document root directory, virtual directories, default documents, and new virtual servers. You should now be able to add functionality to your website by mapping additional file extensions using MIME and adding web applications that use ASP and CGI that build web documents dynamically. You should also be able to connect your web server to a database by using a web application and be able to install and configure a streaming media server.

Exam Essentials

Know when to use IIS and when to use Apache as your web server.
IIS is more expensive, has a GUI, is easier to configure, and integrates with Microsoft web applications such as ASP and ISAPI. Apache server is the

most popular web server, however, and is free. Apache runs on Unix and Linux. CGI web applications will run on IIS and Apache.

Know how to configure virtual servers.   A virtual server is an additional instance of a web server program that resides on the same physical server. Dedicated virtual servers have additional NICs with additional IP addresses; simple virtual servers have one or more additional IP addresses on the same NIC; and shared virtual servers have a single NIC with a single IP address, but additional ports.

In IIS and Apache, know how to change the document root directory and default document and how to create additional virtual directories. Only files and folders in the document root directory and files and folders in virtual directories are accessible to web server clients. Virtual directories are shortcuts to folders that do not exist in the document root directory, but may exist in one of three places: a redirection to another URL, a share on another computer, or a directory on the same computer.

Understand how to enable directory browsing.   When a user connects to a web server, three things can happen: the default document is displayed; a directory listing is displayed if browsing is enabled; or an error message is displayed.

Be able to configure directory security and control access to your web server.   The primary authentication methods for Windows 2000 are anonymous access, basic authentication, and integrated Windows authentication. For additional security, you can restrict access by IP address or domain. Finally, for data encryption, you should enable Secure Socket Layer (SSL) when sensitive data such as a credit card number is being transmitted.

Understand that web applications enable e-commerce.   E-commerce sites use sophisticated web applications to connect web servers to databases. Server-side applications can be part of a three-tier client/server communication scheme. The first tier is the user interface; a middle tier runs on a separate application server and processes the data against business rules; and a third tier is a database management system that runs on a database server. Application servers that enable database connectivity and apply business rules include Allaire ColdFusion, IBM Websphere, Microsoft Transaction Server, and Microsoft IIS 5 Active Server Pages (ASP) engine. Understand that ODBC provides a way for ASP to transfer data between a client and a database. Know how to access the ODBC Data Source Administrator from Windows 2000 Administrative Tools and know how to add a system DSN.

Be able to connect to RealServer steaming media mount points.   For instance, if you want to create a link to a RealMedia file that is a live broadcast called `concert.rm`, and you are hosting this concert on a server named `www.ciwcertified.com`, your URL appears as follows:

`http://www.ciwcertified.com:8080/ramgen/encoder/concert.rm`

The default port for real server is 8080.

Key Terms

Before taking the exam, you should be familiar with the following terms:

access.conf file	Internet Database Connector (IDC)
anonymous access	Internet Server Application Programming Interface (ISAPI)
bandwidth throttling	Multipurpose Internet Mail Extensions (MIME)
basic authentication	Red Hat Package Manager (RPM)
dedicated virtual servers	shared virtual server
httpd.conf file	simple virtual server
integrated Windows authentication	three-tier

Review Questions

1. Jim is creating a website for a brick-and-mortar travel agency. Jim is both a Unix systems administrator and a Windows 2000 MCSE. He is told to minimize costs and maximize performance. Which web server should Jim implement?

   A. IIS 5

   B. Oracle Web

   C. Apache

   D. SQL HTTP

2. Jim is creating a website for a brick-and-mortar travel agency. Jim is both a Unix systems administrator and a Windows 2000 MCSE. He is told that after the website is created that he needs to train Edith, one of the secretaries, to modify server properties. Which web server should Jim install?

   A. IIS 5

   B. Oracle Web

   C. Apache

   D. SQL HTTP

3. On one server, using multiple IP addresses, Jim sets up multiple websites for different opticians. They have some common links to general optometry information, and they have common links to account maintenance information. How can Jim most efficiently create these links to common directories? Choose the best answer.

   A. Create virtual servers using the same home directory

   B. Create virtual directories on each virtual server

   C. Place shortcuts to CGI scripts in a common directory

   D. Place shortcuts to CGI scripts in each home directory

4. Brad creates an `index.htm` file that should be the first web page that a user sees when connecting to the `www.radio-flyer.com` website. This file will be placed in the default location on an IIS 5 server. Where should Brad place this file and what must he do so that it will display whenever a user connects to `www.radio-flyer.com`? Choose two.

   A. Place the file in `C:\winnt\drivers\etc`

   B. Place the file in `C:\inetpub\wwwroot`

   C. Change the default directory

   D. Change the default document

   E. Delete other `*.htm` files in the directory

5. Frank connects to the `www.ebay.com` website, which is hosted on an Apache server. He receives a directory listing of ebay stores. What two events in combination might have caused this problem?

   A. The default document has been deleted.

   B. Directory browsing has been enabled.

   C. The Active Server Pages for this application has crashed.

   D. The DNS server record for this host header has been corrupted.

   E. This website has been redirected.

6. Frank is concerned that many users connect to his IIS 5 website for stock quotes and stay connected throughout the day, preventing other users from connecting. What should Frank do? Choose the best answer.

   A. Disable HTTP keepalives

   B. Set the number of connections to unlimited

   C. Set a connection timeout

   D. Disable bandwidth throttling

7. Brenda is concerned that a new ASP script might crash other ASP scripts on her website. She is also concerned that there might be a security weakness in this new ASP script that was not discovered in beta testing. What should Brenda do? Choose the best answer.

    A. On the Home Directory tab in the Default Web Site Properties dialog box, use the Application Protection drop-down list box to set the ASP script to run in a separate memory space

    B. On the Home Directory tab in the Default Web Site Properties dialog box, use the Application Protection drop-down list box to set the ASP script to run at a lower priority than the other ASP scripts and CGI applications

    C. Put the ASP application in a separate directory and allow only NTFS execute permissions on that directory

    D. Put the ASP application in a separate directory and allow only NTFS read permissions on that directory

8. Peter has been using host headers to host multiple low traffic e-commerce websites. One of the websites experiences remarkable growth. For what reason might this website be moved to another IP address that doesn't need host headers to differentiate that website from others?

    A. Forms are not supported by host headers.

    B. A shopping cart is not supported by host headers.

    C. SSL is not supported by host headers.

    D. Load balancing is not supported by host headers.

9. Peter hosts 20 virtual web servers for Washington DC Political Action Committees (PACs) on one Windows 2000 Advanced Server with four processors and 2GB of RAM. Occasionally, when one PAC has a mass mailing encouraging supporters to log on to that PAC's website, the performance of the other PAC websites suffers tremendously. What should Peter do? Choose the best answer.

    A. Limit the number of users that can connect

    B. Enable bandwidth throttling

    C. Enable processor throttling

    D. Put each website on a separate NIC

10. Ralph wants to host multiple websites on an Apache web server. What options does Ralph have?

    A. Dedicated virtual servers

    B. Simple virtual servers

    C. Complex virtual servers

    D. Shared virtual servers

11. Ralph creates multiple new websites. What must be updated on Internet DNS servers before these websites may be accessed by their host names?

    A. CNAME record

    B. PTR record

    C. MX record

    D. A record

    E. SOA record

12. Mark notices that when he connects to some websites, he ends up in the /cgi-bin directory. What does this tell Mark?

    A. He is connecting to a Microsoft server.

    B. He is connecting to a Linux or Unix server.

    C. He is running an executable file.

    D. He is connecting to a virtual directory.

    E. He is connecting to the document root directory.

13. Brad wants to install the latest Apache server that he just downloaded for use on his Linux server. What command should Brad execute?

    A. cd /var/cgi-bin. Ssh apache-1.3.12.25.i386.ssh

    B. kill all httpd

    C. rpm

    D. ps aux | grep httpd

14. Brad wants to change the Apache server root from the default of /home/http. He also wants to create aliases, virtual directories, and virtual servers. Which file should Brad edit?

   A. `/etc/httpd/conf/httpd.conf`

   B. `/etc/httpd/conf/access.conf`

   C. `/etc/httpd/conf/srm.conf`

   D. `/etc/httpd/conf/conf.httpd`

15. Ben is creating a new website on an Apache server. Using the default file locations, in which directories should he place the following three files: `default.html`, `dearfield.exe`, and `paradise.jpg`?

   A. `/var/html`

   B. `/var/webfiles`

   C. `/var/bin`

   D. `/var/cgi-bin`

   E. `/var/images`

   F. `/var/icons`

16. Frank is a webmaster. He reviews the server logs when he comes in on Monday morning. What series of HTTP reply messages would be of greatest concern to Frank?

   A. 1xx

   B. 2xx

   C. 3xx

   D. 4xx

   E. 5xx

   F. 6xx

17. Mark wants to create a web application that will run as fast as possible on both Windows and Linux servers. What should Frank use? Choose the best answer.

   A. ODBC

   B. ISAPI

   C. ASP

   D. CGI

18. For added security on his web server, Mark has allowed only script permissions on ASP, ISAPI, and CGI files. What is the most salient effect?

   A. None of these applications will run.

   B. CGI applications will not run.

   C. ASP and ISAPI will only run if they have execute permissions.

   D. Security will be diminished.

   E. Security will be enhanced.

19. Peter is writing an ASP web application to transfer data between a web client and multiple databases at a bank. What should Peter do? Choose two.

   A. Use ODBC as the API to transfer data

   B. Use JDBC as the API to transfer data

   C. Add a user DSN

   D. Add a system DSN

20. Ralph wants to connect to a RealMedia file called `acoustic.rm` that is broadcast live on the `www.audio.com` website. Which URL should Ralph use?

   A. `www.audio.com:8888/acoustic.rm`

   B. `www.audio.com/ramgen/encoder/acoustic.rm`

   C. `www.audio.com:8800/ramgen/encoder/acoustic.rm`

   D. `www.audio.com:8080/ramgen/encoder/acoustic.rm`

Answers to Review Questions

1. C.   Apache sits on Unix or Linux, is virtually free, and has better performance than IIS.

2. A.   Because of its GUI, IIS is much easier to use.

3. B.   Each Virtual website should have a unique document root directory, but have virtual directories (shortcuts) to directories that contain common, non-customized information.

4. B, D.   Brad should put index.htm in the document root directory of C:\inetpub\wwwroot, and on the Documents tab of the Default Web Site Properties dialog box, Brad needs to add and make index.htm the default document.

5. A, B.   If the default document is not present and directory browsing is enabled, then the client's browser will receive a directory listing. Apache servers do not use Active Server Pages or host headers.

6. C.   Given the goal of disconnecting inactive users, Frank should set a connection timeout on his website.

7. A.   Brenda should run the ASP script in a separate memory space.

8. C.   Host headers do not support SSL.

9. B.   To solve this particular problem in the least intrusive and most effective way, enable bandwidth throttling.

10. A, B, D.   Ralph can use multiple NICs with separate IP addresses (dedicated virtual servers), multiple IP addresses on one NIC (a simple virtual server), or additional port numbers on one NIC with one IP address (shared virtual server).

11. D.   A (address) record must be registered on the Internet and added to DNS servers.

12. B, C.   The /var/cgi-bin directory holds executable web files on a Unix/Linux server.

13. C.   Brad should execute the RPM command, for example, rpm-ivh apache-1.3.12-25.i386.rpm.

14. A.   Ben should modify the /etc/httpd/conf/httpd.conf file, which is the main Apache server configuration file.

15. A, D, F.   The default locations for web files on an Apache server are as follows: /var/html, which holds HTML files; /var/cgi-bin, which holds executable files; and /var/icons, which contains images used by the server.

16. E.   The 5xx HTTP messages indicate a server error—that the server failed to fulfill an apparently valid request.

17. D.   CGI programs run on both Windows and Linux servers. ASP and ISAPI are faster than CGI but only run on Windows servers.

18. B.   CGI applications need the execute permission to run. CGI programs generally refer to scripts written in Perl.

19. A, D.   Peter should use Open Database Connectivity (ODBC) and add a system Data Source Name (DSN).

20. D.   Ralph should use www.audio.com:8080/ramgen/encoder/acoustic.rm.

Chapter 12

Enabling Secure Sockets Layer

THE CIW EXAM OBJECTIVE GROUPS COVERED IN THIS CHAPTER:

✓ Perform Secure Sockets Layer (SSL) transactions.

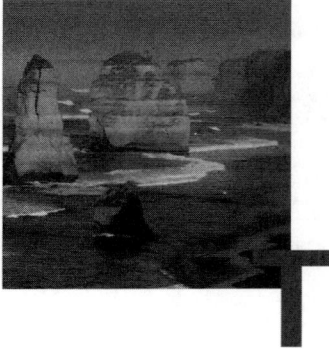

he advent of e-commerce and business-to-business transactions has required the widespread use of encryption with Internet servers. In fact, it would be hard to imagine e-commerce without encryption. Although developers have proposed many standards, Netscape's *Secure Sockets Layer (SSL)* has become the most common form of encryption. E-commerce customers with a variety of browsers on a variety of operating systems routinely use SSL to safely pass millions of credit card numbers across the Internet. In this chapter, you will learn about the services provided by SSL. You will learn that that an SSL session is established using a six-step handshake that provides connection security which has three basic properties:

- The connection is private due to symmetric encryption.

- The peer's identity can be authenticated using asymmetric cryptography.

- The connection is reliable due to secure hash functions.

In this chapter, you will learn to use the IIS 5 snap-in to generate an SSL certificate request, and you will learn how to deploy the Certificate Authority snap-in to sign certificate requests.

Secure Sockets Layer Architecture (SSL)

Netscape developed SSL to provide a security protocol for communications between a web server and a web browser. SSL is a leading technology in secure network communication and provides authentication, data encryption, and message integrity. SSL is implemented in the Application layer of the TCP/IP (Transmission Control Protocol/Internet Protocol) architectural model, though it acts much like a standalone layer between the Transport and Application layers. Figure 12.1 shows the network architecture model with SSL.

FIGURE 12.1 The network architecture model showing SSL

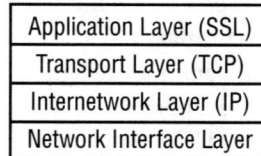

Application Layer (SSL)
Transport Layer (TCP)
Internetwork Layer (IP)
Network Interface Layer

The SSL protocol is composed of two separate processes:

- The SSL handshake
- The SSL record

During the *SSL handshake*, the web server and the client browser exchange and negotiate a secure communications link. The handshake occurs in six phases:

- Hello
- Key Exchange
- Session Key Production
- Server Verify
- Client Authentication
- Finished

In a later section in this chapter, we'll look at each phase in detail.

During the SSL record process, the data communication is transmitted. The *SSL record* is composed of three data parts:

- Message Authentication Code (MAC)
- ACTUAL
- PADDING

Architecturally, SSL can be viewed as an additional layer between the Transport and Application layers of the four-layer IP stack. SSL uses services of the Transport layer; however, applications running at the Application layer cannot determine that a secure communication is being used. SSL uses TCP (Transmission Control Protocol) as its transport mechanism because it needs a reliable transport. Connectionless transports such as UDP (User Datagram Protocol) cannot use SSL.

The primary advantage of using SSL is that it provides encryption, authentication, and message integrity services to the Application layer. Therefore, higher-level protocols that use TCP, such as Telnet, FTP (File Transfer Protocol), or HTTP (Hypertext Transfer Protocol), can use SSL for secure communications. Application-layer protocols that use UDP for transport cannot use SSL, because UDP does not check for transmission loss. The strategy of SSL being an additional layer between the Application and Transport layers allows it to operate independently of the Internet application protocols. Because SSL is implemented on both the client and the server, Internet communications are transmitted in encrypted form, ensuring privacy. Figure 12.2 shows the architectural interaction of the top three layers when SSL is employed.

FIGURE 12.2   The SSL architecture

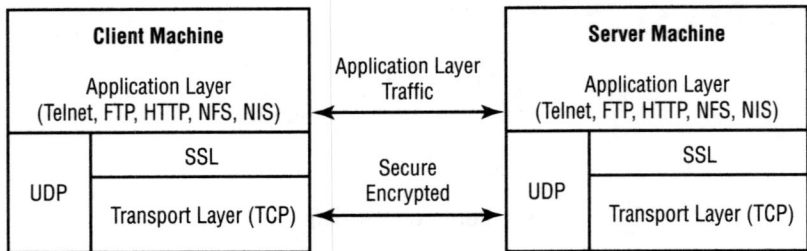

SSL authenticates the server and (optionally) the client. SSL can negotiate an encryption algorithm and a session key and can authenticate the server before the application protocol transmits or receives its first byte of data. Therefore, all Application-layer traffic is transmitted over a secure, encrypted channel.

The current version of SSL is version 3. Compared with the previous version, version 3 provides improved key-exchange algorithms, including Diffie-Hellman.

The SSL protocol provides data security by encrypting the data channel. This process is called channel security. Channel security has three basic properties:

The channel is private.   All messages are encrypted after a simple handshake is used to define a secret key. Data is encrypted (for example, DES and RC4) using symmetric cryptography.

The channel is authenticated.   The server endpoint of the session is always authenticated, and the client endpoint is optionally authenticated. Asymmetric public-key cryptography is used for authentication. Because the server is always authenticated, servers using SSL require a digitally signed certificate. Without this certificate, the server can operate only in a non-secure mode. Server administrators should submit a certificate request to a well-known *Certificate Authority (CA)*, a third-party organization that issues certificates.

The channel is reliable.   The message transport includes a message integrity check using a Message Authentication Code (MAC). Secure hash functions such as MD2 or MD5 are used for MAC computations.

The SSL Handshake

For two SSL peers to communicate, several phases must occur before the first byte of data is transmitted. The first and most important phase is the SSL handshake, which negotiates security enhancements for data to be sent over SSL. The security enhancements consist of authentication, symmetric encryption, and message integrity. Symmetric encryption is facilitated using a key-exchange algorithm. Figure 12.3 illustrates the SSL handshake. The following sections define each phase in detail.

NOTE   Three basic types of handshakes are defined in the SSL handshake process. The first type occurs with no recently pre-existing session (this creates a short delay). The second type uses a set of session identifiers, and the third type is initiated by a server seeking client authentication.

FIGURE 12.3   The SSL handshake process

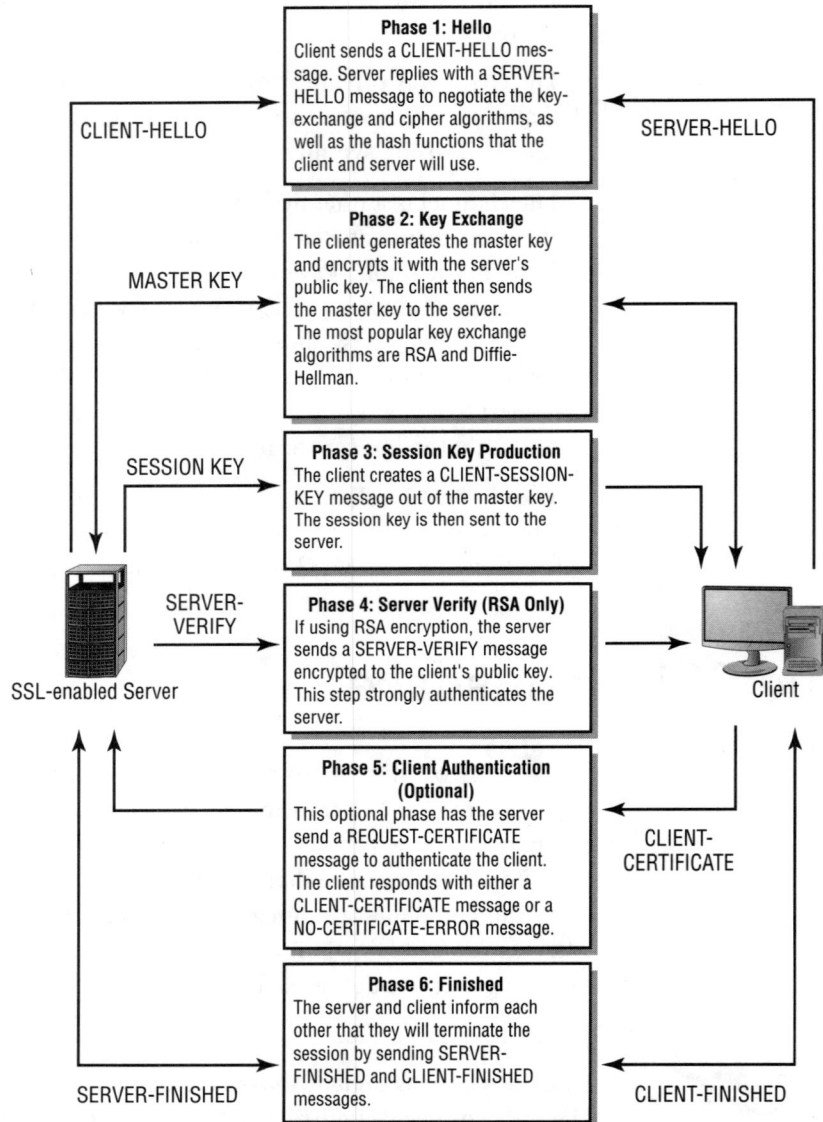

Phase 1: Hello
Client sends a CLIENT-HELLO message. Server replies with a SERVER-HELLO message to negotiate the key-exchange and cipher algorithms, as well as the hash functions that the client and server will use.

CLIENT-HELLO

SERVER-HELLO

Phase 2: Key Exchange
The client generates the master key and encrypts it with the server's public key. The client then sends the master key to the server.
The most popular key exchange algorithms are RSA and Diffie-Hellman.

MASTER KEY

Phase 3: Session Key Production
The client creates a CLIENT-SESSION-KEY message out of the master key. The session key is then sent to the server.

SESSION KEY

SSL-enabled Server

SERVER-VERIFY

Phase 4: Server Verify (RSA Only)
If using RSA encryption, the server sends a SERVER-VERIFY message encrypted to the client's public key. This step strongly authenticates the server.

Client

Phase 5: Client Authentication (Optional)
This optional phase has the server send a REQUEST-CERTIFICATE message to authenticate the client. The client responds with either a CLIENT-CERTIFICATE message or a NO-CERTIFICATE-ERROR message.

CLIENT-CERTIFICATE

Phase 6: Finished
The server and client inform each other that they will terminate the session by sending SERVER-FINISHED and CLIENT-FINISHED messages.

SERVER-FINISHED

CLIENT-FINISHED

The Hello Phase

In the Hello phase the capabilities of the client and server are defined, and the client and server agree on a set of algorithms to use for the privacy and authentication enhancements. At the end of the Hello phase, the following encryption enhancements are resolved:

- The key-exchange algorithm and certificates for each endpoint (the client's certificate is optional)

- The symmetric cipher algorithm, the session key(s) for it, and any key argument data

- The hash function used for MAC computation, handshake hash computation, and session key production

During the Hello phase, the client sends a CLIENT-HELLO message. The CLIENT-HELLO message consists of the SSL version number, a list of all cryptographic algorithms the client is willing or able to support, some challenge data used in a later phase to authenticate the server, and the session identifier data. The session identifier data is sent only if recent connections have occurred (that is, if the client found a valid session identifier in its cache for a particular server). If the client has a valid session identifier, the handshaking process is faster because the previous encryption enhancements can be used. The CLIENT-HELLO message is sent unencrypted in cleartext format.

Upon receipt of the CLIENT-HELLO message, the server examines it to verify that it can support the SSL version being requested, as well as one of the client's cryptographic specifications. If the client sent a session identifier, the server checks its cache to see if it can bypass the negotiations. Assuming that a session identifier was not sent by the client, the server packs its certificate, the cryptographic specifications it can support, and a connection identifier to send to the client in a SERVER_HELLO response. The connection identifier is a string of randomly generated bytes (from 16 to 32) used by the server and client at various points in the protocol. The SERVER-HELLO message is sent unencrypted in cleartext format.

The Key Exchange Phase

When the client receives the SERVER-HELLO message, it chooses a cryptographic specification common to itself and the server. It also generates a master key that is a shared secret between the client and the server. The master key is generated randomly and then encrypted with the server's public key (part of the server's certificate passed to the client in the SERVER-HELLO message). The client packs the cryptographic specification it chose, the master key, and some other attributes to create a message that will be sent to the server. If the RSA key exchange algorithm was used, the client sends a CLIENT-MASTER-KEY message. If a Diffie-Hellman–style key exchange was used, the client sends a CLIENT-DH-KEY message, which includes some random data to generate a master key. Both messages are sent primarily in cleartext, although some portions are encrypted, such as the master key for RSA key exchanges.

The Session Key Production Phase

During this phase, a CLIENT-SESSION-KEY message is sent from the client to the server. This message is used to establish one or two *session keys* with the server. These keys are derived from the master key already sent in the CLIENT-MASTER-KEY or CLIENT-DH-KEY message.

The Server Verify Phase

The Server Verify phase occurs only when the RSA key exchange algorithm is being used. This phase occurs after a pair of session keys have been agreed upon either by a session identifier or by explicit specification with the CLIENT-MASTER-KEY message. During this phase, the server sends an encrypted SERVER-VERIFY message to the client. This message contains an encrypted copy of the challenge data sent to the server in the CLIENT-HELLO message. The SERVER-VERIFY message verifies the server as follows.

A legitimate server will have a private key corresponding to the public key contained in the server certificate that was transmitted to the client in the SERVER-HELLO message. Accordingly, a legitimate server can extract and reconstruct the pair of session keys encrypted by the client using the server's public key as part of the Key Exchange phase.

Finally, if the server encrypts the client's challenge data using its private key, only its public key will decrypt the challenge data. The client should already have this public key. Thus, if the client can successfully decrypt the challenge data, the server has the correct private key that corresponds to the public key in the server's certificate.

The Client Authentication Phase

The Client Authentication phase is optional and occurs only if key exchange algorithms do not authenticate the client (for example, the RSA key exchange algorithm). This phase results in a REQUEST-CERTIFICATE message sent from the server to the client asking for the client's certificate. The client immediately responds with a CLIENT-CERTIFICATE message if it has one or with a NO-CERTIFICATE-ERROR if it does not.

The Finished Phase

In this phase, the server and the client exchange their respective Finished messages. The client sends an encrypted CLIENT-FINISHED message. This message contains, among other information, the original connection identifier it received in the SERVER-HELLO message. The server in turn sends a SERVER-FINISHED message, also encrypted, that contains a session identifier and other information. This session identifier is used by the client and server to add entries to their respective session identifier caches for possible future use. At this point, the SSL handshake is terminated.

Once the SSL handshake is complete, normal Application-layer data can flow through the Transport layer. The data is now encrypted using a cryptographic algorithm negotiated during the handshake process, which is completely transparent to the end user. End users who participate in SSL sessions are guaranteed complete privacy during the session. The security features built into SSL protect Internet communication in three ways:

- Server authentication (thwarting imposters)

- Privacy using encryption (thwarting eavesdroppers)

- Data integrity (thwarting vandals)

Applying SSL Encryption

SSL encrypts data using either a 40-bit or a 128-bit secret session key. A message encrypted with a 40-bit key requires an average of 64 MIPS over a year to break. For example, a 64-MIPS computer would require a year of dedicated processing time to break a single key. The 128-bit version provides exponentially larger protection, because instead of 2^{40} possible keys, it uses 2^{128} possible keys.

The Internet Assigned Numbers Authority (IANA) has reserved the following port numbers for encrypted SSL communications:

- 443 for SSL

- 465 for *SSMTP (Secure Simple Mail Transfer Protocol)*

- 563 SNNTP (Secure Network News Transfer Protocol)

Requesting and Installing a Certificate

HTTP, NNTP, and SMTP servers use certificates to begin SSL sessions. You can obtain a valid certificate in three ways:

- Create the certificate in-house, which means that your company acts as its own CA. You will create an in-house certificate later in this chapter in Exercise 12.1.

- Create a certificate request and get it signed by a third-party CA, such as VeriSign.

- Relay information to a CA so that it can conduct the entire process.

Following is a discussion of the types of certificates available and the elements that all SSL certificates must contain.

Certificate Types

Four types of certificates are currently in use:

Certificate authority   Used by organizations such as VeriSign to sign other certificates.

Server   Used on web servers to identify the web server and the company running it and to allow for encrypted SSL sessions between the server and browsers. Server certificates are also necessary for a server to participate in transactions using the SET (Secure Electronics Transactions) protocol.

Personal   Issued to individuals to allow them to be strongly authenticated and to engage in S/MIME, SSL, and SET.

Software publisher   Used by software authors to sign and identify their released code. This certificate verifies the identity of the author and the integrity of the code.

The X.509v3 Standard

All four certificate types use the *X.509v3 standard*, which establishes the format and contents of the physical certificate file. X.509v3 is an International Telecommunications Union (ITU) standard issued as a corollary of the X.500 messaging standard. Table 12.1 summarizes the elements that certificates should contain as set forth in the X.509v3 standard.

TABLE 12.1 Certificate Elements

Field	Description
Version	The version number of the certificate.
Serial number	A unique serial number for the certificate file.
Signature algorithm ID	Indicates which message digest algorithm was used to sign the certificate file so that it can be verified using the same message digest.
Issuer name	The company name of the certificate issuer; most often VeriSign for public certificates.
Validity period	The start and end dates for which the certificate file is valid. This range is usually one year from issuance. Once a certificate expiration has been reached, the certificate has no value.
Common Name (CN)	Contains the server's ID, which is usually the server's DNS or NetBIOS name. Whenever you generate a certificate, be sure that the CN you specify is the same as your computer name. Internet servers often specify their FQDN for their CN.
Subject public key information	Contains the holder's actual public key, usually 1024 bits long.
Issuer-unique identifier (v2 and v3)	Contains a unique number identifying the issuer, most often VeriSign's unique ID.
Subject-unique identifier (v2 and v3)	Similar to the issuer-unique identifier, but specific to each certificate holder.
Extensions (v3)	This non-standard field allows for additional information, such as date of birth.
Signature	A cryptographic signature of the contents of all previous fields. When certificate files are viewed in the Windows environment, this field is most often referred to as the fingerprint.

Revocation Lists

CAs such as VeriSign maintain *revocation lists* that identify certificates that have been revoked after their release. Most protocols that support certificates allow real-time verification of the certificates. This process involves sending the certificate information electronically to the CA for verification. In this step, the CA checks the certificate against a revocation list. The advantage of using this optional step is the additional verification of certificate validity. The disadvantage is that this verification process takes a few seconds, which can be an unacceptable delay on busy electronic-commerce servers. Carefully consider the need for additional verification on a site-by-site basis.

Reasons for revocation include private key compromise, wrong certificate issuance, issuance for an individual or service that is no longer valid, and CA compromise. All these problems are serious and invalidate the certificate. All CA applications, including those by Microsoft and OpenSSL (`www.openssl .org`), provide the ability to obtain revocation lists that help people learn quickly about expired or compromised certificates.

The Advantages and Disadvantages of Certificates

Both advantages and disadvantages are associated with the use of certificates. You need to consider both when deciding how to use certificates.

Identification, Not Proof

Certificates significantly assist authentication but do not provide absolute proof of identity. For example, the files might have been stolen from a user's hard drive and the password broken. The password assigned when creating a certificate is actually a symmetric key for encrypting the private key on the physical hard drive. Therefore, a good password significantly raises the private key's protection level. If the private key is physically copied, it is still useless without the key to decrypt and use it. However, loss of this key compromises your own ability to use the certificate, so protect this information.

Identical Usernames

If a certificate user is named James Dean, the CA's verification process will attempt to verify that someone claiming to be James Dean is indeed James Dean.

However, this process will not guarantee that it is the correct James Dean for your system. In this case, a subject-unique identifier could be used, but the identifier would have to be known in advance for comparison.

Specialized Information

Certificates are not the solution if you want to establish an e-commerce site for a specialized user group. Imagine that your e-commerce site provides services only for red-haired women. The certificate does not store information such as user gender or hair color. The Extensions field can be used for extraneous information, but this is not a viable solution because the information must be included initially in the certificate, and CAs do not currently include that type of information. A certificate cannot be modified after it is issued because modification renders the signature invalid, thereby nullifying the entire certificate.

No Selective Disclosure

What if you want to reveal only certain fields of the certificate and not the entire contents? Currently, limited disclosure is not possible. All contents of the certificate are sent, and any information contained therein is seen.

Easy Data Aggregation

Organizations currently use information such as social security numbers or e-mail addresses to track users' usage and spending habits. This method is not particularly reliable because it can be easily falsified. Also, errors can occur while data is being entered. These problems all contribute to unreliable data aggregation. With the advent of digital certificates, the ability to achieve privacy-invading levels of information becomes easy. The unique identifiers, combined with the fact that all information is sent electronically and is cryptographically secured, mean that misinformation and user errors can be eliminated.

Certificate Lending

Currently, if you need a coworker to retrieve your e-mail for you, you need supply only your password. If certificates are used for identification, this legitimate activity will no longer be possible. Much of the intention of certificates is to allow only the actual user to access the data. Portable technologies such as smart cards and similar physical storage methods are being used to store certificates, but the use of theses technologies is not standardized or widespread.

Certificate Concerns

As you create certificates, you must consider the following logistical concerns:

- Creating a certificate request requires that you create a text file. This file must be password-protected. You must not forget the password used to generate your certificate request. If you do, the only way to use SSL will be to create and process another request. Therefore, keep the password safe.

- In IIS 5, you can bind a certificate to all IP addresses or to a single IP address. If you want to use multiple certificates, you must bind each certificate to specific IP addresses to use them with your HTTP or NNTP server.

- Study the CA you plan to use. Make sure that it is respected and as secure as possible.

- Do not be overly confident. SSL sessions help guard against data sniffing and tampering; however, they are not a complete security solution.

- The Computer Name (CN) field in the certificate given by the server to the client must be the same as the server computer. Otherwise, a client's browser will warn the client that the certificate has the wrong name.

EXERCISE 12.1

Becoming a CA

In this exercise, you will install the Windows 2000 certificate server. Before you begin, you need to check the NetBIOS and DNS names for your computer. To check the NetBIOS name, follow these steps.

1. On the Desktop, right-click My Computer and choose Properties from the shortcut menu to open the System Properties dialog box.

2. Click the Network Identification tab.

3. Take note of the value identified as Full Computer Name.

To check the DNS name, follow these steps:

1. At a command prompt, enter **ipconfig /all** and press Enter.

2. Take note of the value identified as Host Name.

3. Write your computer's NetBIOS and DNS names here:

   _____.

These steps are necessary because you will need to synchronize all names for all exercises to proceed smoothly. Although problems will not cause fatal errors, the exercises will not be as instructive on how a certificate helps prove the identity of a computer. It is important to verify and, if necessary, change this information because after you install Certificate Services, you will not be able to change this information unless you first uninstall Certificate Services.

1. At a command prompt, issue the **certreq** command:

2. If the Open Request File dialog box opens, Certificate Services is installed, and you do not have to finish this exercise. If you receive an error message, continue with the remaining steps to install Certificate Services.

3. Choose Start ➢ Settings ➢ Control Panel to open Control Panel.

4. Double-click the Add/Remove Programs icon to open the Add/Remove Programs window.

5. Click the Add/Remove Windows Components icon, and then select the Certificate Services check box.

6. Click Yes to indicate that you understand that you will not be able to change the computer name or join another domain as long as this service is installed.

7. Click Next to open the Certificate Authority Type screen. Choose the Stand-alone Root CA radio button, as shown in the following graphic:

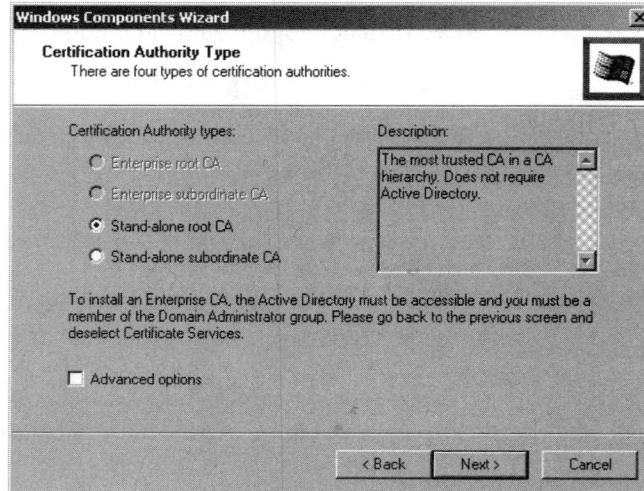

8. Click Next and enter the full DNS name of your computer in the CA Name field. For example, if your computer is named server1.ciw.com, enter this value.

9. Enter your first name in the Organization field, and then enter **training** in the Organizational Unit field.

10. Enter the relevant information for your own city, state or province, and country. Be sure that you enter the full name of your city and state/province. In the country field, use the accepted two-digit abbreviation, such as UK for the United Kingdom or US for the United States. Do not enter characters such as commas or semicolons in any of these fields. Use only standard alphabetic characters.

11. Enter the following e-mail address in the E-mail field: **ciw@ciw.com**.

12. In the CA Description field, enter **Certificate Authority for <*Yourfirstname*>**, making sure to substitute your name.

13. Leave the Valid For field at its default setting.

14. Click Next to continue through the wizard.

15. Leave the defaults as they are in the Data Storage Location field, and click Next.

16. You will be informed that IIS is running and will be shut down for installation to continue. Click OK.

17. If asked for the installation disk, insert your Windows 2000 installation CD in your computer drive, click OK, and wait while the needed files are copied.

18. When the Certificate Services are installed, click Finish.

19. Close the Add/Remove Programs window.

20. At a command prompt, issue the **certreq** command again. You should see the Open Request File dialog box. Certificate Services are now installed on your system.

EXERCISE 12.2

Requesting an SSL Server Certificate

In this exercise, you will use the IIS 5 snap-in to generate an SSL request.

1. Open the Internet Information Services/IIS 5 snap-in and expand your server to display the Default Web Site.

2. Right-click Default Web Site, and choose Properties from the shortcut menu to open the Default Web Site Properties dialog box.

3. Click the Directory Security tab.

4. In the Secure Communications section, click the Server Certificate button to start the IIS Certificate Wizard.

5. At the Welcome screen, click Next to open the Server Certificate screen:

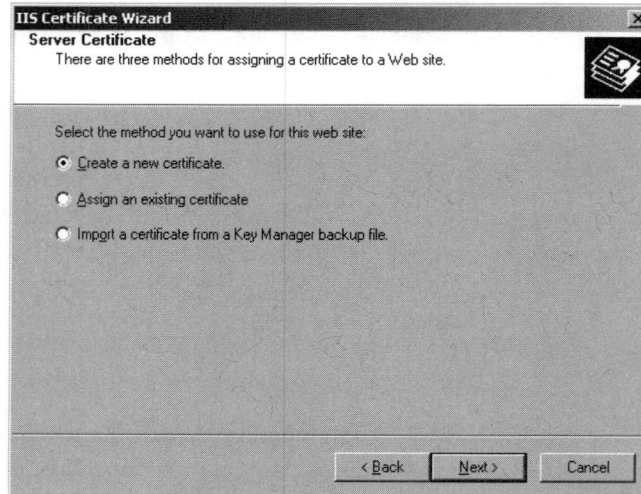

6. You can choose to create a new certificate, assign an existing certificate, or import a certificate from a Windows NT 4 Key Manager backup certificate. Click the Create a New Certificate radio button, and then click Next to continue through the wizard.

7. Make sure the Prepare the Request Now, But Send It Later button is selected, and then click Next to continue moving through the wizard.

8. Enter your name in the Name field. Leave the bit length at its default setting of 512, and click Next to continue moving through the wizard.

9. In the Organization field, enter **ciw**. In the Organizational Unit field, enter **training** and click Next to continue moving through the wizard.

10. In the Common Name field, enter your computer's NetBIOS name (you wrote it down in Exercise 12.1) if not already present.

11. Click Next, and in the Country/Region field, enter your country. In the State/Province and City/Locality fields, enter that information. Be sure to enter the entire name and not an abbreviation. Do not use any characters such as semicolons or commas. When you are finished, click Next.

12. You will be asked to enter a file name for your certificate request. The wizard will enter a file name by default. Enter the directory and file name of the certificate request here:

_____

The location and file name will likely be `C:\certreq.txt`, if the system was installed on the C:\ drive.

13. Leave the default location and file name, and click Next to open the Request File Summary screen. (If a previous request has been made, you will see a dialog box informing you that this file already exists and asking if you want to replace it. Click Yes.)

14. Review your settings and click Next.

15. 15. Click Finish to complete your certificate request.

Signing and Processing a Certificate Request to Create an SSL Certificate

Normally, you receive a certificate from a widely known CA, such as VeriSign, or a specially designated intranet CA for your company. For this exercise, you will act as your own CA.

EXERCISE 12.3 *(continued)*

1. At a command prompt, enter the **certreq** command and press Enter to open the Open Request File dialog box, as shown in the following graphic:

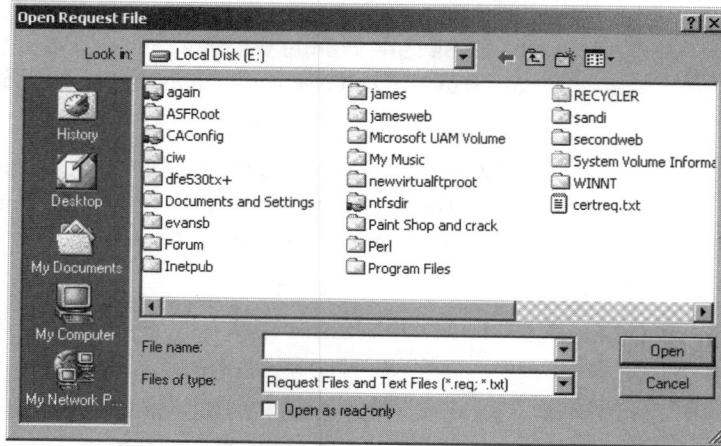

2. Your certificate request should be visible after navigating with the Look In drop-down list box to your C: drive.

3. Once you find the proper file (probably C:\certreq.txt), select it and click Open to open the Select Certification Authority dialog box.

4. Select your own system as the Certificate Authority, as shown in the following graphic, and click OK.

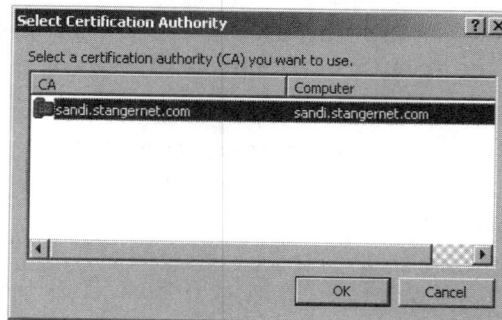

5. Choose Start ➢ Programs ➢ Administrative Tools ➢ Certification Authority to open the Certification Authority snap-in and expand your server.

6. Select the Pending Requests icon. You should see that your request is pending. You will see an entry similar to the one shown in the following graphic:

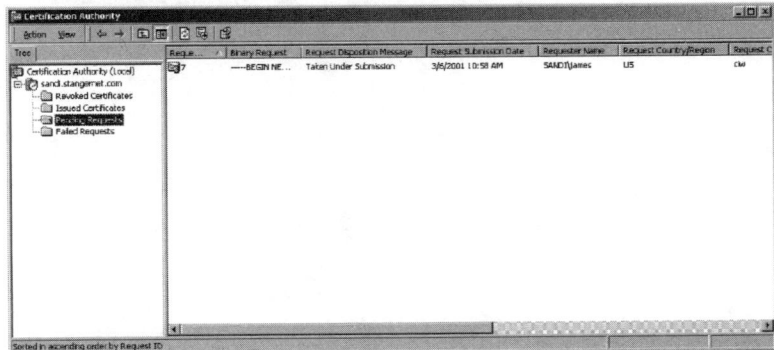

7. Right-click the pending certificate, and choose All Tasks ➢ Issue from the shortcut menu.

8. Click the Issued Certificates icon to display your certificate. You are now going to save (that is, export) this certificate to your disk so that you can apply it to your web server using the IIS 5 snap-in. Right-click your newly issued certificate, and choose Open from the shortcut menu to open the Certificate dialog box.

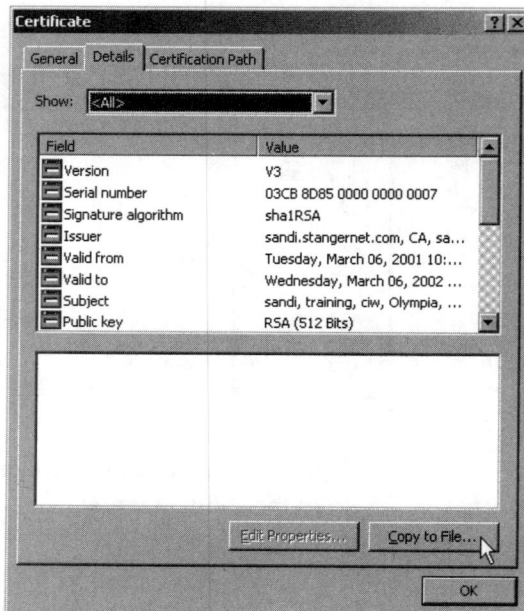

9. Click the Details tab.

10. Review the details concerning your certificate, and then click the Copy to File button to start the Certificate Export Wizard.

11. Click Next, and make sure that the DER Encoded Binary X.509 (.CER) radio button is selected (it should be by default), and then click Next to continue moving through the wizard.

EXERCISE 12.3 *(continued)*

12. You will be asked to supply a file name and location. Use your name as the file name and do not enter a file extension. Click Next to complete the wizard.

13. Review your settings, and then click Finish. Click OK to acknowledge that your export was successful.

> **NOTE** In Unix/Linux systems, the OpenSSL project allows systems to act as certificate authorities. Go to `www.openssl.org` to learn more about how to use the CA.pl script in conjunction with openssl.

Summary

In this chapter, you learned that SSL was developed by Netscape to provide secure communications between a web server and a web browser. SSL is implemented above the Transport layer and below the Application layer of the network architecture model; therefore, SSL can support multiple applications. You learned that SSL provides a private, authenticated, reliable channel using a six-step SSL handshake. You learned that the first phase, Hello, is the most important phase of this handshake and is where security algorithms and strength are negotiated. You also learned that SSL uses TCP port 443 and can use 40-bit or 128-bit encryption.

You learned that you can obtain a valid certificate for use with SSL by creating your own certificate in-house by creating a certificate request and getting it signed by a third-party CA, such as VeriSign; or by relaying the information to a third-party CA so that it can conduct the entire process. You learned that there are four certificate types: certificate authority, server, personal, and software publisher. You also learned about the advantages and disadvantages of using certificates.

In the exercises, you saw that SSL can create immediate encryption between parties that do not know each other, thus enabling secure e-commerce.

Exam Essentials

Be able to describe the functions of Secure Sockets Layer (SSL).   SSL protects Internet communications in three ways: server authentication (thwarting imposters), privacy using encryption (thwarting eavesdroppers), and data integrity (thwarting vandals).

Identify the SSL handshake process.   During the SSL handshake the web server and the client browser exchange and negotiate a secure communications link. The handshake occurs in six phases: Hello, Key Exchange, Session Key Production, Server Verify, Client Authentication, and Finished.

Describe how an IIS 5 server certificate is requested from a Windows 2000 Certificate Server, installed, and used.   On a Windows 2000 server, you install Certificate Services using the Add/Remove Programs applet. You use the IIS 5 snap-in or a web browser to generate an SSL server certificate request for your IIS 5 server. You then use the Certification Authority MMC to approve your own certificate request and to export your server certificate to a file.

Key Terms

Before taking the exam, you should be familiar with the following terms:

certificate authority (CA)	server certificate
certificate authority certificate	session key
personal certificate	software publisher certificate
revocation lists	SSL handshake
SSMTP (Secure SMTP)	SSL record
Secure Sockets Layer (SSL)	X.509v3 standard

Review Questions

1. Jonathan is director of Human Resources for Great Escapes. He wants to know if SSL can be used with Novell NetWare. Choose all the true answers to his question.

   A. SSL is designed to work with TCP/IP.

   B. SSL easily works with the WAN protocols TCP/IP and IPX/SPX, but not with the LAN protocol NetBEUI.

   C. SSL will most easily work with Novell NetWare if Novell is using TCP/IP.

   D. SSL is a security layer between TCP/IP and other application protocols, including HTTP, LDAP, and FTP.

   E. SSL is a security layer that sits on top of the Network Access layer. Therefore, it has greater speed than higher-level protocols and is compatible with all higher-level protocols.

2. Mary runs `MostGifts.com`, which provides website hosting with a shopping cart for independent gift shops that use a variety of computers, including Windows 98 and Apple PowerBook clients. The independent gift shops must upload their price lists to their individual websites. Mary is concerned that a hacker will try to upload bogus price lists to a gift shop's website. What should she implement on her FTP server? Select the best answer.

   A. Anonymous authentication

   B. Basic authentication

   C. Integrated authentication

   D. Secure Sockets Layer

3. Edward is making a presentation to potential angel investors in a new web-hosting company. He is touting the benefits of using SSL to upload web content. Which benefits should he cite? Choose all that apply.

   A. Speed

   B. Privacy

   C. Authentication

   D. Reliability

4. Jason has recently established an SSL session that includes the RSA key exchange algorithm. Which phase of the SSL handshake can be abbreviated? Choose the best answer.

   A. Phase 1: Hello

   B. Phase 2: Key Exchange

   C. Phase 4: Server Verify

   D. Phase 5: Client Authentication

5. Heather wants to use a strong SSL key in the United States. What strength SSL key should Heather use?

   A. 40-bit Master Key.

   B. 40-bit Session Key

   C. 128-bit Master Key

   D. 128-bit Session Key

   E. 1024-bit Master Key

   F. 1024-bit Session Key

6. Jim knows that there are six phases to the SSL handshake. Which phase is the most important phase and the phase in which the encryption algorithms and strength of encryption are negotiated?

   A. Phase 1: Hello

   B. Phase 2: Key Exchange

   C. Phase 3: Session Key Production

   D. Phase 3: Master Key Production

7. Jason has just installed a firewall to protect his website. He has opened port 80 for HTTP and port 25 for SMTP, yet when users try to send secure e-mail or use SSL, they are blocked. Which ports on the firewall does Jason need to open for SSL and Secure SMTP?

   A. 119

   B. 20

   C. 443

   D. 465

   E. 21

8. Mike wants to conduct secure e-commerce with customers around the world. He wants to request and install a certificate that will be used for SSL and universally trusted. Which of the following options will work?

    A. Create the certificate in-house

    B. Create a certificate request and get it signed by a third-party CA, such as VeriSign

    C. Relay information to a third-party CA, such as VeriSign, so that it can conduct the entire process

    D. Use the client's server certificate

9. Mike wants to allow executives and sales people who travel to communicate securely with corporate headquarters using SSL. He wants maximum control over this process, and he wants to minimize costs. What should Mike do? Select the best option.

    A. Create the certificate in-house

    B. Create a certificate request and get it signed by a third-party CA, such as VeriSign

    C. Relay information to a third-party CA, such as VeriSign, so that it can conduct the entire process

    D. Use the client's server certificate

10. Steve needs to use S/MIME to bid securely on training contracts with the Central Command. What type of certificate does Steve need to install?

    A. Certificate authority

    B. Server

    C. Personal

    D. SMTP

    E. Software publisher

11. Denise is a global network engineer and has set up her servers to allow installation of signed drivers only. A vendor for a new fiberoptic NIC that operates at incredible speed wants to allow Denise to test his NIC for free. What kind of certificate does the vendor need to sign the NIC driver?

    A. Certificate authority

    B. Server

    C. Personal

    D. Enterprise certificate

    E. Software publisher

12. Fred wants to use SSL on his web server. What type of certificate does Fred need?

    A. Certificate authority

    B. Server

    C. Personal

    D. Internet server

    E. Software publisher

13. Rajesh wants his web server's certificate validated so that just about any client will be able to conduct SSL sessions with his website. What type of certificate is needed?

    A. Certificate authority

    B. Server

    C. Personal

    D. Enterprise certificate

    E. Software publisher

14. The www.OmniSky.com website filed for Chapter 11, and a year later, the assets were bought by another company. Which of the following events can invalidate the server certificates of OmniSky? Choose all that apply.

    A. VeriSign revokes its server certificates.

    B. The validity period expires.

    C. The DNS names of the servers change.

    D. The MAC address of the servers change.

15. Mary is trying to explain Secure Sockets Layer to her husband. Mary should say that Secure Sockets Layer is the most common method of which of the following? (Choose the best answer.)

    A. Securing communications between a web server and a web browser

    B. Providing communications between businesses

    C. Enabling commerce across the Internet

    D. Transferring money across the Internet

16. Hank is trying to understand SSL. What are the three types of handshakes in the SSL process?

    A. When no previous session exists

    B. When a previous session exists

    C. When a server seeks client authentication

    D. When a client seeks server authentication

17. Tom runs a consulting firm. He wants to use SSL and understand the SSL handshake process. What happens during or immediately after the Finished phase? Choose all that apply.

    A. The SSL session is terminated.

    B. Normal application-layer data is allowed to flow through the Transport layer.

    C. The server caches the session identifier for possible future use.

    D. The client caches the session identifier for possible future use.

    E. The server caches the client's private key for possible future use.

18. Dennis is presenting the benefits of SSL to higher management. Which of the following are benefits? Choose all that apply.

   A. SSL certificates provide a fingerprint that is used to distinguish even among users with identical names.

   B. SSL may be used with all application layer protocols including UDP.

   C. SSL provides data integrity.

   D. SSL provides privacy using encryption.

   E. SSL provides server authentication.

19. Jessica is attempting to explain how SSL works to her supervisor. He wants to know how many of the upper layers SSL operates with when implemented. What answer should she give?

   A. One

   B. Two

   C. Three

   D. Four

20. Willy administers a Windows 2000 network that is used for e-commerce with the general public. Willy wants to make the SSL certificate as secure as possible. What should Willy do? Choose two answers.

   A. Put a strong password on the certificate request

   B. Bind the certificate to a particular IP address

   C. Use SSL for all web pages

   D. Use Microsoft as the CA

Answers to Review Questions

1. A, C, D.   SSL sits between the Transport layer and the Application layer of the four-layer network architecture model.

2. D.   SSL works with all Application-level protocols including FTP, LDAP, and HTTP. See www.ipswitch.com for an FTP server that uses SSL. Without SSL, a password is sent in cleartext to an FTP server and can be hacked.

3. B, C, D.   SSL provides privacy, authentication, and reliability. Reliability is provided by a hash that verifies that the data have not been corrupted in transmission or cooked by a hacker.

4. A.   If the client has a valid session identifier, the handshaking process is faster because encryption enhancements negotiated during the previous Hello phase can be used.

5. D.   A 128-bit Session Key is billions of times stronger than a 40-bit Session Key.

6. A.   In the Hello phase, the encryption algorithms and strength of encryption are negotiated.

7. C, D.   SSL uses port 443; Secure SMTP uses port 465.

8. B, C.   A third-party certificate, such as one from VeriSign, is universally trusted. An in-house certificate will work internally and with trusting partner organizations.

9. A.   A third-party certificate, such as one from VeriSign, is universally trusted, but is costly. An in-house certificate will work internally and with trusting partner organizations.

10. C.   The personal certificate is issued to individuals to allow them to be strongly authenticated and engage in S/MIME, SSL, and SET.

11. E.   A driver is software that requires a software publisher certificate if the identity of the author and the integrity of the code is to be verified.

12. B. A server certificate is used on web servers to identify the web server and the company running it and to allow for encrypted SSL sessions between the server and browsers.

13. A. A certificate authority certificate is used to sign other certificates.

14. A, B, C. Certificates can be revoked, or they can expire. You should also make sure that whenever you generate a certificate that the Common Name (CN) is the same as the computer name. Changes in the CN can invalidate the certificate.

15. A. Secure Sockets Layer is the most common method of securing communications between a web server and a web browser.

16. A, B, C. Three basic types of handshakes are defined in the SSL handshake process. The first type occurs with no recently preexisting session (this creates a short delay); the second type uses a set of session identifiers; and the third type is initiated by a server seeking client authentication.

17. B, C, D. During the Finished phase of the SSL handshake, the client and server add entries to their respective session identifier caches for possible future use. At this point, the SSL handshake is terminated. Once the SSL handshake is complete, normal application-layer data can flow through the transport layer.

18. C, D, E. SSL provides identification, not proof of identity, and may not be able to resolve identical user names. SSL encrypts data in transmission, but not on the hard drive. File and folder security should be applied. SSL does not provide for selective disclosure of data. SSL uses TCP, not UDP. UDP is not an application layer protocol. SSL does provide data integrity, privacy, and server authentication.

19. C. SSL interacts with the top three layers when employed.

20. A, B. Willy should place a strong password on the certificate request and bind the certificate to a single IP address. The use of SSL for all web pages would slow down a website and not create substantially greater security. Microsoft is not currently a third-party CA whose certificate is preloaded into browsers.

Configuring and Connecting to News and E-mail Servers

THE CIW EXAM OBJECTIVE GROUPS COVERED IN THIS CHAPTER:

✓ Configure and manage news servers and e-mail servers.

Most business organizations have an e-mail server and couldn't function without it, but not many have a news server. A news server can be an excellent way to disseminate information without increasing network traffic. In this chapter, we'll look at how to configure and manage both a news server and an e-mail server. We'll start by looking at the Network News Transfer Protocol (NNTP), and then we'll look at how to configure newsgroups in Windows 2000 and Linux.

Our discussion of e-mail servers will begin with a look at how e-mail servers and clients process messages using the e-mail protocols, and then we'll describe the masquerading, aliasing, and forwarding processes. In conclusion, we'll look at how to configure a domain name server with MX (mail exchange).

The Network News Transfer Protocol (NNTP)

Unlike e-mail servers, news servers post only one instance of a message and then keep that message on the server for all users to read. Clients log on to the news server to read or download posted messages.

Newsgroups can be accessed by the entire company or secured to allow access only to certain users. You can place limitations on the messages posted to the newsgroups and on those who post them, and you can configure newsgroups with a variety of options, ranging from message size to expiration policies.

The NNTP service defaults to using TCP port 119. NNTP also supports SSL (Secure Sockets Layer). If SSL-enabled, the NNTP server will listen on port 563. The NNTP service supports Usenet-style newsgroups. *Usenet* is a collection of topically named Internet discussion groups, or newsgroups, including information on the computers that run the protocols and the people who read and submit postings. The IIS 5 NNTP service supports other NNTP clients and servers, but it does not support Usenet feeds. You can use Microsoft Exchange Server or other newsfeed software. Other Usenet sites can retrieve newsgroups from the IIS NNTP service, but they cannot receive the newsgroups directly. The Linux INND server does, however, support Usenet feeds.

Private and Usenet NNTP Servers

You will probably be tasked with configuring an NNTP server and various groups for a specific business purpose. The NNTP server you configure can be used on your company's intranet or over the Internet. This section focuses on creating an intranet news server.

You can configure your news server to receive feeds from Usenet. Thus, your system becomes part of thousands of systems on the Internet that compose Usenet. If your server is Usenet-enabled, clients who log on to your server can access all newsgroups, as long as your server has connected to another Usenet server and downloaded the most recent Usenet list, which is updated daily.

The Expires Header

NNTP clients can send messages that have a special header called the *Expires header*. This header contains information that tells the news server it can delete a particular message from a newsgroup after a certain period of time. All of today's news servers honor this heading; however, the server has the final say over when a message will be deleted from a newsgroup.

Creating a Newsgroup in Windows 2000

As mentioned earlier, you can use a news server in your company as a forum for exchanging information among employees. The first task is to install the NNTP service. To do so, follow these steps:

1. Choose Start ➢ Settings ➢ Control Panel ➢ Add/Remove Programs to open the Add/Remove Programs window.

2. Click Add/Remove Windows Components to open the Add or Remove Windows Components window.

3. In the Components list, select Internet Information Services (IIS), and then click the Details button to open the Subcomponents of Internet Information Services dialog box.

4. Click the NNTP Service check box, and then click OK.

5. Click Next to start the installation. A progress bar will appear while components are configuring.

6. Click Finish. You may have to restart your computer.

Now, you need to verify that the Default NNTP Virtual Server has been installed. Follow these steps:

1. Choose Start ➤ Programs ➤ Administrative Tools ➤ Internet Services Manager to open the IIS 5 snap-in.

2. Expand the icon that represents your computer, and then expand the Default NNTP Virtual Server. You should see the Newsgroups, Expiration Policies, Virtual Directories, and Current Sessions icons, as shown in Figure 13.1.

FIGURE 13.1 Viewing the Default NNTP Virtual Server

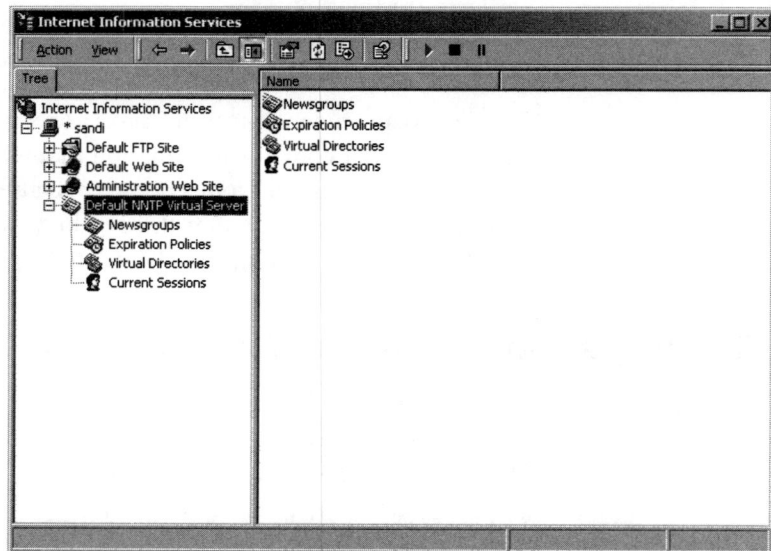

3. Select the Newsgroups icon. Notice that the news server has a few default newsgroups installed.

4. Right-click the Newsgroups icon, and choose New ≻ Newsgroup from the shortcut menu to start the New Newsgroup Wizard.

5. In the Name field, enter your first name, and then click Next to open the Welcome to the New Newsgroup Wizard screen.

6. In the Description field, enter My Newsgroup Server, and enter your first name in the Newsgroup Pretty Name field.

> **NOTE** The Newsgroup Pretty Name field is used to provide an alternative name for the newsgroup to particular NNTP clients that support pretty names, which allow newsgroups to use a name such as Site News instead of `company.site.news`.

7. Click Finish.

EXERCISE 13.1

Configuring Outlook Express as a News Client

In this exercise, you will create a news account using Outlook Express and then access the newsgroup you created earlier.

1. Open Outlook Express. If the Internet Connection Wizard appears, this is the first time Outlook Express has been opened. Create an e-mail account, and then exit the wizard.

2. In Outlook Express, choose Tools ≻ Accounts to open the Internet Accounts dialog box.

3. Click the News tab, then choose Add ≻ News to start the Internet Connection Wizard.

4. In the Display Name field, enter your full name. Click Next to open the Internet News E-mail Address screen.

5. Enter a fictitious e-mail address and click Next to open the Internet New Server Name screen.

6. In the News (NNTP) Server field, enter your computer name. (You can enter your own IP address instead of a DNS name.) Select the My News Server Requires Me to Log On check box, and then click Next to open the Internet News Server Logon screen.

7. In the Account Name and Password fields, enter a valid username and password. The password cannot be blank.

8. Click Next, and then click Finish.

9. Click Close to exit the Internet Accounts dialog box. You will immediately be asked if you want to download the newsgroups from the news account you just added. Click Yes.

10. In the Newsgroup Subscriptions dialog box, select all the newsgroups (your own name will appear as the last entry) and then click the Subscribe button:

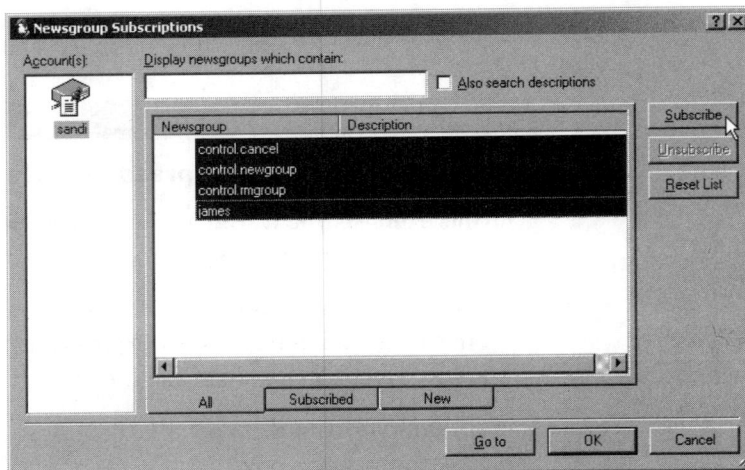

11. Click OK. In the main Outlook Express window, you will see your new account at the bottom of the left pane, along with a list of newsgroups. This list will include the newsgroup you just created. Highlight the newsgroup you created. In the right pane, you will see that no messages have been posted.

12. Post a message on your newsgroup. Select New Post to open a blank message window, already addressed to your newsgroup.

13. In the Subject field, enter **This is a test**. In the message body, enter **Hello World!** and then click the Send button.

14. Click OK to acknowledge that this post is being sent and that it may not appear immediately. If you want, select the Don't Show Me This Again check box.

15. When the message is sent, highlight your newsgroup, and then press the F5 key. You will see your new message. Highlight the message in the right pane of Outlook Express to view it. Double-click the message.

16. Select Reply Group, and then compose a reply.

17. When you are finished writing, click the Send button.

18. Highlight the message you replied to in steps 15 and 16 and press the F5 key. You should see that the message from you has begun a newsgroup tree. Expand the tree to see that your reply has a + sign next to it.

Creating a News Server Expiration Policy in Windows 2000

1. Open the IIS snap-in if it is not open already.

2. Expand Default NNTP Site.

3. Right-click Expiration Policies, and choose New ➤ Expiration Policy from the shortcut menu to start the New NNTP Expiration Policy Wizard.

4. In the Expiration Policy Description field, enter **policy1**. This name allows you to identify the expiration policy in the IIS snap-in.

5. Click Next to open the next New NNTP Expiration Policy Wizard screen.

6. Click the Only Selected Newsgroups on This Virtual Server radio button, and then click Next to open the next screen of this wizard.

7. Click Add to add the *your_first_name* newsgroup, and then enter your name. Click OK, and then click Next to move to the next screen.

EXERCISE 13.2 *(continued)*

8. The number you enter in the Remove Articles Older Than (Hours) field will cause your NNTP server to hold articles for a certain number of hours. After the number of hours you specify expires, the server deletes the articles. For example, if you enter 1, the articles are held for one hour and then deleted. Enter 48 to keep articles for two days, and then click Finish.

Creating a Newsgroup in Linux

Newsgroups are a convenient way to share information among computer users. Those users can be running any operating system; the functionality remains the same, although the implementation differs. In the previous section, we examined how to add a newsgroup in Windows 2000. In this section, we will look at the process of creating a newsgroup in the Linux operating system. To create a newsgroup in Linux, follow these steps:

1. Boot into Linux.

2. Use the `host# cd /etc/news/` command to change to the `/etc/news/` directory.

3. Make a copy of the `innd.conf` file.

4. Using vi, open the `innd.conf` file.

5. Scroll down to the Organization field, and then delete the following text: A poorly installed InterNetNews site.

In vi, you delete text by entering command mode (press Esc, place your cursor in front of the text you want to delete, and press the d key.

---

6. Press i to enter insert mode, and then replace the text you deleted with the following text: A CIW site.

7. Enter command mode, scroll down to the server entry, and delete the existing entry. Enter Insert mode, and enter your own FQDN (for example, `student1.classroom.com`).

8. In the domain field, enter your domain name (for example, `classroom.com`).

9. Press Esc, and then enter **ZZ** to exit vi and save your changes.

10. For security reasons, this server does not allow anyone access to the service by default. To allow all users on your network to access your server, open the `nnrp.access` file in vi.

11. Scroll down to the bottom of the file, enter Insert mode, and enter the following lines:

```
192.168.2.0/24:Read Post:::*
192.168.3.0/24:Read Post:::*
192.168.3.0/24:Read Post:::*
```

> **NOTE** These lines allow anonymous access from the 192.168.2.0, 192.168.3.0, and 192.168.4.0 networks. If your network is using a different set of IP addresses, substitute the appropriate IP addresses. The syntax for these entries is as follows: hosts:permissions:username:password:patterns. The hosts entry allows you to specify IP addresses or DNS names. The second field allows you to specify whether users can only read entries or can post entries. The third field can contain a username or can be blank. A blank field causes INND to not check for a username. The fourth field is for the password. As with the username, a blank field means that INND will not ask for a username and will allow anonymous access. You specify newsgroups that will use this rule in the last field.

12. Exit this file, making sure to save your changes.

13. Now, start INND using its System V initialization script using the following command:

```
/etc/rc.d/init.d/innd start
```

14. You have started your news server. However, your news server currently has no newsgroups in it. You need to create at least one newsgroup for this server. You do this using the `/usr/bin/ctlinnd` command, once INND has started. Add a new group named ciwcertified to this news server as shown below:

```
host# /usr/bin/ctlinnd newgroup ciwcertified
```

15. You will see a message that reads Ok to indicate that you have created a new newsgroup.

16. Now, start the X Window System using the `startx` command.

17. Open a terminal, and then enter **host# netscape &** to launch Netscape Navigator

18. Several icons are at the bottom-right of Netscape Navigator. One of these is the mail and newsgroups icon. Click it to open the Netscape Mail and Newsgroups window.

19. Choose Edit ➢ Preferences and expand the Mail & Newsgroups icon.

20. Select the Identity section.

21. Enter your name and any e-mail address.

22. Select the Newsgroups Servers icon.

23. Delete any existing entries.

24. Click the Add button and add your own server, either by using its DNS name or its IP address, and then click OK twice to return to the main window.

25. Expand the server you created, right-click it, then choose Subscribe to Newsgroups from the shortcut menu to open a list of newsgroups for your server.

26. Select the ciwcertified newsgroup.

27. Click the Subscribe button.

28. Click OK.

29. You will see that this newsgroup has been added. Right-click this newsgroup and choose New Message from the shortcut menu to open the Compose window.

30. Enter **test** in the Subject field, enter **Hello World** in the body of the text, and then click Send.

31. After several minutes, refresh your screen by highlighting another server icon or e-mail icon in your news client. Highlight the Linux news server again. You can then see your new message.

Sending and Delivering E-mail

Approximately ten years ago, e-mail became a convenience. It allowed communication to transpire in a medium that had not been widely used before. As more companies, and more users, started using the Internet as a regular business component, e-mail changed from a convenience to a staple. Whereas at one time a downed server would cause a few eyes to roll, it now attracts the attention of management and can bring some businesses to their knees.

In this section, we will examine e-mail and how the behind-the-scenes process works. Figure 13.2 shows the process required to send e-mail from one host to another.

FIGURE 13.2   The e-mail delivery process

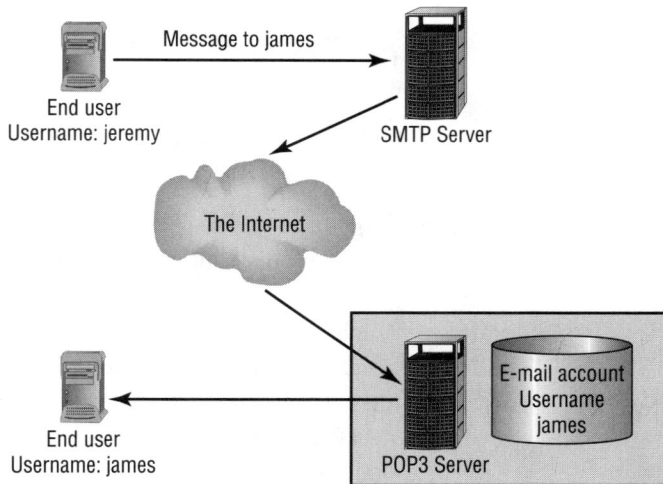

Following is a summary of the e-mail delivery process:

1. Jeremy composes a message to James and clicks the Send button on his e-mail client. The message is sent on its way.

2. Jeremy's e-mail message is routed through an SMTP server, which directs it to the Internet.

3. Jeremy's e-mail message travels from computer to computer across the Internet until it reaches its destination host (possibly a POP3 or IMAP server), where the intended recipient, James, has an account.

4. After the message arrives at the destination host, the SMTP e-mail service (or daemon) delivers it to a mailbox file owned by James.

5. James either accesses the file by logging onto the system locally or accesses the POP3 or IMAP server to access his mailbox file and reads the new message.

E-mail servers use agents to handle each step of this process.

E-mail Agents

An e-mail system has one goal: to deliver a message from the sending client to the recipient. All e-mail systems use three agents that create, send, store, and download e-mail messages:

- Mail Transfer Agent (MTA)
- Mail Delivery Agent (MDA)
- Mail User Agent (MUA)

The *Mail Transfer Agent (MTA)* is a server responsible for delivering mail between hosts until it arrives at an MDA. This server is also known as an SMTP server. The Unix sendmail daemon is an example of an MTA. An MTA is also responsible for formatting messages correctly so that different platforms (such as a Microsoft Exchange Server, a Lotus Notes server, and an MDaemon server) can all cooperate. Finally, an MTA server can rewrite SMTP headers to simplify e-mail addressing. (You will learn more about rewriting SMTP headers shortly.) An MTA is responsible for Steps 2 through 4 of the e-mail delivery process outlined earlier.

> **NOTE** In this section, we'll use sendmail and the SMTP services provided by MDaemon as example MTAs.

Whenever an MTA server receives a message, it stores this message in a dedicated directory, the *drop directory*. Usually, each message accepted by the MTA is placed into individual text files named after the recipient. For example, when sendmail receives a message addressed to james@ciwcertified .com, it saves this message in a file named james in the /var/mail/ directory. This file can contain many e-mail messages.

SMTP servers store outgoing messages in a particular directory. Sendmail, for example, stores its outgoing messages in the `/var/spool/mqueue/` directory. This directory is often called the *message queue*. You can check this queue to see how well the service is sending messages.

The *Mail Delivery Agent (MDA)* is a server responsible for storing e-mail messages that a client can download. An MTA server can be either a POP3 or an IMAP daemon. An MDA server is responsible for Step 5 of the e-mail delivery process outlined previously.

Generally, an MDA contains the following elements.

A drop directory   Also called a mail drop or an inbox, depending on the server, this directory is owned only by the end user. The drop directory stores incoming e-mail messages and is usually the same directory as the SMTP drop directory discussed earlier. Upon authentication, the end user can read, download, or delete the messages in this directory.

A valid user account   This account allows the user to log on to obtain messages from the drop directory.

A limited logon shell   An IMAP or a POP3 server provides a limited logon shell that allows users access to the inbox (that is, the drop directory).

The *Mail User Agent (MUA)* can be any e-mail client application with which end users compose, send, and retrieve e-mail, including the `mail` or `pine` programs in Unix or Windows applications such as Outlook Express or Netscape Messenger. An MUA is responsible for Step 1 and Step 5 of the e-mail delivery process outlined earlier.

It is common for a single application to assume multiple functions. For example, the mail program in Unix acts as both an MUA and an MDA; it allows you to create e-mail, and it also stores e-mail sent between local users on a system.

E-mail Server Terminology

E-mail agents perform several tasks, including the following:

- Masquerading
- Aliasing
- Relaying

Masquerading is the practice of altering the *SMTP header* of a message so that a user can appear to be sending e-mail from a different computer. The SMTP header is routing information placed at the front of an e-mail message. Masquerading offers many benefits, including the following.

- Masquerading conceals your company's DNS structure from outsiders.

- Masquerading eases the administration of e-mail messages.

- If you have multiple e-mail servers, you can use masquerading to ensure that all recipients of company e-mail see a unified e-mail address (for example, james@ciwcertified.com as opposed to james@mail4.ciwcertified.com).

For example, suppose that a user named Patrick has an e-mail account on a host named `metallica` and that `metallica` is part of the `ciwcertified.com` domain. The `metallica` host is an e-mail server. Any message from Patrick actually originates from patrick@metallica.ciwcertified.com. However, if the MTA service on `metallica` supports masquerading, Patrick could configure the service to rewrite the SMTP header so that all messages appear to be from patrick@ciwcertified.com.

Aliasing is a renaming practice for accounts on a local host that creates an alternative address for a specific user. Any MTA can maintain a database of local address aliases. Aliasing allows users to refer to other users by simple nicknames or by names other than their Unix user names. Aliasing is different from masquerading because it works with the MTA service on the local host. Unlike masquerading, aliasing does not rewrite message headers to change the computer name. Following is an example of aliasing:

```
sjstanger@ciwcertified.com:  mom@ciwcertified.com
djstanger@ciwcertified.com:  dad@ciwcertified.com
drstanger@ciwcertified.com:  brother@ciwcertified.com
sstanger@ciwcertified.com:  sister@ciwcertified.com
jstanger@ciwcertified.com:  sister2@ciwcertified.com
jastanger@ciwcertified.com:  me@ciwcertified.com
```

The second half of each of these lines constitutes an alias. The syntax is straightforward: The first address is the original account name, and the address following the colon is the assigned e-mail alias that SMTP uses. The benefit of aliasing is that it helps keep e-mail addresses unique. For example, the user with the account of jastanger@ciwcertfied.com now has another e-mail address of me@ciwcertified.com. Yet all e-mail messages sent to either address can be downloaded from the same account.

You can create any number of aliases. For example, you are responsible for administering the e-mail server and the web server at your company. Your only e-mail account is *yourname*@ciwcertified.com. Using aliasing, you can create two additional e-mail addresses named web@ciwcertified.com and e-mail@ciwcertified.com. These additional addresses are not accounts; they are simply aliases that allow you to easily understand and organize the nature of each message you receive.

Another use of aliasing is to provide easier-to-read names, as well as full names. For example, you could use aliasing to assign jstanger@ciwcertified .com the full-name alias of james.stanger@ciwcertified.com.

> **NOTE** RFC 2821 states that all e-mail servers should have at least one alias: postmaster.

As you know, an MTA forwards e-mail to its destination using SMTP. *Relaying* is the practice in which Host A is updated as an intermediary by Host B for a message that is meant for Host C. For this transaction to work, Host A needs to serve as a relay host. Many e-mail hubs act as relay hosts because they receive e-mail from many users and then forward it to other e-mail servers for delivery. An e-mail hub is an e-mail server that transfers and stores e-mail for multiple clients. Such arrangements are popular in LANs and intranets.

Suppose that a host is named `relay.ciwcertified.com` and that another computer on the network is named `mail.ciwcertified.com`. The `relay .ciwcertified.com` host is the relay host for a particular LAN. The `mail.ciwcertified.com` host is the e-mail server with access to the Internet. Mail sent from a user to `relay.ciw.certified.com` destined for a host on the Internet travels the following path:

1. The user's MUA contacts the MTA service on `relay.ciwcertified.com`.

2. The MTA on `relay.ciwcertified.com` contacts the MTA on `mail.ciwcertified.com`.

3. The `mail.ciwcertified.com` host contacts the remote mail server (usually a POP3 server) and delivers the message.

If the remote user responds to this e-mail message, incoming mail is first delivered to `mail.ciwcertified.com` and then to the relay server (`relay.ciwcertified.com`), which is then responsible for routing the mail to the proper POP3 or IMAP server acting as an MDA.

> **NOTE**
>
> For this scenario to work, `relay.ciwcertified.com` must allow relaying.

Many sites connected to the Internet control or even deactivate relaying to help thwart spamming. In fact, recent versions of sendmail (the SMTP server used in Linux) deactivate relaying by default.

Whenever you change ISPs or accounts on e-mail servers, you can use aliasing to help ensure that you make the transition from one platform to another smoothly.

Understanding E-mail Protocols

There are three primary protocols used with e-mail. Simple Mail Transfer Protocol (SMTP) is used to send e-mail between hosts, and retrieval is accomplished through the use of either POP (Post Office Protocol) or IMAP (Internet Messaging Application Protocol). The primary difference between the latter two, as explained in the following section, is whether the mail is removed from the server (POP) or left there (IMAP) after being viewed by a client.

Simple Mail Transfer Protocol (SMTP)

Simple Mail Transfer Protocol (SMTP) is designed to transfer messages from host to host. An MTA using SMTP listens on port 25.

Following are some of the relevant SMTP commands used during a session.

- `helo`: begins a session. For example, a client from the domain name of `ciwcertified.com` would enter: `helo ciwcertified.com`.

- `ehlo`: roughly equivalent to `helo`. Some SMTP servers use this command to provide additional SMTP services. RFC 2821 provides a detailed explanation of these extensions, which include `help`, `send`, and `soml` (used to send mail directly to a terminal if the session is active). See RFC 2821 for more details.

- `mail from:` identifies the name of the sender. For example, if the sender's name is Denise, Denise's MUA enters the following command:

  `mail from: denise@ciwcertified.com.`

- `rcpt to:` specifies the recipient of the e-mail message. If Denise wants to send an e-mail to liam@ciwcertified.com, her MUA enters the following command:

  `rcpt to: liam@ciwcertified.com.`

- `data:` informs the SMTP service that it will receive any data that follows. When the MUA is ready to finish a particular message, it leaves a single dot (.) on a blank line. The service can then begin sending additional messages.

- `quit:` ends the session.

NOTE Many RFC sites exist. A popular site is www.rfc-editor.org.

Generally, an e-mail client (MUA) processes all these commands without the user's participation. In the process of forwarding mail, an MTA (SMTP server) attaches a series of headers to the top of the message. These headers contain routing information, including the following:

- The path that the message takes to its destination
- The sender
- The intended recipient
- The date and time that the message was sent

For the exam, it is important to know that sendmail is a service (and implemented as a daemon in Linux) that allows for the transfer of electronic mail between hosts using SMTP. Because SMTP is the protocol and because any number of programs can communicate with it (sendmail being but one), sendmail is said to be an *agent* of SMTP—a *mail transfer agent*, to be exact. This is an important point because sendmail is not—nor was ever intended to be—what the user interacts with. The user interacts with an e-mail program (such as mail), and sendmail is merely a service running in the background that sends completed e-mail from one location to another. Always remember that sendmail is a mail transfer agent (MTA) and not a mail user agent (MUA). The sendmail service moves mail between hosts; MUAs (discussed in the next two sections) allow users to retrieve/read their mail from/on a host.

Post Office Protocol 3 (POP3)

Post Office Protocol (POP3) is one of the protocols an e-mail client uses to obtain e-mail. POP3 is the latest version of POP. The purpose of a POP3 server is to provide a limited logon shell. According to POP3, this shell allows only a limited set of commands, including the following.

- `user:` allows the client to specify a logon name.
- `pass:` allows the client to specify a password.
- `list:` lists any e-mail messages in the inbox (that is, the mail directory).
- `retr:` allows you to read messages.
- `dele:` deletes a message that you specify.
- `quit:` ends the session.

Clients authenticate with this shell and then issue commands as needed. Normally, end users never see the commands because MUAs such as Eudora and Outlook Express issue them invisibly. POP3 uses port 110.

NOTE You can read more about POP3 in RFC 1225.

Internet Messaging Application Protocol (IMAP)

Internet Messaging Application Protocol (IMAP) is a more sophisticated version of POP3. The primary differences between IMAP and POP3 are that IMAP does the following:

- Allows users to read, search, organize, and manipulate e-mail messages without first downloading them to the server.

- Allows users to add and rename mail directories, assuming that they have the permission to do so.

IMAP listens on port 143.

NOTE You can read more about IMAP in RFC 2060, as well as additional RFCs that extend the protocol.

Recent e-mail clients, including Netscape Messenger, Eudora Pro, and Microsoft Outlook Express, support IMAP. When creating an e-mail account, you can choose between POP3 or IMAP. Most clients allow you to specify multiple IMAP accounts.

Lightweight Directory Access Protocol (LDAP)

Lightweight Directory Access Protocol (LDAP) does not send e-mail. However, it enables e-mail servers to store multiple directories as if they were one large directory. LDAP has many uses, including the following:

- Provide updated, centralized lists of e-mail users
- Store e-mail databases across several e-mail hosts or servers
- Replicate drop lists from one e-mail server to another

NOTE You can learn about LDAP version 1 in RFC 1777. You can learn about LDAP version 3 in RFC 2251.

Web Mail

Many e-mail services allow you to create a web interface that allows users to send, check, and download e-mail. Hotmail (`www.hotmail.com`) is one of the more popular web mail services.

Many e-mail servers provide web-based access by opening an ephemeral port to which clients can connect. For example, the MDaemon e-mail server opens port 2000. For an end user to access this port, they must specify it in a browser and then authenticate with the server as follows:

```
www.emailserver.com:2000
```

It is also possible to change this port so that the logon interface is presented at port 80.

List Servers

A *list server* automates collecting and distributing messages from an authorized group of participants, allowing collaboration among multiple users. A group of participants is often called a list group. Each participant is required to send an e-mail to the list server in order to join a specific group. Once subscribed, the user is placed on a mailing list, which is a collection of users authorized to receive messages from the list server. Some list server groups allow any and all users to join, and the joining process is automated. To be added, all an Internet user need do is subscribe. List server administrators can restrict access to certain users; any unauthorized user who attempts to participate in a restricted list server group will be denied access. When a list server receives a message from a list group participant, it stores the message until it distributes it according to its mailing list.

A user who wants to join a list server group simply uses their e-mail client to send an e-mail message to the list server. This request is often a blank e-mail message with a simple request in the Subject field. A request can be formatted as follows:

```
subscribe ciw
```

Some list servers also request that the same message be placed in the body of the e-mail message. If the list server is configured to allow this user to join, the list server sends a confirmation message to the subscriber. Occasionally, users will sign other people up to list server groups. To prevent this practice, list servers often require the user to confirm subscription before they add a user to the mailing list.

MX Records and E-mail Servers

Before you can install and configure an e-mail server, you must configure a *Mail Exchange (MX) record* on your domain name server so that e-mail destined for your domain can find your e-mail server.

Electronic mail relies on DNS to properly deliver messages. But how does an MTA determine exactly where to send e-mail intended for a particular DNS domain? Most e-mail messages are addressed to only a user and a DNS domain (for example, james@ciw.com), so a specific machine name is not mentioned in an e-mail address. DNS uses MX records to inform the DNS server about the exact location of the machine that acts as an e-mail server (for example, the server `pop3.bigcompany.com`). The MX record essentially provides a map for e-mail destined to a domain so that it can reach a specific system. Whenever an e-mail message is delivered to a domain name, the MX record points the message to the correct server.

MX records (also called MX entries) are contained in the forward DNS zone file. MX entries can redirect e-mail for your server or for an entire domain. If you are using DNS in your LAN and you want to use e-mail, you must have an MX record for your server and/or domain in order for your domain to send and receive e-mail messages between DNS domains. The sendmail service also requires DNS resolution to communicate with all other sendmail daemons in a LAN environment.

Suppose that your POP3 server is named `pop3.bigcompany.com`. All your e-mail accounts are on this system, including the accounts james, sandi, and susan. A remote user named Patrick wants to send e-mail to the susan account. However, you do not want to force Patrick to enter susan@pop3 .bigcompany.com. Rather, you want e-mail addressed to susan@bigcompany .com to be delivered to the `pop3.bigcompany.com` machine.

The following entry in the DNS forward zone file will accomplish this task:

```
bigcompany.com. IN MX 1 pop3.bigcompany.com.
```

Now, your DNS server knows exactly where to deliver e-mail addressed to `bigcompany.com`. Notice that you must specify names, not IP addresses.

NOTE You also need to add an A (host record) in the DNS forward file for the server name pop3.

Intradomain E-mail

Intradomain e-mail is e-mail that stays within one DNS domain. Figure 13.3 shows the role a DNS server plays in helping to locate the e-mail server for a particular LAN.

FIGURE 13.3   DNS MX records and intradomain e-mail

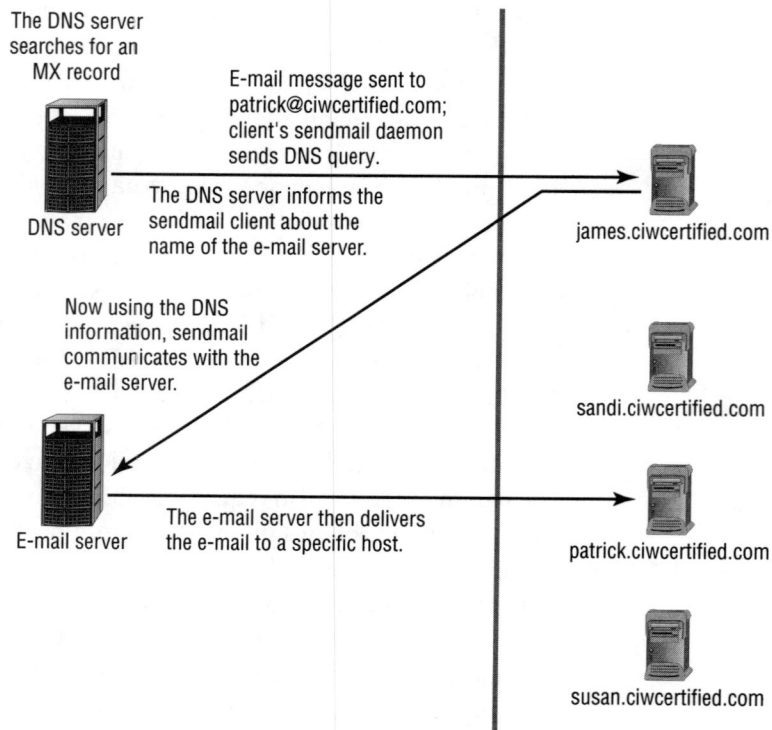

The DNS server searches for an MX record

E-mail message sent to patrick@ciwcertified.com; client's sendmail daemon sends DNS query.

DNS server

The DNS server informs the sendmail client about the name of the e-mail server.

james.ciwcertified.com

Now using the DNS information, sendmail communicates with the e-mail server.

sandi.ciwcertified.com

E-mail server

The e-mail server then delivers the e-mail to a specific host.

patrick.ciwcertified.com

susan.ciwcertified.com

The MX record specifies the name of a computer that will handle all e-mail messages directed to a particular domain (in this example, `ciwcertified.com`). This implementation of an e-mail server is known as an e-mail hub.

Interdomain E-mail

Most often, you enable clients to send e-mail between DNS domains. This activity is called sending interdomain e-mail, which requires an MX entry to identify the destination domain and host of a particular e-mail server. As long as a client is configured to participate in the DNS hierarchy that contains the MX record, the client can send and receive e-mail between different domains. Figure 13.4 shows the method by which an e-mail message from the `stanger.com` domain finds the e-mail server for `lane.com`.

FIGURE 13.4 DNS MX records and interdomain e-mail

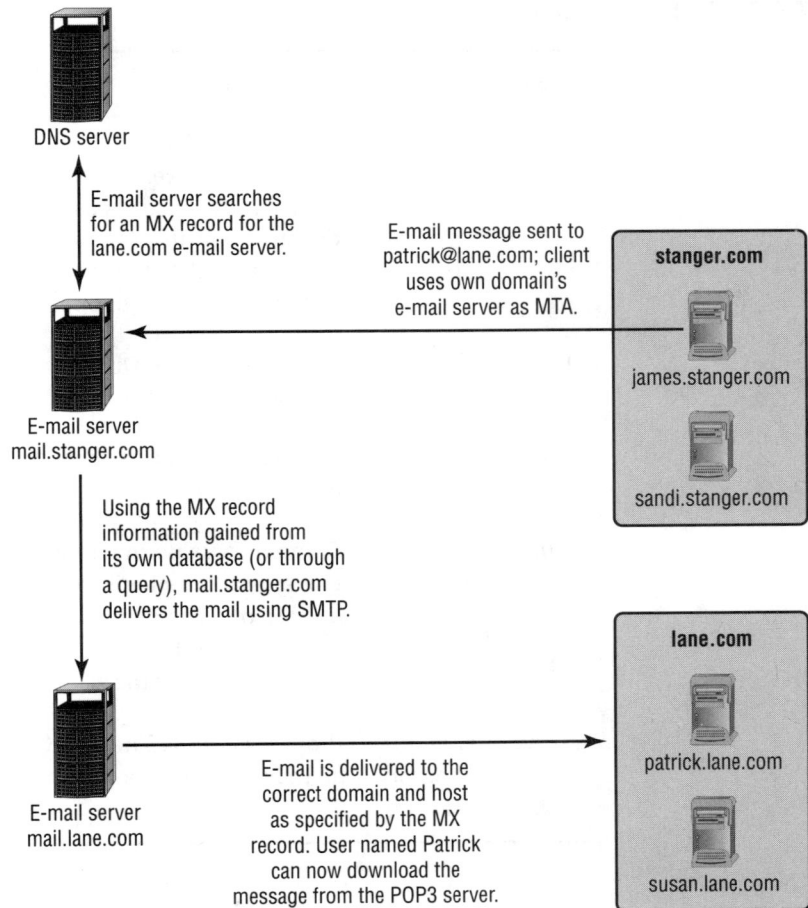

DNS server

E-mail server searches for an MX record for the lane.com e-mail server.

E-mail message sent to patrick@lane.com; client uses own domain's e-mail server as MTA.

stanger.com

james.stanger.com

sandi.stanger.com

E-mail server mail.stanger.com

Using the MX record information gained from its own database (or through a query), mail.stanger.com delivers the mail using SMTP.

lane.com

patrick.lane.com

susan.lane.com

E-mail server mail.lane.com

E-mail is delivered to the correct domain and host as specified by the MX record. User named Patrick can now download the message from the POP3 server.

The DNS server in Figure 13.4 can belong to any domain. For example, it can belong to `lane.com`, or it can belong to the DNS domain of the ISP. As long as an MX entry exists and all hosts are part of the DNS domain structure, resolution can occur and the e-mail message will be delivered.

For anyone in the lane.com domain to reply to this e-mail message, the e-mail server for lane.com (mail.lane.com) requires access to a valid MX record for stanger.com. This record could exist in any DNS database or server, provided that the lane.com server can eventually query that database. An MX record has five fields, as described in Table 13.1.

TABLE 13.1 MX Record Fields

Field	Description
	Specifies the domain to which all e-mail will be sent. This entry can be a server. In many DNS implementations, forward DNS records use the $ORIGIN directive. This directive puts the domain name, such as ciwcertified .com., after all names in the left column that do not end in a dot. Blank fields repeat the $ORIGIN directive.
IN	Indicates that the DNS record is for a host running TCP/IP.
MX	Indicates that the redirection is for a host that is an e-mail server.
Numerical value (for example, 10)	Contains a value that indicates the entry's priority. Lower numbers indicate a higher priority. Therefore, a value of 1 assigns higher priority for a host than a value of 20. A host with a value of 0 in this field has priority over all others.
Server name (for example, mailserv .ciwcertified.com)	Provides the DNS name of the e-mail server to which all messages will be directed.

Following are three sample MX entries that redirect all e-mail sent to the ciwcertified.com domain to specific e-mail servers, depending on priority:

```
ciwcertified.com IN MX 0 mail.ciwcertified.com.
ciwcertified.com IN MX 1 mail1.ciwcertified.com.
ciwcertified.com IN MX 20 mail2.ciwcertified.com.
```

Following is a sample zone file containing MX records. This zone file is for the ciwcertified.com domain. Before you read it, remember that $ORIGIN adds ciwcertified.com. after names in the left column that do not end in a dot and that blank fields repeat the $ORIGIN directive. For this reason, the following example does not contain ciwcertified.com in front of the IN entry.

Also in the following example, notice that mail.ciwcertified.com has an MX record (with the preference of 0), pointing to the server named mail.courseware.ciwcertified.com. When offered a message addressed to james@courseware.ciwcertified.com, the MTA (the server running SMTP) looks for an MX record and receives mail.courseware.ciwcertified.com. Once this happens, the MTA contacts the SMTP server on mail.ciwcertified.com and delivers the message.

```
$ORIGIN com.
ciwcertified      IN      SOA      dns.ciwcertified.com.
james.courseware.ciwcertified.com.

(19990707 1800 300 604800 1800)

                  IN      NS       dns.courseware.ciwcertified.com.
                  IN      NS       page.courseware.ciwcertified.com.

                  IN      MX       10 mail2.courseware.ciwcertified.com.
                  IN      MX       0 mail.courseware.ciwcertified.com.
                  IN      MX       20 pop3.courseware.ciwcertified.com.
```

In the previous example, the MX entry with a 0 will be given priority and will send mail to the host that handles e-mail for the **courseware** subdomain. If this action fails, the MTA queries the next MX record (mail2) and then pop3. If no MX records or a working e-mail server exist, DNS then queries any CNAME and A records (if present), in that order.

NOTE The order of MX entries in a file does not matter. Priority is always assigned according to the number in the record.

Once the SMTP server forwards the message, the message goes to an MDA, such as a POP3 or an IMAP server.

Suppose that you want to stop all e-mail servers and use the `imap.yourisp` `.com` server for all e-mail. You can use the following syntax to create an MX record that redirects all e-mail to `imap.yourisp.com`:

```
$ORIGIN com.
ciwcertified      IN      SOA      dns.ciwcertified.com.
james.courseware.ciwcertified.com.

(19990707 1800 300 604800 1800)

                  IN      NS       dns.courseware.ciwcertified.com.
                  IN      NS       page.courseware.ciwcertified.com.

                  IN          MX      0 imap.yourisp.com.
```

Summary

In this chapter, you learned how to configure NNTP servers in both Windows 2000 and Linux. The NNTP service is ideal for establishing group discussions, such as project development. You also learned about some of the fundamental settings you can impose for expiration policies and maximum newsgroup size.

You should now be able to create newsgroups in both Windows 2000 and Linux, configure newsgroup expiration policies, and control client access to a news server through IP address filtering and user-based authentication. Using Outlook Express, you should now be able to connect to a news server, subscribe to newsgroups, and be able to download and post messages.

In this chapter, you also learned about e-mail server essentials such as the process of sending an e-mail message from one host to another using the Mail Transfer Agent (MTA), Mail Delivery Agent (MDA), and the Mail User Agent (MUA). You learned that a user composes a message on their e-mail client and clicks the Send button. The message is relayed to the Internet by an MTA (SMTP server) to an MDA (POP3 or IMAP server) to an MUA (e-mail client).

You also learned about key e-mail concepts such as masquerading, aliasing, and forwarding. You learned that masquerading is the practice of modifying the SMTP header of a message so that it appears to come from a different user. On the other hand, you learned that aliasing does not modify the SMTP header of a message, but is implemented on an e-mail server to provide an alternate name for e-mail accounts, sometimes to provide a shorter name. RFC 2821 requires that e-mail severs have the postmaster alias. Finally, in this section, you learned about relaying in which an MTA forwards e-mail to its destination using SMTP. You learned that many sites control or disable relaying in order to thwart spamming.

In the next sections, you looked at the benefits of SMTP, POP3, IMAP, LDAP, web mail, and list servers. SMTP is used to send mail. It uses port TCP 25. POP3 is the most popular protocol for downloading e-mail. It uses port 110. IMAP allows you to read, search, organize, and manipulate e-mail messages without first downloading them. It uses port 143. LDAP enables e-mail servers to store multiple directories as if they were one large directory. LDAP uses port 389. Web mail is firewall friendly because it uses port 80. List servers automate the collection and distribution of messages from users that self-subscribe. In the remaining sections of this chapter, you learned how to construct MX records for your LAN. You learned how DNS can deliver mail to a specific machine, even though the message is mailed to a domain name.

Exam Essentials

Understand the benefits of newsgroups.   Newsgroups are a good way to get information. They are global message boards that cover a broad range of topics. They let people from around the world share information, swap tips, and get advice. Usenet is the preeminent collection of Internet-based newsgroups. Usenet feeds can be implemented on Linux INND news servers. This is not possible using IIS 5, but you can create Usenet-like newsgroups.

Be able to create newsgroups in Windows 2000.   In Windows 2000, you must install the NNTP Service. To do so, open the Add/Remove Windows Components dialog box. Select Internet Information Services (IIS). Click the Details button to open the Subcomponents of Internet Information Services dialog box and click the NNTP Service check box. Then, using the Internet Services Manager snap-in, under the Default NNTP Virtual Server, right-click the Newsgroups icon, and choose New ➢ Newsgroup from the shortcut menu.

Be able to create newsgroups in Linux. In Linux, edit the /etc/news/ innd.conf file to create an INND news server. Start the INND with the following command: host# /etc/rc.d/init.d/innd start. Finally, to add a Sybex.ciw.admin newsgroup, use the following command: host# /usr/bin/ctlinnd newgroup sybex.ciw.admin.

Understand how and why you configure newsgroup expiration policies. Newsgroup expiration policies remove stale messages from a news server in order to remove outdated information and save space on the news server. In IIS 5, you set expiration policies by expanding the Default NNTP Virtual Server, right-clicking the Expiration Policies icon, and choosing New ➢ Expiration Policy from the shortcut menu to start the wizard. You can set policies on all newsgroups or on a specific newsgroup. The most restrictive policy applies. The number in the expiration policy is the number of hours before a message is removed from the news server.

Understand how users access newsgroups and how you can control that access. Using Outlook Express as an example of a newsreader program, you add a news server using the Internet Connection Wizard. After connecting to a news server, you need to subscribe to the newsgroups that interest you. You can then download information or post your own messages. The administrator of the news server can control your access through IP address filtering and/or user-based authentication.

Describe the process of sending an e-mail message. The client sends e-mail though the MTA agent, which is also known as the SMTP server, to the MDA, which is either a POP3 or an IMAP server that is downloaded by client software that functions as an MUA.

Explain key e-mail concepts such as forwarding, masquerading, and aliasing. Spammers can use a fake SMTP header on their messages to masquerade the true source address so that it is not blocked. Unwitting e-mail servers can relay spam if relaying is not controlled. You can use aliasing to shorten a long e-mail address. The syntax for an alias is name@domain.com: alias@domain.com.

Describe the functions of e-mail protocols such as SMTP, POP3, IMAP, and LDAP and e-mail servers such as list servers. SMTP sends mail. POP3 is the most popular protocol for downloading e-mail. IMAP allows you to manipulate e-mail on the server without downloading it. LDAP enables transparent sharing of directories among e-mail servers. A list server (mailing list server) is a program that handles subscription requests for a mailing list.

Understand the functions of DNS and MX records in simplifying access to e-mail servers. E-mail recipients can be addressed by their IP address (for example, mary@63.211.12.4). If you create an address (A) record on a DNS server for your e-mail server, recipients can be addressed by FQDN (for example, mary@pop3.mailmax.com). If you create a Mail Exchanger (MX) record on your DNS server, recipients can be accessed by a shortened address (for example, mary@mailmax.com).

Key Terms

Before taking the exam, you should be familiar with the following terms:

aliasing	Mail User Agent (MUA)
drop directory	Mail Exchange (MX) record
expiration policy	masquerading
Expires header	Network News Transfer Protocol (NNTP)
INND news server	newsgroups
Internet Messaging Application Protocol (IMAP)	Post Office Protocol (POP3)
Lightweight Directory Access Protocol (LDAP)	Pretty Name field
list server	relaying
Mail Delivery Agent (MDA)	Simple Mail Transfer Protocol (SMTP)
Mail Transfer Agent (MTA)	Usenet

Review Questions

1. Bart is trying to remember the function of e-mail agents in delivering e-mail. He knows that this agent is also called an SMTP server and that it is responsible for delivering mail between hosts until it arrives at its destination. What is the name of the e-mail agent that Bart is trying to recall?

   A. Mail Transfer Agent (MTA)

   B. Mail Delivery Agent (MDA)

   C. Mail User Agent (MUA)

   D. Mail Acceptance Agent (MAA)

2. Before a new firewall was installed, users at Barclay Spirits could connect to Usenet newsgroups. This is no longer the case. Which port number on the firewall should be opened for the NNTP?

   A. 80

   B. 443

   C. 21

   D. 119

3. Jerry is studying how spammers circumvent inbox rules and seem to have an unlimited number of source e-mail addresses. What method do spammers use to hide their true e-mail address?

   A. Masquerading

   B. Aliasing

   C. Relaying

   D. Ghosting

4. Mark is a developer working on Xbox virtual reality games. He wants to use a newsgroup to research undocumented glitches with Xbox. Which of the following represents a valid newsgroup name?

   A. www.microsoft.com:technet

   B. www.microsoft.com/support

   C. www.microsoft.com/xbox

   D. alt.games.video.xbox

5. James is concerned that spammers are using his e-mail server as a transit point for their spam. What can James eliminate on his server to solve this problem?

   A. Masquerading

   B. Aliasing

   C. Ghosting

   D. Relaying

6. Joshua wants to restrict access to his company's news server in order to limit posting of extraneous content. How can Joshua control client access? Choose two answers.

   A. Use IP address filtering.

   B. Password protect newsgroups.

   C. Impose expiration policies.

   D. Configure user-based authentication.

7. Spencer is configuring his firewall and needs to make sure that POP3 traffic is allowed out. What is the default port used by the POP3 protocol?

   A. Port 80

   B. Port 110

   C. Port 21

   D. Port 25

8. Due to popular demand, Frank sets up a news server. After a year, the news server is running out of space. What should Frank do? Select the best option.

   A. Set a group policy that forbids attachments.

   B. Set a message size limit.

   C. Set up newsgroup expiration policies.

   D. Set up disk quotas.

9. Which of the following scenarios depicts the process of sending e-mail from one client to another over the Internet?

   A. SMTP Server → Sender → Internet → SMTP → Server → POP3 server → recipient

   B. Sender → POP3 Server → recipient

   C. Sender → IMAP Server → SMTP server → recipient → IMAP server

   D. Sender → SMTP server → Internet → SMTP Server → POP3 server → recipient

10. Management of www.dating.com wants to set up a server that will allow interchanges between clients. Which protocol should www.dating.com implement? Select the best option.

    A. NNTP

    B. SMTP

    C. HTTP

    D. POP3

    E. IMAP4

11. Frank wants to configure his domain name server so that e-mail to users in corp.com will be routed to the correct e-mail server. Which type of record should Frank configure?

    A. SOA

    B. MX

    C. HINFO

    D. PTR

12. Management of www.dating.com wants more security on their newsgroups, so they implement SSL with NNTP. Which port should be opened for SSL in this scenario?

    A. 119

    B. 443

    C. 80

    D. 563

13. Evan is configuring the company firewall and has been told by his supervisor that IMAP traffic must be allowed through. What is the default port used by the IMAP protocol?

A. Port 143

B. Port 389

C. Port 110

D. Port 25

14. Peter is using a search engine; Copernic (`www.copernic.com`), to look for information on topically named Internet discussion groups. Which keyword should Peter use for his search?

A. News

B. Usenet

C. Outlook Express

D. IIS 5

15. Brad wants to complain about an e-mail user, lisa@phonecard.com, who is spamming him. To whom should Brad complain?

A. webmaster@phonecard.com

B. postmaster@phonecard.com

C. administrator@phonecard.com

D. CustomerService@phonecard.com

16. Ralph works for Medical Automation International. He wants to set up Usenet feeds on his IIS 5 NNTP server so that selected medical and research Usenet newsgroups will be available to his clients. What should Ralph do?

A. Buy a Linux INND server.

B. Set up round-robin DNS.

C. Upgrade clients from Outlook Express to Outlook.

D. Set up a Kerberos trust with a Usenet realm.

17. Frank is attempting to configure the Mail Exchange (MX) record on his domain name server so that e-mail intended for his domain can find the e-mail server. Which of the following is a correct syntax for this resource record?

    A. `bigcompany.com MX IN 1 pop3.bigcompany.com`

    B. `bigcompany.com. IN MX 1 pop3.bigcompany.com`

    C. `pop3.bigcompany.com MX IN 1 bigcompany.com`

    D. `pop3.bigcompany.com. IN MX 1 bigcompany.com`

18. Frank wants to use Usenet newsgroups to offer imported gift products for sale. He collects orders for two weeks and then places his bulk order with the distributor. He wants any postings that he makes to expire after two weeks. What should Frank do?

    A. Set an expiration policy.

    B. Use a moderated newsgroup.

    C. Use an Expires header on his postings.

    D. Use an auction newsgroup.

19. Mark wants a totally authoritative, vendor-neutral source for information about the Network News Transport Protocol (NNTP). Where can he best research NNTP?

    A. `www.microsoft.com/technet`

    B. `www.rfc-editor.org`

    C. `www.tucows.com`

    D. `www.linux.org`

20. Ralph hosts nearly 100 e-mail domains on his MDaemon servers. He wants to enable these e-mail servers to store multiple directories as if they were one large directory so that he can search an updated, centralized list of e-mail users. What protocol should Ralph enable?

    A. SMTP

    B. LDAP

    C. IMAP

    D. POP3

Answers to Review Questions

1. A. The MTA is also known as an SMTP server.

2. D. NNTP uses port 119.

3. A. Masquerading is the practice of cooking the SMTP header of a message so that it appears to come from a different computer.

4. D. The `alt.games.video.xbox` newsgroup has more than 8,000 postings.

5. D. James can eliminate the relaying of messages. Many sites connected to the Internet control or even deactivate relaying to help thwart spamming.

6. A, D. You can control client access to a news server through IP address filtering or user-based authentication.

7. B. The default port used by the POP3 protocol is 110.

8. C. Frank should set up newsgroup expiration policies so that old newsgroup postings are automatically deleted.

9. D. The correct sequence is as follows: sender → SMTP server → Internet → SMTP Server → POP3 server → recipient.

10. A. The NNTP allows interchanges between clients.

11. B. Frank should configure an MX record to point toward his e-mail server.

12. D. If SSL is enabled, the NNTP server will listen on port 563.

13. A. The IMAP protocol uses port 143 by default.

14. B. Usenet is a collection of topically named Internet newsgroups.

15. B. The postmaster alias is required by RFC 2821.

16. A. IIS 5 NNTP does not support Usenet feeds, but Linux INND does.

17. B. The correct syntax is `bigcompany.com. IN MX 1 pop3.bigcompany.com`.

18. C. NNTP clients can send messages that have a special header called the Expires header. This tells the news server that it can delete the message after a certain period of time.

19. B. Mark should research RFC 977 at `www.rfc-editor.org`.

20. B. Ralph should enable Lightweight Directory Access Protocol (LDAP), which uses TCP port 389.

Chapter

14

Logging Activity

THE CIW EXAM OBJECTIVE GROUPS COVERED IN THIS CHAPTER:

✓ Analyze server and service logs.

f your company wants to expand its business on the Internet, a good first step is to log information about visitors to your website and then use that information to make business decisions. Effective logging and analysis can result in the following business benefits:

- Decrease the acquisition costs for new customers

- Increase the conversion rate from visitor to customer

- Improve customer retention

- Build customer loyalty

As a systems administrator, you can check system and service logs to determine a system's ability to meet demands. Logs can also inform you about security issues. In this chapter, you will learn about the nature of HTTP and FTP server logs, as well as system logs. We can't stress enough that you need to look at your log files. They are a systems administrator's best friends.

Logging Information

As a systems administrator, log files can be your best friend or your worst enemy. They can monitor the system and report on administrative and security issues 24/7, creating fingerprints that allow you to see what is happening and by whom. If improperly implemented, log files monitor so much information that you spend days looking through thousands of lines of unneeded entries trying to find a single item. They eat up precious disk space and serve little purpose.

The experience of a colleague illustrates how improperly implemented log files can have a negative impact. She once worked in support for an electronic-monitoring corporation that sold computer systems to law-enforcement departments. When making the purchase, most departments had to scrape together the money to buy the system and cut corners where they could, usually saving money by buying small hard drives or minimal RAM. Given the sensitive nature of house arrest, log files recorded everything that happened—every time a modem was accessed (thousands of times a day), every time a change was made to a person's information, and so on. The machines constantly ran out of hard-drive space, and on a weekly basis customer support had to dial in remotely and delete the log files—defeating the whole purpose of having them.

On the other hand, one of our personal experiences illustrates how properly implemented log files can have a positive impact. We once consulted for a company that had problems no one else had ever encountered. As soon as one problem was fixed, another occurred. The problems did not seem to make sense; instead of showing file corruption, the databases would completely disappear from the system—seemingly out of the blue without rhyme or reason. Users who could log on one day would come in the next and discover that their profiles contained variables that caused one error after another. Frustration was reaching an all-time high. A quick look at the logs showed that a disgruntled employee had figured out a number of passwords, logged in as other users, did some damage, and then exited and acted as confused as everyone else.

The key to using log files effectively is to know what each of them does. Once you know that, you can realistically set your expectations and look for necessary data without being overwhelmed.

Using your logs effectively, you can be informed of any or all of the following:

Server efficiency   You can keep track of how efficient your system is and determine whether you need to add additional hardware or software components. Within the Microsoft server family of operating systems (Windows 2000 and Windows NT), the primary tool for viewing log files is Event Viewer. Within the Linux operating systems, similar data is found in the `/var/log/messages` file. Each can notify you of failed services or services that are experiencing problems, within their respective operating systems.

Usage rate   Logs can help you determine the amount of work a server is handling. If you find out that a server has a particular bottleneck, you can use this information to make the system more efficient. For example, if the logs show that a processor is rarely utilized more than 50 percent, and the same is true of the hard drive, yet memory is always near 100 percent utilization, you can reasonably assume that adding more RAM would increase the efficiency of the server.

Revenue generation   Your business may be able to sell information derived from your logs. For example, if you sell shareware, the logs can indicate the number of downloads over a period of time. Barring extraneous factors, increases in the percentage of downloads from one month to the next should also be reflected as a percentage increase in the number of purchases over the same time period. To fully understand and appreciate this type of data, you'll often need to use other programs, such as spreadsheets.

Security   Logs can alert you to possible security problems. For example, a failed logon attempt might be the sign of an intruder trying to break into your system. Just as finding these events is important, so too is protecting your log files to keep others from covering their tracks. When security is involved, make your log files owned and readable only by root and assign them to their own special group. Create a dummy user in that group and have all log checking programs run as that user.

Scanning and accessing log files can take a fair amount of time if done manually. There are many tools out there to automate the task. Some have their own faults and create a hole somewhere else. Use these tools only after investigating whether their creation and use justifies their legitimacy.

We must also point out, however, that while creating logs is an essential task for system administrators, logging has a direct effect on system performance. The more events you log, the harder your system will have to work. It is advisable to log only selected events for your server. Because your resources are limited, you will have to set priorities. Here are some guidelines:

Mission criticality and service type   As an administrator, determine the most important servers and services for your particular business, such as e-mail and e-commerce web service. Once that has been ascertained, check those logs daily for abnormalities and apparitions that could signal a need for proactive interaction. As a general rule, check web, e-mail, and database server logs often because these servers handle large loads of traffic. If you check the logs infrequently, there will be so much data that it may be difficult to find the items that warrant your attention. These type of services are also those that hackers tend to target frequently, and thus you need to scrutinize them carefully for unusual activity.

Server location   Many organizations place their web servers outside the system firewall. A *firewall* is a security barrier that controls the flow of information between the Internet and private networks. It prevents outsiders from accessing an enterprise's internal network, which accesses the Internet indirectly through a proxy server. If a server resides outside your company's firewall, consider viewing its logs for failed logons and other problems more frequently than you check servers behind the firewall.

Recent installations   After you upgrade a system, check for any problems that may occur afterward.

Your security policy should determine how often you check server logs, but as you do so, evaluate the following:

Peak usage rates   We mentioned usage rates earlier, but peak usage is different from usage rates. Peak usage rates are spikes that occur for short periods of time. Evaluating peak usage rates can help you determine how to adjust system performance and, if necessary, when to obtain a more powerful server. When the peaks start lasting for longer and longer periods, they no longer qualify as peaks and begin to represent normal usage.

Error messages   Errors reported by the server or one of its services might be evidence of an overburdened server, a faulty executable file, or an unstable operating system. You want to react to errors as soon as possible to prevent infrequent occurrences from becoming common.

Failed logon attempts   Although failed logon attempts can signal an attempted break-in, they can also indicate that users need more training on their systems. Examine these log files routinely, and if users are experiencing frequent problems, investigate to see if they need more training or assistance.

HTTP and FTP Server Log Files

Probably the most important sources of information about the stream of HTTP and FTP requests and responses are the server log files, which record the time of each transaction, along with the number of bytes transferred. Analysis of these files provides a complete picture of each transaction handled by the server.

Keep in mind that this information does not show definitive information about users and visitors to your sites. Internet protocols are stateless, so there cannot be sustained connections between clients and servers.

One major advantage of server logs is that you can analyze them offline. More intrusive performance analysis tools complicate performance issues because the tools themselves use system resources. This problem will not occur if the logs are analyzed on a computer other than the server.

Because so many types of web servers exist, it is difficult to write a log analysis program tailored to every server's log file. Instead, almost all servers produce access log files in a standardized form called *National Center for Supercomputing Applications (NCSA) Common Log File Format*, but other choices are usually offered. In IIS, for example, the four choices are as follows:

Microsoft IIS Log Format   A fixed ASCII format that records basic logging items, including username, request date, request time, client IP address, number of bytes received, HTTP status code, and other items. This format is a comma-delimited log file, which is easier to parse than other ASCII formats.

NCSA Common Log File Format   A fixed ASCII format endorsed by NCSA. The data it logs includes remote hostname, username, HTTP status code, request type, and the number of bytes received by the server. Spaces separate logged items.

ODBC Logging   A fixed format that is logged to a database. This log includes client IP address, username, request date, request time, HTTP status code, bytes received, bytes sent, action carried out, and the target. When you choose this option, you must specify the database for the file to be logged to. In addition, you must set up the database to receive that log data.

W3C Extended Log File Format   A customizable ASCII format endorsed by the World Wide Web Consortium (W3C). This format is the default setting. You can set this log format to record a number of settings, such as request date, request time, client IP address, server IP address, server port, HTTP status code, and more. Data is separated by spaces in this format.

The following is an example of an access log from Apache server (stored in the /var/log/httpd/ directory) created in the NCSA Common Log File Format:

```
[root@server1 logs]# cat access_log
192.168.4.1 - - [10/Jan/2002:19:06:08 -0800] "GET /
↪index.html HTTP /1.0" 400 285
192.168.4.1 - - [10/Jan/2002:19:06:33 -0800] "GET
↪index.html HTTP/1.0" 400 265
192.168.4.1 - - [10/Jan/2002:19:07:18 -0800] "GET /
↪index.html HTTP/1.0" 200 1945
192.168.4.1 - - [10/Jan/2002:19:55:33 -0800] "GET / HTTP/
↪1.0" 200 1945
192.168.4.1 - - [10/Jan/2002:19:55:33 -0800] "GET /
↪poweredby.gif HTTP/1.0" 200 1817
192.168.4.1 - - [10/Jan/2002:19:55:33 -0800] "GET /icons/
↪apche.gif HTTP/1.0" 200 2326
[root@server1 logs]#
```

EXERCISE 14.1

Configuring HTTP Logging for IIS 5

1. Choose Start ➢ Programs ➢ Administrative Tools ➢ Internet Services Manager to open the IIS 5 snap-in.

2. Expand your computer name. Right-click Default Web Site, and choose Properties from the shortcut menu to open the Default Web Site Properties dialog box.

3. On the Web Site tab, the Enable Logging check box should already be checked by default. In the Active Log Format text box, make sure that the W3C Extended Log File Format option is selected.

4. In the Enable Logging section, click the Properties button to open the Extended Logging Properties dialog box:

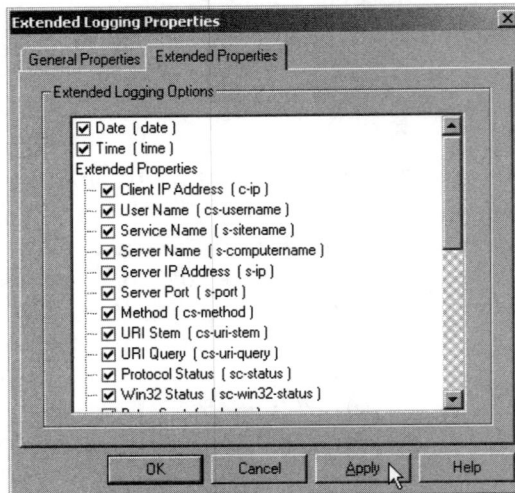

5. Click the Extended Properties tab, place a check in every box in both the Extended Properties and Process Accounting sections, and then click Apply.

6. Click OK twice to close the Default Web Site Properties dialog box and continue.

7. Access your website. Enter **http://127.0.0.1** in the Address bar in your browser. Doing so will generate some logging information.

8. Now view your own log files. Open Windows Explorer and select C:\WINNT\system32\LogFiles\. If Windows 2000 is installed on a different partition, change the path accordingly.

EXERCISE 14.1 *(continued)*

9. You may see a list of several subdirectories for the FTP, NNTP, and HTTP services. Depending on how long this server has run and how busy it is, several subdirectories may exist for the same service. The directories that start with MSFTPSVC are for the FTP service. The directories that start with NNTPSVC are for the NNTP service, and the directories that start with W3SVC are for the HTTP server. The W3SVC1 directory contains the latest log files. Click this directory and find the latest file.

10. Open this file and view its contents.

Table 14.1 shows the various options for the W3C Extended Log File Format Logging.

TABLE 14.1 W3C Extended Log File Format Logging Options

Option	Description
Date	Date the activity occurred
Time	Time the activity occurred
Client IP Address	IP address of the client attaching to your server
Username	Username who accessed your server
Service Name	Client computer's Internet service
Server Name	Server name where the log entry was created.
Server IP	Server IP address where the log entry was created
Server Port	The port number to which the client is connected
Method	The action the client was performing
URI Stem	The resource the client was accessing on your server, such as an HTML page, CGI program, and so on

TABLE 14.1 W3C Extended Log File Format Logging Options *(continued)*

Option	Description
URI Query	The search string the client was trying to match
HTTP Status	The status (in HTTP terms) of the client action
Win32 Status	The status (in Windows terms) of the client action
Bytes Sent	The number of bytes sent by the server
Bytes Received	The number of bytes received by the server
Time Taken	The amount of time to execute the action requested by the client
User Agent	The browser used by the client
Cookie	The content of any cookies sent or received by the server
Protocol Version	The protocol used by the client to access the server (http or ftp)
Referrer	The URL of the site from where the user clicked to get to your site

Not only do access logs exist, but web servers also create error logs (for when things go awry), referrer logs, and agent logs. The *error log* file records any errors that occur, including the following:

- Server startup and shutdown
- Malformed URLs
- Erroneous CGI scripts

Following is an example of an error log in Apache server:

```
[root@server1 logs]# cat error_log
[Sun Jan 9 04:02:05 2002] [notice] Apache/1.3.9 (Unix)
↳(Red Hat/Linux) configured -- resuming normal operations
```

```
[Sun Jan 9 04:02:05 2002] [notice] suEXEC mechanism
↳enabled (wrapper: /usr/sbin/suexec)
[Mon Jan 10 19:06:08 2002] [error] [client 192.168.4.1]
↳request failed: error reading the headers
[Mon Jan 10 19:06:33 2002] [error] [client 192.168.4.1]
↳Invalid URI in request GET index.html HTTP/1.0
[root@server1 logs]#
```

It is important for many web administrators to know how people found out about their site. The *referrer log* provides this information. Whenever you browse from Page A to Page B by clicking a hyperlink, Page A is said to "refer" Page B. An HTML page can also refer images, other HTML documents, and any other file that page needs so that it can render completely. A referrer log can show the number of files one page requires to render in a browser.

The format of the referrer log is:

URI -> Document

A document's Universal Resource Identifier (URI) references the server document. The document's path is relative to the server root. Following is an example of a single hit to a default page (represented by /) on an Apache server, which then shows that the root document refers the images `james.gif`, `sandi.gif`, and `joel.gif`:

```
http://192.168.4.1/
http://192.168.4.1/ -> /images/james.gif
http://192.168.4.1/ -> /images/sandi.gif
http://192.168.4.1/ -> /images/joel.gif
```

The *agent log* file records the version of any user agent that accesses your site. A *user agent* is client software used to browse a website. User agents can include web browsers and spiders used by search engines. All agents send a special header that identifies them. If you configure the agent log properly, the web server can record this information. The following example shows that this particular website was visited by end users using Netscape Navigator 4.7 and Microsoft Internet Explorer 5:

```
[root@server1 logs]# cat agent_log
Mozilla/4.7 [en] (Win98; I)
Mozilla/4.0 (compatible; MSIE 5.0; Windows 98; DigExt)
```

You can track this information to gather statistics and trace any possible problems with your site's ability to serve documents to various browsers.

Configuring System Logs

Most of the discussion within this chapter, up to this point, has been in regard to logging Internet activity. Just as it is important to know what is going on there, it is also important to monitor the general status of the system.

Most applications have their own logging features, but in Linux and Windows NT/2000, one log service runs only for the operating system. The service responsible for adding entries to the log files in Linux is `syslogd`–the system log daemon—which is spawned by the `init` daemon. When started, `syslogd` reads the `/etc/syslog.conf` file to see what to monitor. Very descriptive in nature, each line consists of the item you want to monitor followed by a period (.), the priority, white space, and the location of the log file.

You can use a comma (,) to separate multiple entries. You can also use a semicolon (;) to denote exceptions to the rule. The syntax is as follows:

```
item.priority;exceptions log_file
```

By default, messages are sent to `/var/log/messages` unless otherwise redirected. Messages regarding news, mail, and authentication are almost always redirected and recorded elsewhere. Private authorization messages (but not those for regular login) are often sent to `/var/log/secure`, mail messages to `/var/log/main`, and news messages to `/var/log/news.all`.

> **NOTE** A kernel log daemon on many systems—`klogd`–can be running for the sole purpose of logging kernel messages.

In Windows NT/2000, the System log (viewable with Event Viewer) holds all information about system events, including errors and warnings.

You should recognize a number of log files that exist by default. Table 14.2 shows the locations of frequently used logs in Windows 2000 and Linux.

TABLE 14.2 Log Locations

Log	Windows 2000 Location	Linux Location
DNS	The DNS Server log in Event Viewer	/var/log/messages
NNTP	C:\WINNT\system32\LogFiles	/var/log/innd and /var/log/news/
SMTP	Depends on your e-mail service	/var/log/maillog and /var/log/messages
File Sharing (Samba)	Event Viewer	/var/log/samba/
POP3	Depends on your e-mail service	/var/log/messages

Summary

In this chapter, you learned about logs and how they can help you analyze system events, system performance, and bandwidth requirements. You configured and viewed log files for your server.

With this information, you should now be able to explain the need for logging activity generated by servers and services; configure web server logs and explain the need for logging activity generated by servers and services; identify the need to check logs; and view information from a web server log file.

Exam Essentials

Be able to list the advantages of logging.   Logs inform you of server efficiency, usage rate, and security, and you may be able to sell information derived from your logs. The proper use of this information could decrease the acquisition costs for new customers, increase the conversion rate from visitor to customer, improve customer retention, and build customer loyalty.

Know what to log and how to set priorities for reading logs. Don't log too much; logging affects performance. Evaluate HTTP logs offline. The NCSA Common Log File Format works for IIS and Apache. Factors to consider in setting priority for reading logs are mission criticality, service type, server location, and recent installations. Your security policy should determine how often you check server logs.

Know the information contained in the log files. When reading log files, evaluate and take appropriate corrective measures based on peak usage rates, error messages, and failed logon attempts. Know the contents of the access log, error log, referrer log, agent log, and FTP log files.

Know the default log file locations. The default location for IIS log files is C:\WINNT\system32\LogFiles\. The directories that start with MSFTPSVC are for the FTP service. The directories that start with NNTPSVC are for the NNTP service, and the directories that start with W3SVC are for the HTTP server. The W3SVC1 directory contains the latest log files. Click this directory to find the latest file. The default location for Apache log files is /var/httpd/log/. Know the location of the logs for additional services such as DNS, which is the DNS Server log of Event Viewer in Windows 2000 and /var/log/messages in Linux.

Key Terms

Before taking the exam, you should be familiar with the following terms:

access log	National Center for Supercomputing Applications (NCSA)
agent log	Common Log File Format
error log	referrer log
firewall	user agent
FTP log files	

Review Questions

1. Which of the following can you track using standard operating system log files? Choose four.

   A. Server patch levels

   B. Usage rate

   C. Security

   D. Revenue generation

   E. Server efficiency

2. Jim is creating a website for a brick-and-mortar travel agency. Jim is considering installing a third-party log analysis tool. He needs to justify its cost to the owner of the travel agency. Which four benefits to the bottom line can the travel agency expect?

   A. Customers will have an easier time navigating the website.

   B. The travel agency will be able to decrease the acquisition costs for new customers.

   C. The travel agency will be able to increase the conversion rate from visitor to customer.

   D. Customers will have an easier time finding the website.

   E. The travel agency can expect to improve customer retention.

   F. The travel agency can expect to build customer loyalty.

3. Jim maintains 10 websites for different timeshare properties. How might Jim make additional revenue?

   A. Sell information derived from the logs

   B. Use third-party logging tools

   C. Enable NCSA logging

   D. Buy the best timeshare

602 Chapter 14 · Logging Activity

4. Brad is concerned about the security of his Unix log files. Which of the following courses of action should he take?

A. Stop creating log files of security events

B. Make the log files owned and readable only by root

C. Redirect the logging activity to a terminal

D. Remove permissions from the log files

5. Brad reviews the access log for his company's Apache server. Which of the following elements are included in the Apache server access log by default? Choose four.

A. Login name of client accessing the server.

B. Client IP address

C. Name of the URL

D. HTTP request

E. Date and time the connection occurred

6. Frank is an extremely busy systems administrator. Frank should give high priority to which logs based on which factors?

A. Recent installations

B. Third-party installations

C. Behind the firewall

D. High traffic

E. Low traffic

F. Outside the firewall

7. Brenda wants to protect her web servers from hackers. What should Brenda install? Choose the best answer.

A. Proxy server

B. Firewall

C. WebTrends

D. Access logs

8. Tony is the systems administrator of Delta Hospitals. He checks the error log for Apache server. Which of the following activities are reported by default in the Apache server error log? Choose three.

    A. Server startup and shutdown

    B. Authentication methods

    C. IP address and domain name errors

    D. Malformed URLs

    E. Erroneous CGI scripts

9. Peter is a busy senior systems administrator with two junior administrators that work for him. How should Peter convey to them how often they should check server logs?

    A. Brainstorming session

    B. Security policy

    C. Weekly task list

    D. Job description

10. Ralph checks server log files for error messages. What evidence might Ralph find? Choose three answers.

    A. Evidence of attempted break-ins

    B. Evidence of an overburdened server

    C. Evidence of a faulty executable file

    D. Evidence of an unstable operating system

11. Frank checks log files for failed logon attempts and peak usage rates. What information might Frank glean?

    A. When to obtain a more powerful server

    B. That users need more training

    C. That someone is attempting a break-in

    D. That the server is unstable

12. Mark wants to find the Apache server log files. Where should he look?

    A. `/etc/httpd`

    B. `/sbin/apache`

    C. `/home/logs`

    D. `/var/log/httpd`

13. Brad is analyzing the FTP log files. Which five pieces of information are contained in these files?

    A. Client IP address

    B. Client username

    C. Referring URL

    D. Date and time connection was made

    E. Server IP address

    F. Commands issued

14. Brad wants to know who modified the company policy document on his FTP server. How can Brad glean this information?

    A. Directly from the FTP logs.

    B. By correlating the FTP logs to the server access log.

    C. From a third-party utility.

    D. This information is not logged by FTP.

15. Ben reads the term "user agent" in a technical paper. Which of the following are examples of user agents?

    A. Browsers

    B. Logging software

    C. Spiders

    D. List servers

16. George uses third-party software to analyze IIS log files. He does not obtain the rich set of reports that were promised. What is the most likely problem?

    A. He has not registered the product.

    B. He doesn't have enough hits on his web server.

    C. He is analyzing the wrong log.

    D. He hasn't configured extended logging.

17. Mark is presenting to his boss the three ways that log files can be viewed and evaluated. What are these ways?

    A. Directly

    B. Commercial log analysis software

    C. A third party who can log activity for you

    D. Via SNMP from a Network Management Station.

18. If your web server is located outside a firewall, what specific problem should be your highest priority when checking the server's log file?

    A. Peak usage patterns, to adjust system performance, throttle bandwidth, and control connections

    B. Error messages, indicating a faulty executable file or indicating that permissions have been set incorrectly on that directory

    C. Traffic volume, to determine a potential bottleneck in the web server's performance

    D. Failed logon attempts, indicating problem areas in the site, as well as possible hacking activity

19. Which default directory would you check to manually view logs for your FTP service in IIS 5?

    A. FTPLOG

    B. W3SVC1

    C. FTPSVC1

    D. MSFTPSVC1

20. Mike is considering paying a third party to log activity on www
.smart-money.com's website. What advantages might there be to
this approach to logging? Choose three.

A. Real-time monitoring

B. Alerts when the website is down or saturated

C. Website load balancing

D. Improved website performance

E. Slightly lower costs than internal logging and analysis

Answers to Review Questions

1. B, C, D, E.   You can review standard operating system log files to track usage rate, security, revenue generation, and server efficiency.

2. B, C, E, F.   The proper use of third-party logging software can decrease acquisition costs, increase conversion rates, improve retention, and build customer loyalty. See www.webtrends.com for details.

3. A.   Jim can use the logs to generate revenue.

4. B.   Make the log files owned and readable only by root. To further increase security, assign the log files to their own special group, create a dummy user in that group, and run all log-checking programs as that user.

5. B, C, D, E.   The Apache server access log reports by default the IP address of the client accessing the server, the date and time the connection occurred, the name of the URL, and the HTTP request.

6. A, D, F.   Frank should give priority to reading the logs of servers that are recent installations, have high-traffic, or reside outside the firewall.

7. B.   Brenda should install a firewall.

8. A, D, E.   The Apache server error log reports server startup and shutdown, malformed URLs, and erroneous CGI scripts.

9. B.   Your security policy should determine how often you check server logs.

10. B, C, D.   Error messages contain evidence of an overburdened server, a faulty executable file, or an unstable operating system.

11. A, B, C.   Failed logon attempts may signal that users need training or that someone is trying to break in. Peak usage rates can signal that system performance needs to be adjusted or that you need to obtain a more powerful server.

12. **D.** Apache server stores its log files in `/var/log/httpd`.

13. **A, B, D, E, F.** FTP log files contain the server IP address, client username, client IP address, commands issued, and connection date and time.

14. **A.** FTP log files contain the commands issued, including files obtained, deleted, and created.

15. **A, C.** Browsers and spiders used by search engines are examples of user agents.

16. **D.** George needs to configure extended logging so that the third-party log analysis program has enough types of information to analyze.

17. **A, B, C.** Log files can be viewed and evaluated directly, via commercial log analysis software, or by a third party who can log activity for you.

18. **D.** If your web server is outside the firewall, you should be concerned about security.

19. **D.** The directory name for the FTP log files in IIS 5 is `MSFTPSVC1`.

20. **A, B, D.** Third parties can log activity on your web servers in real time and send alerts when your website is down or saturated. You pay a price for this, but your website's security and reliability improves without degrading performance.

Chapter

15

Monitoring and Optimizing Internet Servers

THE CIW EXAM OBJECTIVE GROUPS COVERED IN THIS CHAPTER:

✓ Evaluate system performance, including but not limited to: server monitoring and optimization, maximizing performance, disaster assessment, data recovery.

You want your Internet server to load pages for your users quickly enough so that you don't lose 10 percent of your potential customers because they click away before your page loads. So what do you do? Optimize your web server.

In this chapter, we'll look first at how to identify problems that can cause slow performance, and then we'll look at the tools you can use in both Windows 2000 and Apache server to analyze performance and then speed it up. Before we get into that, though, here are some general questions to ask about your site. Dealing with the answers could do a great deal to optimize your server:

- Does your hardware have enough memory, enough CPUs of sufficient speed, a fast enough RAID array of hard drives, and enough bandwidth to satisfy your users?

- Are you doing anything to slow performance, such as logging too much information, running backups over the network on the same network card you use to serve web pages, not defragging your hard drives, using reverse DNS lookups, not having a big enough swap file, or using a very slow firewall?

- Have you designed your graphics so that they load quickly? Do they contain only needed colors, and in the most efficient format, and do you reuse common images so they only have to load once?

Understanding Queues and Bottlenecks

To understand server performance, you need to understand queues and bottlenecks. A *queue* is a sequence of requests for services from one or more servers. These requests arrive one at a time and wait to be processed.

A queue grows as more service requests arrive and shrinks as the requests are processed. If the server handles requests almost as fast as they arrive, the queue remains small. If requests continually arrive faster than the server can process them, the queue grows.

In a web server, HTTP requests are processed in the primary input queue. One factor that affects the efficiency with which requests in this queue are processed is how well the network device driver manages its queue of received packets. This factor, in turn, is affected by the efficiency with which the operating system manages its queue of processes waiting for CPU time. These queues are all directly affected by the amount of available memory and disk resources and by how well the queues for these resources are managed.

When the number of requests on these resources is small or when requests are widely spaced, the resources needed to handle the requests are available on demand. As the number of requests increases, users can experience wait times when trying to access server resources. If the system is working efficiently, wait time is consistently short. However, if the rate of incoming requests exceeds the rate at which the system can service them, queuing begins and wait time increases.

If the requests continue to queue up until there is no more space in the queue, a bottleneck results. At this point, other parts of the system will slow down to block new requests, and wait time can become unacceptable. A *bottleneck* is the weakest link or the limiting resource that causes the entire process to slow down or stop. Bottlenecks occur when one or several hardware resources are being used too much. The term "bottleneck" comes from the narrow part of a bottle used to slow the flow of liquid so it doesn't escape too fast.

To improve Internet server performance, first optimize what you have by eliminating bottlenecks. You can do so in four ways:

- Reconfigure the service or daemon software to use existing resources more efficiently. The software might be causing the problem because it is limiting what your hardware can do. You might, for example, have to update a NIC driver or install a service pack to derive the maximum performance from your machine.

- Update the server's hardware to replace the component causing the bottleneck.

- Move files to another server so that it can assume some of the load. You might have to create virtual FTP and/or web servers to help distribute the load.

- Obtain additional servers. Sometimes, you must replicate the component (or components) causing the bottleneck by distributing the demand for a service across multiple servers. For example, you might want to use a cluster server, which distributes processor load across several systems.

Finding a bottleneck can often be a slow and laborious task. You must often monitor the site over a long period of time to be able to identify where the slowdowns are occurring and to try to determine the cause.

> **NOTE** Solving one bottleneck can often reveal another. Make sure you test your system once you eliminate a bottleneck so that you have a clear idea of the server's new behavior.

> **NOTE** In a later section in this chapter, you'll see how to use System Monitor in Windows 2000 to identify bottlenecks. In Windows 2000, you can also use Task Manager and Event Viewer to identify bottlenecks.

Optimizing Hardware

Optimizing your hardware will always improve Internet server performance. To optimize hardware, you can do the following:

- Increase RAM
- Improve the quality of the NIC
- Upgrade the TCP/IP stack
- Upgrade to a faster CPU
- Update the I/O card driver or replace the card
- Upgrade to a motherboard with a faster system bus
- Upgrade to a multiple-CPU system or add another CPU
- Use the latest SCSI hardware
- Use disk striping (RAID 0)

The most important consideration for web server performance is the amount of RAM. Once a server runs out of dedicated RAM, it can obtain it through other sources, for example, by caching the hard drive. Caching the hard drive is often referred to as swapping.

Swapping diminishes the web server's ability to serve requests. A slow web server can cause many problems; primarily, a slow response time can cause end users to repeatedly attempt to reload pages. This activity puts further demands on the server, causing a chain reaction that could lead to further slowing and even system overload.

Understanding Optimization Tools

When you analyze the performance of a service, you must also analyze the operating system on which the service runs. For a service to function properly, the underlying operating system must operate at peak efficiency.

You can measure server performance using several methods and tools. The following are your three main resources:

- Server and service log files
- Protocol analyzers (for example, packet sniffers)
- System performance tools.

You learned about how to review logs in the previous chapter. In this section, we'll look at how to use one type of protocol analyzer, packet sniffers. In the following sections, we'll look at the tools available in Windows 2000 and Apache server.

Packet sniffers capture packets as they cross the network. Examples of *packet sniffers* include `tcpdump` (all flavors of Unix), Ethereal (many flavors of Unix and Windows 2000), Network Monitor (Windows 2000), as well as Sniffer Portable WAN and Sniffer Wireless by Network Associates (Windows 9x, Me, and 2000). A packet sniffer operates by placing a host's NIC into promiscuous mode, from which it can capture packets from the network wire.

You can capture packets for a particular host or port. For a web server, for example, you can monitor port 80 to collect statistics on failed and successful connections.

Packet sniffers can produce sizable amounts of data that might place a load on the packet-capturing host. Thus, the results you see during monitoring can be skewed by the additional load. Always be cognizant of this additional load and factor it into your analysis if possible.

Using System Monitor in Windows 2000

In Windows 2000, *System Monitor* is the primary tool for identifying server bottlenecks and problems on that system. This tool monitors "objects that belong to the server," including Physical Disk, Server Work Queues, Active Server Pages, Processor, TCP, Server, Logical Disk, Web Service, and FTP Service.

Each object contains at least one counter. For example, the Physical Disk object contains the Avg. Disk Bytes/Write counter, which helps you determine the average number of bytes written to the hard disk over a certain period of time. You track elements of your operating system by adding a specific object counter. For example, the Web Service object uses the CGI Requests/sec counter, which allows you to determine how many times your server processes a particular CGI script. Once added, the counter tracks the usage of that particular object.

The best way to monitor performance on a Windows 2000 computer is to monitor how often the operating system accesses the hard drive. Like many operating systems, Windows 2000 uses a portion of the hard drive as RAM. The hard drive space devoted to RAM is called the *paging file*. In Linux, this space is called the *swap file*.

Windows 2000 is unique among many operating systems because it relies heavily on the hard disk to operate. When a Windows 2000 system gets overburdened, it constantly hits the system's hard disk(s). The term for constant access of a hard disk is "thrashing." Disk thrashing is one of the primary reasons for bottlenecks in Windows 2000.

Table 15.1 shows some of the objects and counters you can use to monitor hard disks.

TABLE 15.1   Some Hard Disk Objects and Counters

Object	Counter	What It Does
Physical Disk	Disk Reads/sec	Measures how much of the system is reading information from the disk.
Physical Disk	Disk Writes/sec	Measures how quickly information is being written to the disk.
Physical Disk	Average Disk Queue Length	Measures the number of requests the Input/Output (I/O) card has made to the hard disk. If the counters average 90% for a sustained period, you have a bottle-neck. You can also measure the Current Disk Queue Length, if you want to obtain real-time information.
Physical Disk	% Disk Time	Measures the amount of time the disk is being accessed in a given period. The counter should not approach 90%.
Logical Disk	LogicalDisk Object % Free Space	Helps you determine if drive space is becoming too small.
Paging File	% Usage	Gives you the real-time usage statistics for the paging file. If usage is constantly over 95%, you need to increase the size of your paging file or consider a way to decrease the load on your server.
Paging File	% Usage Peak	Gives you the total peak usage of the paging file. Tells you the time the paging file has been accessed most.

The disk counter objects are not activated in Windows 2000 by default, because they can degrade system performance. To activate them, use the `diskperf` command, which has the options shown in Table 15.2.

TABLE 15.2 Options for the diskperf Command

Option	What It Does
-y	Activates all disk performance counters
-n	Disables all disk performance counters
-yd	Enables disk performance counters only for physical drives on the system
-nd	Disables the disk performance counters for physical drives
-yv	Enables disk performance counters only for logical drives on the system
-nv	Disables the disk performance counters for logical drives

It is often a good idea to monitor a server's disk access from a remote system. Remote monitoring ensures that your monitoring activity, which can significantly affect system performance, will not be included in the statistics you gather. If you have the correct permissions, you can also set disk counters on remote systems. For example, if you wanted to set all disk counters for a system named student10, issue the following command:

```
diskperf -y \\server1
```

You must restart your system after using diskperf. Otherwise, the objects will not activate. You must also reboot after disabling disk counters; otherwise, they will remain enabled and can slow performance.

Some additional counters are relevant to Internet-based servers, and they are listed and described in Table 15.3.

TABLE 15.3 Counters for Internet-Based Servers

Object	Counter	What It Does
Processor	Server Work Queues	Measures the number of processes waiting to be addressed by the CPU. The number of queues should not remain consistently high.

TABLE 15.3 Counters for Internet-Based Servers *(continued)*

Object	Counter	What It Does
Processor	Queue Length	Displays the number of processes in a queue. A queue of more than four processes for a sustained time indicates that your CPU may need an upgrade.
Web Service	CGI Requests/sec	Provides the number of CGI requests occurring at any given time.
Web Service	Current Anonymous Users	Determines the number of anonymous users currently on the system.
Memory	Pages/sec	Helps you determine how many times the system attempted to cache the hard drive for RAM, but found that the particular memory (i.e., page) was already in use or had moved. A high page-faults-per-second rate indicates an over-worked system.

EXERCISE 15.1

Using Windows 2000 System Monitor

In this exercise, you will learn how Internet-based connections to your system affect performance. Specifically, you will view two different types of web-based connections to see how they require Windows 2000 to allocate memory differently.

1. Log on as administrator.

2. At a command prompt, enter **diskperf -y** to activate all physical counters on your system.

3. Reboot your system.

4. Log back on as administrator, and choose Start ➢ Programs ➢ Administrative Tools ➢ Performance to open the Performance snap-in. The System Monitor snap-in will open by default.

5. Click the Add button (+) to open the Add Counters dialog box:

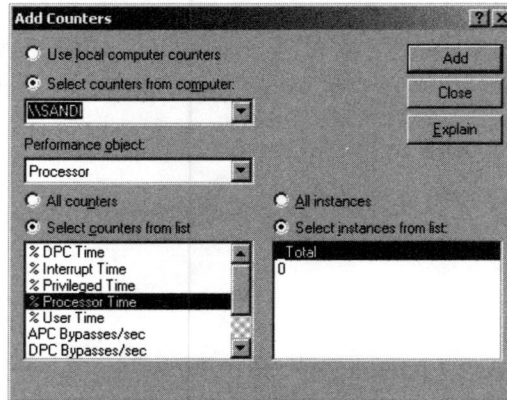

6. Click the Performance Object drop-down box, and select the PhysicalDisk object.

7. Hold down the Ctrl key, and then in the Select Counters from List section, select % Disk Time, Avg Disk Queue Length, and Disk Bytes/sec.

8. Click the Add button.

9. Click Close.

10. If your web server is not started already, start it now. Make sure you do not have any conflicts with a proxy server that may be using the same port.

11. Access your website and FTP site to generate a load that the Performance snap-in can monitor, and/or copy larger folders to your Desktop and then delete them. Depending on your server's load, you will see activity similar to that shown in the following graphic:

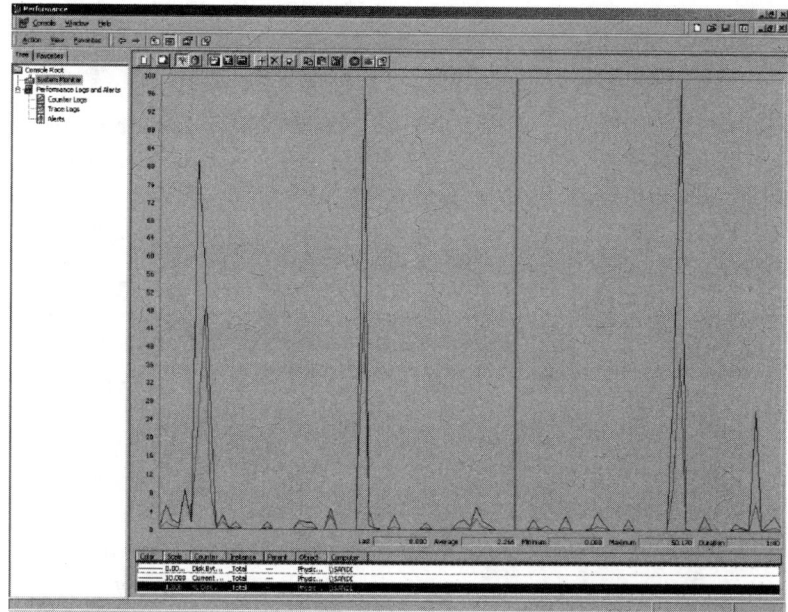

12. You have just viewed the physical disk activity for your server. Delete these counters by highlighting each counter and pressing the Delete key. You will now add a list of new counters. Click the Add Counter button to open the Add Counters dialog box.

13. Select the Server Work Queues object, select the Queue Length counter, and click Add. The counter should appear in the System Monitor main window.

14. Follow the process in Step 13 to select the Web Service object and add the CGI Requests/sec and Current Anonymous Users counters. Select the Memory object, and then select the Page Faults/sec and Pages/sec counters. Select the Paging File object, and then select the % Usage and % Usage Peak counters.

15. Click Close to close the Add Counters dialog box.

16. Access your own web server opening multiple browser windows.

17. Check the Performance snap-in to view statistics concerning your website. Notice that the paging counters give you a continuous line. If this line is above 90 percent, you need to take corrective action.

18. Close the System Monitor. At a command prompt, use the diskperf -n command to deactivate all disk counters. Reboot your system.

Optimizing Internet Information Services

The amount of time a web connection is active can directly affect the performance of a web server. You never want active connections to time-out, yet you also don't want to allot too many resources to connections that are sitting idle on a user's screen while they have left their desk to perform another task. Choosing the right trade-off between the two is a difficult task, but one that an administrator must try to balance.

For example, if you configure a machine to be able to handle fewer connections than are regularly concurrently serviced, the result will be faster connections and improved server performance for each of those connections that is able to establish a connection. More resources are allocated to fewer connections.

On the other hand, if you set the host to be able to provide a number of connections that is much higher than the actual number of connections, you will notice a decrease in server performance because server memory is being wasted (not being utilized). Compare your daily hit logs with the server settings to ensure that your configuration closely matches the actual connections to your site

One of the easiest configurations is to adjust the amount of time a web application will keep a connection active. IIS refers to this setting as "enabling session state." You can adjust this setting from the Home Directory tab in the Properties dialog box for your web server, as illustrated in the following exercise.

EXERCISE 15.2

Adjusting Web Server Performance in IIS 5

In this exercise, you will use IIS 5 to adjust server performance for your web server. Specifically, you will adjust performance for the following scenario: You are the administrator of a web server that receives 4,000 hits a day. The nature of this traffic is that each user establishes contact and then almost immediately leaves for another location. The site uses several web applications, and the average session length for these web applications is 10 minutes. At peak times, the network experiences traffic at 1,800KBps. However, you want your web server to refuse traffic at 1,500KBps. Finally, this web server uses Microsoft SQL Server; and you want to set a maximum limit on the amount of CPU time IIS can take.

1. Open the IIS snap-in and expand your server. (Choose Start ➤ Programs ➤ Administrative Tools ➤ Internet Services Manager.)

2. Expand the listing beneath your computer name. Right-click Default Web Site and choose Properties from the shortcut menu to open the server's Properties dialog box.

3. Select the Performance tab.

4. Change the Performance Tuning value from its default (Fewer than 100,000) to Fewer Than 10,000.

5. Click the Enable Bandwidth Throttling check box, and then set it for the appropriate value (1,500KBps).

6. Click the Enable Process Throttling check box, and then set the limit to 50%.

7. Click the Enforce Limits check box.

8. Click the Web Site tab, and clear the HTTP Keep-Alives Enabled check box. By clearing this check box, clients with slower connections can be prematurely closed (thus requiring them to re-establish connections), but you are not keeping connections open unduly.

9. In the Connections section, select the Limited To radio button, and limit the number of simultaneous connections to 500. The default is Unlimited, but choosing a smaller number optimizes resources better, as mentioned earlier.

10. Change the Connection Timeout value from its default of 900 seconds to 600 seconds.

11. Click Apply, and then click OK to return to the IIS snap-in.

Optimizing Apache Server

You can use several tools in Linux to monitor system performance. Some tools, such as top, can be run in real time or in a batch mode, collecting data for offline analysis later. You can use programs such as vmstat to determine a host's use of virtual memory.

The top program places the most CPU-intensive programs at the top of a list of processes running on your Linux system. It also determines the amount of memory being used by each process.

The top program reports on several values, including the following.

- The PID of the process you are querying
- The user account that started the process
- The priority of the task (PRI)
- The "nice" value of the task
- The size of the executable
- The percentage of CPU time
- The percentage of memory used by the process
- The command used to run the process

You can also use top in interactive mode. Once top is running, you can issue the commands shown in Table 15.4, among others.

TABLE 15.4 top Commands

Command	What It Does
s	Allows you to specify, in seconds, the intervals at which top updates its information. By default, top updates every five seconds.

TABLE 15.4   top Commands *(continued)*

Command	What It Does
S	Toggles cumulative mode on and off.
H	Enables help.
P	Sorts information according to CPU usage.
U	Allows you to search for processes owned by a specific user.
K	Allows you to kill a task, using any signal (including –HUP and –9) you prefer.

For more information on top commands, consult the man file (man top).

The vmstat program classifies all processes using fields and field values, which are listed in Table 15.5. Each field lists the values for the processes that use memory.

TABLE 15.5   Process Categories Used by vmstat

Field	Value	Description
Procs	r	The number of processes waiting in a queue
	b	Sleeping processes
memory	swpd	Virtual memory used, in kilobytes
	free	The amount of idle memory, in kilobytes
	buff	Memory used in buffers, in kilobytes
swap	si	Memory swapped from the hard drive
	so	Memory swapped to the hard drive
io	bi	Memory blocks sent to a device

TABLE 15.5 Process Categories Used by vmstat *(continued)*

Field	Value	Description
	bo	Blocks received from a device
system	in	Interruptions per second
	cs	The number of context switches per second
CPU	us	The percentage of total CPU time occupied by user process
	sy	The percentage of total CPU time occupied by system process
	id	The amount of time CPU is idle

If the r value in the Procs field begins registering values approaching 100, your system is running low on virtual memory. If you begin to see that the id value in the CPU field is running below 50 percent, your CPU has become overburdened.

> **NOTE** The vmstat program does not count its own memory usage in its statistics.

To adjust server performance in Apache server, you edit the http.conf file to alter keepalive requests, timeout times, and the number of servers that Apache server can start. For example, if you are the administrator of a web server that receives many hits from clients that remain at the server for an average of 500 seconds, and you expect that as many as 300 users connect simultaneously, with each visitor generating as many as 200 requests per connection, here is how you can edit the /etc/httpd/conf/httpd.conf file.

1. Log on as root.

2. Use the cd /etc/httpd/conf command to change to the /etc/httpd/conf/ directory.

3. Use the vi httpd.conf command to open the httpd.conf file.

4. Scroll down until you see the Timeout, KeepAlive, and MaxKeep-AliveRequests entries. Adjust the Timeout setting to 500.

5. Scroll down and set the MaxKeepAliveRequests value to 500.

6. Scroll down and set the MaxClients value to 300.

7. Exit vi, making sure to save your changes by pressing the Escape key and entering **ZZ**.

8. Use the `/etc/rc.d/init.d/httpd restart` command to completely stop and restart.

9. Test your work by reconnecting to the server to see if it is running correctly.

10. Issue the `cat /var/log/messages | grep httpd` command to view the log entries for httpd.

11. Read the `/etc/httpd/logs/error_log` file. If you find no recent messages, you have properly adjusted Apache server's performance.

Summary

In this chapter, you learned that we want to optimize web server performance so that our web pages load quickly. You also learned how to monitor the performance of your operating system and its servers. You learned that the three main resources for measuring server performance are server and service log files; protocol analyzers, and system performance tools. You used applications such as `top`, `vmstat`, and Windows 2000 System Monitor to analyze the nature and effect of various connections. You also learned how to adjust server performance in both Windows 2000 and Linux using various programs and configuration files.

With the knowledge gained in this chapter, you now understand the need for server monitoring and optimization; you can utilize tools when monitoring and optimizing servers; you can identify key Internet server elements to monitor; and you can adjust Internet server settings to meet expected workload.

Exam Essentials

Know the three main resources for measuring server requests and responses. The three main resources are server and service logs, protocol analyzers such as packet sniffers, and system performance tools.

Use tools when monitoring and optimizing servers.   Packet sniffers capture and analyze packets. Know the names of the packet-sniffer programs and that a packet sniffer places a host's NIC in promiscuous mode.

Know how to identify bottlenecks.   A queue is a waiting line for a resource. When the waiting line is too long, you get a bottleneck. The resource that is in shortest supply is the bottleneck. Look for bottlenecks on Internet servers caused by a slow disk system, not enough memory, not enough processing power, or not enough bandwidth due to network card or Internet connection bandwidth restrictions. Use Windows 2000 System Monitor and Linux `top` and `vmststat` to identify bottlenecks.

Know how to eliminate bottlenecks.   You can eliminate bottlenecks four ways. (1) Reconfigure the service or daemon software to use existing resources more efficiently. The software might be causing the problem because it is limiting what your hardware can do. You might, for example, have to update a NIC driver or install a service pack to derive the maximum performance from your machine. (2) Update the server's hardware to replace the component causing the bottleneck. (3) Move files to another server so that it can assume some of the load. You might have to create virtual FTP and/or web servers to help distribute the load. (4) Obtain additional servers. Sometimes, you must replicate the component (or components) causing the bottleneck by distributing the demand for a service across multiple servers. For example, you might want to use a cluster server, which distributes processor load across several systems.

Key Terms

Before taking the exam, you should be familiar with the following terms:

bottleneck	queue
packet sniffers	swap file
paging file	System Monitor

Review Questions

1. Jonathan is director of Human Resources for Great Escapes. He is thinking about upgrading some Internet servers and replacing others in order to satisfy a projected 20 percent increase in hits. What is the first step he should take to improve performance?

   A. Identify bottlenecks

   B. Identify the oldest servers

   C. Consult the business plan

   D. Look at revenue projection to determine the budget

2. Mary runs MostGifts.com, which provides website hosting using a server farm. There has been a slight downturn in business in the last year, which has been turbulent. She has lost some clients that are hosted on some servers; on the other hand, some clients are outgrowing their servers. She uses tools to identify bottlenecks. Which strategy to correct bottlenecks will probably work best for Mary?

   A. Reconfigure the service of daemon software to use existing resources more efficiently

   B. Update the hardware on any servers that have bottlenecks to replace the component causing the bottleneck

   C. Move the files to another server so that it can assume some of the load

   D. Obtain additional servers

3. Edward is briefing a junior systems administrator on the three main resources for measuring server requests and responses. What are they?

   A. SNMP

   B. Server and service log files

   C. Protocol analyzers

   D. System performance tools

4. Jason has a consulting firm analyze system performance on his Internet server farm. After they leave to prepare their report, he notices that performance is even slower. What is the most likely problem?

   A. A NIC is operating in promiscuous mode.

   B. Disk counters have been enabled.

   C. Memory counters are enabled.

   D. A packet sniffer has not been disconnected.

5. Heather wants to capture packets coming into her Apache server. What is the near-universal tool in all flavors of Unix that captures packets?

   A. grep

   B. PAM

   C. vi

   D. tcpwrappers

   E. perfmon

   F. tcpdump

6. Jim wants to watch the data in server log files in real time to look for spikes of activity on his Windows 2000 server. What is the most economical method or tool he can use to accomplish this task?

   A. SNMP

   B. rconsole

   C. Packet sniffer

   D. System Monitor

7. Jason wants to quickly determine the number of connections to his Windows system. Which TCP/IP utility should he use?

   A. top

   B. bottom

   C. vmstat

   D. qstat

   E. netstat

8. Mike wants to optimize requests to his Apache web server so that they are handled efficiently. What can Mike do?

    A. Upgrade the NIC or network device driver

    B. Increase the queue length

    C. Eliminate the primary input queue

    D. Use offsite queuing

9. Mike wants to enable disk performance counters on a web server. What two things must Mike do?

    A. Enter the `diskperf -y` command

    B. Enter the `diskperf \\127.0.0.1` command

    C. Flash the BIOS

    D. Reboot the computer

10. Steve is evaluating CGI scripts that provide a shopping cart for his IIS 5 website. He wants to track usage of this particular script. What should Steve do?

    A. Add a CGI Requests/sec counter to System Monitor

    B. Put the script on a separate disk and enable disk counters for the disk using the `diskperf -y` command

    C. Use a sniffer

    D. Program the script with a counter

    E. Use the loopback function

11. Denise notices that Apache web server response slows in the summer. She suspects that one of the summer interns is abusing the web server in some way. Which switch can Denise use with the **top** command to identify the culprit?

    A. s

    B. o

    C. P

    D. u

    E. k

12. Denise notices that Apache web server response has slowed. She wants to use **top** to troubleshoot but can't remember all the switches. Which command should she try first?

    A. m

    B. S

    C. h

    D. u

    E. k

13. Denise notices that Apache web server response has slowed. She identifies the process that is hogging CPU time. Which switch can Denise use with the **top** command to stop the process?

    A. s

    B. o

    C. P

    D. u

    E. k

14. The www.OmniSky.com website filed for Chapter 11, and the assets were bought by your company. Your company is moving their website to your web server farm. What is the best way to optimize Internet server performance in this case?

    A. Reconfigure the software running the daemon

    B. Replace bottlenecked components

    C. Integrate the additional systems

    D. Buy new servers

15. Using `top` and `vmstat`, Mary determines that performance has suffered as additional services have been added to her Apache server website. Which three options for improving performance are available to Mary?

A. Reconfigure the software running the daemon

B. Replace a component on the machine

C. Obtain additional systems

D. Increase the size of the primary input queue

16. Frank wants to improve Internet server performance. What are some of the techniques? Choose five.

A. Increase RAM size

B. Improve the quality of the NIC

C. Upgrade the TCP/IP stack

D. Use a volume set

E. Upgrade the motherboard with a faster system bus

F. Use disk striping (RAID 0) for temporary files

G. Decrease the size of the paging file.

17. Which of the following performance monitoring tools classifies all processes using fields and field values?

A. `top`

B. `vmstat`

C. `ntop`

D. System Monitor

18. A bottleneck develops when which of the following occurs?

   A. A web server receives HTTP requests faster than it can process them, using all space in the queue.

   B. A system cannot handle all the print requests received, consuming too much network traffic.

   C. An e-mail client cannot process all the incoming messages and begins refusing them.

   D. A streaming media server forbids access to anonymous users, allowing access to only a few.

19. To adjust the number of clients Apache Server will allow, which of the following lines would you edit in `httpd.conf`?

   A. `MaxClients`

   B. `MaxRequests`

   C. `ServerReq`

   D. `MaxReq`

20. Willy administers an Apache web server. He wants to find out if he has a big enough swap file. Which three field values of the `vmstat` command output could be helpful?

   A. `memory: swpd`

   B. `memory: free`

   C. `memory: buff`

   D. `swap: si`

   E. `swap: so`

Answers to Review Questions

1. A.   The first step in improving Internet server performance is identifying bottlenecks.

2. C.   The load needs to be redistributed.

3. B, C, D.   The three main resources for measuring server requests and responses are server and service log files, protocol analyzers, and system performance tools.

4. B.   Disk counter objects are not activated in Windows 2000 by default because they can degrade performance. The disk counters needed to be on in order to do the reporting, but now the additional load of logging this information is slowing the performance even more.

5. F.   You can use `tcpdump` in all flavors of Unix to capture packets coming into a web server.

6. D.   Windows 2000 System Monitor is capable of real-time monitoring.

7. E.   You can use simple TCP/IP utilities such as `netstat` to determine the number of connections to your system.

8. A.   In a web server, HTTP requests are processed in the primary input queue. Factors affecting the efficiency with which requests in this queue are processed include how well the network device driver manages its queue of received packets.

9. A, D.   Mike must enter the `diskperf -y` command and reboot the computer to enable disk counters.

10. A.   You can monitor CGI scripts using the CGI Requests/sec counter in System Monitor.

11. D.   The u command used with `top` allows you to search interactively for processes owned by a specific owner.

12. C.   The h command used with `top` interactively displays help.

13. E.   The k command used with `top` interactively kills a process.

14. C.   Your company should integrate the additional systems.

15. A, B, C.   The three methods to correct a bottleneck are reconfigure the software running the daemon, replace a component on the machine, and obtain additional systems.

16. A, B, C, E, F.   To improve Internet server performance, you can increase the RAM size; improve the quality of the NIC; upgrade the TCP/IP stack; upgrade to a motherboard with a faster system bus; and use disk striping (RAID 0).

17. B.   The `vmstat` tool classifies all processes using fields and field values.

18. A.   A bottleneck occurs when a web server receives HTTP requests faster than it can process them, using all space in the queue.

19. A.   To adjust the number of clients Apache Server will allow, edit the `MaxClients` line in `httpd.conf`.

20. A, D, E.   The `memory:swpd` field value shows the virtual memory used. The `swap:si` field value shows the memory swapped from the hard drive. The `swap:so` field value shows the memory swapped to the hard drive.

Chapter

16

Fault Tolerance and System Backup

THE CIW EXAM OBJECTIVE GROUPS COVERED IN THIS CHAPTER:

✓ Evaluate system performance, including but not limited to: server monitoring and optimization, maximizing performance, disaster assessment, data recovery.

ault tolerance is the ability of a system to continue to operate after an unexpected hardware or software problem. If you run a web-hosting company, the fault tolerance of your systems is a major selling point. If you are looking at taking an Internet-based company public, during a due-diligence inspection of your operation you must show that it will survive equipment and software malfunctions.

The context of fault tolerance is system dependability and the means to achieve it. A fault-tolerant computer system or component is designed so that a backup procedure or component can immediately take its place in the event of failure.

A fundamental part of administering servers is ensuring that the data they serve is protected. This chapter discusses how to ensure data integrity and provide fault tolerance. You will learn how to increase fault tolerance on specific systems, plan a backup strategy, and archive information on these systems. You will also learn how to implement offsite storage and recover from system crashes.

Fault Tolerance

Fault-tolerance measures are efforts to keep a server crash from denying services to customers. The true definition of fault tolerance is the ability for a server to continue to run and function in the event of a failure. You can implement fault tolerance using software, hardware, or a combination of software and hardware. In this section, we'll look at some of the most common ways to provide fault tolerance on individual servers.

Redundant Array of Inexpensive Disks (RAID)

Redundant Array of Inexpensive Disks (*RAID*, which is also known as Redundant Array of Independent Disks) was developed when hard drives of 1GB or more were prohibitively expensive. RAID can increase storage by making multiple smaller drives act as one logical drive, resulting in cost savings.

You can implement RAID support using hardware or software. In a hardware implementation, a RAID-capable hard-disk controller controls the physical disks. This controller normally has its own microprocessor and RAM dedicated to handling read and write requests. RAID-capable hard-disk controllers are much more expensive than standard hard-disk controllers.

Some network operating systems provide RAID software support. The operating system itself configures RAID, and you can use standard hard-disk controllers to lower costs.

RAID is used today to protect data and is categorized by levels. The most frequently used RAID levels are as follows:

- Level 0
- Level 1
- Level 4
- Level 5

In this section, we'll look at these common RAID levels as well as some others.

RAID 0: Disk Striping

RAID 0 uses disk striping but does not provide fault tolerance. A *stripe set* is a collection of physical disks that are configured to act as one logical set. In *disk striping*, each file that is written to the stripe set is divided into pieces; each piece is then written to a separate physical disk in the stripe set, as shown in Figure 16.1.

> **NOTE** Disk striping by itself is not a fault-tolerant solution. It does, however, provide improved read and write access speeds because each drive can be read from or written to independently.

Disk striping is the fastest of the RAID technologies, but it does not provide system redundancy. It is nevertheless defined as a RAID technology because it provides a set of physical disks that act as a single entity.

FIGURE 16.1 Disk striping

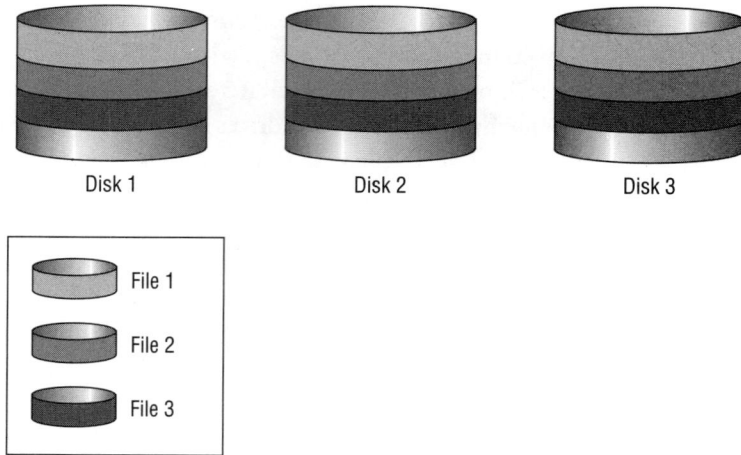

Disk 1

Disk 2

Disk 3

File 1

File 2

File 3

RAID 1: Disk Mirroring

RAID 1, the most often used form of RAID, uses disk mirroring and does provide fault tolerance, though not to the extent of RAID 5. In *disk mirroring*, two sets of writes occur for each write procedure. A mirror set is established between two physical hard disks (or partitions on two physical disks), as shown in Figure 16.2.

FIGURE 16.2 Disk mirroring

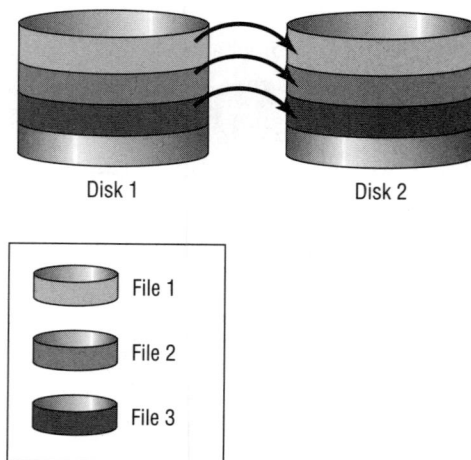

Disk 1

Disk 2

File 1

File 2

File 3

Data is written to the primary disk when a write request is issued. Data is then copied to the mirrored disk, providing a mirror image of the primary disk. If one of the hard disks fails, all data is protected from loss.

Most network operating systems (using a software implementation of RAID) allow any portion of a disk to be mirrored, including the operating system files, which protect the entire system.

You can implement mirroring using the same physical hard-disk controller for both disks. However, if the single controller fails, neither disk is accessible. Often when a hard-disk controller fails, the hard disks attached to it are damaged as well.

> **NOTE** *Disk duplexing* eliminates the problem of a single controller failure. Disk duplexing functions the same way as disk mirroring, but provides a separate controller for each hard disk.

RAID 4: Disk Striping with Large Blocks

Although not common, RAID 4 uses a single disk to store parity information (error-checking calculations) and multiple disks to store data. The data from a single file is written in its entirety to a single disk, and the parity information for that data is stored on a separate parity disk.

Storing complete files on a single disk (versus storing portions of a file on multiple disks, as in RAID 0) produces high performance when large blocks of data must be read. Additionally, multiple reads can be conducted simultaneously. For example, one simultaneous read occurs for each data disk in the system. Figure 16.3 shows how RAID 4 works.

RAID 5: Disk Striping with Parity

RAID 5, the most often used form of fault-tolerant RAID, uses *disk striping with parity*, which becomes fault tolerant because the stripe set includes parity information.

In a RAID 5 implementation, a portion of each write request is written to a separate physical disk in the stripe set. However, parity information is calculated on the entire file and is written to a completely separate physical disk. For each file written, parity information never resides on the same physical disk as file information for which the parity is calculated. Figure 16.4 shows how RAID 5 works.

FIGURE 16.3 RAID 4 disk striping with large blocks

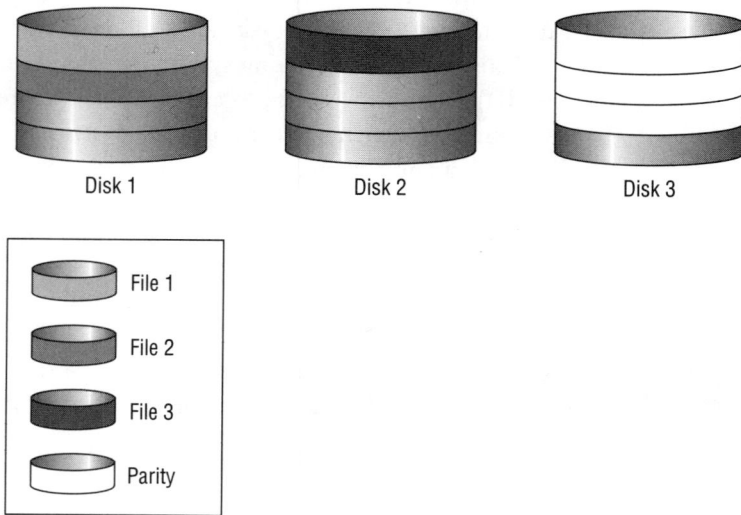

FIGURE 16.4 Disk striping with parity

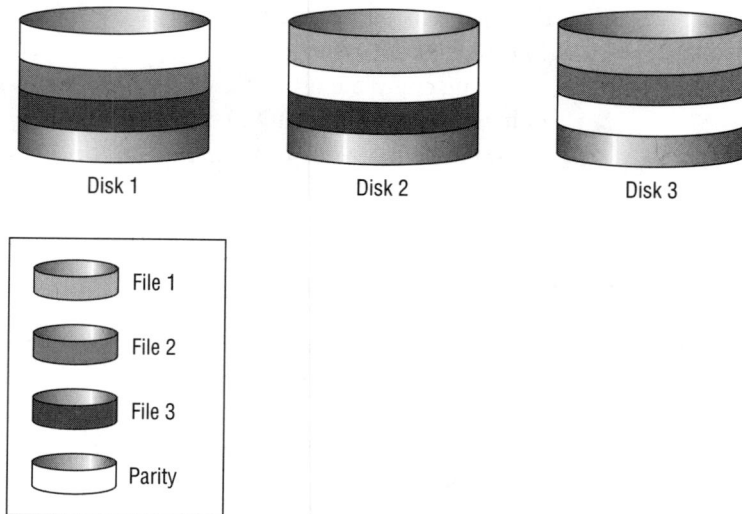

RAID 5 requires a minimum of three disks.

For each subsequent write procedure to the stripe set, parity information is rotated to another disk so that each disk eventually contains file and parity information for files not on that disk.

Because information for each write request is spread across multiple disks and because error-checking information is stored on another physical disk, RAID 5 configurations can survive a single disk crash without losing information. In RAID 4, if any one disk fails, either one-half of the data and the parity information survive, or all the data survives but the parity information is lost. If you have one-half of the data and the parity information, you can regenerate the missing portion of the data. If you have all the data, you can recalculate the parity information.

In software implementations of RAID 5, the operating system files are restricted from inclusion in the stripe set. When a system boots, the operating system is loaded into memory. The operating system is stored on the hard disk, and a hard-disk controller delivers the read operation commands to the physical disk. If the operating system (instead of a hardware controller) is controlling a stripe set (thereby issuing the read commands), the operating system must be loaded to issue the read commands. Placing the operating system files in the stripe set would prohibit the system from booting.

Additional Levels of RAID

Additional RAID levels include RAID 6 and RAID 10. RAID 6 differs from RAID 5 in that RAID 6 uses a second parity stripe distributed among the disks. This technology delivers higher fault tolerance than lower levels of RAID. RAID 10 provides an array of stripes in which each individual stripe is itself a RAID 1 array of disks. Although much more costly than the other RAID types, RAID 10 provides additional fault tolerance.

Automatic RAID

Recent implementations of RAID can automatically recover from a disk failure. Traditionally, when a disk failure occurred, an IT professional manually "broke" and then restored the array after replacing the failed disk. Many high-end systems now have software that automatically detects most RAID failure. This software can break the RAID array, deactivate the failed disk, and then activate the waiting replacement disk. The software can then create a new RAID array and, if necessary, reboot the system.

High-Availability Disk Subsystems

When a disk fails in a RAID configuration, you must replace the bad disk and restore the mirror or stripe set. Excluding RAID 0, data is not lost for a single disk failure.

For environments in which rapid regeneration of stripe sets is necessary to avoid downtime, administrators implement hot-swappable disk subsystems, also known as hot-pluggable drives. These specialized disks are installed in drawer-like mountings that allow you to remove them while the machine is on. If a disk fails, you can remove and replace it without shutting down the machine. The RAID controller automatically detects the new disk and regenerates the stripe set. Hot-swappable PCI cards and power supplies are also available.

> A server might require you to first stop a service or to use software to prepare the system before replacing a component. When software configuration is required before a swap, the condition is referred to as a "warm swap."

System performance will degrade during the regeneration process because the computer is recalculating parity information and re-creating lost pieces of files. Hot-swappable disks must be implemented with a hardware solution and support only RAID 5 or higher.

Additional Fault-Tolerance Options

Many other types of data protection are available, including the following.

- Uninterruptible power supply (UPS)
- Folder replication
- Offsite storage and site mirroring
- Removable media

Uninterruptible Power Supply

Power problems are the greatest cause of computer data loss; a typical PC can experience more than 120 power problems a month. An *uninterruptible power supply (UPS)* offers a steady stream of power to critical servers and workstations if electric power supplies fail or are inadequate.

A UPS is powered by internal batteries. A battery is charged when normal power is available, and the system attached to the UPS uses the battery when power is inadequate or unavailable. Additionally, most UPSs can regulate the power sent to the attached system. The power flows from the wall into the UPS, and the UPS delivers a steady stream of power to the system. This feature is beneficial when a power surge or brownout occurs.

Folder Replication

You may sometimes want to copy folders or key files to a separate location. Whenever you change a folder, replicate it to a temporary location on the hard disk or to another physical hard disk if possible. *Folder replication* is normally a manual process, but many network operating systems can automatically copy specified files and folders to a different location at specified times.

Offsite Storage

Most large organizations store key information offsite, including copies of backup files. If you consider offsite storage, be sure the location is secure. Imagine the consequences if an unauthorized person were to access information on your backup tapes or CDs. Some organizations allow designated employees to keep a copy of the latest set of tapes. Such a practice may be suitable for a small business but is not feasible for a large organization, mainly because of security concerns and the sheer bulk of media required to back up a large amount of information.

Site Mirroring

Site mirroring is the ability to duplicate any part of an existing website on remote hosts. For example, the main Apache server distribution site (`www.apache.org`) allows anyone to mirror the contents of its file download area. Sites such as TUCOWS (`www.tucows.com`) also engage in site mirroring. Because of its duplication feature, site mirroring provides fault tolerance and data security.

Site mirroring also provides load balancing, because users can obtain the same information from several sites. Site mirroring tends to decrease wait time experienced by users who connect to geographically distant sites. For example, an international company such as IBM can establish mirrors of its most popular web pages for clients all around the world.

The most efficient way to mirror sites is through software that provides incremental file transfers. Available Windows and Linux software includes the following:

- VERITAS products, including NetBackup and Foundation Suite (www.veritas.com).

- PowerSync (www.linkpro.com).

- rcp, the traditional Unix utility for copying files between hosts.

- rsync, a more advanced Unix utility that allows non-root users to transfer files.

- cvsupd, a freeware group of programs designed to be faster and more flexible than rcp or rsync. The cvsupd program requires the cvsup client. More information is available at www.polstra.com/projects/freeware/CVSup/faq.html.

More ambitious mirroring options, such as those provided by Omni-FORCE (www.storage.com), use proprietary operating systems.

To use most site-mirroring software in Linux, you must also use a remote shell (rsh) or a secure shell (ssh). The rsh command is similar to telnet, but is used only to execute commands on a remote host. For example, you can use rsh if Host A wants to list a file on Host B and then transfer it to Host A. Of course, you must set the appropriate permissions for these programs to work properly. Many IT professionals prefer using ssh because it incorporates encryption, which makes it more secure than programs such as rsh or rlogin.

Most current software has its own automation features, although you can automate site mirroring by using cron in Linux or the Task Scheduler service in Windows 2000.

Site Redirection

Although not technically a fault-tolerance solution, site redirection can help you recover from system outages and denial-of-service attacks. A *denial of service attack* is a security intrusion that incapacitates the service of a particular entity, allowing a hacker to engage in IP spoofing; a denial-of-service attack can also be responsible for an entity performing abnormally. You can redirect any Internet service that you want, including entire sites. A crude way to redirect a website, for example, is to place a default page on the disrupted site that informs users of a move and then automatically sends users to the new site.

More sophisticated redirection services are available from most ISPs, including sites such as www.redirection.net, shown in Figure 16.5.

FIGURE 16.5 The Redirection.net home page

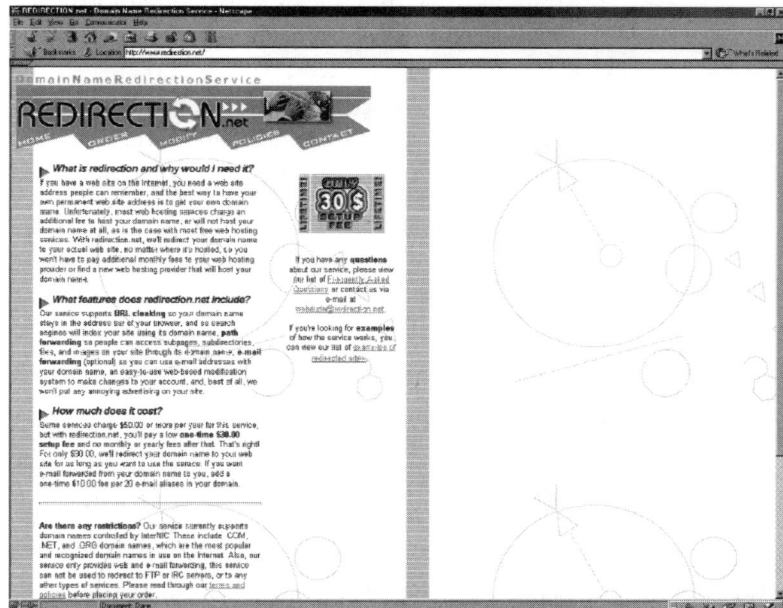

Services such as Redirection.net usually require a nominal setup fee and an additional monthly or yearly fee to continue the service. Such services can automatically redirect the following:

- E-mail (SMTP, POP3, and IMAP); the practice of redirecting e-mail is often called e-mail forwarding.

- Web traffic.

- News server traffic.

- List server traffic.

The most critical steps in site redirection are creating a DNS entry for your site and then informing your ISP about the change. Your ISP can offer redirection for any Internet service.

Tape and Removable Media Backup

Although RAID systems are beneficial and often essential, they do not take the place of a backup strategy. The best solution for total data protection is a combination of RAID and tape backup. Remember that if a RAID configuration loses one disk, you do not lose data. If it loses two disks, all data is lost. After a second simultaneous disk failure, the importance of tape backup becomes evident.

Several types of removable media are available today. Each type has its own role and storage capacity, and several types can be valuable components in an administrator's toolkit. These include the following:

- Floppy disks
- Zip disks
- CD-ROMs
- Tapes

Floppy disks provide a simple method for backing up small amounts of data or key files and for transferring files from one non-networked computer to another. They can store 1.44MB of data.

WARNING Because floppy disks are often used to transfer files from one system to another, they are frequently responsible for virus infection. A high percentage of viruses are written to replicate themselves to floppy disks and then to the hard disk of the machine that accesses the infected diskette.

Some vendors produce floppy disks that can hold 100MB or 120MB of data. These disks use the LS-120 technology. A popular brand is the Imation SuperDisk. Although these SuperDisks offer increased storage capacity, they also require a special floppy drive. A benefit of the SuperDisk Drive from Imation is that it can utilize both SuperDisks and standard floppy disks.

Iomega Corporation developed the Zip drive. This device can store 100MB of data on a single cartridge that is slightly larger than a standard 3.5-inch floppy disk. Several models are available, including internal and external drives. The drives offer an IDE, a SCSI, or a parallel port interface. Iomega also produces a Zip drive that can store 250MB on a single Zip disk and is backward-compatible with 100MB Zip disks.

Technology for creating CD-ROMs has evolved dramatically. With each CD capable of holding 700MB of information, CDs are becoming a popular choice for offline storage. You can use single-write discs (CD-Rs) or multiple-write discs (CD-RWs). Many systems administrators prefer using CR-RW discs because they can be less expensive.

Many sites deploy systems that write to multiple CD-ROM drives simultaneously. These systems, often called jukeboxes, allow you to create a backup system that is fault tolerant as well as fully automated.

Until recently, tapes were the only media available for storing files. Today, tape storage is still the most-often-used method for storing large numbers of files or for backing up an entire system.

Planning a Backup Strategy

Backing up your system is a requirement even if you use data-protection technologies such as RAID. A good backup strategy includes the following five steps:

1. Determining which files to back up

2. Choosing local or network backup types

3. Selecting a backup method

4. Planning and practicing restoration procedures

5. Ensuring that you have verified all backup files

You must carefully choose which files to back up. Backing up unnecessary files requires additional time and storage, but if you neglect to back up critical system files, you may not be able to recover a system after a failure.

Each installation will vary in its backup requirements, but generally always back up any files you deem critical, all system files, and the Registry on Windows 2000 machines. You may choose to occasionally back up non-critical files or files that change infrequently. Backing up temporary files wastes storage space and time.

If you are using a tape backup system, you must choose between backing up the tape drive in each computer and using a single tape drive to back up all required computers. Having a tape drive in each computer allows each machine to be backed up independently from the others, thus eliminating a single point of failure. However, purchasing multiple tape drives and backup software is expensive.

Using a single tape drive to back up multiple computers can reduce costs, but a single tape drive generates network traffic during the backup process, which may actually cost a company money over time. This method also creates a single-point-of-failure vulnerability. Many administrators choose a combination of local and network backup types.

Most backup methods use a file's archive bit. An archive bit indicates whether a file has been changed. When a new file is created or an existing file is modified, the archive bit is set to on, indicating that a backup is necessary. You can view the archive attribute in Windows Explorer when viewing file details. The archive bit displays as a capital A for any file that has changed since the previous backup.

When you back up files or a system, you must choose from one of the following backup types:

- Normal or full

- Differential

- Incremental

- Copy

A *full or normal backup* is also known as a level 0, an archival, or an epochal backup. A full backup copies every selected file on the system to whatever backup device you are using. During the full backup, the archive bit for each file is reset, indicating that an archive (backup) is not needed. This type of backup requires the most storage space and the most time to perform. This option is a necessary part of both the differential and incremental types.

The differential and incremental backup types are similar in one respect: each file that has its archive bit set to on is backed up. However, in a differential backup, the archive bit is not reset; thus the storage size and time requirement increase with each differential backup.

A *differential backup* is usually the easiest to implement and is therefore the most popular. If you are using tape backup, two sets of tapes are necessary. The first tape set contains the full backup as of a certain date. The second set contains a backup of all files created or changed since the full backup, which are resaved with new changes each day. The second tape set will contain increasingly more information, but will probably not accrue as much as the epochal (that is, full) backup tape. This option saves backup time, but requires more time during restoration because you use two tapes.

For example, if you do a normal backup on Friday night (archive bit is reset) and differential backups on Monday, Tuesday, Wednesday, and Thursday, the tape used for Thursday's differential backup contains all the data that has changed since last Friday.

An *incremental backup* strategy uses several sets of tapes (if you are using tape) to archive only those files created or modified since the last backup. A new tape (or set of tapes) is used for each day. Each new tape (or set of tapes) contains only files created or changed that day. The incremental method relies heavily on the archive bit. With this method, the backup program scans the hard disk for files with the archive bit set to on. These files are copied to tape, and the archive bit is reset.

An incremental backup is more complex than a differential backup. When restoring, you must use the archival tape and then restore each tape for each day. This option allows you to spend the least amount of time backing up, but the most amount of time restoring. Also, incremental backups pose the threat of operator error and can force administrators into searching each tape for the proper archive. This option is suitable for slower backup equipment or when archiving many large files.

The *copy method* of backup is similar to the full backup. All selected files on the system are copied, but the archive bit is not reset. This method is frequently used to duplicate data on the system without interfering with the backup strategy (for instance, to send data to a business partner).

Because the archive bit is essential to both the incremental and differential methods, performing a backup without affecting the archive bit may be necessary. The copy method allows you to perform a backup for any reason without resetting the archive bit, thereby not affecting the backup strategy.

In practice, many administrators perform full backups nightly or some combination of the backup types previously mentioned. Here are some examples.

Full backup nightly   This method copies all selected files and requires the most storage space and time to complete. If the system fails, only the most recent full backup is required to completely restore the system.

Full and incremental backups   In this scenario, a full backup is done on Monday, for example, and incremental backups are done on Tuesday through Friday. This method requires less time to back up than the full method, but more time to restore. Incremental backups copy only changed files and reset the archive bit, so a failure on Friday would require all backup archives beginning with Monday for a complete restoration.

Full and differential backups This method involves a full backup on Monday, for example, and differential backups the rest of the week. This method requires more time to back up than the full and incremental combination, but less time to restore. Because a differential backup does not reset the archive bit, if the system fails on Friday, only Monday's full backup and Thursday's archive (containing all changes since Monday) are required to restore the system.

It is vital that you have plans and procedures for reconstructing corrupted data. Your particular restoration procedures will depend on the backup method you use. Plan your restoration procedures according to your backup strategy, and perform trial restorations periodically to a test system or a temporary directory. Although the backup program error log states that the backup was performed successfully, you cannot be sure of success until you actually try a restoration.

> **NOTE** Be careful not to overwrite your production system when performing a trial restoration.

No backup is ever worthwhile unless you have actually verified that the media has accepted the data. As you verify your backup, ensure that your backup media is working properly and is not ready to fail.

Backup software varies from platform to platform. Windows 2000 contains a native utility named Backup. Additional backup utilities exist, including those sold by VERITAS (www.veritas.com).

It is also possible to make simple backups using Windows programs such as WinZip and the Linux tar and gzip utilities.

EXERCISE 16.1

Backing Up and Restoring in Windows 2000

1. Place a floppy disk in your disk drive.

2. Create a folder named C:\backuptest.

3. Open Notepad, and type the word **Important**, and then save the file to the C:\backuptest folder.

4. Choose Start ➢ Programs ➢ Accessories ➢ System Tools ➢ Backup to launch the Backup utility and open the main Backup interface:

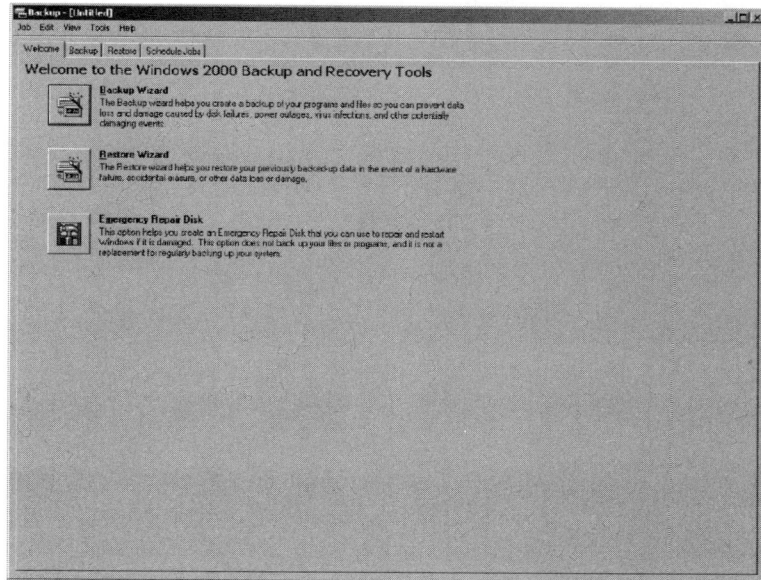

5. Click the Backup Wizard button to open the Welcome to the Windows 2000 Backup and Recovery Tools screen. Click Next to open the What to Back Up screen.

6. Select the Back Up Selected Files, Drives, or Network Data radio button, and then click Next to open the Items to Back Up screen.

7. Your Desktop should appear automatically. Double-click My Computer to open the My Computer folder, and then double-click the C:\ drive. Do not just place a check next to the C:\ drive. If you do so, Backup will try to back up the entire C:\ partition to your floppy drive.

8. Find the C:\backuptest folder you created in Step 2 of this exercise and place a check mark next to the file, as shown in the following graphic:

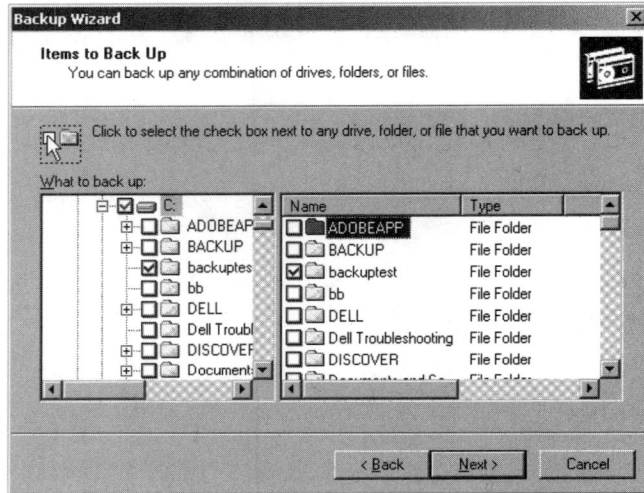

9. Click Next to open the Where to Store Backup screen.

10. In the Backup Media or File Name: text box, enter **A:\ciw.bkf**, and click Next to open the Completing the Backup Wizard screen.(If you do not have a floppy disk handy, you can save this information to your local disk. However, doing so does not allow you to recover from a system fault.)

11. Review your settings, and then click Finish. View the Backup Progress window as the file is archived.

12. Click the Report button to view the report. In all backups, it is vital that you verify that the backup has actually taken place and that the archive is valid.

13. When you have finished viewing the report, close the report and click the Close button.

14. Delete the C:\backuptest folder. Deleting this folder represents a catastrophic event in which important information has been lost.

15. Using the Backup utility main interface, click the Restore Wizard icon. When the Welcome to the Restore Wizard screen appears, click Next to open the What to Restore screen.

16. Expand the File icon, expand the media created icon, and select the C: icon, as shown in the following graphic:

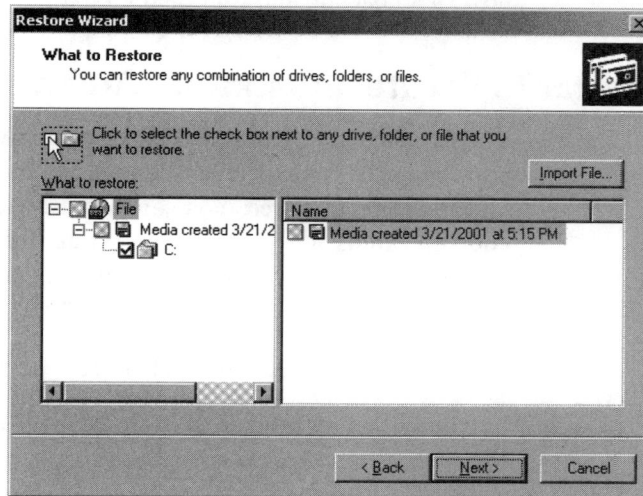

17. Click Next to open the Completing Restore Wizard screen. Review the settings and then click Finish to open the Enter Backup File Name dialog box. Enter **A:\ciw.bkf** and click OK.

18. The restore will proceed. The Restore Progress window will inform you that the backup is finished. Click the Report button to see if the restore was successful. Click Close. Close the main Backup interface. If the restore was not successful, delete the C:\backuptest folder before trying to restore again. By default, restore will not overwrite an existing folder.

19. Use Windows Explorer to verify that the C:\backuptest folder has been restored.

Backing Up in Linux

The fundamentals of backing up and restoring files and systems are universally true regardless of the operating systems used. The implementation details, however, differ from operating system to operating system depending on the tools and utilities used. Earlier, we walked through the backup and restore process in Windows 2000. In this section, we will examine how to do backup and restore in Linux.

Using *tar* to Create and Extract Archives

The tar program creates and extracts archive files. It is a simple tool that you can use to implement a backup program. The tar command can archive an entire directory tree. You can also use the –c option to create archives, and you can use the –x option to extract them back into original form. To create an archive file called archive.tar in the current directory, use the following syntax:

```
host# tar -cf archive.tar top_of_tree_to_be_archived
```

You can extract the archive file archive.tar with the following syntax:

```
host# tar -xf archive.tar
```

> The tar program does not compress archives; it simply creates them. The tar program is valuable as a way to preserve entire directory structures.

The –v option (verbose) is useful because it allows you to monitor how tar works. To list the contents of an archive file without extracting, use the –t option. Table 11.1 summarizes the options for tar.

TABLE 16.1 Options for tar

Option	Purpose
-x	Extracts the archive file
-f file	Specifies the name of the archive file

TABLE 16.1   Options for tar *(continued)*

Option	Purpose
-c	Creates the archive file
-v	Verbose; provides information about the operation taking place
-t	Lists the archive file without extracting

EXERCISE 16.2

Using the *tar* Program in Linux

In this exercise, you will use tar to archive an entire directory.

1. Log on as root.

2. Use the host# cd / command to change to the root directory.

3. Use the host# mkdir backup command to create a new directory off the home directory called backup.

4. Use the host# mkdir /backup/important command to create a subdirectory called important.

5. Copy an assortment of files you would like to archive into the important directory. For example, to copy the /etc/passwd file into the important directory, enter the host# cp /etc/passwd /backup/ important command.

6. Use the *host# tar -cvf backup.tar /backup* command to archive the /backup directory into a file called backup.tar.

7. Use the host# tar -tvf backup.tar command to list the contents of your archive file.

8. Use the mkdir restore command to create a new subdirectory named restore.

9. Use the cp backup.tar /restore command to copy backup.tar into the restore directory.

10. Use the cd restore command to change to the restore directory.

EXERCISE 16.2 *(continued)*

11. Use the host# `tar -xvf backup.tar` command to extract the archive.

Notice that `tar` extracted the entire path so that a subdirectory of your new `_dir` called backup was created.

Using *compress/uncompress* and *gzip/gunzip*

To save space on backup media, you may want to compress files. The `compress/uncompress` and `gzip/gunzip` programs actually compress files and directory structures. These programs are the Linux counterpart to programs such as WinZip. Combined with `tar`, these programs can help ensure that the archives you create will not consume too much space.

The `compress` program uses a patented algorithm, whereas `gzip` uses an open-source algorithm. The `gzip` program is distributed with Linux; it is another example of software available through the GNU project (`ftp://prep.ai.mit.edu`). Given a choice, use `gzip`; it is free from copyright restrictions and is more efficient at compressing files.

Files compressed with the `compress` utility have a `.Z` file name extension, and files compressed with `gzip` have a `.gz` extension. Following is a sequence that uses the `compress` and `gzip` programs:

```
host# compress backup.tar
host# ls
host# backup.tar.Z
host# uncompress stuff.tar
host# ls
host# backup.tar
host# gzip stuff.tar
host# ls
host# backup.tar.gz
host# gunzip backup.tar.gz
host# ls
host# backup.tar
```

Notice that the distinguishing file name extensions (`.Z` and `.gz`) are added and removed by the compression utilities.

EXERCISE 16.3

Compressing and Decompressing Files

In this exercise, you will experiment with gzip and compress to learn more about compressing tar archives.

1. As root, locate the backup.tar archive.

2. Use the host# ls -l backup.tar command to list the archive.

3. In the space provided, write the size of the archive: _____

4. Use the host# gzip backup.tar command to compress the archive.

5. List the file again. What is the size of the file now? Write your answer in the space provided: _____.

6. Decompress the archive with gunzip.

7. Repeat these steps using compress and uncompress, and compare your output.

Using *dump* and *restore*

The dump and restore programs are common to many flavors of Unix, including Linux. The dump command creates archives that you can save to Zip disks, tapes, and CD-ROM jukeboxes.

The syntax for using dump is as follows:

```
dump epoch number options
```

The epoch number tells dump whether to perform a full, differential, or incremental backup. When you first use dump to create an archive, this number should always be 0. For subsequent differential updates, you can specify 1, 2, and so forth. (For more information, see the man files on dump.)

The common options for dump include u and f. The u option updates the etc/dumpdates file, which informs you about the last time you used the program. The f option allows you to specify a device. For example, a tape drive often has a file name of /dev/ht0. For example, to dump the /etc/ directory to the /dev/ht0 drive for the first time, enter the following:

```
host# dump -0uf /dev/ht0 /etc/
```

The `restore` command is interactive. Once you begin a restore session, you can specify commands to list the contents of a dump archive, change directories, and extract specific archive elements.

The syntax for the restore program is as follows: `restore if device`. The letters `if` specify interactive mode (which allows you to issue various commands once in the restore program), and `f` specifies the name of the device file. For example, if you have a tape device named `/dev/ht0`, enter `restore if /dev/ht0`. Once in the restore program, you can issue various commands, including the following.

- `cd` (changes directories)

- `ls` (lists the contents of a dump file)

- `add` (adds a specific archive that you must name to a list of files to be extracted)

- `extract` (tells `restore` to extract the file to the hard drive)

- `help` (provides information on how to use restore)

- `delete` (allows you to delete contents from a dump archive)

- `quit` (stops the restore session)

By default, the `restore` program restores files to the directory in which you issued the command.

Disaster Assessment and Recovery

When a file, or group of files, is lost, you can always turn to your backup set and recover what you need. What do you do, however, when the problem you are faced with is exponentially greater than just a lost folder? When a natural disaster, such as a fire or flood, takes away your server(s)?

This is the realm of planning and administration known as disaster assessment and recovery. In this section, we'll look at how to recover—so that data can then be restored—in a variety of ways.

Creating and Using a Boot Disk

The Windows 2000 boot disk starts a Windows 2000 system that has missing or corrupted files in the system partition and therefore will not boot properly. Each floppy disk is specific to each Windows 2000 computer, so you must create a separate boot disk for each physical server or workstation.

To create a Windows 2000 boot disk, follow these steps:

1. Insert a floppy disk in drive A.

2. Open Windows Explorer, right-click the A drive, and choose Format to open the Format dialog box.

3. Format the floppy disk.

4. Once the disk is formatted, copy the following files from your C:\ directory to your floppy drive:

   - Ntldr
   - Ntdetect.com
   - Boot.ini
   - Ntbootdd.sys (if it appears)

> **NOTE** The bootsect.dos file enables dual-boot machines to choose operating systems. If you have a SCSI disk, you will also have to copy the ntbootdd.sys file. You can copy these files from any working Windows 2000 system, as long as the boot information is the same. If the information is different, you can use a text editor to change the required values.

5. With the boot disk in drive A, restart the system and log on as administrator.

6. Remove the boot disk from drive A and restart the system. Log on as administrator.

The best way to recover from a Linux bootup problem is to use the installation CD. This bootable CD contains all the files you need to investigate common problems. Should you want to create a Linux emergency boot disk on a floppy disk, use the mkbootdisk program. The mkbootdisk program needs to know the exact kernel image from which your Linux system has booted. You can discover this by reading the /etc/lilo.conf file or by using the uname -a command and reading the output. When using this program, you must make sure that you have not previously mounted the disk.

If, for example, you have a Linux system with the 2.4.16-22 kernel, issue the following command:

```
/sbin/mkbootdisk –device /dev/fd0 2.4.16-22
```

This command runs mkbootdisk and specifies the device (in this case, the floppy disk) and the kernel version. The system will then find the existing partitions, and the boot process will continue until you reach a command prompt.

1. Follow these steps to build a Linux boot disk:

2. Boot into Linux as root.

3. Use the host# uname -a command to learn your kernel version.

4. Using the kernel version, use the /sbin/mkbootdisk –device /dev/ fd0 *kernel_version* command to create a boot floppy.

5. Once the disk is created, leave it in your floppy drive and reboot your system.

6. As the system reboots, enter CMOS to make sure that your system is configured to boot from your floppy disk.

7. When the system reads your disk, you will see a LILO prompt. Type **linux** and then press Enter. The system will boot from the floppy, then go directly to the operating system.

Windows 2000 System State Data

Windows 2000 uses the term "system state data" to refer to the configuration and database files necessary for the system to run properly. All system state data files are crucial to a backup of a Windows 2000 server. System state data includes the following.

- All boot files
- System files (for example, io.sys)
- The Registry
- The Certificate Server database (if the server is a certificate authority)
- All Active Directory databases, if applicable

- Cluster server databases (if the server is acting as a cluster server)
- The COM+ Registration database
- The SYSVOL directory (if the system is acting as a domain controller)

You can back up system state data using the Windows 2000 Backup utility. System state data can occupy hundreds of megabytes, so you must back it up to a tape drive or to another system. You will probably need this information to fully recover if Windows fails to start.

The Windows Emergency Repair Disk

You use the Windows Emergency Repair Disk (ERD) to restore the Registry or critical files that have been corrupted. Create an ERD when a Windows 2000 system is installed and then regularly update it, particularly after major changes (program installations, added or deleted users, and so forth).

To create an ERD and back up the user accounts database, follow these steps:

1. Launch the Backup utility.
2. Click the Emergency Repair Disk button to open the Emergency Repair Diskette dialog box.
3. Insert a floppy disk into the floppy drive.
4. Select the check box that also lets you back up your Registry.
5. Click OK.
6. The disk will be formatted, and files will be copied.
7. You will be informed that the disk was created successfully. Click OK.
8. You now have a disk that can help you recover from a catastrophic Windows 2000 crash. To fully recover, you may also need to obtain the system state data, as well as additional files.

Windows 2000 Safe Mode

Windows Safe Mode lets you start your system with a minimal set of device drivers. If you've recently installed drivers that are preventing your system from starting, for example, you can start the computer in Safe Mode and then remove the guilty drivers. To enter Safe Mode, press the F8 key as Windows begins to load; the Windows 2000 Advanced Options menu will appear. Table 16.2 shows the Safe Mode options available. Use the arrow keys to highlight the appropriate option, and then press Enter.

TABLE 16.2   Safe Mode Options

Safe Mode Option	Description
Safe Mode	Loads Windows 2000 into a crude GUI display. No networking is enabled.
Safe Mode with Networking	The same as Safe Mode, except the system can communicate on the network.
Safe Mode with Command Prompt	Places Windows 2000 into command line–only mode. The display is still somewhat graphical, but this mode is easier for administrators with experience using the command line.
Enable VGA Mode	Allows you to install a new video driver.
Enable Boot Logging	Allows the system to log all successful and unsuccessful device driver attempts into the C:\ntbtlog.txt file.
Last Known Good Configuration	Causes Windows 2000 to use a stored copy of the Registry that does not contain any problematic device drivers. This option is designed to allow you to log on successfully. You must still resolve the problem with the device driver, but at least the system will function without requiring a full restoration.
Directory Services Restore Mode	Allows you to restore Active Directory, if installed.
Debugging Mode	Enables you to send boot logging information to another computer using a serial cable.

Troubleshooting Linux

You have seen how to create boot disks and then rescue your Windows 2000 system from a catastrophic failure. In Linux, you have several recovery options. Three of the more handy options are as follows.

Booting into single mode If you can boot the system, but a dysfunctional service hangs the logon process, you can go into Linux single mode and disable that service. Linux single mode is also helpful when you want to troubleshoot broken X server (graphics) installations. In many ways, Linux single mode is the same thing as Windows Safe Mode.

Using Linux Interactive mode When the system boots, press Shift+I, and you will be asked to confirm whether you want to start each service.

Using the installation CD as a rescue disk If the system will not boot, insert the installation CD-ROM, type **linux rescue,** and then mount the system to perform the repair. For example, if you have a sound card that is causing a boot problem, use the rescue disk to mount the disk.

Summary

In this chapter, you learned about fault tolerance and data-protection concepts, including hard drive redundancy, power protection and RAID, removable media, and backup options. You learned how to reconstruct data that has been corrupted or deleted and how to implement procedures for disaster assessment. Backup methods were discussed, and steps for planning a backup strategy were detailed.

Backup strategies include using `tar`, `gzip`, `dump`, and `restore` and the Windows 2000 Backup utility.

You also learned how to recover from boot errors by creating and using emergency boot disks. You learned how to restore a Windows 2000 system to its last known usable boot settings and how to troubleshoot a failed Linux system. Using tools and techniques such as these, you will be able to protect against and recover from system failures.

With this knowledge, you should now be able to identify ways to create fault tolerance in a network host; explain the concept of offsite storage; implement procedures for disaster assessment; follow a data-recovery strategy; and implement recovery procedures to repair corrupted data.

Exam Essentials

Know the levels of RAID and when to use them. RAID 0, disk striping, is not fault tolerant but provides the fastest speed for temporary files and doesn't waste any space for redundancy. It uses two or more disks. RAID 1, disk mirroring, uses 50 percent of the space for redundancy and uses two disks. For a small business, this level is preferable because it requires the fewest disks to achieve fault tolerance. The only software RAID solution that can be used with the system and boot partition of Windows 2000 is RAID 1. RAID 5, disk striping with parity, uses three or more disks with the parity stripe distributed in turn among the disks. The equivalent of one disk's worth of data is used for fault tolerance. RAID 5 has excellent read performance and is commonly used for data and programs. Windows 2000 supports RAID 0, 1, and 5 in software. Hardware RAID solutions provide better performance, and often the disks are hot-swappable in the event of a failure; however, the cost is higher, the solution is proprietary, and you are locked into a vendor.

Understand when to implement additional fault-tolerant measures. A UPS is essential to fault tolerance, not only for servers but also for any critical computers, such as a web developer's computer. Buy motherboards that have redundant power supplies that are hot-swappable if possible, and consider hot-swappable PCI cards, such as NICs. If your website has problems, you might want a backup set of folders for your website and then redirect your website to a backup folder that has a copy of your website. As your business grows, you might have multiple websites that mirror one another and provide fault tolerance and load balancing.

Know that even if you have RAID, you need backups. Your hard disks may be intact, but what if the data is corrupted, a user maliciously or unintentionally deletes a critical directory, or you get a virus? You need backups. Back up each workday of the week and archive a backup for each week of the month, for each month of the year, and possibly for a few years. When you follow such a procedure, you have the best chance to recover a file that was corrupted or deleted and not noticed for a long period of time. Store a backup offsite in case of a natural disaster, and test your backups to verify that they actually work.

Know when to use a normal, a differential, or an incremental backup. Always start with a normal backup that backs up everything and clears the archive bit that marks a file as needing to be backed up. If your business is small and backups can be scheduled and completed off-hours, you might do only normal backups. As your business grows, and the time to back up intrudes on work hours, you might start with a normal backup the last day of the week and do differential backups the other days. Differential backups back up all files that have the archive bit set and do not clear the archive bit. If you do a differential backup on a Monday and a Tuesday, the Monday backup backs up all files since the last full backup, and the Tuesday file does the same, overlapping the Monday file. The size of the differential backups grow throughout the week until you do a normal backup. Using this method, if a file is corrupted, you have to search at most two tapes, the latest differential backup and the normal backup. A yet faster backup method is an incremental backup, which backs up the files with the archive bit set and clears the archive bit. Using this method, if you do an incremental backup on a Monday and a Tuesday after a full backup on a Friday, the Monday backup gets the files that changed since the full backup, and the Tuesday backup gets only the files that changed since Monday's backup. An incremental backup is quicker to back up, but possibly slower to restore. You might have to go through all the incremental backups for the week and the last normal backup to find a file.

Know the Linux backup and compression utilities. You can use the `tar` program to archive and extract files in Linux. Know the switches. The `dump` and `restore` programs are common to many flavors of Unix and Linux, and you can also use them to archive and extract files from tapes, Zip disks, and CD-ROM jukeboxes. To save space on backup media, you might want to compress directories. You can use the `gzip` program to compress files, and you can use the `gunzip` program to uncompress files.

Key Terms

Before taking the exam, you should be familiar with the following terms:

denial-of-service attack	fault tolerance
disk duplexing	folder replication
disk mirroring	Redundant Array of Inexpensive Disks (RAID)
disk striping	site mirroring
disk striping with parity	uninterruptible power supply (UPS)

Review Questions

1. Jim wants to keep a server crash from denying services to customers. What should he implement?

   A. A backup strategy

   B. A recovery strategy

   C. Fault-tolerance measures

   D. A firewall

2. Mike creates a boot disk and a rescue disk. Which type of measures is Mike implementing?

   A. Fault tolerance

   B. Disaster recovery

   C. Backup

   D. RAID

3. Brad wants to implement fault tolerance for the SQL 2000 database files. Which level of RAID should Brad use?

   A. RAID 0

   B. RAID 1

   C. RAID 4

   D. RAID 5

4. Jim downloads gigabyte-sized graphics files from the Hubble telescope. He wants the fastest fault-tolerant solution for his Unix server that stores these files. What should Jim implement?

   A. Software RAID 5

   B. Hardware RAID 5

   C. Software RAID 4

   D. Hardware RAID 4

5. Brad is using Windows 2000 Advanced Server in a cluster in which two servers are using one RAID array. If one server fails, the other server picks up the load. Brad wants the most fault-tolerant RAID array for this cluster. Which RAID level should Brad implement?

A. RAID 0

B. RAID 1

C. RAID 4

D. RAID 5

E. RAID 10

6. Mike wants to create an Emergency Repair Disk. Which command or utility can he use to create an Emergency Repair Disk in Windows 2000?

A. Start ➤ Run ➤ rdisk

B. The Windows 2000 Backup Utility

C. Active Directory Users and Computers

D. Disk Management MMC

7. Sandy wants the fastest disk performance for temporary database files. Which RAID level should Sandy implement?

A. RAID 0

B. RAID 1

C. RAID 4

D. RAID 5

E. RAID 10

8. The ability to use hardware or software to increase storage and/or access speed by making multiple smaller disks act as one logical disk is called what?

A. Compression

B. Site mirroring

C. Backup

D. RAID

9. Brad wants to implement fault tolerance for a small business. Which fault-tolerant solution uses the fewest disks?

   A. RAID 0

   B. RAID 1

   C. RAID 4

   D. RAID 5

   E. RAID 10

10. What is the most important step to take after you create a backup?

   A. Remove the tape so it is not overwritten.

   B. Read the backup log.

   C. Take the backup offsite.

   D. Verify the data.

11. Which two measures should Mike take to ensure continuous power to his Internet server?

   A. Install a UPS.

   B. Isolate the circuit that supplies power to the server room.

   C. Install a transformer-rectifier (TR).

   D. Use a motherboard with two redundant power supplies.

12. Jody's company, San Francisco Style, buys New York Designs. For fault tolerance, load balancing, and speedier access to their websites over the Internet, what should Jody consider?

   A. Site mirroring

   B. Site redirection

   C. Folder replication

   D. A reverse proxy array

13. Frank needs to back up 500MB of transactions each evening and keep the backup for a year. What is the best backup medium?

   A. Hard drive

   B. Tape

   C. Zip disk

   D. CD

14. You have just loaded a new video driver into your Windows 2000 Server system. Now your system boots, but you cannot use the display. Which of the following options uses a copy of the Registry that does not include the new device driver to start your machine?

   A. Safe Mode

   B. Last Known Good Configuration

   C. Safe Mode with Command Prompt

   D. Enable VGA Mode

15. Mandy wants to use a backup strategy that usually takes no more than two tapes to perform a restore for any missing file. Which two backup strategies would work?

   A. Normal backups Monday through Friday

   B. Normal backup on a Friday and incremental backups Monday through Thursday

   C. Normal backup on a Friday and differential backups Monday through Thursday

   D. Differential backups Monday through Friday

16. A good backup strategy includes which elements? Choose five.

   A. Determining the medium to use

   B. Determining which files to back up

   C. Choosing local or network backup types

   D. Selecting a backup method

   E. Planning and practicing restoration procedures

   F. Verifying the data

17. GreatDomains.com has 20 Linux servers. Which fault-tolerant measures should GreatDomains.com implement? Choose two.

   A. Backups

   B. UPS

   C. RAID

   D. Recovery Console

   E. Using the Linux CD as a rescue disk

18. You are planning a data recovery strategy. Your site specializes in Computer Aided Design (CAD) and thus creates many very large files. You want to create backups quickly and are not concerned with the time to restore the backup. Which method should you choose?

   A. Full

   B. Mirror

   C. Incremental

   D. Differential

19. Peter wants to extract the Linux archive file archive.tar. Which command should Peter issue?

   A. host# tar -xf archive.tar

   B. host# tar -cf archive.tar

   C. host# tar -t archive.tar

   D. host# tar -e archive.tar

20. The Master Boot Record on your Linux system has been overwritten. You know that the operating system is fine, but you cannot get to it. What should you do?

   A. Enter into Linux single mode.

   B. Use a Linux boot disk.

   C. Use an Emergency Repair Disk.

   D. Use the mkbootdisk command.

Answers to Review Questions

1. C. Fault-tolerance measures are efforts to keep a server crash from denying services to customers.

2. B. Disaster recovery is a procedure used to repair machines and data after a problem has occurred.

3. D. RAID 5 provides the fastest read performance for data files and uses the least space for redundancy.

4. D. Hardware implementations of RAID are faster than software implementations. RAID 4 uses a single disk to store parity information and provides the highest read performance when large blocks of data are stored.

5. E. RAID level 10 is two mirrored RAID 5 arrays.

6. B. Start ➤ Run ➤ rdisk worked in NT 4, but in Windows 2000 you use the Backup Utility to create an Emergency Repair Disk.

7. A. RAID level 0 is not a fault-tolerant solution, but it provides the fastest performance.

8. D. Redundant Array of Inexpensive disks (RAID) uses hardware or software to increase storage and/or access speed by making multiple smaller disks act as one logical disk.

9. B. RAID level 1 provides disk mirroring, which uses two disks.

10. D. The most important step to take after you create a backup is to verify the data.

11. A, D. Mike should install a UPS and use a motherboard with redundant power supplies.

12. A. Jody should consider having both websites mirrored at both locations so that if one location goes down, customers can still buy from the other location.

13. D. For up to 700MB of data, CDs are the least expensive medium and take the least space to archive; also the write speeds are respectable.

14. B. You can use the Last Known Good Configuration to point toward the old driver as long as it has not been overwritten and the user has not logged on after rebooting.

15. A, C. A series of normal backups take only the most current tape to restore a missing file. A normal backup followed by a series of differential backups should have any missing file on the latest differential of the latest normal backup tape.

16. B, C, D, E, F. A good backup strategy includes these five elements: determining which files to back up; choosing local or network backup types; selecting a backup method; planning and practicing restore procedures; and verifying the data.

17. B, C. Redundant Array of Inexpensive Disks (RAID) and UPSs are fault-tolerance measures.

18. C. Incremental backups take the least time to make and the most time to restore.

19. A. The host# `tar -xf archive.tar` command extracts `archive.tar`.

20. B. A Linux boot disk has a copy of the Master Boot Record.

Chapter

17

Proxy Servers and Security Overview

THE CIW EXAM OBJECTIVE GROUPS COVERED IN THIS CHAPTER:

✓ Install and configure proxy servers and Internet servers.

✓ Identify internal and external security risks, including but not limited to: operating system features and vulnerabilities, firewalls, log file analysis.

Everyone agrees that security is a good thing, in much the same way everyone agrees that stray dogs can be dangerous. Once you move beyond the generalization and into specifics, however, the consensus begins to fade, and it becomes clear that what security means to one administrator is different from what it means to another.

The CIW exam focuses only on web technologies and methods for implementing security on those technologies. The primary focus is on proxy servers (which provide caching, filtering, and network address translation [NAT]) and firewalls, with some coverage of web servers. A proxy server is a type of firewall and one of the most commonly implemented types of firewalls.

This is the last chapter in the book, but hopefully the beginning of a safe Internet experience.

Proxy Servers

A *proxy server* is a server that acts as an intermediary between client computers and the Internet and that processes many types of network traffic, including HTTP, FTP, Telnet, and POP3. You can use a proxy server to do the following:

Reduce costs   A proxy server allows a private network to share one Internet connection among many hosts. This connection can be anything from a slow dial-up shared between two or three employees, to a high-speed DSL (Digital Subscriber Line) connection servicing the entire office.

Enforce security   A sophisticated proxy server can invoke access control, allowing only specific users into or out of the private network. A proxy server also allows end users to use essential business protocols, such as web browsers and e-mail clients, without the risk of a direct connection to the Internet.

Increase bandwidth efficiency   A web proxy server can store retrieved pages for web clients to use later. A competent proxy server updates its cache regularly to ensure that clients receive current information. Because web proxy servers store current information, less traffic has to pass through network routers, which helps to eliminate network congestion and to speed connectivity.

Improve logging   A proxy server can log activity, which helps you learn about the nature of traffic going into and out of a particular subnet. The logs created can be invaluable when attempting to find the source of immoral attempts by external users to access data.

Network Address Translation (NAT)

Because a proxy server performs *Network Address Translation (NAT)*, a proxy server needs only one public IP address that is valid on the Internet. It can translate this one public IP address to all the private internal network addresses in use by an enterprise. Every enterprise can use private IP addresses, even though other enterprises are using them, because Internet routers ignore packets from these addresses. NAT gives a proxy server the ability to act as a mediator between a public and private network. RFC 1918 discusses the use of the following private IP addresses that are not routable to the Internet:

- 10.0.0.0 (subnet mask of 255.0.0.0).

- 172.16.0.0 to 172.31.255.255 (subnet mask of 255.240.0.0).

- 192.168.0.0 (subnet mask of 255.255.0.0).

Although it is not necessary to use these IP addresses for your LAN, doing so is useful because you do not need to register these addresses. You will need a registered IP address for your proxy server, however, so that all internal clients can access necessary services (HTTP, FTP, POP3, and so forth).

To engage in NAT, advanced proxy servers require that you define a pool of valid internal IP addresses. Microsoft Proxy Server calls this pool of addresses a local address table (LAT).

When a user on a private network requests web pages from the Internet, the client host forwards the requests to a proxy server, as shown in Figure 17.1. The proxy server can then relay the request to the Internet and hide the internal IP address, serve the page from a cached file, or simply deny access.

FIGURE 17.1 Connecting to proxy server

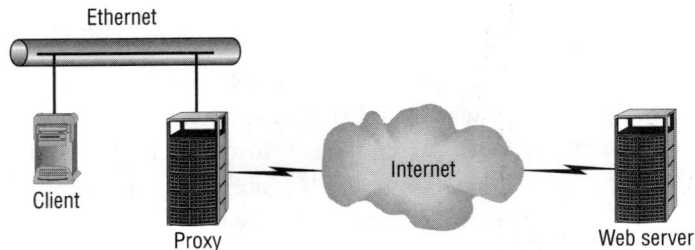

Modifying Clients

One of the benefits of a proxy server is that it protects clients. A proxy server client is not directly connected to the Internet; the client communicates with the Internet via the proxy server. The process of configuring a client to communicate with a proxy server is called client modification.

You can modify a client in two ways.

- By adding a service onto the client's operating system so that it captures and forwards requests to the proxy server.

- By configuring applications on the client to forward requests to the host acting as the proxy server. For example, most web browsers and e-mail clients contain settings that allow you to configure proxy support on an application-by-application basis.

Generally, modifying a client involves specifying the following:

- The location of the proxy server by its DNS name or IP address

- The port of the proxy server

In Internet Explorer, to connect to a proxy server using port 88, follow these steps.

1. Double-click the Internet Explorer icon on your Desktop to open Internet Explorer.

2. Choose Tools ➢ Internet Options to open the Internet Options dialog box.

3. Click the Connections tab, and then click the LAN Settings button to open the Local Area Network (LAN) Settings dialog box.

4. In the Proxy Server section, click the Use a Proxy Server for Your LAN check box.

5. In the Address box, enter the IP address of your proxy server, and in the Port box, enter 88.

6. Click OK to close the Local Area Network (LAN) Settings dialog box, and then click OK again to close the Internet Options dialog box.

7. Close and reopen Internet Explorer. You should now connect to websites through your proxy server.

Advanced users may try to bypass your proxy server by discovering your default gateway and using it directly. One way to prevent such access is to configure your default gateway so that it rejects connections from all hosts except your proxy server.

As you plan your proxy server, be aware that you will need a software license that allows enough connections for all your users. If you choose a license with fewer connections than the number of users you have, be sure that you study your usage patterns carefully. Otherwise, users will become frustrated if they cannot access the Internet during peak hours.

Finally, the single largest cause of proxy server problems is client misconfiguration. Usually, the server functions well once you configure it properly. As you install new systems, be sure that you take the time to properly configure all e-mail, news, and web clients to access the proxy server.

EXERCISE 17.1

Configuring Apache Server as a Web Proxy Server

In this exercise, you will configure Apache Server 1.3.12-25 to cache HTML documents.

1. Boot into Linux and log in as root.

2. Use the host# `cd /var/cache/httpd` command to change to the /var/cache/httpd directory.

3. List the contents of this directory. If this server has never been used as a proxy server, the contents of this directory will be empty.

4. Use the `vi httpd.conf` command to open the /etc/httpd/conf/httpd.conf file.

5. You must uncomment several lines before you can activate the server. First, find the LoadModule proxy_module modules/libproxy.so line and uncomment it. This line loads the proxy server module.

6. Now, find the line that reads AddModule mod_proxy.c. and uncomment it. This line enables the actual authentication portion of Apache's proxy server. (Failure to uncomment either of these lines will cause Apache server's proxy server to fail.)

7. You are now ready to uncomment the entries that will allow users to access the proxy server. Find the <ifModule mod_proxy.c> section, and then uncomment and modify the lines so that you have the following:

```
<IfModule mod_proxy.c>

ProxyRequests On


<Directory proxy:*>

    Order deny,allow

    Deny from none

    Allow from all

</Directory>


ProxyVia Full




CacheRoot "/var/cache/httpd"

CacheSize 5

CacheGcInterval 4
```

CacheMaxExpire 24

CacheLastModifiedFactor 0.1

CacheDefaultExpire 1

NoCache a_domain.com another_domain.edu joes.garage_
sale.com

</IfModule>

Uncomment only the lines given above. You will only need to change the Deny from all line *to* Deny from none.

The first section enables the proxy server. The second line, ProxyVia Full, allows your proxy server to handle all browser requests. The last section (CacheRoot) enables the server to store cached files from clients in the /var/cache/httpd directory.

8. Exit vi, making sure to save changes by pressing Esc and typing **ZZ**.

9. Use the /etc/rc.d/init.d/httpd restart command to completely stop and restart httpd.

10. On a client computer, boot into Windows 2000 and configure a browser to use your Linux system as a proxy. When configuring your client, specify port 80. Apache server can serve documents and act as a caching server on this port. In Internet Explorer, choose Tools ➤ Internet Options to open the Internet Options dialog box. Click the Connections tab. Click the LAN Settings button to open the Local Area Network (LAN) Settings dialog box. Click the Use a Proxy Server check box, enter the IP address of the Apache server, and enter 80 as the port number. Use your browser to investigate some websites.

11. To test whether the cache is working on the Apache server, view the files in the /var/cache/httpd directory. Do this only after a client has used your proxy server to view some websites. This directory should be populated with directories and documents.

System Security

The best way to achieve effective systems security is to implement a combination of systems and security products and protocols. Today's networks have become so complex that you can never really be sure a web server is secure. Therefore, the first principle of security is to be more cautious than you think is necessary. Subsequently, if you properly secure the operating system, the web service running on it will be more secure. If the web server's security is circumvented, the operating system's security settings will help mitigate the damage. Because the web server and operating system run at different levels, you can implement an effective redundant security model.

Regardless of which operating system you are running (Unix, Windows 2000, NetWare, and so forth), the operating system is vulnerable in several areas. Every operating system has security-related problems. When you implement your security solution, however, you can identify specific security issues and regularly analyze your servers to look for problems.

Operating system upgrades offer a way to address specific security problems. Frequently, the latest version of an operating system will solve some problems of the previous version. However, this new version may have new problems, often in completely different areas. For this reason, consider operating system security on an area-by-area basis:

Carefully analyze all permissions granted to users and groups. Your goal should be to allow the most restricted level of access for each user and/or group that still allows users to perform their jobs. Carefully examine any default accounts and remove, reset, or rename them as appropriate. When deciding which accounts to create on a particular host, determine the role that host will play in your network. If your host is an internal computer with no direct access to the Internet, you can create many user and group accounts without a security risk. If your host has direct access to the Internet, limit the number of accounts you create. Crackers often try to gain access to a host through a poorly secured user account.

Create special accounts for your public servers. For example, your web server should have its own account that the web service or daemon uses to access resources. By creating a special account, you can restrict the web service or daemon to particular areas on the server.

When you create accounts for system services, be sure to divide them by resource, and restrict them to the minimum access needed to accomplish their tasks. For example, if a server acts as both a web server and an FTP server, create two special accounts. The FTP service will use one account to access resources through the operating system, and the web server will use the other account. This technique increases security by restricting access to only the resources needed by each service. If a cracker obtains the account for the FTP service, they cannot access any of the resources owned by the web server.

When first installed, most operating systems allow users nearly unlimited access to files. Secure individual directories and programs on your system as quickly as possible. Do not take shortcuts with your file system. Tools are available to help you with this process.

You can often enhance security by partitioning the physical disk on your server. Restricting a service's or a daemon's access to a specific partition protects the operating system and other daemons in case one service is compromised or the partition's disk space is filled to capacity. The drawback to this solution is that it requires a great deal of preliminary planning and additional administrative costs. Still, the resulting increase in security is worth your time and resources. Typically, you can configure a hard disk so that one partition is used for the operating system only, another is used for the services or daemons running on the server, and a third is used for data storage only.

Crackers often try to penetrate sites as legitimate users. If a cracker obtains a valid user account and the corresponding password, they can bypass security mechanisms and open any resource to which the user account has access. Given enough time, any password can be cracked. The risk of this threat is greatly reduced by establishing proper operating system policies.

Operating system policies help users work securely by enforcing choices that guard against system attacks. For example, many policies require a minimum password length, maximum password age, restricted logons, and so forth. Such limitations help users create and maintain proper passwords and are enforced at the operating system level.

Do as much work as you can using a nonadministrative account. In Linux, for example, assert root privileges using the su command only when necessary, such as when you have to restart a daemon or edit a root-owned configuration file. You will find that working as a nonadministrative user has few limitations, as far as doing most of your user-level work is concerned (for example, checking e-mail and the like). Also, you will find that many user-oriented system features, such as screen savers, become available to you.

System defaults are the out-of-the-box settings the system uses if you do not alter them upon installation. Most systems are preconfigured with defaults because the manufacturer wants to make it easy for administrators and users to initialize and run the system. Competent crackers have comprehensive lists of system defaults for each operating system. If a systems administrator leaves the setting of an account at the default, a cracker can access the account without logging on to the system.

Many operating systems have support accounts designed to grant the manufacturer access in case of a problem. Because crackers know the location, configuration, user name, and password of such accounts, leaving your operating system configured with default settings is an invitation for unauthorized entry.

For example, in Windows 2000, the administration account is set to Administrator by default. You cannot lock out this account due to incorrect logon attempts because it is designed to allow new administrators to learn the logon process. This default also helps prevent denial-of-service attacks, in which a cracker logs on as the administrator with the wrong password and thereby prevents the true administrator from logging on. Unfortunately, the default setting also allows a cracker to assault your system with a brute-force attack. For this reason, change all default settings. You can change the name of the administrator account using the Local Security Policy snap-in. The actual setting that changes the Registry is found in the Security Options section. Exercise 17.2 walks you through this process.

EXERCISE 17.2

Changing the Name of the Administrator Account in Windows 2000

1. Make certain you are logged in with administrative permissions.

2. Choose Start ➤ Programs ➤ Administrative Tools ➤ Local Security Policy to open the Local Security Policy snap-in.

3. Expand Local Policies, and then expand Security Options.

4. Double-click Rename Administrator Account, which has a default of Not Defined.

5. In the Local Policy Setting text box, enter the name of the account to be used in place of Administrator as the new top-level user account.

6. Click OK to exit the setting, and then close the Local Security Policy snap-in.

Almost all operating systems have well-documented problems that allow illicit users an opportunity for malicious activity. Such bugs range from very minor to extremely dangerous. Whenever you load an operating system for the first time or upgrade an existing one, contact the vendor for a list of known problems. In many cases, you can also obtain patches, fixes, and workarounds for various problems. Stay informed about an operating system's weaknesses by monitoring the vendor's website to learn whether any new security holes have been discovered. Vendors usually respond quickly when a new exploit is found for a particular piece of software; however, vendors do not usually contact their customers with such information. Each security administrator must stay current with all security-related issues.

To stay informed, subscribe to industry magazines and frequently visit the vendor's website. Regularly scanning security-related newsgroups and security websites is also helpful. For example, the mailing list for the NTBugtraq site (`www.ntbugtraq.com`), shown in Figure 17.2, keeps users informed about the latest Windows 2000 issues.

FIGURE 17.2   The NTBugtraq website

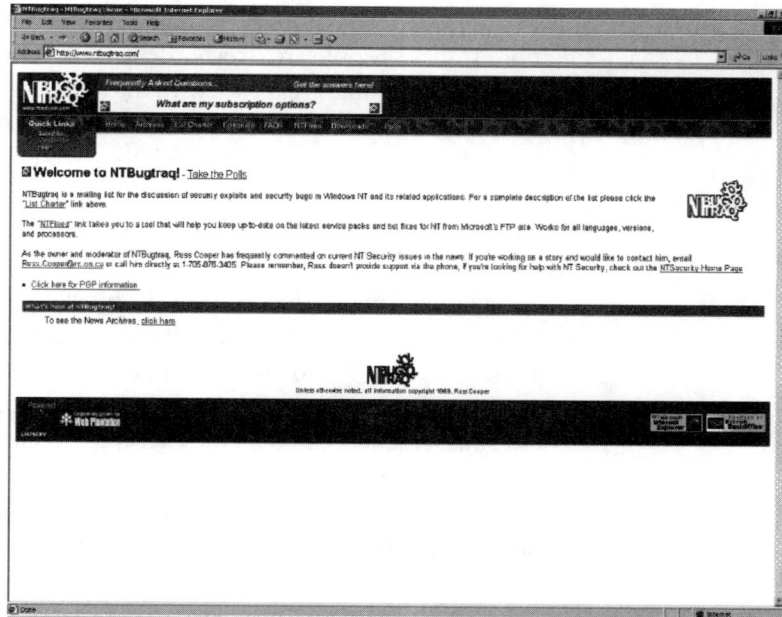

Some additional websites that contain news about the latest system bugs include the following:

- Microsoft Web Security Advisor (www.microsoft.com/security)

- Linux Security (www.linuxsecurity.com)

- Red Hat Bugzilla (http://bugzilla.redhat.com)

Enhancing Server Security

You can strengthen even areas of the server that are not problematic. You can audit your system, secure the Windows 2000 Registry, enable shadow passwords, and remove unnecessary services from your system.

As you have already learned, auditing is critical to your security infrastructure. Without it, you cannot determine whether your security is effective or if dangerous breaches have occurred. Most operating systems require you to explicitly enable the auditing function. Choose the systems you will audit carefully. If you audit too little activity, unacceptable activity can go undetected. If you audit too much, you place an undue burden on the system and create extra work for the administrators who must interpret the information. If these people are overburdened, they might miss illicit activity.

You must also take great care with the log files themselves. A cracker who penetrates your system will immediately attempt to destroy evidence of their activities by locating the log files and destroying or modifying them. Secure log files so that only the most privileged accounts of the operating system can access or write to them. Also change the default location where log files are stored.

In older versions of Unix, one of the most common problem areas is the file that contains the user account database: the passwd file. This file contains an encrypted version of all user account passwords on the system. The permissions for this file must allow all accounts to read for various operations. Thus, crackers can read the encrypted version of a user's account and then run the encrypted value through a brute-force attack, in which the cracker tries every possible password combination and compares the results to the encrypted version. Once a match is found, the cracker has the password for that account.

Newer Unix systems now use a shadow file for password storage (Red Hat Linux enables shadow passwords by default). The password information has been removed from the passwd file and is now stored in a special file, often called the `/etc/shadow` file. The control permissions for the shadow file allow access to only the most privileged account. Check your version of Unix to make sure that password shadowing is available and enabled.

After you implement security on your operating system, remove any services that you do not specifically require. Removing unnecessary services gives potential crackers fewer targets. If you were going to use a building for a secure purpose, you would not choose one with many doors and windows. Unnecessary services or daemons on a server are comparable to these excess openings. For example, if you are running a web server on Windows 2000, you can eliminate such items as the OS/2 and POSIX subsystems, and you can disable the NetBIOS server services. These actions increase security without affecting your web server's operations.

Firewalls, Intrusion Detection Systems, and Server Log Files

Use firewalls to prevent intrusions in so far as possible, and use intrusion detection systems and/or analyze the server log files to recognize any intrusions that make it past your firewall. For example, most snooping on your network is done by employees, and even those outside the network that are determined and expert crackers will generally have some success. Nevertheless, firewalls are an essential element of any security package and, in general, deter all but the best crackers.

The primary purpose of a firewall is to create a perimeter that protects your private network from other public networks. A firewall can also do the following:

- Enhance logging and authentication
- Encrypt transmissions between hosts and/or networks by means of a Virtual Private Network (VPN)
- Provide enhanced security to dial-up customers

Firewalls generally default to one of two types of behavior:

- Reject all traffic unless it is explicitly permitted
- Allow all traffic and then explicitly deny specific types

Table 17.1 describes firewall types.

TABLE 17.1 Firewall Types

Type	Description
Packet filter	A router or other device that inspects the source IP address, destination IP address, and TCP/UDP source and destination ports. Suitable for high-volume networks.
Application-level gateway proxy	A proxy-oriented device that delves more deeply into the IP packet. This type of firewall is generally considered more secure, but can encounter performance problems when used in high-volume networks.
Circuit-level gateway proxy	Mostly suitable for Network Address Translation (NAT); allows only incoming and outgoing traffic specifically addressed to the network. This firewall requires all clients that want to connect to it to undergo modifications. The most common example of a circuit-level gateway is a SOCKS server. You can learn more about SOCKS at www.socks.nec.com.

Some of the more popular firewall products include the following:

- Raptor Firewall from Symantec Corporation (www.symantec.com)
- FireWall-1 from Check Point (www.checkpoint.com)
- Gauntlet from Network Associates (www.nai.com)
- Squid Proxy Server (www.squid-cache.org)

Squid was originally designed for Unix systems, but you can compile it on Windows NT/2000 systems, as long as you have installed compilation software, such as the GNU-Win32 package.

Unix systems support the Ipchains and Iptables commands, which you use to create packet-filtering rules.

A router is a specially designed host that connects one LAN to another. Therefore, a host acting as a firewall has at least one *internal interface* and at least one *external interface*. Firewalls are specially designed to accept all traffic (including malicious packets) on the external NIC and then safely pass acceptable packets to the internal NIC, where they travel on to the rest of the network.

A *demilitarized zone (DMZ)* is a partially protected network that resides between the router used to connect the entire network and a host acting as a firewall. Another name for a DMZ is a service network. Many organizations place hosts (such as web, DNS, and e-mail servers) in the DMZ rather than behind the firewall. This common practice is not secure because it exposes the hosts to many different types of attacks.

A *rule* is an entry in a firewall database designed to control access into and out of a network. A rule also determines which protocol is allowed into or out of the network. Rules can be very specific. For example, you can create a rule that allows a certain protocol, such as ICMP, into your network only from certain external hosts.

Similarly, you can create firewall rules that forbid internal hosts access to all outside networks, including the Internet. For example, with the exception of a web proxy server, you can deny external access to all internal hosts. You can then connect all internal hosts to the web proxy server. The result of this arrangement is that all internal users must use the proxy server. You can then use this server to filter and monitor all traffic. Additionally, end users cannot use e-mail, network newsgroups, or FTP or telnet to external hosts. As you implement new services and hosts, you will probably need to adjust existing rules or create new ones to accommodate new traffic.

A *bastion host* uses firewall software that has at least one internal NIC and one external NIC. A bastion host can act as either a packet or a proxy filter. Proxy-oriented bastion hosts generally house services or daemons that mediate protocols such as SMTP, POP3, NNTP, HTTP, secure HTTP, and so forth.

Firewalls are the primary means of protecting networks from outside attacks; however, a firewall has no way of detecting inside attacks. Attacks from behind the firewall are the most common. Disgruntled employees and corporate spies can infiltrate network assets unless you deploy an *intrusion detection system (IDS)*. An IDS uses various types of applications residing on various network hosts to monitor all internal network traffic. You can use filters and rules on these applications to log and filter selected traffic, much like a firewall.

Several types of IDS applications exist, as follows.

Network-based IDS   An application that scans all internal network traffic passed over the wire. Software sets a NIC into promiscuous mode and then captures packets. Depending on its rules, an IDS can block certain traffic, including unproductive web surfing or actual attacks. A network-based IDS usually resides on a single host dedicated to scanning the network. This form of application is useful in non-switched Ethernet networks.

Host-based IDS   An agent that resides on a host. This agent scans the host's log files and then compares these files with its own rules. This application is ideal for monitoring highly sensitive hosts, such as databases or exposed web servers.

Hybrid IDS   An application designed to combine the strengths of both network-based and host-based IDS applications.

NOTE   IDS logging is an ideal way to supplement individual server logs.

Examples of IDS applications include the following:

- Snort (`www.snort.org`)

- Intruder Alert (`www.symantec.com`)

- NetProwler (`www.symantec.com`)

- ISS RealSecure (`www.iss.net`)

Except for Intruder Alert, each of these IDS applications is network-based. The primary way to determine a security breach is to view your server log files. From a security standpoint, truly useful log files might require you to adjust your auditing levels so that they report only the activity you want. As you study your logs, look for the following types of activity.

- Failed logons

- Unexplained or common system shutdowns and restarts

- Changes in user privileges

- Added or removed accounts

- System processes that have been shut down, activated, or restarted

- Changes in file permissions

When you identify such events, communicate them to your manager or to the party specified in your security policy.

Security Tradeoffs

In an IT environment, security settings that you enable will probably have a tangible effect on users' ability to perform their duties. Enforcing security always has associated tradeoffs and drawbacks, including the following.

Complexity   Users often do not want to modify their behavior when they encounter a firewall or new operating system setting. You must train users to cope with new settings and procedures.

Host performance degradation   Although most vendor products are designed to operate efficiently, placing an IDS or other software on a host can affect its performance. For example, an improperly configured host-based IDS application can cause an unacceptable performance drain on a system. Whenever you reconfigure a host or install a software agent, be sure to monitor the host's performance carefully.

Unintended denial of service   A security setting you create might negatively affect an employee's ability to do their job. Carefully consider all changes to a host's configuration, and then be sure to consider the effect of each change on users.

Summary

 The thrust of this chapter is to protect your server's security while maintaining the highest possible performance. As a systems administrator, you must make intelligent security tradeoffs. The cost associated with installing security devices and monitoring hardware, training users, and monitoring performance is high, but the cost associated with opening your Internet systems to intrusion is even higher. In the first part of this chapter, you saw that a proxy server not only provides some security but also enhances performance by caching web pages.

You learned about the function of proxy servers and how they use public and private IP addressing to provide NAT and mediate between public and private networks. You learned that NAT has the security benefit of hiding internal network addresses. You also learned how to modify clients so that they properly access the proxy server. For security, clients should not have direct network access to the router that your enterprise uses to get on the Internet, but should use the proxy server for Internet access.

You learned that a proxy server is a type of firewall. It is also a form of Application-level gateway because it helps translate Application-layer traffic, such as HTTP, FTP, and so forth. However, much more powerful firewall products exist. Some are Application-level gateways, such as the Axent Raptor firewall. Others are packet-filtering firewalls, such as the CheckPoint Firewall-1. In the second half of this chapter, you looked at firewalls and other security systems.

Your operating system is the central element of your network; securing it enhances and complements other security measures. In this chapter, you learned how to mitigate damage to individual users and groups, protect file systems, implement access control, and change system defaults. You also learned how system bugs can affect security and how elements such as the Windows 2000 Registry and other operating system–specific issues warrant special attention when securing your system.

With this information, you should be able to identify vulnerabilities commonly found in various operating systems; list the steps to counteract operating system weaknesses; define firewall and intrusion detection concepts; discuss the effect of security measures on employees and system hosts; and recognize security breaches.

Exam Essentials

Understand the benefits of a proxy server.   Proxy servers reduce costs, enforce security, increase bandwidth efficiency, and improve logging. Proxy servers increase security by hiding internal network addresses by doing Network Address Translation (NAT) and by acting as a packet-filtering firewall in which IP packets can be filtered based on source and destination IP addresses and ports.

Know the private IP networks that are not routable on the Internet and that can be used by any enterprise without registering these addresses on the Internet.   These IP addresses are on the following networks: 10.0.0.0 (subnet mask of 255.0.0.0), 172.16.0.0 to 172.31.255.255 (subnet mask of 255.240.0.0), and 192.168.0.0 (subnet mask of 255.255.0.0).

Know how to connect to a proxy server.   Configure clients with the IP address or the domain name of the proxy server, plus the port of the proxy server. You might have to configure these items separately for the client's browser and e-mail client. Clients should be able to connect to the Internet router only by using a proxy server. They should not be able to bypass the proxy server. You can put only the proxy server on the physical segment with the Internet router, or you can configure the Internet router to talk only to the proxy server.

Know how best to achieve system security.   Carefully limit user and group permissions. For example, configure a separate system account for the web server and the FTP server. Be sure that these system accounts have very limited privileges. Multiple partitions with the appropriate access permissions should separate the operating system, the services or daemons running on the server, and data storage. Enforce operating system policies such as minimum password length. Users with administrative privileges should also have a regular user account and use the regular account when performing nonadministrative duties. Eliminate system bugs, and install the latest security patches. Enable auditing and shadow passwords, and remove any unnecessary system services.

Know firewall types and terminology.   The three firewall types are a packet filter, an Application-level gateway proxy, and a circuit-level gateway proxy. You need to create firewall rules before a firewall will be effective. A bastion host uses firewall software and has at least one internal NIC and one external NIC. The area between a screening router and a firewall is partially protected. It is called a DMZ, and you can place web servers, e-mail servers, and DNS servers there while isolating your internal network behind a firewall.

Understand intrusion detection systems (IDSs).   A firewall cannot detect an internal attack such as employee snooping. Internal attacks are more common that external attacks. Intrusion detection systems monitor internal traffic. You can use filters and rules on these applications to log and filter selected traffic. The three types of IDS are network based and monitor all traffic, but they can't work in a switched Ethernet environment; a host-based IDS is ideal for monitoring highly sensitive hosts, and hybrid IDs.

Understand the tradeoffs that you make in enforcing security.   Security systems are complex and involve training. Host performance sometimes degrades, and some security settings can deny services to legitimate users.

Recognize security breaches. Study logs and look for the following: failed logons; unexplained or common system shutdowns and restarts; changes in user privileges; added or removed accounts; system processes that have been shutdown, activated or restarted; and changes in file permissions.

Key Terms

Before taking the exam, you should be familiar with the following terms:

Application-level gateway	Network Address Translation (NAT)
circuit-level gateway	packet filter
filter	proxy server
firewall	security breach

Review Questions

1. Jonathan is director of Human Resources for Great Escapes Theme Park. He needs to add 5000 IP addresses for workers at a new European theme park. These workers need access to the Internet. Which network should he use to add these addresses in the most economical way?

   A. 10.0.0.0 (subnet mask of 255.0.0.0)

   B. 127.0.0.0 (subnet mask of 255.240.0.0)

   C. 254.0.0.0 (subnet mask of 255.0.0.0)

   D. 131.107.2.0 (subnet mask of 255.255.0.0)

2. Jonathan is director of Human Resources for Great Escapes Theme Park. If he uses a proxy server to connect to the Internet, in what two ways can he enhance security?

   A. By hiding internal network addresses from the Internet

   B. By caching requests so that clients do not directly connect to web servers

   C. By creating rules that filter Internet traffic

   D. By implementing a reverse proxy array with stealth port mapping

3. Brian works at Red Hat. He teaches training classes on the road. He wants to use a subnet that will not conflict with any other subnet on the Internet. Which private IP subnets could Brian use for his training classes? Choose three.

   A. 10.0.0.0 (subnet mask 255.0.0.0)

   B. 131.107.2.0 (subnet mask 255.240.0.0)

   C. 172.16.0.0 (subnet mask 255.240.0.0)

   D. 192.168.0.0 (subnet mask 255.255.0.0)

4. Jason is configuring Internet Explorer to use an Apache server that is acting as an HTTP proxy server. Which port should Jason use?

   A. 80

   B. 8800

   C. 8000

   D. 88

5. Which of the following is true of web proxy servers?

   A. They decrease a connection's throughput.

   B. They enable clients to connect directly to the Internet.

   C. They eliminate the need for other security practices.

   D. They store requests for later use to enhance bandwidth efficiency.

6. Using Network Address Translation (NAT) requires that you do which of the following?

   A. Define a pool of valid internal IP addresses

   B. Use certain private IP addresses that are not routable to the Internet

   C. Register every IP address that you use

   D. Use only certain proxy servers

7. You just installed a new Windows Me machine for an employee. You verify that this system can communicate with other computers on the network, including the default gateway, which is the machine that allows access to the Internet. After some time, you receive a telephone call from the employee. She tells you that she cannot use her e-mail client to send or receive messages. She can, however, browse the Web and access her newsgroups. You test the e-mail server, and it is up and processing messages to and from remote clients. What is the most likely cause of the problem?

   A. The employee's e-mail software is faulty.

   B. You have not reconfigured the e-mail proxy server.

   C. You have not reconfigured the firewall.

   D. You have not configured the employee's e-mail client to use a proxy server.

8. Mike has several proxy server help desk calls from four new users in his 200-user LAN. What is the most likely problem?

    A. The proxy server has intermittent problems.

    B. The proxy server does not have a scope of IP addresses valid for the new clients.

    C. The clients do not have valid user accounts on the proxy server.

    D. Client misconfiguration.

9. Mike is a consultant. This week, he is working at `Internet-Investigation.com`. He wants to get on the Internet using the company's proxy server. Mike configures his laptop to obtain an IP address automatically and can see other computers on `Internet-Investigation.com`'s LAN. What two additional steps must Mike take?

    A. Configure his proxy client with the proxy server's IP address or DNS name

    B. Configure his proxy client with the port of the proxy server

    C. Configure the proxy server as the default gateway

    D. Disable dial-up networking

10. Clients at `Freeway.com` were connecting to the Internet through a router. For security, a proxy server is installed that will act as a firewall. How should the network be configured? Choose all the valid answers.

    A. The Internet router should be disabled.

    B. The clients should be configured to use the proxy server.

    C. The proxy server should have two network cards installed, one to connect to the Internet router and the other to connect to the clients.

    D. The proxy server should be the only host on the segment that is used to connect to the router.

11. Because of recent cracker activity, Denise wants to bolster security. What is the first step she should take?

    A. Install a firewall

    B. Install an intrusion detection system

    C. Increase security logging

    D. Implement complex passwords

    E. Install the latest security patches, fixes, and workarounds.

12. Jim is the webmaster for a small business that has a website and an FTP site. What reasonable measure should Jim take to increase security?

    A. Put the website and the FTP site on separate servers

    B. Use nondefault ports for the website and the FTP site

    C. Use different versions of IIS for the website and the FTP site

    D. Create separate, restricted system accounts for the website and the FTP site

13. Rajesh wants to enforce operating system policies to increase security. How might this increase security?

    A. By defining penalties for Internet abuse

    B. By forcing users to use strong passwords

    C. By forcing users to use a firewall

    D. By installing the latest security patches

14. Hank is installing SQL 2000. What can Hank do to increase security? Select the best answer.

    A. Use a custom install

    B. Change system defaults

    C. Increase security logging

    D. Delete the administrative account

15. Hank is installing a firewall on a Windows 2000 server. What should he do to increase security? Choose the best answer.

   A. Put the web server on the same computer so that it can be directly protected

   B. Put the web server on a separate computer to make the firewall a harder target

   C. Increase system services such as NetBIOS support so that crackers can be identified

   D. Decrease system services to the minimum required

16. Jessica wants to increase security by installing a firewall. She learns that she has to select a type of firewall. What are Jessica's three main choices?

   A. Internal firewall

   B. External firewall

   C. Packet filter

   D. Application-level gateway proxy

   E. Circuit-level gateway proxy

17. Tom wants to at least partially protect web servers, DNS servers, and e-mail servers while providing a higher degree of security for database servers and file and print servers. Where should Tom place his publicly accessible servers?

   A. In the DMZ

   B. On a bastion host

   C. In front of a proxy server

   D. Between proxy servers

18. Dennis has purchased a firewall. Before it becomes operational, what must Dennis do? Choose the best answer.

   A. Create procedures

   B. Create rules

   C. Create a security policy

   D. Install the latest security patches, fixes, and workarounds

19. Jessica is implementing a bastion host. What are two requirements?

   A. Intrusion detection software

   B. Two or more processors

   C. Two or more NICs

   D. Firewall software

20. Willy wants to protect against employee snooping from inside the firewall on a switched Ethernet network. Specifically he wants to protect the database server that contains highly sensitive information. What should Willy install? Choose the best answer.

   A. Internal firewall

   B. Host-based intrusion detection system

   C. Network-based intrusion detection system

   D. Firewall appliance

Answers to Review Questions

1. A. Jonathan should use private IP addressing. The 10.0.0.0 network supports private IP addressing.

2. A, C. Using a proxy server, client computers do not connect to the Internet directly; thus their IP address remains essentially hidden. Proxy servers can also filter out requests that are embedded in the packets.

3. A, C, D. The private IP addresses that are not routable on the Internet are on the following subnets: 10.0.0.0, 172.16.0.0, and 192.168.0.0.

4. A. Apache server, acting as a web proxy server, uses port 80.

5. D. Proxy servers cache web pages for later use, which reduces bandwidth consumption.

6. A. Using NAT requires that only one valid public IP address be used to communicate with the Internet. The Internal IP addresses can be private IP addresses, or they can be other valid addresses that were previously used by a corporation that perhaps was not originally connected to the Internet. In either case, these addresses are hidden from the Internet, because the proxy server has the only address that is exposed to the Internet.

7. D. The e-mail client needs to be configured to use a proxy server.

8. D. The single most frequent cause of proxy server problems is client misconfiguration.

9. A, B. Mike should configure his proxy client with the IP address or DNS name of the proxy server and the port used by the proxy server.

10. B, C, D. For security, the proxy server should be the only computer that has a physical connection to the Internet router so that the proxy server's security cannot be bypassed.

11. E. Denise should search various security-related sites or contact the vendor for the latest patches, fixes, and workarounds.

12. D. Jim should use separate system accounts for the web and the FTP services and restrict what these accounts can do, so that if one account is cracked, it can do limited damage.

13. B. Operating system policies guard against security threats by enforcing choices (such as password selection) that guard against system attacks.

14. B. Hank should change system defaults. For example, the administrative account is the SA user with a blank password. Hank should change the name of that account and set a password.

15. B, D. Firewall and other servers should be optimized so they are running the minimum number of services and applications to perform their job. Each additional service and application is an additional potential entry point for a cracker.

16. C, D, E. The three firewall types are packet filter, Application-level gateway, and circuit-level gateway proxy.

17. A. A demilitarized zone (DMZ) is a partially protected network that resides between a screening router and a stronger firewall.

18. B. A rule is an entry in a firewall database designed to control access into and out of a network.

19. C, D. A bastion host uses firewall software and has at least one internal NIC and one external NIC.

20. B. A host-based IDS is ideal for monitoring highly sensitive hosts and can work on a switched Ethernet network.

Glossary

acceptable use policies   Rules or regulations regarding authorized network and computer use and activities, including e-mail content.

access control list (ACL)   A list that defines the permissions for a resource by specifying which users and groups have access to the resource.

Access log   An HTTP server log that contains information about URL requests, including the IP address of the client accessing the server, the time the connection occurred, the name of the URL (for example, /index.html), and the HTTP request.

access.conf   An Apache server configuration file that allows you to create virtual hosts, set error documents, and configure access to the server's files.

Active Directory   Microsoft's directory service that is an integral part of Windows 2000 architecture. It stores user, computer, group, and other data used to manage a Windows 2000 domain in a centralized and automated database that enables interoperation with other directory services in a distributed computing environment.

Active Server Pages (ASP)   A set of technologies developed by Microsoft for developing and hosting networked database applications.

ActiveX   An open set of technologies for integrating components on the Internet and within Microsoft applications.

ActiveX Data Objects (ADO)   The Microsoft model for creating applications that can work together across a network even though they were created using different computer languages. ADO uses the Microsoft Object Linking and Embedding Database (OLE DB) model to access the database or other information. ADO is part of the Component Object Model (COM).

adapter   A device that provides connectivity between at least two systems.

Address Resolution Protocol (ARP)   A Network layer protocol used to convert a numeric IP address into a physical address, such as a MAC address. Used for direct routing.

Agent log   An HTTP server log file that records the version of any user agent that accesses your site. A user agent is client software used to browse a website. User agents can include web browsers and spiders used by search engines.

aliasing   A renaming practice for accounts on a local host that creates an alternative address for a specific user.

anonymous access   Allows any anonymous user access to resources on a web or FTP server. IIS uses the Windows 2000 IUSR account to provide a limited logon shell that allows users to access web server files. You can change this account, if you want.

anonymous FTP   A method for legitimately accessing an FTP server without an assigned username or password.

antivirus software   Applications that scan, detect, repair, and remove virus infections on a computer.

Apache server   A freely available web server that runs under Unix and Linux. Apache is the most popular web server on the Internet.

applets   Small programs, written in Java, that are downloaded as needed and executed within a web page or a browser.

application   An executable program typically used to perform functions on data including retrieval, transmission, display, editing, and formatting.

Application layer   1. Layer 7 in the OSI Reference Model, responsible for presenting data to the user. 2. The top layer of the Internet architecture, corresponding to the Application and Presentation layers of the OSI Reference Model.

application-level gateway   A firewall component that filters packets on a program-by-program basis and provides strong authentication.

application-level gateway proxy   A type of firewall. A proxy-oriented device that delves more deeply into the IP packet. This type of firewall is generally considered more secure, but can encounter performance problems when used in high-volume networks.

applications programming interface (API)   A method that allows a programmer to make requests of an operating system or application.

asymmetric-key encryption   An encryption method that uses a pair of keys, one of which is made public and the other kept private.

asynchronous transfer mode (ATM)   A fast packet-switching technology that uses fixed-sized cells (instead of frame relay's variable-length packets) and PVCs (permanent virtual circuits) to support data as well as real-time video and voice. Both LANs and WANs can use ATM, but ATM is primarily used as an Internet backbone.

auditing   The ongoing process of examining systems and procedures to determine their efficiency, including the ability to withstand cracker activity. Involves both manual and automated analysis.

authentication   The ability to determine a user's or a computer's true identity.

backbone   Network part that carries the majority of network traffic; usually a high-speed transmission path spanning long distances, to which smaller networks typically connect.

backbone services   Services that operate in the background and provide the foundation for a working LAN or WAN. Backbone services provide naming services, address management, directory services, central logon, and routing.

bandwidth   The amount of information, sometimes called traffic, that can be carried on a network at one time. Measured in bits per second (bps).

bandwidth throttling   A setting that controls the amount of bandwidth a web server can use; measured in kilobits per second (Kbps).

basic authentication   A way to gain access to resources on an IIS server by providing your username and password. You must use NTFS permissions with this option, which requires IIS to first check with the Windows 2000 SAM. The danger of basic authentication is that it allows user names and passwords to be transmitted across networks in cleartext. The benefit to basic authentication is that anyone with a browser can authenticate with IIS and gain access to a directory.

bastion host A computer that houses various firewall components and services. A bastion host uses firewall software that has at least one internal NIC and one external NIC. A bastion host can act either as a packet or as a proxy filter. Proxy-oriented bastion hosts generally house services or daemons that mediate protocols such as SMTP, POP3, NNTP, HTTP, secure HTTP, and so forth.

bind The act of attaching a networking protocol to a computer's operating system.

boot sector A dedicated portion of a disk that contains the first parts of an operating system's startup files.

bottleneck Any element (a hard drive, an I/O card, or a network interface card) that slows network connectivity rates. A bottleneck is the weakest link or the limiting resource that causes the entire process to slow down or stop. The term "bottleneck" comes from the narrow part of a bottle used to slow down the flow of liquid so that it doesn't flow too fast.

broadband A transmission method that uses frequency division multiplexing (FDM) to transmit multiple signals over a single transmission path.

broadcast address An IP address used to send messages to all network hosts and used only as a destination address. Usually includes the number 255.

browser An application that displays a document for viewing and printing. Typically used to refer to web-browsing applications.

browser cache An area kept by a web client on a hard drive to store downloaded web documents and images for later viewing.

brute-force attacks A method of network invasion that repeatedly tries different possible passwords from a dictionary program that contains obvious passwords and names in order to gain unauthorized access to network assets. Also called a *front door attack*.

buffer A cache of memory used by a computer to store frequently used data. Buffers allow faster access times.

cable modem A hardware device that connects a computer to a WAN, such as the Internet, using cable television lines. A cable modem works by demodulating transmissions from the cable network, modulating the computer's transmissions to the WAN, and using one or more channels on the cable television line for these transmissions.

cache An area of RAM or disk storage used to store frequently accessed information for speedy retrieval.

caching-only server A DNS server that does not maintain its own database files (called zone files), but gathers information from client requests that it fulfills and stores in its cache. Caching-only servers fulfill requests by asking other servers for information and then passing that information to the initial requesting client and any subsequent clients that request the same information.

canonical name (CNAME) A DNS record that creates an alias for a specified host. For example, suppose the name of a web server is `server1.company.com`. A CNAME record can create an alias to the `server1.company.com` host so that it is known as `www.company.com`.

cd A command to change the working directory. This command is also used in FTP.

central logon   A single logon point that allows access to additional resources (such as servers, printers, and the Internet). A service of this type lets users maintain a single username and password and yet have access to multiple resources.

Central Processing Unit (CPU)   The brains of a computer. The central unit in a computer that performs the instructions of a computer's programs.

certificate authority (CA)   A trusted third-party organization that issues digital certificates used for SSL authentication. Servers using SSL require a digitally signed certificate. Without this certificate, the server can operate only in a non-secure mode. Server administrators can submit a certificate request to a well-known CA.

certificate authority (CA) certificate   A type of digital certificate used for SSL. Trusted third-party organizations such as VeriSign use a CA certificate to sign other certificates.

certificate server   An internetworking server that validates or certifies keys.

channel service unit/data (or digital) service unit (CSU/DSU)   A hardware device that terminates physical connections and is required when using dedicated circuits, such as T1 lines. Converts digital network signals to a format that is suitable for line transmission.

circuit-level gateway proxy   A type of firewall that monitors and transmits information at the Transport layer of the OSI Reference Model. It hides information about the network; a packet passing through this type of gateway appears to have originated from the firewall. Mostly suitable for Network Address Translation (NAT); allows only incoming and outgoing traffic specifically addressed to the network. This firewall requires all clients that want to connect to it to undergo modifications.

Class A address   An IP address that uses the first byte for the network portion and the last three bytes for the host portion. Class A addresses range from 0.0.0.0 through 127.255.255.255.

Class B address   An IP address that uses the first two bytes for the network portion and the last two bytes for the host portion. Class B addresses range from 128.0.0.0 through 191.255.255.255.

Class C address   An IP address that uses the first three bytes for the network portion and the last byte for the host portion. Class C addresses range from 192.0.0.0 through 223.255.255.255.

Class D address   An IP address that supports multicasting and is targeted to a group that is identified by a network address only. No host portion exists in the address. The first byte can range from 224 through 239.

Class E address   An IP address that is reserved for future use. The first byte can range from 240 through 247.

client   A system or an application that requests a service from another computer (the server).

client/server model   A distributed computing system in which computing tasks are divided between the server and the client.

client-side applications   Web applications that are downloaded by the client from the server and executed by the client's browser or operating system. Client-side applications include JavaScript and VBScript embedded in HTML pages, as well as ActiveX controls and Java applets.

client-side script   Code embedded in the HTML and downloaded by a user; it resides on the client and helps process a form. Common client-side scripting languages include JavaScript and VBScript.

co-location   The placement of third-party equipment, such as servers and other networking hardware, in a company. The hosting company provides infrastructure support, such as electrical power and bandwidth.

command-line interface   A common method for accessing computers and operating systems that requires users to type and enter commands on a keyboard or console.

Common Gateway Interface (CGI)   A program that processes data submitted by the user. The applications used by web servers to create documents dynamically in order to present server resources are called Common Gateway Interface applications, or CGI scripts.

cookie   A small text file created by a web server that resides on a client's computer and preserves the state of a client-server session. May be used to store data, settings, and other information.

cracker   In *The New Hacker's Dictionary* a distinction is made between a cracker who cracks the security of a system and a hacker who is a clever programmer.

daemon   A Unix program that is usually initiated at startup and runs in the background until required.

database   A file or a series of files used to organize information by storing data in a consistent format so that users can search the files for specific information.

database management system (DBMS)   Software that manages a flat file database.

dcpromo   Windows 2000 command to promote a Windows 2000 server to a domain controller and in so doing install Active Directory. This command is also used to demote a domain controller.

dedicated virtual server   A virtual FTP or HTTP server that uses a separate NIC for each virtual server.

default gateway   The IP address of the router on your local network.

demilitarized zone (DMZ)   A partially protected area between an external and internal router where public servers can be hosted outside the firewall.

denial of service (DoS) attack   An attack meant to deny authorized users access to a network, usually by flooding one or more network assets with packets or messages that consume server resources.

dictionary program   A program specifically written to break into a password-protected system. It has a relatively large list of common password names it repeatedly uses to gain access.

differential backup   A backup type in which each file that has its archive bit set to on is backed up. In a differential backup, the archive bit is not reset; thus the storage size and time requirement increase with each differential backup.

digital   A data representation format that uses a series of two integers, 1 and 0, to store the data.

digital certificate   A digital ID issued by a certificate authority to authenticate and validate Internet data transfers. A digital certificate is a specific form of an asymmetric key.

Digital Subscriber Line (DSL)   A high-speed direct Internet connection that uses all-digital networks.

Direct Memory Access (DMA)   A computer bus architecture that allows data to be sent directly from the hard drive to the memory on the computer's motherboard, bypassing microprocessor involvement.

directory services   These services centralize system resources such as servers, printers, and Internet access. Examples of directory services include Novell Directory Services (NDS), the Windows NT Directory Services (NTDS) in Windows NT 4, and the Windows NT Active Directory in Windows 2000.

disaster recovery   Measures taken beforehand to expedite the repair of machines and data after a problem has occurred. Ensuring that you have a boot or rescue disk is an example of a disaster recovery measure.

disk cache   A storage space on a computer hard disk used to temporarily store downloaded data.

disk duplexing   A separate hard disk controller is used for each of two disks that are paired with writes to each occurring in tandem. If either disk fails, the other has a complete set of data. Disk duplexing functions the same way as disk mirroring, but provides a separate controller for each hard drive.

disk mirroring   Two disks are paired, with writes to each occurring in tandem. If either disk fails, the other has a complete set of data. A mirror set is established between two physical hard drives (or partitions on two physical drives). This is RAID Level 1.

disk striping   Disk striping, which is RAID Level 0, causes each file written to the stripe set to be divided into pieces; each piece is written to a separate physical drive in the stripe set. A stripe set is a collection of physical drives that have been configured to act as one logical set. They provide the fastest read and write performance of any RAID implementation by sharing the load among disks, but provide no fault-tolerance.

disk striping with parity   This is RAID 5, in which a portion of each write request is written to a rotating separate physical drive in the stripe set. Disk striping with parity becomes fault tolerant because the stripe set includes parity information that can be used to reconstruct the data if a disk drive is lost.

dmesg   A command that reports in detail how Linux configured all recognized devices on the system at startup. If you use the command by itself, it will likely give you more information than you need. Instead, use it in combination with a pipe (the | character) and grep.

DNS domain   A DNS domain is an entity that controls the naming of all network resources by resolving names to IP addresses. The hierarchical naming system consists of three levels: root, top, and secondary.

domain controller A Windows 2000 server that controls logon to a domain and access to resources, hosting the Active Directory database. If multiple domain controllers exist within a domain, they are peers, each with read-write copies of Active Directory that is replicated among them.

Domain Name System (DNS) A system that maps uniquely hierarchical names to specific Internet addresses.

dotted quad Common term for describing an IPv4 address, such as 127.0.0.1.

drop directory A dedicated directory on an MTA that stores incoming e-mail messages.

dual-homed bastion A firewall that funnels traffic through a computer with two or more NICs with their IP forwarding features disabled. Software-imposed firewall rules help forward valid packets between subnets.

dynamic Constantly changing.

Dynamic DNS (DDNS) Allows DNS automatic name-to-IP address mapping changes.

Dynamic Host Configuration Protocol (DHCP) An Application-layer protocol designed to assign Internet addresses, DNS servers, and gateway addresses to nodes on a TCP/IP network during initialization. Commonly used to configure workstations and computers on an ISP, an IAP, or a LAN.

E1 A European digital carrier standard for synchronous data transmission at a speed of 2.048Mbps.

E3 A European digital carrier standard for synchronous data transmission at a speed of 34.368Mbps.

e-commerce (electronic commerce) The integration of communications, data management, and security capabilities to allow organizations to exchange information related to the sale of goods and services.

e-mail (electronic mail) A system for transferring messages from one computer to another over a network. Messages can include data in text-only format or text with attachments.

Emergency Repair Disk (ERD) A disk created and used in Windows 2000 to restore the Registry or critical files that have been corrupted. You should create an ERD when installing a Windows 2000 system and then update it regularly, particularly after major changes (program installations, added or deleted users, and so forth).

encryption The encoding, or scrambling, of information to a scrambled (unreadable) form by using specific algorithms, usually a string of characters known as a *key*.

enterprise networks Networks that provide connectivity among all nodes in an organization, regardless of their geographical location, and run the organization's mission-critical applications. Enterprise networks can include elements of peer-to-peer and server-based networks. An enterprise network can consist of several different networking protocols.

ephemeral ports Temporary, operating-system–assigned ports.

Error log   An HTTP server log file that is used to record any errors that occur, including, server startup and shutdown, malformed URLs, and erroneous CGI scripts.

Ethernet   A set of hardware technologies and networking protocols for LANs, including MAC and CSMA/CD. Also defined as IEEE 802.3. First developed at Xerox PARC in 1972.

expiration policy   Specifies the number of hours that a news server will retain copies of posted messages. Expiration policies also allow you to specify the amount of disk space the newsgroup can use. If you do not designate expiration policies for your newsgroups, your server's hard disk space will fill up with newsgroup postings quickly.

expires header   A special NNTP header that tells the news server it can delete a particular message from a newsgroup after a certain period of time. All of today's news servers honor this heading. The server, however, has the final say about when a message will be deleted from a newsgroup.

external interface   A NIC that is connected only to the external network or Internet. A host acting as a firewall has at least one internal interface and at least one external interface. Firewalls are specially designed to accept all traffic (including malicious packets) on the external NIC and then safely pass acceptable packets to the internal NIC, where they travel on to the rest of the network.

extranet   A network that connects enterprise intranets to the global Internet. Designed to provide access to selected external users to expedite the exchange of products, services, and key business information.

fault tolerance   Fault tolerance is the ability of a system to continue to operate after an unexpected hardware or software problem. The context of fault tolerance is system dependability and the means to achieve it. A fault-tolerant computer system or component is designed so that a backup procedure or component can immediately take its place.

File Transfer Protocol (FTP)   An Application-layer protocol used to transfer files between computers; FTP allows file transfer without corruption or alteration.

finger   A protocol to find out about users on local and remote Windows 2000 and Unix systems. For example, you can use finger to get more information about a user on a Linux/Unix system such as the full name of the user, the user's home directory, whether the user is logged in, and if so, since when.

firewall   The collection of hardware, software, and corporate policies that protects a LAN from the Internet. A firewall is a security barrier that controls the flow of information between the Internet and private networks.

folder replication   Copying folders or key files to a separate location. Folder replication is normally a manual process, but many network operating systems can automatically copy specified files and directories to a different location at specified times.

forward lookup zone   A DNS zone file that contains entries that map names to IP addresses.

forwarding-only server A DNS server that has no other zones and offers no caching, but fulfils client name resolution requests by passing them on to another DNS server.

frame relay A streamlined version of X.25 that uses variable-length packets and allows high-speed connections using shared network facilities and permanent virtual circuits (PVCs).

FTP log files Log files on an FTP server. They contain the IP address of the client connecting to your server; the client's user name; the date and time that the connection was made; the IP address of the server; and the commands issued, including files obtained, deleted, and created.

full backup A complete backup of all files. A full backup copies every selected file on the system to whatever backup device you are using. During the full backup, the archive bit for each file is reset, indicating that an archive (backup) is not needed. This type of backup requires the most storage space and the most time to perform. This option is a necessary part of both the differential and incremental strategies.

fully qualified domain name (FQDN) The complete domain name of an Internet computer, such as www.CIWcertified.com.

gateway A device that converts signals from one protocol stack to another. Also called a protocol converter.

get An FTP command that downloads a file.

global groups Windows 2000 provides two group types: global and local. *Global groups* are designed to contain users. *Local groups* contain

resources. You can place global groups into local groups, which provides anyone in the global group with access to the resources in the local group.

GNU A variety of non-proprietary Unix-compatible software and operating systems. GNU software formed the basis for Linux. The acronym stands for "GNU's Not Unix."

graphical user interface (GUI) A front-end or shell used as a substitute for a command-line interface in operating systems such as Windows, MacOS, and many varieties of Unix and Linux. Provides visual navigation with menus and screen icons, and performs automated functions at the click of a button.

group ID (GID) The default group for a given user. This group owns files that the user creates.

hacker A computer user who knows an application, operating system, or hardware very well.

home directory A directory on a server in which, by default, all work is saved. This function helps organize files. Home directories are important because they allow a server administrator to back up user files easily. A home directory can exist on a local drive or on a remote drive.

home page 1. The web document that a web client opens when it is first executed. 2. The initial page of a website.

host A computer that other computers can use to gain information; in network architecture, a host is a client or a workstation.

hosts A file that links IP addresses to alphanumeric names, such as nicknames and domain names. Before the DNS was developed, hosts files on each Internet computer contained a complete mapping of all registered Internet node names to their IP addresses.

hot fix   A vendor solution for a specific problem. Most vendors issue hot fixes as problems are discovered and solved.

hot swapping   The ability to replace system components without first powering the system down. Common hot-swap components include hard drives, power supplies, and PCI cards.

httpd.conf   An Apache server configuration file that allows you to determine the port number, declare the server's name and type, and declare the user under which all processes will run. Apache server reads this file first when it starts. Other settings also operate this function.

hyperlink   Embedded instructions within a text file that link it to a separate file. Also called *link*.

hypertext   Electronic text that, unlike static text in a book, contains links to other text or to various media, including sound, video, animation, and images.

Hypertext Markup Language (HTML)   The standard authoring language used to develop web pages.

Hypertext Transfer Protocol (HTTP)   An Application-layer protocol for transporting HTML documents across the Internet. HTTP requires a client program on one end (a browser) and a server on the other, both running TCP/IP.

Hypertext Transfer Protocol Secure (HTTPS)   An Application-layer protocol used to access a secure web server.

ifconfig   A program that displays TCP/IP network settings on the Linux operating system.

incremental backup   A backup type in which each file that has its archive bit set to on is backed up. In an incremental backup, the archive bit is reset; thus, the next incremental backup will back up only those files that changed since the last incremental backup.

inetd   The internet daemon, a Unix application that responds to received requests and starts an appropriate Internet service.

Information Technology (IT) department   An in-house computer and network systems department entrusted with the setup, operation, and maintenance of all computer systems within an organization.

INND news server   A daemon that runs on a Linux or a Unix computer to provide a news server.

insider attacks   An attack against a network asset mounted by an internal user of a computer network.

integrated drive electronics (IDE)   A disk drive controller built into the motherboard of a computer. The American National Standards Institute name for IDE is Advanced Technology Attainment (ATA).

Integrated Services Digital Network (ISDN)   An international standard that defines the transmission of data, voice, and video over digital lines at 64Kbps. An ISDN line consists of several 64-Kbps channels, which can be combined for faster speeds.

714 Glossary

integrated Windows authentication A way to gain access to resources on an IIS server by using your username and password. Windows 2000 detects a connection request and then issues an encrypted challenge to the browser. The browser then decrypts the challenge, allowing you to respond with a password.

internal interface A NIC that is connected only to the internal network. A host acting as a firewall has at least one internal interface and at least one external interface. Firewalls are specially designed to accept all traffic (including malicious packets) on the external NIC and then safely pass acceptable packets to the internal NIC, where they travel on to the rest of the network.

Internet The global wide area network that uses TCP/IP and other protocols to interconnect WANs, LANs, and computers.

Internet architecture A four-part model that provides a reference to the internal workings of the Internet and TCPI/IP networks. See also *Application layer*, *Transport layer*, *Internet layer*, and *Network Access layer*.

Internet Control Message Protocol (ICMP) The troubleshooting Network-layer protocol of TCP/IP that allows Internet hosts and gateways to report errors through ICMP messages that are sent to network users.

Internet Corporation for Assigned Names and Numbers (ICANN) The international organization responsible for domain name registration. In 1998, ICANN inherited responsibilities originally performed by InterNIC. ICANN allocates Internet address space, assigns protocol parameters, and manages root servers. It can be found on the Web at www.icann.org.

Internet Database Connector (IDC) A file that accesses a database to give users requested information.

Internet Information Services (IIS) Microsoft's web, FTP, and news server that comes with Windows 2000.

Internet layer The OSI Reference Model layer responsible for addressing and routing packets, using a protocol such as IP: Layer 3 of the OSI Reference Model. Also known as the Network layer of the OSI Reference Model.

Internet Message Access Protocol (IMAP) Provides the same services as POP, but is more powerful. Allows sharing of mailboxes and multiple mail server access. The latest version is IMAP4.

Internet Network Information Center (InterNIC) Until 1998, the cooperative organization formed by an agreement between the United States Department of Commerce and Network Solutions that registered domain names for the .com, .net, and .org top-level domains.

Internet Protocol (IP) The data transmission standard for the Internet. Every computer connected to the Internet has its own IP address, which allows a packet or unit of data to be delivered to a specific computer.

Internet server applications programming interface (ISAPI) A web server extension that allows the server to execute programs and scripts without the expensive processing associated with

CGI. Supported on Microsoft operating systems and some third-party gateways.

Internet Service Provider (ISP)   An organization that maintains a gateway to the Internet and rents access to customers on a per-use or subscription basis.

Internet standard   A protocol designated as an official standard by the Internet Engineering Task Force (IETF). Also called full standard.

intranet   An internal network, using Internet technology, that is not accessible to Internet users at large.

intrusion detection system (IDS)   Various types of applications residing on various network hosts that monitor all internal network traffic in order to detect intrusions. You can use filters and rules on these applications to log and filter selected traffic, much like a firewall. Firewalls are the premier means of protecting networks from outside attacks. However, a firewall has no way of detecting inside attacks. Attacks from behind the firewall are the most common. Disgruntled employees and corporate spies can infiltrate network assets unless you deploy an IDS.

IP address   A numeric address that identifies a computer or device on a TCP/IP network. IPv4 addresses are 32 bits in length, and arranged in a dotted quad such as 127.0.0.1. IPv6 addresses are 128 bits in length and uses eight sections of hexadecimal numbers each delimited by a colon. Here is an example: 12AB:0:0:CD30:123:4567:89AB:CDEF.

ipconfig   A program that displays TCP/IP network settings on the Windows NT, 2000, and XP operating systems.

Java   An object-oriented programming language developed by Sun Microsystems that is fully cross-platform functional.

JavaScript   An interpreted, object-based scripting language developed by Netscape Communications that adds interactivity to web pages.

Java servlet   A dedicated Java program that resides on a server. Java servlets extend a server's functionality.

Java Virtual Machine (JVM)   A small, efficient operating system that resides on top of other operating systems. It creates an environment that supports Java programs.

Kerberos   A secure method of providing a central logon. *Kerberos* authentication does not allow passwords to travel across the network and provides granular access to resources on a timed basis.

kernel   The essential part of an operating system; provides basic services; always resides in memory.

key   A string of numbers used by software that scrambles your message from plaintext, readable by anyone, into encrypted text. Some software encrypts and decrypts with the same key, whereas other software relies on a pair of keys.

lastlog   A Unix/Linux command that allows you to check when a user last logged on.

legacy applications   Applications that have existed for years and may not support current technologies without manipulation or upgrades.

license   A credential issued by an entity that gives one permission to perform a set of defined acts.

Lightweight Directory Access Protocol (LDAP)   A protocol based on X.500 for transmitting data from a directory server to a client.

list server   A server that automates collecting and distributing messages from an authorized group of participants, allowing collaboration between multiple users. A group of participants is often called a list group. Each participant is required to send an e-mail message to the list server in order to join a specific group. Once subscribed, the user is placed on a mailing list, which is a collection of users authorized to receive messages from the list server.

links   See *hyperlink*.

Linux   A popular version of the Unix operating system, designed for personal computers under the supervision of Linus Torvalds. Linux is an open-source network operating system licensed under the GNU framework. Many Linux distributions include a graphical user interface. Pronounced LIH-nucks.

linuxconf   A program that provides a graphical interface that you can use to create user accounts and take care of many other administrative tasks. One version of linuxconf runs from the command line, and another runs under the X Window System.

lmhosts   A file that contains IP address to NetBIOS name mappings.

load balancing   The process of distributing processing and communications activity evenly across a computer network so that no single device is overwhelmed.

local area network (LAN)   A group of computers connected within a confined geographic area so that their users can share files and services.

local groups   Windows 2000 provides two group types: global and local. *Global groups* are designed to contain users. *Local groups* contain resources. You can place global groups into local groups, which provides anyone in the global group with access to the resources in the local group.

local profile   Connects a user's permissions to a computer's interface. In Windows 2000 systems, you can create a local profile that restricts user access to certain areas of the operating system. For example, most users do not need access to network configuration commands. You can, therefore, create a local profile that forbids access to this element of the operating system.

logon account   A user account in a database that is used in conjunction with a password to verify that a user will be granted access to resources on a computer or a group of computers. In a user-level security environment, a logon account with a secure password grants universal access to resources based on permissions. To make permissions easier to track and to facilitate administration, you add logon accounts to groups that are assigned permissions.

logon script   A special application designed to customize a user's work environment. Generally, a logon script runs specific programs that enable an individual user to work more efficiently.

loopback   A set of IP addresses used to test and diagnose network connections. The common loopback address is 127.0.0.1.

ls A Unix/Linux command to list files that is also used in FTP.

MAC address See *Media Access Control address.*

Mail Delivery Agent (MDA) An e-mail server responsible for storing e-mail messages that a client can download. This server can be a POP3 or an IMAP server.

mail exchange (MX) record Entries in the forward DNS zone file that identify the e-mail server responsible for sending and receiving e-mail for the specified domain. MX entries can redirect email for your server or for an entire domain. If you are using DNS in your LAN and you want to use e-mail, you must have an MX record for your server and/or domain in order for your domain to send and receive e-mail messages between DNS domains.

Mail Exchanger (MX) A DNS record that identifies a server used for processing and delivering e-mail for the domain.

mail server An internetworking server that stores and/or transmits e-mail messages.

Mail Transfer Agent (MTA) An e-mail server responsible for delivering mail between hosts until it arrives at a Mail Delivery Agent. This server is also known as an SMTP server. The Unix sendmail daemon is an example of an MTA.

Mail User Agent (MUA) An e-mail client application with which end users compose, send, and retrieve e-mail.

masquerading The practice of altering the SMTP header of a message so that a user can appear to be sending e-mail from a different computer.

master server A DNS server loads its database from a file on a local disk. This server is used for adding the master domain, subdomains, and hosts for those domains. Another name for a master server is a primary server. Microsoft, for example, uses the term "primary" as opposed to master.

Media Access Control (MAC) address A unique hardware address that is assigned and burned by the NIC manufacturer and can be used to identify a specific computer on a network.

message queue The directory in which outgoing e-mail is stored.

mget An FTP command that allows you to download multiple files or directories.

Microsoft Management Console (MMC) A standard interface for managing Windows 2000 servers. You can use preconfigured MMCs such as Active Directory Users and Computers, or you can add various snap-ins to an MMC interface to manage various aspects of Windows 2000.

middleware Software that extends the capabilities of a web server. *Middleware* can include Java servlets, application servers, and other servers that let you organize and direct information between an end user and a web server.

mirroring A process that causes two sets of disk writes to occur for each original disk write that takes place. Uses a mirror set that is established between two or more physical hard drives or partitions.

mission-critical applications Applications that are absolutely essential for the day-to-day operation of a business environment.

modem A device that enables a computer to communicate with other computers over telephone lines by translating digital data into audio/analog signals (on the sending computer) and then back into digital form (on the receiving computer). The term is derived from the device's functions as a modulator/demodulator.

modprobe Command to find out detailed information about Linux modules that are loaded. For example, if you have a 3c509 adapter, you can issue the following command, which displays information about the IRQ (interrupt request) and memory address: modprobe 3c509.

module An extension to the Linux operating system that does not require recompiling the Linux kernel. Adding a device driver to a Linux machine requires either extending the Linux kernel by incorporating a device driver code or by installing a new module.

mput An FTP command that allows you to upload multiple files or directories.

Multipurpose Internet Mail Extension (MIME) type Identifies the contents of a file in the MIME encoding system using a type/subtype format; examples are image/jpg and text/plain. The MIME standard identifies the many types of documents and applications that various Internet services must manage when servicing a client request. Different document types are classified under broad headings (text, audio, video) and then subclassified by exact type. For example, an HTML document has the following MIME type: text/html. Plain text documents have the following type: text/plain. MIME was originally intended to work with Internet mail, but has been adopted by HTTP.

name resolver Commonly called a DNS client. Technically, a name resolver is the client software component that uses the services of one or more name servers.

name server A server application that supports name-to-address translation. Typically, the system on which the name server resides is called the name server system or DNS server. Many types of name servers exist.

named pipe Also known as first in, first out (FIFO). A way for one process to pass information to another process.

naming services These services include the Domain Name System (DNS), the Windows Internet Naming Service (WINS), and Samba (Samba enables Unix systems to participate in Windows networking). Naming services also include Dynamic DNS (DDNS), which allows DNS automatic name-to-IP address mapping changes.

nbtstat (NetBIOS over TCP/IP statistics) A Windows command, the NetBIOS equivalent of the nslookup command. The nbtstat command helps determine NetBIOS names when only an IP address is available. It also displays protocol statistics and TCP/IP connections on networks running NetBIOS over TCP/IP.

NetBIOS Enhanced User Interface (NetBEUI) An extension of NetBIOS that uses a different format for data frames.

NetBIOS name cache Resolved IP address to NetBIOS name mappings stored in a computer's memory.

NetBIOS names Sixteen-character computer names. In Microsoft networking, the 16 characters designate the service provided by the computer or the computer's domain or workgroup.

netstat A utility that displays the contents of various network-related data structures, such as the state of sockets.

network A group of two or more computer systems linked together.

Network Access layer A layer of the Internet architecture that corresponds to the Physical and Data Link layers of the OSI Reference Model. Includes the operating system's device driver, corresponding network interface card (NIC), and physical connections.

network adapter card See *network interface card (NIC)*.

Network Address Translation (NAT) Using one public IP address to talk on the Internet on behalf of internal computers that have multiple IP addresses that are hidden from the Internet. Using NAT conceals the actual IP address of any computers behind the firewall. NAT is the ability of a proxy server to act as a mediator between a public and a private network.

network analyzer A software program that can intercept and decode network transmissions, including packets.

Network Basic Input/Output System (NetBIOS) An interface that allows systems to communicate on a LAN. NetBIOS runs over TCP/IP in much the same way that SMB runs over TCP/IP.

network interface card (NIC) A hardware device installed in a computer that serves as the interface between a computer and a network. When using a cable modem, an additional cable connects a computer's NIC to the modem. Also called a network adapter card.

Network layer Layer 3 of the OSI Reference Model, responsible for addressing and routing packets, using a protocol such as IP. Also known as the Internet layer of the Internet architecture.

Network News Transfer Protocol (NNTP) An Application-layer Internet protocol that allows the exchange of newsgroup articles. It is used to post and share single instances of messages using TCP port 119.

network operating system (NOS) An operating system that manages network resources.

New Technology File System (NTFS) This file system is supported in Windows NT, Windows 2000, and Windows XP. It provides security, stability, and scalability.

newsfeed A source that transmits newsgroup information and messages to NNTP servers.

newsgroups An Internet discussion group that allows users to read and post messages using NNTP. Newsgroups are global message boards that cover a broad range of topics.

Network File System (NFS)   A client-server application that allows you to read and optionally write files on a remote Unix/Linux computer.

nmbd daemon   Samba consists of the `nmbd` daemon that provides NetBIOS names over the network and the `smbd` daemon that provides file and print shares. Samba also uses the SMB protocol to create shares.

nonrelational database   A database format in which all related information is contained within a single table. Also called a flat file database.

nonroutable   Uses predefined, or static, routes that cannot be changed.

normal backup   A complete backup of all files. A normal or full backup copies every selected file on the system to whatever backup device you are using. During the normal or full backup, the archive bit for each file is reset, indicating that an archive (backup) is not needed. This type of backup requires the most storage space and the most time to perform. Both differential and incremental backup strategies start with a baseline of a normal backup.

Novell Directory Services (NDS)   A utility that displays the contents of various network-related data structures, such as the state of sockets.

Novell NetWare   A network operating system developed by Novell to provide file and print services for LANs, servers, and personal computers. Versions 1 through 4 used IPX/SPX as the default protocol. Later versions use TCP/IP.

nslookup   A standard TCP/IP utility that probes and queries DNS servers for DNS records. It is the primary DNS troubleshooting tool. You can use it to view examples of DNS record types. Also, it generates name server queries on command.

NT Directory Services (NTDS)   Windows NT 4 directory services that contain users, computers, groups and permissions, and other properties assigned in a domain to provide central management.

ntsysv   A Linux program used to select daemons for startup upon system boot. The ntsysv command determines the run level at which services (that is, daemons) will run the next time the system reboots.

one-way encryption   An encryption method that is used for information that is not meant to be decrypted. The encrypted message can be checked against a hash table of hexadecimal numbers to confirm its validity. Also called hash encryption.

open-source movement   A largely informal gathering of developers who create freely available applications, services, and operating systems.

Open Standards Interconnect Reference Model (OSI/RM)   A seven-layer networking model used to break down the many tasks involved in moving data from one host to another. For more information see `http://www.tml.hut.fi/Opinnot/Tik-110.250/1999/Kalvot/NMedia030399/sld006.htm`. See also *Application layer, Presentation layer, Session layer, Transport layer, Network layer, Data Link layer,* and *Physical layer.*

operating system (OS)   A program that after being loaded on a computer using a boot program manages all computer resources and all the other programs.

operating system policies   Policies that help users work securely by enforcing choices that guard against system attacks. For example, many policies require a minimum password length, maximum password age, restricted logons, and so forth. Such limitations help users create and maintain proper passwords and are enforced at the operating system level.

packet   Data processed by protocols so that it can be sent across a network.

packet filter   A type of firewall. It can be implemented as a router or as a device that inspects the source IP address, destination IP address, and TCP/UDP source and destination ports. Suitable for high-volume networks.

packet filtering   A function of routers and firewalls that screens packets based on their contents and discards offending packets.

packet sniffer   Software that captures packets as they cross the network. Examples of packet sniffers include tcpdump (all flavors of Unix), Ethereal (many flavors of Unix and Windows 2000), Network Monitor (Windows 2000), and Sniffer Portable WAN and Sniffer Wireless by Network Associates (Windows 9x, Me, and 2000). A packet sniffer operates by placing a host's NIC into promiscuous mode, from which it can capture packets from the network wire.

paging file   The hard drive space devoted to virtual RAM is called the paging file. In Red Hat Linux, this space is called the swap file.

passive mode   The most prevalent FTP mode. It is firewall friendly. In passive mode, which has become the industry standard, the FTP client opens two ephemeral ports and then connects to port 21 of the server to create the control connection. Embedded within this connection is a PASV command that allows a passive-enabled FTP server to open an ephemeral port. The FTP client then establishes a connection between its second ephemeral port and the server's ephemeral port to create the data channel. The server then creates a passive TCP connection on an ephemeral port back to the client.

password   A secret string of characters used as a credential to verify the authenticity of a user.

password sniffing   A method of intercepting the transmission of a password during the authentication process. A *sniffer* is a program used to intercept passwords.

pathping   A Windows 2000 command that combines the features of `tracert` and `ping`. The `pathping` command sends packets to each router on the way to a final destination over a period of time in order to locate congested or malfunctioning routers.

peer-to-peer network   A network formed by two or more computers that are linked to each other without centralized controls. Each computer can have as much control as the other over the network.

Performance Monitor The primary Windows 2000 graphical utility for determining server bottlenecks and problems on the system. This tool monitors objects that belong to the server. These objects include Physical Disk, Server Work Queues, Active Server Pages, Processor, TCP, Server, Logical Disk, Web Service, and FTP Service.

permissions 1. Instructions given by an operating system or server (or a combination thereof) that restrict or allow access to system resources, such as files, user databases, and system processes. 2. An owner's granting of the rights to another for the use of copyrighted or licensed intellectual property.

personal certificate A type of SSL certificate. It is issued to individuals to allow them to be strongly authenticated and to engage in S/MIME, SSL, and SET.

ping A utility that tests Internet connectivity by using ICMP to send packets to a host. From the term Packet Internet Groper.

plaintext Unencrypted text that can be easily viewed by the sender, receiver, or an intermediary.

Pluggable Authentication Module (PAM) Allow integration of various authentication technologies such as Unix, Kerberos, RSA, smart cards, and DCE into system entry services such as login, passwd, rlogin, telnet, ftp, and su without changing any of these services. Pluggable means that you do not have to recompile the operating system to use the technology.

plug-in A program installed as part of the browser to extend its basic functionality. Allows different file formats to be viewed as part of a standard HTML document.

Point-to-Point Protocol (PPP) An improved version of SLIP (Serial Line Internet Protocol) that allows a computer to connect to the Internet over a phone line. If an ISP offers you a choice of a SLIP or a PPP connection, choose PPP.

Point-to-Point Tunneling Protocol (PPTP) Encapsulates protocols and transmits them over the Internet, using encryption, which allows Virtual Private Networks (VPNs) to be established over the Internet.

pointer (PTR) A DNS record that helps map IP addresses to names (the opposite of a standard, forward lookup).

port number An address contained in the header of TCP and UDP packets that identifies the appropriate communication process.

Post Office Protocol (POP) A protocol that resides on an incoming e-mail server. Sorts e-mail messages into the correct user mailbox for the user to download. The latest version is POP3.

prettyname field A news server field that allows an alternative name for the newsgroup. For instance, company.site.news might have a prettyname of Company News.

protocol Communication rules that define and describe how computers and networks can communicate with each other.

proxy server An intermediary server that stands between a network host and other hosts outside the network. Provides enhanced security, manages TCP/IP addresses, and speeds access to the Internet by providing caching-server functions for frequently used documents.

public key encryption   The use of a pair of keys that allows two or more systems to encrypt transmissions to each other. The resulting encryption is difficult to unencrypt without the key and allows systems to communicate with confidence.

put   An FTP command that uploads a file

queue   A sequence of requests for services from one or more servers. These requests arrive one at a time and wait to be processed. A queue grows as more service requests arrive and shrinks as the requests are processed. If the server handles requests as fast as they arrive, the queue remains small. However, if requests arrive faster than the server can process them, the queue grows.

random access memory (RAM)   Stores data and programs in volatile (it is erased when the computer is shut off), fast-access memory in the computer. It is called "random access" because memory locations can be directly accessed.

RealOne Player   A streaming media client application developed by RealNetworks. Real-One combines individual programs that were previously named RealAudio, RealVideo, and RealPlayer.

Redundant Array of Inexpensive Disks (RAID)   A disk system in which multiple disks act as a single unit. RAID is used today to provide higher disk read performance and/or to protect data. It is categorized by levels. The most frequently used RAID levels are as follows: Level 0: disk striping (does not provide fault tolerance); Level 1: disk mirroring (provides fault tolerance and enhanced read performance, but not the higher read performance of RAID 5); Level 5: disk striping with

parity (RAID 5, the most often used form of fault-tolerant RAID).

Referrer log   An HTTP server log that provides information about how people found out about a site. Whenever you browse from Page A to Page B by clicking a hyperlink, Page A is said to "refer" Page B. An HTML page can also refer images, other HTML documents, and any other file the page needs in order to render it completely. A Referrer log can show the number of files one page requires to render in a browser.

registered port number   Port numbers form 1024 to 65535 that can be used by any process.

relational database   A database that is stored in a series of related tables and allows data to be linked based on the records in these tables.

relational database management system (RDBMS)   An application that manages relational databases, including the editing and saving of records and fields by one or more concurrent users.

relaying   The practice in which Host A is updated as an intermediary by Host B for a message that is meant for Host C. For this transaction to work, Host A needs to serve as a relay host.

Requests for Comments (RFCs)   Published documents of the IETF that detail information about standardized Internet protocols and those in various development stages.

reserved IP addresses   Address ranges reserved by ICANN for use on private networks, including ISPs and LANs. These include 10.0.0.0 through 10.255.255.255, 172.16.0.0 through 172.31.255.255, and 192.168.0.0 through 192.168.255.255.

reverse lookup zone   A DNS zone file that contains entries that map IP addresses to names. A reverse zone is also known as the loopback network.

revocation list   A list of SSL certificates that have been revoked by a CA such as VeriSign. Most protocols supporting certificates allow real-time verification of the certificates. This process involves sending the certificate information electronically to the CA for verification. In this step, the CA checks the certificate against a revocation list.

roaming profile   This profile type is the same as a local profile, except that a roaming profile travels with the user. For example, you assign a roaming profile to an employee named Joel. As soon as Joel authenticates, regardless of the location, the server downloads his profile.

robot   A program that automatically searches web pages and indexes them for searches. See also *spider*.

root-level DNS domain   This level is at the top of the hierarchy. Root uses a null label that is expressed by a period (called a dot). This trailing period is usually removed from domain names.

root server   A DNS server that can identify all top-level domains on the Internet. Root servers provide authoritative information for the location of authoritative top-level domains.

routable   An indication that data can be forwarded through a router.

router   A network device that determines the best path across a network for data.

RPM (Red Hat Package Manager)   A powerful package manager that can be used to build, install, query, verify, update, and uninstall individual software packages on Red Hat Linux computers. RPM files are pre-compiled services and applications created especially for Red Hat Linux.

rule   An entry in a firewall database designed to control access into and out of a network. A rule also determines which protocol is allowed into or out of the network. Rules can be very specific. For example, you can create a rule that allows a certain protocol, such as ICMP, into your network only from certain external hosts.

run level   In Linux, a run level describes the current state of the system, including the number of services the system can run. Lower run levels start minimal services and accommodate few or no additional users, whereas higher run levels can start additional services.

Samba   A network file system that can be installed on a variety of clients, including Unix/Linux, to connect to and share resources that are offered using the Server Message Block (SMB) protocol that is used in Microsoft networking.

Samba Web Administration Tool (SWAT)   A GUI that is used to administer Samba using a browser.

search engine   A powerful software program, usually hosted on a website, that searches a database of other websites and Internet resources for user-specified information.

second-level DNS domain   This level is one level below the top-level domain. Second-level domains are usually named after the organization (for example, W3C) or business (for example, CIW).

Secure MIME (S/MIME)   Secure version of MIME that adds encryption to MIME data. See also *Multipurpose Internet Mail Extension (MIME)*.

Secure SMTP (SSMTP)   A standard for encrypting and decrypting e-mail using digital certificates. It uses TCP port 465. See also *Simple Mail Transfer Protocol*.

Secure Sockets Layer (SSL)   A technology embedded in web servers and browsers that encrypts traffic. SSL is the most common form of encryption. An SSL session is established using a six-step handshake that provides connection security that has three basic properties: The connection is private due to symmetric encryption. The peer's identity can be authenticated using asymmetric cryptography. Finally, the connection is reliable due to secure hash functions.

security   Concerns the safety and protection of network assets, especially from unauthorized users.

Security Accounts Manager (SAM)   The database of local users and their permissions stored on a Windows 2000 computer. In contrast, domain controllers store domain user accounts, groups, and permissions in Active Directory.

server   A computer that provides information or connections to other computers on a network.

server-based network   A configuration of nodes, some of which are dedicated to providing resources to other hosts on the network.

server certificate   A type of digital certificates used for SSL. It is used on web servers to identify the web server and the company running it and to allow for encrypted SSL sessions between the server and browsers. Server certificates are also necessary for a server to participate in transactions using the SET protocol.

Server Message Block (SMB)   A Microsoft-specific protocol for communicating across networks. Microsoft uses SMB to establish file and print shares, as well as execute commands and named pipes using TCP-based connections.

server-side applications   Web applications that reside on the Internet server itself. The server must execute them.

service   A program that runs on a server or a client full-time in the background. For example, to place a Windows 9*x* or Me system on a network, you must first install Client for Microsoft Networks, as well as File and Printer Sharing for Microsoft Networks. Other operating systems use different services to make a resource available across a network.

service pack   A self-contained, all-inclusive patch designed to bring the Windows 2000 operating system up to the latest vendor specifications. Most vendors issue service packs.

session key   A shared secret derived from the master key that is used for symmetric encryption during an SSL session. The third phase of the SSL handshake process is the Session Key Production phase. During this phase, a CLIENT-SESSION-KEY message is sent from the client to the server. This message is used to establish one or two session keys with the server. These keys are derived from the master key already sent in the CLIENT-MASTER-KEY or CLIENT-DH-KEY message.

shadow passwords Encrypted passwords stored in the /etc/shadow or similar file that only the root user can read. Newer Unix systems use a shadow file for password storage. (Red Hat Linux enables shadow passwords by default.) The password information has been removed from the passwd file and is now stored in a special file, often called the /etc/shadow file. The access control permissions for the shadow file allow access to only the most privileged account.

share A file, folder, or disk on a host that can be accessed over the network. In Windows 9x/Me/2000, you establish a share using Windows Explorer.

shared virtual server An additional FTP or HTTP server created on a computer using the same NIC and IP as an existing server of the same type, but using a different port assignment.

shell A command-based interface, usually for an operating system.

shell account The command-line interface of a Unix server at the ISP. Shell accounts require users to enter commands to access and navigate the Internet.

shell program The program that is executed when the user logs on. Usually, the shell program is the user's preferred interactive environment (/bin/sh, /bin/ksh, /bin/csh, or /bin/bash, for example), but it can also be a special-purpose shell with limited capabilities.

Simple Mail Transfer Protocol (SMTP) An Application-layer protocol for transferring Internet e-mail messages. Specifies how two mail systems interact, as well as the format of control messages they exchange to transfer mail.

simple virtual server An additional FTP or HTTP server created on a computer using the same NIC as an existing server of the same type, but using a different IP address.

single-homed bastion A firewall that uses one computer that acts as both a firewall component and the network interface.

site mirroring The ability to duplicate any part of an existing website on remote hosts. For example, the main Apache server distribution site (www.apache.org) allows anyone to mirror the contents of its file download area. Sites such as TUCOWS (www.tucows.com) also engage in site mirroring. Because of its duplication feature, site mirroring provides fault tolerance and data security.

slave server A DNS server that receives its authority and database from the master server. The slave server provides fault tolerance and load distribution. When the slave server first starts, it requests all the data for a given zone from the master server. The process of pulling information from the master server is called a zone transfer. The slave server then periodically checks with the master name server to determine whether it needs to update its data. Another name for a slave server is secondary server, which is the term Microsoft uses.

Small Computer System Interface (SCSI) Small Computer System Interface allows computers to communicate with peripheral hardware such as disk drives, tape drives, CD-ROM drives, printers, and scanners faster and more flexibly. As many as 15 devices can be connected in parallel on a daisy-chained cable to a single controller. The latest SCSI standard is Ultra-3, which increases the maximum data transfer burst rate to 160Mbps.

smart card   A credit-card–sized device that includes an embedded computer chip for storing and processing data.

smbd daemon   Samba also uses the SMB protocol to create shares. Samba consists of the nmbd daemon that provides NetBIOS names over the network and the smbd daemon that provides file and print shares.

snap-in   In Windows 2000, a tool you can use to administer network applications and to control elements of the system that are added to the Microsoft Management Console (MMC). See also *Microsoft Management Console (MMC)*.

socket   The end point of a connection (either side), which usually includes the TCP or UDP port used and the IP address. Used for communication between a client and a server.

software publisher certificate   A type of SSL certificate. Software authors use the software publisher certificate to sign and identify their released code. This certificate verifies the identity of the author and the integrity of the code.

spam   1. Popular term for unsolicited commercial e-mail. 2. A delicious yet unfairly maligned luncheon meat product of the Hormel Corporation.

spider   A program that automatically searches web pages and indexes them for searches. See also *robot*.

srm.conf   An Apache server configuration file that allows you to configure the document root (in conjunction with access.conf), as well as aliases and other settings.

SSL handshake   A process in which a web server and the client browser exchange and negotiate a secure communications link. The handshake occurs in six phases: Hello, Key Exchange, Session Key Production, Server Verify, Client Authentication, and Finished.

SSL record   Data transmitted during an SSL session. The SSL record is composed of three parts: Message Authentication Code (MAC), ACTUAL, and PADDING.

Start of Authority (SOA)   A DNS record that identifies the DNS server with the best source of information for the DNS domain. Because several backup DNS servers may exist, this record identifies the master server for the specified DNS domain.

static mapping   An entry made manually in the WINS database so that WINS clients can find a non-WINS client such as a Linux computer not running Samba.

streaming audio and video   Audio and video files that travel over a network in real time.

streaming media   A continuous flow of data, usually audio or video files, that assists with the uninterrupted delivery of those files into a browser.

strong authentication   The process of identifying an individual, usually based on a username and password, in which the requirements for selection and application of the username and password are designed to enhance the security of the authentication method.

subnet mask   A 32-bit number similar to an IP address with a one-to-one correspondence between each of the 32 bits in the Internet address. Distinguishes the network and host portions of an IP address, and specifies whether a destination address is local or remote. Also called a net mask.

swap file   The hard-drive space devoted to virtual RAM is called the swap file in Red Hat Linux. In Windows 2000, this space is called the paging file.

symmetric-key encryption   An encryption method that uses a single key to encrypt and decrypt messages. All parties must know and trust one another completely and have confidential copies of the key.

system bugs   Computer operating system or application problems that allow illicit users an opportunity for malicious activity. Such bugs range from very minor to extremely dangerous. Whenever you load an operating system for the first time or upgrade an existing one, contact the vendor for a list of known problems. In many cases, you will also be able to obtain patches, fixes, and workarounds for various problems.

system defaults   Out-of-the-box settings the system uses if you do not alter them upon installation. Most systems are preconfigured with defaults because the manufacturer wants to make it easy for administrators and users to initialize and run the system. Competent hackers have comprehensive lists of system defaults for each operating system. If a systems administrator leaves the setting of an account at the default, a hacker can access the account without logging on to the system.

system state   Windows 2000 configuration and database files necessary for the system to run properly. All system state data files are crucial to a backup of a Windows 2000 server.

T1   A North American digital carrier standard for synchronous data transmission at a speed of 1.544Mbps.

T3   A North American digital carrier standard for synchronous data transmission at a speed of 44.736Mbps.

table   A file or unit in which records are stored.

TCP   See *Transmission Control Protocol*.

TCP wrappers   A package you can use to monitor and filter incoming requests for the SYSTAT, FINGER, FTP, TELNET, RLOGIN, RSH, EXEC, TFTP, TALK, and other network services. The package provides tiny daemon wrapper programs that can be installed without any changes to existing software or to existing configuration files. The wrappers report the name of the client host and of the requested service; the wrappers do not exchange information with the client or server applications and impose no overhead on the actual conversation between the client and server applications.

Telnet   An Application-layer protocol that is the Internet standard for remote terminal connection service. Telnet is a terminal emulation protocol that is part of the TCP/IP suite of protocols. Telnet operates on port 23. Windows 2000 and Red Hat Linux include native Telnet servers and clients.

testparm A command that reads the /etc/samba/smb.conf file and displays a list of existing file and print shares.

three-tier A three-tier solution is a client/server communication scheme that involves a web browser, a web server, an interpreter/application server, and a database. An application server is an advanced method for enabling communication between web servers, clients, and databases. As such, this configuration is called a three-tier solution.

throughput The amount of data that can successfully be moved from one place to another in a given time period. Throughput is often the most telling measurement as it stacks up the data to be moved against the capacity of the channel, yielding a time to move a given amount of data through a channel with a given bandwidth.

top A Linux/Unix command that displays the most CPU intensive programs at the top of a list of processes running on the system. It also displays the amount of memory being used by each process.

Top-level DNS domain This level contains organizations (.org), businesses (.com), universities (.edu), and so forth. Most Internet users are familiar with this level.

top-level domain (TLD) The group into which a domain is categorized, by geography (country, state, and so on) and/or common topic (company, educational institution, and so on).

tracert A utility that can display the path between the source and destination systems.

traditional mode A legacy FTP mode of operation. Traditional mode FTP uses two ports: TCP 20 and TCP 21. Port 20 is the data connection (it transports the file you have requested); port 21 is the control connection for the FTP session (it allows commands such as LIST, DIR, PUT, and GET). In traditional mode, the FTP client opens two ephemeral ports. Ephemeral ports are temporary, operating-system assigned ports that the FTP server can detect. The FTP client uses one ephemeral port to connect to the server's port 21 and uses the PORT command to establish the command connection on port 20. The server then connects to the client's second ephemeral port using its own port 20 to transfer data.

Transmission Control Protocol (TCP) A stateful Transport-layer protocol that ensures reliable communication and uses ports to deliver packets. TCP/IP fragments and reassembles messages, using a sequencing function to ensure that packets are reassembled in the correct order.

Transmission Control Protocol/Internet Protocol (TCP/IP) The standard protocol suite for breaking up data for transmission to another computer, using TCP, and for specifying the destination address, using IP. See also *Transmission Control Protocol* and *Internet Protocol*.

transmission medium A method or device for interconnecting all networking elements and allowing the transmission of data. May use physical methods (cable, wire), optical means (fiber), or other technologies (wireless).

Transport layer A layer of the Internet architecture that corresponds to the Session and Transport layers of the OSI Reference Model. Also known as the host-to-host layer, the end-to-end layer, or the source-to-destination layer.

Ultra ATA (Advanced Technology Attainment) Although not a true I/O card, Ultra ATA is an important extension to IDE devices. Ultra ATA allows higher data-transfer speed between a hard drive and the IDE I/O card. Generally, IDE cards communicate at a rate of 16.6Mbps. Ultra ATA allows data to travel at a maximum speed of 133Mbps.

Uniform Resource Locator (URL) A text string that supplies an Internet or intranet address, and the method by which the address can be accessed. For example, the URL for the Sybex website is www.sybex.com.

uninterruptible power supply (UPS) A device that provides a steady stream of power to a computer if electric power supplies fail or are inadequate. UPSs are powered by internal batteries. A battery is charged when normal power is available and is used by the system attached to it when power is inadequate or unavailable. Additionally, most UPSs can regulate the power sent to the attached system. The power flows from the wall into the UPS, and the UPS delivers a steady stream of power to the system. This feature is beneficial when a power surge or brownout occurs.

Unix A high performance network operating system that supports multi-user and multi-tasking operations. Unix uses a command-line interface by default. Some varieties of Unix also have a graphical user interface. There are many different varieties of Unix systems, including Linux.

unnecessary system services Services that are not necessary for the functioning of your server and that you should remove so that they are not compromised by hackers. After you implement security on your operating system, remove any services that you do not specifically require. Removing unnecessary services gives potential hackers fewer targets. If you were going to use a building for a secure purpose, you would not choose one with many doors and windows. Unnecessary services or daemons on a server are comparable to these excess openings.

Usenet (User Network) A collection of topically named Internet discussion groups or newsgroups, including information on the computers that run the protocols and the people who read and submit postings. Usenet is a public access network consisting of newsgroups and group mailing lists.

user accounts database The standard term for an access list in the user-level access security model. A user accounts database is also an application of an access control list (ACL).

user agent The W3C term for any application, such as a web browser or a help engine, that renders HTML for display to users. A user agent is client software used to browse a website. User agents can include web browsers and spiders used by search engines.

User Datagram Protocol (UDP) A connectionless Transport-layer protocol designed for broadcasting short messages on a network. UDP does not support acknowledgment. Also used for streaming media.

user ID (UID) Identifies a file's owner in Linux, and it's stored in the kernel's process table to identify the owner of a process. The UID is stored internally in 32-bit fields, so it can be any reasonable size. It is used to assign permissions.

user-level access security model Allows users to obtain access to resources only if they belong to a centralized access list. This access list can be central to a particular server or to an entire network. User-level access is quite different from share-level access because it can be used to authenticate specific users.

uuencode A method for converting binary file attachments to text prior to transmission. The encoded attachments can be uudecoded.

virtual FTP server Additional instance of a software FTP server that is created on the computer. See also *dedicated virtual server*, *simple virtual server*, and *shared virtual server*.

virtual private network (VPN) A method for allowing secure network access to external users through a firewall using tunneling protocols.

virus A program that replicates itself on computer systems, usually through executable software, and causes damage.

vmstat A Linux/Unix command that provides information on computer resource use by processes. The vmstat program classifies all processes using fields and field values.

web application Any executable file that enhances the normal function of a web server. A web application can be a simple script, or it can be a much more complex set of files and programs. E-commerce sites use sophisticated web applications to connect web servers to databases.

web browser A client application that downloads World Wide Web documents and displays them. May also serve as a client for other services, including FTP and Gopher.

well-known port number Port numbers 1 through 1023 that are registered by ICANN and linked to specific services.

wide area network (WAN) A group of computers connected over an expansive geographic area, such as a state or country. The Internet is a WAN.

Windows The brand name for several personal computer and network operating systems developed by Microsoft, all featuring graphical user interfaces.

Windows Internet Naming Service (WINS) Microsoft's NetBIOS name service that resolves NetBIOS names to IP addresses.

Windows Media Player A streaming media application developed by Microsoft.

winipcfg A program that displays TCP/IP network settings on the Windows 95, 98, or Me operating system.

workgroups The organization of computers that participate in a particular peer-to-peer network. All members of a workgroup have equal access to all shares depending on the password. This access is the reason that the workgroup members are called peers.

workstation A terminal or personal computer on a network; usually refers to a client.

World Wide Web (WWW) The universe of resources and users accessible on the Internet using Hypertext Transfer Protocol (HTTP).

World Wide Web Consortium (W3C) An international industry consortium founded in 1994 to develop common standards for the World Wide Web.

X.509v3 standard A standard governing SSL certificates. The X.509v3 standard is an International Telecommunications Union (ITU) standard issued as a corollary of the X.500 messaging standard. It establishes the format and contents of the physical certificate file.

xinetd A super daemon because it controls how other daemons operate.

X Window System A windowing system used with Unix, Linux, and other operating systems.

zone file A database file that contains DNS records. A zone file helps define a branch of the DNS name space under the administrative control of a master DNS name server. Many IT professionals use the terms "domain" and "zone" interchangeably; however, they are not the same. A zone is a specific file that resides on a server.

zone transfer The process of pulling information from the master DNS server.

Index

Note to the reader: Throughout this index **boldfaced** page numbers indicate primary discussions of a topic. *Italicized* page numbers indicate illustrations.

Symbols & Numbers

A

Execute permission (NTFS), 128
Execute permission (Unix), 131
execution rights, for web scripts, 500
Exit message, for FTP site users, 392
expiration date, for user accounts, 239, 249
expiration policy, 711
    for news server, 557–558
Expires header, **553**, 711
Extended Logging Properties dialog box, Extended
    Properties tab, *594, 594*
external interface, 711
extract command (Unix restore), 658
extranet, 10, 711

F

failed logon attempts, logs to determine, 591
Failsafe mode, 49
Fast Ethernet, 29
Fast SCSI, 28
FAT (File Allocation Table)
    conversion to NTFS, 190
    features, 189
    and Windows 2000, 188
fault tolerance, **449, 636–645**, 711. *See also* backup
    and DNS resolution, 280
    exam essentials, **664–665**
    folder replication, 643
    offsite storage, 643
    RAID (Redundant Array of Inexpensive Disks),
        637–642
      automatic, 641
      disk mirroring, *638*, 638–639
      disk striping, 637, *638*
      disk striping with large blocks, 639, *640*
      disk striping with parity, *639, 640*, 641
      high-availability disk subsystems, 642
    site mirroring, **643–644**
    site redirection, **644–645**
    UPS (uninterruptible power supply), **642–643**

fields in database, 438–439
File Replication Service log, 193
File Scan right (NetWare), 134
File Transfer Protocol (FTP), 711. *See also* FTP
    (File Transfer Protocol)
files and folders. *See also* permissions
    Access Control Settings for, 197
    ownership, **202–207**
    replication, 643, 711
    selecting for backup, 647
    sharing in Samba, **363–366**
    in Unix, 131
finger, 381, **418–419**, 711
Finished phase, in SSL handshake, **527**
firewall-friendly FTP, 382
firewalls, 444, **687–688**, 711
    attacks inside, 689
    and linuxconf, 242
    logging and, 591
FireWire, 28
floppy disk
    for backup, 646
    for booting to install NOS, 61
folder Properties dialog box
    Security tab, *168,* 168–169, *169, 200*
    Sharing tab, 116
folders. *See* files and folders; permissions
forward lookup zone, 294, 711
forward-only server, 712
forward zone file, 282, 283, 313–314
    DNS records for, 298–299
forwarding-only server in DNS, 281
forwarding server in DNS, 281
foundation services, **435–447**
    data and resource sharing, 436
    database server, **438–441**
    e-commerce server, **441**
    e-mail server, **443**
    exam essentials, **452–453**
    HTTP Server, **436–438**
    name resolution, 435

G

H

TELL US WHAT YOU THINK!

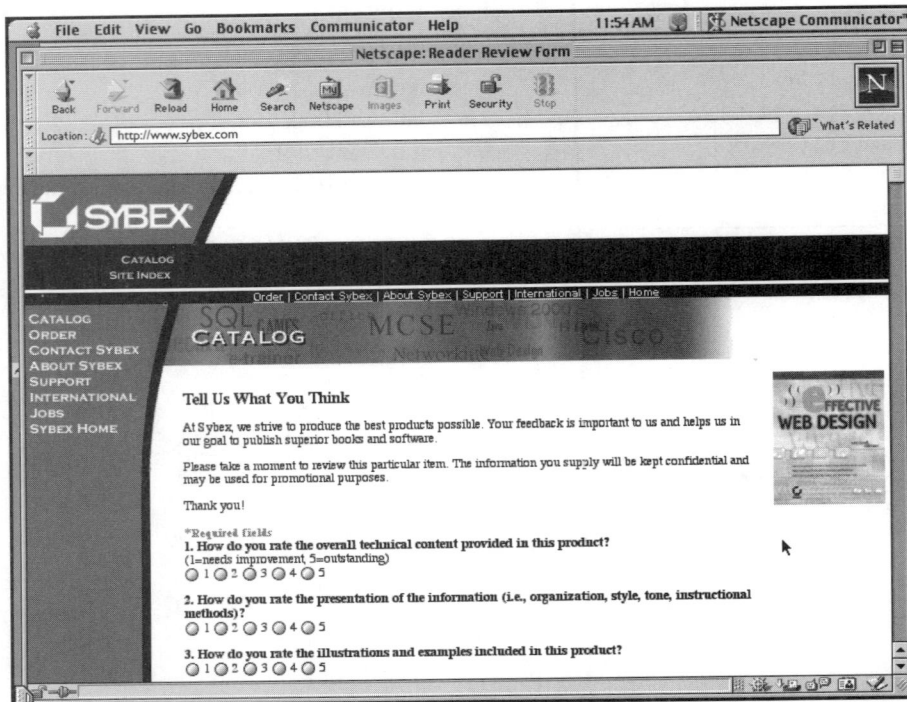

Your feedback is critical to our efforts to provide you with the best books and software on the market. Tell us what you think about the products you've purchased. It's simple:

1. Visit the Sybex website
2. Go to the product page
3. Click on **Submit a Review**
4. Fill out the questionnaire and comments
5. Click **Submit**

With your feedback, we can continue to publish the highest quality computer books and software products that today's busy IT professionals deserve.

www.sybex.com

SYBEX Inc. • 1151 Marina Village Parkway, Alameda, CA 94501 • 510-523-8233

Sybex + ProsoftTraining=CIW Success!

The CIW (Certified Internet Webmaster) program from ProsoftTraining™ is the most widely recognized Internet-specific certification. Sybex and ProsoftTraining™ have teamed up to bring you high quality Study Guides that will provide you with the skills and knowledge you need to approach the exams with confidence!

Endorsed by ProsoftTraining™, each CIW Study Guide from Sybex® is based upon the official ProsoftTraining.com courseware and comes packed with additional study tools for your benefit.

CIW Associate

The CIW Associate certification is the entry point for those pursuing the "Master" CIW designations. The Foundations exam validates the basic hands-on skills and knowledge that an Internet professional is expected to understand and use. Foundations skills include basic knowledge of Internet technologies, network infrastructure, and Web authoring using HTML.

Exam Name	Exam #	Sybex Products
Foundations	1D0-410	*CIW: Foundations Study Guide* ISBN: 07821-4081-5

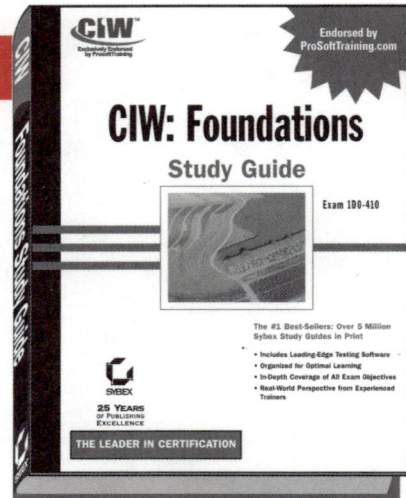

Master CIW Designer

The Master CIW Design certification requires candidates to pass two exams in addition to Foundations. The Site Design exam validates skills relevant to designing, implementing, and maintaining web sites using authoring languages and content creation tools. The E-commerce exam tests knowledge of web marketing and purchasing methods, inventory control, shipping and site performance.

Exam Name	Exam #	Sybex Products
Site Designer	1D0-420	*CIW: Site and E-Commerce Design Study Guide* ISBN: 07821-4082-3
E-Commerce Designer	1D0-425	

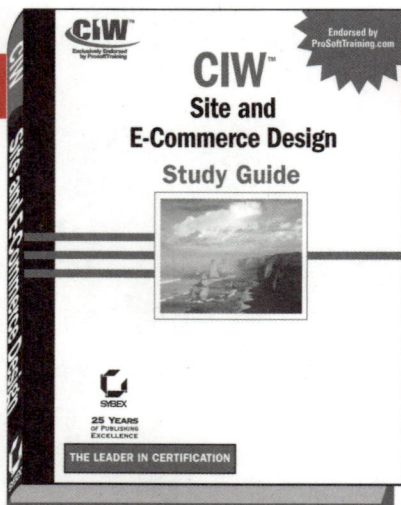